Visual J++ 1.0 Publisher's Edition

Microsoft© Corp Visual J++™ Publisher's Edition included on the accompanying CD-ROM allows you to create your own Visual J++™ programs without purchasing the commercial version. The Publisher's Edition does differ from the commercial version in some ways. These include: No database support for SQL and ODBC databases through Data Access Objects (DAO) and Remote Data Objects (RDO). No JET engine for creating programs that work with Access and other DAO databases. No Zoomin and WinDiff Tools. No third-party tools and libraries that integrate with Visual J++™. No redistribution of Java Virtual Machine and Internet Explorer. No code samples. No Microsoft technical support. No free or discounted upgrades to later versions of Visual J++™ Professional Edition.

Microsoft Corporation Visual J++™ Publisher's Edition requires the following to operate:

- Personal computer with a 486 or higher processor running MS Windows® 95 or Windows NT® Workstation version 4.0 or later operating systems
- 8MB of memory (12MB recommended) if running Windows 95; 16MB (20MB recommended) if running Windows NT Workstation
- Hard-disk space:

  Typical installation: 20MB

  Minimum installation: 14MB

  CD-ROM installation (tools run from the CD-ROM): 14MB

  Total tools and information on CD-ROM: 50MB
- A CD-ROM drive
- VGA or higher resolution monitor (super VGA recommended)
- Microsoft Mouse or compatible point device

NOTE

The material in this book was written to cover the commercial release of Visual J++. The following chapters discuss features not available in the Publisher's Edition:

- Chapter 10: Windiff
- Chapter 30: Querying databases with Data Access Objects (DAO)

Visual J++™

Bryan Morgan, et al.

201 West 103rd Street
Indianapolis, IN 46290

UNLEASHED

Copyright © 1997 by Sams.net Publishing

FIRST EDITION

International Standard Book Number: 1-57521-161-0

Library of Congress Catalog Card Number: 96-69064

2000 99 98 97   4 3 2

Interpretation of the printing code: the rightmost double-digit number is the year of the book's printing; the rightmost single-digit, the number of the book's printing. For example, a printing code of 97-1 shows that the first printing of the book occurred in 1997.

Composed in AGaramond and MCPdigital by Macmillan Computer Publishing

Printed in the United States of America

Trademarks

Publisher and President   *Richard K. Swadley*

Publishing Manager   *Greg Wiegand*

Director of Editorial Services   *Cindy Morrow*

Managing Editor   *Kitty Wilson Jarrett*

Director of Marketing   *John Pierce*

Assistant Marketing Managers   *Kristina Perry, Rachel Wolfe*

Acquisitions Editor
Sharon Cox

Development Editor
Jeffrey J. Koch

Software Development Specialist
Brad Myers

Production Editor
Kitty Wilson Jarrett

Copy Editors
Kimberly K. Hannel
Marilyn J. Stone
June Waldman

Indexer
Tom Dinse

Technical Reviewer
Greg Guntle

Editorial Coordinator
Katie Wise

Technical Edit Coordinator
Lynette Quinn

Resource Coordinator
Deborah Frisby

Editorial Assistants
Carol Ackerman
Andi Richter
Rhonda Tinch-Mize

Cover Designer
Tim Amrhein

Book Designer
Gary Adair

Copy Writer
Peter Fuller

Production Team Supervisor
Brad Chinn

Production
Jenaffer Brandt
Sonja Hart
Brad Lenser
Chris "Bud" Livengood

Overview

Contents

Part IV Activating the Internet with Visual J++

Acknowledgments

Special thanks go out to the following people, without whom this book would have been much, much more difficult to complete: Sharon Cox, Chris Denny, Jeff Koch, Kitty Wilson Jarrett, Mike Nygard, David Blankenbeckler, Vince Mayfield, and Jeff Perkins. Also thanks to TASC for providing a work environment in which special projects outside of work are encouraged and appreciated.

Dedication

This book is dedicated to my wife, Becky, and our beautiful new baby who hasn't entered the world yet. Thank you both for allowing me to share my hopes and dreams with you.

—*Bryan Morgan*

About the Authors

Bryan Morgan

Bryan Morgan is a software engineer with TASC, Inc., in Fort Walton Beach, Florida. He holds a bachelor's degree in electrical engineering from Clemson University and has also authored material for several other books by Sams.net Publishing, including *Java Developer's Reference*. Bryan and his wife, Becky, are anxiously awaiting the arrival of their first child in November 1996.

David Blankenbeckler

David Blankenbeckler received a bachelor of science degree in electrical engineering from Clemson University in 1991. After graduation, David worked for AT&T's Workstation Products Division as the primary software engineer for AT&T notebook products. David moved to Oregon in 1995 to work for Intel Corporation as a senior software engineer. His programming experience includes Java, C/C++, JavaScript, VBScript, HTML, Visual Basic, and Delphi. David currently lives in Oregon with his wife, Kimberly, and new son, Logan.

Mike Cohn

Mike Cohn is the director of information technology at Access Health, Inc., the leading provider of personal health management. Before that he was with Andersen Consulting and the Adler Consulting Group in New York. He holds a master's degree in computer science from the University of Idaho and has been programming for 16 years. Mike lives in Cameron Park, California, with his wife, Laura, and their daughter, Savannah.

David Hanley

David Hanley is a professional Java programmer working out of Chicago, where he was born. He is currently completing his master's degree in computer science. When he is not working or studying, he enjoys running, bicycling, martial arts, playing chess, or relaxing with a book.

Mahendra Palsule

Mahendra Palsule is a software professional born and raised in Mumbai, India. With an engineering diploma in computer technology from Bombay in 1991, he is also a Microsoft Certified Professional in Windows Operating Systems Services & Architecture. He has worked as a software consultant for the past four years, and has experience in software development, networking, and multimedia authoring on Windows and Macintosh platforms. He has contributed to multimedia projects in Europe and the Middle East. He is currently involved in Web Publishing at Radan Multimedia Limited, Mumbai. Apart from his obsession with computers and the Internet, he has diverse interests from astronomy to epistemology. He loves to work on multimedia projects where he can synthesize his creative and technical skills. You can reach him at `mahendra@radanmedia.com`.

Hiro Ruo

Hiro Ruo was born in Taichung, Taiwan. He has lived in Tokyo, Japan, and did most of his growing up in Skokie, Illinois (a suburb of Chicago). Hiro received a bachelor of science degree in electrical engineering from Northwestern University and a master of science degree in electrical engineering from Purdue University. He worked for more than five years at NCR (eventually AT&T, and back to NCR). Currently, he is a software engineer with Intel Corporation.

Mark Seminatore

Mark Seminatore has a master's degree in mechanical engineering and has been programming for more than 15 years. When not programming killer Java applets, Mark likes to work on high-performance graphics and optimization. Mark was one of the co-authors of *Tricks of the Game-Programming Gurus* and *More Tricks of the Game-Programming Gurus*. Mark has also written several articles for *Dr. Dobb's Journal*, including "A Raycasting Engine in C++" and "A 2D Gaming Engine in C." He can be reached via the Internet at `72040.145@compuserve.com`.

Tell Us What You Think!

As a reader, you are the most important critic and commentator of our books. We value your opinion and want to know what we're doing right, what we could do better, what areas you'd like to see us publish in, and any other words of wisdom you're willing to pass our way. You can help us make strong books that meet your needs and give you the computer guidance you require.

Do you have access to CompuServe or the World Wide Web? Then check out our CompuServe forum by typing GO SAMS at any prompt. If you prefer the World Wide Web, check out our site at http://www.mcp.com.

> **NOTE**
>
> If you have a technical question about this book, call the technical support line at 800-571-5840, ext. 3668.

As the publishing manager of the group that created this book, I welcome your comments. You can fax, e-mail, or write me directly to let me know what you did or didn't like about this book—as well as what we can do to make our books stronger. Here's the information:

Fax: 317-581-4669

E-mail: programming_mgr@sams.mcp.com

Mail: Greg Wiegand
          Publishing Manager
          Sams.net Publishing
          201 W. 103rd Street
          Indianapolis, IN 46290

Introduction

Visual J++ is the name of Microsoft's Java development tool. Using Visual J++, you can create powerful applets and embed them within a Web page for distribution across the Internet or a local intranet. In addition, standalone applications can be written in Java that can run on any operating system that supports the Java Virtual Machine. If Microsoft had stopped here, Visual J++ would probably be noted for its excellent integrated development environment (IDE) and its extremely fast compiler.

However, Microsoft also extended the Java Virtual Machine and Visual J++ to support the integration of Java with the Microsoft object model, the component object model (COM). Tools included with Visual J++ allow Java objects to call ActiveX objects and, likewise, ActiveX objects can call Java objects. In fact, it is even possible to create a COM object in Java. This is important to the Java developer because of the huge installed base of COM objects already existing in the form of OLE objects and OCX or ActiveX controls. In short, Visual J++ allows the Java developer to truly choose the best tool for the job at hand, whether that tool be ActiveX or Java.

It is important to remember that pure Java bytecodes produced by the Visual J++ compiler will run unmodified in any Java-enabled browser on any platform. Therefore, the majority of the focus of this book is on building traditional Java applications. Specific topics that are examined in this book are

- Building powerful, interactive Web applications with VBScript and JavaScript
- Performing networking operations in Java
- Database access using Java Database Connectivity (JDBC) and Microsoft's Data Access Objects (DAO)
- Multimedia development using Java
- ActiveX and why it is important to the Web developer

 Throughout this book, examples are given to illustrate relevant topics. The majority of these examples are included on the CD-ROM accompanying this book and can be compiled and run unmodified using Visual J++.

Conventions Used in This Book

TIP

Tips appear in text blocks like this; they give hints and ideas for how to use Visual J++.

> **NOTE**
>
> Sections like this identify noteworthy features or highlight key points being covered in the text. This draws your attention to something that should not be overlooked.

> **WARNING**
>
> A Warning box cautions you against making a mistake you could make either by overlooking an important step or by doing something that you might otherwise try to do. A mistake here could cause problems later.

Text that you type and text that should appear on your screen is presented in monospace type:

```
It will look like this to mimic the way text looks on your screen.
```

Placeholders for variables and expressions appear in *monospace italic*.

How to Use This Book

This book contains introductory information that will be of interest to the beginning Java developer as well as a large amount of advanced information that is designed to help intermediate to advanced Java programmers. Although the focus of this book is on Visual J++, the majority of the topics in this book provide technical information of interest to the Web developer such as Java, ActiveX, and VBScript/JavaScript. Therefore, anyone interested in building interactive Web applications using the latest technologies should find this book to be an invaluable resource.

Visual J++ Unleashed introduces and thoroughly examines Microsoft's exciting new Java development tool: Visual J++. Due to the capabilities of Visual J++, Web programming techniques using Java, ActiveX, VBScript, and JavaScript are examined in great detail. In addition, useful sample programs are given in each chapter to illustrate the power of these technologies.

For readers new to the Java language, the book begins with an introduction to Java programming fundamentals in Part I, "Introduction to Java Programming Using Visual J++." Special attention is given to object-oriented programming with Java and advanced Java programming topics such as multithreading, exception handling, and networking.

Following this introduction to the Java language, the Visual J++ development environment is examined in Part II, "The Visual J++ Development Tools." Visual J++ includes a powerful integrated development environment, Microsoft's Developer Studio, and a number of time-saving wizards and programming tools.

Because the Microsoft Java Virtual Machine included with Visual J++ and Microsoft's Internet Explorer browser supports the integration of ActiveX controls and Java applets, ActiveX and its underlying technology COM are explained in Part III, "The Foundation for Visual J++: The Component Object Model." This part of the book explains COM and ActiveX in great detail and focuses on building Web-based applications using Java and ActiveX. Interesting examples are given each step of the way to help explain these critical technologies.

Because much of the growth in popularity of the Java language can be attributed to its use to build applets for display within Web pages, Part IV, "Activating the Internet with Visual J++," focuses on Web programming topics. Included in this section are chapters that compare the capabilities of popular Web browsers, explain the latest versions of HTML, and illustrate the construction of active Web pages using VBScript and JavaScript.

Part V, "Visual J++ Development Topics," focuses on real-world Java programming issues. Included in this section are chapters on network programming, database access using JDBC, Microsoft's Data Access Objects, and multimedia programming with Java.

I

PART

Introduction to Java Programming Using Visual J++

Visual J++: What It Is and Why It Is Unique

by Bryan Morgan

IN THIS CHAPTER

CHAPTER 1

Visual J++ is Microsoft's first Java development tool. It was originally internally dubbed Jakarta after the largest city on the island of Java, but Microsoft decided to refrain from using yet another coffee- or Java-related name for this product. The name *Visual J++* can be taken to mean several different things:

- Visual J++ is a visual tool that makes use of standard GUI development techniques such as resource builders, syntax-aware editors, and graphical debuggers.
- Visual J++ is integrated with Microsoft's "Visual" family of tools, which includes Visual C++ and Visual Basic.
- Visual J++ allows the developer to extend the capabilities of the Java language (that's where the ++ comes in).

At its most basic level of operation, Visual J++ provides a high-performance Java compiler, an integrated development environment (with a resource editor, visual debugger, and visual editor), programming wizards, and extensive online help capabilities. Standard Java applets and applications built using the Microsoft Visual J++ toolset will run unmodified on any machine on Earth that includes a copy of the Java Virtual Machine (more on this later).

Had Microsoft stopped at that point and released the tool with just these capabilities, Visual J++ would be highly regarded for its excellent development environment and extremely fast compiler. It uses the Developer Studio environment, which is also used by the Visual C++ and FORTRAN PowerStation products. The compiler can compile up to one million lines of Java code per second (on a standard Pentium-based computer), which should place it near the top of the heap in compilation speed.

As stated earlier, had Microsoft stopped with these features, this book would focus primarily on the Java language and its use in the development of applets and applications (a topic that has produced over 100 books in Java's first year alone!). However, as you probably know by now, Visual J++ is much more than an extremely nice development environment. Microsoft has worked for several years to produce an object-based framework for the Windows platform with the eventual goal of making this framework distributed and cross-platform.

> **NOTE**
>
> The term *distributed* here means that objects can be shared across multiple computers. In other words, if an application were running on your local machine, it could call other objects running on machines elsewhere across the network. This allows applications to be partitioned across multiple machines in order to improve performance and improves maintenance time because only one machine needs be updated in the case of software updates.
>
> The term *cross-platform* is used throughout this book to represent computers sharing information or programs even when the computers are running different operating systems. An example of a cross-platform environment is a network of Windows 95 and Apple Macintosh computers using programming objects stored on a UNIX server.

Microsoft's object standard is known as the *component object model* (COM), and an implementation of this standard can be found in a group of technologies known as *ActiveX*. One ActiveX technology that will be familiar to Windows developers is *ActiveX controls*. These components (formerly known as OCX, or OLE, controls) are industry-standard programming tools now used by many, if not most, Windows programmers. A partial list of products that support the use of ActiveX controls is as follows: Microsoft Visual C++/Visual FoxPro/Visual Basic/ Access, Borland C++/Delphi, Powersoft PowerBuilder, and Oracle PowerObjects.

Why is ActiveX being discussed in a book about a Java compiler? This is what separates Visual J++ from every other Java tool on the market. The Visual J++ toolset, in combination with the Microsoft Windows Virtual Machine for Java, allows Java programmers to use ActiveX controls along with Java applets. In addition, standard Windows applications can be built using Visual J++, ActiveX, and the underlying COM. This allows Windows developers to utilize the full power and elegance of the Java language along with the huge existing base of COM objects that many developers have already invested in.

What Is ActiveX?

ActiveX is the name of a group of related technologies from Microsoft that is designed to allow developers to provide active Web content. Although ActiveX is currently a Windows-only technology, implementations for the Macintosh and UNIX operating systems are slated for release in the near future. When this platform independence is a reality, ActiveX will allow software developers to choose their language and tools, reuse existing inventories of objects, and develop extremely powerful distributed applications for use on a variety of operating platforms. It will do this using a variety of technologies that exist under the ActiveX umbrella, including

- ActiveX documents
- ActiveX controls
- ActiveX scripting
- ActiveX-enabled Internet protocols
- ActiveX APIs
- ActiveX server framework
- Microsoft Windows Virtual Machine for Java

ActiveX Documents

ActiveX documents can be thought of as Internet-aware OLE2 compound documents. An ActiveX-enabled Web browser such as Microsoft Internet Explorer can download a Word document from a Web browser and immediately know how to display that file through the use of ActiveX documents. This technology continues Microsoft's information-centric approach, which allows users to concentrate more on an application's content than on the application itself.

ActiveX Controls

ActiveX controls are extensions of the OLE controls mentioned earlier in this chapter. In fact, in many instances there is no difference at all between an ActiveX control and an OLE control. Microsoft simply reduced the number of interfaces that an ActiveX control is required to implement. Potentially, this allows ActiveX controls to be much smaller than their OLE counterparts. However, in many situations the control is required to implement the same interfaces.

ActiveX Scripting

ActiveX scripting extends the concept formerly known as OLE automation by adding scripting capabilities to Web pages, programs, and even server applications. ActiveX scripting allows scripts to be written in a variety of languages because it uses two components: a scripting host and a scripting engine. The *scripting host* is an application that is responsible for creating the scripting engine. The *scripting engine* in turn is responsible for processing and performing the script commands. Here are a few examples of scripting hosts:

- Microsoft Internet Explorer
- Future Microsoft server products
- Various Web authoring tools, including Microsoft FrontPage

Scripting engines are currently available for Visual Basic for Applications (VBA); Visual Basic, Scripting Edition (VBScript); and JavaScript.

ActiveX-Enabled Internet Protocols

Common Internet protocols such as FTP and HTTP can make use of ActiveX technologies such as monikers (which are equivalent to OLE monikers). These monikers can server as pointers to applications and can be interpreted by ActiveX server products in order to link applications to the Internet.

ActiveX APIs

An entire suite of ActiveX APIs is available through the ActiveX Software Development Kit (SDK). These APIs allow software developers to extend traditional Windows-based programs with Internet capabilities such as file transfer and Web server access.

ActiveX Server Framework

The ActiveX server framework is actually an entire class of ActiveX technologies that can be used to provide server-side functions. Some examples of components within the ActiveX server framework are the Internet security framework (which includes items like the CryptoAPI, code signing, and Microsoft Wallet), database access using dbWeb, and the Normandy commercial service provider platform.

Microsoft Windows Virtual Machine for Java

The final component of ActiveX to be discussed here is the Microsoft Windows Virtual Machine for Java. This Java Virtual Machine is designed both to run standard Java applets and to expose Java applets as COM objects for their use in ActiveX applications. The Windows Virtual Machine for Java also allows Java applets to coexist with ActiveX controls because, to the programmer, both are just objects composed of properties, methods, and events. The Microsoft WindowsVirtual Machine for Java is discussed in greater detail in Chapter 18, "The Microsoft Java Virtual Machine."

Java + ActiveX = A Unique Development Tool

What does this mean for Windows and Java programmers? First, it means that these two groups can now be one and the same. Just as there are Windows VB developers and Windows C++ developers, soon developers will be able to select Java as the development language for new projects. In short, Microsoft is elevating Java from its already lofty status as a Web programming tool to that of *the* Web programming tool and also a Windows programming tool. Actually, in the near future it may become inaccurate to refer to Visual J++ as simply a "Windows tool" because COM is gradually becoming a cross-platform object model.

Had Microsoft chosen to simply make Visual J++ a graphical layer over the standard Java tools, the Visual J++ programmer could use Java to do the following:

- Develop Java applets that can run within any Java-capable Web browser
- Develop Java applications that can run on any platform containing the Java Virtual Machine (JVM)
- Develop Java applications that make use of native methods to call existing code written in other languages such C or C++

As you probably know, these capabilities are included with virtually every Java tool on the market today. With the extra features that Microsoft has added to Visual J++, the Visual J++ programmer can take advantage of the previously listed features as well as the following four:

- Develop ActiveX controls in Java (in an upcoming release of Visual J++)
- Build powerful Web-based applications using a combination of Java applets and ActiveX controls that can be scripted together using any ActiveX scripting language such as JavaScript or VBScript
- Develop Windows 95 label-compliant applications in Java, making use of the growing libraries of Java applets and the already extensive library of ActiveX controls
- Develop Windows executables consisting of true binary code that can run at native machine speeds and make use of the elegance of the Java language

Despite many Java programmers' fears that Microsoft would release a proprietary tool that would somehow pollute the Java waters, these fears are unfounded. A key point that will be reinforced throughout this book is that Visual J++ is a great tool to use for both non-ActiveX and ActiveX Java development. After all, despite the explosive growth and potential of the World Wide Web, it will be quite some time before the majority of applications developed are designed to run only within a Web browser.

As mentioned earlier, the Visual J++ programmer can take advantage of both Java and ActiveX when building applications in the Java language. This is what separates Visual J++ from other Java compilers currently on the market. The remainder of this chapter provides an overview of both the Java and ActiveX technologies and prepares the reader for more detailed topics covered throughout the remainder of the book. The goal of this book is to leave the reader with two primary skills:

- The ability to develop Java applets for deployment as active Web content. These applets will take advantage of Java's unique capabilities and will run unmodified on all popular operating platforms and Web browsers that support Java applets.

- The ability to integrate Java and ActiveX objects in a seamless manner in order to provide end users with the most powerful application possible.

Microsoft's Component Object Model and ActiveX

Many developers may wonder: Exactly what is ActiveX and where did it come from? Although it was announced by Microsoft in 1996, believe it or not, it has actually been around for several years, and nearly all Windows developers have used some form of it at one time or another. Before diving into ActiveX, however, you need to take a look at the history of the component object model (COM) and object linking and embedding (OLE).

The Birth of ActiveX: An Overview of COM

COM provides the basis for nearly all of Microsoft's new products. It is, in theory, a platform-independent, vendor-independent, and language-independent model for developing applications using intercommunication among binary objects. These objects communicate with each other using a set of predefined interfaces that each object chooses to implement.

> **NOTE**
>
> An *interface* is a set of related functions that can be implemented by an object. If an object chooses to implement an interface, all of the functions specified by that interface must be implemented.

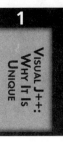

Each object is defined by which interfaces it is programmed to implement. (For instance, if an object wanted to be able to be saved to disk, it could implement what is known as a *structured storage interface.* This interface is defined by Microsoft to give objects the capability of saving their contents off to a file using a structured file format.)

Note that I used the words *in theory* in the first paragraph to describe the COM standard's cross-platform capabilities. Although a COM infrastructure could be written for any operating system, the fact remains that at the present time it is only available for the Windows family of operating systems. Microsoft has recently announced plans to assist Metrowerks in porting COM to the Apple Macintosh, and the company is currently working with Bristol and MainSoft to port COM to UNIX. However, at the current time, developers should realize that using COM objects in an application will limit the platforms on which the application will run. This possible drawback is discussed later in this chapter in the section "Advantages and Disadvantages: A Close Look at Java and ActiveX."

COM: Specification and Implementation

COM is both a specification and an actual implementation. The COM specification specifies a language-independent binary standard for implementing objects. Therefore, a COM object could be written using Delphi, Visual Basic, C++, or, you guessed it, Java. All that is required is that a specific set of functions be provided by your object so that the object's provided interfaces can be queried.

The COM implementation is provided in the form of a Windows dynamic link library (DLL). This DLL exports a small number of API functions that allow the programmer to instantiate a component object using a unique class identifier known as a *class ID*. These topics are discussed in greater detail in Chapter 16, "Java and the Component Object Model," in the section titled "Identifying COM Objects"; what is important to realize now is that COM, by itself, simply provides the "rules" by which objects can be instantiated and communicate among themselves. A group of COM objects can be combined to make an application. With the advent of distributed COM (DCOM), these objects can be located anywhere on a network. This functionality is currently provided as a core part of Windows NT 4.0.

Using COM Objects

Although COM is destined to be an integral part of future Microsoft operating systems, it has never been an active topic of discussion among most Windows developers. This is because COM, by itself, does not specify any applicable, real-world objects that can be used by developers to create applications. Instead, COM is the object *model* that developers can use to integrate any number of objects into a working application. These objects could come from a variety of sources. Here are some examples:

■ A COM object could be written in C++ and provide spell-checking if given a large string of text. A Visual Basic programmer could then instantiate the spell-check object, pass it a string of text, and reuse that functionality without having to write his own spell checker. Now imagine that the word-processing software installed on all machines in your office was made up of a set of COM objects, one of which was a spell-check object. One nice thing about this model is that shrink-wrapped applications can in turn become programmable objects themselves, therefore making it possible to reuse powerful functionality already existing in desktop software products.

- A geographical information system (GIS) residing on a remote server could be used to store mapping and statistical data for your enterprise. If that GIS were built using DCOM objects, an application could be written so that users across the network could reuse those DCOM objects to display custom maps within local applications.

- COM-enabled applications such as spreadsheets and word processors could allow COM objects to be inserted directly into a document. This would allow multiple applications to be integrated together so that the document would be the focus, rather than the application. This has long been a "Holy Grail" of personal computing, and COM allows those to be done today using OLE.

Although it is completely possible to write COM objects from scratch that are fully compliant with the binary specification, most Windows developers have never done this. Instead, programmers wanting the functionality provided by the COM object model have historically relied on OLE, a framework that lies on top of COM. OLE stands for *object linking and embedding* and is the parent of what is now known as ActiveX.

ActiveX: Activating the Internet

The wary reader may by this point be wondering where this discussion is headed. After all, on one hand I have discussed the Web and Java's use in building networked, platform-independent applications. On the other hand, I have discussed OLE and its capabilities for building object-based applications on the Windows platform. Now you'll learn how the two technologies can be brought together through the magic of COM and the Windows Virtual Machine for Java.

In 1995 all Microsoft projects were issued a well-publicized edict to Internet-enable every product if possible. The results of that request are beginning to be seen now as Microsoft is releasing a flood of products aimed at corporate and independent Web developers. (Visual J++ is one of the products leading this charge.) While OLE2 was introduced to address the needs of desktop software developers and system integrators, the previous section discussed many topics that could clearly be applied to networked applications. Like all other Microsoft products, OLE2 was thoroughly examined from an Internet point of view; the resulting set of transformed technologies has been named ActiveX. Many pieces of this technology are portions of OLE2 that have been completely reworked for maximum performance benefits for Web usage, while others are OLE2 pieces that have basically been renamed and remarketed as ActiveX technologies.

Like its parent, OLE2, ActiveX cannot be summed up as one simple technology. Instead, it must be broken into several parts, all of which can be thought of collectively as Microsoft's ActiveX architecture. The following discussion highlights the key ActiveX technologies and attempts to draw a parallel between them and their parent OLE2 technologies.

Comparing Java and COM

Visual J++ is the first product to combine two extremely popular technologies: Java and COM. This can be done because, in fact, the two are extremely similar on many levels. This section summarizes the capabilities of Java and COM and discusses why they fit together so well.

Java and COM: Some Differences

From the outset, it is obvious that in some ways Java and COM are very different technologies. Most notably, Java is a programming language, whereas COM is an object model that specifies how objects created in *any* programming language must interact. However, it is fair to say that Java *objects* and COM *objects* can be compared.

Java objects are not distributed. Although it is true that Java objects can be stored on remote servers, these objects must actually be uploaded to the client machine before they can be used to run an applet within a browser. DCOM objects, meanwhile, can be stored on a remote machine and then be called from that remote machine using a remote procedure call (RPC).

Java applets are designed with specific security restrictions, including the inability to call code on any server other than the originating server and the inability to make local operating-system calls. COM objects, on the other hand, have full access to the underlying operating system and rely on a completely different security model that revolves around a concept known as *code signing*.

Java classes are not required to implement *interfaces* (groups of related functions that can be thought of as a unit). The Java programmer can choose to implement zero or more interfaces for each Java class. COM objects are required to implement at least one interface: IUnknown. This interface is then used to determine specific information about the object and to acquire new interfaces if necessary.

Java also uses a technique known as *garbage collection* for automatic memory management. When the system knows that an object is not going to be used any longer, the Java runtime system automatically frees that object from memory. Memory management with COM also uses runtime tracking of objects to free them from memory when they are no longer used. Instead of garbage collection, however, COM tracks the *reference count*, or the number of instances that are using an object. When the reference count drops to zero, that object is freed from memory.

Java and COM: Surprising Similarities

Despite the differences mentioned in the previous section, the number of similarities between Java and COM is very interesting (and an excellent sign that both technologies benefit from a good design!). This is probably not surprising if one stops to really think about what both Java and COM were designed to solve. They both were intended to be

- Platform independent
- Object oriented
- Multithreaded
- Dynamic

Java and COM both require a foundation underneath them to support their platform-independent claims. Java's foundation is known as the Java Virtual Machine, while COM requires an implementation of the component object model for each specific platform. Once this foundation is in place, both systems rely on objects that are created on-the-fly and are dynamically linked together at runtime.

Even the way that the objects are defined is similar in some respects. Java uses a `.class` file format that is well documented. The `.class` file defines the contents of the internal class and any interfaces it implements. COM uses a `.tlb` (type library) file to define the contents of the COM object and any interfaces it implements. A key factor in the operation of the Windows Virtual Machine is its capability to create type libraries from Java classes and likewise create Java classes from COM object's type libraries.

As you may have noticed by now, both rely heavily on the use of interfaces. Interfaces allow objects to implement a related set of functions for an object. The intent of these interfaces is generally documented; thus the interface serves as a sort of contract between one object (the implementor of the interface) and another (the user of the interface). Java and COM both use classes (a concept familiar to object-oriented programmers) to group together related functions and data.

One feature of many systems and languages is *exception handling*, which allows the developer to trap errors and handle them accordingly so that the program will not simply crash. Java handles exceptions through the use of the `Throwable` interface. COM handles exceptions through the use of the `IErrorInfo` interface.

Advantages and Disadvantages: A Close Look at Java and ActiveX

Because of the excitement surrounding Java since its introduction in 1995, the software-development community has enthusiastically supported Java and pushed it to the forefront of Web development. However, like all new technologies, it has some advantages as well as

disadvantages. ActiveX is no different than Java in this respect. These strengths and weaknesses are discussed here so that you, the reader, are well aware that no technology by itself can solve every problem out there. As with all complicated undertakings, a variety of issues need to be weighed before decisions are made.

Java Is Platform Independent

Java's greatest advantage may be that it is the most powerful, ubiquitous programming language that allows developers to create *platform-independent* code. Unlike most other cross-platform tools, the Java developer actually has to make an effort to *add* platform-dependent code to the application at hand. Java programmers can thank the availability of the Java Virtual Machine for this feature. This is because all the platform-specific code is contained in the Java Virtual Machine distribution for a particular platform. This means that all the platform-specific work has already been done for you by the creator of the virtual machine. The Java programmer can simply concentrate on programming in Java.

> **NOTE**
>
> Although it is true that Java is not truly platform-independent without the availability of a Java Virtual Machine, the fact is that the JVM is available now (or will be soon) on nearly every popular operating system in widespread use today.

Java Is Object Oriented

Java is also *object oriented*. This is truly an advantage because of the large effort made over the last few years to train programmers to think in terms of objects and design systems. Object-oriented programming has repeatedly been demonstrated to improve productivity through a systematic approach to object design and analysis.

Java's object-oriented structure and platform independence are also enabling it to be quickly retrofitted to common object request brokers (ORBs) for use in building distributed applications. In fact, the Netscape Navigator 4.0 Web browser will include ORB client software by Visigenix for use in building distributed, object-based applications using the Netscape Open Network Environment (ONE) platform.

Although Java was introduced by Sun Microsystems, it remains largely a *vendor-neutral* architecture. Sun Microsystems originally developed the JVM for Sun Solaris, Apple Macintosh, and Windows 95/NT, but JVMs have now been developed by many other corporations including IBM, Microsoft, and Netscape. Developers deciding to develop applications using Java can choose from a broad range of tools from a variety of vendors and are not tied exclusively to Sun Microsystems's line of products.

The Importance of Broad Support

Java also has the advantage of widespread *acceptance* and near *ubiquity*. It is rapidly becoming the programming language of choice for Web solutions and is being used for actual product development now for things like Web server software, collaboration systems, and desktop applications. Business analysts often discuss the topics of market share and mind share. Market share is, of course, the universal indicator used to judge the success or failure of a product; mind share is a much more difficult and subjective indicator to measure. For developers trying to decide whether to implement a pure Java solution or an ActiveX solution, the decision becomes extremely difficult because of these two measuring sticks. In terms of product support and existing lines of code, ActiveX is the market share leader because it effectively existed as OLE for several years already. However, developers who try to keep a finger on the pulse of the computing community realize that Java has captured an ever-increasing mind share of the programming audience. For Sun Microsystems, the maturation of Java and the company's role in it will determine whether that mind share can be converted into market share at a future time for Sun's software and hardware products.

ActiveX Has a Large Developer Base

A lack of existing code and experienced programmers are drawbacks in some ways to implementing standard Java applications. Although advanced class libraries, thousands of existing controls, and several excellent tools exist for the ActiveX developer, the Java programmer is often forced into the "roll-your-own" mode of development. Naturally, it is through this trial by fire that beginning Java developers turn into expert Java developers, but in some situations the business case (or return on investment) for new Java development may be hard to sell when compared to existing partial solutions that already exist in the form of ActiveX. For instance, several ActiveX controls currently exist that allow developers to create impressive charts and graphs that appear to the user as full-featured mini-applications. These controls are relatively inexpensive ($99–$299), and many employ internal object models for ease of development. To date, there is no Java applet available that approaches the sophistication of these controls, and because of Java applets' security restrictions, some features of these applets may never be implemented to compete directly with their ActiveX counterparts.

The huge interest in Java and its related technologies has also made it increasingly difficult for businesses to find truly qualified programmers. It is common to hear HTML designers who haven't done more than include an applet within a Web page refer to themselves as Java programmers. The truly seasoned Java developer, however, can use the Web to his or her advantage by publishing work samples on the Web for all to see. A well-placed URL on a résumé can go a long way toward quieting a potential employer's anxiety when he examines your résumé.

Security Limitations

Perhaps Java's biggest drawbacks come in the area where it is the most visible: the Web browser client. Due to the possibility of rogue applets damaging a user's system, Java's designers built it around a *strict security model* that treats applets extremely carefully within most Web browsers. This security model prevents applets from

- Accessing the local hard drive
- Communicating with any server other than the originating server
- Making any calls to the local operating system

Java applets also have *no persistence.* Because Java is object oriented and each class can derive from another class and implement several interfaces (more on this in Chapter 3, "Object-Oriented Programming with Java"), when an applet is uploaded to a Web browser, it may require the uploading of 1, 2, or maybe 20 other class files with it. Because these applets are not persistent, the next time the user visits that Web site, this same group of applets will need to be reloaded all over again. In an intranet setting where users will continually upload the same Java applets over and over, it is possible that the users could install local versions of these applets, but Java provides no "self-installation" capabilities.

Java Is an Interpreted Language

One final weakness of Java that should be pointed out is that it is an *interpreted* language and suffers from poor performance without the existence of a *just-in-time compiler.* Just-in-time (JIT) compilers actually compile Java code into native machine code on-the-fly, after the applets have been downloaded, so that the applets can have improved performance. This feature is included in the Netscape Navigator 3.0 and Microsoft Internet Explorer 3.0 browsers. Even with the existence of a JIT compiler, Java code still runs slower than comparable C code, and this is an important point to be considered. A general rule of thumb is that whenever a task is I/O-bound (such as user-interface operations), the slower language probably will not make a difference. However, in tasks that are CPU-bound (such as mathematical operations), the interpreted language will force your code to take a performance hit.

Native ActiveX controls are *natively compiled, dynamically linked* code modules that run without the aid of an interpreter. This allows them to boast a performance advantage over comparable Java applets. Although it is easy for us as developers to say that machines today are fast enough so that performance differences don't matter much, we should keep in mind that we are often writing for the lowest common denominator. I have been in many situations when software ran just fine on my souped-up development machine only to suddenly crawl on a user's less-capable box.

Object Persistence

ActiveX controls also are, for better or worse, *persistent* on clients' local systems after being downloaded the first time. At the current time, Microsoft Internet Explorer does not automatically remove these controls when the browser exits. Instead, these controls reside indefinitely until the user deletes them. Microsoft has stated that control removal will be an option in later versions of Internet Explorer.

Some ActiveX technologies such as ActiveX controls also benefit from the *large existing code base.* Well over 1,000 ActiveX controls currently exist that will run within an Internet Explorer or Netscape Navigator page. This is a double-edged sword, however, because the Windows platform is the only platform on which these controls can be used. *Platform dependence* is without a doubt the primary drawback to implementing ActiveX Web sites. Until COM becomes available for other popular operating systems such as Macintosh and UNIX, ActiveX may remain primarily an intranet development technology. This is because within an intranet, Web designers are usually able to pinpoint exactly which machines will be using a Web-based application and can plan their design accordingly.

Language Independence

ActiveX controls have a truly distinct advantage: *language independence.* These controls can be built using a variety of popular products including Visual Basic 5.0, Visual C++, Delphi, and future versions of Visual J++. Another benefit is that they are not simply a Web-only solution. As mentioned earlier, ActiveX controls are currently being used by Delphi, Visual Basic, C++, and even COBOL developers worldwide. The capability to build controls in any language alone ensures that ActiveX will continue to grow in the future regardless of the success of Java and other technologies.

The *lack of browser support* could possibly slow the adoption of ActiveX for Web-based development. Because Netscape Navigator is the market leader (remember the discussion on market share earlier?), and because Netscape has chosen not to implement ActiveX support within its browser, users are being forced to decide between the two market leaders: Microsoft and Netscape. Although users can download an ActiveX Netscape plug-in from NCompass Labs that will allow Netscape to use ActiveX controls, very few users (relative to the total number) have chosen to do so. Once again, the topic of mind share versus market share is brought up! If the Microsoft Internet Explorer suddenly experienced a dramatic increase in mind share among power users, it could only help ActiveX and its related technologies. One can only hope that the end user will be the eventual winner of the browser wars, and that the best technologies will survive in the long run.

Summary

Visual J++ is an extremely powerful development tool that can be used for a wide variety of undertakings. Java applets and applications can be created using this product, making it a valuable resource for the World Wide Web programmer who decides to program using the Windows platform. In addition to these capabilities, Visual J++ is the first tool to allow Java and the component object model (COM) to be combined in the application-development process. The Windows Virtual Machine for Java allows Java classes to be treated as COM objects. Because of this, Java classes can be used for interactive Web content as well as for building powerful Windows-based applications.

Visual J++ will also allow the reverse process to take place. In other words, COM objects can be used side by side with Java objects to produce the most powerful (and flexible) application possible. Capabilities within Microsoft's Internet Explorer browser allow this functionality to be carried over to the Web as well. COM objects that act as plug-and-play programming tools are known as ActiveX controls. These controls are distant descendants of the popular VBX controls introduced in Visual Basic 3.0 and direct descendants of OLE controls. ActiveX controls are programming objects that expose a set of properties, methods, and events that can be used by the programmer to construct applications from others' code. Because COM is a language-independent standard, ActiveX-enabled Java classes can now be used in common Windows programming environments such as Visual J++, Visual C++, Delphi, PowerBuilder, Visual Basic, Access, and many others. ActiveX-aware applications such as the Microsoft Office suite (Word, Access, Excel, and PowerPoint) can also make use of ActiveX controls for the creation of powerful, custom-built applications.

In short, Visual J++ satisfies the needs of Web developers and also introduces Java to a much broader programming audience. Using this tool, Java may soon be the Windows programming language of choice as well as the unquestioned programming language of choice for the World Wide Web.

This chapter included a discussion of the strengths and weaknesses of the Java and ActiveX technologies. Issues such as performance, platform independence, and vendor support will apparently continue to be key factors in designers' decisions despite the early promise of the World Wide Web. The purpose of the remainder of this book will be to educate you, the reader, on the capabilities of the Visual J++ tool in hopes that you can then use this newfound knowledge to make good decisions.

The following chapter introduces the Java runtime environment. This environment is comprised of several interrelated parts, including a Web server, a Web client, the Java Virtual Machine, and additional components. The chapter is a must-read for any programmer new to the World Wide Web and Java in particular.

The Visual J++ Development Environment

by Bryan Morgan

IN THIS CHAPTER

CHAPTER 2

The Visual J++ development environment is unique among Java tools because it is also used by several other Microsoft development tools. In appearance, it is the same integrated development environment (IDE) used by Microsoft's Visual C++, FORTRAN PowerStation, Test, and Development Network software packages. This IDE—named the Microsoft Developer Studio—is an extremely popular, award-winning environment and should be a hit in the Java world. Because the look and feel of the IDE is common to an entire suite of Microsoft development tools, thousands of developers can use Visual J++ with little or no additional learning above the standard Java learning curve.

This chapter examines the capabilities and options of the Developer Studio and pays special attention to the features only used by Visual J++.

Because Microsoft has chosen to include Visual J++ in the Developer Studio family, J++ developers can be certain that this tool will not be ignored or subject to haphazard IDE changes. This positioning is also a good indication that Microsoft perceives this tool to be extremely important. For years, Windows programmers have relied on two general-purpose Microsoft tools: Visual Basic and Visual C++. Visual J++ allows Microsoft to enter the world of cross-platform development and to continue to use the technology it has worked on for more than five years (namely, ActiveX).

The first section in this chapter introduces the Developer Studio and explains the general features of the IDE. The remainder of the chapter focuses on the many capabilities and options of Visual J++.

The Microsoft Developer Studio

After Visual J++ has been installed, run the Developer Studio tool to enter Visual J++. The opening screen shows the Developer Studio tools and highlights the toolkits currently installed on your machine. Figure 2.1 shows the Microsoft Developer Studio with no project loaded.

Although Visual J++ projects are covered in detail in Chapter 9, "Managing Visual J++ Projects," I'm explaining them briefly here because the word *project* is used throughout this chapter.

What Is a Project?

Nearly all graphical user interface (GUI) development tools today group related files together within units known as *projects*. In contrast, earlier C++ programming projects contained C++ source code files only; a file (known as a *makefile*) held the compiler instructions to compile and link the individual C++ files. In a contemporary GUI environment, however, files above and beyond the source code files are integrated into the development project. These files include elements such as bitmaps, dynamic link libraries (DLLs), and controls (for example, ActiveX controls). Tools such as Visual C++, Visual Basic, and Delphi group the disparate files into a *project file*. The project file may also contain overall project information such as the application name, compiler flags to be used, and debugger settings.

FIGURE 2.1.

The Developer Studio IDE.

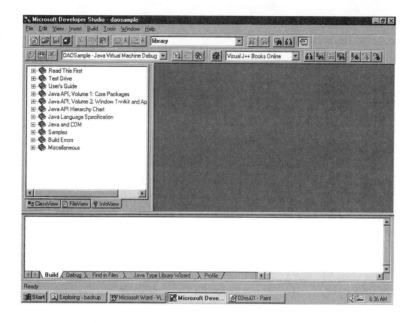

Visual J++ allows you to keep all the files used to build a program in a single project. In fact, if you try to create a simple class and compile it, Visual J++ will inform you that a project workspace is *required* before a class can be compiled. In other words, all Java applets or applications created with Visual J++ must be contained in a Visual J++ project workspace.

Exploring the IDE Interface

In order to fully explore the IDE interface, you need to create a new project. The first step is to select File|New…|Project Workspace…. Figure 2.2 shows the New Project Workspace dialog box.

FIGURE 2.2.

The New Project Workspace dialog box.

Type in a project name and select Java Virtual Machine in the Platform box. A new subdirectory will be created in the location you specify in the Location edit box, and your project workspace files will be created within this subdirectory. Once a project workspace has been created and opened, its files will appear in the project workspace window. The Developer Studio IDE comprises three primary windows:

- Project Workspace window
- Application window
- Output window

You can resize the windows to create an environment that is comfortable for you. These three windows have a Docking View option that causes the window to be *docked,* or frozen, in place. If the Docking View option is unselected, the window is free to be moved. Click the right mouse button within any main window to display a pop-up menu from which you can select the Docking View option.

The Project Workspace Window

The Project Workspace window is used to present project information as well as information about Visual J++ in general. Figure 2.3 shows the Animator example and how it appears in the ClassView frame of the Project Workspace window.

FIGURE 2.3.

The Project Workspace window.

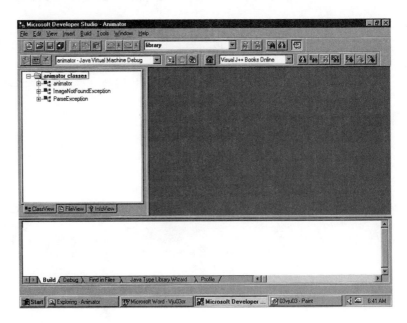

Notice the three tabs at the bottom of the window: ClassView, FileView, and InfoView. Clicking on any tab will display a frame containing more information about the current project.

The ClassView Frame

The ClassView frame displays all of the classes used in this project and illustrates relationships between classes and interfaces in that project. This view is very useful because it does not force you to remember which class is in which file. In addition, all members of a class (variables and methods) are displayed underneath the class name. A small icon next to the class gives some information about the class, such as public, private, or static. For now, don't worry about what these keywords mean. They are explained in Chapters 3, "Object-Oriented Programming with Java," and 5, "Elements of the Java Language."

ClassView can be used to perform the following operations:

- Add methods to the selected class
- Add variables to the selected class
- Add a new class to the project
- Set a breakpoint on a method

To add a method to a class, right-click over a class, select the Add Method... option, and complete the Add Method dialog box, shown in Figure 2.4.

FIGURE 2.4.
The Add Method dialog box.

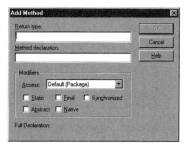

To add a variable to a class, right-click over a class, select the Add Variable... option, and complete the Add Variable dialog box, shown in Figure 2.5.

FIGURE 2.5.
The Add Variable dialog box.

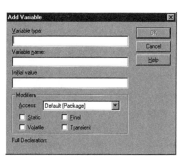

To add a new class to a project, right-click over the Projectname-classes parent node on the class tree and select the Create New Class... option. (Another way to add a class is to right-click over an individual class file.) Complete the information in the Create New Class dialog box, shown in Figure 2.6. A new class (with its associated Java file) will be created in the project directory.

FIGURE 2.6.

The Create New Class dialog box.

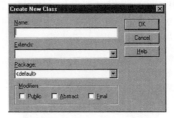

To set a breakpoint on a specific method in a class, right-click over the method name in the ClassView and select the Set Breakpoint option. A breakpoint will then be set at the method definition in the application frame.

The FileView Frame

The purpose of the FileView frame is to show relationships among files in the current project (just as the ClassView frame illustrated relationships among Java classes and interfaces in the project). Figure 2.7 shows the Animator sample applet project loaded in the FileView frame.

FIGURE 2.7.

The FileView frame.

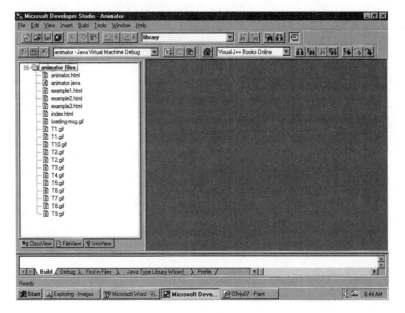

Note that the relationships shown in FileView are not physical relationships. That is, the trees presented in FileView do not correspond to directory trees on your hard disk. Instead, the relationship tree is used to demonstrate the relationships among the contents of the individual files.

Each file in Visual J++ has a corresponding property sheet. You can view the properties sheet by selecting the file in the FileView pane and doing any of the following:

- Press Alt+Enter
- Right-click to display a pop-up menu and select the Properties option
- Choose Properties from the Edit menu

Figure 2.8 shows the properties sheet for the `Animator.java` file in the Animator sample project.

2

THE VISUAL J++
DEVELOPMENT
ENVIRONMENT

FIGURE 2.8.

A project file's properties sheet.

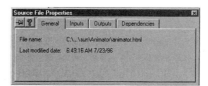

The General tab of the Source File Properties sheet shows the filename and the date it was last modified. The Inputs and Outputs tabs show the relative pathnames of the input and output files of the project, as well as the tool that will be used to compile this file. The Dependencies tab shows the list of files that this file is dependent on, as well as the tool that will be used to compile this file.

You can also set some project-level options in the FileView frame. Right-click over the project name (the root node of the file view tree) and select the Settings... option from the pop-up box. The Project Settings dialog box (see Figure 2.9) allows you to set CLASSPATH directories, debugging information, and compiler switches.

FIGURE 2.9.

Setting project properties within FileView.

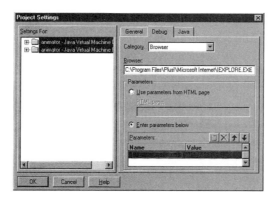

You can also set these options by selecting main menu choices. (See Chapter 9 for details.)

The InfoView Frame

The InfoView frame contains information about the Visual J++ tool, including all online books, class library documentation, and Java language documentation, as well as readme and release notes. Although putting this information on the main screen right next to a project's object and file information may seem a bit odd, within a matter of minutes you probably won't be able to imagine working without it.

> **NOTE**
>
> Listing all the information about Visual J++ in one place makes the Developer Studio environment an excellent tool for the person who spends hours a day writing code.

The 1.0 release of Visual J++ lists the following online documentation in InfoView:

- Release Notes
- Test Drive (An Introduction To Visual J++)
- The Visual J++ User's Guide
- Java API, Volume 1: Core Packages
- Java API, Volume 2: Window Toolkit and Applets
- Java API Hierarchy Chart
- Java Language Specification
- Java and COM
- Visual J++ Programming Samples
- Build Errors Documentation
- Miscellaneous

The Visual J++ programming samples include all the standard Java programming samples provided in the Java Developer's Kit (JDK) as well as samples from Microsoft written in Java that use ActiveX controls.

Viewing Online Documentation

All Microsoft Developer Studio–aware products feature online documentation in the form of *online books*. Topics within these books are displayed in a list view within the InfoView frame of the Project Workspace window. To view any of the topics, double-click on that topic in the Project Workspace window. The topic will then be displayed within the Application window (see Figure 2.10).

FIGURE 2.10.
A Books Online topic.

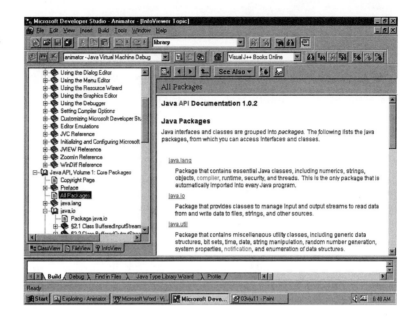

Several interesting options are available via the right-button pop-up menu. The Search option allows you to search through all topics for keywords or to query topics for information. Selecting the Options item displays an Options dialog box from which you can completely configure the display and operation of the Help system. Like the text editor, the text within the Help window can be highlighted, depending on the context, to provide the reader with more information. The Docking View option can be turned on or off to display the topic in one of two modes. If Docking View is turned on (denoted by a check mark), the window containing the topic will "pop out" of the Application window and appear as a modeless window that can be minimized, maximized, or closed. If the window containing the topic is minimized, it will appear to be "docked" at the bottom of the Developer Studio environment.

The Application Window

The contents of the Application window depend on the context in which you are working. If you double-click on a class (or any of its members) in the ClassView frame, that class will be opened in the Application window. If you select a topic from the Online Books list in the InfoView frame, that topic will also be displayed in the Application window. Resource file contents are also displayed in this window when a resource file is being edited (this is discussed later in this chapter).

Basically, the Application window is used for the real work you do on a project. The Project Workspace window is used by you and Visual J++ to provide tools for managing your project. The Output window at the bottom of the screen is used by Visual J++ to display feedback to you as it is doing its work (compiling, debugging, searching, and so on).

The next two sections discuss the options available in the Application window for editing code and viewing the online book topics.

Editing Code Within the Application Window

Visual J++ features a powerful text editor that is completely configurable by the user. The various capabilities of this editor are discussed here; the configuration options are explained later in the chapter.

The Visual J++ editor uses syntax-aware color highlighting to highlight Java keywords, operators, and comments. This feature means that you can, for example, configure the editor to display all Java keywords in red, all comments in blue, and everything else in purple—and that rainbow is just the foreground colors! You can also change background colors. (You should use some restraint, though, to avoid going blind after staring at brilliant colors while hacking code in the wee hours of the morning.)

Highlighting keywords and comments helps you find key attributes within the Java code. The unique aspect of Visual J++ is that you use highlighting to customize virtually every bit of text in the entire environment—Java source files, HTML source files, debugging output, call stacks, watch windows, and so forth.

Visual J++ also supports recording and playing back a series of keystrokes. In addition to reducing the risk of repetitive stress injuries, record and playback is useful when you need to repeat a set of keyboard operations within a class. Some restrictions apply to keystroke recording:

- Keystrokes can be played back only into the editor view that was current when recording began.
- All mouse-driven selections are disabled while keystroke recording is taking place.

To begin recording a series of keystrokes, select Tools | Record Keystrokes or press Ctrl+Shift+R. A small dialog box displays the standard Pause and Stop buttons. Perform the desired keystrokes and then click the Stop button. To play back your keystrokes, position the cursor at the desired location and select Tools | Playback Recording or press Ctrl+Shift+P.

Right-clicking within the text editor will display a pop-up menu. In addition to the normal cut, copy, and paste functionality, this menu provides some other useful operations. Use the Insert/Remove Breakpoint selection to add or remove a breakpoint at the current cursor location. Use the Enable/Disable Breakpoint to enable or disable a breakpoint at the current cursor location.

Selecting Insert File into Project displays a File Select dialog box. You can select a file from this dialog box to add it to the current project. One really cool feature is the Open menu option, which you can enable by selecting an `import` *filename* statement in a Java source file. The following code snippet shows some `import` statements:

```
import java.io.InputStream;
import java.awt.*;
import java.awt.image.ImageProducer;
```

```
import java.applet.Applet;
import java.applet.AudioClip;
```

Selecting any one of these statements and then selecting the Open menu option will open that file in the IDE. Cool, don't you think?

Selecting the Properties item from the pop-up menu displays the dialog box shown in Figure 2.11.

FIGURE 2.11.

The Source Window Properties dialog box.

Changing the Language selection will affect the color highlighting chosen for the text display of this file. Note that the tab size and indent size can be modified from this dialog box.

Using Bookmarks in Source Files

You can use bookmarks to mark a position within a file; then, after scrolling through that file, you can return directly to the bookmark. This feature greatly reduces the amount of time you spend searching for text when you need to move back and forth in a file. You can remove a bookmark when it is no longer needed.

Visual J++ supports two types of bookmarks. *Named bookmarks* are given a name by the user and persist between editing sessions. *Unnamed bookmarks* are temporary bookmarks that are removed as soon as the source file is closed.

Named Bookmarks

To create a named bookmark, select the Bookmark option from the Edit menu; then enter the name of the bookmark into the Bookmarks dialog box. Because named bookmarks store a bookmark's name as well as the cursor's current row and column location, even if characters or entire lines of code are deleted, the bookmark will always be set to the exact location where the cursor is at the time of the bookmark's creation.

To delete a named bookmark, open the Bookmarks dialog box (select Edit|Bookmark...), select the desired bookmark or bookmarks, and press the Delete button. To jump to a bookmark, click the Go To button in this dialog box.

Unnamed Bookmarks

Unnamed bookmarks are temporary bookmarks that disappear once a source file is closed. Unlike named bookmarks, however, they provide visual notification (a cyan-colored square, by default) that a bookmark exists at the current line. To create an unnamed bookmark, select the

Bookmark toggle button from the Edit toolbar. (For more information on adding and removing toolbars such as the Edit toolbar, see the section titled "Using and Configuring the Visual J++ Toolbars" later in this chapter.) When this button is clicked, a small cyan square should appear in the current line's left margin.

To remove an unnamed bookmark, click the Bookmark toggle button again. Other buttons in the Edit toolbar allow the developer to jump to the next or previous bookmark as well as clear all bookmarks within the current file.

The Output Window

The Output window, by default, appears at the bottom of the Developer Studio environment. (Because the Output window is a dockable window, you can drag it to another portion of the screen.) The Output window, like the Project Workspace window, contains a number of tabbed frames that correspond to the tools you can use to display output. These tabs are Build, Debug, Find in Files, Java Type Library Wizard, Profile, and Source Control (if it is being used). For example, when a project is being compiled, compiler messages are forwarded to the Build frame.

Messages in these frames are not simply "dumb" text messages. When an error triggers a compiler message, for example, double-clicking on that compiler message will immediately highlight the line in the source code that caused the error. Features like this combined with the lightning-fast speed of the Visual J++ compiler make it an ideal tool for rapid application development (RAD). With products like Visual J++ and the upcoming Symantec Visual Café setting a new standard for visual development, Java programmers don't have to worry about using clunky, command-line tools any longer.

> **NOTE**
>
> Although C++ tool vendors have worked for years to make their tools easier to use and quicker to compile, these vendors have never really been able to turn the corner and compete head-to-head with true RAD tools such as Visual Basic and Delphi.

When you right-click in any of the Output windows, a pop-up menu displays several options:

- Copy the current selection to the Clipboard.
- Clear the output of the current Output frame.
- Go To Error/Tag moves the cursor to the line containing the current error.
- Docking View enables or disables this window's docking behavior.
- Hide closes the output window; it will reappear the next time any tool tries to output to it.

If you select the Hide option or close a dockable window and are unable to figure out how to bring the window back, don't worry. The View main menu contains a list of all the dockable windows under Visual J++, including Project Workspace, InfoViewer Topic, Output, Watch, Variables, Registers, Memory, Call Stack, and Disassembly. If the window is currently showing, selecting its View menu option will have no effect; however, if the window has been closed, selecting its View menu option will display it in its last known state.

The Watch, Variables, Registers, Memory, Call Stack, and Disassembly windows have not been mentioned in this chapter. Because these options relate to viewing Java runtime information, they are examined in detail in Chapter 10, "The Visual J++ Compiler," Chapter 12, "Debugging with the Visual J++ Debugger," and throughout the remainder of the book.

The Full Screen View

You'll find another really cool Visual J++ feature by selecting the Full Screen option from the View menu. This option blows up the current source code text to fill the entire screen. That's *entire* as in no menus, no window title bar, no system menu, and so on. Click the small button at the top of the screen to return the IDE to its normal mode. Using the Full Screen option enables you to view a few more lines of code than normal and removes all other visual distractions from the screen.

This concludes the description of the three primary windows most often visible in Visual J++. The following section examines the different Visual J++ menus and toolbars; the chapter concludes with a look at customizing the IDE.

Using and Configuring the Visual J++ Toolbars

The Visual J++ toolbars duplicate functionality that can be found in main menu (or submenu) selections. Experience has shown that many users prefer visual toolbars to menus. Toolbars have become even easier to use since the introduction of ToolTips. To see a ToolTip in action, hold your mouse over a toolbar button. A little rectangle should appear within a second or so that displays text describing the purpose of that button. Like the main windows in the Developer Studio environment, toolbars are dockable, which means that you can drag them to different parts of the screen. This feature allows you to completely customize the look of the environment without losing any functionality.

You will find the most commonly used features in Visual J++ on a variety of toolbars. In fact, as you will see shortly, you can not only assign every single menu selection in Visual J++ to a toolbar of your choice but also *create* new toolbars. (When I said Visual J++ was really, really configurable, I meant it!)

Table 2.1 lists the toolbars (and the corresponding functionality) that are available to the Visual J++ user.

Table 2.1. Visual J++ toolbars and their functionality.

Toolbar	Functionality
Standard	Performs the most common file operations: File New, File Save, Save Project, Cut/Copy/Paste, Undo/Redo, and Search.
Project	Contains the most commonly used project-specific options: Compile, Build, Set Breakpoint, Debug Go, and Default Project Settings.
Resource	Used in the creation and viewing of resource information. Examples of resources that can be created from this toolbar are dialog, menu, cursor, icon, bitmap, accelerator, string, and version resources.
Edit	Contains options that are most useful when editing source files: the ability to create new windows containing the same source file, the ability to tile a window within itself so that different parts of a file can be viewed simultaneously within one window (cool if you've got a big monitor), Find in Files, and bookmarks. Find in Files is a feature that allows a developer to search through one or more files for a keyword. This feature is similar to the grep command familiar to many programmers.
Debug	Contains the commonly used debugger commands: Start debugging, Stop debugging, Step into/over/out/to, and options to show/hide the Watch, Variables, Registers, Memory, Call Stack, and Disassembly windows.
Browse	Provides commonly used options for viewing symbol definitions and references. Included in these options are selections to display the current/next/previous symbol definition and reference as well as options to view the call and callers graph of a selected method.
InfoViewer	Allows the user to quickly switch among installed documentation and includes Search and Bookmark options when viewing online documentation.
InfoViewer Contents	Allows the user to filter the contents that are displayed in the InfoView window. Options include a Define Subset button and a drop-down list that shows the current information that may be displayed in InfoView.

Displaying and Hiding Toolbars

All toolbars can be displayed and hidden using functionality built into the Developer Studio IDE. You can access the Toolbars dialog box, shown in Figure 2.12, by selecting the Toolbars option from the View menu.

Figure 2.12.

The Toolbars dialog box.

As you can see, this dialog box lists all the toolbars mentioned in Table 2.1. Selecting a check box will cause that toolbar to be displayed in an undocked state. To dock the toolbar, simply drag its frame to the desired location. Here are two ways to hide a toolbar:

- Double-click the frame of a docked toolbar to put it in an undocked state. Then click the Close button in the window's top-right corner.
- Select View | Toolbars… and hide the toolbar by unselecting its check box in the Toolbars dialog box.

Note the two selection boxes at the bottom of the dialog box in Figure 2.12. These two selection boxes are used to turn ToolTips off or to display the ToolTip with/without the shortcut. Displaying the ToolTip with the shortcut gives you some idea of which shortcut key can perform the same function.

Creating and Modifying Toolbars

In addition to being able to turn toolbars on and off, you also have complete control over the contents of toolbars. You can also build and name custom toolbars from the Toolbars dialog box in Figure 2.12.

To modify an existing toolbar, select the Customize… button. The Customize dialog box contains a list of all the main menu selections along with buttons that are equivalent to the individual menu options (see Figure 2.13).

To modify a toolbar, grab any of the buttons displayed in the dialog box and drag it onto the toolbar you want to modify. This step makes the button part of that toolbar until you remove the button or reset the toolbar to its default settings. To remove a button from a toolbar, simply grab it, drag it off, and release it anywhere but over another toolbar. To reset a toolbar to its default settings, select the Reset button in the Toolbars dialog box.

FIGURE 2.13.

The Customize dialog box.

After using Visual J++ for a while, you'll recognize the top 10 or top 20 commands you use over and over. You can save yourself time and energy by building your own toolbar and keeping it displayed (if the extra screen space required won't interfere with your work environment). Select the View|Toolbars... menu option to display the Toolbars dialog box. Click the New... button. Enter the name of your toolbar in the next dialog box. A small, empty toolbar should appear on your screen. If the dialog box is in front of the new toolbar, move it over to the side or, better yet, dock it underneath your current toolbars.

Now that you have created an empty toolbar, review the menu selections in the Toolbar dialog box and drag the ones you want onto your new toolbar.

Figure 2.14 shows a toolbar named The Visual J++ Unleashed Top Ten that contains 10 of my favorite commands.

FIGURE 2.14.

A custom toolbar.

Configuring the Visual J++ Menus

You can also configure the Visual J++ main menus, although not to the degree of detail that you can achieve with customized toolbars. With the menus, you can

- Change the shortcut keys used to activate a menu selection
- Customize the Tools menu by adding your own tools to it

The shortcut keys can be modified by selecting Tools|Customize.... The Customize dialog box (refer to Figure 2.13) will appear. To modify shortcut keys for a variety of editors, select the Keyboard tab. Clicking on the different commands will display their current shortcut keystrokes at the bottom of the dialog box. To modify any of these shortcuts, enter your own shortcut keystroke in the Press new shortcut key text field.

To add your own tools to the bottom of the Tools menu, select the Tools tab in the Customize dialog box. The current contents of the menu will be displayed, as well as pushbuttons for adding, relocating, and removing tools from the menu. Any tool that was added using this method will appear above the Java Resource Wizard... menu option.

Customizing the Other IDE Options

As you probably realize by now, the Visual J++ environment is completely customizable. In addition to modifying toolbars and menus and relocating dockable windows, you can customize many other items, including

- The default editor to emulate (Developer Studio, Epsilon, or Brief)
- The display of the status bar (on or off)
- Compiler options
- File locations (both input and output)
- Default fonts used by Developer Studio
- Text Editor appearance and functionality
- Java and HTML syntax coloring

The rest of this chapter discusses some of these customization options. The compiler options and file location paths are examined in detail in Chapter 10.

You can use the Options dialog box to modify most of the IDE options. (Select Options from the Tools menu.) The Options dialog box uses tabbed controls to essentially display the equivalent of six different dialog boxes; the tabs—except for Debug and Directories, which are saved for later chapters on the debugger and compiler (Chapter 10 and Chapter 12)—are explained in the following subsections.

The Editor Options Page

The Editor tab (Figure 2.15) contains several settings that customize the appearance of the Text Editor window.

FIGURE 2.15.

The Editor Options page.

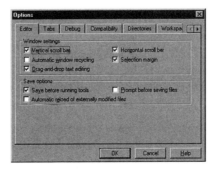

Options within this page allow you to toggle the vertical and horizontal scrollbars, drag and drop, and the use of automatic window recycling. Convenient options at the bottom of the page force the saving of files and the automatic reload of externally modified files. The last feature is particularly useful when using source-code control software because it forces the automatic reloading of all externally modified files. Often, a file may be updated that was modified by another user, but your project may not be aware that that file was modified because it wasn't done by you.

The Tabs Options Page

The Tabs Options page (see Figure 2.16) is where you can modify tab and indent sizes.

Note the Smart Indent Option. Selecting this option forces the IDE to indent based on the program language element.

FIGURE 2.16.

The Tabs Options page.

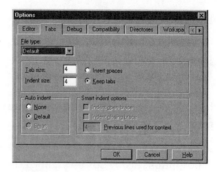

The Compatibility Options Page

The primary purpose of the Compatibility Options page (see Figure 2.17) is to determine the default editor style to be used by Visual J++.

FIGURE 2.17.

*The Compatibility
Options page.*

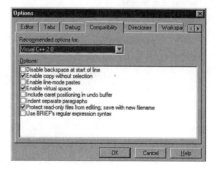

Nearly all development environments come with a default text editor that most programmers feel comfortable with. However, popular third-party editing tools are also available:

- Programmer's File Editor (PFE)
- Lugaru Epsilon
- Borland Brief

Therefore, in addition to the default Developer Studio editing tool, emulations are provided for both Epsilon and Brief as well as Visual C++ 2.0 (which didn't use the Developer Studio IDE). One area in which these three editors differ is in their search expressions. For information on the specific syntax used in each editor's search expressions, see the Visual J++ documentation.

The Workspace Options Page

The Workspace Options page (see Figure 2.18) is where you can configure the workspace.

This page gives you the capability to enable or disable the Visual J++ windows' docking characteristics. By default, the Output, Watch, Variables, Registers, Memory, Call Stack, and Project Workspace windows are dockable. The InfoViewer Topic and Disassembly windows are, by default, not dockable.

FIGURE 2.18.
The Workspace Options page.

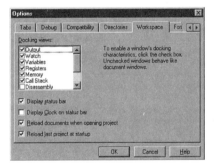

The Format Options Page

The Format Options page (Figure 2.19) contains configuration options for various categories of foreground color, background color, font types, and font size.

FIGURE 2.19.
The Format Options page.

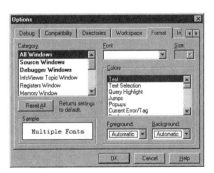

You can make changes to code elements in a particular window or apply the changes to all Visual J++ windows from the Format Options page. This page enables you to modify the environment colors to suit your exact tastes. Elements whose colors and fonts can be modified include

- Text
- Text Selection
- Bookmark
- Breakpoint
- Keyword
- Comment
- Number
- String
- Operator
- HTML Element Name
- HTML Attribute
- HTML Comment
- HTML String
- HTML Tag Delimiter and Tag Text
- Assembly Code

The InfoViewer Options Page

The final page is the InfoViewer Options page (see Figure 2.20). This page allows you to modify the appearance of the InfoViewer (which is the Developer Studio Online Help System).

FIGURE 2.20.

The InfoViewer Options page.

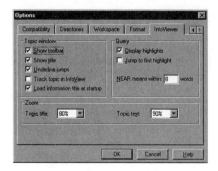

The Zoom features on this page control the size at which the topic title and text are displayed. The larger the number, the larger the title or text will be displayed in the topic's window.

Summary

By now you should be impressed with the wide range of features and options available to the Visual J++ programmer. None of the options mentioned in this chapter affect the actual Java applications produced by Visual J++. Instead, this chapter describes the many configurable items in Visual J++ and explains how you can modify their appearance or behavior to create a comfortable working environment. (Specific compiler and Virtual Machine features that utilize ActiveX [and thereby force Java to be platform dependent] are introduced in Chapter 10.)

The Developer Studio contains three primary windows in which nearly all development work is done:

■ The Project Workspace window

■ The Application window

■ The Output window

Each window has a specific purpose and can contain an extremely large amount of information. However, because each window can be completely customized and placed anywhere on the screen, you have complete control over your working environment. (User control of the working environment is the goal of nearly all modern development tools; unfortunately, although many have tried to achieve this goal, few have succeeded.)

The Project Workspace window contains three tabbed frames. Each frame presents a different view of the information that is currently used to develop Visual J++ projects. These views are

■ ClassView

■ FileView

■ InfoView

ClassView displays information about each class in a project. FileView displays any relationships that may exist among the files in the current project. InfoView lists all online documentation, samples, and associated information that is provided with the Visual J++ installation.

Toolbars and menus within the Developer Studio perform specific context-sensitive operations. Toolbars are completely configurable, can be created from scratch, and can be located anywhere on the screen. Menus, on the other hand, allow their shortcut keys to be modified, but little else. (The Tools menu is an exception in that you can add new tools to the bottom of the list.)

Another item that you can modify is the syntax highlighting of source code.

Although this chapter deals with the Visual J++ product, before you can use Visual J++ to build an actual program (see Chapter 6, "Creating Programs with Java"), you need to learn the nuts and bolts of the Java language. The following two chapters discuss object-oriented programming with Java and the basic elements of the Java language.

Object-Oriented Programming with Java

by Bryan Morgan

CHAPTER 3

IN THIS CHAPTER

One of the most overused words in the field of software development is *object*. Because developers realize the value of object-based design and development, tool makers and other manufacturers continually market themselves as *object based* or *object oriented*. Fortunately for the Visual J++ programmer, the Java language truly is a full-featured, object-oriented language. This chapter presents the basic tenets of object-oriented programming and gives examples that show how Java supports these basic principles.

What Is Object-Oriented Programming?

Before delving into the specifics of Java's object-oriented nature, you need to understand what object-oriented programming (OOP) is and why it is important. OOP is, at its highest level, the process of building applications or systems with objects. To a mechanical engineer or construction supervisor, this concept may seem like an obvious way to do things. In fact, examining the process of building a house, you can draw some interesting parallels between home construction and object-oriented software construction.

Before you begin to build a house, you must complete several steps, such as purchasing bricks, roofing materials, and wood for framing and laying a foundation. You also have to decide how to acquire the bricks:

- Should you set up your own kiln, get a lot of sand, and go to work over a furnace?
- Should you purchase bricks through a local brick supplier?

The builder will be forced to make similar choices throughout the building process. Although you could go to a forest, cut down some trees, and produce lumber for your construction project, you probably would not choose to do so. Because the most commonly used building objects are used by so many people, the building industry has established a widely accepted set of properties and potential uses for various objects. This system allows you to avoid "reinventing the wheel" and concentrate on actually constructing the house. When a particular object such as a door has a problem (that is, it won't lock), it is quite simple to locate that object, repair it, or replace it.

Object-oriented programming is used to build applications out of building blocks, or objects. These objects can be either source code objects (as is the case with Java or C++ classes) or binary objects (such as ActiveX or CORBA objects). A true object-oriented programming language supports the following properties:

- Encapsulation
- Inheritance
- Polymorphism

These properties are explained in detail in the following sections.

Encapsulation

The goal of object-oriented programming is to allow the software developer to construct software in the same way that the builder builds a house. No matter what type of system is being developed, programmers can always group together common functionalities and features in the form of software objects. For instance, graphical user interfaces repeatedly use a common group of objects such as buttons, dialog boxes, and menu items. Each of these objects has a set of properties (Color, Font, Height) and methods (Show, Close, Create, Resize). Because these features are grouped together within an object named Button, for instance, programmers are not forced to think of an item's data separately from that item's behavior. This feature is known as *encapsulation.*

Inheritance

Suppose now that you have chosen to redesign an application written for your local public library. This application was written in a procedural language such as C, FORTRAN, BASIC, or Pascal. After analyzing your application, you see that a large group of objects share the same properties. Things such as science fiction books, computer books, history books, and cookbooks all have a common set of features: an author, a publisher, a price, and an identification number used by the library. Each book can also be checked out, checked in, purchased, or sold.

Ideally, a programmer developing in an object-oriented language could define a parent object named Book that contains these properties. Each individual book type then could be implemented as a child of the parent object Book. This hierarchy would allow all the common functionality of each book to reside in one place without being repeated for each object that shares the functionality. Each specific book type would also then appear to be much simpler to anyone viewing your code. This is because each type of book inherits from the "parent" Book and therefore inherits all of that object's public member variables and methods. The new "child" object gains all this underlying functionality without writing any new code!

Object-oriented programming implements this process through a feature known as *inheritance.* Inheritance allows child objects to be derived from parent objects, which ultimately means that programmers can reuse code. For instance, the CheckIn or CheckOut methods for a ScienceFiction book probably do not differ in any way from the methods for a History book. By making these methods part of the parent Book class, they would automatically be inherited by the Book class's children.

Polymorphism

In many situations, however, all aspects of the parent's behavior may not be passed on to the child. (We all know that this happens in real life, so why not in programming?!?) The parent Book object could have a method called Catalog that was used to place a book on a shelf. Because the shelf location of this book depends on what type of book it is, the Book object would probably specify a default behavior that was intended to be overridden. In a procedural language, the programmer might write something like the following:

```
if Book = ScienceFiction then
 PutOnScienceFictionShelf()
else if Book = History then
 PutOnHistoryShelf()
else if Book = Cooking then
 PutOnCookingShelf()
else if Book = Computer then
 PutOnComputerShelf();
```

if...then...else statements like this result in unnecessarily large amounts of code to be maintained, particularly when all the methods (such as PutOnScienceFictionShelf) produce the same basic result: putting a book on a shelf. Object-oriented programming allows child classes to provide new implementations of their parent's properties and methods if so desired. This feature is known as polymorphism. *Polymorphism* is a big word that means a child can change its inherited behavior without changing the primary intent of that behavior. Using OOP, if the Book object contained a method known as PutOnShelf, the child objects ComputerBook, HistoryBook, CookingBook, and ScienceFictionBook would all inherit this method. However, thanks to OOP, each child object implements its own PutOnShelf method that overrides the parent's behavior. Therefore, when a child object's PutOnShelf methods are called, the child's—not the parent's—implementation will be called.

Some programming languages (such as Java and C++) take the concept of polymorphism a step further. Java allows programmers to duplicate behavior *within* an object, not just via inheritance. Recall the method named PutOnShelf in the previous example. In Java and C++, a single object can provide several methods named PutOnShelf that can all reside within the same object as long as each method accepts different arguments. The following methods would all be legal within a C++ class:

- int PutOnShelf(char* str)
- int PutOnShelf(int I)
- int PutOnShelf(long l)

The concept of polymorphism allows the programmer to build an object that can be reused within an application or across multiple applications. The base class (or parent object) could have a default implementation consisting of actions and data. Each of these actions would specify a specific set of parameters. These sets of parameters define the protocol that is used to interact with other objects within a program. If child objects were derived from this parent object, these actions could be redefined to meet the child objects' purposes.

Information Hiding and Object-Oriented Programming

As you are now aware, every object-oriented language allows programmers to model real-world attributes as programming objects. Although syntax varies from language to language, the key feature of object-oriented languages is that programmer-created objects can be reused throughout an application as a new data type.

The ability to create new data types that can be reused is the characteristic that makes object-oriented programming languages special. In Java and C++, a new object is known as a *class*. In Object Pascal (used by Borland Delphi), a new object is known as a *type*. All object-oriented languages share the features of encapsulation, inheritance, and polymorphism.

> **NOTE**
>
> In the case of C++ and Java, the words *class* and *object* are often used interchangeably. The convention most often used is to refer to a type that has been defined within source code as a "class." Once this class has been instantiated and resides in memory within a program, most developers refer to it as an "object."

Some object-oriented languages also allow the creator of an object to restrict access to that object's attributes. This feature allows the designer of an object to hide variables or methods from other objects or, as is more common, to force other objects to access data in a standard way. Suppose, for instance, that you want a flag to be set whenever a variable is updated. The way to ensure that the flag is set correctly within your object is to force another object to call a Set() method.

Restricting Access to Members

Restricting access to an object is accomplished through the use of keywords such as public, protected, and private. (Both Java and C++ support the use of these keywords.) The meanings of these restrictions are as follows:

- public—A variable or method defined as public is freely available to other objects.
- protected—A variable or method defined as protected can be accessed only by members of this object or objects derived from this object.
- private—A variable or method defined as private can be accessed only by members within this object.

Java also allows objects themselves to be created as `public` or `private`. Only one public object can be created within a single source file, although multiple `private` objects can be created within that same source file. The catch is that because these objects are designated as `private`, they can only be used by the public class within that source file. The following example shows a `public` and `private` class that could be created within the same source file:

```
public class Class1
{
  int x;
  DoSomethingWithX(int x);
}

private class Class2
{
  int y;
  DoSomethingWithY(int y);
}
```

This brief introduction to the basic concepts of encapsulation, inheritance, polymorphism, and access restriction should help you understand the following discussion of objects, as well as the object-oriented specifics of the Java language.

An Object-Oriented Example

This brief demonstration of encapsulation, inheritance, polymorphism, and access restriction builds a set of objects to represent employees within a company. Each employee is an autonomous object that can stand alone. However, for a company to be successful, the employees need to be able to interact in a meaningful fashion.

> **NOTE**
>
> Keep in mind that the following objects are built using what is often called *pseudocode*. Try to focus on the concepts being discussed and rest assured that the Java syntax will be covered in detail later.

The People Object

Although many different types of employees work within a company, this example assumes that all employees are people. (I realize that this may be a stretch in certain cases, but some generalizations have to made to simplify this example.) Therefore, the `People` object should encapsulate the common information and behavior of a standard employee. Using the pseudo-language, the first step is to add the data that should apply to every employee:

```
Object People  {
string Name;
string Address;
int Age;
long SSN;
long Salary;
char Sex;
bool Married;
int YearsOfService;
}
```

The preceding set of properties should look very familiar to most programmers—even to some-one who is new to object-oriented programming. In fact, the structure could be created in just about every programming language in existence today. However, data alone is not enough to accurately model the typical person. In addition to the set of data that provides information about the person, each person also performs a set of routine actions throughout the day. Object-oriented languages allow programmers to use *encapsulation* to mix information and ac-tions together. The next step is to use the pseudo-language to add some behavior to the `People` object:

```
Object People  {
string Name;
string Address;
int Age;
long SSN;
long Salary;
char Sex;
bool Married;
int YearsOfService;
void DriveToWork(int TimeLeft);
void DriveBackHome(int TimeLeft);
String DoWork();
void GoToLunch();
}
```

Through encapsulation, the object's variables and methods have been combined into a single, autonomous entity. This object could be used to apply to every employee within a company, but it is very generic. Although identifiers like name, address, or salary may mean the same thing for every employee, the method `DoWork()` could be dramatically different depending on an employee's job title. This set of common features coupled with individual differences can be represented best using *inheritance.*

Now you can use the `public`, `private`, and `protected` keywords to take advantage of the object-oriented pseudo-language's information-hiding features. The following object is simi-lar to the `People` object created earlier, only now the `Salary` variable is hidden from all other objects:

```
Object People  {
string Name;
string Address;
int Age;
```

```
long SSN;
private long Salary;
char Sex;
bool Married;
int YearsOfService;
void DriveToWork(int TimeLeft);
void DriveBackHome(int TimeLeft);
String DoWork();
void GoToLunch();
}
```

After this change has been made, all classes deriving from the People class are unable to access the Salary class. In many cases, it is considered good programming style to hide all variables from public view by making them private. Data access methods are then provided as public methods so that other objects can have access to an object's data. The following class provides access to a member variable through the use of data access methods:

```
Object People  {
string Name;
string Address;
int Age;
long SSN;
private long Salary;
char Sex;
bool Married;
int YearsOfService;
void DriveToWork(int TimeLeft);
void DriveBackHome(int TimeLeft);
String DoWork();
void GoToLunch();
public void SetSalary(long newSalary);
public long GetSalary();
}
```

Using access methods (such as SetSalary() and GetSalary()) prevents users from inadvertently modifying data. In addition, using access methods makes your code more readable and also allows the creator of an object to fully control access to an object's data. For example, you might want to store a boolean value in the object that would be true if the person received a raise. To do so, add the following line to the SetSalary() method: ReceivedRaise := True;. This line adds functionality to your object without changing a single line of code anywhere else within the application.

Using the People Object to Create Employees

Most technical organizations have three primary types of employees: support, technical, and managerial. Each of these primary types of employees is responsible for performing specific tasks. If any of these groups is missing, the organization cannot function in an optimal fashion. Therefore, the next step in this example is to create three new employee objects: Support, Technical, and Managerial. To provide these objects with some basic functionality, they will be derived from the existing People object.

The process of creating the Support object demonstrates the concepts of inheritance and polymorphism. This type of employee can be thought of as performing work that is not directly turned into profit for the company. Examples of support personnel are secretaries, receptionists, and accountants. Obviously, the work an accountant does is a necessity, but an accountant's output cannot be sold to a customer. Therefore, support personnel are generally classified by whom they support and by the services they offer. The following Support object inherits from the People class:

```
Object Support Inherits From People {
string Department;
void ReceiveInstructions();
void ReportFindings();
void DoWork();
}
```

Notice that the Support object is designated to inherit all of People's attributes. Also note that the DoWork() method is listed in order to override the default DoWork() behavior of the People object. In an actual implementation, the People object's DoWork() method will probably be left blank. Each child object would then be responsible for providing the functionality for this method.

Java: Fully Buzzword Compliant

One of the creators of Java, James Gosling, has stated that Java is fully buzzword compliant; in other words, Java is an object-oriented, thread-safe, distributed, secure, and platform-independent language. Although much has been made of Java's platform independence, Microsoft has publicly stated that Java is also a great programming language. Java's designers included nearly every feature valued by developers and intentionally left out many extraneous, more cumbersome programming features. This section focuses on how Java supports object-oriented programming.

Encapsulation Using a Class

Unlike languages such as C++ and Object Pascal, every line of code written in Java must occur within an object (known as a *class*).

> **NOTE**
>
> Although C++ provides the ability to encapsulate data and methods together within a class, it allows programmers to use data and methods outside a class, as well.

Introduction to Java Programming Using Visual J++

The syntax used to create a new class in Java is

```
Modifier class className [extends ParentClass] [implements Interfaces]
{
/* Provide class variables and methods */
}
```

`Modifier` can be any of the following keywords:

- `public`—A class declared as `public` can be used by any object. Keep in mind that a source file can have only one `public` class. That source filename must be `className.java`.

- `private`—A class declared as `private` can be used only within a source file. A source file can contain only one `public` class, but the file can contain multiple `private` classes.

- `<empty>`—If the modifier is left blank, the class is known as a "friendly" class; all other classes within a friendly class's package can reach it. (You'll learn more about packages later in this chapter in the "Interfaces and Packages" section.)

- `synchronizable`—The `synchronizable` keyword is used to synchronize statements.

- `abstract`—A class declared as `abstract` is declared to be used only as a base class. An abstract class contains only methods without implementations.

- `final`—A `final` class cannot be subclassed from. This means that a class declared as `final` cannot be inherited from in Java using the `inherits` keyword.

Because Java supports encapsulation, variables and methods can be combined within a class. Listing 3.1 should give you some idea of how to create classes in Java.

Listing 3.1. Sample Java classes.

```
public class Animal  {
String Species;
int Age;
int NumberOfLegs;
int IQ;
int Run(int speed);
}

public final Automobile  {
String Manufacturer;
int Year;
int Price;
int Doors;
int Drive(int speed);
}

private class Button  {
Color FaceColor;
String Caption;
private int Size;
int Press(int velocity);
}
```

The classes in Listing 3.1 illustrate the creation of some simple Java classes. The first class, `Animal`, is declared as a `public` class. The second class, `Automobile`, is declared as a `public final` class. Therefore, other classes can access the `Automobile` class, but no other class can derive from it. The final class, `Button`, is declared with the `private` modifier, which means that it can be used only by other classes within its source file. Note that the final member variable, `Size`, was itself declared as `private`.

Just as classes can be declared using a variety of modifiers, Java also allows the class designer to use a variety of method and field modifiers to control access to class members. Each method and variable within a class can be prefixed with any of the following modifiers:

`public`—A method or variable declared as `public` can be accessed by any class.

`protected`—A method or variable declared as `protected` can be accessed only by subclasses.

`private`—A method or variable declared as `private` can be accessed only by other methods within this class.

`<empty>`—If no modifier is given, the method or variable can be accessed by any other class within this class's package.

`static`—The `static` modifier designates a method or variable that is shared globally by all instances of this class.

`native`—The `native` modifier denotes a native method that is implemented in another language, such as C. Native methods are discussed in detail in Chapter 7, "Advanced Java Programming."

`final`—`final` specifies a method or variable that is constant (for a variable) or cannot be overridden by a subclass (for a method). A constant variable is a variable whose value cannot be changed at runtime. Once the variable is initialized to some value, that value is set for the duration of the application.

`synchronized`—The `synchronized` keyword locks this object when a method is entered and unlocks it when this method exits. A method is entered when it is called by some other method. You can exit a method by issuing the `return` statement or by completing all the statements within that method.

It is possible to create a simple class using the information just presented. However, one of the most important features of object-oriented programming is reuse of code through inheritance.

Inheriting from Other Classes

Java supports inheritance through the use of the `extends` keyword. In Java-speak, if a class `Dog` is derived from a parent class `Animal`, `Dog` extends `Animal`. The example in Listing 3.2 shows you how to extend objects through inheritance.

Listing 3.2. Extending objects through inheritance.

```
public class Animal extends LifeForm  {
String Species;
int Age;
int NumberOfLegs;
int IQ;
int Run(int speed);
}

public final Automobile extends Vehicle  {
String Manufacturer;
int Year;
int Price;
int Doors;
int Drive(int speed);
}

private class Button extends Component {
Color FaceColor;
String Caption;
private int Size;
int Press(int velocity);
}
```

Unlike C++, Java supports only *single inheritance*—that is, an object can inherit from only one other class. Although single inheritance may seem restrictive, most classes that you create only need to derive from one other class. Java does allow programmers to extend the functionality of a class in another way: through the use of *interfaces*. In addition, you can group related classes and interfaces to form *packages*.

Interfaces and Packages

An *interface* is a declaration of a set of methods whose implementation is not provided. You can think of an interface as a contract between the interface designer and the "implementor" of the interface (the class designer). The class that implements the interface is responsible for providing the actual implementation of the interface's methods. Java is interesting in that it allows classes to be typecast as interfaces; that is, a class can be passed as an interface argument as long as the class actually implements the interface. This implementation is done through the use of the implements keyword. Interfaces can be derived from one or more other interfaces. Keep in mind also that although a class can inherit only from one other class, it can implement as many interfaces as it chooses!

Listing 3.3 includes an example of an interface (the Behavior interface). Behavior specifies a group of methods that collectively make up the behavior of some form of life. The implementation of these methods is left to the implementor of the interface.

Listing 3.3. Extending an object using inheritance and interfaces.

```
public interface Behavior  {
void Eat();
void Breathe();
void Sleep();
}

public class Animal extends LifeForm implements Behavior {
String Species;
int Age;
int NumberOfLegs;
int IQ;
int Run(int speed);

void Eat() {
/* Provide implementation here */
  };

void Breathe()  {
/* Provide implementation here */
  };

void Sleep()  {
/* Provide implementation here */
  };
}
```

Once you have built up a library of classes and interfaces that have something in common, you can place the group of objects into a *package* by adding the following line to the beginning of each source file:

```
package PackageName;
```

Imagine that you have created an entire library of classes to represent living creatures, including the following:

- class LifeForm;
- class Animal;
- interface Behavior;
- class Zebra;
- class Tiger;
- class Bear;

You can group these classes and interfaces together into a package named Creature by placing the text package Creature; at the beginning of each source file containing the classes and interfaces.

3

OBJECT-ORIENTED
PROGRAMMING
WITH JAVA

As you may be aware, Visual J++ comes with a large number of packages, each of which contains many classes and interfaces. Because a primary focus of object-oriented programming is the reuse of objects created by you or by others, this chapter includes an explanation of the packages (also referred to as the *class library*) that ship with Visual J++. First, however, take a look at an interesting example of classes and interfaces within the java.applet package that is a standard package in every runtime Java environment.

Case Study: The `java.applet` Package

No matter which platform you are running your Java code on, installed somewhere with the Java Virtual Machine is a package known as the java.applet package. You can find it by locating a java subdirectory and then by locating the applet subdirectory under it.

> **NOTE**
>
> A Java convention is to create package names based on their underlying directory structure. For instance, to create a subpackage named Package1.Package2.Package3, a directory named Package1 would be created followed by a subdirectory Package2 and a sub-subdirectory Package3. All of subpackage Package3's files would be stored in the Package3 subdirectory.

The java.applet package contains a number of classes and interfaces. This java.applet package provides the basic set of classes used to create an actual Java applet. (A *Java applet* is a small program that is capable of running within a Web page. Java applets are discussed in great detail throughout this book.)

The java.applet package contains the Applet class as well as three interfaces: AppletContext, AppletStub, and AudioClip. The various interfaces were designed by Sun to be used by Web browsers. It is left up to each browser manufacturer to provide its own implementations of these interfaces. For example, the AudioClip interface defines the following methods:

```
public interface AudioClip {
public abstract void play()
public abstract void loop()
public abstract void stop()
}
```

Because AudioClip is an interface, the implementation of these methods is left to the class developer. Therefore, if the developers of the Netscape Navigator browser decide to support WAV sound files, they simply need to provide a class that implements the AudioClip interface that is capable of playing, looping, and stopping WAV sound files.

A better example of interfaces in use is the `Applet` class itself. The `Applet` class looks like this:

```
public class Applet extends Panel {
public final void setStub(AppletStub stub)
public boolean isActive()
public URL getDocumentBase()
public URL getCodeBase()
public String getParameter(String name)
public AppletContext getAppletContext()
public void resize(int width, int height)
public void resize(Dimension d)
public void showStatus(String msg)
public Image getImage(URL url)
public Image getImage(URL url, String name)
public AudioClip getAudioClip(URL url)
public AudioClip getAudioClip(URL url, String name)
public String getAppletInfo()
public String[][] getParameterInfo()
public void play(URL url)
public void play(URL url, String name)
public void init()
public void start()
public void stop()
public void destroy()
}
```

Notice that the `setStub` method accepts an `AppletStub` interface as a parameter. The `AppletStub` interface allows the `Applet` class to retrieve information from its surrounding environment (known as the *applet context*). Because `AppletStub` was defined as an interface, the designers of the `java.applet` package did not need to write an implementation for each environment that a Java applet would ever run in. Instead, this environment can be described in terms of an interface that the developers of Web browsers, such as Microsoft and Netscape, can implement.

Here are the methods defined by the `AppletStub` and `AppletContext` interfaces:

```
public interface AppletStub {
public abstract boolean isActive()
public abstract URL getDocumentBase()
public abstract URL getCodeBase()
public abstract String getParameter(String name)
public abstract AppletContext getAppletContext()
public abstract void appletResize(int width, int height)
}

public interface AppletContext {
public abstract AudioClip getAudioClip(URL url)
public abstract Image getImage(URL url)
public abstract Applet getApplet(String name)
public abstract Enumeration getApplets()
public abstract void showDocument(URL url)
public abstract void showDocument(URL url, String target)
public abstract void showStatus(String status)
}
```

The Visual J++ Class Library

Most of this discussion of object-oriented programming with Java focuses on the creation of new objects for use in application development. However, most of the objects that you will create during your Java programming experiences will probably inherit from existing objects. These existing objects may be among the hundreds of classes included with Visual J++, or you may have purchased them from a Java-object vendor. (A burgeoning market currently exists for Java classes such as spreadsheets, charts, editors, and other common programming objects.)

The classes included with Visual J++ allow you to inherit from a large body of existing classes used for

- Graphics programming
- Networking
- Web server access
- Multimedia
- Database access
- Debugging
- Utility functions
- COM applications

Packages containing all these classes are located in the CLASSES.ZIP file that was installed when you installed Visual J++. The default location for this file is the \windows\java\classes directory. To determine the exact location of the file, examine the HKEY_LOCAL_MACHINE\ SOFTWARE\Microsoft\Java_VM\ClassPath registry key in the Windows Registry. The following sections discuss the primary packages included in the CLASSES.ZIP file.

The com.ms Package

The com.ms package contains a number of subpackages that are useful in developing COM applications.

> **NOTE**
>
> Microsoft provides the com.ms package on Microsoft machines only. You will not find this package on non-Microsoft Java Virtual Machine installations.

Subpackages included in the com.ms package include the com, applet, awtX.directx, awtX.win32, and net.wininet subpackages. The com subpackage provides the basic COM functionality for the Iunknown, IID, and IExternalConnectionSink interfaces as well as the definitions of CLSID, GUID, and the Variant COM data type. The DirectX subpackages provide the Java implementations for Microsoft's DirectX graphics API.

The `java.applet` Package

The `java.applet` package contains the classes used to create and work with Java applets. Each Java applet is derived directly from the `java.applet.Applet` class in this package. Interfaces specified in this package are `AudioClip`, `AppletContext`, and `AppletStub`.

The `java.awt` Package

The `java.awt` package contains the classes and subpackages that make up the Java Abstract Windowing Toolkit (AWT). The AWT provides the core user interface objects that allow a GUI application written in Java to run on any platform. Examples of classes included within the `java.awt` package include `Button`, `List`, `Menu`, `Checkbox`, and `Color`.

The `java.io` Package

The `java.io` package contains the classes used to provide programmers with input/output capabilities in Java. Classes within this package allow developers to read and write from streams to standard input/output, files, and byte arrays. Examples of classes within the `java.io` package are `FileInputStream`, `FileOutputStream`, `PrintStream`, and `DataInputStream`.

The `java.lang` Package

The `java.lang` package contains the classes that correspond to the Java primitive data types (`int`, `float`, `boolean`, `char`, `byte`, `long`, `short`, and `double`). Also included in this package are the `System` and `Thread` classes. The `System` class provides access to system information such as operating system name and vendor and Java Virtual Machine version and vendor. The `Thread` class provides multithreading capabilities to applets or applications.

The `java.net` Package

The `java.net` package includes classes that can be used to open sockets for communication between processes on remote machines. Also included in this package are the `URL` and `InetAddress` classes. These classes are used to encapsulate World Wide Web addresses and information.

The `java.util` Package

The `java.util` package provides the developer with a large number of utility classes. These classes include common data structures such as `HashTable`, `Dictionary`, `Stack`, and `Vector`. Also included in the `java.util` package are the `Date`, `Properties`, and `Random` classes. Each of these classes provides a number of useful methods and properties that may be of interest to developers.

The sun Package

Like the `com.ms` package, the `sun` package is not guaranteed to be a part of every Java Virtual Machine installation. However, many items currently in the `sun` package are slated to become permanent parts of the Java package at a later date, so it will continue to be a "test bed" for internal packages developed by Sun Microsystems. Developers should remember that classes within this package are not guaranteed to appear on every user's local machine. Subpackages available within the sun package are `applet`, `audio`, `awt`, `misc`, and `net`.

Summary

After being touted in academic circles and large development projects as the development paradigm of choice, object-oriented programming has finally entered the mainstream. This acceptance is partly associated with the popularity of rapid application development environments that speed routine development tasks by providing easy-to-use user interfaces for accomplishing those tasks.

For a language to be considered truly object oriented, it must support inheritance, encapsulation, and polymorphism. Java supports all three of these and in many ways is very similar to the object-oriented C++ language. Classes in Java are used to encapsulate member data and methods. These members can be granted different access levels (public, private, protected, or friendly) depending on the goals of the class designer. Java supports single inheritance of classes but allows multiple implementations of interfaces.

Anyone using J++ needs to become acquainted with the capabilities of the Visual J++ class library, which contains literally hundreds of thousands of lines of prewritten source code. The library includes all popular GUI objects as well as objects to be used in COM, networking, and database access applications.

Chapter 4, "Understanding the Java Base Platform," introduces the Java packages that comprise the Java Base platform. These packages are included with every certified Java Virtual Machine installation. Chapter 5, "Elements of the Java Language," introduces the basic elements of the Java language. This introduction to Java constructs, combined with your knowledge of object-oriented programming, should enable you to design and build Java programs by the time you have finished reading Chapter 6, "Creating Programs with Java."

Understanding the Java Base Platform

by Bryan Morgan

IN THIS CHAPTER

CHAPTER 4

Before beginning to consider the loftier concepts of the Java language and its use in application development, the new Visual J++ programmer needs to understand the environment in which all Java code runs. The foundation of this environment is referred to as the *Java Base Platform,* which comprises the following elements:

- A runtime engine responsible for receiving and checking Java code
- The Java Virtual Machine
- The Java API

This chapter explains in detail the constituents of the Java Base Platform, its use, and its location on your machine. This discussion covers a variety of topics, including

- Bytecodes
- The Java security model
- The Java Virtual Machine's responsibilities
- Java API capabilities

Although the Java language has many benefits, perhaps the primary reason for Java's quick success is its promise of platform-independent application development. Since its beginnings, the computer industry has had to accommodate many incompatible computing platforms. Because of these inherent differences, users who shared similar interests generally migrated to similar platforms. In the late 1990s, four primary computing platforms dominate the personal computer market:

- The Microsoft Windows family of operating systems, which runs on the 80x86, PowerPC, Alpha, and MIPS microprocessors
- The IBM OS/2 operating system, which runs on the Intel 80x86 microprocessor
- The Apple Macintosh operating system, which runs on Motorola microprocessors and the PowerPC microprocessor line (made by a consortium of Motorola, IBM, and Apple)
- Many flavors of the UNIX operating system, which runs on a large variety of RISC-based chips from Sun, Hewlett-Packard, Digital, IBM, and others

Factors such as cost, ease of use, availability, and existing software applications have attracted different groups of users to each of these operating environments. The UNIX operating system is popular in academic environments and many scientific applications are available for it. UNIX is also popular for use as a server because of its scalability and communications features. The Apple Macintosh is popular with a wide range of users, but it is in widest use in the publishing, arts, and education fields because of its intuitive graphical user interface and existing library of software applications. OS/2 is also in wide use, especially in organizations that require seamless connectivity to other IBM computing environments. Microsoft Windows is the leader in terms of number of users and is available in two primary versions: Windows 95 and Windows NT.

As a result of the popularity of these four incompatible operating systems, corporate networking designers have had to deal with a bewildering array of integration problems. Software developers faced with the task of producing applications for use under all of these platforms have had a very limited set of tools to work with. What's more, once developers chose their cross-platform development tools, they were committed to that vendor's cross-platform toolkit and had little opportunity to turn back.

Java eliminates the platform-dependence problem by providing a runtime environment known as the Java Base Platform that is guaranteed to be the same on each operating system. The Java Base Platform resides on each client computer and interprets files containing Java *bytecode* that can be retrieved from the local machine or from any other computer on the Internet. You will need to understand what bytecodes are before you go on to read about the Java Base Platform later in this chapter.

The Java Runtime Environment

As mentioned in Chapter 1, "Visual J++: What It Is and Why It Is Unique," Java was being developed as the World Wide Web was introduced and the Internet began to grow at a much faster rate than it had ever grown in the past. Because of Java's lofty goals (of being networked and platform independent), Java's designers came to the conclusion that delivering a set of bytecodes to the client machine would result in the best solution.

What is a bytecode, you ask? *Bytecodes* are the intermediate result when Java source code is compiled. All compilers go through three basic processes: compiling, linking, and executable creation.

FIGURE 4.1.

The Java compilation process.

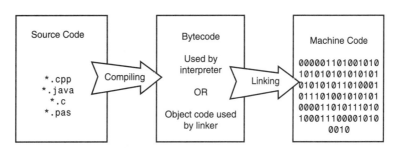

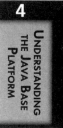

The compilation process examines source code for syntax errors. As you are probably well aware, if any syntax errors are found, the compilation process ends with an error. After checking the syntax, the compiler checks to make sure that all objects, variables, and methods that the code references are what the code says they are. If the compiler is unable to determine what an object is, it will issue another error and cease to compile. After performing the error-checking routine, the compiler goes through the code again and tries to figure out the best way to convert it into instructions that the computer can understand. Entire books and careers have been built on this topic, so I won't attempt to go into detail. However, the end result of this process is a new version of your source code called *bytecode*! The Java compiler's job is finished as soon as it writes the bytecode.

> **NOTE**
>
> The result of this compilation process is a *class file* in Java. This file is denoted by a `.class` extension to the source code's original filename. The subject of Java classes was introduced in Chapter 3, "Object-Oriented Programming with Java," and will be discussed in much greater detail in Chapter 5, "Elements of the Java Language," and Chapter 6, "Creating Programs with Java."

The linking process links all the newly compiled code modules within the application. In other words, if object A uses object B, object A and object B are initially compiled separately. The objects are combined during the linking stage, which ultimately produces an actual executable program consisting of machine code to be executed by the microprocessor.

Because Java is an interpreted language, the linking and executable file creation processes are deferred until runtime (they will be discussed later in the section titled "The Bytecode Verification Process"). The term *interpreted* means that an interpreter reads each individual bytecode within the class file and then converts these bytecodes into actual machine instructions. Java uses approximately 250 different bytecodes to denote the basic set of executable instructions. Just as an Intel Pentium or DEC Alpha chip has its own instruction set that represents every instruction built into the chip's silicon, the Java runtime environment has its own instruction set called *bytecodes*. However, because the Java bytecode specifications (and the class file format) are defined and controlled by Sun, they are exactly the same on every platform that Java runs on.

The Java Class File Format

Each Java class file contains the bytecodes required to implement a specific object in the Java language. Each class file contains the following individual sections:

- Magic (4-byte header)
- Class file version number (4-byte value)
- Constant pool (used to store all constants)
- Access flags (2-byte value)
- This class index (2-byte value)
- Super class index (2-byte value)
- Fields (2-byte count field plus an array of field structures)
- Methods (2-byte count field plus all methods)
- Attributes (2-byte count field plus individual attributes)

Although the contents of most of these individual sections are self-explanatory, a few need to be examined in a little more detail. I will answer the most pressing question first: What is "magic"? Interestingly enough, the Magic header represents the first 4 bytes of every class file. To designate that the field being read is in fact a class file, the contents of the Magic number should be 0xCAFEBABE. (Supposedly, this designation refers to certain individuals at a local coffee shop frequented by the Java team and was chosen even before the name "Java.")

The next 4-byte value, the version number, represents the version number of the class file itself. Each Java Virtual Machine (JVM) is cognizant of the maximum version number that it is capable of loading. Should the class file's version number be greater than the JVM's capability, the class file will be rejected.

Because class files are generated and placed on a remote server, in the case of Web applets, the client-side Java runtime system needs to have some methodology for ensuring that the applets being loaded obey all Java security restrictions. Runtime processes known as the *bytecode verifier* and the *class loader* do this job.

How Security Is Maintained at Runtime

Once Java bytecodes have been produced in the form of .class files, these bytecodes are ready to be run as an applet or application. Because Java was designed to be a networked language using classes retrieved at runtime from remote servers, security is an integral part of the Java runtime system. Java's designers handled security on three separate levels:

- The elimination of pointers from the language eliminates an entire class of security problems. Programmers in C, for instance, can fake objects in memory because it is loosely typed and allows pointers.

- The bytecode verification process forces uploaded Java applets to undergo a rigorous set of checks in order to run on the local system. In other words, this process will foil "bad" users who decide to write a hostile compiler. Keep in mind that no matter what features are built into the language, a rogue compiler could still produce Java applets capable of circumventing the Java security model. Bytecode verification will be explained later in the chapter.

- Client-side precautions add another layer of security. Most Web browsers preclude Java applets from performing file access or communicating with any computer on the Internet other than the computer that the applet was uploaded from. The Java class loader assists in this process.

Features needed to be built into the entire runtime system to prevent specially compiled applets from invading remote systems. In other words, nothing could stop an individual from writing a Java compiler that produced bytecodes designed to circumvent the JVM in some way. Remember that Java is an interpreted language. This means that actual memory management for the application is put off until runtime (it is not built into the compiled Java classes). This feature allows Java to run on many different platforms, thanks to the installed JVM. However, it also allows the Java runtime engine to verify that the bytecodes being loaded are, in fact, good bytecodes. This is done using a part of the Virtual Machine known as the *verifier*.

The Bytecode Verification Process

The bytecode verifier has the unenviable task of checking each bytecode before it is executed (interpreted) to make sure that it is not going to perform an illegal operation. After the bytecode has been verified, the applet is guaranteed to do the following:

- Obey access restrictions such as public, protected, private, and friendly. No class will be allowed to access data that goes against these restrictions.
- Never perform illegal data conversions. Because Java is a strongly typed language, automatic conversions from arrays to pointers, for instance, are not allowed.
- Conform to all return, parameter, and argument types when calling methods.
- Live within its allocated stack. An applet that overruns its memory will not be loaded.

The verification process checks many of the things that a good Java compiler will check, but it is important to recognize that the verification process takes place on the *client's* computer. Security on the server side is virtually meaningless to Internet clients because of the unknown nature of most servers. (This concept clashes with Microsoft's own ActiveX security model that uses "code signing" to give a stamp of approval to a vendor and their ActiveX objects being downloaded. This is discussed in more detail in Chapter 24, "Distributed Component Object Model."

The Java Runtime Class Loader

The set of precautions enforced by the client Web browser (or other applet loader) is done by a part of the Java runtime engine known as the *class loader*. The class loader does what it says: It loads classes.

NOTE

The class loader can vary from browser to browser. Security features in Sun's HotJava Web browser allow the user to control security restrictions and even remove them altogether. The Netscape Navigator and Microsoft Internet Explorer browsers offer no user-controlled security measures. Instead, applets are forced into a very rigid set of rules. Therefore, it is probably wise to plan to write applets to conform to the most restrictive case because this will allow them to run on every user's computer.

The class loader can recognize three possible worlds:

- The local system (highest level)
- The local network within a firewall (middle level)
- The Internet at large (lowest level)

The class loader implements defined rules that allow it to intelligently prevent an applet from wreaking havoc on your system. It does this by never allowing a class loaded from a lower level to replace a class existing on a higher level. Although much of the information presented on Java has stated that applets cannot write to a local hard drive or connect to remote computers other than the originating host, this statement is not necessarily correct. For instance, the HotJava Web browser allows users to configure these security restrictions (see Figure 4.2).

FIGURE 4.2.

The Java applet security screen in HotJava 1.0.

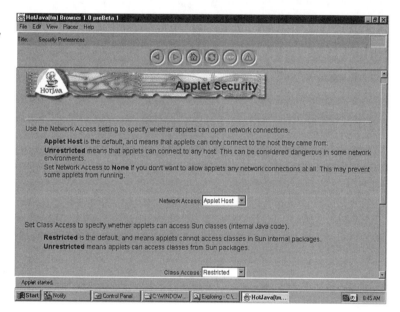

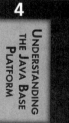

Figure 4.2 allows the HotJava user to loosen or even drop all security restrictions so that applets can do whatever they want when uploaded to your machine. This may be useful in an intranet setting where machines are never connected directly to the Internet, but be very careful otherwise. Undoubtedly, devious applets will be written to do damage to unsuspecting systems. This is why the Netscape Navigator and Microsoft Internet Explorer developers left configurable security features completely out of their product.

Are Java Applets Safe?

As discussed, Java handles security at several different levels. The language is designed in a manner that removes many security holes because it does not allow pointer manipulation. The bytecode verifier is used to verify each uploaded Java class to ensure that it obeys all Java language rules. The class loader enforces security on another level by controlling applet operations at runtime. It is important to realize that the bytecode verifier and class loader both exist on the local system and are part of the Java runtime environment. Because these two components are critical to the success of the Java security model, the user must rely on these components to ensure that Java applets are secure. As the number of third-party virtual machines increases, it is critical that these virtual machines be verified by some independent source to ensure that they operate according to the JVM specification. Sun is currently working on a test suite to do just this. In short: Yes, the Java environment is safe and secure. Vendor-specific implementations, however, must be validated to ensure that they comply with the Java specifications.

Whether developing a standalone application, Web applet, or embedded code, however, two things remain constant no matter where Java runs: the JVM and a standard group of Java classes known as the Java API.

My experience has been that many people are a little intimidated by the JVM, perhaps due to the use of the word *machine*. The following section explains exactly what the JVM is and what responsibilities it has.

The Java Virtual Machine

Just as a C++ compiler targets code for an Intel microprocessor or a FORTRAN compiler targets binary code to run on a DEC Alpha chip, Java code can be thought of as being targeted to run on the JVM. For this reason, it can be helpful to think of the JVM as a "soft CPU." Although Java is truly platform independent, Java bytecode cannot simply be dropped onto a blank machine and be expected to run. Instead, a virtual computer (thus the name virtual machine) must be available to execute those bytecodes. This virtual computer is, you guessed it, the JVM. In practical terms, the JVM is a piece of software that resides on the machine where Java code is to be run.

The next topic for consideration is the specification for the JVM, which Sun Microsystems controls. Because it isolates Java code from the underlying hardware and software platform, the JVM itself can be explained using a computing platform metaphor. To Java code being executed, the JVM performs both as the operating system and as the hardware platform. Therefore, JVM is described in this context.

The JVM Specification

This specification provides details on exactly what functionality the JVM is to provide so that companies who choose to build JVMs can convert the specification into actual code. Note here that even though Sun controls the specification, it does not create the JVM for every platform. The first JVMs that Sun released were initially available for the Sun Solaris and Microsoft Windows 95/NT operating systems. Since that time, other vendors have provided their own virtual machines for their respective platforms. In some instances, such as Windows 95/NT, several virtual machines are available from different vendors. Information on how to obtain a copy of the JVM for a platform appears later in this chapter. Table 4.1 contains a partial list of platforms that the JVM is available on and the vendors that are officially responsible for providing that platform's reference implementation.

Table 4.1. Reference implementation providers for the Java Virtual Machine.

Company	Operating System
Microsoft	Windows 95, Windows NT
IBM	Windows 3.1
Apple	Macintosh
IBM	OS/2
Hewlett-Packard	HP UX
Hitachi	Hitachi OS
IBM	AIX
SGI	Irix
Sun	Solaris
SCO	UNIXWare
Tandem	Non-Stop Kernel
Novell	NetWare 4.0
IBM	MVS

Table 4.1 shows only the companies that have officially contracted with Sun to provide the reference implementation of the JVM for their specific platform. In fact, many other companies including Netscape Communications currently provide their own versions of the JVM for use with their products. For instance, Microsoft has agreed to provide the reference implementation of the JVM for Windows 95 and Windows NT. This implementation is officially called the *Windows Virtual Machine for Java* and is the focus of Chapter 18, "The Microsoft Java Virtual Machine."

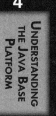

With Emphasis on the Word *Machine*

As mentioned earlier, when Java code runs on a computer, it does so "on top" of the JVM. Actually, this virtual machine in many ways mimics a hardware device. Other portions of its architecture can be thought of as resembling an operating system. This section examines the internal workings of the JVM by comparing it to hardware and software platforms.

All microprocessors come with a basic list of possible operations that the microprocessor can perform. Each operation appears to the programmer as a single, atomic unit of work, although in actuality several operations may be occurring "behind the scenes" within the microprocessor. This finite number of operations is known as the microprocessor's *instruction set.* This instruction set varies from microprocessor to microprocessor and is usually documented in manuals that you can obtain from the chip's vendor.

Programs that use this set of instructions are often referred to as *assembly language* programs, although these instructions can also be passed directly to the computer using common languages such as C and C++. Like computer hardware, the JVM supports its own finite set of instructions. In fact, a direct parallel can be drawn between a hardware instruction set and the JVM instruction set.

The terms *JVM instruction set* and *bytecodes* are synonymous. The JVM supports approximately 250 bytecodes, and each bytecode supports zero or more operands (arguments passed with the instruction). As a compiled Java class runs on the JVM, these bytecodes are processed one line at a time and are eventually converted to machine code to be executed by the actual hardware. Several other interesting parallels can be drawn between the JVM and computer hardware. These parallels are explained in the following paragraphs.

Computer architecture designers often refer to the size of memory that a processor can address as that machine's *address space.* A chip that uses 16 bits to store memory addresses can address 64KB of memory. The JVM uses a 32-bit value to store addresses and therefore can address 4GB of memory. The size of a single block of memory maintained by the JVM is one byte. A machine's *word size* is the amount of storage used to transfer data. The JVM uses 32 bits to store a word; therefore, its word size is (surprise!) 32 bits. Unlike actual hardware implementations, the JVM supports a small number of data types. (Many microprocessors' instruction sets simply transfer memory values from location to location without worrying about the actual *types* of this data.) The JVM supports the following data types:

- Byte—An 8-bit value
- Short—A 16-bit value
- Int—A 32-bit value
- Long—A 64-bit value
- Float—A 32-bit floating-point value
- Double—A 64-bit floating-point value
- Char—A 16-bit value

Coincidentally, you will find in Chapter 5 that this basic set of data types is identical to the set of data types supported by the Java language except for the boolean data type (which is actually a byte value to the JVM).

As a microprocessor executes instructions one by one, it maintains a type of scoreboard that always represents the current state of the machine. The actual values, or scores, of program variables are maintained using temporary storage areas located within the microprocessor. Examples of storage elements used to manage this imaginary scoreboard are registers and the stack.

Registers are used to store the results of various operations and also memory addresses. The hardware stack stores the parameters and the results of all instructions. Values that are added and removed from the stack are said to be "pushed" and "popped." By now, you shouldn't be surprised to find out that the JVM maintains its own internal registers and stack to perform bytecode operations.

Although the term *machine* may seem somewhat blunt when referring to what, at first glance, seems like an interpreter, the JVM is in effect a full-featured software microprocessor.

Taking Out the Trash Using Garbage Collection

So far in this chapter, you've seen how the Visual J++ compiler converts your Java source code to bytecodes. These bytecodes are then sent over a wire (either from your hard drive to the JVM or from a Web server's hard drive to the JVM) and are validated by the Java runtime system. Once the code has been verified, the JVM breaks down the bytecodes into a set of machine instructions and executes it.

Believe it or not, because Java is designed to run within a garbage-collecting environment, the JVM's job is not yet done. The term *garbage collection* refers to the process of automatically cleaning up unused memory when the program is done with it. Most languages that allow programmers to allocate new memory in the form of objects also require the programmer to free the memory. Large amounts of memory that are allocated and never freed can eventually cause a system to slow down to a crawl or halt completely.

Java removes this memory-management chore from the hands of programmers by using the JVM to monitor memory usage at all times during a program's runtime. Java provides this feature for two primary reasons:

- Garbage collection is popular with developers and makes the Java language even more powerful and easy to use.
- Without garbage collection, a rogue programmer could potentially crash the JVM by freeing invalid sections of memory. This type of maneuver could permit a breach of security and has been disallowed.

The JVM specification in no way specifies how the JVM should free unused memory. Instead, this implementation decision is left up to individual JVM designers. The important feature is that the JVM provides support for runtime garbage collection, which is a two-step process.

The first step in garbage collection requires the JVM to monitor memory usage and determine which objects are subject to being "taken out with the trash." An object is determined to be garbage if it cannot be reached by any currently active branches, or "roots," within the program code. Once these objects have been determined, the JVM must free the memory they are occupying.

Two popular algorithms used to free memory at runtime are the *mark-and-sweep* and *stop-and-copy* algorithms. These algorithms are discussed briefly in the following sections because they are excellent examples of different design philosophies and because the Microsoft JVM uses the stop-and-copy approach.

Garbage Collection Using Mark and Sweep

The mark-and-sweep algorithm traverses the entire list of objects available within a program. The algorithm determines which objects are currently active and marks them as such (see Figure 4.3).

FIGURE 4.3.

Step 1: Mark all active objects.

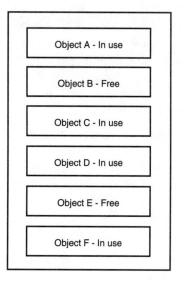

Once this traversal is complete, all unmarked objects are deleted (see Figure 4.4).

FIGURE 4.4.

Step 2: Delete all unused objects.

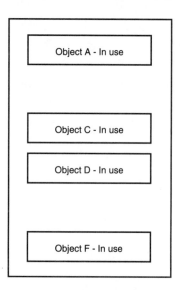

Unfortunately, when objects are dynamically deleted, memory becomes fragmented. To solve the fragmentation problem, the final stage of the mark-and-sweep algorithm compacts the objects in memory by moving objects around in memory (see Figure 4.5).

Figure 4.5.
Step 3: Defragment memory by moving objects.

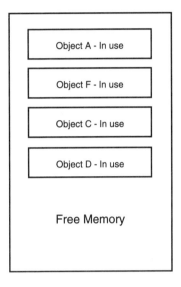

Many JVM implementations use the mark-and-sweep algorithm. It has the disadvantage of having a high performance overhead because of the large number of object accesses involved. However, this algorithm can operate within a small memory space and is ideal for embedded implementations of the JVM.

Garbage Collection Using Stop and Copy

The stop-and-copy algorithm arrives at the same result as the mark-and-sweep algorithm but usually does so more quickly. However, stop and copy has the disadvantage of requiring a larger amount of heap memory than mark and sweep for its operation because this algorithm requires two equal-sized areas of heap memory at all times. The first area contains all objects used by the program. The second area is used as a "copy buffer." The stop-and-copy algorithm begins by traversing the object list and examining all objects. As soon as an object is determined to be active, it is immediately copied to the second memory area (see Figure 4.6).

Once the JVM reaches the end of the active objects, it switches its focus to the second memory area for all future memory accesses.

The Microsoft Windows Virtual Machine for Java uses the stop-and-copy algorithm to perform garbage collection. This methodology results in much higher performance (compared to the mark-and-sweep algorithm), but it requires twice as much memory as the mark-and-sweep method. From Microsoft's desktop-centric viewpoint, performance is a more important benchmark than memory usage; therefore, this choice makes sense.

FIGURE 4.6.

Move active memory objects.

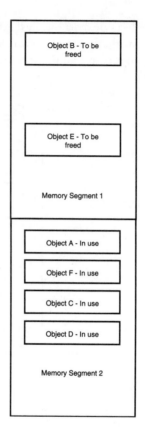

This section concludes the discussion of the Java runtime operating environment. The following section examines the Java API in detail and explains the Java Base Platform, its constituents, and its system-level capabilities.

The Java API

The Java Application Programming Interface (API) provides a standard set of objects that all Java programmers can use when developing software. Portions of the Java API are guaranteed to exist in every Java runtime installation. These portions make up what is known as the Java Base API. One of the exciting features of Java is its dynamically linked nature. As has been discussed throughout this chapter, when Java code is compiled, it produces a set of bytecodes that exist in one or more files. One of these class files corresponds to each public Java class implemented in the applet or application. (Don't concern yourself now with the word *public*. The important point here is that one class file is equivalent to each Java object used throughout your program.)

In the case of a Web-based Java applet, all of the class files that collectively make up your applet could reside together in a directory on a remote Web server. When a client browser loads your applet, all of these class files are transferred over the network to the user's browser (which, by the way, is running an implementation of the JVM). If you have loaded applets in the past into a Web browser, you know that some time was spent downloading these class files before the applet was actually displayed and executed. The Java API greatly reduces this download time because the API probably includes the majority of the objects that your applet uses.

For instance, imagine an applet that contains a list box, a button, and text on the screen. Because Java is an object-oriented language, this screen is created using the List, Button, and Label objects contained within the Java Base API. When your code is compiled, one class file will be generated to be placed on the Web server. After a user loads a page containing your Java applet, your solitary class file will be downloaded to his or her machine and will be linked with local copies of the List, Button, and Label class files.

The beauty of this process is that Java programmers can not only produce *bytecodes* that run on all operating platforms, but also produce *source code* that does not need to be modified for any particular platform. Developers can distribute applets or applications with the knowledge that each machine using their software will contain a common base set of Java bytecodes known as the Java Base API.

The Java Base API

The Java Base API is currently defined as the full set of APIs that is distributed with the Java Developer's Kit, or JDK, version 1.0.2.

> **NOTE**
>
> The JDK contains the Java Base Platform and a rudimentary set of development tools that can be used for Java development. More information on the JDK is provided in the section titled "Obtaining the Java Base Platform."

The Java Base API provides an incredibly useful code base for Java developers. Classes in the Base API, or Java Applet API as it is also called, provide the functionality used for common input/output, networking, graphical user interfaces, and applet operations. These classes are part of the java *package*. (A *package* is simply a Java construct for an object used to group a set of related classes.) The java package contains the following subpackages:

- java.lang
- java.util
- java.io
- java.net
- java.awt
- java.applet

Each package contains a myriad of classes that are most commonly used by Java developers. Brief discussions of the individual packages follow. For more detailed information on the java package, see Chapter 13, "The Standard Java Packages," which is dedicated to this topic.

This list of packages collectively make up the Java Base API. As Java expands, more and more classes will be added to the different packages so that enhanced functionality can be passed on to the end user. Many future packages are currently contained in the Java Standard Extension API.

The Java Standard Extension API

The Java Standard Extension API provides a standard API that is published and open. Because members of the Extension API are not included with the Java Base Platform, individual vendors are encouraged to implement their own versions of these APIs as long as they conform to Sun standards. Sun is currently considering adding some of the more popular Extension APIs to the Base API. (These APIs are noted in the following sections.)

The Java Security API

The Java Security API is being designed to provide a modular approach to implementing security for Java applications. Consequently, security models will be able to be swapped in and out should better methods be chosen. For instance, a plug-in architecture such as this would allow developers to quickly switch between different encryption schemes should more superior schemes be introduced in the future. The Java Security API will provide digital signatures, encryption, and authentication of Java code. The Java Security API is being considered for migration to the Java Base API.

The Java Media API

The Java Media API is being designed to provide complete multimedia capabilities for use in Java application development. It includes APIs for animation, collaboration, 2D and 3D graphics, video, audio, and telephony. The 3D API is eagerly awaited by many because it provides support for VRML. Tools for collaboration will be provided with the Share API, which should allow developers to add collaboration capabilities to their applications. Portions of the Java Media API being considered for addition to the Java Base API include the Audio, 2D, and Animation APIs.

The Java Commerce API

The Java Commerce API provides secure commerce capabilities through the use of Java. A key component of the Java Commerce API is the Java Wallet. This object will allow clients to use a digital wallet containing identification information, credit cards, and cash. Powerful security features are naturally part of this API, and their implementation is essential to the success of secure commerce using Java. This API is being considered for addition to the Java Base API.

The Java Server API

The Java Server API will provide capabilities that can be used for the creation of Java-based Internet and intranet servers. This API includes libraries for system administration, security, and resource monitoring.

The Java Enterprise API

The Java Enterprise API is arguably the most eagerly awaited of all the Java standard extensions. Included in the Enterprise API is a group of frameworks that support Java database connectivity (JDBC), Interface Definition Language (IDL), and Remote Method Invocation (RMI).

JDBC is currently available and is the Java equivalent of Microsoft's open database connectivity (ODBC) API. JDBC will provide database connectivity and uses a driver-based system to communicate with SQL database servers such as Oracle, SQL Server, and Informix.

IDL is a language-independent way of exposing an object's methods and properties to other object models on different platforms. The IDL is used by common object request brokering architecture (CORBA) to define properties of objects.

RMI is the object world's equivalent of remote procedure calls (RPCs). RMIs are used to call objects located on remote machines.

Of the three APIs included within the Java Enterprise API, JDBC is the only one currently being considered for inclusion with the Java Base API.

Obtaining the Java Base Platform

By now you should have a good understanding of how the Java runtime system operates through the combination of the Java Base API and the underlying JVM. You can obtain the Java Base Platform in three different ways:

- Install a Java-capable Web browser, such as Sun HotJava, Microsoft Internet Explorer, or Netscape Navigator.
- Download and install Sun's JDK from Sun's Web or FTP sites.
- Purchase and install a commercial Java compiler such as Microsoft Visual J++.

If you are reading this book, you are probably most interested in the Java Base Platform provided with Visual J++, which is discussed in the next section. If you are interested only in viewing Java applets, install a Java-capable Web browser. Once this installation is complete, a copy of the Java Base Platform will exist somewhere on your system. (The exact location depends on which browser you install.) However, if you do not yet have a copy of Visual J++ but are interested in developing Java code, you can use the JDK to compile and run many of the examples in this book. This toolkit is freely provided by Sun Microsystems and is currently available for Windows 95/NT, Apple Macintosh, and Sun Solaris.

Let me stress that the tools and documentation included in the JDK are rudimentary at best. A tremendous effort will be made throughout this book to point out the many strengths and capabilities of the Microsoft Visual J++ compiler. In fact, all discussions and examples involving Microsoft COM or ActiveX technologies are applicable *only* to Visual J++. In the future, other tools will undoubtedly be released that support these technologies, but for now Microsoft leads the pack. Of course, it certainly doesn't hurt to have the ActiveX, Windows Virtual Machine for Java, and Visual J++ designers working within the same organization!

Assuming that you have already chosen to install the Visual J++ development platform, the next section discusses the physical components on your machine. Examining the Java Base Platform in detail should remove some of the mystique surrounding Java and its runtime execution environment. Other items installed as part of Visual J++ are also explained briefly. Many of these items will be explained in much greater detail throughout the remainder of this book.

Examining the Visual J++ Installation

As mentioned earlier, the Java Base Platform has three basic components:

- A runtime engine responsible for receiving and checking Java code
- The Java Virtual Machine
- The Java API

Visual J++ installs all three components onto your local machine in different forms.

The runtime interpreter is installed in the form of the JVIEW.EXE application. JView can be located in the Visual J++ \bin directory. This interpreter accepts a Java class name as its command-line input (jview classname). If the class is a valid Java application class (see Chapter 8, "Developing Applets and Applications," for more information on Java applications), JView will act as the runtime interpreter for the application. For Java applets and ActiveX controls embedded in Web pages, the Web browser itself supplies the runtime interpreter. This runtime component varies from browser to browser.

The Microsoft Windows Virtual Machine for Java is actually distributed throughout the c:\windows directory. However, several Windows Registry keys can be examined to determine the location of required components. To examine the Registry under Windows 95, run REGEDIT.EXE. Under Windows NT, run REGEDT32.EXE. Examples of keys that can be found in the HKEY_LOCAL_MACHINE\Software\Microsoft\Java VM Registry entry are

- ClassesBuild
- ClassPath
- LibsDirectory
- TrustedClasspath
- TrustedLibsDirectory

The Windows Virtual Machine also examines the CLASSPATH environment variable in addition to the ClassPath Registry key to determine the location of all class files.

The Java Base API is also included with the Visual J++ installation. The classes in the Base API are zipped into a file named CLASSES.ZIP located in the c:\windows\java\classes directory. If for some reason the CLASSES.ZIP file is not located in that directory, examine the ClassPath Registry key to get an idea of where it might be located.

Summary

The Java Base Platform is a well-defined subset of Java technologies that is guaranteed to be the same on every platform. This sort of standardization is extremely important in a world where every company is racing to add features to "standardized" technologies. Any application or applet that is written to run using the Java Base Platform will be guaranteed to run on every Java-enabled operating system.

The Java Base Platform is composed of a runtime engine that is responsible for validating Java bytecodes as they are received. The JVM then translates these bytecodes into machine code. When Visual J++ is installed, the user also receives the Sun-certified copy of the Microsoft Windows Virtual Machine for Java. This JVM is the reference implementation for the Windows platform. Any changes Microsoft makes to this JVM can then be licensed back to Sun for inclusion in JVMs on all other platforms.

In addition to the Java Base API, Sun is continually developing new Java APIs in the hope that Java can gain enough broad support to become the programming language and environment of choice for all development. The key point of this chapter is that Visual J++ is fully compatible with all capabilities of Java. Bytecodes produced by Visual J++ will run on any platform that contains a JVM (unless Java is combined with ActiveX). The following chapter introduces the basic syntactical elements of the Java programming language. Following Chapter 5, the concepts introduced in the first five chapters will begin to be applied to developing actual Java applets and applications through the remainder of Part I, "Introduction to Java Programming Using Visual J++."

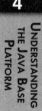

Elements of the Java Language

by Bryan Morgan

IN THIS CHAPTER

CHAPTER 5

Programmers who have experience writing code in C or C++ will find that Java borrows heavily from these languages. The languages are so similar that the Java language specification (from Sun Microsystems) actually mentions that in any case where Java syntax is not specifically explained, the ANSI C specification should be consulted. Although the previous chapters introduced the Visual J++ development environment and object-oriented programming, you still need to learn basic Java syntax before you can write full-featured programs. This chapter introduces the elements of the Java language. Then you will be ready to create Java programs, as you will do in Chapter 6, "Creating Programs with Java."

Like all programming languages, Java executes commands in the form of statements that tell the computer what to do. Programmers can use three basic forms of variables to perform work within a statement:

■ A basic Java data type

■ An array of values

■ A class

As you have already seen, a set of statements grouped together can be used to form a method, which in turn (when grouped with variables) can form a Java class. This chapter starts out by describing the data types, operators, and control flow statements of the Java language, then discusses arrays and classes, and concludes with the creation of a class.

Java's Unit of Work: The Statement

Every Java program is made up of statements that are used to accomplish tasks. All code used to form a statement is case sensitive in Java, which means that you can use two similar variables (for example, I and i) to perform some task without receiving a compiler error. Like statements in C and C++, every Java statement must end with a semicolon (;). Leaving a semicolon off the end of a statement can lead to horrific amounts of compiler errors (depending on which compiler you use). Even if you have never worked with a language that terminates statements in this way, you can be sure that over time, terminating statements with semicolons will become an automatic task.

The following statements are all legal Java statements:

```
Font theFont = new Font("Helvetica", Font.BOLD, 20);
String String1, String2;
if (evt.target instanceof Button) theList.addItem(theText.getText());
import java.awt.Button;
package visual.jplusplus;
```

Notice that four of the five statements consist of a single line of text terminated with a semicolon. These statements are known as single statements. The `if` statement is known as a compound statement because it actually uses more than one line to accomplish its task. In this case the `if` statement checks to see if some condition has been met. If the condition is true, then some text is added to a list box on a screen.

Compound statements are statements that contain operations within a block that can be surrounded by braces ({...}). Examples of compound statements are the control flow statements (such as if...then...else, do...while, and for).

In some cases, a statement simply declares a variable or provides the compiler with information. It does not return any information to the program for later use. Examples of statements that do not return data are

float Frequency;—Declares a floating-point variable named Frequency.

import sun.debug.*;—Imports all of the classes within the sun.debug package.

paint(graph);—Calls a method named paint and passes the variable graph as an argument.

Expressions

No truly useful program can possibly be written, however, without using statements that return values. These statements are also known as *expressions*. Here are some examples of useful expressions:

float Frequency = 5.538;—Declares a floating-point variable named Frequency and initializes it to 5.538.

if (checkVal = 999)...—Compares the variable checkVal to the number 999. If this comparison is true, it returns a boolean true to the if statement.

return true;—Exits a method and returns a value of true to the calling method.

Adding Comments to Your Source Code

All modern programming languages provide ways for programmers to leave helpful notes, reminders, or documentation within their source code. These reminders are known as *comments*. Comments are not actually statements because they are skipped by the compiler and do not exist at runtime. Although the compiler ignores comments, you—the software developer—should not ignore them. Java provides developers with three separate ways to add comments to their code. (With so many options, you have no excuse for not properly documenting your software!) The following symbols are used to denote comments in Java:

■ /* ... */—These delimiters, like delimiters in C and C++, are used to surround single- or multiple-line comments.

■ //—Borrowed from C++, this delimiter denotes a single-line comment.

■ /** ... */—Comments used by javadoc, a Java documentation tool provided with the Java Developer's Kit (JDK) from Sun Microsystems. (Visual J++ makes no special use of these comments.)

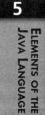

Two things should be noted about comments:

- Source code can appear on the same line as a comment as long as it appears outside of the comment's delimiters.
- If the delimiters do not match up, a compilation error will occur.

For instance, the following lines show some invalid comments:

```
int I = 3; /* We left one hanging! -->*/  /*

//This is a valid comment, but the code is ignored! int I = 3;
```

The next two snippets are perfectly valid comments (although not particularly helpful):

```
int I= 3;  /* Set I = 3 */
```

and

```
/*
    Created by Bryan Morgan
    Special thanks to:
    Dave Matthews Band,
    Oasis,
    and, of course ... caffeine
*/
```

You should always make sure that your comments are for someone else (or for you at a later date) to understand.

Legal Syntax for Identifiers

The Java language specification details exactly which characters can and cannot be used to create identifiers (such as variable names, method names, and so on). The basic rules for identifiers are

- Identifiers must start with a letter, underscore, or dollar sign.
- Any letter other than the first letter can be a digit (0–9).
- Any character can be in the following ranges: a–z, A–Z, and Unicode values above 00C0. (Unicode is discussed later in this chapter.)
- The identifier must not be one of the Java keywords.

Java Keywords

The Java language specification lists a group of keywords that can be used only for their intended purpose as listed in the specification. These keywords are listed in Table 5.1.

Table 5.1. Java keywords.

abstract	continue	for	new	switch
boolean	default	goto	null	synchronized
break	do	if	package	this
byte	double	implements	private	threadsafe
byvalue	else	import	protected	throw
case	extends	instanceof	public	transient
catch	false	int	return	true
char	final	interface	short	try
const	finally	long	static	void

Where Are the `ifdefs`, `pragmas`, and `includes`?

Veteran C and C++ programmers should feel comfortable with Java's syntax. C++ programmers, in particular, have a very short learning curve because Java's object-oriented features are so similar to those of C++. However, C and C++ both use keywords to provide compiler directives. The following are some examples of these directives:

```
#ifdef
#define
#pragma
#include
```

Java was intentionally designed to remove the more complicated or redundant features of C++ without sacrificing any of its power. In doing so, some features of other languages were borrowed, and many other features were ignored. For instance, C and C++ use the `#include` directive to specify header files containing variable, structure, and function specifications. Java source files contain *only* Java classes. All code used to create class members is contained within that class, which means that you don't have to maintain separate header files. C or C++ programmers that fault Java for deleting certain syntactical elements should remember that Java is still a full-featured, extremely powerful language. In short, anything that can be coded in C/C++ can be written with Java.

Java Data Types

As was discussed in Chapter 3, "Object-Oriented Programming with Java," Java classes can contain member variables that coexist with class member methods. Variables can also be created within a method, and a variables scope extends within that method only. Variables can be any one of three types: an array, a class, or a Java primitive data type. Programming with array and class variables is discussed later in the chapter; this part of the discussion focuses on the eight primitive data types included with the Java language.

You can use these data types in a program without allowing for the coding overhead associated with Java classes. (All Java classes must specifically be created and imported by the programmer. Otherwise, they are unknown entities to the Visual J++ compiler.)

> **NOTE**
>
> If you have ever done cross-platform software development, you probably know that data type sizes can change between platforms. For instance, in a 16-bit Windows program written in C, an `int` is a 2-byte value. For a UNIX program written in C, an `int` is a 4-byte value. Java, as part of its platform-independent philosophy, guarantees that all primitive data types will be the same size regardless of the underlying platform.

Table 5.2 describes the eight basic data types.

Table 5.2. Java data types.

Data Type	Description
`boolean`	Boolean value that can be either `true` or `false`
`byte`	8-bit signed value
`char`	16-bit Unicode character
`double`	64-bit floating-point value
`float`	32-bit floating-point value
`int`	32-bit signed value
`long`	64-bit signed value
`short`	16-bit signed value

These primitive data types can be used to declare a variable for use within a program. Once the variable has been declared, the programmer can use it immediately without worrying about allocating or deallocating memory for that variable.

As you can see in Table 5.2, a `boolean` variable can be either `true` or `false`. Unlike many other programming languages, character values are not simply ASCII values. Instead, they are Unicode values. Because the ASCII character set restricts a character to one of 255 values, it is practically useless for displaying languages such as Chinese with its hundreds or thousands of possible characters. A Unicode character is a 16-bit value and can store one of 64K different values.

Like C/C++, Java allows programmers to use character escape codes when performing string operations. For example, you can use the following statement to print the string `"Hello World!"` to the screen:

```
System.out.println("Hello World!");
```

Now assume that you want to place a tab character at the end of this string so that your text would appear properly formatted on the screen. The best way to do so is by including a special character escape code at the end of that string. (The escape code for a tab character is `"\t"`.) To print the string correctly with a tab out to the screen, use the following statement:

```
System.out.println("Hello World!\n");
```

The escape codes that can be used in Java are

- `\n`—Newline
- `\r`—Carriage return
- `\t`—Tab
- `\b`—Backspace
- `\f`—Form feed
- `\\`—Backslash character (requires two backslashes)
- `\'`—Single-quote character
- `\"`—Double-quote character
- `\ddd`—Octal-bit pattern
- `\xdd`—Hexadecimal-bit pattern
- `\udddd`—Unicode character

At first glance, representing a backslash as `"\\"` or a double quote as `"\"` may seem odd. However, in a statement such as

```
System.out.println("Howdy,"pardner"");
```

the compiler would throw an error saying it expected a `");"` after the second double quote because the second double quote closes a string literal value. The escape code enables the compiler to understand the following:

```
System.out.println("Howdy, \"pardner\"");
```

When this statement is executed, the following would appear on the user's screen:

```
Howdy, "pardner"
```

Converting Among Types

Nearly every Java data type can be converted to any other Java data type. The only exception to this rule is that a boolean value can not be converted (or "cast," as it is commonly called) to any other value. A general rule of thumb is that when going from a smaller bit-value type to a larger bit-value type (such as from byte to float), you don't need to make an explicit cast. An example of this type of cast is

```
byte TinyBite;
float BigChomp;
TinyBite = 17;
BigChomp = 42.568;
BigChomp = TinyBite;
```

These statements are perfectly legal. At the end of these statements, the value of BigChomp would be 17.00.

To go from a larger bit-value type to a smaller bit-value type, some data will be lost. Therefore, Java requires you to explicitly cast the type so that the compiler is sure that you know what you are doing. Here is the syntax to explicitly cast a type:

```
(new type name) oldvalue;
```

Here is an example of an explicit typecast:

```
byte TinyBite;
float Bigchomp;
TinyBite = 17;
BigChomp = 42.568;
TinyBite = (byte) BigChomp;
```

Following the execution of these statements, TinyBite would be equal to 42.

Now that you know about Java statements, variables, methods, and classes, you are ready to use operators in Java in order to perform operations on variables. Examples of the types of operations that can be performed are bit-shifts, mathematical operations, and logical comparisons.

Java Operators

All Java statements and expressions are made up of two things: operands and operators. To compare a Java statement to an English sentence, operands are the nouns (or direct objects) and operators are the verbs. For example, if X is divided by Y (X / Y), X and Y are the operands and the division sign is the operator. Operators assign values, do arithmetic, and perform comparisons. Every operator uses two operands (one on either side of it). The result of the operation is then forwarded for use in the next operation. The following statements illustrate operators at work:

```
int i = 2 * x; /* Two operators:  "=" and "*" */
x += y;        /* One operator: "+=" */
if ((x == 3) = True) … /* Four operators:  "(…)" (twice) and "==" and "=" */
```

The Java language specification describes the exact order in which multiple operations are evaluated. The evaluation order is discussed throughout this section.

Assignment Operators

The most commonly used assignment operator is the operator =, which takes the operand on its right side and assigns it to the operand on its left side. The following shows the assignment operator being used:

```
x=3;
y=x;
String name="Billy Bob";
```

NOTE

One interesting bit of information concerning operators is that the result of an operation becomes the operand of the next operation. For instance, in (x + y) + (a * b), the (x + y) operation occurs first, the (a * b) operation occurs second, and then the results of these two operations occurs third. This sequence applies also to multiple assignment operators within the same statement. Therefore, the statement a = b = c = d = e = f = g is a perfectly valid statement that assigns the value of the variable g to the variables a, b, c, d, e, and f.

The remainder of the assignment operators borrow from C/C++. They are as follows:

- a += b (equivalent to a = a + b)
- a -= b (equivalent to a = a - b)
- a *= b (equivalent to a = a * b)
- a++ (equivalent to a = a + 1)
- a-- (equivalent to a = a - 1)

Note that an operation such as a = a + b is not illegal. The assignment operators listed above simply make your code more compact and perform the same operations in a fewer number of keystrokes. In fact, these assignment operators are often referred to as the *shorthand assignment operators.*

The Comparison Operators

The purpose of the comparison operators is to perform comparison operations between two operands. Typical operations include greater than, less than, and equal to. These operators are as follows:

- == (equals)
- != (not equal)

- ■ < (less than)
- ■ <= (less than or equal to)
- ■ > (greater than)
- ■ >= (greater than or equal to)

CAUTION

When using the == operator to test for equality, make sure to always use two equals signs! A common coding mistake is to attempt to perform a comparison using one equals sign (=), which actually performs an assignment. Therefore, the code "if (x = 3)..." will always return true because when x is *assigned* 3, it returns a boolean True. The correct way to perform this comparison is "if (x == 3)..."

Comparison operators are commonly used in control flow statements such as if-then-else branches or for loops. These statements are discussed later in this chapter.

The Logical Operators

Programmers with some training in digital logic will be familiar with computer circuitry such as AND, NAND, OR, and NOR gates. The premise behind these circuits is that two signals are input through the circuit to produce one output. For instance, an AND gate will take two binary 1s and produce a 1. It will also take a 1 and a 0 and produce a 0.

The Java language provides logical operators that perform exactly the same function on two operands. These operators are

- ■ &—Returns true only when both operand tests are true. Both left and right operands are tested.
- ■ &&—Returns true only when both operand tests are true. The left side is evaluated first, and if it is false, the right side is never evaluated.
- ■ ¦—Returns true if either operand test is true. Both the left and right operands are tested.
- ■ ¦¦—Returns true if either operand test is true. The left side is evaluated first, and if it is true, the right side is never evaluated.
- ■ !—The NOT operator is used with only one operand. If the operand is true, this operator returns false; if the operand is false, this operator returns true.
- ■ ^—Returns true if one operand is false and the other true; if both are true or both are false, this operator returns false.

The following code snippets illustrate the usage of the logical operators:

```
boolean a = true;
boolean b = false;
boolean result;
result = a && b; // Returns false, both a and b are tested
result = a ¦ b;  // Returns true
result = a ¦¦ b; // Returns true, b is never evaluated
result = a ^ b;  // Returns true
result = !a;      // Returns false
result = !b;      // Returns true
result = !(a && b) // Return true
result = ((a ^ b) ^ b) && a; // Returns true
```

Notice that in the last two example statements, more than one operation actually occurs. In the next to last example, a & b is evaluated first and returns false. The NOT operator is then applied to it and returns true.

The final example statement has three separate evaluations. The internal parentheses— (a ^ b)—is evaluated first, which returns true. This expression is then XORed with b and returns true. This result is then ANDed with a to return a true result.

Arithmetic Operators

Regardless of your level of computer programming experience, you are undoubtedly familiar with most or all of the arithmetic operators (except for perhaps the modulus operator). Here is a list of arithmetic operators:

- + (Addition)
- - (Subtraction)
- * (Multiplication)
- / (Division)
- % (Modulus)

The modulus operator may be new to you and therefore requires some explanation. In short, a modulus operation returns the remainder of the division of two operands. Therefore, 14 mod 7 = 0 because 14 divided by 7 returns 2 (with no remainder). Likewise, 100 mod 40 = 20 because 100 divided by 40 returns 2 with a remainder of 20. The following example snippets illustrate the use of these operators.

```
int I = 3;
int J = 10;
int result;
result = I * J; // result = 30
result = I + J; // result = 13
result = I / J; // result = 0
result = J % I; // result = 1
```

Notice that in the I / J operation that the result is actually 0 because both I and J are integer values. When a floating-point value is stored to an int in Java, the result is truncated.

One additional use of the addition operator (+)in Java is to add strings together. Using the addition operator, the statement

```
Name = "George" + " Washington";
```

would result in the Name variable equaling "George Washington". This is much simpler than using methods to concatenate two strings together and greatly improves the readability of code. Also note that the "+=" assignment operator can be used to add a string together such as in the following sample code:

```
Name = "George";
Name += " Washington";
```

These two statements would return the same result as the previous single-line statement returned.

The Bitwise Operators

The final set of operators are the bitwise operators, which perform what engineers lovingly refer to as "bit fiddling." In other words, these operators do not operate on the operand's decimal or string values; instead, bitwise operators work at the actual binary level (that is, a byte value of 8 isn't treated as an 8—it's treated as a 00001000.) Before discussing what the operators actually are, the following examples should help explain their purpose.

To perform a bitwise AND, the binary values of two operands are ANDed together, bit by bit. Keeping in mind that 0 AND 0 = 0, 0 AND 1 = 0, and 1 AND 1 = 1, then:

```
00001000 AND 00000100 = 00000000
```

Likewise

```
10001001 AND 11101000 = 10001000
```

To perform a bitwise OR, the binary values of two operands are ORed together, bit by bit. Keeping in mind that 0 OR 0 = 0, 0 OR 1 = 1, and 1 OR 1 = 1, then:

```
00001000 OR 00000100 = 00001100
```

and

```
10001001 OR 11101000 = 01110001
```

A bit shift is exactly what it sounds like. All bits are moved over one position in the direction of the shift. The bit on the end that is "bumped off" is shifted around to the opposite end of the chain. For instance, if 00001000 were left shifted, the value would become 00010000.

The Java operators for bitwise operations were borrowed directly from C and C++. They are as follows:

■ & (bitwise AND)

■ ¦ (bitwise OR)

- ^ (bitwise XOR)
- - (bitwise complement)
- << (left shift)
- >> (right shift)
- >>> (zero fill right shift)
- >>>= (zero fill right shift with assignment)
- <<= (left shift with assignment)
- >>= (right shift with assignment)
- a &= b (AND with assignment)
- a ¦= b (OR with assignment)
- a ^= b (XOR with assignment)

The bitwise operators are extremely useful in operations in which a binary value may represent a number of different channels or inputs and a variety of these values need to be manipulated in some way.

Order of Operator Evaluation

Just as mathematical operations are evaluated in terms of precedence, operators as a whole are also evaluated by the Visual J++ compiler from highest to lowest precedence. The Java operators are evaluated in the following order (from highest to lowest):

```
. [] ()
++ — ! ~ instanceof
* / %
+ -
<;<; >;>; >;>;>;
<; >; <;= >;=
== !=
&;
^
¦
&;&;
¦¦
?:
= op=
,
```

It is necessary to define an operator evaluation order so that the compiler will know which portions of a statement to execute first. As an example, the following uses the +, ==, and ¦¦ operators in a single statement:

```
boolean Value = x+y==6 ¦¦ x+y==5;
```

In this statement, the + operator is evaluated first, followed by ==, and then ¦¦, according to the operator evaluation order shown earlier. If some order was not defined for Java, the compiler would simply evaluate statements from left to right. In this situation, you could receive a far different result than the desired one.

5

ELEMENTS OF THE
JAVA LANGUAGE

Before examining control flow statements in Java, take note that any operators not mentioned above are identical to their corresponding operators in C or C++. Examples of operators not discussed in the following sections are the ternary (?:) and bitwise complement (-) operators.

Java Control Flow Statements

The Java language supports the exact same type of control flow statements that are found in C and C++. These are the `if` conditional statement, the `while`, `do-while`, and `for` loops, and the `switch` statement. Some subtle differences do exist between the Java and C implementation, however. In some cases these differences give the J++ programmer additional control; in other cases J++ is more restrictive than C or C++.

The basic concept behind a control flow statement is controlling the flow of a program. Although the simple statements discussed so far execute only one line of code at a time, control flow statements contain multiple statements within a block of code surrounded by braces (`{ ... }`). In general, all of these "block" statements check for a boolean condition in order to execute the block of code. In the case of loops, the condition is checked each time through the loop. Once the condition returns `false`, the loop exits. Remember that the condition being checked must return a boolean value. Some languages, such as C, allow this conditional check to simply return *any* value (an integer, float, and so on). Java forces this condition to be either `true` or `false`.

One other difference between the C language syntax and Java's is that any variable declared for use within a loop cannot be used outside of that loop's statement block. Consequently, the final statement in these pseudo-statements is invalid:

```
for (int i = 0; i<100; i++)
{
.
.
.
}

i = 5;
```

The `if` Conditional Statement

One programming construct that is no doubt familiar to programmers is the `if` statement. This statement can be found in virtually every programming language. The `if` statement has two basic steps:

1. A condition is checked.
2. If that condition is true, a block of statements is executed.

The syntax for the `if` statement is as follows:

```
if (boolean condition)
{
   /* block of statements */
}
else if (boolean condition)
{
   /* block of statements */
}
else if (boolean condition)
{
   /* block of statements */
}
.
.
.
else
{
   /* block of statements */
}
```

The `else` clause at the end `if` is optional. This clause is used to provide a default statement block should all of the preceding `if`s prove to be false. In some cases, no default processing is required. (The same principle also applies to `else if...` statements.) Notice also that the block of statements within each clause is surrounded by braces (`{...}`). In situations where the block of statements is a single line, the braces are not required. The removal of the braces surrounding a block of code helps reduce the size of the code you have to stare at on the screen.

The `if` statement is demonstrated with two samples: one invalid and one valid. The following sample is invalid because the condition returns an integer value, not a boolean:

```
int i = 75;
int j = 120;

if (i * j)
   System.out.println("Greater than zero!");
else
   System.out.println("Equals zero!");
```

In C, `i * j` returns an integer value, which satisfies a condition. In Java, a boolean *must* be returned here. Therefore, the proper way to test this statement to see if it is greater than zero is

```
int i = 75;
int j = 120;

if (i * j > 0)
   System.out.println("Greater than zero!");
else
   System.out.println("Equals zero!");
```

Listing 5.1 makes full use of the `if` statement to execute entire blocks of code. This listing uses the `String` and `Float` classes, which have not been covered yet. Unlike all other classes, a `String` object can be assigned a value without the programmer needing to explicitly allocate memory for it. The `Float` class is useful for converting floating-point values to other data types.

NOTE

You will learn later in this chapter that for every primitive data type, Java also provides a corresponding class. These classes provide helper methods that are useful when dealing with the primitive data types. While C and C++ simply include helper functions such as `floattostr()` as global functions, everything in Java must be in a class. Therefore, classes that correspond to each data type are part of the `java.lang` package.

In addition to noting the class types when you read Listing 5.1, you will see that you can already begin to build a fairly powerful group of statements. Control flow statements allow you to accomplish many complicated tasks in a relatively small amount of code.

Listing 5.1. Calculating the area of a shape.

```
String shape;
int x = 10;
int y = 5;
int radius = 25;
float area;
float circumference;

shape = "Circle";

if (shape.equals("Square"))
{
  area = x * x;
  circumference = 4 * x;
  System.out.println("The area is " + Float.toString(area) + "\n");
  System.out.println("The circumference is " + Float.toString(circumference)
      + "\n");
}
else if (shape.equals("Circle"))
{
  area = (float)(3.14 * radius * radius);
  circumference = (float)(3.14 * 2 * radius);
System.out.println("The area is " + Float.toString(area) + "\n");
  System.out.println("The circumference is " + Float.toString(circumference)
      + "\n");
}
else if (shape.equals("Rectangle"))
{
  area = x * y;
  circumference = (2 * x) + (2 * y);
  System.out.println("The area is " + Float.toString(area) + "\n");
  System.out.println("The circumference is " + Float.toString(circumference)
      + "\n");
}
else
  System.out.println("Don't known how to compute!!\n");
```

Listing 5.1 uses the `if` statement to test the equality of a `String` variable and a character string value. If the two are equal, then the area and circumference are computed and printed out to the console.

The `while` Loop

The `while` loop is used to continually execute a statement block while a condition is true. If the condition is initially false, the statement block is never executed. This is what separates the `while` loop from the `do-while` loop. In a `do-while` loop, the statement block is executed once before the condition is initially tested.

The `while` loop in Java looks like the one found in C:

```
while (boolean condition)
{
   /* block of statements */
}
```

Listing 5.2 uses a `while` loop to continually print the area of a rectangle out to the console as long as that area stays less than `200`.

Listing 5.2. Incrementally calculating the area of a square.

```
int x = 5;
int y = 5;
float area = (float)0.0;

while (area < 200.0)
{
  area = x * y;
  System.out.println("The area is " + Float.toString(area) + "\n");
  x++;
  y++;
}
```

This `while` loop should print out until x and y each are 15. At that point 15 * 15 = 225 and the loop will end. In other words, the output will be

```
The area is 25
The area is 36
The area is 49
The area is 64
The area is 81
The area is 100
The area is 121
The area is 144
The area is 169
The area is 196
The area is 225
```

The do...while Loop

The do...while loop performs a similar function to the while loop. The only difference is that the do...while loop tests the condition at the end of the statement block. Therefore, even if the condition is false, the loop will execute at least one iteration instead of simply exiting before executing the statements within the loop. The do...while loop looks like this:

```
do
{
   /* block of statements */
}
while (boolean condition);
```

Listing 5.3 uses the do...while loop to print out the area of a rectangle. (This listing is similar to Listing 5.2.)

Listing 5.3. Using a do...while loop to calculate area.

```
int x = 15;
int y = 15;
float area = 0.0;

do
{
   area = x * y;
   System.out.println("The area is " + Float.toString(area) + "\n");
   x++;
   y++;
}
while (area < 200.0);
```

This loop will print out the following:

```
The area is 225
```

The for Loop

The for loop is used to loop through a block of statements as long as a condition is true. This loop is, in concept, the same as a while loop except that a for loop allows the programmer to specify how to increment values within the loop. A basic for loop has three parts:

■ A variable initialization

■ A conditional test to return a boolean value

■ A calculation, expression, or anything else that you want to perform for each iteration of the loop

The for loop separates each of these parts with a semicolon as follows:

```
for (init; condition; operation)
{
   /* block of statements */
}
```

Listing 5.4 produces the exact same result as Listing 5.2. The only difference is that it uses a
for loop to produce these results.

Listing 5.4. Using a for loop to calculate area.

```
for(int x = 5, int y = 5, float area = 0.0; area < 200.0; x++, y++)
{
  area = x * y;
  System.out.println("The area is " + Float.toString(area) + "\n");
}
```

This for loop should print out until both x and y are 15. At that point 15 * 15 = 225, and the
loop will end. In other words, the output will be as follows:

```
The area is 25

The area is 36

The area is 49

The area is 64

The area is 81

The area is 100

The area is 121

The area is 144

The area is 169

The area is 196

The area is 225
```

Note that multiple operations occur in the different parts of the for loop. These operations are
legal operations separated by the comma operator.

The switch Statement

In some situations, one variable may require testing for 1, 2, or maybe 200 values. Although it
is possible to perform if...else statements over and over again, Java provides a switch statement that is nearly identical to the switch found in C. The switch statement checks one variable for a variety of values. If any of these values are equal, J++ will execute the statement block
associated with that value. Unlike C, however, this variable must be a "small" data type such as
int, short, char, or byte. The syntax for the switch statement is

```
switch (test_expression)
{
  case Value1:
```

```
      /* block of statements */
      break;
   case Value2:
      /* block of statements */
      break;
   case Value3:
      /* block of statements */
      break;
...
   default:
      /* block of statements */
}
```

The `break` keyword forces the execution to break out of the `switch` statement so that the values below do not even need to be evaluated. This `break` is optional. If you want to continue to check for conditions, omit the `break`. Listing 5.5 illustrates how to use the `switch` statement.

Listing 5.5. Checking for a condition using the `switch` statement.

```
char FirstLetter;
FirstLetter = 'b';

switch (FirstLetter)
{
   case 'a':
      System.out.println("Your name begins with an a.");
      break;
   case 'e':
      System.out.println("Your name begins with an a.");
      break;
   case 'i':
      System.out.println("Your name begins with an a.");
      break;
   case 'o':
      System.out.println("Your name begins with an a.");
      break;
   case 'u':
      System.out.println("Your name begins with an a.");
      break;
   default:
      System.out.println("Your name doesn't begin with a vowel.");
}
```

The `switch` statement is convenient in some circumstances. However, the fact that this statement is limited to only evaluating ints, booleans, bytes, and chars keeps it from being useful all of the time. Remember that any operation that can be performed with a `switch` can also be performed with an `if`. In addition, the `if` statement can deal with any data type as long as the condition it checks returns a boolean value.

Forcing the Direction of Code Using break, continue, return, and label

As you saw in the switch statement, sometimes you want to force the execution of your code to go in a specific direction. Java provides several statements that can be used to exit a loop or method or cause the execution of your program to jump to another location in your code.

The break keyword is used to "break out" of a loop or switch. Whenever the break keyword is encountered, execution automatically drops out of the loop and continues with the next line of code immediately following the end of the loop. The break keyword can also be used in conjunction with a label (see the explanation that follows) to force the execution to jump to the labeled statement.

The continue keyword is also used with loops. However, instead of forcing the loop to automatically end, continue causes only this iteration to end. Therefore, if your code is on iteration 51 (out of 100) and it encounters the continue keyword, the loop automatically jumps to iteration 52, ignoring any statements that remain in the body of the loop. The continue keyword can also be used in conjunction with a label to force the execution to jump to the labeled statement.

The return keyword's usage is identical to its usage in C or C++. This keyword forces the method to exit immediately. When used with an operand, the return keyword returns the operand as that method's result. Keep in mind that the type of the returned value must match the return type of the method.

Finally, the label keyword can be used with any statement in this manner:

```
label: statement
```

This label can then be used by a break or continue to cause program execution to jump to the labeled statement.

The label keyword concludes this discussion of the basic elements of the Java language. By now you should have a good understanding of the following topics:

- Primitive data types
- Control flow statements
- Comments
- Class and interface syntax (from Chapter 3)
- Common Java operators

You are now ready to tackle the final topics that will allow you to create an actual Java class in this chapter and a real, live Java program in Chapter 6. The remainder of this chapter discusses the usage of arrays in Java and, finally, how to put all of these elements together into a single Java class that can be used in any Java application.

Creating and Using Arrays

On the surface, arrays in Java look identical to arrays in C. Individual array elements are accessed using an identifier within brackets such as [n], and all elements in an array must be of the same data type. Programmers familiar with C and C++ should remember that, in these languages, array syntax is in reality another way of doing pointer arithmetic. In C and C++ the zeroth element in an integer array is actually an integer pointer to an address in memory. The first element in an integer array is pointed to by the memory address plus one and so on. In other words, C/C++ compilers simply treats array variables as pointers. Treating arrays as pointers unfortunately allows the programmer to easily overrun the limits of an array's size, which results in an extra burden being placed on the programmer to make sure array index values are valid. "Overrunning" memory in this way also opens the door for security breaches of a system.

Java's designers recognized these pitfalls and changed the way arrays are handled. In Java, arrays are first class objects that can be created and passed to other methods as the objects they are. Like all other objects, memory for an array must be allocated before the array can be used. Failure to specifically create a new array object will result in an error. As the next section explains in more detail, the following two steps are required before you can use an object:

1. The variable must be declared.
2. A new object must be created and then assigned to the variable declared in step 1.

The most common syntax used to declare array variables is as follows:

```
Data type variable_name[];
```

The brackets after the variable name tell the compiler that an array will be allocated at some later point, and all elements in the array will be of the specified data type. Another way to write this statement is

```
Data type[] variable_name;
```

The following sample statements declare array variables of various data types:

```
int[][] numbers;
float degrees[];
Color rainbow[];
String[] people;
Button FormElements[];
```

Creating Arrays

As you can see, any type of data can be stored in an array. Although an array variable has been declared, it has not yet been instantiated. It is possible to instantiate the array variable either by allocating a new array of objects (filled with default values) or by filling the array with a group of values.

The new operator is used to assign an array object to the array variable. The new operator is discussed in detail in the next section, "Working with Objects"; using this operator will allocate the requested array of objects and assign that array to the variable you have declared. The following statements use the new operator to instantiate arrays for the variables listed previously:

```
numbers = new int[10][10];
degrees = new float[360];
rainbow = new Color[7];
people = new String[1000];
FormElements = new Button[10];
```

You can also use the = assignment operator to declare and create the array within a single statement. The following statements demonstrate this technique:

```
int[][] numbers = new int[10][10];
float degrees[] = new float[360];
Color rainbow[] = new Color[7];
String[] people = new String[1000];
Button FormElements[] = new Button[10];
```

When an array is created using the new operator, the array is filled with default values if the data type is a primitive data type. This value depends on the data type of the array, but it is a blank value (such as 0 for numbers, '\0' for char, and so on). However, for actual objects stored in an array (such as the array of Color objects created above), the array is filled with nulls. Each individual array element then needs to be set to an instantiated object. If this procedure is omitted, you will receive a "null pointer exception" at runtime if a null array element is accessed.

As mentioned earlier in this chapter, arrays can also be created by specifying a group of values to fill the array with. This method accomplishes two things at once:

■ Sets the size of the array

■ Initializes all of the array elements

These values are grouped within braces({...}) and must be separated by commas. The following statements initialize the array variables declared previously:

```
int[][] numbers = {{1, 2, 3, 4, 5}, {6, 7, 8, 9, 10}};
float degrees[] = {1.7, 4.1, 9.8, 11.2};
Color rainbow[] = {Color.red, Color.green, Color.blue};
String[] people = {"Katie Berry", "Baby Blankenbeckler", "The President"};
Button b1 = new Button();
Button b2 = new Button();
Button b3 = new Button();
Button FormElements[] = {b1, b2, b3};
```

Using the Created Array

Array elements can be accessed using an index value in the array. The following statements show array elements being accessed and used:

```
int x = numbers[0][5];
degrees[2] = 5.67;
rainbow[0] = Color.black;
String name = people[2];
Button btnExit = FormElements[0];
```

An important thing to remember when using arrays in Java is that they are zero based. Unlike C, if the array is of known size at compile time and you accidentally step past its upper limit, the compiler will flag this error and report it to you. In C, most compilers ignore errors of this type; they eventually show up as segmentation faults (or GPFs, to Windows programmers) at runtime. As an example, the following statements would generate a compile time error:

```
float degrees[] = new float[5];
degrees = {0.0, 1.0, 2.0, 3.0, 4.0};
float temp = degrees[8];
```

That example may seem obvious. If only five elements were allocated, trying to access the eighth element *should* cause a compilation error. However, suppose that the array was dynamically allocated at runtime, as in the following example:

```
int ArraySize = GetUserInput();
float degrees[] = new float[ArraySize];
float temp = degrees[8];
```

If the GetUserInput() method returned a value of 50, then the assignment in the last statement would execute just fine. However, if the GetUserInput() method returned a value of 3, then the final assignment would cause an exception. This error could not be caught at compile time because the ArraySize variable is assigned dynamically at runtime.

Working with Objects

During the discussion of arrays, I mentioned that arrays are actually objects "beneath the surface" (unlike arrays in C, which are simply pointers to memory locations). In fact, arrays have properties, such as length, that can be examined at runtime. Like all other objects, they are created using the new operator. Although objects were introduced in Chapter 3, this section focuses on combining your knowledge of the Java class with your understanding of the syntax of the Java language.

As you will recall, classes in Java are made up of member variables and methods. A class can inherit from a parent class (known as the superclass) and can also choose to implement any number of interfaces. An *interface* is an object that specifies a related group of methods, but does not provide an implementation. Instead, the class that implements the interface must also provide the behavior for the methods. As a review, remember that the syntax for a Java class declaration is as follows:

```
Modifier class className [extends ParentClass] [implements Interfaces]
{
  /* Provide class variables and methods */
}
```

The `Modifier` can be any of the following keywords:

- public
- private
- <empty>
- synchronizable
- abstract
- final

The data type of the variables within the class can be any one of the eight primitive data types introduced in this chapter. In addition, the data type of a variable can be any Java class that was imported into this class's source file. Methods declared as members of a class can either be new to that class or can override a method that exists in the parent class. If the class implements an interface, all methods from that interface *must* be implemented by the class. As a refresher, the modifiers for variables and methods are as follows:

- public
- protected
- private
- <empty>
- static
- native
- final
- synchronized

For more information on any of the keywords listed above, see Chapter 3.

Accessing Java Class Members

When a Java object is used as a variable in a method, its available member variables and methods can be accessed using the object name, the dot (.) operator, and the member being accessed. The syntax is as follows:

```
objectname.variablename
```

or

```
objectname.methodname(arguments)
```

If the variable or method being used by a class belongs to that class, the *objectname* is not required. Before discussing scope issues, examine Listing 5.6 to see variables and methods being accessed.

Listing 5.6. Accessing variables within a Java class.

```
class Computer
{
  public int Price;
  public Color CaseColor;
  public boolean Tower;
  public String Manufacturer;

  public void create(String Company, int dolares)
  {
    int size;
    Manufacturer = Company;
    CaseColor = new Color(255, 255, 255);
    Tower = true;
    Price = dolares;
    CaseColor = CaseColor.brighter();
    CaseColor = CaseColor.darker();
    size = Manufacturer.length();
  }
}
```

Listing 5.6 illustrates a simple class named Computer. This class inherits from no other class and implements no interfaces. However, it does contain four member variables and one member method. Notice that the member variables can be accessed anywhere from within the class. When the brighter(), darker(), and length() methods are called, the objectname must be specified because CaseColor and Manufacturer variables are class data types themselves. If you omit the objectname from these method calls, the compiler will automatically think that these methods are members of the Computer class.

Accessing Inherited Class Members

Assume now that you have another class called Laptop that derives from the Computer class in Listing 5.6. If a method in the Laptop class accesses the Price variable, it does not have to specify Computer.Price because the compiler is smart enough to realize that the Laptop class inherited the Price member variable. Listing 5.7 illustrates this concept.

Listing 5.7. Inheriting from the Computer class.

```
class Laptop extends Computer
{
  float Weight;
  int ScreenArea;

  public float PricePerPound()
  {
    return (Price/Weight);
  }
}
```

What happens if the Laptop class supplies its own Price variable? Which one will be accessed if another object uses the Laptop class? The answer is that if the objectname is not specified, then the variable or method is assumed to have come from the current class. If the variable or method is not found in the current class, the superclass (the class inherited from) is then examined. In cases where a method name or variable name is used in both the parent and child class, the super keyword is used to access the superclass's member. This technique is illustrated in Listing 5.8.

Listing 5.8. Accessing a superclass's member method.

```
class Laptop extends Computer
{
  float Weight;
  int ScreenArea;

  public float PricePerPound()
  {
    return (Price/Weight);
  }

  public void create(String Company, int dolares, float Pounds)
  {
    super.create(Company, dolares);
    Weight = Pounds;
  }
}
```

Notice that by using the super keyword, we were able to reuse the functionality in the Computer superclass. Another way to write the Laptop.Create() method follows:

```
public void create(String Company, int dolares, float Pounds)
  {
    int size;
    Manufacturer = Company;
    CaseColor = new Color(255, 255, 255);
    Tower = true;
    Price = dolares;
    CaseColor = CaseColor.brighter();
    CaseColor = CaseColor.darker();
    size = Manufacturer.length();
    Weight = Pounds;
  }
```

The code above has the same effect as the create() method in Listing 5.8. However, using the super.create() method call directly means that if the Computer.create() method is ever changed, it will be changed for all of its children. This reuse of code helps illustrate the beauty of object-oriented programming.

Constructing and Destroying Objects

In a code snippet given earlier in the chapter, buttons were created using the following lines of code:

```
Button b1 = new Button();
Button b2 = new Button();
Button b3 = new Button();
```

In Listing 5.8, however, you created a new Color object like this:

```
CaseColor = new Color(255, 255, 255);
```

Notice that the two methods that are used here accept completely different parameters. The Button() method takes no arguments, whereas the Color() method accepts the Red, Green, and Blue color values that constitute an RGB color. Despite these differences, these two methods perform the same basic task; they both create new objects.

The type of method used to create an object is known as a *constructor*. A constructor for a new class can be created by creating a method that has the following properties:

■ The name of the constructor method must be the same as the name of the class. (In fact, Java uses this method to identify a constructor.)

■ A constructor returns no values.

Because design decisions occasionally require multiple ways to create an object, Java classes are allowed to have multiple constructors as long as each one accepts different arguments. For instance, the Color class supplies several different constructors. One of these constructors accepts three separate RGB color values; one constructor accepts a single integer and then breaks the first 24 bits of the integer into three separate values. The final Color constructor creates a color based on floating-point values that may range from 0 to 1.

The new Operator

The new operator has already been used several times in this chapter, but so far I haven't explained it. The new operator performs several tasks in Java:

■ Allocates memory for the specified object.

■ Calls the object's constructor.

■ Initializes the object to a default value. For classes being created, this value is always null.

Listing 5.9 rebuilds the Computer class that was created in Listing 5.6. The class created in Listing 5.6 contained a method named create() that performed the same function that a constructor should.

Listing 5.9. Creating a constructor for the Computer class.

```
class Computer
{
  public int Price;
  public Color CaseColor;
  public boolean Tower;
  public String Manufacturer;

  Computer(String Company, int dolares)
  {
    int size;
    Manufacturer = Company;
    CaseColor = new Color(255, 255, 255);
    Tower = true;
    Price = dolares;
    CaseColor = CaseColor.brighter();
    CaseColor = CaseColor.darker();
    size = Manufacturer.length();
  }
}
```

Now that the Computer class contains a constructor method, we could allocate a new Computer this way:

```
Computer MyTool = new Computer("DELL", 2500);
```

> **NOTE**
>
> Although constructors are a convenient way for the class designer to initialize a class's values, constructor methods are *not* required. If a class is created with the new operator, and no constructor exists, memory for the object is still allocated. However, all variables within the constructor will be set to their default values (0 for numbers, false for booleans, null for objects, and so on).

The new operator must be used in conjunction with an object's constructor. Likewise, a constructor must be called in conjunction with the new keyword and cannot be called as a normal method except for one special case.

That special case occurs when an object needs to call the constructor of the superclass. This occurrence is common, and in most cases is recommended. By calling the constructor of the superclass first, you can ensure that any initialization that the constructor needs to perform will be accomplished. Then, after it has been called, you can initialize your class as you see fit. To call the superclass's constructor, use the super keyword with the parameters of that class's constructor. The super keyword has to be used because, as you recall, a constructor cannot be called by name as a standard method call. In Listing 5.8, the `create()` method of the Laptop class called the `create()` method of the superclass Computer. Listing 5.10 modifies the Laptop class by adding a constructor and calling the superclass's constructor within the Laptop constructor.

Listing 5.10. Calling a superclass's constructor.

```
class Laptop extends Computer
{
  float Weight;
  int ScreenArea;

  public float PricePerPound()
  {
    return (Price/Weight);
  }

  Laptop(String Company, int dolares, float Pounds)
  {
    super(Company, dolares);
    Weight = Pounds;
  }
}
```

Although the Laptop constructor does have some initialization of its own to do, it first calls the constructor inherited from the Computer class. This constructor initializes all of the Computer class's member variables. The only function left for the Laptop class is to initialize its Weight variable.

Now that you know how to create an object, you may be wondering how to destroy that object when you are finished with it. Programmers in C, C++, Delphi, and any other language that allows the programmer to allocate memory for objects will be glad to learn that Java does not require you to deallocate that memory when you are done with an object. In fact, Java does not have a "deallocate," "free," or "destroy" keyword because this language uses a *garbage collection* scheme to determine when an object is no longer being used. For more information on garbage collection in Java, and the Windows Virtual Machine for Java in particular, see the section "Taking Out the Trash Using Garbage Collection" in Chapter 4, "Understanding the Java Base Platform." Java does allow programmers to perform cleanup tasks, however, using a `finalize()` method.

The `finalize()` method will be called whenever an object is deallocated by the Java Virtual Machine. Please note that only the JVM really knows when an object is truly going to be deallocated. Therefore, don't assume that a `finalize()` method has been called just because an object "went out of scope," or is no longer in use. A `finalize()` method can be created in any class using the following syntax:

```
void finalize()
{
  /* Insert cleanup code here! */
}
```

Unlike constructors (which can be called by any method as long as they are public), `finalize()` cannot be called like any normal method. Instead, the `finalize()` method is called by the Java Virtual Machine when the object is freed from memory. The vast majority of classes do not even supply a `finalize()` method, but it can be useful in some instances to verify that an object has been removed from memory.

Using the `this` Keyword

Assume for the moment that you are writing an application that will display colors on a screen. For this application, you have created several classes including a `Pixel` class and a `PixelColor` class. The `Pixel` class represents a pixel on the screen and includes a method named `Draw()`. Here is a snippet of the imaginary `Pixel` class:

```
class Pixel
{
  …
  public void Draw(PixelColor);
  …
}
```

The `PixelColor` class represents the color of a specific pixel. This `PixelColor` class performs various operations; it also contains a `Pixel` object that represents the actual pixel that will be set to this `PixelColor`. The following example shows a portion of the `PixelColor` class:

```
class PixelColor extends Color
{
  …
  Pixel thePixel;
  …
}
```

Now suppose that you want to call the `Pixel.Draw()` command and pass the current `PixelColor` object to it. You wouldn't be able to do so using what you have learned so far. The following code snippet would not compile because it tries to pass a class name, *not* a created object:

```
thePixel.Draw(PixelColor);
```

Fortunately, Java provides the `this` keyword for exactly this purpose. A class can use the `this` keyword to refer to itself.

Another possible situation in which the `this` keyword could be used is when a constructor wants to call another constructor within the class. (Remember, an object's constructor can't be called by name within that object's own methods!) A class's own constructors often need to be called within classes that supply multiple constructors that differ only by one or two arguments. Instead of duplicating code in each constructor, one "base" constructor can perform initializations required by all of the other constructors. Then each individual constructor can call the base constructor before continuing with its own initialization. The `this` keyword is also required when a local variable within a method has the same name as a class member variable. In addition, the `this` keyword can always be used to refer to the class instance variable, although you should try to avoid this problem altogether by simply giving method variables names that won't conflict with class variables. Listing 5.11 demonstrates these situations.

Listing 5.11. Using the `this` keyword to refer to an object.

```
class PixelColor extends Color
{
  int red;
  int green;
  int blue;
  boolean flashing;

  PixelColor(int red, int green, int blue, boolean flashing)
  {
    this(red, green, blue);
    this.flashing = flashing;
  }

  PixelColor(int red, int green, int blue)
  {
    this.red = red;
    this.green = green;
    this.blue = blue;
    flashing = false;
  }
}
```

Because the constructors accept arguments whose names are the same as the class member variables, `this` must be used to differentiate between the two. The `this` keyword is also used to call the `PixelColor` (int, int, int) constructor from within the `PixelColor` (int, int, int, boolean) constructor.

What Class Is This?

Every now and then, you may be required to determine the class of an object at runtime. You can use either of two methods using Java. The first method can be applied to any Java class, regardless of its derivation. This method uses the `instanceof` operator, which returns a boolean value and is used in the following manner:

```
boolean_variable = object instanceof classname
```

For example, the following statement could be used to determine if an object variable is of type `Frame`:

```
isFrame = ScreenBox instanceof Frame;
```

Another possible way to determine the class of an object requires that the object be derived from the `Object` class found in the `java.lang` package. Nearly all classes in the standard Java libraries are derived from `Object`, and this class provides some extremely useful functionality. However, it is not required that a new class derive from the `Object` class.

The `java.lang.Object` class contains a method named `getClass()` that returns a class of type `java.lang.Class`. The `Class` class (pardon the redundancy) includes a method called `getName()` that will return a `String` containing the name of the class. The following statement uses this method to determine a class's name:

```
String classname = myClass.getClass().getName();
```

Keep in mind that nearly all classes available in the Visual J++ class library derive from the `Object` class. Therefore, functionality found in this class will be available to you when you use the majority of the Visual J++ classes.

Converting Object Types

Earlier in the chapter you learned how to typecast variables from one primitive data type to another, using the syntax:

```
variable2 = (typename) variable1;
```

The process required the type of `variable2` to be the same as the typename used within the parentheses. The type of an object can also be cast to another type with one restriction: Both objects must share a common class through inheritance. If both objects share a common class, the member variables within the class on the left side of the assignment operator will be set equal to the member variables within the class on the right side of the assignment operator. For instance, if you derived a class named `PDA` and inherited it from `Computer`, you could typecast a `PDA` class to a `Laptop` class like this:

```
PDA myNewton;
Laptop myLaptop;
…
myNewton = (Computer) myLaptop;
```

After the above statements have been executed, all of the member variables in `myNewton` will be set equal to those like variables in `myLaptop`.

Summary

The Java language is similar in many respects to C++. The majority of the operators, keywords, and syntax were borrowed from C++, although many additional, more esoteric features were left out for simplicity's sake. Like C++, Java uses the concept of a class to encapsulate variables and methods. Unlike C++, a class can inherit only from one other class (called single inheritance). Java also provides the concept of an interface so that classes can, in effect, inherit functionality from multiple sources. Interfaces are groups of methods that are not implemented. When a class implements an interface, the class implements a "contract" with the interface by implementing all of its methods.

Java operators can be broken into several primary groups: comparison, logical, arithmetic, assignment, and bitwise. Like C++, Java includes a `for` loop, `do...while` loop, `while` loop, `if` statement, and `switch` statement. These statements are used to control code flow.

Arrays are dynamically allocated objects that contain rows and columns of data. An array's size can be determined at runtime, but an element within an array must be initialized before that element can be accessed. Memory for objects is also allocated at runtime using the `new` keyword and, in some cases, a class's constructor. Memory for all objects in Java does not need to be freed up because of the garbage collection performed by the Java Virtual Machine.

All the primary elements of the Java language have now been introduced. Chapter 6 will formally acquaint you with the Visual J++ compilation process. The knowledge gained in this book's first five chapters will be used throughout the remainder of the book to build Java applets and applications using Visual J++.

Creating Programs with Java

by Bryan Morgan

IN THIS CHAPTER

Chapter 5, "Elements of the Java Language," introduced you to the syntax, requirements, and capabilities of the Java programming language. Java's syntax, combined with proper object-oriented design, allows programmers to build flexible, extensible systems. However, writing code in Java does not always result in good solutions. Although building procedural applications forces programmers to at least determine which variables and methods to use to reach some result, object-oriented applications require much more planning.

C++ veterans probably realize that it is possible to write a C++ program that is not object oriented. C programmers making the switch to C++ often fall into this trap. They create one or two extremely large objects to contain all of the application's GUI, logic, and database access layers. When the application is completed, none of its components can ever be reused by other programmers or projects. In addition, new C++ programmers often forget to define their operations and properties clearly. Therefore, any bug left in the software can be difficult to track down and correct. Likewise, correcting that bug often means changing identical lines of code dozens of times throughout multiple code modules. Doing a proper object design before the implementation can limit the severity of some of these problems. In addition, a proper design should result in a set of objects that can be reused in other applications.

A variety of language features in Java (discussed later in this chapter) help programmers create objects. Java also enforces object-oriented programming by requiring that every single line of code within an application must exist within an object (be it a class or an interface). C++ also makes use of a similar object type (also known as a class); however, C++ also borrows the C language convention that allows variables and methods to be declared "globally" outside of a class.

Although the designers of C++ undoubtedly had good reasons for adopting this technique, the end result is that C++ source code can be difficult to interpret. Although similar in syntax to C++, Java greatly streamlines the look and feel of source code by removing header files and by forcing all variables and methods to be declared within a class. To provide an even cleaner interface, each Java source file can contain only one publicly accessible class. This source file must have the same name as the public class within the file. This simple feature allows a developer to quickly identify the source file in which a particular class is defined.

The Goals of This Chapter

This chapter walks through the steps required to design a standalone Java package named `Politics`. The classes contained in this package are used to model elected officials within the American political system. The demonstration uses Java's object-oriented features to design objects in a flexible manner (the object-identification stage) so that virtually any type of politician can be "built" using these components (the object-construction stage). The politicians can be combined into a group (such as the Senate or House of Representatives), which can also be represented as an object. The demonstration also builds and runs several small applications that show these political objects hard at work (the application-assembly stage).

Object-Oriented Design

Object-oriented design is a superset of the object-oriented programming process. It deals with the "before" and "after" portion of the software-development process—an aspect of development that many development teams often ignore. Typical stages in the object-oriented design process include

- Object identification—The stage in which the designer identifies and models the real-world objects that will be used throughout the application. If the application is a mapping application, map objects will probably be identified here. If the application is a financial application, a variety of objects (including markets, currencies, charts, and calculations) will be described here. Note that no actual coding takes place during this stage.

- Object construction—The stage in which actual classes (in Java's case) are created to accurately model the objects described during the identification stage. Efforts are usually made at this point to stratify the different layers that the application will use (GUI, application logic, and data access layers).

- Application/system assembly—The stage in which objects are assembled to create the actual application. At this time objects are often modified as implementation details become more apparent.

Once the application is completed successfully, it will continue to be extended or modified as requirements continue to evolve. The success of your object design will become readily apparent at this time. One other "offshoot" of the design process is that many objects created during the application design and construction process can be reused within new applications. For example, suppose you construct a set of financial trading objects for use in an application for Company X. If you design and implement these object cleanly, you can reuse them weeks or months later when you start to write a similar application for Company Y. This illustrates the beauty of a good object design.

Thinking in Terms of Objects

Generally speaking, every application can be broken down into a core set of objects that are used repeatedly throughout the program. Many of these objects are supplied with Java (buttons, dialogs, threads, menus, and so on), and many other objects can be purchased from third-party developers (spreadsheets, charts, database queries, and so on). You, the developer, can also create objects in order to encapsulate a set of properties and methods within a data type. This data type, known as a *class*, can inherit from other existing classes and can possibly be reused later in other applications if it is generic enough.

Obviously, you cannot reuse all objects across multiple applications. For instance, classes created to encapsulate common geographical information system (GIS) operations will likely never be reused by corporate MIS programmers writing accounting applications. However, programmers who make the mistake of mixing GUI functionality with the internals of a non-GUI object have been known to create a GIS class that cannot be reused by other GIS applications! Listing 6.1 illustrates a Map class that does not lend itself to code reuse.

Listing 6.1. A poorly designed class.

```
class Map
{
float scale;
float top_Lat;
float top_Long;
String Title;
String Units;

void DrawMap(MapDialog dialog)
  {
/* Add Drawing Code Here */
  }
}
```

Because it passes arguments to the DrawMap() method, this Map class can be drawn only on the surface of a MapDialog dialog box. Therefore, if you had another application that required some type of mapping, you would probably have to modify or rebuild this Map class before you could reuse it (chances are, the next application won't use the MapDialog class). Listing 6.2 shows a better way to build the Map class.

Listing 6.2. A correctly designed class.

```
class Map
{
float scale;
float top_Lat;
float top_Long;
String Title;
String Units;
}

class MapDialog
{
Map theMap;
... /* Provide other member variables and methods */
  ...
  ...

void DrawMap()
  {
/* Add Drawing Code Here That Uses theMap Member Variable */
  }
}
```

Creating Programs with Java

CHAPTER 6

117

6

CREATING
PROGRAMS WITH
JAVA

Notice that in Listing 6.2, the GUI is completely separate from the implementation of the Map class. Now this class can be reused in any application that requires some type of Map object, and it can be inherited from where needed.

A Brief Review of Object-Oriented Programming

The primary features of object-oriented programming were introduced in Chapter 3, "Object-Oriented Programming with Java." They are as follows:

- Encapsulation
- Inheritance
- Polymorphism

Encapsulation is the process of grouping related properties and methods within a single object. If a class named Animal contains a property known as Species and a method named Run(), both of these attributes can be addressed as members of the Animal class:

```
String temp = Animal.Species;
if (BeingChased = true)
{
Animal.Run();
}
```

Using encapsulation to group class members allows you to think of a data type as a true "object." The data type has a set of visible properties and actions that collectively give that object some behavior.

Inheritance allows the software developer to build objects that inherit the attributes of another class. These attributes can be overridden, where required, to give the child class a set of unique attributes that differentiate the child from the parent. The child can also have new attributes to give it capabilities that were nonexistent in the parent. To allow inheritance from another class, a Java class must use the extends keyword:

```
class Dog extends Animal;
class GermanShepherd extends Dog;
class SeeingEyeDog extends GermanShepherd;
```

Polymorphism means different things to different people. At its simplest, polymorphism allows an object to change the implementation of some attribute without modifying that attribute's definition within the program. For example, the Dog class can override the Animal class's Run() method without changing the method's definition.

The following code uses polymorphism to override the Animal class's Run() method:

```
Class Animal
{
void Run()
  {
return;
  }
}
```

```
class Dog extends Animal
{
void Run()
  {
/* Provide implementation here */
  }
}
```

Declaring a class of type Dog and calling its Run() method will call the method defined in the Dog class (not the Run() method defined in the Animal class). In a procedural language, only one method could be named Run(). Any attempts to create another method with this name would result in a compile-time error.

Polymorphism also allows entire classes or interfaces to be cast in terms of their parent classes. For instance, the following code is perfectly valid in Java:

```
Dog Fido = new Dog();
Animal thing = Fido;
```

The Fido variable is of type Dog, but can be assigned to an Animal class because Dog derives from Animal. Calling the thing variable's Run() method will in turn call the Run() method that was defined in the Dog class.

These three primary features (encapsulation, inheritance, and polymorphism) allow the developer to build a complete application using existing and new objects based on a preliminary object design. This design process models the real-world objects that will be used by the application. It is necessary to model these objects first and use them as a basis for all other objects in the application (GUI, database, and so on).

The Object-Identification Stage

This section begins the object-identification stage mentioned earlier in the chapter. The purpose of this stage is to identify and outline the primary objects that will be modeled in Java code. This discussion uses the theme of American politics to illustrate the object-identification process.

This example assumes that every elected office is held by some type of politician. The definition of a *politician* is someone who campaigns for public support and who runs against other politicians in an election. The winner of the election is allowed to hold a public office for some amount of time. Each politician must have an opinion on a variety of issues (for example, environment, crime, economy, defense, social issues). Many politicians (no matter what their individual opinions are) can be grouped into a voting body to approve or disapprove of new laws. Because politicians seem to be involved in virtually every stage of politics, the first step is to design a Politician object that will be reused throughout the Politics package.

Creating Programs with Java

CHAPTER 6

119

6

CREATING
PROGRAMS WITH
JAVA

The Politician Object

When designing the `Politician` object, a number of properties immediately spring to mind:

- Name
- Age
- Sex
- Married?
- Good hair?
- Personality

All of these properties indeed describe a generic politician. Another possible property to add to the list might be Republican or Democrat. Because we're accustomed to thinking of politics in terms of these two parties, this option is tempting. However, throughout this country's history, many political parties have come and gone, and new parties are very likely to continue to emerge in the future. Therefore, hard-wiring the `Politician` object to one of these two parties limits its flexibility. A better technique is to build a generic `Politician` object and then derive the specific parties' politicians from the base `Politician` class. This method uses Java's inheritance capabilities and yields an extensible design.

In addition to a common set of properties, every politician also performs a few common actions while in elected office:

- Campaigns
- Kisses babies
- Debates
- Votes
- Speaks
- Meets with constituents

All these actions will be implemented as methods in the object-construction stage.

The Issues Objects

Now that you have identified the basic characteristics of a `Politician` and made fundamental design decisions (ignore party affiliation for now), it is time to think about the different issues that define a politician's voting tendencies. Some of the hot-button issues that always seem to dominate political discussions are crime, economics, religion, and international relations. Each of these issues can be broken down into separate sub-issues that each politician is either for or against. (This is necessary because, of course, all politicians are for crime control, a good economy, freedom of religion, and strong foreign policy. How each politician proposes to deal with each of these issues is another matter!) Examples of some of these topics include

- Gun control
- Longer prison terms
- Capital gains tax cut
- Increased taxes
- Support for the United Nations

Java provides two separate ways for the object designer to add features such as these to classes. The first option allows you to add all the related methods to a single class (such as our `Politician` class). The second option is to group all the related methods into an *interface*. If the methods are members of an interface, any class that chooses to do so can implement that interface. Because Java supports only single inheritance of classes but allows implementations of multiple interfaces, classes that choose to implement an interface gain functionality missing from their parent class. In addition, thanks to polymorphism, once the interface has been implemented, the class can then be type cast to an interface object.

As the example expands to actually build these objects, all of the "issues" methods will be grouped together into related interfaces. Although the base `Politician` class will not necessarily need to implement these interfaces, other children of `Politician` will be required to. The following section discusses the object-construction stage in detail.

The Object-Construction Stage

The previous section discussed the overall premise for the design of a set of objects related to politics. These objects will be grouped together within the `Politics` package once they are built. The purpose of this section is to construct the objects using what you know about the Java language and the Visual J++ development environment. Because classes are the building blocks of Java, the first step is to lay out some of the `Politics` classes.

Building Classes

To accurately model the political process, a large number of objects are required, many of which contain hundreds (or thousands) of members. At its simplest, though, the driving force behind all of the committees, parties, and lobbying organizations is the politician. For this example, the rest of the general public is placed into one of two possible categories: voters and activists. Voters are average citizens who have opinions on issues, but never feel the need to attempt to affect public policy outside the polls. Activists, meanwhile, are actively involved with some political issue and vigorously defend their position.

With these assumptions, three primary base classes should jump out: `Politician`, `Activist`, and `Voter`. Every individual in the political process can be derived from one of these three classes. The examples in this chapter focus on the `Politician` class and its corresponding responsibilities. Based on the previous discussion of a `Politician` object, Listing 6.3 provides a good start for the construction of a `Politician` class.

Listing 6.3. The Politician class.

```java
package Politics;
/*
 *
 *   Politician Class
 *
 */
public abstract class Politician
{
  private String Name;
  private int Age;
  private String Gender;
  private boolean Married;
  protected boolean GoodHair;
  protected int Personality; // on a scale of 1 to 10

  abstract public boolean Vote(String bill);

  public void KissBabies()
  {
    return;
  }

  public void setName(String newName)
  {
    Name = newName;
  }

 public void setAge(int newAge)
  {
    Age = newAge;
  }

 public void SetMaritalStatus(boolean newStatus)
  {
    Married = newStatus;
  }

  public String getName()
  {
    return Name;
  }

  public int getAge()
  {
    return Age;
  }

  public boolean GetMaritalStatus()
  {
    return Married;
  }
}
```

To create this class using Visual J++, do one of the following:

- Open the POLITICS.MDP project workspace file located on the CD-ROM included with this book. Opening this file will give you access to all of the source code used within this chapter.

- In Visual J++, select the New | Project Workspace option by selecting Java Workspace when prompted for the project type. When prompted for the name of the workspace, enter Politics. After the workspace has been created, build a new class either by right-clicking over the project and selecting Create New Class... or by selecting the Insert | New Class menu option.

Notice that the Politician class was defined to be an *abstract public* class. This designation means that at least one method in the class was defined as an abstract method. *Abstract methods* are methods that are defined by a superclass, but carry no actual implementation. Any class that inherits from the superclass is required to provide an implementation for the method. In this first example, the Vote() method was declared to be abstract. The KissBabies() method was implemented within this class because, in effect, it carries very little weight or influence in the entire political process. (Any politician from any party can be seen in a picture with a baby and look good; therefore, no other classes will probably want to override this method.)

Data Hiding and Access Methods

Notice also that a set of helper methods was provided to give other classes access to the Politician's member variables. These methods are setName(), setAge(), SetMaritalStatus(), getName(), getAge(), and GetMaritalStatus(). Hiding data and providing these access methods is considered good object-oriented programming practice. It prevents child classes from inadvertently accessing or modifying class member variables. It also allows the programmer to perform other operations each time one of its member variables is set. For example, suppose that before getting a divorce, a politician wants to determine whether his public-opinion rating would be damaged in any way. Adding the following methods and variables to the class would track public opinion and perhaps allow the politician to get a divorce:

```
private boolean RatingsUp = true;
private double publicOpinion = 1.00;
  .
  .
  .
protected void SetPublicOpinion(double newValue)
{
  if ((newValue <= 1.00) && (newValue >= 0.00))
  {
    publicOpinion = newValue;
    if (publicOpinion < newValue)
      RatingsUp = false;
    else
      RatingsUp = true;
  }
}
```

Creating Programs with Java

CHAPTER 6

123

6

CREATING
PROGRAMS WITH
JAVA

```
protected boolean GetDivorce()
{
  if (RatingsUp)
  {
    SetMaritalStatus(false);
    return true;
  }
  else
    return false;
}
```

Both the GetDivorce() and the SetPublicOpinion() methods perform double duties. They set internal class variables, and they also perform additional logical checks on the input data. If these variables (Married, RatingsUp, and publicOpinion) were all made public, any class that used the Politician class or inherited from it could modify these variables in any way. In short, always try to hide as much data as possible using the protected and private keywords within objects. This method allows the design to be extremely flexible down the line and may allow you to reuse large amounts of code without modification.

Using Hidden Helper Classes

As we are well aware, no politician acts completely alone. Instead, politicians are generally surrounded by campaign managers, policy advisers, assistants, and other aides. Because these support personnel exist primarily to support the politician, the next step is to implement a helper class within the POLITICIAN.JAVA source file. This class, named PoliticalAssistant, will be visible only to the Politician class. (Remember that only one public Java class can be declared per source file!) Adding a private class within a public class's source file will demonstrate an effective example of using hidden helper classes. The private PoliticalAssistant class models the real-world political process in that no one in the public is usually concerned about who a politician's advisers are or what they do. This assistant is instead most important to the politician alone. In general, any discussions with the assistant usually take place through the politician in the form of a news conference or an interview.

Listing 6.4 shows the PoliticalAssistant class and changes that were made to the Politician class.

Listing 6.4. The Politician and PoliticalAssistant classes.

```
package Politics;
/*
 *
 *   Politician Class - Uses PoliticalAssistants and public
 *   opinion to make "informed" decisions.
 *
 */
public abstract class Politician
{
```

continues

Listing 6.4. continued

```
    .
    .
    .
  private PoliticalAssistant[] assistants;

  public Politician()
  {
    /* Hire some political assistants */
    assistants = new PoliticalAssistant[6];

    assistants[0] = new PoliticalAssistant("CRIME");
    assistants[1] = new PoliticalAssistant("ENVIRONMENT");
    assistants[2] = new PoliticalAssistant("ECONOMICS");
    assistants[3] = new PoliticalAssistant("SOCIALISSUES");
    assistants[4] = new PoliticalAssistant("EDUCATION");
    assistants[5] = new PoliticalAssistant("FOREIGNPOLICY");
  }

  public boolean MakeDecision(String Area, String Issue)
  {
    boolean returnValue = false;

    for (int i = 0; i <= 5; i++)
    {
      if (assistants[i].GetExpertise().equals(Area))
        returnValue = assistants[i].MakeDecision(Issue);
    }
    return returnValue;
  }
}

class PoliticalAssistant
{
  private String AreaOfExpertise;

  PoliticalAssistant(String Expertise)
  {
    AreaOfExpertise = Expertise;
  }

  public GetExpertise()
  {
    return AreaOfExpertise;
  }

  public double MeasureRisk(String Issue)
  {
    /* Return a constant value for now!
    The actual implementation of this method might
    go out and query a database to determine the level
    of political support for some issue.  This value would
    range from 0.0 to 1.0 and would be returned to the
    Politician. */
    return 0.5;
  }
}
```

Creating Programs with Java

CHAPTER 6

6

CREATING
PROGRAMS WITH
JAVA

125

Some interesting changes were made to the `Politician` class in Listing 6.4. A `private` array of `PoliticalAssistant` classes was added so that the politician could have someone to consult before making a decision. To create and initialize an array of `PoliticalAssistants`, a `Politician` constructor was added. This constructor initializes an array of assistants of constant size. Each one of these assistants is a specialist in a certain political area. The politician's opinion on an issue can be determined by calling the `Politician.MakeDecision()` method and indicating a specific issue. Note that this method was identified as a `public` method so that anyone (a voter, fellow politician, or lobbyist) can determine the politician's opinion on any issue at any time. (Maybe that's why they get paid the big bucks!)

Adding Other Classes to the Project

Listing 6.4 illustrates the addition of a class within the `POLITICIAN.JAVA` file. Building the `POLITICIAN.JAVA` source file using Visual J++ should have resulted in two class files being created on your drive: `POLITICALASSISTANT.CLASS` and `POLITICIAN.CLASS`.

> **NOTE**
>
> If you used the project workspace file supplied with the CD-ROM in this book, these class files will be located in the `.\POLITICS` folder. The files are output to this folder because these classes were declared to members of package `Politics`. If the first line of the `POLITICS.JAVA` source file were changed to package `Politics.BaseClass`, the files would have been output to the `.\POLITICS\BASECLASS` folder. Java converts the `.` between names in the `import` and package statements to the file system directory separator, which is `\` in the case of Windows 95/NT. Visual J++ then utilizes the `CLASSPATH` environment variable to determine where (in which directories) to search for the package or imported classes.

Many programmers do not approve of the practice of passing `String` values around as parameters for examination. For instance, in Listing 6.3, the `Vote()` method was defined as

```
abstract public boolean Vote(String bill);
```

Passing a `String` value for the `bill` parameter probably will not allow the `Politician` class to make an informed choice based on its current capabilities (that is, Which bill? What is it for? When is the vote?).

The Legislation Class

Suppose now that a new class named `Legislation` is defined that contains a number of useful parameters including

- The date of the vote
- The area this bill deals with (economy, crime, and so on)

- The specific issue this bill examines
- The owner of the legislation (who drafted it)

If a class such as this existed, a politician could receive a Vote() request using an instantiated class of this type as a parameter. This type of information would enable the Politician class to make a more intelligent decision when voting. Listing 6.5 shows an initial implementation of the Legislation class.

Listing 6.5. The Legislation class.

```java
package Politics;

import Politician;

/*
 *
 * Legislation
 *
 */
public final class Legislation
{
  private String DateOfVote;
  private String PrimaryArea;
  private String PrimaryIssue;
  private String LegislationText;
  private Politician LegislationOwner;

  public Legislation(String Date, String Area, String Issue, String Text,
    Politician Owner)
  {
    DateOfVote = Date;
    PrimaryArea = Area;
    PrimaryIssue = Issue;
    LegislationText = Text;
    LegislationOwner = Owner;
  }

  public String GetDateOfVote()
  {
    return DateOfVote;
  }

  public String GetPrimaryArea()
  {
    return PrimaryArea;
  }

  public String GetPrimaryIssue()
  {
    return PrimaryIssue;
  }

  public String GetLegislationText()
  {
    return LegislationText;
  }
}
```

Using the Legislation class, we can modify the Politician class's Vote() method to return an "intelligent" vote on a piece of legislation based on the legislation's issues (see Listing 6.6).

Listing 6.6. Modifying Politician to use the Legislation class when voting.

```java
import Legislation;

public class Politician
{
  .
  .
  .
  public boolean Vote(Legislation bill)
  {
    return MakeDecision(bill.GetPrimaryArea(), bill.GetPrimaryIssue());
  }
  .
  .
  .
}
```

In Listing 6.6, the Vote() method was changed from an empty abstract method to an actual method within this class. The new Vote() method takes a Legislation object as an argument and, based on the Legislation's area and issue, returns a boolean true or false value.

> **NOTE**
>
> At first glance, you might think that some redundancy is occurring within the Politician class because the Vote() method simply issues a call to the MakeDecision() method. Why not just get rid of one of these methods?
>
> The answer is that although a politician may rarely be required to vote on an issue, members of the media, staff, colleagues, and the general public will continually ask for his or her opinion. Therefore, separating the Vote() method from the MakeDecision() method allows the designer to extend the MakeDecision() method with additional capabilities without ever changing the Vote() method (or vice versa).

Now that the Politician and Legislation classes have been somewhat finalized, only one last "base" class remains before we can begin to extend the class library. The purpose of this class is to group related sets of politicians and legislation together. Because a group of politicians that passes laws is commonly known as a *legislative body*, the name of the final base class is LegislativeBody.

The LegislativeBody Class

As was the case during the design of Legislation and Politician, the primary goal in designing the LegislativeBody class should be to make it as generic as possible. Thinking back to the Politician class, notice that nothing in the class specifically ties it to a representative, mayor, or councilman. In fact, nothing even ties it directly to an *American* politician! (The Politician could be the prime minister of France...Politician doesn't care.) Therefore, LegislativeBody should be as generic as possible, yet implement as much functionality as possible. Listing 6.7 shows a simple LegislativeBody class that will be extended later in the chapter.

Listing 6.7. The LegislativeBody class.

```
package Politics;

import Politician;
import Legislation;

/*
 *
 * LegislativeBody - Used To Group Related Politicians Together
 *
 */
public class LegislativeBody
{
  protected String Location;
  private Politician[] Members;

  // Return Location of Body (Washington, Richmond, Sacramento, etc.
  public String GetLocation()
  {
    return Location;
  }


  //Return number of politicians in body
  public int GetNumberOfMembers()
  {
    return Members.length;
  }

  //Set Number of members in array of Politicians
  public boolean SetNumberOfMembers(int newNumber)
  {
    if (Members == null)
    {
      Members = new Politician[newNumber];
      return true;
    }
    else
      return false;
  }

  //Add a politician to the LegislativeBody
  public boolean AddPolitician(Politician official)
  {
    boolean retValue = false;
```

Creating Programs with Java

CHAPTER 6

129

6
CREATING
PROGRAMS WITH
JAVA

```java
    if (official != null)
    {
      for (int i = 1; i <= Members.length; i++)
      {
        if (Members[i - 1] == null)
        {
          Members[i - 1] = official;
          retValue = true;
        }
      }
    }
    return retValue;
  }

  //Remove a politician from office
  public boolean RemovePolitician(Politician official)
  {
    boolean retValue = false;

    for (int i = 1; i <= Members.length; i++)
    {
      if (Members[i - 1].getName() == official.getName())
      {
        Members[i - 1] = null;
        retValue = true;
      }
    }
    return retValue;
  }

  /* Perform a vote on some piece of legislation */
  public boolean Vote(Legislation bill)
  {
    int Yeas = 0;
    int Nays = 0;
    boolean retValue;

    for (int i = 1; i <= Members.length; i++)
    {
      if (Members[i - 1] != null)
      {
        retValue = Members[i - 1].Vote(bill);
        if (retValue == true)
          Yeas++;
        else
          Nays++;
      }
    }

    if (Yeas >= Nays)
      return true;
    else
      return false;
  }
}
```

The LegislativeBody class makes extensive use of the existing Politician and Legislation classes. All legislative bodies are generally made up groups of politicians. The U.S. Senate has 100 members, for instance. Therefore, LegislativeBody contains an array of Politicians. The size of this array is set in the SetNumberOfMembers() method. Once the number of members in this legislative body has been set, you can use the AddPolitician() and RemovePolitician() methods to add or remove Politicians from this array. The Vote() method accepts a Legislation object as an argument and returns either a true or false based on the opinion of each politician. (Note that in this case, a tie wins.)

By this point, the design contains four separate classes that allow us to roughly model the political process. The remainder of the chapter focuses on inheriting from these classes to build more specific political classes (Congress or President, for instance). Listing 6.8 demonstrates the use of the classes that have been created thus far.

> **NOTE**
>
> Before entering and compiling this example, make sure that the source code for the Politician, PoliticalAssistant, Legislation, and LegislativeBody and class files are available. If you have chosen not to use the files located on the CD-ROM accompanying this book, create a new project named Listing8 and then create the class listed in Listing 6.8. In Visual J++ select the Build | Settings... menu item to select the output and class path directories. (Set the class path directory to the directory containing the Politics class files.) Because Listing8 is a standalone application and not a Java applet, select Stand-alone interpreter when Visual J++ asks how you would like to run this class.

Listing 6.8. Using the political classes.

```
/*
 *
 * Example8: Creates legislative body of five members
 *           and forces a vote.
 *
 */
import Politics.LegislativeBody;
import Politics.Legislation;
import Politics.Politician;

class Listing8
{
  public static void main(String args[])
  {
    LegislativeBody CityCouncil = new LegislativeBody();
    CityCouncil.SetNumberOfMembers(5);

    Politician politico1 = new Politician();
    Politician politico2 = new Politician();
    Politician politico3 = new Politician();
    Politician politico4 = new Politician();
    Politician politico5 = new Politician();
```

```
    System.out.println("Adding politician...\n");

    CityCouncil.AddPolitician(politico1);
    CityCouncil.AddPolitician(politico2);
    CityCouncil.AddPolitician(politico3);
    CityCouncil.AddPolitician(politico4);
    CityCouncil.AddPolitician(politico5);

    System.out.println("Number of politicians = " +
    CityCouncil.GetNumberOfMembers() + "\n");

    Legislation bill = new Legislation("Today", "CRIME", "PRISONS",
      "BUILD MORE", politico1);
    System.out.println("Date of vote: " + bill.GetDateOfVote() + "\n");
    System.out.println("Area:   " + bill.GetPrimaryArea() + "\n");
    System.out.println("Issue: " + bill.GetPrimaryIssue() + "\n");

    boolean retValue = CityCouncil.Vote(bill);

    System.out.println("The result of the vote was: " + retValue + "\n");
  }
}
```

The `Listing8` program initially creates a new `LegislativeBody` class named `CityCouncil`. Five `Politician` objects are added to the `CityCouncil` class, and a vote is taken on whether to build more prisons. Because the `PoliticianAssistant` class is hard-wired at this point to always return `false`, the output of the `Vote()` method is `false`. When this class is run in Visual J++, the following output should be displayed:

```
Adding politician...

Number of politicians = 5

Date of vote: TODAY

Area: CRIME

Issue: PRISONS

The result of the vote was:  false
```

One way to make these classes a little more useful is to replace the contents of the `PoliticalAssistant.MeasureRisk()` method with a database query (or a request for user input). At this point, however, the objects that have been created do a good job of showing basic object-oriented design and development.

Using Inheritance

The classes created thus far are sufficient to write and run a basic program, as shown in Listing 6.8. This section explains how to use the object-oriented programming feature known as *inheritance* to create new classes that extend the existing classes so that they more accurately model real-world political environments.

Recall that Java uses the `extends` keyword to inherit from a superclass. Superclasses are also commonly called *parent classes*. A superclass that has children but inherits from nothing else can also be referred to as a *base class*. Examples of base classes are the `LegislativeBody`, `Legislation`, and `Politician` classes created earlier in this chapter. The `LegislativeBody` and `Politician` classes will be extended to more accurately model the American political system.

Inheriting from Politician

The `Politician` class was originally created to model the typical attributes and duties of a politician. A politician also has the following features:

- `Name`, `Age`, `Gender`, `Marital Status`, `Good Hair`, `Personality`, and other attributes
- A set of advisors in the form of `PoliticalAssistant` objects
- The ability to vote and make decisions with the help of a staff of advisors

One basic premise of the design was that all politicians, no matter who they are or where they reside, share this basic feature set. This broad generalization works fine for this example.

However, depending on the type of politician, this set of variables and methods may not allow the politician to perform his or her job completely. For instance, the President of the United States must meet with foreign leaders, converse with members of Congress, attend sporting events, and speak in public regularly. A senator must travel often to visit constituents from the home district, meet with special interest groups, and attend committee meetings. Therefore, in order to provide greater flexibility to the builder of political software applications, new classes must be inherited from `Politician`. Two new classes are be created here: `President` and `Senator`. These classes will inherit from `Politician`. Both of these classes will add new capabilities that are not found in the `Politician` class. Listing 6.9 creates a `President` class that inherits from the existing `Politician` class.

Listing 6.9. The President class.

```
package Politics;

import Politician;

/*
 *
 * President
 *
 */
public class President extends Politician
{
  public void MeetWithForeignLeader(Politician leader)
  {
    /*
      Add code to hold meeting with dignitary.
```

```
      */
      return;
    }

    public void TalkWithCongressman(Politician congressman)
    {
      /*
        Add code to hold meeting with U.S. Congressman
      */
      return;
    }

    public void AttendEvent(String location)
    {
      /*
        Add code to travel to, prepare, and attend an event
      */
      GiveSpeech();
      return;
    }

    public void GiveSpeech()
    {
      /*
        Give speech based on some topic
      */
      return;
    }
}
```

Listing 6.10 creates a class designed to simulate a U.S. senator. The Senator class extends the Politician class.

Listing 6.10. The Senator class.

```
package Politics;

import Politician;

/*
 *
 * Senator
 *
 */
public class Senator extends Politician
{
  public String HomeState;
  public int District;
  public String Committee;

  public void TravelToHome()
  {
    /*
      Go to home district and meet with people
    */
```

continues

Listing 6.10. continued

```
    return;
  }

  public void MeetWithGroup(String SpecialInterest)
  {
    /*
      Meet with members of a special interest group
    */
    return;
  }

  public void AttendCommitteeMeeting()
  {
    /*
      Go to committee meeting, listen, and vote if necessary
    */
    return;
  }
}
```

With the creation of these two classes, the Politician class has been successfully reused. Although the implementations of the Senator and President classes appear to contain only a few variables and methods, in reality Senator and President have access to all public and protected members of the parent Politician class. The following statements are possible because of inheritance:

```
President AbeLincoln = new President();
AbeLincoln.SetPublicOpinion(0.85);
AbeLincoln.GiveSpeech();
boolean MaritalStatus = AbeLincoln.GetMaritalStatus();

Senator BobDole = new Senator();
BobDole.SetName("Bob Dole");
BobDole.AttendCommitteeMeeting();
boolean answer = Vote(bill);
```

In addition to the Politician class, one other base class—the LegislativeBody class—is an excellent candidate for inheritance. Like Politician, LegislativeBody does a good job of roughly modeling a group of politicians that meet regularly to vote on various pieces of legislation. However, it was given only generic capabilities to provide maximum reusability.

Inheriting from LegislativeBody

Because the President and Senator classes have already been constructed, the next step is to build two legislative bodies to "hold" the offices of the President and Senators. These classes are the OfficeOfThePresident and Senate classes, shown in Listings 6.11 and 6.12.

Listing 6.11. The `OfficeOfThePresident` class.

```
package Politics;

import LegislativeBody;

/*
 *
 * OfficeOfThePresident
 *
 */
public class OfficeOfThePresident extends LegislativeBody
{
  private Politician VicePresident;

  public OfficeOfThePresident()
  {
    Location = "Washington, D.C.";
    SetNumberOfMembers(1);
  }

  public Politician GetVicePresident()
  {
    return VicePresident;
  }

  public void SetVicePresident(Politician veep)
  {
    if (veep != null)
      VicePresident = veep;
  }
}
```

Listing 6.12 creates a class designed to simulate the U.S. Senate. This class contains a group of senators (represented by the `Senator` class).

Listing 6.12. The `Senate` class.

```
package Politics;

import LegislativeBody;

/*
 *
 * Senate
 *
 */
public class Senate extends LegislativeBody
{
  private int NumberAdded = 0;
  private Politician CrimeCommittee[];
  private Politician EconomicsCommittee[];
  private Politician EnvironmentCommittee[];
  private Politician SocialIssuesCommittee[];
  private Politician EducationCommittee[];
```

continues

Listing 6.12. continued

```java
public Senate()
{
  Location = "Washington, D.C.";
  SetNumberOfMembers(100);
  CrimeCommittee = new Politician[20];
  EconomicsCommittee = new Politician[20];
  EnvironmentCommittee = new Politician[20];
  SocialIssuesCommittee = new Politician[20];
  EducationCommittee = new Politician[20];
}

/* Randomly assign politicians to a committee */
public boolean AddPolitician(Politician official)
{
  NumberAdded++;
  int number = NumberAdded / 5;
  switch (NumberAdded % 5)
  {
    case (0):
      CrimeCommittee[number] = official;
      break;
    case (1):
      EconomicsCommittee[number] = official;
      break;
    case (2):
      EnvironmentCommittee[number] = official;
      break;
    case (3):
      SocialIssuesCommittee[number] = official;
      break;
    case (4):
      EducationCommittee[number] = official;
      break;
  }
  return super.AddPolitician(official);
}
}
```

Inheritance allows the Java developer to continually extend and shape classes to meet the needs of the task at hand. Thus far, inheritance and encapsulation have been used extensively to build what is getting to be a large group of classes. Although you may have not realized it, the Senate class also used the object-oriented programming concept of polymorphism to enhance itself.

Using Polymorphism

By overriding the LegislativeBody.AddPolitician() method, the Senate class reused the name of a method in the subclass while changing its behavior. Now, in addition to adding an elected politician to the list of politicians within the LegislativeBody, Senate will also randomly add a politician to a Committee. Polymorphism, in this instance, allows the functionality of the AddPolitician() method to stay roughly the same and gives it added behavior. Polymorphism

Creating Programs with Java

CHAPTER 6

137

6

CREATING
PROGRAMS WITH
JAVA

can be used when calling AddPolitician() as well. Note that this method accepts a Politician variable as an argument. Using polymorphism, this variable could actually be a Politician object *or* an object of any class that inherits from Politician (such as Senator or President). Listing 6.13 shows this use of polymorphism.

Listing 6.13. Adding Senators to the Senate using polymorphism.

```
/*
 *
 * Example13: Creates Senate of five members
 *
and forces a vote.
 *
 */
import Politics.Senate;
import Politics.Legislation;
import Politics.Senator;

class Example13
{
  public static void main(String args[])
  {
    Senate USSenate = new Senate();

    //Add senators and set names
    Senator BobDole = new Senator();
    BobDole.setName("Bob Dole");
    Senator StromThurmond = new Senator();
    StromThurmond.setName("Strom Thurmond");
    Senator ConnieMack = new Senator();
    ConnieMack.setName("Connie Mack");
    Senator DianneFeinstein = new Senator();
    DianneFeinstein.setName("Dianne Feinstein");
    Senator ChuckRobb = new Senator();
    ChuckRobb.setName("Chuck Robb");

    System.out.println("Adding senators...\n");
    USSenate.AddPolitician(BobDole);
    USSenate.AddPolitician(StromThurmond);
    USSenate.AddPolitician(ConnieMack);
    USSenate.AddPolitician(DianneFeinstein);
    USSenate.AddPolitician(ChuckRobb);
    System.out.println("Number of senators = " +
    USSenate.GetNumberOfMembers() + "\n");

    Legislation bill = new Legislation("Today", "CRIME", "PRISONS",
      "BUILD MORE", ConnieMack);
    System.out.println("Date of vote: " + bill.GetDateOfVote() + "\n");
    System.out.println("Area:    " + bill.GetPrimaryArea() + "\n");
    System.out.println("Issue: " + bill.GetPrimaryIssue() + "\n");
    boolean retValue = USSenate.Vote(bill);
    System.out.println("The result of the vote was: " + retValue + "\n");
    System.out.println("Senator 1 = " + BobDole.getName());
    System.out.println("Senator 2 = " + StromThurmond.getName());
```

continues

Listing 6.13. continued

```
    System.out.println("Senator 3 = " + ConnieMack.getName());
    System.out.println("Senator 4 = " + DianneFeinstein.getName());
    System.out.println("Senator 5 = " + ChuckRobb.getName());
  }
}
```

In Listing 6.13, note that although AddPolitician() accepts Politician objects as a parameter, we are able to pass it Senate objects instead because Senate inherits directly from Politician. Therefore, every public member of Politician is available to the AddPolitician() method through the Senator objects.

Compiling and running this class should result in the following output:

```
Adding senators…

Number of senators = 5

Date of vote: TODAY

Area: CRIME

Issue: PRISONS

The result of the vote was:  false

Senator 1 = Bob Dole
Senator 2 = Strom Thurmond
Senator 3 = Connie Mack
Senator 4 = Dianne Feinstein
Senator 5 = Chuck Robb
```

At this point, an entire of package of reusable objects has been built using the object-oriented concepts of encapsulation, inheritance, and polymorphism. Each of these objects has a quantifiable set of properties and methods that specifically pertain to that object. The access keywords public, protected, and private were used throughout to control access to member variables and methods where needed.

This discussion concludes by demonstrating the use of one last feature of the Java language—the Java interface—to extend the Politics package. An *interface* is a grouping of public abstract methods that separates the design of an object from its implementation.

Adding Interfaces

An effective use of interfaces in the Politics package is to represent a politician's views on a variety of issues. The interfaces themselves comprise a set of public abstract methods and/or public static final variables. Defining the interfaces allows a related grouping of functionality to be self-contained in one unit. Any class can choose to implement an interface as it sees fit. (Recall that if a class implements an interface, it must implement *all* of that interface's methods!) To continue the Politics example, interfaces will be created to group together related

Creating Programs with Java

CHAPTER 6

6

139

CREATING
PROGRAMS WITH
JAVA

sets of issues such as economics, education, social issues, and so on. A `Politician` class can choose to implement any interface as it is needed. Obviously, some issues (such as economics or crime) apply to every politician at every level. Other issues (such as local construction projects or school board decisions) apply only to specific politicians in specific locations. Continuing with the design decisions made earlier, interfaces that apply to all politicians are implemented within the `Politician` class.

The following sample interfaces could be implemented by the `Politician` class if so desired:

```
public interface Crime
{
  public abstract boolean BuildMorePrisons();
  public abstract boolean EducateOffenders();
  public abstract boolean ShowZeroTolerance();
  public abstract boolean ForDeathPenalty();
  public abstract boolean ToughOnDrugs();
  public abstract boolean ForGunControl();
}

public interface Economics
{
  public abstract boolean IncreaseDeficit();
  public abstract boolean TaxAndSpend();
  public abstract boolean SupplySider();
  public abstract boolean CutCapitalGains();
  public abstract boolean HasVotedToIncreaseTaxes();
}
public interface Education
{
  public abstract boolean SpendMoreOnSchools();
  public abstract boolean PayTeachersMore();
  public abstract boolean EducationOverDefense();
  public abstract boolean SetHigherStandards();
  public abstract boolean SupportSchoolChoice();
}
```

Once again, the idea behind interfaces is to separate the design from the implementation of objects. The previous three interfaces (`Education`, `Crime`, and `Economics`) simply specify which methods will be implemented by classes that choose to do so. Keep in mind that Java's polymorphic capabilities allow programmers to type cast classes to the interfaces they implement. Therefore, the following statements are perfectly legal in Java:

```
class Politician implements Crime, Economics, Education
{
  ...
}

Politician politico = new Politician();
Crime crimeMethods = politico;
```

The `politico` variable is created as type `Politician`. However, once created, it can be cast to a `Crime` interface (just as `Senator` can be cast to a `Politician` or as `OfficeOfThePresident` can be cast to a `LegislativeBody`). Because `Politician` in this example implements the `Crime` interface, all methods in `Crime` are guaranteed to be in the `Politician` class.

One final example illustrates how effectively interfaces can be used within an application. Suppose the National Teacher's Union (NTU) is trying to determine the views of each individual politician in order to see that the union's views are represented in an upcoming vote. The NTU (a fictional union) class defines a method named DetermineOpinion() that will be used to determine whether an elected official is friendly toward educational issues. This method could be implemented as follows:

```
public boolean DetermineOpinion(Education opinions)
{
  int tally = 0;

  if (opinions.SpendMoreOnSchools()) then
    tally++;
  if (opinions.PayTeachersMore()) then
    tally++;
  if (opinions.EducationOverDefense()) then
    tally++;
  if (opinions.SetHigherStandards()) then
    tally++;
  if (opinions.SupportSchoolChoice() == false) then
    tally++;

  if (tally >= 3) then
    return true;
  else
    return false;
}
```

The DetermineOpinion() method accepts an Education interface as its argument, which allows this method to be completely flexible. We could call this method in a loop and pass in each member of the Senate to determine his or her opinions (assuming that the Senator class implemented this interface). However, it is just as possible to pass in each member of the general public (all 300-odd million of them!) and determine their opinions on a matter.

Summary

Object-oriented programming should always be preceded by a good object-oriented design. Stopping to consider the problem at hand nearly always results in a more reusable, more extensible set of objects than does programming in an ad hoc fashion. Java programmers have the luxury of an extremely large built-in class library that is part of the java package. Visual J++ programmers have additional capabilities in the Microsoft com package. Any Java programmer can extend all the public classes in these packages.

This chapter demonstrates the concepts of encapsulation, inheritance, and polymorphism by constructing a fairly sophisticated package named Politics. Grouping classes into packages allows these classes themselves to be viewed as a type of object. Any user seeing that a class is included in the Politics package will immediately know that the class has something to do with Politics. All classes in the Politics package can be imported by issuing the following statement:

```
import Politics.*;
```

The Java CLASSPATH environment variable controls where the compiler and Java Virtual Machine "look" for classes. As a Visual J++ developer, you have several options when setting the path to classes used in the application. You can set this class path for the specific project workspace by selecting the Build I Settings menu item and then selecting the General tab. You can also set the class path by modifying the CLASSPATH environment variable in AUTOEXEC.BAT (for Windows 95) or the system environment variables (for Windows NT). Visual J++ will also look in the Windows Registry under the MYComputer\HKEY_LOCAL_MACHINE\SOFTWARE\Microsoft\Java_VM\Classpath Registry key. Modifying the class path using any of these techniques allows the compiler to find class files being imported.

Advanced Java Programming

by Bryan Morgan

IN THIS CHAPTER

CHAPTER 7

Being object oriented is not the only thing that makes Java a powerful language. The Java language also provides native support for a variety of advanced programming constructs that can be used to build virtually any type of application, including the following:

- Exception handling
- Multithreading
- Streamable input and output
- Native methods
- Networking

This chapter introduces and discusses all of these concepts in order to give you the broadest possible knowledge of Java before delving into such concepts as graphical user interface design, ActiveX/COM, scripting, database access, and multimedia. All these programming topics build on the concepts introduced in this chapter. For instance, many classes in the java package contain member methods that are capable of throwing exceptions. Likewise, to do animation or perform simultaneous threads of animations, the developer should possess a basic knowledge of multithreading in Java. The following section discusses exceptions and how they can be handled in Java.

Exception Handling

Exception handling refers to a capability in Java that allows you to plan ahead for potential problems and respond to these problems when they happen. Imagine a situation where you have built a screen asking the user for some type of input. Exceptions can be used to trap invalid user input and send, or *throw*, an exception. The Java programmer can trap, or *catch*, an exception by executing a set of statements within a handler. If any one of these statements causes, or *throws*, some type of problem, your code can catch the problem and handle it accordingly. The syntax provided by the Java language to perform this task is the following:

```
try
{
    //Execute one or more statements
}
catch (SomeException1 error1)
{
    //Handle the error in some way
}
catch (SomeExceptionN errorn)
{
    //Handle the error in some way
}
finally
{
    //Perform mandatory cleanup operations
}
```

Note the use of the `try...catch...finally` mechanism here. This is the basic format used to trap exceptions in code. The `try...catch` portion of this operation is required syntax in Java. The `finally` keyword is used to introduce a set of statements that will always be executed before the method executes. Because exceptions are simply classes derived from the `java.lang.Throwable` class, you are free to define your own set of exception classes complete with member variables and methods. The next section illustrates how exceptions can be used to build elegant applications in Java.

Handling Errors in Java

Java implements exception handling using the base class `java.lang.Throwable`. All classes that derive from this class are objects that can be thrown at runtime whenever an error is encountered. All thrown errors must be accompanied by a catch at some level in the program (in either the current class or the parent classes of the current class). If an exception is not caught, the program will crash.

The `java.lang.Exception` and `java.lang.Error` classes are derived directly from `java.lang.Throwable`. Classes derived from the `Exception` class define normal programming errors that can be caught in an application. Classes derived from the `Error` class define abnormal errors that occur in the Java system. Examples of `java.lang.Error` errors are the `ThreadDeath`, `VirtualMachineError`, `LinkageError`, and the `ClassFormatError`. Chances are good that you will probably never try to catch an `Error`-derived class, because they are designed to signal low-level errors that, as the Java API documentation says, should be handled "only if you know what you're doing." The `Exception`-derived classes represent much more common programming problems such as using a null pointer, dividing by zero, or indexing beyond the end of an array.

> **NOTE**
>
> A class derived from `java.lang.Exception` is generally referred to as an *exception*. A class derived from `java.lang.Error` is generally referred to as an *error*.

Examples of exceptions are `ArithmeticException`, `ArrayIndexOutOfBoundsException`, `ClassNotFoundException`, and `NullPointerException`. Java allows you to define new errors or exceptions and to try to catch existing exceptions and errors. When an error occurs within a method, that method can throw an exception. The Java runtime environment will attempt to determine which method in the call chain handles an exception that most closely matches the thrown exception. If one is found, its exception handler (the `catch` block) is called.

Catching Exceptions Using `try...catch`

To retrieve any error that may occur in a block of code, catch the `Exception` class exception, as in the following example:

```
try
{
   callSomeMethod();
}
catch (Exception e)
{
   System.out.println("An error occurred.");
}
System.out.println("Everything looks OK!");
```

In this block of code, the `callSomeMethod()` method is called. If the code throws an exception anywhere in that method (either through the use of the `throw` keyword or by an invalid operation), the error message is printed and the method is exited.

Performing Default Operations Using the `finally` Keyword

As mentioned in the "Exception Handling" section, you can use the `finally` keyword to execute a block of statements regardless of whether an error was caught. The method shown in Listing 7.1 uses a `try...catch...finally` block to open a database using a fictional `Database` object, perform some operation, and then make sure that the database connection is closed.

Listing 7.1. Catching exceptions using a `try...catch...finally` block.

```
void PerformQuery(String SQL, Database DB)
{
   String results;
   try
   {
      DB.Open();
      results = DB.PerformQuery(SQL);
   }
   catch (DBException e)
   {
      System.out.println("Your query failed, buddy.");
   }
   finally
   {
      DB.Close();
   }
   System.out.println("Query results = " + results);
}
```

In this example, the `DBException` exception is caught by the `PerformQuery()` method. Regardless of what happens, the database is closed using the `DB.Close()` method call in the `finally` clause.

Catching Multiple Exceptions

In Listing 7.1, two statements are executed in the try clause:

```
DB.Open();
results = DB.PerformQuery(SQL);
```

Most database class libraries define two different exceptions for these two operations; let's call them DBOpenException and ExecuteQueryException. With Java, your program can catch and handle multiple exceptions. This allows you to fine-tune error handling so that a variety of problems can be handled effectively. Listing 7.2 illustrates how this is done.

Listing 7.2. Catching multiple exceptions in Java.

```
void PerformQuery(String SQL, Database DB)
{
  String results;
  try
  {
    DB.Open();
    results = DB.PerformQuery(SQL);
  }
  catch (DBOpenException e)
  {
    System.out.println("Database open failed.");
  }
  catch (ExecuteQueryException e)
  {
    System.out.prinln("Query execution failed.");
  }
  finally
  {
    DB.Close();
  }
  System.out.println("Query results = " + results);
}
```

You can handle as many exceptions as you like, but no one wants to write error handlers for all the possible errors that could ever occur. Suppose that the source code for a method was not available to you and you had no idea which exceptions were thrown by that class, if any. The best that you could hope to do is catch the base exception, Exception, and perform some type of generic error handling.

Using the throws Keyword to Identify Possible Exceptions

Fortunately, Java provides a way for the creator of a method to define which exceptions are being thrown by a method: by using the throws keyword in the method definition, as demonstrated in Listing 7.3.

Listing 7.3. Catching and throwing exceptions in Java.

```
void PerformQuery(String SQL, Database DB) throws EmptyResultException
{
  String results;
  try
  {
    DB.Open();
    results = DB.PerformQuery(SQL);
  }
  catch (DBOpenException e)
  {
    System.out.println("Database open failed.");
  }
  catch (ExecuteQueryException e)
  {
    System.out.prinln("Query execution failed.");
  }
  finally
  {
    DB.Close();
  }
  if (results.length > 0) then
    System.out.println("Query results = " + results);
  else
  {
    throw new EmptyResultException();
  }
}
```

In Listing 7.3, the fictional EmptyResultException is thrown if the length of the result string is less than or equal to 0. The caller of this method could then catch this exception in the PerformQuery() method and have some idea of what error occurred, as in the following example:

```
void QueryButtonClick(void)
{
  String SQL = "SELECT * FROM EMPLOYEES";
  try
  {
    PerformQuery(SQL);
  }
  catch (EmptyResultException e)
  {
    System.out.println("No results returned.");
  }
  catch (Exception e)
  {
    System.out.println("An unknown error occurred.");
  }
}
```

Note that if you use the `throws` keyword in the definition of the `PerformQuery()` method, any method that calls `PerformQuery()` is required to try to catch an exception. This error can be caught at compile time. For instance, assume that you compiled the following method:

```
void QueryButtonClick(void)
{
  String SQL = "SELECT * FROM EMPLOYEES";
  PerformQuery(SQL);
}
```

Using Visual J++, the following error would occur:

```
error J0122: Exception 'EmptyResultException' not caught or declared by
  'void DataDlg.QueryButtonClick(void)'
```

When calling any of the methods in the Java API, always be sure to implement an exception handler if the method definition in the online help shows that the method throws an exception.

Creating New Exception Classes

The previous examples demonstrate throwing and catching an exception known as `EmptyResultException`; however, the exception was never actually implemented. As discussed in the section "Handling Errors in Java," exceptions are simply special-case classes derived from the `java.lang.Throwable` class. The `java.lang.Exception` and `java.lang.Error` classes derive directly from this class and are used to implement errors and exceptions. Therefore, to build your own exception named `EmptyResultException`, you must simply build a class that derives from `java.lang.Exception`. The following example creates this exception:

```
class EmptyResultException extends Exception
{
  EmptyResultException() { super(); }
  EmptyResultException(String s) { super(s); }
}
```

This exception simply defines two constructors that are used to call the `Exception` class's constructors.

Exception handling is used extensively throughout the classes in the `java` package to trap common errors. This is much simpler and more reliable than defining a huge set of error codes that are used as return values from method calls. If an exception is thrown and no handler exists to catch it, the program will crash. If the program is actually a Java applet running within a browser, the browser will not crash because most browsers are designed to catch runtime errors to prevent this from happening. Nonetheless, always attempt to catch errors, particularly when performing calculations or operations based on user input or values obtained from a file. Because these types of data are unpredictable, always be sure to check for errors at runtime by implementing exception handlers.

Performing Simultaneous Operations Through Multithreading

A *multithreading program* can perform two or more different threads of operation simultaneously. Examples of multithreaded applications are the 32-bit Windows operating systems, Java applications that perform animation, and applications that allow user actions while some other operation is being performed. The underlying operating system actually controls the extent to which two different threads are allowed to operate. Different tasks can be assigned different priorities to control their operation in the queue.

You may be wondering why threading is necessary. Suppose you wanted to write an application that would allow the user to update a database and continue with the application. At first glance, this may not seem like that big of a deal. However, suppose the database update involves some complex trigger action on the database server that can take more than a minute. This operation can also cause an error about which the user must be aware. In an unthreaded Java application, the only way to do this is to call the method and wait until it finishes execution (see Listing 7.4).

Listing 7.4. An unthreaded database update.

```
void UpdateButtonClick()
{
  try
  {
    Database.Update();
  }
  catch (DBError e)
  {
    System.out.println("An error occurred!");
  }
  System.out.println("Update completed!");
}
```

As mentioned previously, the Database.Update() method call could take up to a minute to execute. Unfortunately, without a separate thread of execution, you have no way of continuing with the program while the Update() method goes off and does its work. The following section explains how to create a multithreaded application using Java so that there is no interruption in the program.

Creating a Threaded Application

The java.lang.Runnable interface and the java.lang.Thread class are used to create and run a separate thread of execution. Any object that is to execute within a thread *must* implement the Runnable interface. This interface defines a single method: run(). It is the responsibility of the developer of the threaded class to provide the run() method. The operations to be performed by the thread should be done in this method.

The Thread class is used to control a thread in a running program. Some of the important methods it defines are listed in Table 7.1.

Table 7.1. Public methods of the java.lang.Thread class.

Method	Description
destroy()	Destroys the thread without cleanup
getName()	Gets the thread's name
getPriority()	Gets the thread's priority (MAX_PRIORITY, MIN_PRIORITY, or NORM_PRIORITY)
getThreadGroup()	Retrieves the thread's threadgroup
interrupt()	Interrupts the thread
interrupted()	true if the current thread has been interrupted
isAlive()	true if the thread is alive
isDaemon()	true if the thread is a daemon
isInterrupted()	true if this thread has been interrupted
join()	Waits for this thread to die
join(long *millis*)	Waits *millis* milliseconds for this thread to die
join(long *millis*, int *nanos*)	Waits *millis* milliseconds and *nanos* nanoseconds for this thread to die
resume()	Resumes a suspended thread
run()	Calls the Runnable object's run() method
setDaemon(boolean on)	Marks the thread as a daemon thread or a normal thread
setName(*String name*)	Sets the thread's name
setPriority(*int* newPriority)	Sets the thread's priority
sleep(long *millis*)	Forces the thread to sleep for *millis* milliseconds
sleep(long *millis*, int *nanos*)	Forces the thread to sleep for *millis* milliseconds and *nanos* nanoseconds
start()	Starts the thread's execution
stop()	Stops the thread's execution
stop(*Throwable obj*)	Stops the thread's execution and throws the throwable object as an exception
suspend()	Suspends the operation of the thread
toString()	Converts the thread's contents to a string
yield()	Yields execution of the thread so others can execute

All these methods can be used to control a thread when it has been instantiated. Threads are commonly created using one of the following constructors (this is a partial listing; see the Visual J++ documentation to learn about the other `Thread` class constructors):

- `public Thread()`—The defined `Thread` object must implement its own `run()` method to accomplish some action.

- `public Thread(Runnable target)`—The `run()` method associated with the `Runnable` interface is called.

Listing 7.5 shows how the `Thread` class and the `Runnable` interface can be used to implement the same operation performed in Listing 7.4. The difference in Listing 7.5 is that the database update can occur in a separate thread, which allows the application to get on with other work.

Listing 7.5. A threaded database update.

```
public class DBUpdate implements Runnable
{
  Thread dbThread;
  DatabaseUpdate Database;

  public DBUpdate(String SQL)
  {
    Database = new DatabaseClass(SQL);  //pass in query
    dbThread = new Thread(this);
    dbThread.start();
  }

  public void run()
  {
    try
    {
      Database.Update();
    }
    catch
    {
      System.out.println("An error occurred!");
    }
    System.out.println("Update completed!");
  }

  public static void main(String args[])
  {
    String name = "Bryan Morgan";
    new DBUpdate("UPDATE EMPLOYEE SET SALARY=1000000 WHERE NAME =" + name);
    /*
      Continue on with other work
    */
  }
}
```

The code in Listing 7.5 will not actually compile because the `DatabaseUpdate` class used in it is purely fictional; however, it serves to illustrate how a thread is created and used. The `DBUpdate` class implements the `Runnable` interface and therefore the `run()` method that performs the Update() method call in Listing 7.5. The difference is that it occurs within a thread. The thread object, dbThread, is created by calling the Thread(*Runnable obj*) constructor. When the dbThread.Start() method is called, the DatabaseUpdate class's run() method is called. While all of this going on, the main() method can continue with its execution. Listing 7.6 can be compiled and run within Visual J++. It uses separate threads of execution to print different outputs to the screen.

Listing 7.6. A multithreaded output example.

```
/*
  This example prints out some of the different baseball teams in the
  National League and the American League.  The printing occurs in separate
  threads to illustrate how two operations can occur simultaneously.
*/
public class BaseballTeams
{
  public static void main(String args[])
  {
    AmericanLeagueTeams AL = new AmericanLeagueTeams();
    NationalLeagueTeams NL = new NationalLeagueTeams();
    NL.start();
    AL.start();
  }
}

class AmericanLeagueTeams extends Thread
{
  int counter = 0;

  public void run()
  {
    while (counter++ < 5)
    {
      switch (counter)
      {
        case 0:
          System.out.println("AL: Cleveland Indians");
          break;
        case 1:
          System.out.println("AL: New York Yankees");
          break;
        case 2:
          System.out.println("AL: Texas Rangers");
          break;
        case 3:
          System.out.println("AL: Baltimore Orioles");
          break;
        case 4:
          System.out.println("AL: Seattle Mariners");
          break;
      }
      try
      {
```

continues

Listing 7.6. continued

```java
            Thread.sleep(500);
        }
      catch (InterruptedException e)
      {
        System.out.println("AL Operation was interrupted");
      }
    }
  }
}

class NationalLeagueTeams extends Thread
{
  int counter = 0;

  public void run()
  {
    while (counter++ < 5)
    {
      switch (counter)
      {
        case 0:
          System.out.println("NL: Atlanta Braves");
          break;
        case 1:
          System.out.println("NL: St. Louis Cardinals");
          break;
        case 2:
          System.out.println("NL: San Diego Padres");
          break;
        case 3:
          System.out.println("NL: Los Angeles Dodgers");
          break;
        case 4:
          System.out.println("NL: Montreal Expos");
          break;
      }
      try
      {
        Thread.sleep(500);
      }
      catch (InterruptedException e)
      {
        System.out.println("NL Operation was interrupted");
      }
    }
  }
}
```

When Listing 7.6 is compiled and run, the following output is printed to the system console:

```
NL: Atlanta Braves
AL: Cleveland Indians
NL: St. Louis Cardinals
AL: New York Yankees
NL: San Diego Padres
AL: Texas Rangers
```

```
NL: Los Angeles Dodgers
AL: Baltimore Orioles
NL: Montreal Expos
AL: Seattle Mariners
```

The National League and American League teams are printed using separate threads. Each of these threads prints one team and then sleeps for 500 milliseconds. While one thread is sleeping, the system takes the opportunity to execute the other thread. The end result is that the threads give the impression of being run simultaneously.

In the previous example, two separate thread objects are implemented with separate run() methods. One printed out a list of hard-coded American League teams, while the other printed out a list of hard-coded National League teams. This worked well because both threads were working with completely different sets of data. However, stop to think what would happen if two threads were implemented within the same class. One of these threads could print data out to the screen, while the other thread could be used to modify data. When either of these threads is run separately, it should work fine. However, when both are run at the same time, data consistency errors will occur. (As one thread is printing data, the other thread is modifying it.) Listing 7.7 is an example of this problem.

Listing 7.7. Reading and writing data simultaneously.

```
/*
  This example prints out some of the different baseball teams in the
  National League.  The printing occurs in separate
  threads to illustrate how two operations can occur simultaneously.
*/

public class BaseballTeams
{
  String[] NLTeams = {"Atlanta Braves",
    "St. Louis Cardinals",
    "San Diego Padres",
    "Los Angeles Dodgers",
    "Montreal Expos"};

  Teams print1, print2;

  public BaseballTeams()
  {
    print1 = new Teams(this, "1");
    print1.start();
    print2 = new Teams(this, "2");
    print2.start();
  }

  public static void main(String args[])
  {
    new BaseballTeams();
  }

  public void printDataOut(String numPrint)
  {
```

continues

Listing 7.7. continued

```
    int counter = 0;
    int counter2 = 0;
    while (counter2 < 50)
    {
      while (counter < 5)
      {
        System.out.println(numPrint + ": " + NLTeams[counter]);
        counter++;
      }
      counter2++;
      counter = 0;
    }
  }
}

class Teams extends Thread
{

  BaseballTeams theTeams;
  String numPrint;

  public Teams(BaseballTeams teams, String number)
  {
    theTeams = teams;
    numPrint = number;
  }

  public void run()
  {
    theTeams.printDataOut(numPrint);
  }
}
```

This application creates two threads of the same type: Teams. These threads run simultaneously, and therefore the printouts switch back and forth between the Team "1" and the Team "2". A sample printout looks something like this:

```
1: Atlanta Braves
1: St. Louis Cardinals
2: Atlanta Braves
2: St. Louis Cardinals
2: San Diego Padres
1: San Diego Padres
2: Los Angeles Dodgers
2: Los Angeles Dodgers
...
```

This random printing happens because both threads were executing at the same time using the same data and method call. This is a problem (with the code written this way) and illustrates the difficulty involved in writing threaded applications.

Writing Thread-Safe Code Using Synchronized Methods

As you might have guessed, the Java designers were well aware of this potential problem and came up with a solution: It can be solved by declaring a method to be synchronized. When this is done, the method cannot be interrupted until it has finished execution. Take the following method declaration for printDataOut():

```
public void printDataOut(String numPrint)
```

Simply changing it to the following solves the problem:

```
synchronized void printDataOut(String numPrint)
```

Because it is now a synchronized method, the printDataOut() method must finish its execution before it can be reentered. Now when the code in Listing 7.7 is run, the output should look like the following:

```
1: Atlanta Braves
1: St. Louis Cardinals
1: San Diego Padres
1: Los Angeles Dodgers
1: Montreal Expos
.../*Repeat 100 times */
2: Atlanta Braves
2: St. Louis Cardinals
2: San Diego Padres
2: Los Angeles Dodgers
2: Montreal Expos
.../*Repeat 100 times */
```

Forcing a method to be synchronized solves the problem of multiple threads calling a single method simultaneously. However, it does not solve the problem that occurs when separate threads modify data directly within the same object. Another common problem occurs when two synchronized methods call each other. A condition known as *deadlock* occurs when this happens because both methods are waiting on the other to finish before they can continue. Multithreaded programming requires you to be extremely careful to prevent errors such as this from happening.

Streaming Input and Output

Like C++, the Java programming language supports the concept of streamable input and output. A *stream* is simply a byte-stream of data that is sent from a sender to a receiver. This data could be generated from a file, a socket connection sending data to a remote computer, or text printed out to the system console. All types of streams can be separated into two basic categories: input streams and output streams. Therefore, the java.io package includes two abstract classes that are used to provide this functionality, conveniently named InputStream and OutputStream. Table 7.2 lists the public methods found in the java.io.InputStream class. This class can be inherited from in order to open a stream for input.

Table 7.2. Public members of `java.io.InputStream`.

Method Name	Description
`available()`	Returns the number of bytes that can be read without blocking
`close()`	Closes the input stream
`mark(int)`	Marks the current position in the input stream
`markSupported()`	Used to determine whether the stream supports mark/reset
`read()`	Reads a byte of data
`read(byte[])`	Reads into an array of bytes
`read(byte[], int, int)`	Reads into an array of bytes based on an offset and a read length
`reset()`	Repositions the stream to the last marked position
`skip(long)`	Skips a specified number of bytes of input

Table 7.3 lists the public methods in the `java.io.OutputStream` class, an abstract class that is inherited from by other classes opening a stream for output.

Table 7.3. Public members of `java.io.OutputStream`.

Method Name	Description
`close()`	Closes the output stream
`flush()`	Flushes the stream
`write()`	Writes a byte of data
`write(byte[])`	Writes a byte array of data
`write(byte[], int, int)`	Writes a byte array of data based on an offset and a write length

There are many types of classes in the java package that are used to open either input or output streams. One of these classes has been used extensively thus far throughout this book: `java.io.PrintStream` is used to send output to the standard output device. (When using Visual J++ with JVIEW as the Java interpreter, this output device will be the MS-DOS command window.) The instance of the `PrintStream` class that has been used extensively thus far is the out member variable of the `java.lang.System` object. Each time that output has been sent to the screen in the examples, the out output stream class has been used. The following statement is an example of this:

```
System.out.println("Printing to the output stream…");
```

In addition to the `PrintStream` class, there are many other stream classes that are used often, such as `FileInputStream`/`FileOutputStream` and `DataInputStream`/`DataOutputStream`. The first two are file-streaming classes used to read and write files. (Keep in mind that file access is available only from a Java application. Most Web browsers disallow file access by a Java applet running in a Web browser.) The `DataInputStream`/`DataOutputStream` classes are handy because they allow you to read the Java primitive data types directly from the string. (The primitive data types are the basic Java data types such as `int`, `char`, `long`, `float`, and `boolean`.)

Listing 7.8 illustrates how streams can be utilized to read a file's contents and then output it to a separate file. This example uses the `FileInputStream` and `FileOutputStream` classes.

Listing 7.8. Copying the contents of a file using streams.

```
/*
 *
 * FileCopy
 *
 */
import java.io.*;

public class FileCopy
{
  public static void main(String args[])
  {
    try
    {
      FileInputStream in = new FileInputStream("Example10.txt");
      FileOutputStream out = new FileOutputStream("COPIED.TXT");
      int input;

      while ((input = in.read()) != -1)
      {
        out.write(input);
      }
      in.close();
      out.close();
    }
    catch (FileNotFoundException e)
    {
      System.out.println("Input file not found!");
    }
    catch (IOException e)
    {
      System.out.println("File could not be created!");
    }
  }
}
```

Running this simple program will verify that the contents of the `Example10.txt` file were indeed copied to `Copied.txt`. The `FileInputStream.read()` method is used to read through the file one byte at a time. The contents of the input file are then written out one byte at a time using the `FileOutputStream.write()` method.

Retrieving Input from the User

Examples in this book have repeatedly used calls to the PrintStream.println() method in order to print some text out to the screen. However, to this point, none of the examples have retrieved any input from the user using the standard input device. (On a personal computer, the standard input device would be the keyboard.) Listing 7.9 is accepting two things from a user: a filename and text to enter into that file. When the user is finished entering the text, pressing the Enter key will cause the text to be saved to the specified file.

Listing 7.9. CreateTextFile outputs user input to a text file.

```
/*
 *
 * CreateTextFile
 *
 */
import java.io.*;

public class CreateTextFile
{
  public static void main(String argv[])
  {
    try
    {
      DataInputStream in = new DataInputStream(System.in);

      System.out.println("Enter a filename: ");
      String filename = in.readLine();
      System.out.println("Enter text to write to the file: ");
      String contents = in.readLine();
      DataOutputStream out = new DataOutputStream(new FileOutputStream(filename));
      out.writeBytes(contents);
    }
    catch (IOException e)
    {
      System.out.println("File could not be created!");
    }
  }
}
```

Note that in this example, the writeBytes() method is used to write a sequence of bytes to an output file. writeChars() is not used in this case because it writes a sequence of two-byte values to the file, which results in an empty space between each character in the output file.

Networking in Java

Because Java was designed from the outset to support sending bytecodes across a network and the capability of these bytecodes to communicate back to a server, its networking capabilities are extremely powerful. Operations that are extremely complicated in languages such as C or C++ have been greatly simplified using the classes and functionality available in the java.net package.

The first thing to realize about writing network software with Java is that it is completely platform independent. Standard TCP/IP networking concepts such as sockets, URLs, and IP addresses are used throughout the networking classes. Nowhere will you find any mention of Windows NT specifics or any references to UNIX kernels. Using the showDocument() method in the java.applet.Applet class, a single line of code can be used to retrieve files from a remote server for display on the local screen. You can use the java.net.URL class to create a connection to a remote URL.

> **NOTE**
>
> Keep in mind that URLs are not just HTTP addresses. They can be FTP, e-mail, Gopher, or any other URL format supported by your local Java runtime environment.

Sockets are used to open a "pipe" between a client and a port on a specified server. When the socket is opened for communication purposes, data can be streamed back and forth between the client and the server. Client-side sockets are implemented in the java.net.Socket class. Server-side sockets are used to communicate with a client socket and can be created using the java.net.ServerSocket class.

Summary

Exception handling is not a concept unique to Java. It is also supported in Ada, Object Pascal, and C++, to name a few. By anticipating a potential error before it happens and coding for it ahead of time, you can prevent unexplained crashes. In addition, errors can be thrown by a method with some assurance that the caller of the method will handle this error gracefully.

Multithreading applications have become more popular as hardware and operating systems have advanced. A thread represents a single path of execution within a program. A multithreaded program is an application that uses more than one thread simultaneously to accomplish some task. Java supports multithreading through the use of the java.lang.Thread class and the java.lang.Runnable interface.

Input/output streams can be used to send streams of data either to or from some source. The concept of a stream as a generic flow of data allows you to build entire classes of objects that are similar in nature. Native methods are Java's way of allowing code written in other languages to be called from within a Java program. Although this may be the only solution for Macintosh and UNIX programmers for the near future, Visual J++ also supports the creation and use of COM objects from a Java application. By encapsulating code in a COM object, you can call an object from a program written in any language.

Because the Java language is designed from the ground up as a distributed language, networking operations that are extremely complicated using other languages are greatly simplified. The vast majority of networking operations are contained in the `java.net` package. The Java programming language and its companion, the Java Base API, provide a variety of tools and features that can be used to build powerful platform-independent, distributed applications. The features presented in this chapter finish the discussions of the capabilities of the Java programming language. Chapter 8, "Developing Applets and Applications," examines the difference between Java applets and applications and is followed by a thorough examination of the capabilities of the Visual J++ development environment in Part II, "The Visual J++ Development Tools."

Developing Applets and Applications

by Bryan Morgan

IN THIS CHAPTER

CHAPTER 8

This introduction to Java programming with Visual J++ concludes with a discussion of Java applet and application development. This chapter is important for several reasons, the most important of which is that by the time you reach the end, you will have created a real, live Java applet and application. You are almost ready to produce some visible Java code to show your friends, boss, cellmates, and so on.

This chapter opens with a discussion of the similarities and differences between applets and applications—a topic of unending confusion. In fact, most *users* of Java applets within Web pages do not know that they can use Java to create standalone applications as well.

A Comparison of Applets and Applications

Many people still think that the words *Java* and *applet* are synonyms that mean a type of interactive program that runs within a Web browser's window. The reason for this misconception is that, despite Java's rapid growth, nearly all visible examples of Java code are in the form of *applets* running within Web pages. However, it is completely possible to build a standalone Java *application* that can run without the help of a Web browser. In fact, Java applications can be written to duplicate standard Windows, Mac, or UNIX applications; that is, Java applications can have a main window; include a GUI that uses menus, buttons, lists, and text boxes; and can access databases in various ways. With the advent of Visual J++, Java applications can even use existing ActiveX controls, the same way that Visual Basic and Delphi applications do today.

On the other hand, don't underestimate the importance of Java applets! Many people believe that the Web browser will be the next generation in user interfaces, and applets play a key role in the success of that interface. An incredible number of corporate applications that were once written in Visual Basic, PowerBuilder, or Delphi are currently being written to run as intranet applications using HTML, Java, and CGI scripts. In addition, the volume of Java applets currently on the Web vastly outnumbers the Java applications in existence today. With the introduction of Visual J++, however, Java should be a viable candidate for rapid application development (RAD) due to its powerful IDE, the numerous wizards available to the programmer, and its support for ActiveX controls. Because of these advantages, the number of people using Java for application development will undoubtedly grow.

Several unique features set Java applets apart from every other type of computer program:

■ An applet must run within a separate display environment. This environment can be a Web browser or any other application written with "hooks" to contain a Java applet.

■ An applet with a browser is subject to security restrictions. In most Web browsers, the applet is not allowed to access the local file system and cannot communicate with any computer other than the originating server.

■ Applets are always visual objects. It is impossible to write an applet that runs without some type of visual display.

Java applications, meanwhile, have none of the above restrictions. An application could be written to run within a window, but it is not required. The first application you will write runs only from the command line and performs simple text input and output. Currently, Java applications have the disadvantage of requiring a runtime Java interpreter, but soon Java applications will be able to be compiled to binary form and run as executables (EXE files).

Building a Java Application

As mentioned earlier, Java applications are programs that can run without the aid of a Web browser (or some other viewing application such as Sun's applet viewer). A Java application is able to read and write local files, display windows, access remote servers, and play multimedia objects.

Java applications have one coding requirement: They must supply a method named `main()` similar to the following:

```
public static void main(String args[])
{
   /* Include statements here */
}
```

C and C++ programmers will recognize that this method was borrowed directly from the C/C++ languages. When the Java application is first started, the interpreter immediately looks for a `main()` method. If none exists, the program cannot run.

The `main()` method is the entry point for the entire application. In general, this method is where the main objects for the application are created and initialized. If the primary application window is to be displayed to the user, it will be created and displayed within the `main()` method. In other words, all other methods and classes within the application feed off the startup code placed within `main()`.

The Inevitable Hello, World! Application

At this point, you are finally ready to begin serious application development using Java. You should feel comfortable with the Visual J++ environment, have a working understanding of the Java language, and be able to run the Java interpreter either within Visual J++ (which requires no special setup) or from the command line (as discussed earlier). The first example illustrates the process of creating a new project, adding source code, compiling the project, and running the application.

Visual J++ does not require you to create new classes and store them within a project. However, the project files will be created for you anyway the first time you try to compile a class.

The goal of the following example is to create a simple Java application that prints the text `Hello, World!` to an output device. In this case the output device is the MS-DOS console window. After starting Microsoft Developer Studio, select the File | New...menu option. The New dialog box contains selections for creating a new text file, project workspace, resource template, and bitmap file. Because this step is the start of a new application project, select Project Workspace.

Within the New Project Workspace dialog box, you will concentrate on creating a Java workspace (the Java Applet Wizard is covered in Chapter 11, "Building a Simple Java Applet with Visual J++"). Name the project "HelloWorld" and select the directory to create the project in. This step creates a subdirectory within the specified directory, which is named HelloWorld and will contain the HelloWorld project workspace files (HelloWorld.mak and HelloWorld.ncb).

Notice also that the HelloWorld project workspace is now loaded in the ClassView and FileView windows (see Figure 8.1), although it contains no source files yet.

FIGURE 8.1.

The empty HelloWorld *project in Visual J++.*

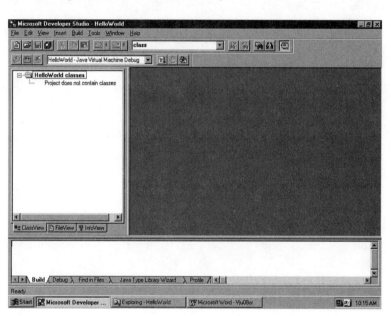

To add a class to the project, right-click over the root note ("HelloWorld classes") in the ClassView and select Create New Class.... In the Create New Class dialog box, enter HelloWorld as the class name and leave everything else blank at this time. Click the OK button, and the following code will be created for you in a source file named HelloWorld.java:

```
/*
 *
 * HelloWorld
 *
 */
class HelloWorld
{

}
```

> **NOTE**
>
> Visual J++ went ahead and named the source file for you because Java source files must be named after the public class within the source file. (Recall that each source file in Java can have only one public class.) Because this source file has only one class, HelloWorld, the file was named HelloWorld.java by default.

To cause the text `Hello, World` to be printed to the screen, you must create a `main()` method. Once this method has been declared, a single line of code will suffice to print to the screen. Modify the `HelloWorld` class by adding the following code:

```
/*
 *
 * HelloWorld
 *
 */
class HelloWorld
{
  public static void main(String args[])
  {
    System.out.println("Hello, World!");
  }
}
```

After saving the source file, notice that `ClassView` was automatically updated with the new `main()` method (see Figure 8.2).

FIGURE 8.2.

The new `main()` *method displayed in* `ClassView`.

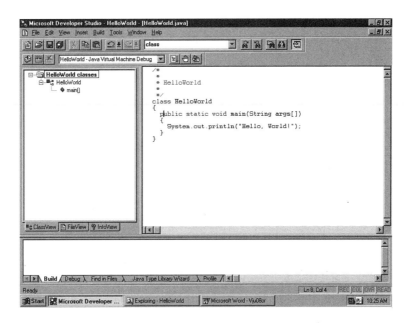

Before compiling and running this project, you will need to modify one project setting. By default, all Visual J++ projects use a Web browser as a debugger. Because, in this case, you want to view the output in the MS-DOS window, select the Build|Settings... menu and then select the Debug tab. Within the Execute project under group box, select Standalone interpreter (applications only) and press OK. Now you're ready to go!

To compile and run this simple application, select the Build | Build HelloWorld menu option or press Shift+F8. If the project compiles with no errors, run the application by selecting the Build | Execute menu option or by pressing Ctrl+F5. When prompted, enter the name of the project's main class file (`HelloWorld.class`) and watch the program run. The following text should appear in the output window briefly before the window closes:

```
Hello, World!
```

You have just built your first Java application using Visual J++. The `System.out` class's `println()` method was used to print a line of text output to the system window. The next section explains where the `System` object came from.

The `java.lang.System` Class

In the `HelloWorld` example, the `java.lang.System` class was used but was never declared anywhere in the `main()` method or in the `HelloWorld` class. It didn't have to be declared because the `System` class is created by default at runtime and is available to all running Java applications and applets. All methods and variables within this class are static; therefore, the `System` class cannot be instantiated or subclassed. It contains three variables used for streaming input and output:

- `err`—The standard error stream
- `in`—The standard input stream
- `out`—The standard output stream

In addition to these member variable classes (and their members), the `System` class provides a number of useful methods including

- `arraycopy()`—Copies the contents of one array to another, beginning at the specified indices
- `getProperties()`—Returns a `java.util.Properties` object that can be used to return information about the Java Virtual Machine (JVM) version and vendor; operating system vendor, name, and architecture; and the user account's name, home directory, and current working directory
- `loadlibrary()`—A system-dependent method used to load a system library

The `in` object is of type `InputStream` and does not need to be created. This class is most commonly used to respond to keyboard input from the user. The `out` object is of type `PrintStream` and is most commonly used to display textual output to some system output device such as the MS-DOS prompt under Windows.

Creating a Graphical Application

The HelloWorld application provides a good opportunity to introduce the steps required to create and build a new project. However, the actual code accomplishes very little from a visibility standpoint. (Below the surface, of course, a lot of work was done. The HelloWorld.class file can be run on any computer in the world with a JVM installed, which includes 3.1/95/ NT, Macintosh, UNIX, and IBM AS/400.) The purpose of this section is to produce a graphical example using menus and graphical output in the form of a Java application. This section is *not* intended to be a tutorial on GUI programming with Java. That topic is discussed in detail in Chapter 14, "An Introduction to GUI Programming."

Listing 8.1 shows the MenuApp application.

Listing 8.1. The MenuApp application.

```
import java.awt.*;
import java.lang.String;

/*
 *
 * MenuApp - A GUI app that prints text to the screen
 *           based on a user's menu selection
 *
 */

class MenuApp extends Frame
{
  MenuBar theMenuBar;
  Menu theMainMenu;
  String PaintString = "MenuApp V1.0";

  MenuApp(String str)
  {
    super(str);
  }

  void SetUpMainMenu()
  {
    /* Create the main menu and add items to it */
    theMenuBar = new MenuBar();
    theMainMenu = new Menu("Print");

    theMainMenu.add(new MenuItem("Hi There!"));
    theMainMenu.add(new MenuItem("Kick Me!"));
    theMainMenu.add(new MenuItem("Coooooool!"));
    theMainMenu.add(new MenuItem("What's Up?"));
    theMainMenu.add(new MenuItem("-"));
    theMainMenu.add(new MenuItem("Exit"));
    theMenuBar.add(theMainMenu);
  }
```

continues

Listing 8.1. continued

```java
public static void main(String args[])
{
  MenuApp theFrame;
  theFrame = new MenuApp("Visual J++ Unleashed MenuApp");
  theFrame.SetUpMainMenu();
  theFrame.setMenuBar(theFrame.theMenuBar);
  theFrame.resize(320,240);
  theFrame.repaint();
  theFrame.show();
}

public boolean action(Event evt, Object arg)
{
  if (evt.target instanceof MenuItem)
  {
    String str = (String)arg;
    if (str.equals("Exit"))
    {
      dispose();
      System.exit(0);
      return true;
    }
    else
    {
      PaintString = str;
      repaint();
    }
  }
  return false;
}

public void paint(Graphics g)
{
  int X = 160;
  int Y = 120;
  int CharWidth;
  int CharHeight;

  FontMetrics metrics = g.getFontMetrics();
  CharWidth = metrics.charWidth('A');
  CharHeight = metrics.getHeight();

  X -= CharWidth * PaintString.length() / 2;
  Y -= CharHeight / 2;

  g.drawString(PaintString, X, Y);  }
}
```

The application in Listing 8.1 (MenuApp) includes the following member methods:

■ SetupMainMenu()—Creates the menu and creates and adds the menu items one at a time. Java menus contain a menu bar (the rectangle along the top of the screen), a menu (each "main menu" element of the menu bar), and menu items (each Menu element which, when clicked, triggers some event).

- `main()`—Creates a new `MenuApp` class, sets up the menus by calling `SetupMainMenu()`, and then displays `MenuApp`. `MenuApp` can be displayed because it inherits this functionality from the `java.awt.Frame` class.

- `action()`—This method is inherited from the `java.awt.Component` class (via the `java.awt.Frame` class). Any time an action occurs within the `MenuApp` frame, this method is called. The object that caused the action is examined in order to determine if it was a menu click. If it was, the `repaint()` method is called after setting the class's `PaintString` variable.

- `paint()`—The `paint()` method also derives from the `java.awt.Component` class. The `action()` method is called whenever the frame's `repaint()` methods are called. In this instance, `action()` simply writes the `PaintString` variable's contents to the middle of the frame's window.

The `MenuApp` application can be seen running in Figure 8.3.

FIGURE 8.3.

The MenuApp *application running in Windows 95.*

This application makes use of quite a few of the classes available in the Java package included with every JVM (including the Microsoft Windows Virtual Machine used by the Visual J++ runtime interpreter, JView). For information on any of the imported classes' member methods called within `MenuApp`, consult the Visual J++ documentation. Classes used within the `MenuApp` class include `java.awt.MenuBar`, `java.awt.Menu`, `java.awt.MenuItem`, `java.lang.String`, `java.awt.Event`, `java.awt.FontMetrics`, and `java.awt.Graphics`. You could have written the following statements to import the classes used by the `MenuApp` class:

```
import java.awt.MenuBar;
import java.awt.Menu;
import java.awt.MenuItem;
import java.lang.String;
import java.awt.Event,
import java.awt.FontMetrics;
import java.awt.Graphics;
```

However, it is easier to simply write the following:

```
import java.awt.*;
```

This tells the compiler to import *all* public classes in the `java.awt` package. Most Java developers import all `java.awt` classes whenever they are programming with the Abstract Windowing Toolkit, that is, GUI programming. This shorthand is much quicker than continually going to the top of a source file and adding class files one by one.

This concludes the section on developing Java applications. The key point is that all Java applications are required to supply one static `main()` method. This method is responsible for initializing and creating objects for use throughout the program.

Running Your Application with the Standalone Java Interpreter

Java programmers already experienced in programming with the Java Developer's Kit (JDK) may be familiar with its Java runtime interpreter. Under Windows 95/NT, this interpreter existed in the form of the file `java.exe` and would run an application using the following command-line command:

```
java main_class_name
```

After you pressed Enter, the application's main class could be run and the application would be started.

Visual J++ provides two different options for running Java applications:

- ■ Running the application directly from the Visual J++ IDE
- ■ Running the application using the Microsoft standalone interpreter, `jview.exe`

These options give the same result, but some users prefer to develop using command-line syntax; therefore, `jview.exe` is discussed briefly here. Even if you plan to develop solely within Visual J++, keep in mind that when you distribute your application, it will not run without the aid of a runtime interpreter such as Microsoft's `jview.exe`. Therefore, if you plan to program in J++, you should understand how to set up the runtime interpreter.

> **NOTE**
>
> When you run a Java application from within Visual J++, no setup needs to be done because Visual J++ calls JView with the correct options. However, calling JView directly requires the user to configure these options manually.

You will find the `jview.exe` file in the `\msdev\bin` directory of the Visual J++ installation. (Don't bother trying to run it at this point. It will not do anything useful without an accompanying Java class name on the command line.) To correctly use JView as a Java interpreter for your application, you need to do two things:

- Set the path to `jview.exe` in your system path.
- Set the path to the Java class libraries, using the `CLASSPATH` environment variable.

Modifying the System Path

To set the path to `jview.exe` under Windows 95, simply open the `AUTOEXEC.BAT` file and modify the `PATH` environment variable. If `jview.exe` resides in the `C:\windows\java\bin` directory, add the following line to `AUTOEXEC.BAT`:

```
SET PATH=%PATH%;C:\WINDOWS\JAVA\BIN
```

(The `%PATH%` setting simply concatenates the current path with the string you are adding to it.) After rebooting, any program within this directory (including `jview.exe`) can be executed from anywhere else on your system.

Modifying the CLASSPATH Environment Variable

Before the interpreter can run any Java application, it needs to know the location of all the Java class libraries you used so that it can link your application's classes together with these additional classes. (For instance, if you derived your application class from the `java.awt.Graphics` class, JView would need to know the location of the `java.awt.Graphics.class` file.)

This information is stored in an environment variable known as `CLASSPATH`. All Java interpreters use the `CLASSPATH` variable to retrieve a search path for class files. As you did for the `PATH` environment variable mentioned previously, you can modify `CLASSPATH` by modifying the variable within the `AUTOEXEC.BAT` file. The Visual J++ class library is included entirely within a file named `classes.zip`.

> **NOTE**
>
> Class files can exist as single files or they can be grouped together within a ZIP file. Java interpreters must be able to locate class files using either method.

If this `classes.zip` file were installed in your `C:\windows\java\classes` directory, the `CLASSPATH` should be set to

`SETCLASSPATH=%CLASSPATH%;C:\WINDOWS\JAVA\CLASSES\CLASSES.ZIP`

If the contents of the `classes.zip` file were extracted into the `C:\windows\java\classes` directory, the `CLASSPATH` could instead be set to

`SET CLASSPATH=%CLASSPATH%;C:\WINDOWS\JAVA\CLASSES`

Now that the path to `jview.exe` and the Java class library have been set, you are ready to run Java applications from within Visual J++ or from the command-line prompt. It is now up to you to decide how to execute any Java applications you create throughout the remainder of the chapter.

Limitations of Java Applets

Unlike applications, Java applets cannot control their own destiny. *Applets*, by definition, are instantiated Java classes that run within another viewing environment. This environment is nearly always a Web browser such as Microsoft Internet Explorer 3.0 (or higher), Netscape Navigator 2.0 (or higher), or Sun's HotJava. Figure 8.4 shows the `BouncingHeads` sample applet running inside Microsoft Internet Explorer 3.0.

FIGURE 8.4.

The `BouncingHeads` *applet.*

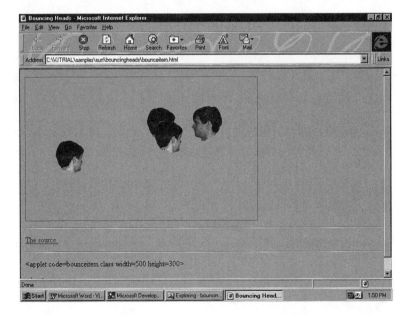

Applet-aware Web browsers are available (or will be soon) on a variety of platforms, including

- Windows 95/Windows NT
- Windows 3.1 (Q4 96)
- OS/2 3.0 (Q4 96)
- Macintosh System 7
- Solaris, Linux, and several other UNIX flavors

Although this list is by no means comprehensive, it does encompass more than 98 percent of the personal computing market. Therefore, you can probably assume that anyone you are writing software for has access to at least one of the operating systems listed. Contrary to what you may think, Java applets (and Web browsers, for that matter) do not require an Internet connection. All sample applets included with Visual J++ and with this book should run fine without a network connection. The only exception to this rule is applets that attempt to do things such as retrieve files from a remote server, perform networking operations, or load new Web pages into the browser.

Applet Security Limitations

Applets do not require the user to have a Web connection; however, most Web browsers put severe restrictions on Java applets to keep them from performing potentially harmful acts on the user's system. For instance, with the power of the classes included in the Java package, a rogue Java applet could retrieve all files from your local file system that begin with the letters *budget* and could send them over the Internet to a remote server. (This action is completely possible with ActiveX controls.) Web browsers such as Netscape Navigator and Microsoft Internet Explorer disallow applets from accessing the local file system. (Both Netscape Navigator 3.0 and Microsoft Internet Explorer 3.0 restrict the user to turning on or off the capability of loading Java applets.)

In addition to Java security features built into popular Web browsers, the Java runtime environment and Java language are both designed to provide an extremely high level of security. Because Java applets can in no way directly access memory through pointers and because they are unable to access the local system, the vast majority of security problems are eliminated.

Inter-Applet Communication Limitations

Java applets are also somewhat limited in that they are, by default, unable to communicate with applets in other browsers, and in some cases, even with other applets on the same page. As you will see, Microsoft ActiveX allows applets and ActiveX controls to be scripted together using JavaScript or VBScript, which enables objects on a Web page to communicate with each other. However, this proprietary solution works only in the Microsoft Web browser. Likewise, Netscape has announced its Open Network Environment (ONE) initiative that will provide a framework for applets to communicate with each other and with distributed CORBA (or Common

Object Request Brokering Architecture) objects, using an Object Request Broker (ORB) that will be packaged with Netscape Navigator 4.0. However, once again this proprietary solution will work only within the Netscape browser. The development community has expressed some concern that the "open" days of the Web may be long gone. Just as the operating system war was beginning to look like a thing of the past, the Web browser has, in effect, become the operating system. If you want your software to provide active content in the form of Java applets or ActiveX controls, you will have to do some careful planning to ensure that your software reaches the broadest audience.

Building a Java Applet

As you already know, from an "external" viewpoint Java applets require two things:

- A Java-aware Web browser capable of displaying and running Java applets.
- A corresponding HTML page containing the <APPLET> tag. This tag tells the browser which Java class file to load.

The rest of this discussion assumes that you have a Java-aware browser. The <APPLET> tag is described in detail in Chapter 11 and Chapter 29, "Embedding Components Within Web Pages."

From an "internal" viewpoint, Java applets must derive themselves from the java.applet.Applet class. The Applet class itself is derived from the java.awt.Panel and therefore by default is always displayed as a plain white rectangle within the boundaries specified for it in the <APPLET> HTML tag. The Applet class contains five methods that are extremely handy when building your own Java applet: init(), start(), stop(), destroy(), and paint(). Keep in mind that applets are not required to supply a main() method. If this method is supplied, it will be ignored by the Java runtime environment and never called.

The init() Method

The init() method is called automatically whenever an applet is loaded within a Web page. This method provides a convenient location for the creation and initialization of applet variables and other setup tasks. The method definition for the init() method looks like this:

```
public void init()
{
  /* Add statements here */
}
```

The start() Method

The start() method is always called after the initialization is completed. Although the init() method is called only when the page is loaded, the start() method is called each time the page is loaded *and* each time the page is restarted. A page can be stopped when a user goes to another page. When the user returns to the original page, the start() method is called again, whereas init() is not. The signature for the start() method is

```
public void start()
{
   /* Add statements here */
}
```

The stop() Method

The stop() method is called whenever the Web browser user leaves a page to go to another page. If you are performing any sort of animation or memory-consuming activity, always be sure to implement the stop() method to avoid wasting system resources. When the user returns to your page, the start() method will be called. The signature for the stop() method looks like this:

```
public void stop()
{
   /* Add statements here */
}
```

The destroy() Method

The destroy() method is called immediately before the applet exits. This exit operation could occur because the applet requested it, or it could occur because the Web browser was being shut down. Unless you need to deallocate some type of resource, you probably will not implement the destroy() method as often as you implement init(), start(), stop(), and paint(). The signature for the destroy() method looks like this:

```
public void stop()
{
   /* Add statements here */
}
```

The paint() Method

The paint() method is used to draw items onto the applet's window. As you saw in Listing 8.1, the paint() method is called each time the repaint() method is called in order to repaint the applet. The signature for the paint() method looks like this:

```
public void paint(Graphics g)
{
   /* Add statements here */
}
```

The Hello, World! Applet

Like the HelloWorld application built at the beginning of the chapter, the HelloWorldApplet applet can be written in just a few lines of code. Follow the same steps to create a project workspace for this applet that you followed to create the HelloWorld application. When the workspace is ready, create a new class named HelloWorldApplet and derive it from the java.applet.Applet class.

> **NOTE**
>
> If you type in the parent class name incorrectly, Visual J++ will prompt you. It quickly scans all the classes available in the CLASSPATH and determines whether the class you asked for is available.

To draw the words Hello world! onto the screen, all you have to do is put the correct draw commands in the paint() method. Therefore, every time the paint() method is called, these words will be drawn to the applet's canvas. Listing 8.2 builds HelloWorldApplet.

Listing 8.2. The HelloWorldApplet applet.

```
import java.applet.Applet;
import java.awt.Graphics;

/*
 *
 * HelloWorldApplet
 *
 */
class HelloWorldApplet extends Applet
{
  public void paint(Graphics g)
  {
    g.drawString("Hello world!", 10, 25);
  }
}
```

Once this code is compiled and run, the text Hello world! will be drawn within the applet (see Figure 8.5).

The default font used by Internet Explorer is almost too small to read. The code in Listing 8.3 uses the Graphics class setFont() method to enlarge the font to a more readable size. This method is called within the applet's init() method and is therefore called when the applet is initialized.

FIGURE **8.5.**

`HelloWorldApplet`
within Microsoft
Internet Explorer 3.0.

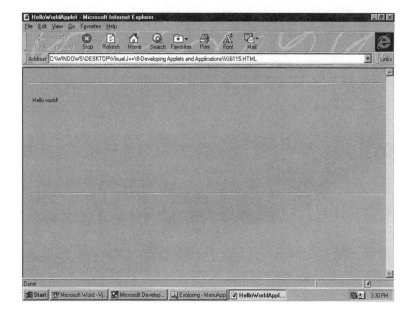

Listing 8.3. The `HelloWorldApplet2` applet.

```
import java.awt.Font;
import java.awt.Graphics;

/*
 *
 * HelloWorldApplet2
 *
 */
public class HelloWorldApplet2 extends java.applet.Applet

{
  Font tempFont;

  public void init()
  {
    tempFont = new Font("Helvetica", Font.PLAIN, 30);
  }

  public void paint(Graphics g)
  {
    g.setFont(tempFont);
    g.drawString("Hello world!", 10, 25);
  }
}
```

Figure 8.6 shows the `HelloWorldApplet2` applet displayed with a much larger font (Helvetica 30-point).

FIGURE 8.6.

The HelloWorldApplet2 *applet says* Hello world! *more clearly.*

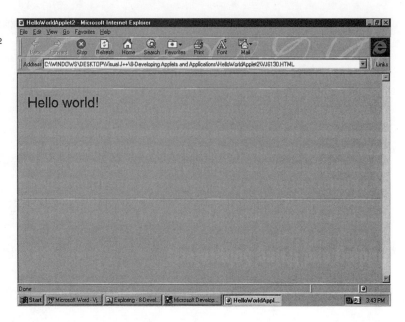

Note that Visual J++ automatically creates default HTML files whenever your default debug viewer is set to Browser. (Remember that tags must exist within an HTML file to tell the browser which class file to load.) The contents of the HTML files and the <APPLET> tag in particular are discussed later in the book. Listing 8.4 shows the contents of the HTM file created for the HelloWorldApplet2 applet by Visual J++.

Listing 8.4. The HTML created by Visual J++ for HelloWorldApplet2.

```html
<html>
<head>
<title>HelloWorldApplet2</title>
</head>
<body>
<hr>
<applet>
code=HelloWorldApplet2
width=200
height=200>
</applet>
<hr>
</body>
</html>
```

This HTML file contains two primary pieces of information: the title to be displayed at the top of the screen and the applet location and size information. Note that the `<title>` tag is `HelloWorldApplet2` . The `<applet>` tag contains three required pieces of information:

- The applet's class filename
- The initial width of the applet
- The initial height of the applet

Chapter 26, "HTML and Web Page Design," and Chapter 27, "Manipulating Web Components Using JavaScript," provide the information you need to modify the HTML generated by Visual J++ in order to enhance your page's appearance.

Summary

Many programmers do not know that they can use Java for purposes other than Web page enhancements. In fact, Java is a full-featured, powerful programming language that is supplied with a large cross-platform class library. Java applications have full access to the local system (no security restrictions) and can use the normal GUI components available to Java applet developers. Java applications are differentiated from applets in that applications must supply a `main()` method.

Java applets, meanwhile, are designed to be run only within Java-aware Web browsers. Because of the security problems inherent in a large network like the Internet, Java applets are commonly subjected to security restrictions. HTML files contain tags to tell the browser which Java class file to access in order to run the applet. Commonly implemented class methods include `init()`, `start()`, `stop()`, `destroy()`, and `paint()`.

This chapter concludes Part I, "Introduction to Java Programming Using Visual J++." Part II, "The Visual J++ Development Tools," focuses exclusively on the many development tools that ship with the Visual J++ product. These tools include an extremely fast compiler, a visual debugger, numerous wizards to aid in development, advanced project management features, and a large library of standard Java classes.

IN THIS PART

II

PART

The Visual J++ Development Tools

Managing Visual J++ Projects

by Bryan Morgan

IN THIS CHAPTER

- Visual J++ Project Workspaces *186*
- Working with the Developer Studio Views *197*

CHAPTER 9

The Developer Studio Integrated Development Environment (IDE) is used by Visual J++, as are Microsoft's Visual C++ and FORTRAN PowerStation development tools. Whereas earlier chapters focus on the usage and configuration of the development environment as a whole, this chapter covers Visual J++ projects in detail. The project workspace, in particular, is presented as a tool for managing complex Java development projects.

Thus far, all of this book's material on the Visual J++ environment has dealt with creating and modifying text files containing Java source code. These files are compiled to produce Java bytecode within `Java.class` files. If the editor were the only feature of Visual J++, it probably would have been named simply J++ (or even J—imagine that!) However, Visual J++ gives the Java developer a full complement of visual development tools that can be used to build graphical user interface (GUI) objects using a variety of components. The standard visual elements of the World Wide Web, GIF, and JPEG files can also be created using the Visual J++ graphics editor. This chapter examines the graphics editor and other Visual J++ resource development tools.

Visual J++ Project Workspaces

Visual J++ uses *project workspaces* to allow developers to group related parts of a project into a single area of work, or workspace. Each project workspace must contain at least one Java project, although it can contain more if necessary. Java source files are contained in each of these main Java projects. Each of these main projects can also contain multiple subprojects, which can contain a Java project or even a project written in another language. (In this case, Java native methods would be used to access code in the subproject.) Within each of these projects is a set of files. These files can be Java source code files, readme documentation files, or even native code used to build Windows dynamic link libraries (DLLs) that your Java application can use.

Project workspaces are also used to maintain configuration information about a Java project. Information typically maintained in a project workspace includes compilation switches, file or class path locations, class file output locations, and compilation settings (such as `Debug` or `Release`). These settings are presented in this chapter. However, for more specific information about compiler options, see Chapter 10, "The Visual J++ Compiler."

Quite often, users of Visual J++ use the words *project* and *project workspace* interchangeably. This is because project workspaces commonly contain only one project. However, the capability to add multiple projects with associated multiple subprojects allows a developer to visually group together an extremely large set of related files. The `Rebuild All` command can even be used to rebuild all these projects at once to ensure that the latest version of your application is being released.

Creating Project Workspaces

You can use two methods to create a default project workspace: open an existing Java source file and compile it, or manually create a project workspace by selecting the appropriate option in Visual J++.

Creating a Workspace Using Existing Source Code

Perhaps you have been developing in Java using Sun's Java Developer's Kit (JDK). The JDK comes with a command-line compiler, debugger, and interpreter that can be used to build Java applications. Of course, because these tools are command line only, they lack many of the sophisticated visual capabilities found in Visual J++. However, until recently, many beginning developers used the JDK as their primary Java development tool because it worked *and* it was free. Let's assume you used the JDK previously to build the sample application found in Listing 9.1. Now that you have bought a version of Visual J++, you would like to use it to compile and build the application from now on.

Listing 9.1. A standalone Java class.

```
class Example1
{
  String Chapters[] =
  {
    "Chapter 1:   Visual J++:  What It Is and Why It Is Special,"
    "Chapter 2:   Understanding the Java Runtime Environment,"
    "Chapter 3:   Object-Oriented Programming with Java,"
    "Chapter 4:   Understanding the Java Base Platform,"
    "Chapter 5:   Elements of the Java Language,"
    "Chapter 6:   Creating Programs with Java,"
    "Chapter 7:   Advanced Java Programming,"
    "Chapter 8:   Developing Applets and Applications,"
    "Chapter 9:   Managing Visual J++ Projects,"
    "Chapter 10:  The Visual J++ Compiler,"
    "Chapter 11:  Building a Simple Applet with Visual J++,"
    "Chapter 12:  Debugging with the Visual J++ Debugger,"
    "Chapter 13:  The Standard Java Packages,"
    "Chapter 14:  An Introduction to GUI Programming,"
    "Chapter 15:  GUI Development Using the Visual J++ Resource Wizard"
  };

  public static void main(String args[])
  {
    Example1 demo = new Example1();
    demo.Completed(8);
  }

  void Completed(int Number)
  {
    for (int i = 0; i <= (Number - 1); i++)
    {
      System.out.println(Chapters[i]);
    }
  }
}
```

9

MANAGING
VISUAL J++
PROJECTS

When this Java file is opened in Visual J++, it loads like a normal Java source file; all the editor features such as syntax highlighting and automatic tabbing are enabled. However, when Visual J++ tries to compile the file, it looks for the file's associated project workspace. Finding none, it prompts the user to determine if he wants to create a default project workspace to be associated with this Java source file (see Figure 9.1).

FIGURE 9.1.

Creating a default project workspace.

It is impossible to compile a Java class within Visual J++ without the presence of a project workspace. Therefore, if No is selected in the dialog box in Figure 9.1, nothing happens.

> **NOTE**
>
> Keep in mind that nothing will physically happen to your .java source code or .class bytecode files if a project workspace is created. These files can still be used by any other Java compiler on any platform. Making a project workspace simply creates a set of additional files used by Visual J++ to maintain project configuration information.

After the project workspace has been created and the class has been compiled, the ClassView, FileView, and InfoView tab screens are available and loaded with your new project workspace (see Figure 9.2).

FIGURE 9.2.

The Java class loaded into the new workspace.

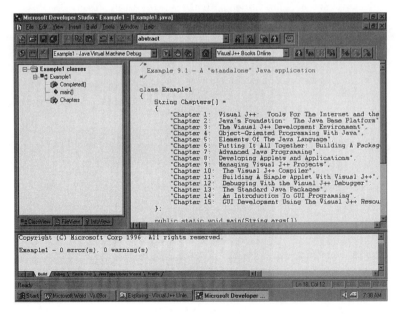

Notice that the ClassView shown in Figure 9.2 already contains the methods and variables contained in the `Example1` class shown in Listing 9.1. For the record, a few additional actions must be accomplished before the `Example1` class can be run. Selecting Build | Execute will cause another dialog box to be shown the first time this class is run. Because this is a Java application, not an applet, select Stand-alone interpreter and enter the class name to be run (`Example1`, in this case). Running this example should produce the following output:

```
Chapter 1:  Visual J++:  What It Is and Why It Is Special
Chapter 2:  Understanding the Java Runtime Environment
Chapter 3:  Object-Oriented Programming with Java
Chapter 4:  Understanding The Java Base Platform
Chapter 5:  Elements of the Java Language
Chapter 6:  Creating Programs with Java
Chapter 7:  Advanced Java Programming
Chapter 8:  Developing Applets and Applications
```

Examining the directory where the `Example1.java` file was located reveals that the following files were created as part of the project workspace:

> `Example1.mdp`—The project workspace file
>
> `Example1.mak`—The project makefile
>
> `Example1.ncb`—The project information file

Now that all your existing Java source files have been imported into Visual J++ and project workspaces have been created, in the future you will most likely create new project workspaces from scratch.

Creating a Workspace from Scratch

New project workspaces can also be created using the File | New menu option. Selecting this option will bring up the New dialog box, which gives the user the option of creating a new source file, project workspace, bitmap, or resource template. Selecting Project Workspace brings up the dialog box shown in Figure 9.3.

FIGURE 9.3.

The New Project Workspace dialog box.

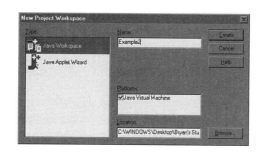

For now, select New | Project Workspace. (The Java Applet Wizard is discussed in detail in Chapter 11, "Building a Simple Java Applet with Visual J++.") Enter the directory in which the project workspace should be created and the name of the new workspace. If a directory does not already exist with the name of the new workspace, a new directory, containing the workspace .mak and .ncb files, will be created for you. By default, the project workspace is created with no member files. Therefore, to do anything useful, you must add new files. Existing files can be added to any project manually, and new files can be added using tools available in Visual J++.

Adding Existing Files to a Project

After copying the Example1.java file into the Example2 directory, this file and any others can easily be added to the Example2 project: Simply choose the Insert | Files Into Project menu and select whichever files you would like to add. Note that these files do not need to exist within the project directory. (The Example1.java file was added to the Example2 directory simply to avoid confusion.) Table 9.1 shows the file types that can be filtered and added using this dialog box.

Table 9.1. Visual J++ file types and descriptions.

File Type	Description
*.java	Java source files
*.rc, *.rct, *.res	Resource files
*.mak	Makefiles
*.bmp, *.dib, *.jpg, *.gif, *.ico, *.cur	Image files
*.exe, *.dll, *.ocx	Executable files and libraries
*.bsc	Browse info files
*.odl	Object description libraries
*.lib	Library files
*.obj	Object files

After a file has been added, it can be viewed in the FileView control under the project name.

> **WARNING**
>
> The Insert | Files Into Project option is very different from the Insert | File option. Whereas Insert | Files Into Project results in the selected files being added to the currently selected project, Insert | File adds the contents of the selected file at the cursor location in the currently selected source code window.

After the desired files have been added to the project, they can be edited, compiled, or run in Visual J++ using the editor, compiler, and standalone interpreter or Web browser.

Creating New Files for a Project

Assuming that you really like Visual J++ and have made it your tool of choice for Java development projects, more often than not you will create new files within a project (rather than adding existing files). Visual J++ provides several ways of adding files to a project.

If the file is not a Java source code file and was created using another application, simply insert the file into the project using the Insert|Files Into Project menu option. If the file to be created is a Java source file, there are two options:

- Create the Java source file using the File|New Text File option. After source code has been added to the file and it has been saved (with a .java extension), add the file to the project using the Insert|Files Into Project menu option.

- Create a new Java class by right-clicking the Example2 project and selecting the Create New Class option or by selecting the Insert|New Java Class main menu option.

The first method has already been demonstrated, so let's add a new Java class by right-clicking the Example2 project. Doing so produces the dialog box shown in Figure 9.4.

FIGURE 9.4.

The Create New Class dialog box.

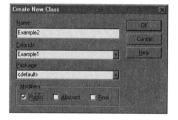

This is the preferred option because filling in the appropriate options in the dialog box creates a skeleton class with the appropriate keywords. Filling in the dialog box with the options shown in Figure 9.4 creates the class in Listing 9.2 and adds it to the Example2 project.

Listing 9.2. The Example2 class generated by Visual J++.

```
import Example1;

/*
 *
 * Example2
 *
 */
public class Example2 extends Example1
{


}
```

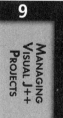

After this class has been added to the project, right-clicking it in the ClassView page of the project workspace will produce a pop-up menu. Within this menu are options to add methods (Add Method) and variables (Add Variable) to the class.

Adding Methods to a Class

Clicking the Add Method pop-up menu option produces the dialog box shown in Figure 9.5. Selecting OK for all the options shown in Figure 9.5 modifies `Example2.java` as shown in Listing 9.3.

FIGURE 9.5.

The Add Method dialog box.

Listing 9.3. The method added by Visual J++.

```
import Example1;

/*
 *
 * Example2
 *
 */
public class Example2 extends Example1
{
  public int GetGoing(boolean StartUp)
  {
  }
}
```

The `getGoing()` method is added with the signature specified in the Add Method dialog box.

Adding Variables to a Class

Clicking the Add Variable pop-up menu option produces the dialog box shown in Figure 9.6. Selecting OK for all the options shown in Figure 9.6 modifies `Example2.java` as shown in Listing 9.4. The variable `StartUp` was added to the `Example2` class using the Add Variable dialog box shown in Figure 9.6.

FIGURE 9.6.
The Add Variable dialog box.

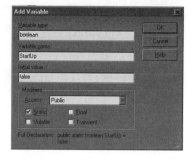

Listing 9.4. The variable added by Visual J++.

```
import Example1;

/*
 *
 * Example2
 *
 */
public class Example2 extends Example1
{
  public static boolean StartUp = false;

  public int GetGoing(boolean StartUp)
  {
  }
}
```

Adding and Using Subprojects

As mentioned earlier, a project workspace can contain multiple projects, and each of these projects can contain multiple subprojects. This allows the developer to create a project containing a reusable library of classes (such as the Politics package created in Chapter 6, "Creating Programs with Java," or a DLL that is called using native methods). The contents of these subprojects are immediately available to the developer, and all the projects and subprojects can be rebuilt at any given time using the Build|Rebuild All menu option. This ensures that the latest versions of all projects and subprojects are used when building an application or applet.

To add a subproject to an existing Visual J++ project, select the Insert|Project menu option. A dialog box similar to that shown in Figure 9.3 comes up. However, this dialog box gives the user the option of creating either a new top-level project or a subproject under an existing project (see Figure 9.7).

9

MANAGING
VISUAL J++
PROJECTS

FIGURE 9.7.

Inserting a new project or subproject.

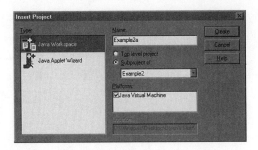

Entering Example2a into the dialog box and selecting a subproject to be created under Example2 creates the Example2a directory under the Example2 directory. Because no source files have been created or added to this new subproject, the directory and associated ClassView and FileView entries under Example2a are empty. (To add files or new Java classes to this subproject, follow the procedures described in the section "Creating New Files for a Project.")

Setting the Default Project

When multiple projects are available in a project workspace, it is important to know which one is the default project; in Visual J++, the default project's name appears in bold text and all other projects' and subprojects' names appear in normal text. Whenever a file is added to a project or the Compile/Build command is selected, these operations will take place on the currently selected default project. To set a project as the project workspace's default, right-click the project's name in the workspace's FileView and select the Set As Default Project option. This project's name will then appear in bold text and Visual J++ will use it as the default.

Deleting Projects or Subprojects from the Workspace

One not-so-obvious operation that you may need to perform from time to time is deleting a project from the workspace. This operation is nowhere to be found in all the menu options in Visual J++. However, it is possible to remove a project or subproject from a project workspace by selecting the Build│Configurations menu option. When chosen, the dialog box shown in Figure 9.8 appears.

FIGURE 9.8.

The Configurations dialog box.

To remove a project or subproject such as Example2 from the project workspace, select it in this dialog box and then press the Remove button. This will cause this project/subproject to be completely removed from the current project workspace. Files and directories associated with this project will not be physically removed from your hard drive, however.

Setting and Using Project Configurations

Each Visual J++ project is created, by default, with two project configurations associated with it: Debug and Release. Carefully examining these project configurations will show that the only difference between them lies in the configuration build settings for the compiler. The Debug configuration uses the /g switch with Generate Debug Info selected, and the Release configuration uses the /O switch with Full Optimization selected.

A project configuration provides an easy way to group a set of related compiler and environment settings together, which can be collectively used to control the final output of the compiler. In many cases, the Debug and Release settings may be adequate. However, many developers like to fine-tune the compiler settings to generate additional information or maintain more control over the compiler's output. (These settings are discussed in Chapter 10.)

To create a new project configuration, select the Build|Configurations menu option. The dialog box shown in Figure 9.8 appears. Now click on the Add button to display the dialog box shown in Figure 9.9.

FIGURE 9.9.

Adding a new project configuration.

Although this dialog box does not allow you to actually specify the settings for the new configuration, it does allow you to copy settings from an existing configuration. It is assumed that future versions of Visual J++ will allow more presetting of configuration options at this stage to reduce the number of steps required to add a new configuration. At any rate, after the new configuration has been added, you can modify its options by selecting the Build|Settings menu option.

Specifying the Default Project Configuration

To set a project configuration to be used as the default for future builds of the current project, select the Build|Set Default Configuration options. A dialog box appears (see Figure 9.10), asking the user to select the configuration to be used as the default.

Selecting Example2-Java Virtual Machine Debug in this example results in the Example2 "Debug" configuration being used whenever this project is built.

FIGURE 9.10.

Setting the default configuration.

Setting Workspace Display Options

In addition to setting the individual project and file settings associated with a project workspace, the actual display of the project workspace can be customized by selecting the Tools|Options menu option and then the Workspace tab (see Figure 9.11).

FIGURE 9.11.

Configuring workspace display options.

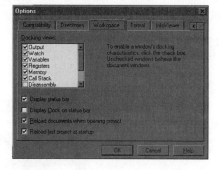

In this dialog box, the display of the following toolbars can be toggled:

Output

Watch

Variables

Registers

Memory

Call Stack

Disassembly

Project Workspace

InfoViewer Topic

Toggle any of these toolbars or select any of the additional options being displayed to make these changes globally for all project workspaces opened in the future. At this time, Visual J++ does not associate display changes with a specific project. Instead, it is assumed that a user feels most comfortable working within one specific environment and that this environment should apply to all project workspaces opened within Visual J++. (This philosophy differs from the IDE of Delphi, which can be customized on a project-by-project basis.)

Thus far, this chapter and this book deal extensively with the views available in the Developer Studio IDE (namely the ClassView, FileView, and the InfoView tab pages). Chapter 3, "Object-Oriented Programming with Java," introduces these views, and they are reintroduced here now that you are more familiar with Visual J++, the Java language, and project workspaces.

Working with the Developer Studio Views

Each view in the Developer Studio IDE gives you a different view of valuable project information. This information is available at the click of one button and can be relocated anywhere on the screen because these views are contained in "dockable" windows. This section discusses each option available in each view. Note that which options are available depends on which item is selected within one of the views. For instance, different options are presented to the user when a project is selected in ClassView than when a class is selected in ClassView.

At a minimum, right-clicking any of the views presents four options that apply to all views:

- Title Tips—Selecting this option toggles a display of Title Tips, which allow the title of a line within a view to be displayed as a floating tip if the view window is minimized so that part of the line is hidden.

- Docking View—Selecting this option toggles a docking view option. If a window is set in docking view mode, it will be "docked" in a corner of the screen. If docking mode is not set, the window floats within the Visual J++ workspace and can be moved or resized as needed.

- Hide—Selecting this option hides the window from view. To redisplay the window, select the View|Project Workspace menu option.

- Properties—Selecting this option brings up the Properties dialog box, showing a set of properties for the selected item.

These primary options apply to each pop-up menu displayed in the project workspace window. The following sections discuss options that are specifically available in the ClassView, FileView, and InfoView pages.

The ClassView Options

The ClassView tab page allows you to view information about projects within the workspace and, specifically, about the Java classes available within those projects. Right-clicking a member in the ClassView page displays a pop-up menu. Table 9.2 lists the menu options available in the ClassView page and their meanings.

Table 9.2. ClassView menu options.

Item	Menu Option	Meaning
Project name	Create New Class	Create a new class within the project
Class name	Go To Definition	Open class file in text editor
Class name	Add Method	Add a method to the class
Class name	Add Variable	Add a variable to the class
Class name	Create New Class	Create a new class within the project
Class name	Group By Access	Group classes by access (public, protected, private, and so on)
Method name	Go To Definition	Go to method within source file
Method name	Set Breakpoint	Set debugging breakpoint at method
Method name	Group By Access	Group methods by access (public, protected, private, and so on)
Variable name	Go To Definition	Go to variable within source file
Variable name	Group By Access	Group variables by access (public, protected, private, and so on)

The ClassView options apply specifically to Java classes. Note that ClassView's contents are updated immediately whenever classes are added, modified, or deleted; in other words, it is not necessary to wait for a class to be compiled to see the contents of ClassView updated.

The FileView Options

Whereas the ClassView page shows only information about Java classes, the FileView page shows information about all files contained in the current project, whether they are Java source files, graphics files, HTML files, documentation, or any other file associated with a project. Table 9.3 lists the options available when the pop-up menu is displayed over a specific FileView item.

Table 9.3. FileView menu options.

Item	Menu Option	Meaning
Project name	Build	Builds the project using the current configuration
Project name	Set As Default Project	Sets the project as the workspace default
Project name	Settings	Displays the Project Settings dialog box

Item	Menu Option	Meaning
Project workspace filename	Settings	Displays the Project Settings dialog box
Filename	Open	Opens the file in an editor window
Filename	Settings	Displays the Project Settings dialog box
Java source code	Compile `filename`	Compiles the selected file

In summary, FileView displays all the files (no matter what their type) within the project workspace. Double-clicking any one of the files opens it within an editor window. If the file is a graphics file (for example, `*.bmp`, `*.gif`, `*.jpg`), the graphics editor is opened. If the file is an HTML or Java source file, the standard Visual J++ editor is opened.

The InfoView Options

The InfoView page is different from the ClassView and FileView pages in that it contains information that applies to all project workspaces in Visual J++. (Even when a project workspace has not been opened, the InfoView page is still shown by default.) The InfoView page is used to display all available information (for example, documentation, help files, samples) that comes packaged with Visual J++. The Visual J++ 1.0 Professional Edition includes the following topics in the InfoView page:

- Read This First—Standard readme documentation
- Test Drive—Includes the online book *Introduction To Visual J++*
- The Visual J++ User's Guide
- Java API, Volume 1: Core Packages—Documentation for all the Java Base API packages (except `java.awt` and `java.applet`)
- Java API, Volume 2: Window Toolkit and Applets—Documentation for the `java.awt` and `java.applet` packages
- Java API, Hierarchy Chart: A graphical depiction of the Java API classes and their relations
- Java Language Specification—The Java Language Specification published by Sun Microsystems
- Java and COM—Contains information on integrating COM and Java
- Samples—Contains information and installation capabilities for the Sun and Microsoft Java samples
- Build Errors—Documentation on all the Visual J++ compiler errors
- Miscellaneous—Contains additional copyright and glossary information

Like in the FileView and ClassView pages, right-clicking any item in the InfoView page will bring up a pop-up menu. Table 9.4 lists the options available for each InfoView item.

Table 9.4. InfoView menu options.

Item	Menu Option	Meaning
Any InfoView topic	Search	Search or query InfoView topics for information
Any InfoView topic	Define Subset	Filter the contents of the help system to display a subset
Any InfoView topic	Set Default Subsets	Define the default subsets to be used as Query, InfoView, and Context-Sensitive Help
Any InfoView topic	Print	Print the selected InfoView topic

Including documentation in the InfoView page provides a handy reference point for an extremely large amount of information. Language, environment, and general Java information topics are within a few clicks of the mouse using the InfoView page.

Summary

With the Developer Studio IDE, Visual J++ allows developers accustomed to working with Microsoft's Visual C++ and FORTRAN PowerStation products to reuse the same environment when programming in Java. All Visual J++ projects are viewed and maintained using a project workspace, which contains project configuration settings and the contents of all projects in the project workspace. A project workspace can contain multiple projects, and each of these projects can contain multiple subprojects.

These projects and subprojects can be located anywhere on the file system (not just in the project workspace directory) and can contain development projects written in languages other than Java. For instance, you could create a subproject containing the information and files needed to build a new DLL used by a Java application. Selecting Rebuild All will rebuild all the projects and subprojects in the project workspace.

The contents of a project workspace can be examined and modified easily using the ClassView, FileView, and InfoView tab pages in the Project Workspace window. ClassView contains information about each class in each project (including class member method and variable information). New methods and variables can be added to a class using pop-up menu options. The FileView page contains information about each file within each project in the project workspace. Files of any type can be added and removed from the ListView (including graphics, HTML, and documentation files). The InfoView page contains Visual J++ and Java documentation topics and help information. All InfoView topics can be searched for information based on a user-defined query. For more information on user-defined queries, consult the Visual J++ documentation.

Visual J++ provides a refined GUI for project management functions and includes convenient help windows and wizards that can automate many routine tasks that otherwise would be done by hand (and therefore would be prone to error). Chapter 10 introduces the Visual J++ compiler and its settings. Although Visual J++ generates projects with default build settings of Release and Debug, these compiler settings may be useful to the developer wishing to adjust the compiler to accomplish a specific task.

The Visual J++ Compiler

by Mark Seminatore

IN THIS CHAPTER

CHAPTER 10

As you learned in earlier chapters, the Visual J++ compiler, like many of Microsoft's latest development tools, is hosted under the Microsoft Developer Studio. The concept of the Developer Studio is very nice. It provides a consistent and comfortable working environment with easy access to online books, class browsers, project-management tools, and optional links to source code revision control. Microsoft has really tried to leverage the strengths of the Developer Studio by hosting Visual C++, FORTRAN PowerStation, Visual Test, and the Microsoft Developer Network in the same environment.

For the most part, when working with Visual J++ most of your interactions are actually with the Developer Studio, which is shown in Figure 10.1. The Developer Studio also contains several other useful utilities, including WinDiff, Zoomin, and JView. Although the integrated environment certainly is convenient, at times the command-line tools can increase your productivity. As an example, if you wanted to create a very simple Java applet consisting of only a single class, it may be more convenient to edit and compile the applet from the command line. The command-line tools are also useful if you want to make only a small change and then rebuild a project using NMAKE. You'll find out more about the command-line compiler and other tools later in the chapter.

> **NOTE**
>
> Don't look for the Visual J++ compiler in this figure. The compiler is not exactly visible because it is called behind the scenes by the Developer Studio.
>
> Of course, a command-line version of the Visual J++ compiler is available.

FIGURE 10.1.

The Visual J++ compiler environment.

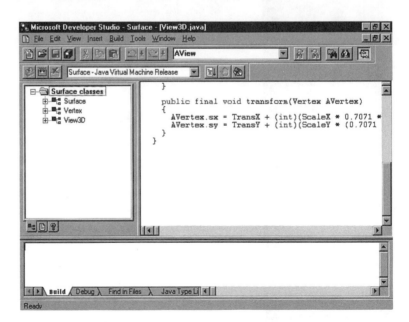

The Visual J++ compiler is really quite fast even with full optimization and debug support enabled. It easily handles the sample programs that Sun provides as part of the Java Developer's Kit (JDK). Microsoft also supplies a number of examples to demonstrate key features of Visual J++. These examples include capabilities such as creating Java links to COM objects, VBScript, and ActiveX controls. One of the Microsoft examples even demonstrates how to implement a COM object in Java that can be called from another application such as Visual Basic.

Code Performance

One of the most important considerations with any development tool is the performance of the resulting code. Programmers tend to spend a great deal of time working with compilers, so they are always happy to work with a fast compiler. However, end users don't care about the speed of the edit-compile-debug cycle. They want fast and responsive software, which, if you think about it, is exactly what the programmer is looking for in a fast compiler. In the end, both end users and programmers want the programs they use to be the result of good code generation. Programmers sometimes deal with this problem by using one compiler for development and another for the final builds. End users seldom have this luxury.

With Visual J++, Microsoft has attacked this problem by separating the development environment from the compiler. This approach allows one development team to focus on developing an environment that can be used in several products while another team focuses on the compiler itself. Other compiler vendors have attacked the same problem simply by providing several compiler back ends, perhaps licensing code generators from other companies.

Performance and Bytecode Interpreters

Does this information have any relation to the Visual J++ compiler and Java programming? Yes, because Java as an interpreted language already has one strike against it with regard to code performance. Getting a bytecode interpreter to execute anywhere near the speed of a compiled language is very difficult. However, as the success of Visual Basic and PowerBuilder proved, applications are spending more and more time executing the user interface code of the operating system. The result is that for most applications, the need for blistering speed is becoming less of a concern than it used to be.

The differences between interpreted code and machine code become readily apparent, however, during complex mathematical calculations. Newer processors such as the Pentium can, in certain situations involving integer and floating-point arithmetic, dispatch multiple instructions per cycle. This is called *superscalar execution*. Superscalar execution allows certain machine code instructions to execute in parallel, which can provide a substantial performance improvement over non-superscalar designs.

The Java Virtual Machine is limited in its capability to take advantage of such advanced processor features. Why? Because the Java compiler and the Java client may run on different hardware, the Java compiler cannot possibly know how to optimally arrange bytecodes for the interpreter. Any performance optimizations targeted at one particular Java platform will usually be offset by significant losses on other platforms. Platform independence is one of Java's greatest strengths, so trying to perform hardware-specific optimizations doesn't make sense.

The Test Program

In order to test the code generation of the Visual J++ compiler, I wrote a test applet. The applet draws an animated 3D wire-frame surface. As such, the applet performs a significant amount of floating-point math while it calculates the vertices of the mesh, transforms the vertices, and then projects the surface to the screen. The applet also tests a compiler's ability to recognize and optimize incremental array accesses.

I compiled the test applet using the Visual J++ compiler and the Sun `javac` compiler that comes with the JDK. I tested both compilers with full optimizations turned on and off. In all four cases I timed the runs in milliseconds by bracketing the animation loop with calls to the `System.currentTimeMillis()` method. When the applet finishes, it displays the resulting frames, duration in milliseconds, and calculated frames per second.

The code for the test applet appears in Listings 10.1 through 10.4. Because programming Java applets isn't the subject of this chapter, only a quick overview of the code follows. The flow of the program is relatively straightforward. It calculates the vertices of a 3D sine surface, draws the surface in an offscreen buffer, copies the buffer to the screen, advances the phase angle of the surface, and then starts again.

The code calculates approximately 1,000 iterations of the surface animation. The grid is 20 by 20, or 400 individual squares. Each square is made up of 4 line segments, giving approximately 1,600 line segments for each frame. All told, the program has to execute a lot of bytecodes.

The first listing is the HTML file that executes the Java applet. The HTML file is very simple and straightforward. The `<APPLET>` tag tells the applet viewer to load and then execute the Java applet contained in `Surface.class`. Listings 10.2 and 10.3 provide the two helper classes, `Vertex` and `View3D`, used by the applet. Listing 10.4 contains the main class, `Surface`, which is a subclass of `Applet`.

Listing 10.1. Surface.html.

```
<HTML>
<HEAD>
<TITLE>3D Surface!</TITLE>
</HEAD><BODY>
<P>Wavy:
<APPLET CODE="Surface.class" WIDTH=320 HEIGHT=200>
```

```
Non-JAVA browser!
</APPLET>
</BODY>
</HTML>
```

Listing 10.2. Vertex.java.

```
public class Vertex        // extends Object implied
{
  // object/world coordinates
  double x, y, z;
  // screen coordinates
  int sx, sy;
}
```

Listing 10.3. View3D.java.

```
public class View3D
{
  double ScaleX, ScaleY;
  int TransX, TransY;

  // default constructor
  View3D()
  {
    ScaleX = ScaleY = 1;
    TransX = TransY = 0;
  }

  // constructor with initializers
  View3D(double sx, double sy, int tx, int ty)
  {
    ScaleX = sx;
    ScaleY = sy;
    TransX = tx;
    TransY = ty;
  }

  public void setScale(double sx, double sy)
  {
    ScaleX = sx;
    ScaleY = sy;
  }

  public void setTrans(int tx, int ty)
  {
    TransX = tx;
    TransY = ty;
  }
```

continues

Listing 10.3. continued

```
public void transform(Vertex AVertex)
{
  AVertex.sx = TransX + (int)(ScaleX * 0.7071 * (AVertex.x - AVertex.z));
  AVertex.sy = TransY + (int)(ScaleY * (0.7071 *
    (AVertex.x + AVertex.z) - AVertex.y));
}
}
```

Listing 10.4. Surface.java.

```
import java.awt.Graphics;
import java.awt.Image;
import java.applet.Applet;

public class Surface extends Applet implements Runnable
{
    final double phaseAngleMax = 150.0;
    final double phaseAngleInc = 0.15;
    Thread runner;
    Image ImageBuffer;
    Graphics OffScreenGraphics;
    double phi;
    View3D aView;
    Vertex[] Vertices;

    // called at each start
    public void start()
    {
      if(runner == null)
      {
        runner = new Thread(this);
        runner.start();
      }
    }

    // called at each stop
    public void stop()
    {
      if(runner != null)
      {
        runner.stop();
        runner = null;
      }
    }

    // run the thread
    public void run()
    {
        long startTime = System.currentTimeMillis();
        while(phi < phaseAngleMax)
        {
            // calculate vertices and transform
            surface();
```

```
                    // show the surface - comment below is intentional
//                       repaint();

                    // advance the phase angle
                    phi += phaseAngleInc;
                }
            long endTime = System.currentTimeMillis();
            System.out.println("Frames: " + phaseAngleMax / phaseAngleInc);
            System.out.println("Millis: " + (endTime - startTime));
            System.out.println("Frame rate: " + 1000*(phaseAngleMax /
              phaseAngleInc)/(endTime-startTime));
        }

    // called once per app
    public void init()
    {
        int i;

        // phase angle is 0
        phi = 0;

        // create 3D view object
        aView = new View3D(30, 30, this.size().width/2, this.size().height/2);

        // allocate an array of object refs
        Vertices = new Vertex[20*20];

        // now we must actually create vertex objs
        for(i=0; i< 20*20; i++)
          Vertices[i] = new Vertex();

        // create an empty image
        ImageBuffer = createImage(this.size().width, this.size().height);

        // get an image buffer
        OffScreenGraphics = ImageBuffer.getGraphics();
    }

    // calculate the vertices
    public void surface()
    {
        double x, z;
        int i,j;

        // calculate vertex coords
        z = -1.5;
        for(i=0; i < 20; i++)
        {
            x = -1.5;
            for(j=0; j < 20; j++)
            {
                Vertices[i*20+j].x = x;
                Vertices[i*20+j].y = Math.sin(x*x + z*z + phi);
                Vertices[i*20+j].z = z;
                x += phaseAngleInc;
            }
            z += phaseAngleInc;
        }
```

10

THE VISUAL J++ COMPILER

continues

Listing 10.4. continued

```
        // translate, transform and project each vertex
        for(i=0; i < 20*20; i++)
          aView.transform(Vertices[i]);
    }

    // don't clear the client area before paint!
    public void update(Graphics g)
    {
        paint(g);
    }


    // paint the screen
    public void paint(Graphics g)
    {
        int i,j;

        // clear our memory buffer
        OffScreenGraphics.setColor(getBackground());
        OffScreenGraphics.fillRect(0,0, this.size().width, this.size().height);
        OffScreenGraphics.setColor(getForeground());

        // draw XZ lines?
        for(i=0; i < 20; i++)
          for(j=0; j < 19; j++)
            OffScreenGraphics.drawLine(Vertices[i*20+j].sx,
                        Vertices[i*20+j].sy,
                        Vertices[i*20+j+1].sx,
                        Vertices[i*20+j+1].sy);

        // draw YZ lines?
        for(j=0; j < 20; j++)
          for(i=0; i < 19; i++)
            OffScreenGraphics.drawLine(Vertices[i*20+j].sx,
                        Vertices[i*20+j].sy,
                        Vertices[(i+1)*20+j].sx,
                        Vertices[(i+1)*20+j].sy);

        // draw image from buffer to Window
        g.drawImage(ImageBuffer, 0, 0, this);
    }
}
```

The results of this very unscientific testing are shown in Table 10.1. They are very interesting not only for what they show but also for what they don't show. You will notice little variation among the examples. In fact, with optimizations turned on, only a slight (but measurable) difference occurs between the javac compiler and Visual J++, with Visual J++ edging out javac. When optimizations are turned off, Visual J++ still produces slightly faster code than the version of javac I tested.

Table 10.1. Test results in seconds for 1,000 frames.

Compiler and Settings	Time (Seconds)
Visual J++ with no optimization	10.82
Visual J++ with full optimization	10.66
Sun javac with no optimization	10.98
Sun javac with full optimization	10.88

What can you take away from this bit of testing? For one thing, it shows, at least for code that involves a lot of math and animation, that using the compiler optimizations doesn't generate a lot of gains. In fact, it's quite likely that all I've been able to measure is the performance of the Java Virtual Machine and not the generated code. Therefore, you might choose to investigate one virtual machine against another.

On the other hand, the test could just as well be showing that both the Visual J++ and javac compilers generate terrific code whether optimizations are selected or not. Either way, as with any programming language, as Java compilers mature the code generation is certain to improve.

One of the more meaningful ways that a C compiler can be benchmarked is by comparing the code generated by the compiler against hand-tuned assembly language. A good assembly language implementation provides an idealized upper bound for performance against which you can measure a compiler. Sadly, Sun does not provide a Java bytecode assembler, or disassembler, with the JDK. As a result, I was unable to create a hand-tuned Java assembly language version for comparison.

In the end, the true performance of any Java application depends on any number of factors. These include the capabilities of the underlying hardware, the operating system, system load, and the browser that implements the Java Virtual Machine. For all the tests, I used the appletviewer program that comes with the JDK. The system I used for testing was running Windows 95 on a 100MHz Pentium system with 16MB of EDO RAM, 256KB of pipelined burst cache, and an S3-based PCI video board. You might want to test the code under other virtual machines to see how well they perform.

Just-in-Time Compilation

If the previous discussion of code performance left you a bit disappointed, take heart. A technique called just-in-time compilation may allow future Java applications to approach the speed of native applications.

Just-in-time compilation (often referred to simply as JIT) is a rather unique approach to dealing with the performance penalties associated with interpreted bytecodes. Rather than try to

10

THE VISUAL J++
COMPILER

optimize the Java Virtual Machine, which is already a game of diminishing returns, JIT takes a radically different approach.

The concept of JIT compilation is generally credited to developers of the SmallTalk language, which is usually implemented as a bytecode interpreter. The idea is very simple: The JIT compiler walks through the stream of bytecodes that make up a Java program. As each Java bytecode is encountered, actual machine code that implements that bytecode is substituted for it. When finished, the result is a program in a machine's native machine code! The benefits of this approach are tremendous, with potential speedups measured in factors of 10.

Even better, because the JIT compiler runs on the client, it has enough information about the client to perform hardware-specific optimizations on the machine code. Explicit knowledge of the client hardware allows a smart JIT compiler to use advanced features of processors such as the Pentium. Expect to see a number of Java Virtual Machines supporting JIT compilation very soon. Microsoft Internet Explorer 3.0, which comes with Visual J++, includes a JIT compiler. Several other browsers have announced this capability as well.

Java Code Optimization

Are there other ways to improve the performance of Java code short of using a Java Virtual Machine with JIT compilation? Sure! In Java, as with most programming languages, performing high-level optimizations is almost always worthwhile. In this case, *high-level optimizations* means optimizations that affect the structure of code (and hopefully generated code) without regard for the CPU. High-level optimizations ignore architectural idiosyncrasies and focus instead on improving code through general features of the programming language. *Lower-level optimizations* are performed by the compiler, and they directly affect the organization of generated code.

Actually, the best high-level code optimization is always performed by the programmer. It involves using the best algorithms and the best data structures for the task at hand. For example, no amount of compiler optimization can make up for the inefficiency inherent in using a linear search when a hash table could be used instead.

As you design new Java classes, you should routinely ask yourself if you are using the best algorithm or data structure. Sometimes, however, you may want to use an inefficient, but easy to implement, algorithm to develop and test a new class quickly. If you later find that you need more performance, you may take advantage of the object-oriented nature of Java to derive a subclass that employs a more efficient algorithm.

An important side note is that the lack of a code profiler as part of the JDK is significant. Of course, this void creates a potentially lucrative market niche for software vendors. A profiler makes code optimization more of a science and less of an art form. Without a profiler, the programmer must rely on intuition and experience to determine the location of performance bottlenecks in Java code. Although determining where a program spends most of its time is usually obvious, having real data as confirmation is helpful. Sometimes, in fact, the profiler reveals bottlenecks that the programmer did not anticipate.

Beyond choosing the proper algorithms, the programmer can manually perform a number of high-level optimizations. As mentioned previously, the interpreted nature of Java bytecodes limits the scope and depth of these types of optimizations. In order to understand how to optimize Java code, you need a basic understanding of how the Java Virtual Machine works.

The Java Virtual Machine and Bytecodes

Just like a CPU, the Java Virtual Machine follows a rather standardized process for executing code in three distinct phases: fetch, decode, and execute. Many of the recent advances in microprocessor design have involved using hardware to execute these phases in parallel with the output of one stage feeding the next. This technique is called *pipelining*. The current Java Virtual Machine does not have this capability.

A unique feature of the Java Virtual Machine is that it employs a stack-based design. This is in contrast to the more common register-based designs found in most CPUs. The purpose behind the register-based design is to allow the CPU to store data in very high-speed units called *registers*, rather than storing data in main memory. The exact configuration of registers is CPU specific and is accomplished via hardware. Therefore, a Java Virtual Machine cannot efficiently use a register-based design. Because all data storage is effectively to main memory, the Java designers felt that the stack-based design would be more appropriate.

The Java Virtual Machine stores all operand data on a last-in, first-out (LIFO) stack. The Java bytecodes represent instructions to push (store), pop (retrieve), and perform mathematical and logical operations on data contained in the stack. Program data is retrieved from user memory and pushed on the stack, manipulated, and then possibly stored back in user memory.

For all the above reasons, optimizing Java code boils down to one simple rule: Minimize the number of bytecodes to be executed. If you ever programmed for the 8086 or the 8088, these optimization techniques should be familiar territory. As with many of the older CPU designs, the overhead in the fetch, decode, and execute pipeline effectively limits the performance of the Java Virtual Machine.

Minimizing the Number of Bytecodes

In order to minimize the number of bytecodes, you should focus your efforts on the most-used code in your application. This category includes heavily looping code and frequently called methods. Reducing the number of operations and therefore bytecodes inside a loop will always produce a performance improvement. For example, look at the following code:

```
// original method
public void foo()
{
    for(int i = 0; i < 100; i++)
    {
```

```
        for(int j = 0; j < 100; j++)
        {
            sum += Math.sin(i*i + j*j);
        }
    }
}

// faster method
public void fastfoo()
{
    int t1;

    for(int i = 0; i < 100; i++)
    {
        t1 = i*i;
        for(int j = 0; j < 100; j++)
        {
            sum += Math.sin(t1 + j*j);
        }
    }
}
```

The first method is implemented in a straightforward manner calculating a sum. The method executes 20,000 multiplies and 20,000 adds. By introducing a temporary variable in the second method, you can pull one of the multiplications outside of the inner loop. The second method executes 10,100 multiplies and 20,000 adds, saving 9,900 multiplies. This method is actually a very old optimization technique called *code motion*. Most compilers employ code motion and loop invariant analysis as a basic optimization technique. The current Java compilers do not appear to use this optimization, but it is easy enough to perform manually.

Also avoid calling methods because each method call has associated overhead. Every method call involves saving the current state, including the return address, and jumping to a new code location. None of these activities results in useful work by the application. They are just necessary to support the structure of the language.

Another way to reduce the number of bytecodes is to only use the int and float data types when appropriate, as opposed to long and double. The Java int and float data types are both 32-bit quantities. Therefore, they are both shorter and more efficient on typical Java client platforms than wider data types. The wider data types have great range and accuracy at the cost of more bytes of data to be processed.

Avoiding or minimizing the number of calls to the Java AWT classes is also desirable, although doing so may not seem intuitive at first. Nearly all the methods in the AWT classes eventually map down to calls to the native operating system. Whether implemented by the Java Virtual Machine or natively by the operating system, these methods tend to be highly unpredictable in their performance. As an example, drawing polygons may be very quick on your Java client due to optimized operating system drivers, but it may be incredibly slow on another system in which such features must be emulated.

Another potential source of poor performance is the use of the generic Java classes such as Stack or Vector. These classes are very useful, but in some circumstances they may not be appropriate. For example, consider an application that requires a stack of floating-point values. To implement this stack using the Java class Stack, you would need to use the Java object-wrapper class Float, as shown in the following code:

```
public foo()
{
    float aValue;
    Float aFloatObj;

    aStack.push(new Float(14.7));
    aFloatObj = aStack.pop();
    aValue = aFloatObj.floatValue();
}
```

The creation of the object-wrapper class does not serve a useful purpose. Rather, it is required because the Stack class can manage only objects, not Java primitives. A better solution in this case is to create a Java class that implements a stack of floating-point values directly:

```
public void foo()
{
    float aValue;

    aBetterStack.push(14.7);
    aValue = aBetterStack.pop();
}
```

One useful method for improving performance is *inlining* frequently called code. This technique is functionally equivalent to manually retyping the body of a method where it is called rather than actually performing a method call. Of course, you would not want to retype the same code in a number of places throughout a Java application. In fact, for most circumstances the data access rules of objects with private data wouldn't allow you to do so.

The member access rules of Java require that certain restrictions be observed for inlining to occur. These restrictions currently permit only static, private, and final methods to be inlined. The following code shows how method inlining would look if it could be done manually:

```
public final int sum(int a, int b)
{
    return a + b;
}

public void Method1()
{
    int result;

    result = sum(1, 2);
}

public void Method2()
{
    int result;
```

```
    // call inlined sum() method
    result = sum(1, 2);
    // code actually executed is result = 1 + 2;
}
```

In Method1() the sum() method is called without inlining. This results in the normal method call overhead. If the sum() method were final, static, or private, it could be inlined by the compiler as depicted by Method2(). Notice how Method2() does not actually call the sum() method. Instead, the code that is executed behaves as if the body of the sum() method were retyped in place of the call.

Visual J++ supports method inlining, and you should take full advantage of this feature for accessor methods. An *accessor method* is a method that does nothing more than retrieve or store a data member of an object. Such methods are common in object-oriented languages, and they can be a source of poor performance. Method inlining was developed to maintain the integrity of private data members while allowing improved performance.

The concept of *synchronized methods* is a feature of the Java language that supports multithreaded applications. The idea is that each object has a lock that must be acquired by a thread that wants to execute a synchronized method. Any other thread that wants to call any synchronized method of the same class will be blocked until the first method completes. Synchronized methods are useful for developing stable, multithreaded code. However, improper use of synchronized methods can result in very poor performance. One thread could enter a synchronized method and block a number of other threads for some time. I won't discuss multithreading any further here, because this complex subject is discussed in detail in Chapter 7, "Advanced Java Programming." Just remember to use synchronized methods only when necessary to avoid the possibility of blocking other threads unintentionally.

The Java programming language supports array bounds checking. This feature is especially useful for locating troublesome bugs. Unfortunately, array bounds checking does impose some runtime overhead on each and every array access. Therefore, you should try to minimize the number of array accesses, particularly redundant ones. You can use temporary variables to do so. Consider these two methods:

```
public void foo()
{
    for(int i=0; i < 100; i++)
        for(int j=0; j < 100; j++)
            A[i] += B[j] + B[j]*C[i];
}

public void better()
{
    float a, c;

    for(int i=0; i < 100; i++)
    {
        c = C[i];
        a = A[i];
```

```
        for(int j=0; j < 100; j++)
            a+= B[j] + B[j]*c;
        A[i] = a;
    }
}
```

The first method shows a hypothetical calculation involving some matrix manipulations. You can improve this method by introducing the temporary variables a and c to hold the values of A[i] and C[i]. This makes more sense once you note that A[i] and C[i] are constants inside the inner loop. This modification results in a savings of approximately 20,000 (actually 19,700) array access calculations.

Many more optimization techniques are available to Java programmers. You may even think that most Java code-optimization techniques are just common sense, as most logical things appear to be once they are understood. Beyond this level of optimization, the next lower level involves manipulations of the actual Java bytecodes generated by the compiler. Current Java compilers do not support very sophisticated transformations of generated code. Visual J++ currently supports only method inlining and jump optimizations. However, Java compilers including Visual J++ will certainly continue to become more sophisticated in their optimization techniques as they mature.

Visual J++ Compiler Options

Several other compiler options can be set through the Developer Studio. Each option can be specified more than once because the Developer Studio maintains parallel debug and release versions of your project by default. The options are accessed via the Build | Settings... menu option. When selected, a dialog box called Project Settings appears. On the left side of the dialog box is a list of the projects that are part of the currently opened workspace. The list is in the form of an expandable outline view of each project. Expanding a project shows the files that make up the project.

On the right side of the screen is a properties sheet with three tabs: General, Debug, and Java. Figure 10.2 shows the General options tab. The items on this tab let you specify a path or paths where additional class files for your project are stored. You could use this option if you have a common network subdirectory that is shared by several users. The output directory lets you specify where the resulting class files are stored.

Several options under the Debug tab, shown in Figure 10.3, tell Visual J++ how to manage debugging tasks. The Category drop-down box selects General, Browser, Stand-alone interpreter, and Additional classes. Each selection enables you specify different debug options. For example, the Browser category contains options such as the browser you want to run for debugging. The Stand-alone interpreter category lets you choose a Java Virtual Machine for running applications.

FIGURE 10.2.

*The Visual J++
compiler General
options tab.*

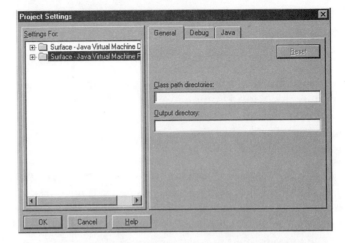

FIGURE 10.3.

*The Visual J++ Debug
options tab.*

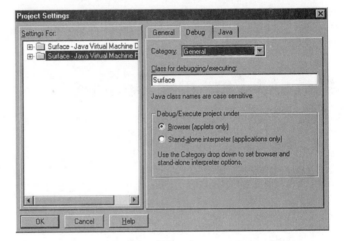

The Java tab, shown in Figure 10.4, lets you specify the Warning Level as well as the optimization and debug level. The Warning Level defaults to 2—1 provides the fewest warning messages and 4 provides the most. The Full Optimization check box either enables or disables full optimization. The only way to set individual optimization options such as method inlining (/O:I) or jump optimizations (/O:J) is to type them in the Project Options text box.

The Generate Debug info check box either enables or disables debug information in your class files. Again, individual debug options such as Generate line numbers or Debug tables are not provided as check boxes, but you may type them in the Project Options text box.

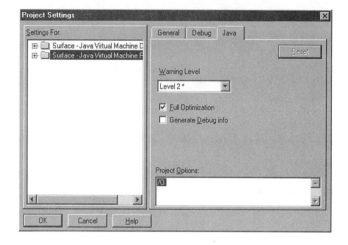

FIGURE 10.4.

*Visual J++ Project
Settings optimization
options.*

The Command-Line Compiler

As mentioned earlier, Visual J++ includes a command-line version of the compiler. The compiler executable is JVC.EXE, and it is located in the \MSDEV\BIN subdirectory. You can run JVC from a DOS prompt or from within a makefile by using the following syntax:

```
JVC [options] <filename>
```

As Table 10.2 shows, a number of command-line options are available.

Table 10.2. The JVC command-line options.

Option	Description
/cp <classpath>	Set class path for compilation
/cp:p <path>	Prepend path to class path
/cp:o[-]	Print class path
/d <directory>	Root directory for class file output
/g[-]	Full debug information (g:l, g:t)
/g:l[-]	Generate line numbers (default is none)
/g:t[-]	Generate debug tables (default is none)
/nowarn	Turn off warnings (default is warn)
/nowrite	Compile only—do not generate class files
/O[-]	Full optimization (O:I, O:J)
/O:I[-]	Optimize by inlining (default is no opt)

continues

10

Table 10.2. continued

Option	Description
/O:J[-]	Optimize bytecode jumps (default is no opt)
/verbose	Print messages about compilation progress
/w{0-4}	Set warning level (default is 2)
/x[-]	Disable extensions (default is enabled)

All options must appear before the Java filename. When the compiler is executed, it reads in the specified Java source file and writes out a class file containing the Java bytecodes. Normally you can specify only a single Java filename on the command line. However, JVC allows you to specify a response file on the command line by replacing the Java source filename with an at symbol (@) followed by the response filename. You can use either an absolute or a relative path name.

A *response file* is a plain text file that can contain only Java source filenames. It cannot contain JVC compiler options, and it cannot be used to invoke the JVC compiler itself. Any compiler options must still be specified on the command line.

The Command-Line Compiler Options Explained

The /cp options allow you to specify a path for class files generated by JVC. Versions exist for specifying absolute class paths or relative class paths. The /d option allows you to specify a root directory for class file output.

The /g option enables or disables generation of debug symbol information in the class files. The suboptions /g:1 and /g:t tell JVC to generate line numbers and debug tables, respectively. Debug information is turned off by default.

The /nowarn message turns off warning messages from the compiler. Warnings are enabled by default. The /nowrite option tells JVC to parse the input file for errors and to produce warning messages, but not to generate any class file output. This option can be used to syntax-check code.

The /O option tells the compiler to perform full optimization, including code movement. The suboption /O:I tells JVC to optimize via inlining small static methods. The suboption /O:J tells JVC to optimize jump bytecode usage. no opt is the default optimization for Visual J++ projects.

The /verbose option tells the compiler to provide additional messages as it compiles source code files. The compiler informs you of every class reference it detects as it parses the source code.

The /w option allows you to specify the warning level. The higher the warning level, the more JVC warnings are produced. A warning level of 2 is selected by default. You should always enable as many warning messages as possible in a compiler to give the compiler the opportunity to suggest possible errors in your code.

The last option, /x, tells JVC to disable any nonstandard Java extensions. It is enabled by default. No such extensions were documented at the time this book was written.

WinDiff

Another useful tool included with Visual J++ is the WinDiff utility, which is a Windows version of the classic UNIX diff utility. The program allows you to compare directories as well as individual files. To run WinDiff, simply double-click the icon in the Microsoft Visual J++ folder or program group. Select either Compare Files or Compare Directories from the File menu.

A typical WinDiff display is shown in Figure 10.5. In the figure, the two versions of the View3D file in Listing 10.3 are being compared. The differences between the files are shown both graphically and using the standard diff notation. In the second version of the code, lines 36 and 37 of the listing were edited to add a call to the Math.floor() method.

FIGURE 10.5.

File comparison using the WinDiff utility.

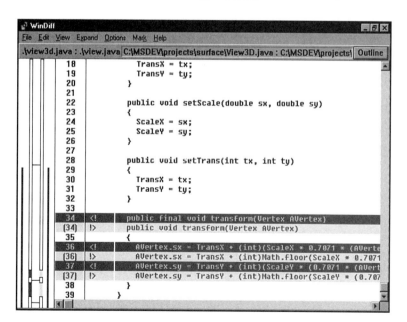

10

THE VISUAL J++ COMPILER

The WinDiff utility can also be run from the command line using the following syntax:

```
WinDiff  path1 [path2] [-s [options] savefile]
```

The options you can enter from the command line are shown in Table 10.3. Specifying only a single path causes WinDiff to compare files in the current directory with those in the path. Specifying two paths compares files in both paths. The command-line switches modify these actions in different ways.

Table 10.3. WinDiff command-line options.

Option	Description
path1	Compares files in *path1* with files in current directory.
path1 path2	Compares files in *path1* with files in path2.
options	Can be any combination of the following options:
/s:	Compares files that are in both paths.
/l:	Compares only files in the first (left) path.
/r:	Compares only files in the second (right) path.
/d:	Compares two different files in both paths.
savefile	Name of text file where comparison results are written.

The WinDiff Options Explained

The /s option tells WinDiff to compare files that appear on both paths. WinDiff shows a list of all the files and identifies which directory has the most recent copy. You can see the file differences by selecting a file and clicking on the Expand button.

The /l and /r options compare only files in the left and right paths, respectively. The last option, /d, compares two different files in both paths. All the options are available as menu options. By specifying the -s option, you can tell WinDiff to save the results of any file comparisons to a file.

When comparing files from one directory, WinDiff shows a list of all the files in the current directory and any subdirectories showing files. You can view the contents of a file by selecting the file and clicking on the Expand button.

When comparing two different directories, WinDiff tells you which files are newer and which are identical. You can show the differences between two versions of a file by selecting the file from the list and clicking on the Expand button.

Summary

The Visual J++ compiler is a great tool for writing Java programs. I had no trouble creating Java applets using the Applet and Class Wizards. The integration of Internet Explorer with Visual J++ as a debugging tool makes development and testing of Java applets even easier. Because both Visual J++ and Internet Explorer support the use of embedded ActiveX controls, you can expect to see a tidal wave of creative Java applets and applications.

Building a Simple Java Applet with Visual J++

by Hiro Ruo

IN THIS CHAPTER

This chapter demonstrates the use of the Applet Wizard to create a simple Java applet. This will give you an introduction to the Visual J++ compiler.

Wizards

When writing a program, you should focus on the requirements of the functionality of the program. The inputs and outputs of the program and the actual processing of information are what differentiate one program from another. In today's programming environment, there is much more to consider when writing code: the correct structuring of the interface to the operating environment; the support of basic operating system features such as mouse control, windowing, and multitasking; and so on. The complexity of the current computing environments has made programming a challenge.

In addition to the capability to build and compile a piece of source code, many modern compilers also provide a more language-independent interface for developers to create programs, called a *wizard*. Wizards will take some of the most common structuring requirements of a typical program and an automated, friendly interface to incorporate these features and requirements into a starting template. After running a wizard, the basic infrastructure of a program is in place, and the developer needs to implement only the differentiating functionality of the planned program. Using wizards greatly reduces time to completion by providing a fairly complete starting point.

Visual J++ Applet Wizard Overview

The Visual J++ development environment's wizard, Applet Wizard, provides a clear, intuitive interface that allows you to select from several key feature supports of the Visual J++ targeted environment:

- Applet versus applet/application
- Source file comments

    Explanatory comments

    TODO comments
- Sample HTML
- Applet workspace dimensions

    Height

    Width
- Multithreading
- Support for animation including sample images

- ■ Mouse event handlers

  `MouseDown()` and `MouseUp()`

  `MouseDrag()` and `MouseMove()`

  `MouseEnter()` and `MouseExit()`

- ■ Applet parameters definition
- ■ Applet `GetInfo()` return values

  Author

  Copyright date

  Other related information

Using the Applet Wizard provides the basis for an applet or application and eliminates the need to manually incorporate lines of code for these functions into the software.

This chapter investigates the use of the Applet Wizard and the features supported in more detail. Let's create a simple Java program to demonstrate the Applet Wizard.

Running the Applet Wizard

Let's start by creating a new program, a template source code. To run the Applet Wizard, you must first create a new project workspace. Under the File menu of the Microsoft Developer Studio–Visual J++ window, select New to create a new project. The dialog box shown in Figure 11.1 appears. Select Project Workspace and proceed. Another dialog box will appear (see Figure 11.2), asking for the type of project workspace and a name of the project.

FIGURE 11.1.

The New Project dialog box.

FIGURE 11.2.

The Project Workspace dialog box.

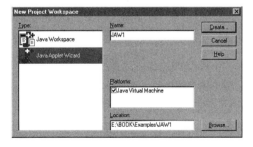

Note that this is the point at which you can elect to use the Java Applet Wizard for Visual J++. Select the Applet Wizard to create the new program workspace with the name JAW1 (Java Applet Wizard 1—not an indication of the type of program you'll be creating). Notice also the Platform option of this dialog box; to create a Java applet, the Java Virtual Machine should be selected. Any additional packages that work with Microsoft Developer Studio may appear here as valid selection options.

Selecting Create after completely filling out the dialog box will take you to the first step of the Applet Wizard.

In step 1 of the Applet Wizard, you will be allowed to select how you want your program to be run: as an applet, a standalone application, or both. (See Figure 11.3.) You will be creating a program to be run as both an applet and application in this example. The lines in Listing 11.1 are what the wizard creates. Note the additional support for parameter definitions needed to run the program as both a standalone application and an applet.

FIGURE 11.3.

Java Applet Wizard, step 1.

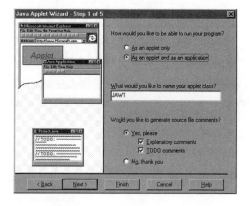

Listing 11.1. An applet and an application.

```
//***************************************************************************
// JAW1.java:    Applet
//
//***************************************************************************
import java.applet.*;
import java.awt.*;
import JAW1Frame;   //This is added as support for application

//===========================================================================
// Main Class for applet JAW1
//
//===========================================================================
public class JAW1 extends Applet implements Runnable
{
    .
    .
    .

    // STANDALONE APPLICATION SUPPORT:
    //       m_fStandAlone will be set to true if applet is run standalone
```

Building a Simple Java Applet with Visual J++

CHAPTER 11

229

11

BUILDING A JAVA
APPLET WITH
VISUAL J++

```
//-------------------------------------------------------------------------
boolean m_fStandAlone = false;
  .
  .
  .

// STANDALONE APPLICATION SUPPORT
//      The GetParameter() method is a replacement for the getParameter()
// method defined by Applet. This method returns the value of the
// specified parameter; unlike the original getParameter() method, this
// method works when the applet is run as a standalone application, as
// well as when run within an HTML page.
// This method is called by GetParameters().
//-------------------------------------------------------------------------
String GetParameter(String strName, String args[])
{
    if (args == null)
    {
        // Running within an HTML page, so call original getParameter().
        //-----------------------------------------------------------------
        return getParameter(strName);
    }

    // Running as standalone application, so parameter values are
    // obtained from
    // the command line. The user specifies them as follows:
    //
    //      JView JAW1 param1=<val> param2=<"val with spaces"> ...
    //-----------------------------------------------------------------
    int     i;
    String strArg    = strName + "=";
    String strValue = null;

    for (i = 0; i < args.length; i++)
    {
        if (strArg.equalsIgnoreCase(args[i].substring(0, strArg.length())))
        {
            // Found matching parameter on command line, so extract its value.
            // If in double quotes, remove the quotes.
            //---------------------------------------------------------
            strValue= args[i].substring(strArg.length());
            if (strValue.startsWith("\""))
            {
                strValue = strValue.substring(1);
                if (strValue.endsWith("\""))
                    strValue = strValue.substring(0, strValue.length() - 1);
            }
        }
    }

    return strValue;
}

// STANDALONE APPLICATION SUPPORT
//      The GetParameters() method retrieves the values of each of the applet's
// parameters and stores them in variables. This method works both when the
// applet is run as a standalone application and when it's run within an HTML
// page.  When the applet is run as a standalone application, this method is
```

continues

Listing 11.1. continued

```java
// called by the main() method, which passes it the command-line arguments.
// When the applet is run within an HTML page, this method is called by the
// init() method with args == null.
//-------------------------------------------------------------------------
void GetParameters(String args[])
{
    // Query values of all Parameters
    //------------------------------------------------------------
    String param;

    // Variable1: Parameter description
    //------------------------------------------------------------
    param = GetParameter(PARAM_Variable1, args);
    if (param != null)
        m_Variable1 = param;

    // Variable2: Parameter description
    //------------------------------------------------------------
    param = GetParameter(PARAM_Variable2, args);
    if (param != null)
        m_Variable2 = Integer.parseInt(param);

    // Variable3: Parameter description
    //------------------------------------------------------------
    param = GetParameter(PARAM_Variable3, args);
    if (param != null)
        m_Variable3 = Boolean.valueOf(param).booleanValue();

    // Variable4: Parameter description
    //------------------------------------------------------------
    param = GetParameter(PARAM_Variable4, args);
    if (param != null)
        m_Variable4 = Double.valueOf(param).doubleValue();

    // Variable5: Parameter description
    //------------------------------------------------------------
    param = GetParameter(PARAM_Variable5, args);
    if (param != null)
        m_Variable5 = Float.valueOf(param).floatValue();

    // Variable6: Parameter description
    //------------------------------------------------------------
    param = GetParameter(PARAM_Variable6, args);
    if (param != null)
        m_Variable6 = Long.parseLong(param);

    // Variable7: Parameter description
    //------------------------------------------------------------
    param = GetParameter(PARAM_Variable7, args);
    if (param != null)
        m_Variable7 = param;

}

// STANDALONE APPLICATION SUPPORT
//     The main() method acts as the applet's entry point when it is run
```

Building a Simple Java Applet with Visual J++

CHAPTER 11

231

11

BUILDING A JAVA
APPLET WITH
VISUAL J++

```
// as a standalone application. It is ignored if the applet is run from
// within an HTML page.
//-------------------------------------------------------------------
public static void main(String args[])
{
    // Create Toplevel Window to contain applet JAW1
    //---------------------------------------------------------------
    JAW1Frame frame = new JAW1Frame("JAW1");

    // Must show Frame before we size it so insets() will return valid values
    //---------------------------------------------------------------
    frame.show();
            frame.hide();
    frame.resize(frame.insets().left + frame.insets().right  + 320,
                 frame.insets().top  + frame.insets().bottom + 240);

    // The following code starts the applet running within the frame window.
    // It also calls GetParameters() to retrieve parameter values from the
    // command line, and sets m_fStandAlone to true to prevent init() from
    // trying to get them from the HTML page.
    //---------------------------------------------------------------
    JAW1 applet_JAW1 = new JAW1();

    frame.add("Center", applet_JAW1);
    applet_JAW1.m_fStandAlone = true;
    applet_JAW1.GetParameters(args);
    applet_JAW1.init();
    applet_JAW1.start();
            frame.show();
}

// JAW1 Class Constructor
//-------------------------------------------------------------------
public JAW1()
{
    // TODO: Add constructor code here
}
   .
   .
   .

// The init() method is called by the AWT when an applet is first loaded or
// reloaded.  Override this method to perform whatever initialization your
// applet needs, such as initializing data structures, loading images or
// fonts, creating frame windows, setting the layout manager, or adding UI
// components.
    //---------------------------------------------------------------
   -
public void init()
{
    if (!m_fStandAlone)
        GetParameters(null);
   .
   .
   .

    // TODO: Place additional initialization code here
}
```

continues

Listing 11.1. continued

```
// Place additional applet clean up code here.  destroy() is called when
// when you applet is terminating and being unloaded.
//-------------------------------------------------------------------------
public void destroy()
{
    // TODO: Place applet cleanup code here
}
.
.
.

    // TODO: Place additional applet code here

}
```

The wizard creates the lines of code in Listing 11.2 to support event handling and frame configuration for running the program as a standalone application.

Listing 11.2. A standalone application frame and event handler.

```
//**********************************************************************************
// JAW1Frame.java:
//
//**********************************************************************************
import java.awt.*;

//================================================================================
// STANDALONE APPLICATION SUPPORT
//      This frame class acts as a top-level window in which the applet appears
// when it's run as a standalone application.
//================================================================================
class JAW1Frame extends Frame
{
    // JAW1Frame constructor
    //-------------------------------------------------------------------------
    public JAW1Frame(String str)
    {
        // TODO: Add additional construction code here
        super (str);
    }

    // The handleEvent() method receives all events generated within the frame
    // window. You can use this method to respond to window events. To respond
    // to events generated by menus, buttons, etc. or other controls in the
    // frame window but not managed by the applet, override the window's
    // action() method.
    //-------------------------------------------------------------------------
    public boolean handleEvent(Event evt)
    {
        switch (evt.id)
        {
```

Building a Simple Java Applet with Visual J++

CHAPTER 11

233

11

BUILDING A JAVA
APPLET WITH
VISUAL J++

```
    // Application shutdown (e.g. user chooses Close from the
    // system menu).
    //---------------------------------------------------------------
    case Event.WINDOW_DESTROY:
        // TODO: Place additional clean up code here
        dispose();
        System.exit(0);
        return true;

    default:
        return super.handleEvent(evt);
        }
    }
}
```

In addition, you can select the commenting options provided by the Applet Wizard. Selecting Yes and individually selecting the Explanatory Comments and TODO Comments check boxes creates an initial piece of code with comments on what the Applet Wizard–created lines do and any space allocated for items to be added to the starting template. Throughout the example, comments are placed to explain the following lines of code and in sections where additional lines of code (TODO) can be added.

At this point as at any throughout the use of the Applet Wizard, if these are all the options you want to have implemented, select Finish to create the starting template. Proceed with Next to investigate the other features of the Applet Wizard.

Selecting Next takes you to step 2 of the Applet Wizard (see Figure 11.4). In step 2, the Applet Wizard provides a selection option to create a sample HTML file for the program being written. Enabling this option provides an HTML file with the applet embedded. This allows you to use HTML to view your program and see how it can be in built into a Web page.

FIGURE 11.4.

*The Java Applet
Wizard, step 2.*

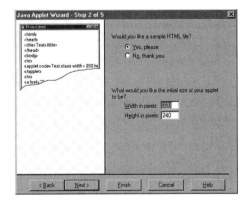

In this step, you can also select the working window size of your program. The default value is 320×240, or one-fourth of the screen in VGA-standard 640×480 mode. Enter the pixel values of the desired applet size in these boxes. In this case, use the default values. The lines of code in Listing 11.3 are added to format the applet size.

Listing 11.3. Applet sizing.

```
// If you use a ResourceWizard-generated "control creator" class to
// arrange controls in your applet, you may want to call its
// CreateControls() method from within this method. Remove the following
// call to resize() before adding the call to CreateControls();
// CreateControls() does its own resizing.
//-----------------------------------------------------------------
        resize(320, 240);
```

Selecting Next takes you to step 3 of the Applet Wizard (see Figure 11.5). Option 1 in step 3 of the Applet Wizard enables multithreading support in your program. Because this program will be run on multiple platforms, some of which may provide multithreading functionality, you should enable this option. (It also demonstrates the full capabilities of the Applet Wizard.) The code in Listing 11.4 is added to the source being created. Note the run() function is called when the thread is started. The code listed is for the support of the default multithreading option.

FIGURE 11.5.

The Java Applet Wizard, step 3.

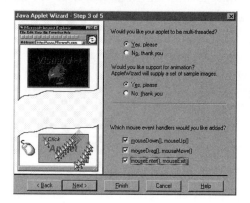

Listing 11.4. Multithreading.

```
// THREAD SUPPORT:
    //      m_JAW1    is the Thread object for the applet
    //-----------------------------------------------------------------
    Thread    m_JAW1 = null;
.
.
.
  //        The start() method is called when the page containing the applet
    // first appears on the screen. The AppletWizard's initial implementation
    // of this method starts execution of the applet's thread.
```

```
//--------------------------------------------------------------------
public void start()
{
    if (m_JAW1 == null)
    {
        m_JAW1 = new Thread(this);
        m_JAW1.start();
    }
    // TODO: Place additional applet start code here
}

//        The stop() method is called when the page containing the applet is
// no longer on the screen. The AppletWizard's initial implementation of
// this method stops execution of the applet's thread.
//--------------------------------------------------------------------
public void stop()
{
    if (m_JAW1 != null)
    {
        m_JAW1.stop();
        m_JAW1 = null;
    }

    // TODO: Place additional applet stop code here
}

// THREAD SUPPORT
//  The run() method is called when the applet's thread is started. If
// your applet performs any ongoing activities without waiting for user
// input, the code for implementing that behavior typically goes here. For
// example, for an applet that performs animation, the run() method controls
// the display of images.
//--------------------------------------------------------------------
public void run()
{
    m_nCurrImage = 0;

// If re-entering the page, then the images have already been loaded.
// m_fAllLoaded == TRUE.
//--------------------------------------------------------------------
    if (!m_fAllLoaded)
    {
        repaint();
        m_Graphics = getGraphics();
        m_Images    = new Image[NUM_IMAGES];

        // Load in all the images
        //--------------------------------------------------------------
        MediaTracker tracker = new MediaTracker(this);
        String strImage;

        // For each image in the animation, this method first constructs a
        // string containing the path to the image file; then it begins
        // loading the image into the m_Images array.  Note that the call to
        // getImage will return before the image is completely loaded.
        //--------------------------------------------------------------
```

continues

Listing 11.4. continued

```java
        for (int i = 1; i <= NUM_IMAGES; i++)
        {
            // Build path to next image
            //---------------------------------------------------------------
            strImage = "images/img00" + ((i < 10) ? "0" : "") + i + ".gif";
            if (m_fStandAlone)
                    m_Images[i-1] = Toolkit.getDefaultToolkit()
                                    .getImage(strImage);
            else
                    m_Images[i-1] = getImage(getDocumentBase(), strImage);

                tracker.addImage(m_Images[i-1], 0);
        }

        // Wait until all images are fully loaded
        //---------------------------------------------------------------
        try
        {
            tracker.waitForAll();
            m_fAllLoaded = !tracker.isErrorAny();
        }
        catch (InterruptedException e)
        {
            // TODO: Place exception-handling code here in case an
            //       InterruptedException is thrown by Thread.sleep(),
            //       meaning that another thread has interrupted this one
        }

        if (!m_fAllLoaded)
        {
            stop();
            m_Graphics.drawString("Error loading images!", 10, 40);
            return;
        }

        // Assuming all images are same width and height.
        //---------------------------------------------------------------
        m_nImgWidth  = m_Images[0].getWidth(this);
        m_nImgHeight = m_Images[0].getHeight(this);
    }
    repaint();
    while (true)
    {
        try
        {
            // Draw next image in animation
            //---------------------------------------------------------------
            displayImage(m_Graphics);
            m_nCurrImage++;
            if (m_nCurrImage == NUM_IMAGES)
                    m_nCurrImage = 0;

            // TODO:  Add additional thread-specific code here
            Thread.sleep(50);
        }
```

```
        catch (InterruptedException e)
        {
            // TODO: Place exception-handling code here in case an
            //       InterruptedException is thrown by Thread.sleep(),
            //       meaning that another thread has interrupted this one
            stop();
        }
    }
}
```

Option 2 in step 3 of the wizard enables support for animation in the program. You should select the option for support of animation. In the lines of added code in Listing 11.5, support for animation, including the default animation of a spinning globe, is implemented in the source code being generated.

Listing 11.5. Animation support.

```
// ANIMATION SUPPORT:
//      m_Graphics          used for storing the applet's Graphics context
//      m_Images[]          the array of Image objects for the animation
//      m_nCurrImage        the index of the next image to be displayed
//      m_ImgWidth          width of each image
//      m_ImgHeight          height of each image
//      m_fAllLoaded        indicates whether all images have been loaded
//      NUM_IMAGES          number of images used in the animation
//-------------------------------------------------------------------
private Graphics m_Graphics;
private Image     m_Images[];
private int       m_nCurrImage;
private int       m_nImgWidth  = 0;
private int       m_nImgHeight = 0;
private boolean   m_fAllLoaded = false;
private final int NUM_IMAGES = 18;
    .
    .
    .


// ANIMATION SUPPORT:
//      Draws the next image, if all images are currently loaded
//-------------------------------------------------------------------
private void displayImage(Graphics g)
{
    if (!m_fAllLoaded)
        return;

    // Draw Image in center of applet
    //-------------------------------------------------------------------
    g.drawImage(m_Images[m_nCurrImage],
            (size().width - m_nImgWidth)   / 2,
            (size().height - m_nImgHeight) / 2, null);
}
```

continues

Listing 11.5. continued

```
// JAW1 Paint Handler
//----------------------------------------------------------------
public void paint(Graphics g)
{
    // ANIMATION SUPPORT:
    //          The following code displays a status message until all the
    // images are loaded. Then it calls displayImage to display the current
    // image.
    //----------------------------------------------------------------
    if (m_fAllLoaded)
    {
        Rectangle r = g.getClipRect();

        g.clearRect(r.x, r.y, r.width, r.height);
        displayImage(g);
    }
    else
        g.drawString("Loading images...", 10, 20);

    // TODO: Place additional applet Paint code here

}
```

Option 3 in this step allows you to enable the support of mouse functions. For this example, you should check all three boxes for mouse support. Doing so will allow the wizard to create the functional infrastructure for support of mouse events in the applet or application. The code in Listing 11.6 is created by the wizard to support mouse events.

Listing 11.6. Mouse functions.

```
// MOUSE SUPPORT:
//          The mouseDown() method is called if the mouse button is pressed
// while the mouse cursor is over the applet's portion of the screen.
//----------------------------------------------------------------
public boolean mouseDown(Event evt, int x, int y)
{
    // TODO: Place applet mouseDown code here
    return true;
}

// MOUSE SUPPORT:
//          The mouseUp() method is called if the mouse button is released
// while the mouse cursor is over the applet's portion of the screen.
//----------------------------------------------------------------
public boolean mouseUp(Event evt, int x, int y)
{
    // TODO: Place applet mouseUp code here
    return true;
}

// MOUSE SUPPORT:
//          The mouseDrag() method is called if the mouse cursor moves over the
```

```
    // applet's portion of the screen while the mouse button is being held down.
    //-----------------------------------------------------------------------
    public boolean mouseDrag(Event evt, int x, int y)
    {
        // TODO: Place applet mouseDrag code here
        return true;
    }

    // MOUSE SUPPORT:
    //        The mouseMove() method is called if the mouse cursor moves over the
    // applet's portion of the screen and the mouse button isn't being held down.
    //-----------------------------------------------------------------------
    public boolean mouseMove(Event evt, int x, int y)
    {
        // TODO: Place applet mouseMove code here
        return true;
    }

    // MOUSE SUPPORT:
    //        The mouseEnter() method is called if the mouse cursor enters the
    // applet's portion of the screen.
    //-----------------------------------------------------------------------
    public boolean mouseEnter(Event evt, int x, int y)
    {
        // TODO: Place applet mouseEnter code here
        return true;
    }

    // MOUSE SUPPORT:
    //        The mouseExit() method is called if the mouse cursor leaves the
    // applet's portion of the screen.
    //-----------------------------------------------------------------------
    public boolean mouseExit(Event evt, int x, int y)
    {
        // TODO: Place applet mouseExit code here
        return true;
    }
```

Selecting Next takes you to step 4 (see Figure 11.6). In this step, you can define the parameters to be passed to your applet or application. The name, member, variable type, and default values of each parameter are defined. At this point, you may not know the complete set of parameters required. These can be added later; however, it is recommended that when determining the scope of the project, you define as many parameters as possible prior to running the Applet Wizard. It is easier to remove extra parameters that are not needed.

Listing 11.7 shows the lines added to the program by the wizard. Note the additional parameter support provided in the previous code entry implemented to support running this program as a standalone application.

The Visual J++ Development Tools

FIGURE 11.6.

*The Java Applet
Wizard, step 4.*

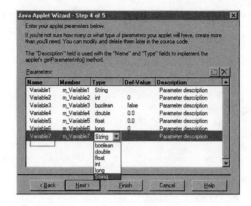

Listing 11.7. Parameter definitions.

```
// PARAMETER SUPPORT:
//          Parameters allow an HTML author to pass information to the applet;
// the HTML author specifies them using the <PARAM> tag within the <APPLET>
// tag.  The following variables are used to store the values of the
// parameters.
//-----------------------------------------------------------------------

// Members for applet parameters
// <type>          <MemberVar>     = <Default Value>
//-----------------------------------------------------------------------
private String m_Variable1 = "";
private int m_Variable2 = 0;
private boolean m_Variable3 = false;
private double m_Variable4 = 0.0;
private float m_Variable5 = 0.0f;
private long m_Variable6 = 0;
private String m_Variable7 = "";

// Parameter names.  To change a name of a parameter, you need only make
// a single change.  Simply modify the value of the parameter string below.
//-----------------------------------------------------------------------
private final String PARAM_Variable1 = "Variable1";
private final String PARAM_Variable2 = "Variable2";
private final String PARAM_Variable3 = "Variable3";
private final String PARAM_Variable4 = "Variable4";
private final String PARAM_Variable5 = "Variable5";
private final String PARAM_Variable6 = "Variable6";
private final String PARAM_Variable7 = "Variable7";
   .
   .
   .

// PARAMETER SUPPORT
//          The getParameterInfo() method returns an array of strings describing
// the parameters understood by this applet.
//
// JAW1 Parameter Information:
//  { "Name", "Type", "Description" },
```

```
//-------------------------------------------------------------------
public String[][] getParameterInfo()
{
    String[][] info =
    {
        { PARAM_Variable1, "String", "Parameter description" },
        { PARAM_Variable2, "int", "Parameter description" },
        { PARAM_Variable3, "boolean", "Parameter description" },
        { PARAM_Variable4, "double", "Parameter description" },
        { PARAM_Variable5, "float", "Parameter description" },
        { PARAM_Variable6, "long", "Parameter description" },
        { PARAM_Variable7, "String", "Parameter description" },
    };
    return info;
}
```

Selecting Next will take you to the final step of the Applet Wizard (see Figure 11.7). A majority of the code is now defined. (Throughout the use of the Applet Wizard, you can select Back to return to a previously decided option to make changes; the current choices will be retained in memory.)

FIGURE 11.7.

The Java Applet Wizard, step 5.

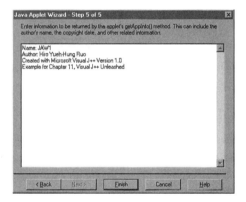

In the final step, enter any information that will be returned by the getAppInfo() method. This should include any information regarding the source code, including but not limited to the author's name, the copyright date (if one exists), the use of this program, and any other information. Listing 11.8 shows the lines of code added to the program by the wizard.

Listing 11.8. GetAppletInfo() return values.

```
// APPLET INFO SUPPORT:
//      The getAppletInfo() method returns a string describing the applet's
// author, copyright date, or miscellaneous information.
    //-------------------------------------------------------------------
public String getAppletInfo()
{
```

continues

Listing 11.8. continued

```
        return "Name: JAW1\r\n" +
               "Author: Hiro Yueh-Hung Ruo\r\n" +
               "Created with Microsoft Visual J++ Version 1.0\r\n" +
               "Example for Visual J++ Unleashed, Chapter 11";
    }
```

The program is now essentially complete. Select Back to make any changes to previous options, or select Finish to complete the code template.

When you select Finish, a summary screen containing some general information regarding the applet/application just created (see Figure 11.8) is displayed. Clicking OK will complete the Applet Wizard and create the program as configured throughout the Applet Wizard.

FIGURE 11.8.

The Java Applet Wizard summary screen.

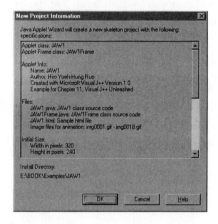

The program is now complete (see Figure 11.9). As you can see, a large portion of the planned project is now completed with a few simple choice selections and a few clicks of the mouse. The created source code is listed in the working window. This program, as it stands, can now be compiled and run as an applet or a standalone application.

Note that the left window displays a directory-like structure to allow you to select specific sections of the source code created. The program can now be modified to add functionality not created with the Applet Wizard.

The following files are created after you select Rebuild All from the Build menu:

```
JAW1.class

JAW1.java

JAW1Frame.class

JAW1Frame.java
```

```
JAW1.mak

JAW1.ncb

JAW1.html

/IMAGES
```

The JAW1.class file is created to run the applet as a Java class in a Web page. As part of the default animation support, a set of images is also created in the subdirectory Images.

FIGURE 11.9.

A Java applet example.

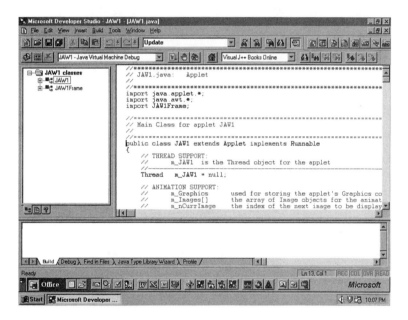

Note that an executable program has not been created. The code has support for running this program as a standalone application, but you must incorporate and compile this program to create an EXE. However, the applet can now be run with JAW1.html (see Listing 11.9).

Listing 11.9. Sample HTML.

```
<html>
<head>
<title>JAW1</title>
</head>
<body>
<hr>
<applet
    code=JAW1.class
    id=JAW1
    width=320
```

continues

Listing 11.9. continued

```
    height=240 >
    <param name=Variable1 value="">
    <param name=Variable2 value=0>
    <param name=Variable3 value=false>
    <param name=Variable4 value=0.0>
    <param name=Variable5 value=0.0f>
    <param name=Variable6 value=0>
    <param name=Variable7 value="">
</applet>
<hr>
<a href="JAW1.java">The source.</a>
</body>
</html>
```

The spinning globe (see Figure 11.10), which otherwise would have taken substantially more time and debugging, is now available for implementation into a Web page.

Figure 11.10.

A Java applet example.

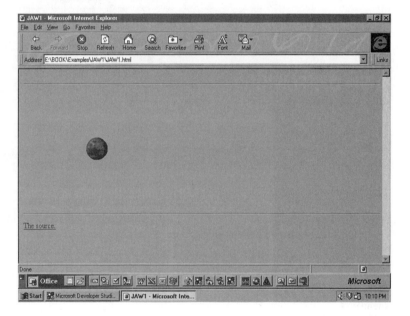

Summary

This chapter demonstrates the power and flexibility of the Visual J++ Applet Wizard. Novice programmers can use this as a method of learning the correct structuring of a fully operational Java applet or simply to create a seemingly complex program to incorporate into a Web page. Advanced developers can use the support provided by the Applet Wizard to get to a better starting point. It's easy to create complex applets by modifying the source code provided. The Applet Wizard is a helpful tool that anyone who wants to write Java using Visual J++ can exploit.

CHAPTER 12

Debugging with the Visual J++ Debugger

by Bryan Morgan

IN THIS CHAPTER

One of the most important and useful tools included with Visual J++ is its integrated visual debugger. This debugger supports conditional and unconditional breakpoints, Watch windows for examining variables at runtime, and a Call Stack window for examining the order in which methods are called within a program. All of these tools make full use of the Windows user interface and are extremely easy to learn and use.

This chapter introduces the many tools that make up the Visual J++ debugging system and presents their configuration and use. Instead of simply presenting the wide variety of dialog boxes, windows, and menu options, this chapter focuses on the fundamental knowledge (such as breakpoints, variables, watches, and call stacks) that is required for debugging. In the course of the explanation of these topics, the specific Visual J++ graphical user interface (GUI) items associated with a topic are shown.

Using Breakpoints to Examine Program Execution

The simplest form of debugging is to print out messages to the screen informing you of the status of variables or a method call within a program. Although this has the advantage of keeping you informed of the internal operations of a program, it is very inflexible and limiting. Whenever you need to examine a new item, you must stop the program, remove println statements, and add new println statements where needed. Using this method completely bypasses the wealth of debugging tools available in the Visual J++ product. Instead of printing a variable's value out to the screen, you could perform this same operation with two mouse clicks using Visual J++ and breakpoints.

Breakpoints are "stop signs" at lines of code within a program that inform the runtime interpreter to halt execution at the breakpoint location. (In fact, some IDEs even display breakpoints using a tiny stop sign in the left margin!) When the program has stopped execution at a breakpoint, the source code of the class containing the breakpoint displays in the Visual J++ editor. At this point, you can use the Visual J++ GUI to examine variables, view which methods have been called and in what order, and then step through the code one line at a time. All of this can be done using either the keyboard or the mouse.

> **NOTE**
>
> If you have had a bad experience using the Sun Java Development Kit jdb debugger, do not be intimidated by the Visual J++ debugger. Whereas the jdb debugger is a character-based, command-line tool, Visual J++ offers a rich set of GUI tools that can be used to examine code at runtime. In other words, the goal of the Visual J++ debugger is to provide an extremely low learning curve so that the developer can instead focus on the task at hand: finding and removing bugs in code.

Because of their importance, breakpoints can be set using a variety of methods within Visual J++.

Setting Breakpoints

The simplest way to set a breakpoint at a line of source code is to use the right mouse button pop-up menu selection Insert/Remove Breakpoint. This option adds a breakpoint at the line of code selected. A breakpoint is denoted by a small red circle in the left margin of the editor window. In Figure 12.1 you can see three breakpoints set in the editor window.

FIGURE 12.1.

Breakpoint symbols in Visual J++.

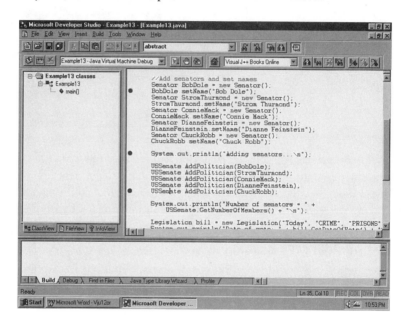

Using the same pop-up menu, you can right-click a line containing a breakpoint to either disable or remove the breakpoint completely. When the pop-up menu appears, you can choose to either Remove Breakpoint or Disable Breakpoint. Disabling a breakpoint leaves a red circle outline in the left margin. Disable a breakpoint when you would like to temporarily go past it but still leave a marker denoting where the breakpoint was set for future sessions. After a breakpoint has been disabled, it can be enabled once again by selecting the pop-up menu option Enable Breakpoint.

One other simple way to set and remove breakpoints is to use the Project. (The Project toolbar can be seen in Figure 12.1 just below the Standard toolbar containing the File Save and File Open buttons.) Holding the mouse over any of the toolbar buttons will display a ToolTip explaining what that button is used for. To add or remove a breakpoint from a line of code, simply position the cursor at the code line of interest, and click on the toolbar button containing the hand icon. (Pressing the F9 key will produce the same result.) Clicking the button containing the crossed-out hands will remove all breakpoints within a file.

Breakpoints can also be controlled from the Edit main menu. Selecting the Edit | Breakpoints... menu option will produce the Breakpoints dialog box shown in Figure 12.2.

FIGURE 12.2.

The Breakpoints dialog box.

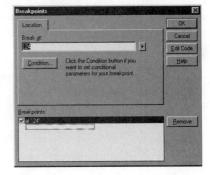

Clicking the Break At: right-arrow button will produce a list containing the current line in the editor window and the Advanced... word. Selecting the current line will add a breakpoint at that point in the editor. (This is equivalent to selecting the Add Breakpoint pop-up menu option, clicking the Add Breakpoint toolbar button, or pressing the F9 key.)

Setting Advanced Breakpoints

Selecting the Advanced... option brings up the Advanced Breakpoints dialog box (see Figure 12.3).

FIGURE 12.3.

The Advanced Breakpoints dialog box.

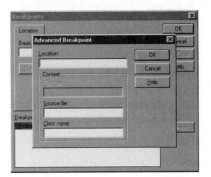

The Advanced Breakpoints dialog box allows you to set breakpoints at specific lines of code within a class in the current source file or any source file. If the source file is not located in the current project workspace directory, you must enter the full pathname and filename in the Source file: text box.

Setting Conditional Breakpoints

After selecting a line of code where you want to set the breakpoint, click the Condition... button (refer to Figure 12.2) in the Breakpoints dialog box to produce the Breakpoint Condition dialog box (see Figure 12.4).

FIGURE 12.4.

The Breakpoint Condition dialog box.

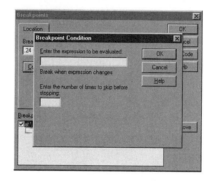

The expression to be evaluated can be a boolean expression or can return a normal value. The following expressions are valid within this text field:

- `i == 0`
- `x <= 5`
- `liar == false`
- `x = (Result * 5) / 26`

If the result of the expression is a boolean value (`true` or `false`), the debugger will stop when the expression evaluates to `true`. If the result of the expression is any other type of value, the debugger will stop execution whenever the value changes. In instances (such as within a loop) in which the debugger may stop hundreds or thousands of times, this dialog box also conveniently lets you set the number of times the expression should be skipped while debugging. If the value is set to `0`, the debugger will stop each time the condition is met. If the value is set to `99`, the debugger will stop each 100th time the condition is met.

You can set or remove breakpoints using the following methods:

- Selecting the Insert/Remove Breakpoint menu option in the editor window's pop-up menu
- Selecting the Insert/Remove Breakpoint button in the Project toolbar

- Selecting a line of code in the editor window and pressing the F9 key
- Selecting a line of code in the Breakpoints dialog box

After a breakpoint has been set, the program can be run in debug or normal mode. If the program is not run in debug mode, the breakpoints will be ignored. If the program is run in debug mode, program execution will be suspended when it encounters a line of code containing a breakpoint. At this point, you can choose to continue or step through the code.

Stepping Through Code at a Breakpoint

After a breakpoint has been set, the program must be run in debug mode for debugging to take place. This can be done using the following operations:

- Pressing the F5 key
- Selecting the Build | Debug | Go menu option
- Selecting the Go button in the Project toolbar

Note that selecting the Build | Execute menu option will run the program but will not run it in debug mode.

> **NOTE**
>
> As soon as a Java program begins to execute in Visual J++, the Build menu will change to the Debug menu. The Debug menu contains a number of commonly executed debugging commands, all of which are duplicated elsewhere using toolbar buttons or pop-up menu options.

After program execution begins, whenever a breakpoint is encountered, the program will be suspended temporarily while awaiting your commands. At this point, you can undertake several actions depending on the task at hand. After examining variables (which are discussed in the section "The Variables Window"), you can continue to run the application, step through the code one line at a time, step into each method encountered on each line, or jump to the current cursor location on a line of code located later in the class.

Controlling Program Execution at a Breakpoint

The easiest of these operations is to continue with the execution of the program after it has been stopped at a breakpoint. Pressing F5, selecting the Debug | Go menu option, or selecting the Go button from the Project toolbar will cause the program to continue with its normal execution. You can also stop or restart the execution.

To stop execution of a program while debugging, select the Debug | Stop Debugging menu option, press Alt+F5, or select the Stop Debugging button on the Debug toolbar. To view the

Debug toolbar, right-click any toolbar to bring up its pop-up menu and then select the Debug option.

There may be times when you want to completely restart the execution of a program. This occurs often when a variable or code has been modified at runtime and the program needs to be restarted to take advantage of this modification. To restart the execution of a program, select the Debug | Restart menu option, press Shift+F5, or select the Restart button on the Debug toolbar.

Stepping Through Code at Runtime

More commonly when execution stops at a breakpoint, you will need to examine the behavior of a block of code or a method at runtime. Because this behavior cannot be truly observed by examining variables at a breakpoint, you'll need to step through the code one statement at a time to observe what is actually going on "under the hood." The Visual J++ debugger allows you to do this. Execution will continue just as it normally would have (except at a much slower pace!). By using the debugger to step through code, you can see exactly how the code is being run by the computer. The following sections explain the different ways you can step through code using the Visual J++ debugger.

Step Over

The Step Over process forces the debugger to execute all method calls and operations in a single line of code and then to step to the next line of code in the current source file. Take the following two lines of code as an example:

```
USSenate.AddPolitician(BobDole);
USSenate.AddPolitician(StromThurmond);
```

If the first line of code is current when Step Over is selected, program execution immediately transfers to the second line of code without stepping into the AddPolitician() method.

You can use the Step Over option by doing any of the following:

- Selecting the Debug | Step Over menu option
- Pressing the F10 key
- Clicking on the Step Over button in the Debug toolbar

There are times when you will need to examine a method *within* a line of code in more detail. Visual J++ also allows you to step into a method.

Step Into

The Step Into process forces the debugger to step into any method calls that are contained at the current line of code. For instance, imagine that the current line of code is the following:

```
USSenate.AddPolitician(BobDole);
```

Selecting the Step Into debugging option will cause the source file containing the AddPolitician() method to be loaded. The AddPolitician() method is the current method in the Visual J++ editor, and the program execution symbol (denoted by a yellow arrow in the left margin of the code) is located at the first line of code in the AddPolitician() method.

You can select the Step Into option by doing any of the following:

- Selecting the Debug | Step Into menu option
- Pressing the F8 key
- Clicking on the Step Into button in the Debug toolbar

Stepping into each method within each line of code allows you to thoroughly view everything that is going on as the program executes. When you're satisfied with the operation of the method you stepped into, you can step out immediately using the Step Out Of option.

Step Out Of

When you have stepped into a method using the Step Into option, you do not have to step through every single line of code within that method before continuing with the program's normal execution. The Step Out Of option allows you to return to the original line of code that contains the method that was stepped into.

You can select the Step Out Of option by doing any of the following:

- Selecting the Debug | Step Out Of menu option
- Pressing Shift+F7
- Clicking on the Step Out Of button on the Debug toolbar

In addition to simply stepping through single lines of code or stepping into a method for one line of code, you can run and step over blocks of code quickly using the Run to Cursor option.

Run to Cursor

The Run to Cursor option allows you to position the cursor on a line of code somewhere beneath the currently executing line of code. When the Run to Cursor option is selected, all lines of code between the current line and the cursor will be executed immediately. Program execution will halt again when the line of code containing the cursor is encountered.

You can select the Run to Cursor option by doing any of the following:

- Selecting the Debug | Run to Cursor menu option
- Pressing the F7 key
- Clicking on the Run to Cursor button in the Debug toolbar

This concludes the discussion of breakpoints and stepping through code at runtime. Although this capability is extremely important to help understand how a program is actually operating while running, developers gain the most value from being able to examine program variables while running the program. Visual J++ provides numerous capabilities that allow you to view variables or code at runtime.

Viewing and Modifying Values at Runtime

The Visual J++ debugger duplicates the functionality found in other Microsoft tools (notably Visual Basic and Visual C++) by providing the capability to view program values at runtime. Using tools such as the Watch window and the Variables window, you can actually see values change on the screen as lines of code are stepped through. This section introduces a variety of tools for examining variable values at runtime, starting with the Watch window.

The Watch Window

By now, you are probably familiar with three commonly used dockable windows in Visual J++: the Project Workspace, InfoViewer Topic, and Output windows. These windows are said to be *dockable* because they can be dragged to different corners of the screen and docked there. The Watch window allows you to specify variables and expressions to be watched during a program's execution. The Watch window displays variables in a spreadsheet window made up of multiple rows and two columns. In each row is a variable to be watched and its associated value(s). The first column is used to store the variable's name. The second column contains that variable's current value. Figure 12.5 illustrates the use of the Watch window while debugging.

FIGURE 12.5.

The Watch window.

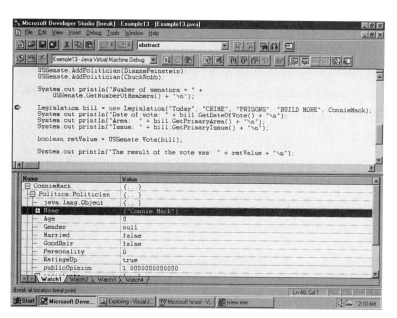

Note that variables that are Java objects contain a small + sign to the left of their name. Clicking on the + will expand the properties of the class and show the values of each of that class's variables. In the example shown in Figure 12.5, the object Politics.Politician contains several variables (including another object, Name). To add a new variable to the Watch list, simply click in the first open row beneath the currently listed rows and type a variable's name (see Figure 12.6).

FIGURE 12.6.

Adding a new variable to the Watch list.

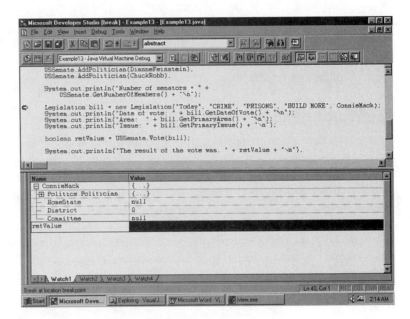

After that variable has been added, you can watch its current value in the Watch window as you step through lines of code within the program.

Removing Variables from the Watch List

The operation required to remove a variable from the Watch window list is very easy. Simply select the row in the Watch spreadsheet containing the variable to be removed and press the Delete key. This will remove the variable from the Watch list.

Modifying Variables Within the Watch List

Just as you can add and remove variables in the Watch window list, you can modify the actual values of these variables. This is useful when you know that a bad value has been returned from a method but you would like program execution to continue just to see what happens. Before continuing, simply modify the value to a "correct" value and continue stepping through the program with the new value.

To modify a variable's value within the Watch window, double-click the value to be modified and type in the new value. This works well for numeric and boolean values, but you are somewhat restricted when modifying String values. This is because a String is actually a class in Java (not a basic data type), and therefore is internally made up of an array of individual characters. Therefore, you must modify each character one at a time before the String itself is modified. In a more generic sense, to modify any object in the Watch window, you must modify that object's individual data members one at a time. The Watch window also contains a set of tabs (Watch1, Watch2, Watch3, and Watch4) that can be used to add related groups of Watch items to a list.

The Variables Window

Like the Watch window, the Variables window is a dockable window available only at debug time. The purpose of the Variables window is to display all variables that are in use in the program's current context (see Figure 12.7).

FIGURE 12.7.

The Variables window.

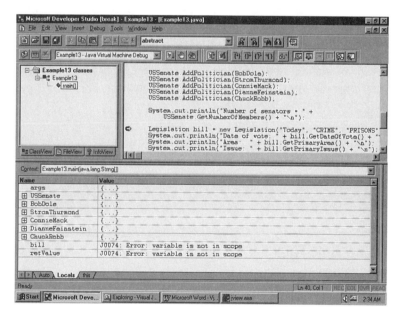

In general, this includes parameters passed to methods, local variables declared within a method, and class variables that are used within the current method. Although the Variables window may sound similar to the Watch window, it differs in several ways. First, new variables cannot be added to the Variables window, and current variables cannot be deleted from it. In addition, whereas the Watch window allows you to watch expressions as well as variables, the

Variables window deals only with variables. However, the Variables window will allow you to modify the values of variables within the window using the same methodology used in the Watch window (double-click or tab, then alter the variable).

Whereas the Watch window contains multiple tabs at the bottom of the window for logically grouping sets of variables or expressions together, the Variables window contains a set of tabs that are used for a different reason. These Variables window tabs (Auto, Local, and this) are used to display different levels of information about the application variables.

The Auto tab page displays all the variables used in the current statement and the next statement as well. The Local tab page displays all the variables used in the current method. The this tab page displays variable information about the object referenced by the this keyword.

> **NOTE**
>
> In the case of a debugging session in the main() method, the this tab page contains the error Error: symbol "this" not found. This is because the main() method is a public, static, void method that is not associated with any object.

When you right-click a variable name and select Properties, a Properties dialog box appears containing the type, name, and value of the current variable. This is an easy way to determine the type of a variable at runtime.

You can also move to a method's source code by selecting the appropriate method within the Variable window's Context box (refer to Figure 12.7). The Context box shows the available methods within a program. Note that changing the selected method in the Context box does not physically change the program's stack or register values; it simply allows you to view the source code of a specific method on the screen and updates the Variables list based on the selected method.

Using DataTips

Tips are small boxes that pop up over an item on a toolbar, within an outline, or within an editor. In the small box is textual information that may be of interest to the user. When debugging, DataTips are available to the programmer. DataTips are enabled by holding the mouse over a variable for a half-second or so. The DataTips box that pops up contains the current value of that variable. Figure 12.8 shows a variable being examined during debugging using DataTips. Using DataTips, you can determine that the value of the retValue variable is false at the current time.

FIGURE 12.8.

Using DataTips while debugging.

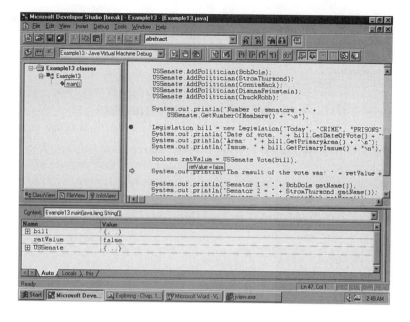

Using QuickWatch

You can use Visual J++'s QuickWatch feature to view the value of a single variable without using the Variables window or the Watch window. When stepping through source code using the debugger, right-click a variable to bring up the pop-up menu. Selecting QuickWatch will bring up the dialog box shown in Figure 12.9. The QuickWatch dialog box can also be displayed by clicking the QuickWatch button in the Debug toolbar (the eyeglasses icon).

FIGURE 12.9

The QuickWatch dialog box.

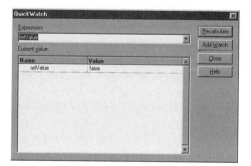

Clicking the Recalculate button will refresh the variable's value in the QuickWatch dialog box. To modify the value of the variable, double-click on that variable's value and change it to the proper new value. Selecting the Add Watch button will add this variable to the Watch window.

By examining variables using the Watch and Variables windows, you can see the value of multiple program variables while the program is running. In addition, the value of these variables is continually updated as you step through the program using the debugger's step functionality.

Using Drag-and-Drop Between Windows

To copy variables between windows (such as the Watch and Variables windows), click a variable to select and, while holding the left mouse button down, drag that variable into the desired window. After lifting the left mouse button, that variable will be copied between the windows and its value updated in both windows as it changes. Because it is not possible to add values to the Variables window, drag-and-drop is most commonly used to drag values from the Variables window into the Watch window for permanent display.

Viewing the Program Call Stack

The *call stack* in a program is a stack containing currently active method calls. To view the call stack of an executing Java program within Visual J++, use the Call Stack window.

The Call Stack Window

The Call Stack window can be displayed during program execution using a variety of methods. To display the Call Stack window while debugging a program, do one of the following:

- Select the View | Call Stack main menu option
- Press Alt+7
- Click on the Call Stack button from the Debug toolbar

The Call Stack shows, in most recently active order, the list of currently active method calls (see Figure 12.10).

The Call Stack window is helpful to determine which methods are calling a method within a program. This is useful in a language such as Java that supports polymorphism. In situations in which a superclass's methods have been overridden within a newly created class, the new class's methods can be called by other methods within the superclass. Because this can be confusing to the unsuspecting developer, the Call Stack window allows you to determine how or why a method was called (and by whom).

To modify the display of the methods in the Call Stack window, two options can be toggled using the right mouse button pop-up menu:

- Parameter Values—Toggle on to display the actual values of the parameters being passed to a method
- Parameter Types—Toggle on to display the data types of the parameters being passed to a method

FIGURE 12.10.
The Call Stack window.

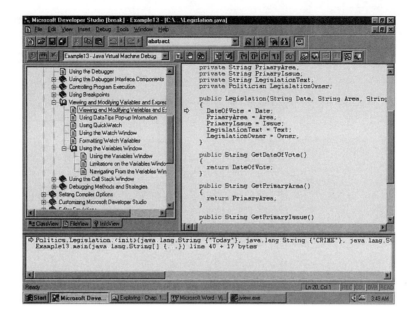

Double-clicking on a method name within the Call Stack window will cause the source code of the method to be displayed. You can also do this by selecting the Go To Code pop-up menu option in the Call Stack window.

You can use standard debugging commands in the Call Stack window as well. Because each method within the window is being currently executed, each method has an associated currently executing line of code. Clicking the Insert/Remove Breakpoint, Enable Breakpoint, or Run To Cursor pop-up menu options will produce the expected results at that method's currently executing line of code.

Debugger Use of the Output Window

As you may have noticed, the debugger continually outputs messages to the Output window's Debug page as new objects are created (see Figure 12.11).

The purpose of this output is to give you some idea as to what objects have been loaded in memory. This output is particularly useful when debugging multithreaded applications because it is used by the debugger to show when specific threads have started or stopped.

FIGURE 12.11.

Debugger output in the Output window.

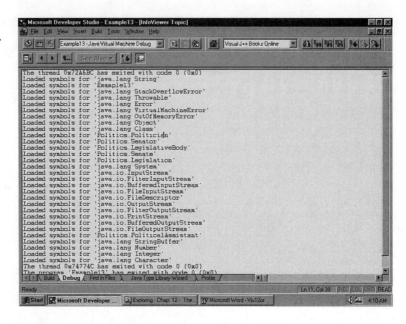

Setting Global Debug Options

Many of the options available in the various debug windows can be set globally for all future debugging sessions. This is done by accessing the Options dialog box from the Tools | Options main menu option. Selecting the Debug tab in this dialog box will display the dialog box shown in Figure 12.12.

FIGURE 12.12.

The Options dialog box (Debug tab).

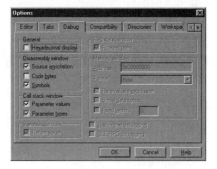

Setting any of the options in this dialog box automatically sets the option to the desired value during the next debugging session.

Debugging the Java Class Libraries

As you delve deeper into Java programming, times will arise when you will be interested in seeing what is going on beneath the surface. Many objects (such as strings, buttons, frames, and threads) are actually declared within the java packages included as part of the Java Base API. If no source code is available for the classes included with these packages, the debugger will be unable to step into methods within these classes. (By default, the standard Visual J++ installation does not install the source code.)

If you have the Visual J++ CD-ROM handy, simply run the Setup program and select the Custom Installation option. Selecting Install Java Class Library Source Code will install the source code for all the standard Java classes to your system. When this has been done, the debugger can step into each of the class's source codes where needed. If you do not have the Visual J++ CD-ROM available, it is possible to extract the source code from the CLASSES.ZIP file using either a ZIP decompression program (such as WINZIP32) or the JAVASRC tool supplied with Visual J++. The JAVASRC.EXE program should be located in the same directory as your CLASSES.ZIP file (in the \WINDOWS\JAVA\CLASSES directory).

If you're using WINZIP, extract all files ending in .java from the CLASSES.ZIP file. Otherwise, re-create the directory structure and the source files included with CLASSES.ZIP by running the following command from the MS-DOS prompt:

```
javasrc classes.zip
```

When this is done, the source code for all the classes included in the sun, java, and com packages can be examined and stepped into while debugging.

Summary

Visual J++ carries on the tradition of Microsoft's family of visual tools (Visual C++ and Visual Basic) by providing a graphical, integrated debugging system for the Java developer. This debugger supports the use of breakpoints, the capability to step through code, and the use of windows to display variable and call stack information.

Variables can be examined at runtime using the Variables and Watch windows. The Watch window gives you the benefit of examining expressions as well as the capability to modify variables on-the-fly while a program is executing. The Call Stack window provides a graphical display of the currently active methods calls within a program. Different options within the Call Stack window allow you to view the data types of parameters passed to a method as well as the actual value of the parameters passed to a method. Several quick tools are available, including DataTips and the QuickWatch window. These tools allow you to quickly examine the contents of variables at runtime by simply moving or clicking the mouse once over a variable.

After becoming acquainted with the Visual J++ developing environment, new Java developers should familiarize themselves with the Visual J++ debugger. Time spent learning these tools will be well worth it the first time you are forced to track down a particularly difficult bug.

This concludes the discussions of the Visual J++ development environment, compiler, and debugger. The remainder of Part II, "The Visual J++ Development Tools," examines the standard Java packages (`java.awt`, `java.applet`, `java.io`, and so on) and introduces GUI programming using the Java Abstract Windowing Toolkit. At the completion of this discussion, you will have been thoroughly introduced to all of the basics of Java programming using Visual J++.

The Standard Java Packages

by Mark Seminatore

IN THIS CHAPTER

CHAPTER 13

The Java programming language, as defined by Sun Microsystems, includes a large library of standard classes. These classes are grouped into several Java packages that are guaranteed to be available in any Java implementation. A summary of the standard Java packages is shown in Table 13.1.

Unfortunately, space limitations don't allow me to explain each method of every class in the standard Java packages. Instead, this chapter contains an overview of the most commonly used classes and methods. For more detailed information about individual classes, complete descriptions of their members and methods, and their roles in the Java class hierarchy, refer to the Visual J++ online help.

> **NOTE**
>
> Visual J++ comes with very extensive online help. Not only is there complete documentation of the Visual J++ compiler, the Developer Studio, and the command-line tools, but there is a complete Java API reference, including code examples and Java object hierarchy diagrams.

Table 13.1. The standard Java packages.

Package	Description
java.lang	The core Java language classes
java.util	Utility classes and data structures
java.io	Input/output classes for streams and files
java.net	Classes for network operations, sockets, and URLs
java.awt	Abstract Windowing Toolkit classes
java.awt.image	Classes for managing bitmap images
java.awt.peer	Platform-specific AWT classes
java.applet	Classes for applet-specific behavior

The java.lang Package

The java.lang package includes the classes and interfaces that make up the core of the Java programming language. The package also includes many individual classes encapsulating the basic behavior of the Java language. A summary of the classes and interfaces is shown in Tables 13.2 and 13.3.

Table 13.2. `java.lang` interfaces.

Interface	Description
Clonable	Defines an object that can be copied or cloned.
Runnable	Provides methods for classes that want to run as threads.

Table 13.3. `java.lang` classes.

Class Name	Description
Boolean	Object wrapper for boolean values.
Character	Object wrapper for character values.
Class	Contains runtime representations of classes.
ClassLoader	Provides abstract behavior for loading of classes.
Double	Object wrapper for double values.
Float	Object wrapper for float values.
Integer	Object wrapper for integer values.
Long	Object wrapper for long values.
Math	Utility class for math intrinsics.
Number	The abstract parent class of all number classes (`Float`, `Integer`, and so on).
Object	Topmost class in Java class hierarchy.
Process	Provides abstract behavior for processes spawned by methods in the `System` class.
Runtime	Provides access to the Java run-time environment.
SecurityManager	Provides abstract behavior for implementing security policies.
String	Java character strings.
StringBuffer	Growable array of characters.
System	Provides platform-neutral access to system-level behavior.
Thread	Provides methods for controlling threads and threaded classes.
ThreadGroup	A group of threads.
Throwable	Base exception class—all thrown exception classes must derive from `Throwable`.

13

THE STANDARD
JAVA PACKAGES

Interfaces

The package includes the interface Runnable, which provides methods for classes that run as threads. Any Java program that wants to execute multiple threads must implement the Runnable interface in one or more classes. You'll find details about the Runnable interface in the discussion of the Thread class.

Classes

The classes in the java.lang package make up the core of the Java programming language. There are classes that provide system-level behavior in a platform-neutral manner, wrapper classes for Java primitives, and math intrinsic functions. Perhaps the most important classes in this package, and the most fundamental to the Java language, are Object, Thread, and Throwable.

Object

The Object class is at the top of the entire Java inheritance hierarchy and is probably the most important class in java.lang. All classes in the Java programming environment (including your own classes) are derived either directly or indirectly from Object.

In fact, if you don't specify a parent or superclass in your class definitions, the Java compiler will *assume* you are inheriting from the Object class. The Object class provides some very basic methods and behaviors that all objects need, but its main purpose is to provide a focal point for the object hierarchy. The following code demonstrates both explicit and implicit inheritance in Java:

```
public class MyApp extends java.applet.Applet     // explicit superclass
{
...
}

public class MotorBoat     // Java assumes "extends Object"
{
...
}
```

Because Java supports only single inheritance, each subclass can trace a single path back to the Object class. This restriction prevents the ambiguous situation that can occur in SmallTalk or C++ whereby a class, through multiple inheritance, finds itself with two (or more!) copies of the Object class.

You need to understand the significance of the Object class and the single inheritance model of Java. These concepts play a key role in how you will design and develop your own Java applets.

Object Wrappers

java.lang also includes several object wrapper classes. These classes provide an encapsulation of the intrinsic data type primitives of the Java language. By design, the basic data types in Java (boolean, char, int, long, float, and double) are *not* classes. This philosophy is in contrast to other "purer" object-oriented languages such as SmallTalk. Rather, for reasons of efficiency, Java's basic data types are implemented as special native data types.

Because of this design compromise, in Java you cannot substitute a primitive data type for an instance of the Object class. For example, you cannot build a list of int values using the Vector class.

The following code shows how the Java primitive data types are not interchangeable with instances of the Object class:

```
// define my new list class
public class MyList      // possibly derived from class Vector
{
    public AddToList(Object AnObject) {...}
}

// some object to add to the list
public class House
{
...
}

List.AddToList(new House);       // ok
List.AddToList(14);              // illegal, 14 is not an object
```

Obviously, it is desirable to have a workaround for situations in which Java primitives must coexist with instances of the Object class. The object wrapper classes provide a solution by allowing you to convert primitive data types to an equivalent object class and then back again at some later time. The following code demonstrates the use of the Integer object wrapper class:

```
// create an Integer object
Integer anIntObject = new Integer(14);

// get the primitive value back
int anInt = anIntObject.intValue();

List.AddToList(new House);       // ok!
List.AddToList(14);              // illegal, 14 is not an object
List.AddToList(new Integer(14)); // ok, object passed
```

String

The String class provides a means of storing and manipulating strings of characters. In Java, strings are not just simple arrays of characters ending in '\0' as they are in C or C++. Rather, all strings in Java are instances of the String class. Because String objects are real objects (inheriting ultimately from class Object), they have methods that make testing the length of a string, adding and deleting individual characters, very easy.

System

The System class provides a platform-neutral way to access to Java's system-level behavior. Important tasks such as reading and writing to standard input and output are found in this class. Methods are also provided for accessing the system garbage collector, loading dynamic link libraries, getting and setting system properties, accessing system environment variables, getting the current system time, and other low-level system activities. The following code provides some sample usages of the System class:

```
// tell the garbage collector to "step back" and clean up
System.gc();

// retrieve system properties
System.initProperties();
System.getProperty("java.version");

// access standard output stream
System.out

// access standard input stream
System.in

// access standard error stream
System.err

// retrieve a reference to the current security manager object
System.getSecurityManager();

// retrieve current GMT time in milliseconds since Jan. 1 1970
long aTimeCount = System.getTimeMillis();
```

Thread

Another class in this package is the class Thread. This class provides methods for managing threads and classes that run in threads. A class that implements the interface Runnable will typically instantiate one or more instances of class Thread. The instances of class Thread may then be used to control execution of these threads.

Throwable

The last class in this package is the class Throwable. This class is a generic exception class from which all exceptions and thrown objects must inherit. That is to say, any exception that is thrown by an application must derive (ultimately) from class Throwable (usually by way of class Exception). The Throwable class encapsulates common exception behaviors such as printing stack traces and returning text messages describing the exception.

The `java.util` Package

The `java.util` package contains numerous utility classes and interfaces. These classes provide behavior such as random number generation, system properties, and common data structures. A summary of the classes and interfaces is shown in Tables 13.4 and 13.5.

Table 13.4. `java.util` interfaces.

Interface	Description
Enumeration	Provides methods for enumerating through sets of values.
Observer	Provides methods for classes to observe descendants of the `Observable` class.

Table 13.5. `java.util` classes.

Class Name	Description
BitSet	A set of bits.
Date	Provides methods to retrieve the current system date, and generate and decode dates.
Dictionary	An abstract class to manage key value pairs.
Hashtable	A subclass of `Dictionary` that implements a hash table.
Observable	An abstract class defining observable objects.
Properties	A persistent hash table for getting/setting properties of a class or the Java system.
Random	Provides methods to generate psuedorandom numbers.
Stack	A last-in, first-out (LIFO) stack.
StringTokenizer	Provides methods for parsing strings into a sequence of tokens.
Vector	A growable list of objects.

Interfaces

The interfaces in `java.util` are provided to allow other Java classes to interact with each other. The `Enumeration` interface provides methods that abstract the behavior of retrieving items (actually `Object`s) from a list in sequential order. The `Observer` interface abstracts the behavior that allows classes to interact with descendants of `Observable` classes. The `Observer` and `Observable` relationship supports the Model-View methodology. Space does not permit a discussion of the Model-View philosophy here, but a good book on object-oriented design concepts should contain an explanation of the concept.

Enumeration and Observer

The interfaces defined by the package include `Enumeration` and `Observer`. The `Enumeration` interface provides methods for enumerating (or counting through) sets of values. Note that the set is consumed or destroyed by use, and its values may be used only once. The following code creates a class that can enumerate a list of `Object`s:

```
// a class which can enumerate sets of values
public class MyEnumerator implements Enumeration     // extends Object implied
{
...
}
```

The `Observer` interface provides methods for allowing classes to observe `Observable` objects. This interface is used in the Java implementation of the model-view paradigm. The following code derives an `Observer` class:

```
public class MyObserver implements Observer     // extends Object implied
{
...
}
```

Classes

The classes in `java.util` provide auxiliary features of the Java language. They include classes that implement basic data structures such as `Dictionary`, `Hashtable`, `Stack`, and `Vector`. The `Date` class provides methods for retrieving and manipulating dates. Lastly, there are classes such as `Properties` and `StringTokenizer`. The former provides methods to store and retrieve property values in a manner similar to the Windows INI files. The latter processes data from a string into a sequence of "tokens."

BitSet

The `BitSet` class provides a hardware independent abstraction of, and a means for, storing and manipulating lists of bits. Methods are provided for getting and setting individual bits, logically comparing and/or combining two sets of bits, and displaying a string representation of the set. The list is implemented so that the list may grow as needed to store more bits. The following code demonstrates the usage of the `BitSet` class:

```
// create an empty set of bits
BitSet bitset = new BitSet();
```

```
// create a set of 100 bits
BitSet bitset = new BitSet(100);

// set bit 23
bitset.set(23);

// clear bit 23
bitset.clear(23);

// get bit 23
boolean bool = bitset.get(23);
```

Date

The Date class provides a wrapper for a date. The class implements a platform independent way of manipulating and parsing dates. The following code shows how the Date class might be used:

```
//  Print today's date
Date d = new Date();
System.out.println("today = " + d);

//  Find out what day corresponds to a particular date:
Date d = new Date(63, 0, 16);   // January 16, 1963
System.out.println("Day of the week: " + d.getDay());
```

Dictionary and Hashtable

The Dictionary and Hashtable classes provide implementations of the common data structures of the same name. A Dictionary can typically store and retrieve key-value pairs from a table. Both the key and the value may be objects. The Dictionary class in this package is actually an abstract class used simply as a base class for Hashtable:

```
// Creates a hashtable of numbers.  Uses the names of the numbers as keys.
Hashtable numbers = new Hashtable();

// add some entries in the table
numbers.put("one", new Integer(1));
numbers.put("two", new Integer(2));
numbers.put("three", new Integer(3));

// Retrieve a number.  Note use of integer object wrapper class
Integer aNumber = (Integer)numbers.get("two");

if (aNumber != null)
{
    System.out.println("two = " + aNumber);
}
```

Properties

The Properties class inherits from the Hashtable class. It provides behavior for setting and retrieving persistent properties (as object key-value pairs) of the system or of a particular class.

The properties may be saved or loaded to or from a stream. If a particular property is not found, an optional list of default properties is searched. The latter provides a means of nesting properties within properties. The following code demonstrates the Properties class:

```
// create property list and define a default set of properties
Properties props = new Properties(defaultProps);

// load the persistent properties
InputStream s = new FileInputStream("properties.dat");
props.load(s);

// retrieve a value
String result = props.get("filepath");
```

Random

The Random class provides various utilities for generating pseudorandom numbers. The class can generate random numbers of various lengths and types including ints, longs, floats, and doubles. The Random class can also generate real numbers approximating a Gaussian probability distribution. The following code shows how the Random class could be used:

```
// create an instance using the system timer as a seed.
Random rand = new Random();

// create an instance with a seed value.
Random rand = new Random(12345678);

// generate some random numbers
int value = rand.nextInt();
long value = rand.nextLong();
float value = rand.nextFloat();
double value = rand.nextDouble();
double value = rand.nextGaussian();
```

Stack

The Stack class implements a last-in-first-out (LIFO) stack or queue. The class is derived from the Vector class and can hold arbitrary lists of Objects. Methods include the typical push(), pop(), and peek() features of a stack data structure. The following code demonstrates the Stack class:

```
// instantiate a Stack object
Stack stack = new Stack();

// fill up our stack
stack.push("Hello");
stack.push("World!");

// results: World! Hello
System.out.println(stack.pop() + " " + stack.pop());
```

StringTokenizer

One of the more significant classes in this package is the StringTokenizer class. This class provides utilities for splitting or parsing strings into sequences of tokens. The class is very general and is useful in many applications. The delimiter defaults to common white-space characters such as tab, space, or newline. The delimiter may be redefined at creation or on a per-token basis. The following code shows a sample of how the StringTokenizer class might be used:

```
String s = "this is a test";
StringTokenizer st = new StringTokenizer(s);
while (st.hasMoreTokens())
{
    println(st.nextToken());
}

// The following is printed on the console
    this
    is
    a
    test
```

Vector

The final class in this package is the Vector class. This class provides an implementation of a "growable" array or list of objects. The list will expand automatically, as required, to contain all of the objects in the list. If no arguments are specified in the constructor, the Vector is instantiated with default values for the capacity and capacityIncrement. The capacity and capacityIncrement members specify the current size of the Vector and how much to grow the Vector, respectively. Methods for common list operations such as addElement(), removeElement(), indexOf(), contains(), and isEmpty() are provided:

```
// instantiate a vector object with default capacity and capacity increment
Vector vector = new Vector();

// instantiate a vector object with capacity of 10
// and the default capacity increment
Vector vector = new Vector(10);

// instantiate a vector object with a capacity of 10
// and a capacity increment of 10
Vector vector = new Vector(10,10);

// add an object to our list
vector.addElement(new Integer(14));
```

The java.io Package

The java.io package provides a number of classes for input and output to streams and files. The classes rely on several interfaces that java.io defines including DataInput, DataOutput, and

FilenameFilter. The classes in `java.io` can be logically separated into two categories: classes that read from streams and classes that write to streams. The following discussion maintains this structure. A summary of the classes and interfaces is shown in Tables 13.6 and 13.7.

Table 13.6. `java.io` interfaces.

Interface	Description
DataInput	Provides methods for reading input streams in a platform-independent manner
DataOutput	Provides methods for writing output streams in a platform-independent manner
FilenameFilter	Provides methods for filtering filenames

Table 13.7. `java.io` classes.

Class Name	Description
BufferedInputStream	An input stream with buffering
BufferedOutputStream	An output stream with buffering
ByteArrayInputStream	An input stream reading from an array of bytes
ByteArrayOutputStream	An output stream writing to an array of bytes
DataInputStream	An input stream that can read Java primitive data types
File	A class that encapsulates a file on the host system
FileInputStream	An input stream reading from a file
FileOutputStream	An output stream writing to a file
FilterInputStream	An abstract class that allows processing of stream bytes as they are read
FilterOutputStream	An abstract class that allows processing of stream bytes as they are written
InputStream	An abstract class that represents reading a stream of bytes—the parent of all input streams
LineNumberInputStream	An input stream that counts line numbers
OutputStream	An abstract class that represents writing a stream of bytes—the parent of all output streams
PipedInputStream	A piped input stream—must be connected to a PipedOutputStream

Class Name	Description
PipedOutputStream	A piped output stream—must be connected to a PipedInputStream
PrintStream	An output stream used for printing
PushbackInputStream	An input stream that can unwrite the last byte read
RandomAccessFile	Provides methods for random-access manipulation of a file
SequenceInputStream	Links several input streams into a single input stream
StreamTokenizer	Parses data from an input stream into a sequence of tokens
StringBufferInputStream	An input stream reading from a StringBuffer object

Interfaces

The DataInput and DataOutput interfaces in java.io provide methods for reading and writing data to streams. They are designed to do this in a completely machine-independent manner. The FilenameFilter interface provides just a single method. The interface provides a means for filtering a list of filenames from a list.

DataInput and DataOutput

The DataInput interface provides methods for reading data from machine-independent typed input streams. Some of the methods that the DataInput interface implements are readBoolean(), readByte(), readChar(), readInt(), and readFloat(). These methods hide the details of the underlying system hardware and allow Java programs to treat all streams identically, regardless of whether they are running under UNIX, Windows, or the MacOS. The following code demonstrates a class that implements the DataInput interface:

```
// a class that can read from input streams
public class MyReader implements DataInput     // implied extends Object
{
...
}
```

Because Java programs also need to write to streams, the DataOutput interface is provided for writing data to machine-independent typed output streams. The methods that this interface includes are analogous to those provided by DataInput. Examples are writeBoolean(), writeByte(), and writeFloat(). These interfaces provide much of the underlying behavior common to the classes in this package. Nearly every class in java.io implements either the DataInput or DataOutput interface.

The following code demonstrates a class that implements the `DataOutput` interface:

```
// a class that can write to output streams
public class MyWriter implements DataOutput      // implied extends Object
{
...
}
```

FilenameFilter

The `FilenameFilter` interface is a very simple abstraction that provides methods for filtering filenames. Only one method is defined: `accept()`. The method takes two parameters, `dir` and `name`, that represent the directory location and filename, respectively. The method returns a boolean value that indicates whether the given file should be included in a file list. The following code shows how simply the `FilenameFilter` interface could be implemented:

```
// essentially the entire interface!
public interface FilenameFilter
{
    boolean accept(File dir, String name);
}
```

Input Stream Classes

The input stream classes in `java.io` provide methods and behavior for reading streams of data. Classes such as `ByteArrayInputStream`, `StringBufferInputStream`, and `FileInputStream` encapsulate different sources of data. Other classes such as `DataInputStream` and `BufferedInputStream` define different methods of reading and interpreting data. Still other classes such as `StreamTokenizer` and `LineNumberInputStream` provide methods for processing the data as it is read.

InputStream and OutputStream

The classes `InputStream` and `OutputStream` are the parent classes for the rest of the `java.io` library. `InputStream` and `OutputStream` are abstract classes that define the basic ways that a stream of bytes moves from a source to a destination. Because the classes are abstract classes (that is, they cannot be instantiated), they know nothing about the source of the bytes or the details of transporting the data from source to destination. I will cover the input streams first and then the output streams.

ByteArrayInputStream

The class `ByteArrayInputStream` is perhaps the simplest class in `java.io`. It is used to create an input stream from an array of bytes. This class essentially allows a Java program to treat an array like any other data source. The following shows two ways to construct a byte array stream:

```
// create a byte array - note an array is _not_ an object
byte[] aBuffer = new byte[256];
```

```
// fill the byte array somehow
fileByteArray(aBuffer);

// instantiate a byte stream
ByteArrayIntputStream byteStream = new ByteArrayInputStream(aBuffer);

// instantiate another byte stream
ByteArrayIntputStream byteStream = new ByteArrayInputStream(aBuffer, 10,100);
```

A class that reads from `byteStream` will "see" a stream of 256 bytes. `ByteArrayInputStreams` do not implement any additional methods beyond those inherited from `InputStream`.

StringBufferInputStream

Another class that is very similar to `ByteArrayInputStream` is `StringBufferInputStream`. This class is identical in every way to `ByteArrayInputStream` except that rather than being constructed from a byte array, it accepts a `String` object. The following shows one possible usage of the `StringBufferInputStream` class:

```
// define a string object
String aString = "A long time ago, in a galaxy far far away...";

// construct our stream
StringBufferInputStream aStream = new StringbufferInputStream(aString);
```

FileInputStream

A `FileInputStream` object attaches a stream to a file in the underlying file system. As such, it is perhaps one of the most commonly used stream classes in Java applications. File stream objects provide a simple streamlike way of reading data from files.

> **NOTE**
>
> Java applets may or may not be allowed to open file streams depending upon the security level of the user's browser. In general, applets should be designed so that file I/O is not required. Information may be stored on servers. Java applications do not have this limitation.

The following code shows how to use the `FileInputStream` class:

```
// instantiate a file stream object
FileInputStream aStream = new FileInputStream("\public\stuff\filename");

// create a buffer to hold data
byte[] aBuffer = new byte[512];

// read some data
String aString = aStream.read(aBuffer);
```

```
// get the file descriptor
int aFileDescriptor = aStream.getFD();
```

> **NOTE**
>
> For most purposes, a convenient way to view a file is as just another type of stream. This philosophy developed under UNIX and was later expanded in C++. Java encourages the programmer to extend the idea even further—to include almost every type of I/O, even URLs!

FilterInputStream

The `FilterInputStream` class is derived from `InputStream` and defines some very unique behaviors. `FilterInputStream`s are constructed with another stream as a parameter. The `FilterInputStream` object contains the passed stream. Any method calls to `FilterInputStream` are passed down to this stream. This nesting relationship of streams is a basic feature of `FilterInputStream`s, and as you will see, it encourages a rather unique way of viewing streams.

Descendants of `FilterInputStream` may, of course, define more complicated methods for determining how to handle bytes as they flow to and from the nested stream. How is this behavior useful? By reinforcing a layered view of streams, it encapsulates, in a very intuitive way, the essential behavior of data filters or translators. In the following code sample a simple class translates data read from a file:

```
// a class that inherits FilterInputStream behavior and translates data
public class MyTranslator extends FilterInputStream
{
...
}

//  setup our translator object
MyTranslator myTrans = new MyTranslator(new FileInputStream("\public\foo.txt"));

// start reading translated data!
myTrans.read(aBuffer);
```

The class above could provide a read method that translates carriage returns into carriage-return line-feed pairs as data is read from the owned `FileInputStream`. The next few classes, which are also descendants of `FilterInputStream`, give a better example of the usefulness of `FilterInputStream`s.

BufferedInputStream

One of the more valuable stream classes in `java.io` is the `BufferedInputStream`. The class is a direct descendant of `FilterInputStream`. This class implements all of the behavior of `InputStream`s while providing the additional capability of buffering or caching data for future reading.

This type of behavior is very useful when data is most efficiently read from a stream in finite blocks or "chunks," for example, disk files or network packets that are often most efficiently read 512 or 1024 bytes at a time. Consider the following examples:

```
// create a buffered file input stream with default buffer size
BufferedInputStream = new BufferedInputStream(new FileInputStream("foo.txt"));

// create a buffered file input stream with a specified buffer size
BufferedInputStream = new BufferedInputStream(new FileInputStream("foo.txt", 512));
```

A `BufferedInputStream` is typically used in conjunction with another stream such as `FileInputStream`. The code above demonstrates one such usage and exemplifies the nested stream behavior that `FilterInputStream` provides.

DataInputStream

The class `DataInputStream` derives from `FilterInputStream` and implements the interface `DataInput`. Therefore, `DataInputStream`s can read any of the primitive data types from a stream. This feature is essential for writing portable Java applets. Consider the problem of reading in complex data from streams such as `FileInputStream`. If you wanted to read, for example, a floating-point number, you would ordinarily need to understand the details of how that number was represented *in binary form* in the file system.

In order to eliminate this difficult situation from Java programs, Sun provided the `DataInputStream` class. Because `DataInputStream` implements the `DataInput` interface, it knows how to read all the primitive Java data types from a stream. By deriving from the `FilterInputStream` class, it also inherits the ability to contain and read from another stream. This means that a `DataInputStream` can be used to postprocess bytes of data read from another input stream, converting them into Java data types such as `int` and `float`. Because reading integers and floating-point numbers from a stream or file is so common, you will find many instances where you will want to derive your own classes from `DataInputStream`. Perhaps the following code, which shows `DataInputStream` in action, will help to clarify things:

```
// construct a data input stream
DataInputStream aStream = new DataInputStream(new FileInputStream("foo.txt"));

// various methods for reading data primitives
boolean aValue = aStream.readBoolean();
byte aValue = aStream.readByte();
int aValue = aStream.readUnsignedByte();
short aValue = aStream.readShort();
int aValue = aStream.readUnsignedShort();
char aValue = aStream.readChar();
int aValue = aStream.readInt();
long aValue = aStream.readLong();
float aValue = aStream.readFloat();
double aValue = aStream.readDouble();

// read an ascii string terminated by carriage-return or line-feed
String aString = aStream.readLine();
```

```
// read a Unicode string
String aString = aStream.readUTF();
```

In this code, you might have noticed that the return types of some of the integer read methods—readUnsignedByte() and readUnsignedShort(), for example—appear to be incorrect. In fact, they are not. Because integer types in Java are signed, an unsigned integer value cannot, for example, fit in an integer variable. Rather, the return value is promoted to the next larger integer size. Therefore, unsigned shorts and unsigned bytes require an integer variable.

LineNumberInputStream

The LineNumberInputStream class is another useful child of FilterInputStream. This class keeps track of line numbers as its stream data is processed. This type of behavior is very useful in subclasses that implement an editor, in a compiler, or perhaps even in a debugger. The most useful method provided by this class is getLineNumber(). The following code shows how a LineNumberInputStream could be used:

```
// create our stream and associate it with a file
LineNumberInputStream aLineStream;
aLineStream = new LineNumberInputStream(new FileInputStream("foo.txt"));

// construct a useful working view of the stream
DataInputStream aStream = new DataInputStream(aLineStream);

// read some data - ultimately from a file
int aValue = aStream.readInt();

// show the current line number
System.out.println("Just read line" + aLineStream.getLineNumber());
```

PushbackInputStream

The class PushbackInputStream is a special purpose class that derives from FilterInputStream—as do many other classes in java.io. This class is commonly used in parsers that often need to "push back" or unread a single piece of the input after reading it. Recursive descent parsers (the easiest to hand-code) frequently require the use of this technique. As you might expect, one of the new methods provided by the class is called unread().

SequenceInputStream

The SequenceInputStream class can be used to glue together two separate streams. It allows the resulting stream to be passed along to another class or method that was designed to handle only a single stream. This programming technique is easier than calling the method once for each stream. Perhaps more useful is the ability to link together an arbitrary number of streams, as shown in the following code sample:

```
// construct a list to hold our streams
Vector aVector = new Vector();
```

```
// call a method which populates our list
aClass.fillTheVectorWithStreams(v);

// presto chango and voila!  The new stream behaves as if it is a single entity
DataInputStream aStream = new SequenceInputStream(v.elements());
```

The preceding paragraphs covered nearly all of the input streams in `java.io`; it is time to discuss the flip side of I/O, output streams. In almost every case, each of the input streams has a companion class that defines similar behavior for output streams.

Output Streams

At the top of the output stream hierarchy is the abstract class `OutputStream`. This class defines the basic ways that a source writes a stream of data. As with the input streams, the specifics of data production, transport, and eventual storage are unimportant. Methods common to all output streams are `write()`, `flush()`, and `close()`. As you would expect, the `write()` method can be expressed in several polymorphic forms.

ByteArrayOutputStream

The `ByteArrayOutputStream` class directs its output to an internal array of bytes. The data in the buffer can then be extracted using one of several methods. The class also provides methods for determining the size of the internal byte array and for clearing the array. These methods are `size()` and `reset()`, respectively. The data can be retrieved from the byte array using methods such as `toByteArray()` and `toString()`, as shown here:

```
// construct our stream
ByteArrayOutputStream aStream = new ByteArrayOutputStream();

// fill up the internal byte array
writeStuffToStream(aStream);

// extract some data to an external byte array
byte[] aBuffer = aStream.toByteArray();
String aString = aStream.toString();
```

FileOutputStream

The class `FileOutputStream` is a direct analogue to `FileInputStream`. As they do with `FileInputStream`, Java applets may experience problems attempting to access files on the host system. Java applications do not have this problem. `FileOutputStreams` can be constructed from a string object representing a filename or from a previously allocated file descriptor.

FilterOutputStream

The `FilterOutputStream` provides nested output streams. Like `FilterInputStream`, this class serves as an anchor for several more specific subclasses. Although data written through a

FilterOutputStream is passed along without modification, the subclasses all perform some sort of additional processing.

BufferedOutputStream

BufferedOutputStream that derives from FilterOutputStream provides, as you might guess, buffered writes of data streams. Data passed through a buffered output stream is collected in an internal buffer until a specified threshold is reached. At this point, the data is "written" to the output. In practice, the output is actually written to the nested stream. As with buffering of inputs, this technique is commonly the most efficient means of writing data to physical devices such as the file system or the network.

DataOutputStream

The DataOutputStream class implements the DataOutput interface, which enables DataOutputStream to write out any of the native Java primitives. This capability is useful for storing application-specific data.

PrintStream

The PrintStream class is used mainly by the System class to provide Java applets and applications with a system-independent way of reading from and writing to the console window. The PrintStream members of the System class are System.err and System.out. On most host systems System.err and System.out are attached to the standard error and standard output, respectively. PrintStream does not have an input analogue. Using System.out is straightforward:

```
// demonstrate use of the PrintStream class
System.out.print(...);
System.out.println(...);
```

Piped Streams

The classes PipedInputStream and PipedOutputStream together support UNIX-style pipe connections, which are usually used to set up a safe means of communication between two threads. One thread would write to a PipedOutputStream while another would read from a PipedInputStream. If each thread has both a PipedInputStream and a PipedOutputStream, then two-way communication between threads is possible.

File

The File class serves as a platform-neutral abstraction of a file. When it's constructed, a File object is passed a physical filename. The File class has methods that return the type, status, and various properties of entities in the file system.

A few other classes in java.io, such as RandomAccessFile and StreamTokenizer, are similar to classes already discussed. For additional information on these classes, refer to the Java API description in the Visual J++ online help.

The java.net Package

The java.net package is quite possibly one of the most exciting packages in the Java class library. It provides a number of interfaces and classes that perform network operations and includes support for UNIX-style TCP/IP sockets and protocols such as FTP and HTTP.

A summary of the classes and interfaces in java.net is shown in Tables 13.8 and 13.9. The rest of this discussion relates to java.net classes only, because these interfaces are not commonly used in typical Java applets.

java.net supports three types of network communication: AppletContext.showDocument(), URL.openStream(), and the UNIX-style Socket classes. By far the easiest way to jump into network programming is to use the showDocument() method. But first you need to understand uniform resource locators (URLs) and the URL class.

Table 13.8. java.net interfaces.

Interface	Description
ContentHandlerFactory	Provides methods for creating ContentHandler objects.
SocketImplFactory	Provides methods for creating socket implementations.
URLStreamHandlerFactory	Provides methods for creating URLStreamHandler objects.

Table 13.9. java.net classes.

Class Name	Description
ContentHandler	Provides abstract behavior for processing data from a URL connection—uses MIME types to construct local objects.
InetAddress	Encapsulation of an Internet host.
ServerSocket	Encapsulation of a server socket.
Socket	Encapsulation of a client socket.
SocketImpl	Abstract class for particular socket implementations.
URL	Encapsulation of a uniform resource locator.
URLConnection	Provides abstract behavior for a socket that processes Web protocols such as HTTP and FTP.
URLStreamHandler	Abstract class for creating and handling Web streams such as HTTP and FTP.

Classes

The classes in `java.net` make network programming in Java relatively painless! Remember, however, that for security reasons Java applets are not (but standalone Java applications are) allowed to read from or write to the hard drive on the host machine. Reading and writing data from the server on which the Java applet resides are allowed. The specific limitations placed on Java applets may sometimes be controlled through settings in the browser.

URL

The URL class encapsulates the notion of a uniform resource locator. If you are familiar with Web pages and the Internet, you already know about URLs. They are the address strings that so often appear as hot links on Web pages. Some examples are `http://www.foo.edu` and `ftp://ftp.foo.com`. An instance of the class URL is needed to create links to Web content in a Java applet.

The constructor for class URL comes in several forms. As you might expect, the different forms are all useful variations on the same theme. The first form is the most generic, allowing you to specify explicitly each component of a URL. The parameters include the protocol, the host address, the port, and a filename. The set of valid protocols includes any that the browser supports, including HTTP, FTP, Gopher, file. The host address is of the form `www.foo.edu`. The port number must be a valid port for the given protocol. For example, Web servers usually listen to port 80 for HTTP requests. The filename represents the file or pathname on the host system.

The second form is identical to the first form except that it leaves out the port number. The third constructor allows a location to be specified as a combination of a base path and a relative path. The base path can either be the results of a call to `getDocumentBase()` for the URL of the current HTML file or a call to `getCodeBase()` for the URL of the Java applet file or an arbitrary URL. The relative path is passed in as a `String` object. It is concatenated to the directory specified by the base path. Note, however, that if the `String` object representing the relative path is actually an absolute address, the absolute address will be used by itself.

The last form of the constructor takes just a single string object as a parameter. The string must specify the complete URL address. Beware that if you pass a `String` that is not a properly formed URL address, you will cause an `Exception` to be thrown that you must handle. Handling a thrown exception requires a `try...catch` clause. The following code shows the various ways to create a URL object:

```
// create a URL given protocol, host, port, and filename
// protocol can be: http, ftp, gopher, file, etc.
// host might be: www.foo.com, etc.
// port is 80 for http, etc.
URL(String, String, int, String);
```

```
// create a URL given protocol, host and filename
URL(String, String, String);

// create a URL using a base path and a relative path
// the URL object represents the base location
//
URL(URL, String);

// create a URL from a complete URL string
URL(String);
```

The code below shows how you might go about creating a URL from a String object. Note the use of the try...catch exception handling in the code:

```
// create a string object
String aString = "http://www.foo.com/";

// instantiate a URL object
try
{
    aURL = new URL(aString);
}
catch( MalformedURLException e)
{
    System.out.println("Error in URL: " + aURL);
}
```

Once you have a valid instance of class URL, you can ask the browser to display the contents of the new page using the following code. The first part of the code is actually a call to a method of class Applet. This method returns an AppletContext object that is an encapsulation of the browser currently running the Java applet. The second part of the code is a call to a method of AppletContext, which tells the browser to display the document or location represented by our URL object. The following code uses showDocument() to display the contents of a URL location:

```
// tell browser to display contents of new URL location
getAppletContext().showDocument(aURL);
```

InetAddress

The class InetAddress encapsulates the properties of an Internet address. The constructor for this class has two forms. The first form creates an empty Internet address object. The internal fields of the object are filled in by a call to the accept() method of class Socket.

The InetAddress class is most often used as an "owned" object by other classes such as Socket(). However, you may find uses for it in your own applets. Given a properly constructed Internet object, you can call methods such as getHostName() and getAddress() that return strings representing the Internet address and the raw Internet address. The following code shows the two forms of the constructor for InetAddress:

```
// parameters provided by Socket.accept()
InetAddress();
```

13

THE STANDARD
JAVA PACKAGES

```
// hostname and IP address () specified
InetAddress(String, byte[]);
```

Network Streams

Network streams are useful for the times when you want to give your Java applet more sophisticated network capabilities. Rather than simply telling the browser to display the contents of Web pages, you might want your applet to somehow process the contents of a file. For example, you might have a set of files on a server that represents some useful data; you want the user to select one of the files and then have your applet display a visual representation of the data. Perhaps you need to display contour plots or a graph.

The URL class provides a method—openStream()—that helps you develop these types of applications. The openStream() method allows you to work with a network file as if it were a stream. This method opens a network connection based upon the contents of the URL object and then returns an instance of the class InputStream (discussed in java.io), as shown here:

```
// create a network stream from a valid URL
InputStream aStream = aURL.openStream();
```

Note that the preceding code, and any code that makes I/O calls, should be wrapped with code to handle any thrown exceptions. Given the instance of InputStream, you can then read data from the stream using any of the stream methods discussed earlier. For example, the following code defines a new class MyStreamClass that is essentially the same as DataInputStream but perhaps defines some additional processing of the data. You can nest a buffered input stream within the new class for better efficiency. Finally, you can use the methods provided by the DataInput interface to read any type of data from this stream. The following code assumes a network stream, aStream, has already been opened:

```
// define a new class
public class MyStreamClass extends FilterInputStream implements DataInput
{
...
}

// create a buffered version of our network stream
MyStreamClass myStream = new MyStreamClass(new BufferedInputStream(aStream));

// read some data from network file
String aString = myStream.readLine();

while(aString != NULL)
{
    System.out.println(aString);
    aString = myStream.readLine();
}
```

The preceding code is an overly simplistic example of how network streams might be used. In a real application large amounts of data might be processed, in which case a better coding technique is to create a separate execution thread to process the data stream. This type of processing prevents the network activities, which might take some time to complete, from monopolizing all of the applet's execution time. Also note that the preceding code does not include any way to handle I/O exceptions. A real Java applet/application code needs a graceful way to handle I/O exceptions.

Socket and ServerSocket

The Socket and ServerSocket classes provide Java programs with a programmatic interface nearly identical to standard UNIX-style sockets. The following code constructs a new socket object:

```
// create a socket object
Socket aSocket = new Socket("hostname", 80);
```

The form of the Socket constructor used here takes a hostname and a port number as parameters. Having created a client-side socket connection, you can now ask the Socket object to provide input and/or output streams for communication through the socket. The methods getInputStream() and getOutputStream() return instances of InputStream and OutputStream classes, respectively. These streams can be nested inside buffered streams and data input streams to provide a simple means of communication across a network connection. The following sample code retrieves input and output streams:

```
// returns instance of InputStream
aSocket.getInputStream();
```

```
// returns instance of OutputStream
aSocket.getOutputStream();
```

After the program finishes with a Socket, you should be sure to close the connection:

```
// close the socket
aSocket.close();
```

You can use server sockets similarly. The main difference is the additional requirement that the ServerSocket must listen to and accept a connection request. The constructor for ServerSocket takes a single parameter representing the TCP port number. After instantiating the server socket, the socket is "bound" to the given port:

```
// create a server socket listening to port 8000
ServerSocket aServer = new ServerSocket(8000);
```

```
// listen to and accept any connection requests on port 8000
aServer.accept();
```

Once the server socket is created, it automatically listens to the TCP port for a connection request. When a request is received, the server socket accepts the request that establishes a link between the client socket and the server socket. As with client-side sockets, the server socket has methods for retrieving input and output streams. When you're finished with the server socket, it must be closed:

```
// close off the server socket connection
aServer.close();
```

Both the Socket and ServerSocket class methods eventually map down to calls to the underlying operating system. In this case calls are made to the TCP/IP stack; Windows accomplishes this task via the WINSOCK.DLL library.

> **NOTE**
>
> Socket programming is a large and diverse topic, and I cannot go into every nuance here. Many good books on UNIX socket programming are available.

The java.awt Package

The java.awt package includes the classes and interfaces that make up the Java Abstract Windowing Toolkit (AWT). The AWT was designed to provide a platform-neutral abstraction of a graphical user interface or GUI. It is hard to overstate the importance of the AWT to the Java programming language. Whether you are writing embedded Java applets or standalone Java applications, avoiding the AWT is nearly impossible.

The appeal of the AWT is that it very effectively hides the implementation details of different windowed operating systems. Consequently, a single Java program written using the AWT has the ability to run with a consistent user interface under any operating system for which a Java virtual machine exists. Currently, that category includes systems such as Windows 95/NT, the MacOS, UNIX/X Windows, or NeXTSTEP.

Introduction to the AWT

The AWT as defined by Sun Microsystems includes classes that provide support for a complete set of user interface components including buttons and check boxes, static text fields, menus, windows, scrollbars, and dialogs. These basic visual objects are called *components;* in fact, they are all derived from a common base class called Component. The class Component forms the root of the AWT class hierarchy and provides the basic functionality common to all AWT objects.

The AWT also introduces the concept of the user interface "container." Objects of this class and its descendants are capable of containing any of the various AWT components. Because the Container class is derived from the Component class, Container objects can also hold other Container objects. This nesting of components and containers creates an environment that allows complex interaction within a coherent recognizable structure. The most important container in the AWT is the Panel, which is a container-component having both a visual representation and the ability to contain other components.

The AWT also provides a complete event-driven system for managing and responding to user events. The event model is very robust and provides the primary basis for communication between various components of the AWT within an application. If you are at all familiar with other GUI event managers, you should have no trouble mastering AWT events.

One of the thornier problems that the AWT elegantly solves is how to manage the layout of graphical screens across so many disparate platforms. Indeed, a wide range of screen resolutions, color depths, and so on may exist within each platform. The model that the AWT uses is rather loosely based on that of the UNIX X-Windows system developed at MIT to solve similar hardware-compatibility problems. Rather than defining component layouts in terms of a fixed, screen-based, x,y grid, layouts are specified in more general terms, such as top or bottom, northeast corner, and so on. This model allows each implementation of the AWT to mask the underlying hardware differences while still providing flexible screen designs.

A summary of the classes and interfaces in java.awt is shown in Tables 13.10 and 13.11. The AWT, although it may sound like an optional, albeit very useful, part of Java is actually very tightly woven into every Java program. For example, the Applet class that forms the basis of every browser-embedded Java program is derived directly from class Panel, which is an integral part of the AWT.

Table 13.10. java.awt interfaces.

Interface	Description
LayoutManager	Provides methods for laying out containers.
MenuContainer	Provides methods for menu-related containers.

Table 13.11. java.awt classes.

Class Name	Description
BorderLayout	A layout manager for arranging components around the borders of a container.
Button	A pushbutton object.
Canvas	Used for drawing graphics.
CardLayout	A layout manager for slideshow-like layouts.
Checkbox	A check box object.
CheckboxGroup	A group of radio buttons.
CheckboxMenuItem	A checkable menu item.
Choice	A pop-up menu.

continues

13

Table 13.11. continued

Class Name	Description
Color	Encapsulates a color representation.
Component	The abstract base class for all components.
Container	Provides abstract behavior for a component that can contain other components or containers.
Dialog	A dialog box window.
Dimension	An object encapsulating a width and height.
Event	An object encapsulating system or user events.
FileDialog	A dialog box for selecting filenames from a list.
FlowLayout	A layout manager that performs a left-to-right and top-to-bottom layout.
Font	Encapsulates a font representation.
FontMetrics	Holds information about a Font object.
Frame	A top-level window.
Graphics	Encapsulates behavior for drawing graphic shapes and objects.
GridBagConstraints	Provides class constants for the GridBagLayout manager.
GridBagLayout	A layout manager that aligns Components using user-supplied constraints.
GridLayout	A layout manager using rows and columns.
Image	Encapsulation of a bitmap image.
Insets	A layout manager helper class—encapsulates Component distances from border of window frame.
Label	A text label object.
List	A list box object.
MediaTracker	Provides a means to track the status of media objects.
Menu	A menu containing menu items.
MenuBar	A menu bar containing Menu objects.
MenuComponent	The parent class of all menu objects.
MenuItem	A single menu item.
Panel	A visible Container object.
Point	Encapsulates x and y coordinates.
Polygon	Encapsulates a set of points defining a polygon shape.

Class Name	Description
Rectangle	Encapsulates x, y, width, and height of a rectangle.
Scrollbar	A scrollbar object.
TextArea	A multiline edit box.
TextComponent	The parent class of all editable text components.
TextField	A single-line edit box.
Toolkit	Provides behavior for binding abstract AWT classes to implementation level objects.
Window	A top-level window—parent of Frame and Dialog.

Interfaces

The LayoutManager interface is used as a "mix in" to provide layout capabilities to the layout managers that are derived from class Object. Layout managers are discussed in depth later in this chapter. If you wanted to create your own layout, you would derive a new class from Object that implements the LayoutManager interface. The new layout could then be used in place of one of the standard layout managers as shown here:

```
// define a new layout manager
public class MyLayout implements LayoutManager     // extends Object implied
{
...
}

// change the layout manager
setLayout(new MyLayout());
```

Component Classes

The component classes in java.awt provide a complete set of platform-independent user interface objects. There are classes for displaying pushbuttons, text boxes, scrollbars, windows, and dialog boxes. Several of the classes, including descendants of Container such as Window, Frame, Dialog, and Applet, may contain other components.

Component

The abstract class Component is derived directly from the Object class. A component represents any object that has a visual representation in the AWT. Components make up the fundamental units with which the majority of AWT classes work. Because Component is an abstract class, it cannot be instantiated; therefore, it serves only as base class for other objects.

Container

As discussed earlier, the AWT introduces the concept of a container. The abstract class Container is a child of class Component. As defined, a Container may add or contain any type of object derived from class Component, meaning that containers can contain other containers. Like Component, the Container class is abstract and therefore cannot be instantiated.

Color

The Color class encapsulates the concept of a color. It does so in a most general way by defining a 24-bit RGB color space with 8 bits of information for each color channel. The actual color used is system dependent. The constructor has three main forms, the first taking an integer value in the range of 0 to 255 for each of the red, green, and blue color channels. The second takes an integer value representing a packed 24-bit number. The third form takes floating-point color channel intensities in the range of 0 to 1.0. All three forms of the constructor are shown here:

```
// create a color from three 8-bit intensities
Color aColor = new Color(int red, int green, int blue);

// create a color from a packed 24-bit number
Color aColor = new Color(int rgb);

// create a color from three intensities in the range of 0 - 1.0
Color aColor = new Color(float red, float green, float blue);
```

Several class variables are also associated with class Color to define commonly used shades. Table 13.12 lists these variables.

Table 13.12. Class variables in class Color.

Color.white
Color.lightGray
Color.gray
Color.darkGray
Color.black
Color.red
Color.pink
Color.orange
Color.yellow
Color.green
Color.magenta
Color.cyan
Color.blue

Dimension

The Dimension class provides an object that has only two properties: width and height. This class is really a helper class used by the rest of the AWT. You may find it a useful addition to your own classes. A Dimension object may be created as shown here:

```
// create a dimension with a width of 50 and a height of 100
Dimension aDimension = new Dimension(50, 100);
```

Point

The Point class provides an object that, like Dimension, is a helper class with only two properties. In this case the properties represent spatial x,y coordinates. By defining methods in your classes to accept a Point object any time you want to pass coordinate values, you will find your code easier to read and understand. A Point object may be created using the following:

```
// create a point at coordinates x=100, y=200
Point aPoint = new Point(100, 200);
```

Rectangle

The Rectangle class provides an object-oriented representation of a rectangle. Note that the Rectangle class is not the same as the rectangle methods of the Graphics class. You might also notice that class Rectangle is *not* a Component. It is a child of Object, which reflects the role of Rectangle not as a visual component, but as a helper class for other classes of the AWT.

A Rectangle has only four integer properties: x, y, width, and height. The Rectangle class has a large number of constructor forms, only a few of which are shown here:

```
// create a rectangle from x, y, width, height
Rectangle aRect = new Rectangle(0, 0, 10, 10);

// create a rectangle from width and height
Rectangle aRect = new Rectangle(10, 10);

// create a rectangle getting x and y from a Point
Rectangle aRect = new Rectangle(new Point(10,10));

// create a rectangle getting width and height from a Dimension
Rectangle aRect = new Rectangle(new Dimension(10,10));
```

The Rectangle class also has methods for computing the union of two rectangles, computing the intersection of two rectangles, growing a rectangle, and more. The Rectangle class is very handy for keeping track of arbitrary regions of space. One use might be to track dirty rectangles as part of an animation class.

Polygon

The Polygon class abstracts the concept of a polygon as a list of x and y coordinates. The Polygon class provides methods for adding additional points, testing whether a point is inside the polygon, and calculating the bounding rectangle of the polygon. An example of how to create a `Polygon` follows:

```
// create an empty polygon
Polygon aPoly = new Polygon();

int xpoints[];
int ypoints[];
int npoints;

fillArraysWithVertexData(xpoints, ypoints, npoints);
// create a polygon from a list of points
Polygon aPoly = new Polygon(xpoints, ypoints, npoints);
```

Font

The `Font` class encapsulates information about a font. This class is used as a helper class by the rest of the AWT. (The exact fonts available on any given system vary.) This class has only one constructor; it takes as parameters a font name, a font style, and a font size. In the current AWT implementation, the font style is the arithmetic sum of up to three class variables. These are `Font.PLAIN`, `Font.BOLD`, and `Font.ITALIC`. You may create a `Font` object as follows:

```
// create a bold, italic helvectica 24-point font
Font aFont = new Font("Helvetica", Font.BOLD + Font.ITALIC, 24);
```

The `Font` class provides some basic methods for determining properties of a given font. These include `getName()`, which retrieves the name of the font; `getSize()`, which returns the size of the font; and `getStyle()`, which returns the arithmetic sum of the font style class variables. Because masking out the bits from the return of `getStyle()` is tedious, the class also provides three additional methods—`isPlain()`, `isBold()`, and `isItalic()`—that return boolean values. Some examples of the more common methods of `Font` are shown here:

```
// get the name of the font
String aString = aFont.getName();

// get the font size
int aSize = aFont.getSize();

// get the sum of the font style types
int aStyle = aFont.getStyle();

// determine font styles
boolean aFlag = aFont.isPlain();
boolean aFlag = aFont.isBold();
boolean aFlag = aFont.isItalic();
```

The `Toolkit` class provides a method, `getFontList()`, that returns an array of strings enumerating the fonts available on the system. Call `getFontList()` as follows:

```
// get a list of available fonts
String[] aFontArray = getFontList();
```

FontMetrics

You are bound to have times when your Java programs need to know some more detailed information about a particular font than the Font class can provide. In these instances, you can use the FontMetrics class. A FontMetric object is created from a Font object using the getFontMetrics() method, as shown here:

```java
// create a bold, italic helvectica 24-point font
Font aFont = new Font("Helvetica", Font.BOLD + Font.ITALIC, 24);
// get information about font
FontMetrics aFontMetric = getFontMetrics(aFont);
```

The methods provided by FontMetrics calculate some useful values relating to the given font. Some examples of these methods are shown here:

```java
// find the width in pixels of a given string in the font
int aPixelWidth = aFontMetric.stringWidth("Hello");

// find the width in pixels of a given character in the font
int aCharWidth = aFontMetric.charWidth('W');

// get font ascent = distance between baseline and top of char
int aAscent = aFontMetric.getAscent();

// get font descent = distance from baseline to bottom of char
int aDescent = aFontMetric.getDescent();

// leading of font = gap between descent of one line and ascent of next
int aLeading = aFontMetric.getLeading();

// height of font = ascent + descent + leading
int aHeight = aFontMetric.getHeight();
```

Canvas

The Canvas class is a child of Component and represents a simple drawing surface. Canvas objects are good for drawing or painting images and other graphics operations. A Canvas object can do very little other than provide a surface on which to draw graphics. It provides a default paint method that simply clears itself to the background color. When you find yourself drawing on a Panel object you should consider adding a Canvas object instead.

Graphics

The Graphics class is an important member of the AWT. It encompasses most of the methods available for drawing graphics. Rather than create instances of Graphics, however, you receive a reference to an already created Graphics object. For example, the paint() and update() methods of Components (including the Applet class) receive an instance of the Graphic class when they are invoked. Where does the instance come from? Ultimately it comes from the Java system as part of the normal event processing. The following code shows how a Graphics object is passed to your applet:

```java
public void paint(Graphics aGraphic)
{
...
}
```

The coordinate system used by Graphics should be familiar if you are familiar with programming microcomputers. The x coordinates increase from left to right across the drawing surface. The y coordinates increase from top to bottom down the drawing surface. So the origin is at the top-left corner.

The Graphics class provides support for drawing a complete suite of graphics primitives including lines, rectangles, polygons, ellipses, and arcs. Drawing lines, rectangles, rounded rectangles, and 3D rectangles is easy. The drawLine() method draws a line using the arguments as x,y pairs of the start and end points. The drawRect() method draws a rectangle using the arguments as left, top, right, bottom coordinates. The drawRoundRect() method is similar to drawRect() except the last two arguments specify the horizontal and vertical diameters of the corner arc.

The parameters passed to the draw3DRect() method are similar to drawRect() with the exception of the final parameter, which is a boolean value. If the boolean variable is true, the rectangle is drawn with a raised 3D effect; if it is false, the rectangle is drawn with a lowered 3D effect. Examples of drawLine(), drawRect(), drawRoundRect(), and draw3DRect() are shown here:

```
public void paint(Graphics aGraphic)
{
    // draw a line from (0,0) - (200,200)
    aGraphic.drawLine(0, 0, 200, 200);

    // draw a rectangle
    aGraphic.drawRect(0, 0, 50, 50);

    // draw a rounded rectangle
    aGraphic.drawRoundRect(0, 0, 50, 50, 5, 5);

    // draw a rectangle with raised borders
    aGraphic.draw3DRect(0, 0, 50, 50, true);
}
```

Drawing filled versions of the same basic shapes (except lines, of course) is just as easy. The shapes are filled using the current foreground color, which can be changed with the setColor() method. Examples of drawing filled versions of rectangles, round rectangles, and 3D rectangles are shown here:

```
public void paint(Graphics aGraphic)
{
    // change the foreground color
    setColor(Color.magenta);

    // draw a filled rectangle
    aGraphic.fillRect(0, 0, 50, 50);

    // draw a filled round rectangle
    aGraphic.fillRoundRect(0, 0, 50, 50, 5, 5);

    // draw a filled raised 3D rectangle
    aGraphic.fill3DRect(0, 0, 50, 50, true);
}
```

Drawing polygons is accomplished with the drawPolygon() method, and it is only a little bit more difficult than drawing rectangles. To define a polygon shape, you need to provide a list of vertices; actually, you need to have two separate lists. One list is an array of integers representing the x coordinates. The other list holds the y coordinates. The final argument is the number of vertices in the polygon. Note that the drawPolygon() method does not automatically close a polygon. Therefore, if you want to draw a closed shape, you must provide an extra vertex (just the first vertex again). The following code draws a polygon and a filled polygon:

```java
public void paint(Graphics aGraphic)
{
    int xpoints[] = {50, 100, 150, 100, 50};
    int ypoints[] = {50, 0, 50, 100, 50};
    int npoints = 5;

    // draw a diamond shape
    aGraphic.drawPolygon(xpoints, ypoints, npoints);

    // draw a filled diamond shape
    aGraphic.fillPolygon(xpoints, ypoints, npoints);
}
```

You can also draw a polygon using an instance of the Polygon class discussed previously. This technique tends to be much easier to work with if you need to manipulate many polygons. It eliminates the need to manage significant numbers of integer arrays. All you need to do is create a Polygon object and call the drawPolygon() or fillPolygon() method. Note the absence of a draw3DPolygon() method. Besides being of questionable utility, it would be a very difficult routine to implement correctly. The following code draws a polygon and a filled polygon using the Polygon class:

```java
public paint(Graphics aGraphic)
{
    // get a Polygon object
    Polygon aPoly = someMethodWhichCreatesPolygons();

    // draw the polygon
    aGraphic.drawPolygon(aPoly);

    // draw a filled polygon
    aGraphic.fillPolygon(aPoly);
}
```

In discussing some of the capabilities of the Graphics class above, I mentioned that methods were provided for drawing nearly every imaginable shape. One shape that was missing was the circle. Was that an accidental omission from the Java language? No. In effect, a circle is just a special case of a more general shape, the ellipse. Now some might argue, and I might agree, that a circle is such a common special case of the ellipse that it deserves its own method.

In any case, the Graphics class does provide drawOval() and fillOval() methods that work just fine for drawing and filling ellipses and circles. Using these methods could hardly be easier. Both methods take four integer arguments. The first two are the x and y coordinates of the top-left corner; the last two arguments are the width and height of the oval. These arguments essentially specify the bounding box of the ellipse. Examples of the `drawOval()` and `fillOval()` methods are shown here:

```
public paint(Graphics, aGraphic)
{
    // draw a horizontally elongated ellipse
    aGraphic.drawOval(100, 100, 150, 100);

    // now draw a circle, radius is 100/2 = 50
    aGraphic.drawOval(100, 100, 100, 100);

    // now fill the circle
    aGraphic.fillOval(100, 100, 100, 100);
}
```

You might be thinking that this syntax is a bit cumbersome because you don't normally think of circles and ellipses in terms of their bounding boxes. If you are like me, you probably think in terms of the center point and horizontal and vertical diameters (or perhaps radii).

Why doesn't the AWT provide a method with these arguments? The reason is that it can't! At least not easily. The explanation goes back to the (reasonable) restriction of Java that polymorphic methods must differ, at a minimum, either in the number or the type of their arguments. Because the proposed method would also take four integer arguments, it would violate that rule.

Are we defeated? No, not really, because the Java AWT *could* provide a `drawOval()` method in the `Graphics` class that *does* take different arguments. Unfortunately, the current AWT does not provide these methods. The following code shows one possible approach. Both the `Point` and `Dimension` classes pass the same basic information to the `drawOval()` method, but each class uses arguments of different types.

```
// possible new methods for Graphics
public void drawOval(Point aPoint, Dimension aDimension);
public void drawOval(int X, int Y, Dimension aDimension);
```

You could simply subclass one of the `Graphics`-derived classes and provide these new methods. Actually, the workaround is a bit more complicated because you would also need to hook into the AWT to make sure that the `paint()` and `update()` methods were passed instances of the new `Graphics` class. I will leave that problem, as they say, as an exercise for the reader. Perhaps Sun will provide these methods in a later release of the Java Developer's Kit (JDK).

Drawing and filling arcs is similar to drawing ellipses; after all, an arc is really just a portion of an ellipse. As it turns out, the implementation of `drawArc()` is a bit harder to work with in practice. The first four arguments are the same as for `drawOval()`—specifying the starting x and y coordinates, width, and height. The last two are a bit tricky. The fifth argument defines the starting angle for the arc, and the sixth is the angle swept out by the arc.

For the starting angle, the AWT defines angles as increasing in a counterclockwise direction with 0 degrees at the 3:00 position. Therefore, 90 degrees is at 12:00, 180 degrees is at 9:00, and 270 degrees is at 6:00. Remember that the sixth argument specifies the angle swept out by the arc *relative* to the starting angle. In the following example, the arc starts out at 0 degrees (that is, 3:00). The arc sweeps through 270 degrees (counterclockwise) to draw three quarters of a circle stopping at 6:00. If the sixth argument had been negative, the arc would have been drawn in a clockwise direction. The drawArc() and fillArc() methods are used in the following code:

```
public paint(Graphics aGraphics)
{
    // draw a 3/4 circle starting at 0 degrees sweeping out 270 degrees
    aGraphics.drawArc(100, 100, 100, 100, 0, 270);

    // fill the same arc
    aGraphics.fillArc(100, 100, 100, 100, 0, 270);
}
```

The fillArc() method connects the two arc end points to the center of the circle or ellipse forming a closed shape. This method is useful for drawing pie wedges and other shapes.

Drawing text is also easy with the Graphics class. The method drawString() draws text using the currently selected font. The first argument is the text string to draw, and the remaining two arguments define the x and y coordinates at which to draw the text. The coordinates specify the bottom-left corner of the string, as shown here:

```
public paint(Graphics aGraphic)
{
    // draw text at coordinates (10, 10)
    aGraphic.drawString("Hello there!", 10, 10);
}
```

Image

The Image class is an encapsulation of a graphic image. Its purpose is to serve as a container for graphic images. The Image class can also provide information about a graphic image. An instance of the Image class is usually retrieved using the getImage() method of the Applet class. The Image class can hold any type of image that is supported by Java and most browsers. Right now that list is limited to GIF and JPG files.

A typical use of an Image object involves retrieving a graphic image using getImage() and then displaying the image using the drawImage() method of the Graphics class. The most common form of the getImage() method takes two parameters. The first is a URL object that points to the base location of the image. The second is a String object representing the path to the image file relative to the base location. Commonly, the Applet class methods getDocumentBase() and getCodeBase()provide the URL object. The following example shows how the getImage() and drawImage() methods may be used:

```
public paint(Graphics aGraphic)
{
    // retrieve an image object
    Image aImage = getImage(getDocumentBase(), "images/redball.gif")
```

```
        // display the image
        aGraphic.drawImage(aImage, 20, 20, this)
}
```

Label

The `Label` class represents the simplest of all the components in the AWT. It represents a static text label. `Label` components don't do very much and are most often used simply to label other components on a panel. A `Label` object is constructed using one of the following constructor forms:

```
// an empty label with no text
Label aLabel = new Label();

// using a String object
Label aLabel = new Label("I am a label!");

// using a String object and an alignment specification
Label aLabel = new Label("I am also a label!", Label.CENTER);
```

The third form of the constructor shown here allows the text alignment of the label to be specified. The class variables `Label.LEFT`, `Label.RIGHT`, and `Label.CENTER` give the allowable values.

Because a label is a component, it provides interfaces that allow the AWT to manage its layout. A label component also knows how to respond to AWT system events such as a request to repaint itself. These types of default behaviors distinguish a component from a simple text string drawn to the screen.

The font of a label is controlled by the setting in its parent class `Component`. By default, every component uses the same font as its parent. The font may be changed, however, by making this call to the `setFont()` method:

```
// change the label font
aLabel.setFont(new Font("Helvetica", Font.BOLD, 12));
```

Remember that every `Applet` is a `Panel` so that we may now display our newly created label object using the following code. The `add()` method of class `Applet` is inherited from class `Container`. Events that are received by the `Applet` are now sent along to the label and any other objects contained by the applet. A `Label` object may be added to a `Container` by calling the `add()` method:

```
// add our label to the applet container
add(aLabel);

// add a label without saving an explicit reference
add(new Label("Another label", Label.RIGHT));
```

Other methods provided by the `Label` class include `getText()`, `setText()`, `getAlignment()`, `setAlignment()`, and any of the methods inherited from `Component`.

Button

Button objects are only a little more complicated than Label objects. In addition to having its own text label, a button must be able to respond to mouse clicks. The way that a button responds to user events is included in the discussion of events a bit later in the chapter.

The constructor forms for the Button class are very simple. The first form creates a plain button with no labeling text. Why would anyone want such a button? One such case is when the text of the button is undefined, but you still want to reserve layout space for a fixed number of button objects. A Button object is created using one of the following constructor forms:

```
// create a blank button
Button aButton = new Button();

// create a button with a label
Button aButton = new Button("OK");
```

Like Label objects, Button objects can be added to a Container and displayed via a call to the add() method.

Check Boxes

A check box is an object that has a label and a single binary state of either on/off, or selected/unselected if you prefer to think of it that way. Changing the state of a check box does not typically result in any action other than updating the state of a program.

Check boxes are also frequently combined into groups of check boxes for the purposes of allowing selection from a set of alternative choices. When used in this manner, the check boxes are often called "radio buttons," referring to the way buttons on a car radio are pushed to select one of several radio stations.

The following code shows the constructors for the Checkbox class. The first form creates an unlabeled and unselected check box. The second form creates a check box using a string object to provide the label test. The third form is a bit more complicated. The first parameter is a string object that specifies the label text, and the second parameter specifies radio button groups (more on that topic later). The third parameter is a boolean argument that specifies whether the check box is initially on or off. All three forms of the Checkbox constructor are shown here:

```
// create an empty, unselected check box
Checkbox aCheckbox = new Checkbox();

// create a checkbox using a string object for a label
String aString = "Show Results";
Checkbox aCheckbox = new Checkbox(aString);

// create a selected checkbox
Checkbox aCheckbox = new Checkbox("Show Results", null, true);

// create some checkboxes and add them to the applet container
add(new Checkbox("Show Results"));
add(new Checkbox("Show More Results", null, true));
```

Some additional methods provided by the Checkbox class are getLabel(), setLabel(), getState(), and setState(). These methods provide a means for getting and setting the label text and check box state. The getLabel() method returns a string object, and setLabel() takes a string object as an argument. The setState() and getState() methods take and return boolean values, respectively. The following code shows how to use each of these methods:

```
// get the checkbox state
boolean flag = aCheckbox.getState();

// set the checkbox state
aCheckbox.setState(true);

// get the checkbox label text
String aString = aCheckbox.getLabel();

// set the checkbox label text
aCheckbox.getLabel("Self Destruct");
```

Radio Buttons

As discussed earlier, when several check boxes are grouped together into a mutually exclusive set they are called radio buttons. If you look at the Java API documentation, however, you won't find a class called RadioButton. How do you create radio buttons then? The answer lies in a special class called CheckboxGroup that manages a set of check boxes so that they behave like radio buttons. Applying CheckboxGroup really is almost as easy as it sounds. The following code is a simple example of grouped check boxes:

```
// create a checkbox group manager
CheckboxGroup aCheckboxGroup = new CheckboxGroup();

// create and display our radio buttons
add(new Checkbox("1st floor",aCheckboxGroup, true));
add(new Checkbox("2nd floor",aCheckboxGroup, false));
add(new Checkbox("3rd floor",aCheckboxGroup, false));
add(new Checkbox("4th floor",aCheckboxGroup, false));
```

Remember that only one radio button can be selected at a time. How does it work? The process is controlled by the CheckboxGroup class. What would happen if you tried to set the state of each checkbox to true in the code above? The Checkbox class contains code that sets itself to be the only active radio button if an instance of CheckboxGroup is passed, rather than null, in the constructor. So in this case, only the last button added would be selected.

The Checkbox class provides two methods to change the group to which it belongs: getCheckboxGroup() and setCheckboxGroup(). The CheckboxGroup class provides the methods getCurrent() and setCurrent() to get or set the selected radio button. These methods are easy to use, as shown by the following code:

```
// assign the checkbox to a newly created group
aCheckbox.setCheckboxGroup(new CheckboxGroup());
```

```
// retrieve the group to which the checkbox belongs
CheckboxGroup aCheckboxGroup = aCheckbox.getCheckboxGroup();

// retrieve the currently selected checkbox
Checkbox aCheckbox = aCheckboxGroup.getCurrent();

// manually set the selected checkbox
aCheckboxGroup.setCurrent(aCheckbox);
```

Choice Menus or Combo Boxes

The Java AWT provides for a visual component called the *choice menu*. I find this name a bit misleading because this component is not a menu as much as a pull-down list of radio buttons. Only one item in the list may be selected at a time, and it is normally the only item visible. When the user clicks on the object, it displays a pull-down list of all the available choices. In the Windows environment this element is called a combo box.

The component class Choice is used to create a choice menu, and the addItem() method populates it. The constructor is very simple, taking no parameters at all, as shown in the following example:

```
// create an empty choice menu
Choice aChoice = new Choice();

// add some items to the menu list
aChoice.addItem("First class");
aChoice.addItem("Business class");
aChoice.addItem("Economy");
aChoice.addItem("Coach");
aChoice.addItem("Baggage Compartment");
```

The only form of addItem() provided by class Choice takes a string object as an argument. Therefore, all menu choices must be string objects. However, the class maintains the list of menu choices in a Vector object that is part of the Choice class, so it is theoretically possible to store any type of object as a choice.

Because of this design, if you wanted to have a set of numeric choices (perhaps airplane models), you could use one of the object wrapper classes to convert the number to a string object. The following code shows several methods for adding numeric data to a list of choices. If you know the set of choices at design time, you can explicitly write the numbers as string objects. However, if you need to add arbitrary numbers to a list, you may have to use an object wrapper to recast the number as a string. The following example shows how to add numeric items to a choice menu:

```
// illegal! Integer primitives are not objects
aChoice.addItem(747);

// ok, all arguments are objects
aChoice.addItem("727");
aChoice.addItem(Integer(727).toString());
```

```
aChoice.addItem(Integer(737).toString());
aChoice.addItem(Integer(747).toString());
aChoice.addItem(Integer(767).toString());
aChoice.addItem(Integer(aNumber).toString());
```

The Choice class provides several additional methods (shown in the next code sample). The getItem() method returns a string object representing the item at a given index. The countItems() method returns the total number of choices in the menu. The getSelectedIndex() and getSelectedItem() methods return the index and string of the currently selected choice. The two forms of the select() method change the current selection based on either the choice index or the string. Each of these methods is demonstrated here:

```
// return the string representing the given choice
String aString = aChoice.getItem(1);

// get the number of items in the menu
int nItems = aChoice.countItems();

// get the index of the selected item
int nSelected = aChoice.getSelectedIndex();

// get the string representing the selected choice
String aString = aChoice.getSelectedItem();

// select the item at index 1
aChoice.select(1);

// select the choice labeled with the given string
aChoice.select("First Class");
```

Text Fields

A text field is a component that provides an editable text field. Windows users might recognize this field as a single-line edit box. Text fields do not have scrollbars and can handle only a single line of text. Also note that the text field is not labeled; it includes only a small frame and the editable text field. Consequently, a Label component is often used in conjunction with a text field to identify its purpose. There are several ways to construct a text field:

```
// create an empty text field
TextField aTextField = new TextField();

// create a text field 10 chars wide
TextField aTextField = new TextField(10);

// create a text field with some default text
TextField aTextField = new TextField("Some text");

// create a text field with some default text, 10 chars wide
TextField aTextField = new TextField("Some text",10);

// add a text field to the display
add(aTextField);
```

You can also create a text field that hides the text entered into it. This technique is used mainly for password fields. The setEchoCharacter() method tells the TextField object to echo a given character rather than the entered text. You must first create the text field:

```
// create a text field with some default text
TextField aTextField = new TextField("Some text");

// set the echo character
aTextField.setEchoCharacter('*');

// display the text field
add(aTextField);
```

TextField provides many additional methods that provide a number of useful capabilities. Some examples of these methods follow:

```
// retrieve the text
String aString = aTextField.getText();

// set the text
aTextField.setText("Some text");

// get width of the text field
in nColumns = aTextField.getColumns();

// select text between start and end columns
aTextField.select(start, end);

// select the entire text field
aTextField.selectAll();

// true or false if field is editable
boolean aFlag = aTextField.isEditable();

// toggle editable state on or off
aTextField.setEditable(true);

// get the echo character
char aChar = aTextField.getEchoChar();

// true of false if echo character is set
boolean aFlag = aTextField.echoCharIsSet();
```

List

The List class represents a scrollable list box component. The list may have a specified number of visible rows. If the list contains more rows than visible rows, a scrollbar is created to allow scrolling through the entire list. A List object may also permit the user to make multiple selections. Both of the List constructor methods are used here:

```
// construct an empty list with no visible lines
List aList = new List();

// construct a list with 10 rows and multiple selections
List aList = new List(10, true);
```

Additional methods are provided to add, replace, and delete items from the list box; they are addItem(), replaceItem(), and delItem().The following code demonstrates how to add items to a list object. After creating a List object and adding items to it, you would normally add() the List component itself to a Panel object, perhaps as in the following code:

```
// add some items to our list
aList.addItem("Pastrami");
aList.addItem("Capicola");
aList.addItem("Corned beef");

// add the List to a Panel object
aPanel.add(aList);
```

TextAreas

The TextArea class represents a multiline editable text region. Unlike TextField objects, a TextArea can handle significant amounts of text. If needed, the TextArea object displays scrollbars to allow the user to browse through the text. Here are the constructors for the TextArea: class

```
// create an empty text area
TextArea aTextArea = newTextArea();

// create an empty text area with a size of 10 rows by 40 columns
TextArea aTextArea = newTextArea(10, 40);

// create a text area with some text
TextArea aTextArea = newTextArea("A little bit of text");

// create a text area with some text and a size of 10 rows by 40 columns
TextArea aTextArea = newTextArea("A little bit of text", 10, 40);
```

Some additional methods provided by TextArea are getColumns(), getRows(), insertText(), appendText(), and replaceText(). Example usage of these methods follows:

```
// get the number of rows
int aColumns = aTextArea.getColumns();

// get the number of columns
int aRows = aTextArea.getRows();

// insert text starting at position 0
aTextArea.insertText("A little bit more text",0);

// append text to end
aTextArea.appendText("This is the end!");

// replace 'A little' with 'A '
aTextArea.replaceText("A ",0,8);
```

Scrollbar

The Scrollbar class is a visual component that is used as a helper class by other classes in the AWT and is not often used by itself. However, sometimes you may want to work directly with an instance of this class. For example, you may want to create a standalone scrollbar, or "slider" as it is sometimes called, to allow users to visually choose from a range of possible values.

The scrollbar range is determined by `minimum` and `maximum` properties. Likewise, the scrollbar horizontal or vertical orientation is determined by an `orientation` property.

Examples of the constructors for class `Scrollbar` follow. The first form creates a vertical scrollbar with minimum and maximum values of 0. The second form creates a scrollbar with an orientation specified by a class variable—either `Scrollbar.HORIZONTAL` or `Scrollbar.VERTICAL`.

The third form is more complicated because it provides the most flexibility. It has a total of five integer arguments. The first argument is the scrollbar orientation, and the second is the initial value of the scrollbar that must be within the minimum and maximum range values. The third argument specifies the total height or width of the scrollbar depending on the scrollbar orientation. The last two arguments are the minimum and maximum range values. Both methods of constructing a `Scrollbar` are shown here:

```
// create a vertical scrollbar with 0,0 min and max values
Scrollbar aScrollbar = new Scrollbar();

// create a vertical scrollbar with 0,0 min and max values
Scrollbar aScrollbar = new Scrollbar(Scrollbar.VERTICAL);

// create a horizontal scrollbar, initial value 0, width of 30
// and a range of 0 to 100
Scrollbar aScrollbar = new Scrollbar(Scrollbar.HORIZONTAL, 0, 30, 0, 100);
```

Window

The `Window` class is a descendant of `Container` (and therefore of `Component`) that provides the ability to create windows. Because windows are container objects, you can add components to them just like you would to a `Panel` object.

These windows exist outside the frame of the browser application. Descendants of class `Windows` may have title bars, menus, sizing frames, and so on. Although not technically an abstract class, it is rare to instantiate an object of this class. More commonly, Java applets and applications will use one of the subclasses that provide additional capabilities.

Frame

The `Frame` class is a subclass of the `Windows` class and provides a more complete implementation of a GUI window. It implements the `MenuContainer` interface that allows it to have pull-down menu bars. `Frames` are initially invisible and, unlike `Panel` objects, their layout manager defaults to `BorderLayout`.

Methods are available for resizing and moving windows. Because a frame window is initially invisible, you must use the `show()` method to display it. The `hide()` method can then be used to hide the window. The following sample code shows how to create a `Frame`, change the size using `resize()`, move the window, and then display it using `show()`:

```
// create a frame window
Frame aFrame = new Frame("I am a Frame Object");

// change window size
aFrame.resize(200, 200);

// move window to 100, 100
aFrame.move(100, 100);

// make window visible
aFrame.show();
```

Dialog

The `Dialog` class is another child of class `Windows`. The `Dialog` class provides behavior common to dialog boxes. `Dialog` objects are similar to `Frame` objects in many ways. The main differences are that dialog boxes tend to be used for displaying messages and for getting inputs from the user. Therefore, dialog boxes do not usually have menus or title bars, although they can have them.

`Dialog` objects may be either modal or nonmodal. A modal `Dialog` blocks or waits until it is completed before allowing input to any other windows. A nonmodal `Dialog` may be hidden behind another `Window` object and does not block user input. A `Dialog` must always have a parent `Frame` so a dialog box cannot exist all by itself. Note however, the parent does not have to be visible. Like the `Frame` class, a `Dialog` is invisible by default, so you must use the `show()` method to display it. The second parameter to the `Dialog` constructor is a boolean value that determines whether the dialog is modal or nonmodal. If the boolean value is true, the dialog is modal; if the value is false, then it is nonmodal. The following code shows how to create both modal and nonmodal `Dialog` objects:

```
// create a modal dialog
Dialog aDialog = new Dialog(aFrame, true);

// create a nonmodal dialog with a title
Dialog aDialog = new Dialog(aFrame, "Warning", false);
```

FileDialog

The `FileDialog` class is a special-case subclass of the `Dialog` class. It provides a dialog box customized for file open and file save dialog boxes. The AWT maps down to the standard operating system dialogs if any exist. The two constructors provided by `FileDialog` allow you to create file dialogs with titles. The first form is used for file open dialogs and specifies the parent `Frame` along with a title string:

```
// create a file open dialog box w/ title
FileDialog aFileDialog = new FileDialog(aFrame, "Open File");
```

The second form also specifies a parent `Frame` and a title string. The third parameter specifies whether the dialog should be a file open or a file save dialog box. The `FileDialog` class provides two class variables—`FileDialog.OPEN` and `FileDialog.SAVE`—to make things easier. By using class variables to define the behavior of the `FileDialog` class, it is possible for future releases of the JDK to support additional standard dialog boxes such as a file save as dialog. The second form is usually used only for file save dialog boxes, but it can create file open dialogs as well:

```
// create a file save dialog using class variable
FileDialog aFileDialog = new FileDialog(aFrame, "Save File", FileDialog.SAVE);
```

Panels and Layout Classes

As discussed earlier, the AWT provides a flexible and platform-independent means of specifying screen layouts. Rather than hard-coding screen x,y coordinates, the AWT supports user interface component layouts using suggested locations and orientations. To this end, the AWT introduces the concept of layout managers.

Layout managers determine the location of individual components within a panel. The layout manager accepts suggestions and hints to help it make the right decisions. The factors that determine just where a component is ultimately located are the order in which it was added to a panel and which layout manager the panel has chosen to use.

Each and every panel can choose its own layout manager. Remember also that panels can contain other panels, each with its own layout manager. This convention provides enough flexibility to describe just about any screen arrangement you can imagine.

The current Java AWT defines four fundamental layout managers. These are `FlowLayout`, `GridLayout`, `BorderLayout`, and `CardLayout`. Each layout manager has a unique way of arranging the components that it manages. The default layout manager for all `Panel`-derived objects is `FlowLayout`. To change the default layout manager, you call the `setLayout()` method inherited from class `Panel`:

```
// change the layout manager
setLayout(new GridLayout());
```

You should normally change the layout before creating any other components. Therefore, you would call `setLayout()` in your `init()` method. You can change the layout manager at other times, but doing so would seldom be useful. The call to `setLayout()` usually occurs during the `init()` method:

```
// some new class
public class MyApp extends Applet
{
    public void init()
    {
      // define new layout manager
      setLayout(new GridLayout());
      ...
    }
}
```

FlowLayout

The `FlowLayout` manager is the default layout manager for all `Panel` and `Panel`-derived objects. It is also by far the simplest layout manager. Components are arranged by the `FlowLayout` manager in rows from left to right across a panel.

When the end of a row is reached, the `FlowLayout` manager simply continues placing components on the next row. Each row is centered by default, but the `FlowLayout` manager class allows the default alignment to be altered. Two forms of the `FlowLayout` constructor follow. The second form specifies an alignment argument:

```
// set the layout manager to FlowLayout
new FlowLayout();

// align each row starting from the right edge of the panel
new FlowLayout(FlowLayout.RIGHT);
```

You can also control the horizontal and vertical spacing used by the `FlowLayout` manager. The default spacing is 3 pixels horizontally and vertically. The defaults can be changed via another form of the constructor:

```
// center align components with 15/15 horizontal/vertical spacing
new FlowLayout(FlowLayout.CENTER, 15, 15);
```

GridLayout

The `GridLayout` manager partitions a panel into a discrete grid made up of a number of equally spaced cells. As components are added to the panel, they are placed in the cells from left to right and top to bottom across the grid. You can also alter the horizontal and vertical spacing between components (cells), as you can do with the `FlowLayout` class. The second form of the `GridLayout` constructor (shown next) demonstrates this process:

```
// create a 4 x 4 grid of cells
new GridLayout(4, 4);

// create a 4 x 4 grid with 10/10 spacing
new GridLayout(4, 4, 10, 10);
```

The default spacing between grid cells is 0 both vertically and horizontally. The additional spacing results in a gap between each cell.

BorderLayout

The `BorderLayout` manager is quite different from the previous two layout managers. In the case of the `BorderLayout` manager, components are placed on the panel according to compass directions such as north, south, east, west, and center. `Component`s that are placed along the edges are given as much space as they need, and the center component is sized to take up the remaining space.

The following code demonstrates one way the `BorderLayout` class might be used:

```
// initialize the Applet class
public void init()
{
    // construct and use a border layout manager
    setLayout(new BorderLayout());
    ...
    // add some components using the new manager
    add("East", new Label("East Side"));
    add("West", new Label("West Side"));
}
```

You might have noticed something peculiar about the form of the `add()` method. A special form of `add()` placed the new components on the panel. The first argument is a string object that represents the compass position to be used by the layout manager in placing the component on the panel.

What happens if you accidentally use this form of `add()` with other layout managers? Nothing! They just ignore the argument if they don't need it. However, as you eventually start to design your own layout managers, you may want to define parameters of your own. You can create a custom layout manager by deriving a new class that implements the `LayoutManager` interface:

```
// define a new layout manager
public class MyLayoutManager implements LayoutManager // extends Object implied
{
    // name is actually our location parameter
    void addLayoutComponent(String name, Component comp)
    {
        ...
    }
}

// our Java applet class
public class MyApp extends Applet
{
    public void init()
    {
        // use the new layout manager
        setLayout(new MyLayoutManager());

        // add some components using string location names
        add("Front", new Label("The Front?"));
        add("Back", new Label("The Back?"));
    }
}
```

As you may have already guessed, another form of the `BorderLayout` constructor allows custom spacing between components. Be aware that the top and bottom (actually north and south) components extend entirely from the left and right edges of the screen. Therefore, increasing the spacing parameters will shrink the vertical size of the components on the east and west edges of the panel. Remember that with all the layout managers, custom spacing affects only the gaps between components. To use custom spacing, construct an instance of BorderLayout providing the spacing parameters and pass it to setLayout():

```
// set custom spacing
setLayout(new BorderLayout(15,15));
```

CardLayout

Like BorderLayout, the CardLayout manager is another very unique layout manager. However, unlike any of the previous layout managers, components added to a CardLayout-managed Panel are not all displayed at the same time. Instead, they are flipped through one at a time, much like a deck of cards. Thus the CardLayout manager can be used to create slide shows of components.

Remember that you can add Panels as components within other Panels. Within the subpanels you can also define different layout managers and place several components. Sound confusing? Perhaps an example will clarify the situation:

```
public class MyApp extends Applet
{
    CardLayout aCardLayout;
    void init()
    {
        // change to card layout
        aCardLayout = new CardLayout();
        setLayout(aCardLayout);

        // this panel uses FlowLayout
        Panel Card1 = new Panel();

        // add label to the card
        Card1.add(new Label("Card one, label 1"));
        Card1.add(new Label("Card one, label 2"));

        // add card to Applet panel
        add("One", Card1);

        // this panel also uses FlowLayout
        Panel Card2 = new Panel();

        // add label to the card
        Card2.add(new Label("Card two, label 1"));
        Card2.add(new Label("Card two, label 2"));

        // add card to Applet panel
        add("Two", Card2);

        // show only the first card
        aCardLayout.show(this, "One");
    }
}
```

When the applet containing the preceding code is executed, several things happen. First the layout manager for the applet changes to CardLayout. Next a new panel called Card1 is created. Because a layout manager isn't specified, this panel will default to flow layout. Next it creates two label components and adds them to Card1. Next Card1 is added to the applet panel, giving it the name "One". The process is repeated for panel Card2, adding two label components as well. Then Card2 is added to the applet panel, giving it the name "Two".

The last statement in the init() method tells the layout manager to display the panel named "One". This step tells the layout manager to flip through the cards in any order. One convenient use for this type of behavior is for implementing wizards or experts that help the user work through a number of screens to provide input and answer questions.

GridBagLayout

The last layout manager is GridBagLayout. It provides the most flexibility at the cost of being the most difficult to use. The space managed by a GridBagLayout is divided vertically and horizontally into a rectangular grid of cells. However, unlike the GridLayout class, the cells here do not have to be the same size. Also, a component does not have to reside in only one cell.

Components added to a GridBagLayout-managed Container use a helper class called GridBagConstraints to describe the desired layout of components. The GridBagConstraints class consists of nothing more than a set of layout option variables and a set of class variables defining the possible states of those variables.

Each component added to a GridBagLayout must have a GridBagConstraints object associated with it. The GridBagLayout class then consults each component's GridBagConstraint object as it decides where to place each component on its container. You must typically set at least one layout-option variable if you want to define a custom layout.

The following code shows how you can use a GridBagLayout manager in a simple Java applet. The example does not demonstrate the complete capabilities of the GridBagLayout class; that topic would require a chapter unto itself. However, you should get a good feel for how you can incorporate the GridBagLayout into your own applications.

```
import java.applet.Applet;
public class MyApplet extends Applet
{
    void addComponent(Component anObj, GridBagLayout aGridBag,
      GridBagConstraints aConstraint)
    {
        // apply constraint to object
        aGridBag.setConstraints(anObj, aConstraint);

        // add it to container
        add(obj);
    }
```

```
void init()
{
    GridBagLayout aGridBag = new GridBagLayout();
    GridBagConstraints aConstraint = new GridBagConstraints();

    // change the layout manager
    setLayout(aGridBag);

    // components fill space in row
    aConstraint.fill = GridBagConstraints.BOTH;
    aConstraint.weightx = 1.0;

    // add some components
    addComponent(new Button("one"), aGridBag, aConstraint);
    addComponent(new Label("two"), aGridBag, aConstraint);

    // next component takes rest of row
    aConstraint.gridwidth = GridBagConstraints.REMAINDER
    addComponent(new Button("three"), aGridBag, aConstraint);
}
}
```

The constraints understood by GridBagLayout are gridx, gridy, gridwidth, gridheight, weightx, weighty, anchor, fill, and insets. The gridx and gridy variables specify the cell at the upper left of the component's display area. The upper-left cell of the grid is at 0,0. The class variable GridBagConstraints.RELATIVE, which is the default for gridx and gridy, specifies that components be added to the right of or just below the last component, respectively.

The gridwidth and gridheight variables specify the number of cells in a row or column. The class variable GridBagConstraints.REMAINDER tells the layout manager to use all the remaining space in a row or column. The class variable GridBagConstraints.RELATIVE specifies that the component should be the next to last one in its row or column.

The weightx and weighty layout variables determine how to distribute the available space. They are also important for determining how components behave during a resize event. The weight parameters, when set to zero (the default), tell the layout manager to put any extra space between its grid cells and the edges of the container. This arrangement results in a component layout centered horizontally and vertically within the container.

The anchor layout variable specifies where to put a component when its desired size is less than the available display area. A number of class variables are defined for this property. They are the names of the eight points of the compass and CENTER, for example, GridBagConstraints.NORTHEAST and GridBagConstraints.SOUTHWEST. The default value is CENTER.

The fill layout variable is also used when the size of a component is less than the available display area. However, this variable determines whether and how a component is resized to fit the available space. The default NONE specifies no resizing. Other class variables include VERTI-CAL, HORIZONTAL, and NONE. Note that the anchor property is meaningless if the fill property is BOTH.

The last layout variable is `insets`. This variable specifies the extra space or "padding" applied to each component and the edge of its display area. This variable is a reference to an `Insets` object, so changing it requires a new instance of `Insets`. The following code shows this implementation:

```
// change the insets
aGridConstraint.insets = new Inset(5, 5, 5, 5);
```

The `GridBagLayout` class is now complete. Using this class really isn't as hard as it might seem at first glance. If you write helper methods such as `addComponent()` from the preceding example, the `GridBagLayout` class is even easier to use.

Insets

Each layout manager discussed previously provides a means for customizing the gaps between components. But what if you want to change the space around the borders of the panel? Not surprisingly, an easy way to do so exists.

Every object descended from class `Container` contains a method called `insets()`. This method returns an instance of class `Insets` that defines the border spacing. The layout managers call the `insets()` method when they need to determine where to place components.

The class `Insets` is a remarkably simple class; it is essentially just a wrapper around four integer constants—the parameters to the constructor. The members of class `Insets` represent the size of the border to reserve around the top, bottom, left, and right edges of the panel. The following code shows an oversimplified example of how to implement class `Insets`:

```
// simplified representation of class Insets
public class Insets  // extends Object is implied{
    // data members
    int top, left, bottom, right;

    // constructor
    public Insets(int aTop, int aLeft, int aBottom, int aRight)
    {
      top = aTop;
      left = aLeft;
      bottom = aBottom;
      right = aRight;
    }
}
```

To change the border spacing for the applet panel, you need to change the values of the `Inset` class returned by the method `insets()`. You can do so just by overriding the inherited `insets()` method and defining your own. The following code shows how:

```
// my custom applet class
public class MyApplet extends Applet
{
    // override the inherited method
    public Insets insets()
    {
```

```
        // 15 pixels on top and bottom, 0 on left and right
        return new Insets(15,15,0,0);
    }
}
```

Events

Up until this point you have learned a great deal about the AWT, but you still don't know how an applet responds to events. The Event class represents events initiated by either the system or the user. Information regarding these events is packaged by the AWT within an instance of class Event and then passed along. The class holds items such as the target of the event, the type of event, the time of the event, the keyboard state, and the x and y coordinates of the event.

If you are familiar with programming event-driven systems, you won't find anything new or mysterious in this class. It just defines a platform-independent representation of system and user events. Defining and responding to events in Java programs is an important topic, and it will be covered in much greater detail in Chapter 14, "An Introduction to GUI Programming."

The `java.awt.image` Package

The java.awt.image package is a subpackage of the abstract windows toolkit. It groups together classes and interfaces for working with bitmap images. Most of the classes exist mainly to support other portions of the AWT, but they can, of course, be used by your own Java programs. A summary of the interfaces and classes in java.awt.image are shown in Tables 13.13 and 13.14.

Table 13.13. `java.awt.image` interfaces.

Interface	*Description*
ImageConsumer	Provides methods for retrieving image data from an ImageProducer.
ImageObserver	Provides methods for creating or loading an image.
ImageProducer	Provides methods for creating and filtering image data.

Table 13.14. `java.awt.image` classes.

Class Name	*Description*
ColorModel	An abstract class for managing color data for images—parent of all color model objects.
CropImageFilter	A filter that crops images to a particular size.

Class Name	Description
DirectColorModel	Implements a true-color color model.
FilteredImageSource	Implements an `ImageProducer` that applies a filter object to an existing image producing a new image.
ImageFilter	Takes image data from an `ImageProducer`, processes the data, and passes the data to an `ImageConsumer`.
IndexColorModel	Implements a palletized color model.
MemoryImageSource	An `ImageProducer` that gets image data from memory.
RGBImageFilter	Abstract class that filters and possibly transforms RGB image data.

Classes

The classes in `java.awt.image` provide additional features for the AWT classes. The color model classes such as `ColorModel`, `DirectColorModel`, and `IndexColorModel` provide an abstraction of the notion of pixel color information. They allow the other classes to ignore the different ways that pixel color data may be represented. The filter classes such as `ImageFilter`, `CropImageFilter`, and `RGBImageFilter` are classes that act as black box filters of image data. Image data is passed to a filter on its way from an `ImageProducer` to an `ImageConsumer`. Along the way the data may be transformed in various ways.

ColorModel

The class `ColorModel` is an abstract class that provides a means for working with image color data. It is an abstract class and cannot be instantiated. The methods provided by the `ColorModel` class allow Java programs to retrieve color information from images. Some of the methods provided by the `ColorModel` class are shown next:

```
// retrieve the pixel color depth
ColorModel.getPixelSize();

// retrieve RGB and Alpha color components for a pixel
int aValue = ColorModel.getRed(aPixel);
int aValue = ColorModel.getGreen(aPixel);
int aValue = ColorModel.getBlue(aPixel);
int aValue = ColorModel.getAlpha(aPixel);
```

DirectColorModel

The `DirectColorModel` class is a subclass of the `ColorModel` class. It works with images in which the pixel data itself contains the color information. In other words, the images are not "palletized." Typically, such direct color images are 24-bit or 32-bit true color images. The model supported by DirectColorModel follows but is not identical to the X11 (for example, UNIX/X-Windows) TrueColor model.

IndexColorModel

The IndexColorModel class is another subclass of the ColorModel class. The IndexColorModel processes images that employ a table lookup to map pixel data to RGB color values. This type of image is common on most platforms. The model supported by this class is similar to the X11 pseudocolor model.

ImageFilter

An ImageFilter is a class that implements the ImageConsumer interface. The ImageFilter object can process image data from an ImageProducer object and send the data to another ImageConsumer. The ImageFilter class is not abstract, but it implements a filter that does not modify the image data in any way. Subclasses of this class provide useful image modifying capabilities.

CropImageFilter

The CropImageFilter class, a subclass of ImageFilter, provides the ability to crop images to an arbitrary rectangular region. The following code shows one way to use a subclass of ImageFilter:

```
// get an image
Image img = getImage(getDocumentBase(), "images/foo.gif");

// create our filter
ImageFilter aCropImageFilter = new CropImageFilter(x, y, width, height);

// create new filtered (ie. cropped) image
Image aNewImage = createImage(new FilteredImageSource(img.getSource()),
  aCropImageFilter);
```

FilteredImageSource

The FilteredImageSource class is an ImageProducer that takes an image from another ImageProducer and applies an ImageFilter. The result is a new image. The preceding source code demonstrates how this class is typically used.

MemoryImageSource

The MemoryImageSource is an ImageProducer that can create images from an array of pixel data. The pixel data is in packed RGB format. The following code shows how you can create an Image from an array of pixel data. Note how the color values are packed into an integer using shifts and the bitwise OR operator:

```
int pixels[] = new int[100*100];
int counter =0;
```

```
// create image fading from red and green to yellow
for(int red=0; red < 100; red++)
    for(int green=0; green < 100; green++)
        pixels[counter++] = (green <<24) ¦ (red << 16);
Image aImage = createImage(new MemoryImageSource(100, 100, pixels, 0, 100));
```

RGBImageFilter

The `RGBImageFilter` class is an abstract class that provides the basic capabilities needed to filter RGB images. A typical use would be to create a subclass of `RGBImageFilter` that provides some specific behavior, for example, to swap the red and green channels in an image, to convert a color image to grayscale, or to form the color negative of an image.

The java.awt.peer Package

The `java.awt.peer` package is a subpackage of the AWT. It provides the hidden platform-specific AWT classes, one for each component class in the AWT. Table 13.15 lists the classes in this package, but they are not discussed here because a Java program usually has no need to work with instances of these classes. Each of the `java.awt` classes is sent an `addNotify()` message when it is created. The `addNotify()` method does nothing more than construct one of the `java.awt.peer` classes. The `java.awt.peer` class typically maps to a system-specific call to the operating system. Under Windows this would probably be a call to a routine in either USER.EXE or GDI.EXE. A summary of the classes in `java.awt.peer` is shown in Table 13.15.

Table 13.15. Classes in java.awt.peer.

Class Name	Description
LabelPeer	Creates a peer label object.
ListPeer	Creates a peer list box object.
ScrollbarPeer	Creates a peer scrollbar object.
TextFieldPeer	Creates a peer edit box object.
MenuItemPeer	Creates a peer menu item object.
MenuPeer	Creates a peer menu object.
TextAreaPeer	Creates a peer multiline edit box object.
FramePeer	Creates a peer framed window object.
ChoicePeer	Creates a peer pop-up list object.
MenuBarPeer	Creates a peer menu bar object.
FileDialogPeer	Creates a peer file dialog box object.
ComponentPeer	Creates a peer component object.

continues

13

THE STANDARD JAVA PACKAGES

Table 13.15. continued

Class Name	Description
WindowPeer	Creates a peer window object.
DialogPeer	Creates a peer dialog box object.
PanelPeer	Creates a peer panel object.
CanvasPeer	Creates a peer drawing surface object.
ContainerPeer	Creates a peer container object.
CheckboxMenuItemPeer	Creates a peer combo box object.
TextComponentPeer	Creates a peer generic edit box object.
CheckboxPeer	Creates a peer check box object.
MenuComponentPeer	Creates a peer generic menu object.
ButtonPeer	Creates a peer pushbutton object.

The `java.applet` Package

The `java.applet` package contains the classes used by every embedded Java applet. In fact, every Java applet *must* be derived from the class `Applet` because it provides some of the capabilities required to embed Java programs in a browser. Note that the main class in Java applications is rarely derived from the `Applet` class. A summary of the interfaces and classes in `java.applet` is shown in Tables 13.16 and 13.17.

Table 13.16. `java.applet` interfaces.

Interface	Description
AppletContext	Provides methods for referencing the applet context.
AppletStub	Provides methods for applet viewers.
AudioClip	Provides methods for playing audio files.

Table 13.17. `java.applet` classes.

Class Name	Description
Applet	The base Java applet class.

Interfaces

The interfaces provided by java.applet are used primarily by Java itself. It is relatively uncommon that a user class would implement an interface other than AudioClip. However, there are a number of times when an applet's AppletContext is referenced to learn details about the environment in which the applet exists.

Classes

The only class in the java.applet package is the Applet class. This is no trivial class, however, because it supplies the default behavior for all Java applets that run in a browser. Java applications, however, are not required to be descendants of the Applet class.

Applet

Perhaps not surprisingly, the Applet class is the only class in the java.applet package. Applet is a subclass of the class Panel. Because an Applet is a panel, it has a drawable surface. This characteristic also makes Applet a Container, so you can add() other components to an applet and they will appear on the applet's surface. Although the Applet class is not declared as abstract, you would rarely instantiate an object of this class. The most common use of Applet is to provide a base class for your own applet classes.

The Applet class provides a number of methods that are used by all Java applications. The paint() and update() methods inherited from class Component are commonly overridden to provide your own specific behaviors.

The following code shows a complete Java applet. The applet first subclasses Applet so that it can provide its own paint() method. Then it overrides the paint() method to draw a text string on the applet panel.

```
import java.awt.Graphics;
import java.applet.Applet;

// subclass Applet class
public MyApplet extends Applet
{
    public void paint(Graphics aGraphic)
    {
        aGraphic.drawString("Hello World!",10, 10);
    }
}
```

Most of the methods defined by the Applet class are just calls to an AppletContext. The AppletContext is an object that represents the environment hosting the applet, which will usually be either a browser or the AppletViewer application. The getAppletContext() method can retrieve a handle to the applet's context. This method gives an applet some ability to control its environment.

The resize() method can request a change in the applet's size. The method comes in two forms—one taking integer width and height values, and the other taking a Dimension object. Note that this method is just a request; it is not guaranteed to succeed:

```
// request the applet be resized.
resize(320, 200);

// same as above
resize(new Dimension(320, 200));
```

The showStatus() method requests that a string message be displayed in the status bar of the host environment. The host support for this method varies somewhat, so you shouldn't write applets that depend on this capability:

```
// display a message on the host status bar
showStatus("I am busy...");
```

The getImage() method (discussed earlier) returns an instance of an Image object. Two forms of this method exist. The first form takes an instance of a URL object representing the absolute path to an image. The second form takes an instance of a URL object representing a base path along with a string representing a path to the image relative to the base URL. The two examples below get the same image. The second form is generally more flexible because it does not depend on an absolute Internet address:

```
// get an image
Image aImage = getImage(new URL("http://www.foo.com/images/foo.gif"));

// same as above
Image aImage = getImage(getDocumentBase(), "images/foo.gif");
```

The getAudioClip() method behaves just like the getImage() method with the exception that the former returns an instance of an AudioClip object. As with getImage(), this method has two different forms. In addition, you can use the play() method for simply playing the audio clip, rather than retrieving it. The following code shows getAudioClip() and play() in action:

```
// get an audioclip
Audioclip aAudioclip = getAudioclip(new URL("http://www.foo.com/audioclips/
foo.au"));
play(new URL("http://www.foo.com/audioclips/foo.au"));

// same as above
Audioclip aAudioclip = getAudioclip(
play(getDocumentBase(), "audioclips/foo.au");
```

The init(), start(), and stop() methods are simply stubs in the Applet class. They exist solely to be overridden in subclasses. Java executes the init() method once when an applet is first created. Java calls the start() method when an applet starts executing and calls the stop() method when the applet is no longer on the screen. Note that whereas the init() method of an applet is called only once, the host system can call the start() and stop() methods, in pairs, any number of times.

Summary

Whew! That is it; you are finished. This chapter covers nearly all of the classes and interfaces in the standard Java packages. However, the coverage of many methods and a few classes is not thorough. You are encouraged to explore the Java API documentation and the Visual J++ online books to learn more about each class as you use them in your own applications.

Better yet, get a copy of the latest JDK from Sun Microsystems (`http://javasoft.sun.com`) because it includes the source code to the standard Java packages. The JDK also includes many sample Java applets that are another good source of information. The best way to learn a new programming language and its subtle nuances is to examine code written by other programmers.

An Introduction to GUI Programming

by David Hanley

IN THIS CHAPTER

In this chapter you will learn to create graphical user interfaces in the Java programming language. These user interfaces are the means by which Java programs interact with their users. Mastering the use of Java's approach to graphical user interfaces will allow you to write easy-to-use interfaces that are platform independent.

The Goals of the AWT

Java comes with a predefined and powerful set of objects for constructing graphical user interfaces (GUIs) for your Java programs. It is called the AWT, which is short for *Abstract Windowing Toolkit*. The AWT allows Java programs to make user interfaces that are simple, robust, and visually attractive. Moreover, it abstracts the details about a specific platform so that the graphical interface can run on all computers on which Java runs. This flexibility is a huge advantage because graphical programs created on one platform are typically completely incompatible with other systems.

The Java philosophy also stipulates that what a user sees on the screen should be familiar—that is, a Windows user should see Windows controls and buttons, a Macintosh user should see a typical Macintosh interface, and so forth for all platforms. The Java button that you create is mapped to the analogous component on the machine on which that code is actually executing.

These two benefits—portability and familiarity—necessarily impose some restrictions on the kinds of components that Java can utilize. Java cannot utilize components available on only one machine and cannot use graphical tricks available only on one platform. Also, as a result of the stripped-down controls and design limitations, Java controls typically are not *quite* as nice as the controls that a good designer creates for a specific platform. This situation is being rectified, however, by the introduction of better design toolkits and a more comprehensive AWT slated for the 1.1 release of Java.

Programmers used to other windowing environments will face a steep learning curve when first encountering the Java AWT, as will programmers unused to event-driven or object-oriented programming. However, this learning curve is lessened by the clean, object-oriented design of the graphics package. Although Sun's documentation is somewhat thin, it is easy to read and describes how the various components function together. The Java SDK, downloaded during J++ installation, provides many examples of the AWT in action. The J++ Books On-Line, on the J++ CD-ROM, has a brief explanation of the AWT classes, and provides a cross-reference to each of the methods of each class. This chapter gets you started with an overview of AWT, a brief explanation of the key classes in the AWT, and some coding.

The AWT Object Categories

The object classes used for constructing interactive windowing user interfaces contain three basic types of entities:

- Containers—Containers are visual objects into which components can be placed so that several can be grouped together in a consistent fashion. For example, a frame is a container, as is a radio button group, and a panel. All these containers are discussed shortly.

- Components—Components are the visual entities with which the user specifically interacts. Components must be placed in some kind of container in order to be visible. You access them later as members of this container. Examples of components are buttons, text fields, and scrollbars.

- Layout managers—You use a layout manager to arrange the components in a container in a desired fashion. Layout managers enable you to align buttons along the left edge of a window in one program and arrange them in a grid in the next.

Plunging Right Into the First AWT Java Program

The easiest way to explain these concepts is by examining some code that creates GUI components using the AWT classes. Enter the code shown in Listing 14.1, set your workspace options to execute it as a standalone application, and then run it.

Listing 14.1. The AWTTest class.

```java
import java.awt.*;

class AWTTest extends Frame
{
    Button ok , exit;

    AWTTest()
    {
        setTitle( "The very first frame" );

            setLayout( new FlowLayout() );

        List list = new List();
        list.addItem( "This" );
        list.addItem( "that" );
        list.addItem( "the other" );

        add( list );

            ok = new Button( "OK" );
        add( ok );

        exit = new Button( "Exit" );
        add( exit );
        show();

    }
```

14

AN INTRODUCTION
TO GUI
PROGRAMMING

continues

Listing 14.1. continued

```
        public boolean action( Event evt , Object o )
        {
                if ( evt.target == exit )
        {
            System.exit( 1 );
        }
        return true;
    }

    public static void main( String [] args )
    {
        AWTTest t = new AWTTest();
    }
}
```

Figure 14.1 shows what the program looks like upon execution.

FIGURE 14.1.

*A simple Java program
demonstrating a frame.*

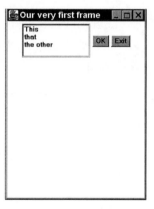

Let's see how this code works. The first line in the program tells the Java compiler that the program may use all the components available in the java.awt package:

```
import java.awt.*;
```

You could import only the specific components you are using, but importing everything is simpler and doesn't add any overhead to you code.

This line declares that your class, AWTtest, extends the Frame class, which means that your class is an child of the Frame class:

```
class AWTTest extends Frame
{
```

Therefore, you gain access to all of the public methods that are associated with the `Frame` class and its ancestors. Just as important, you are allowed to overload the default methods that are supplied with the `Frame` class. This allows you to intercept resize events, tell when the mouse has entered the frame, and accomplish other important tasks. You will see how this works later in the chapter.

The following line sets the title of the window to the string contained in the parentheses:

```
setTitle( "Our very first frame" );
```

If you do not set the title of the windows you create, the system will name the windows `"untitled"`.

This method sets up the layout manager that is used inside this container:

```
setLayout( new FlowLayout() );
```

The flow layout manager governs where the components you add to this container will be located. In this case, with the flow layout manager, objects are laid out in order from left to right and from top to bottom, much as text is read in English. The layout manager also centers lines of components if they do not completely fill the line. You will see other layout managers that let you specify where in a region a particular component should reside in relation to the others in the next cash register example later in the chapter.

To create the list box shown in Figure 14.1, you create a new list object:

```
List list = new List();
```

The list object can reside in the container, in this case the frame `AWTTest`, and allows the user to pick one or more lines of text out of a collection. A list can be set to allow either multiple simultaneous selections or only one selection at a time. The program using the list object can be notified when an entry is picked, or it can check on all the selected items later.

`List` has a method called `addItem` that you use to populate the list box:

```
list.addItem( "This" );
list.addItem( "that" );
list.addItem( "the other" );
```

A list object starts life empty. The `addItem` method is the key to making the list useful.

Once the list object is created, you need to place it on the `AWTTest` frame. To do that, use the `add` method inherited from the `Frame` class:

```
add( list );
```

The flow layout manager will only work on an object that has been added. If you did not add the list, it would not appear on the screen. Try commenting out `add( list )`. Notice that the list box is not visible. Try putting the add(list) back in, but move it to the line after the add(ok) line. Note that the list box will appear between the two buttons. There are two important things to remember here:

- Remember to add your components to the container you want them on, in this case AWTTest.

- When using the flow layout manager, add your components in the order in which you want them to appear.

To create and add the OK and Exit buttons to AWTTest, you write the following:

```
ok = new Button( "OK" );
add( ok );

exit = new Button( "Exit" );
add( exit );
```

Once again, the layout manager specifies how to add each object to the frame. Notice how OK and Exit are declared outside the constructor AWTTest(). In this example OK could have been declared the same way the list is:

```
Button OK = new Button("OK");
```

But this would not work for the Exit button because the Exit button is referenced inside the action subroutine. If Exit were declared inside the constructor, AWTTest, it would not be visible in the action subroutine. Try declaring both buttons in the constructor, AWTTest. The compiler will complain that it doesn't know what Exit is.

The visual elements of a Java screen start out hidden. The show() method instructs the frame to show itself:

```
show();
}
```

Windows are created in an invisible state and depend on the user to eventually show them. This delay prevents the user from seeing the components being laid out into the window area as well as seeing the window change sizes. Such a display would be both unattractive and slow.

The next method overrides one of the methods that is defined by the Frame class:

```
public boolean action( Event evt , Object o )
{
```

This method allows you to access the events that the user generates by interacting with the interface and to take the appropriate actions. In the AWTTest example you want the program to end when the user pushes the Exit button. To do this you use the arguments that come with the action method. The action method contains a field that is a handle to the object that was manipulated, generating the event that triggers the action method. You need to recognize the event and shut down the program:

```
if ( evt.target == exit )
{
```

```
System.exit( 1 );
}
```

In this case you are testing to see whether the object is the Exit button. If the object is the Exit button, you exit the program.

The `main()` function, required when a program is run as a standalone, creates an instance of your new class:

```
public static void main( String [] args )
    {
        AWTTest t = new AWTTest();
    }
```

Run this program, resize the windows, and so on to get a feel for how Java AWT components look and how you can interact with them. Experiment with the title and the order of the add statements. To prove that an event is generated when the OK button is pressed, add this line:

```
list.addItem(o.toString());
```

Place this line in the `action` subroutine. Remember to declare the `list` at the top of the class, along with the OK and Exit buttons. Declaring it outside the constructor will make the `list` visible inside the `action` method. Pressing the OK button while the program is running will cause OK to be added to the list. This is an example of how an event-driven program works.

How does an event-driven program differ from other types of programs? An event-driven program does not execute a series of instructions and exit when finished. Rather, an event-driven program sets up a GUI interface and exits. The system has the responsibility for calling the appropriate part of your program when the user clicks a button. Instead of your program calling the system to conduct I/O, I/O by the system triggers your program.

Components, Containers, and Layouts

The following sections highlight the three principal groups of objects that are available in the AWT class library: components, containers, and layouts.

Component Classes

Common controls that are part of the component class include

- Button
- Canvas
- Check box
- Choice
- Label
- List

14

AN INTRODUCTION TO **GUI** PROGRAMMING

- Scrollbar
- Text area
- Text field

These are the primary controls you will use over and over in your programs to enable user interaction.

As a derivative of the Component class, these controls can be added to containers and arranged by layouts. In addition, you can derive new controls from the classes that are available to you. This allows you to customize the behavior of the controls you derive from the basic AWT classes. You can also assign any component object you have allocated to an object array of type component. This type of assignment enables you to handle component objects in a consistent fashion in your code through the common members and methods of the Component class. Therefore, an array of components might have as its members buttons, text fields, or any user-defined class derived from a component. This technique is very useful when processing collections of display objects. Let's look at the controls available to you through the Component class of the AWT library.

Buttons

Buttons are components that a user can press to activate a certain reaction on the part of your program. Buttons can be labeled or unlabeled; although, clearly, an unlabeled button is not terribly useful. (See Figure 14.2.)

FIGURE 14.2.

Java buttons.

Pressing a button calls the action() method of the container in which it resides. The call can help you determine which button was pressed. One way, which we have already seen, is to compare the target member of the Event object that gets passed to the action() method of the button objects that we have created and added to the container. This technique is very fast and efficient, and the method I prefer, but it may not be practical in all cases. The action() method receives a second parameter, as well as an object. This object, in the case of a button action, is equal to the label of the button. You can use the equal() method of the argument object of the button labels to determine which button was actually pressed. For example, the code inside the `action()` method in the AWTTest program would be changed to look like this:

```
if(o.equals("Exit"))
{
System.exit( 1 );
}
```

This technique enables you to test for the press of a button to which you no longer have the pointer. Try declaring the Exit button inside the constructor in the AWTTest example. If you use the `o.equals()` method you can still catch and react to the fact that the Exit button was pushed even though the variable Exit is not visible to the `action()` method. The method you choose in a particular application will depend on the structure and needs of your code.

Some of the methods that buttons inherit from the Component class allow you to do some interesting things with the buttons that you create. For example, you can change the font that is used on a button with `setFont()` and change the color of the button with `setBackground()`. These methods allow you to incorporate extra pizzazz and attractiveness in your visual displays.

Canvases

Canvases serve several very important functions that would otherwise be difficult to achieve in the AWT paradigm. You can place a canvas in the GUI area and draw on it. Using a canvas in this way is much safer then drawing directly onto the window because you cannot accidentally overdraw the area that is reserved for graphics and overwrite the components. Moreover, drawing on the canvas requires less work than drawing on the component area because drawings made to the canvas are already adjusted to the location of the canvas in the GUI area. If the canvas is later moved to another place in the component layout, drawings made to the canvas will be adjusted to the new location. This technique reduces code dependency on exact locations of components and enables you to update your design without breaking your code.

The canvas also serves another important function: receiving messages. Because it receives all the messages that a regular control receives, by subclassing a canvas you can create new controls and widgets. You could, for example, create a graphing component and place it on the screen. You might also create a button that uses an image for its visual display area, allowing you to create attractive graphical buttons. An example of this approach appears later in the chapter.

Check Boxes

A *check box* is similar to a button but differs in some important aspects. Clicking a normal button causes a message to be sent; then the button reverts to its previous state (unpressed). Clicking a check box causes its state to be toggled (see Figure 14.3). Clicking an unchecked check box sets it to the checked state. Conversely, clicking a checked check box causes it to revert to an unchecked state. Toggling is very useful for applications in which a user can pick many options. For example, in an application in which someone is selecting components for a computer, the customer could toggle on or off check boxes to indicate which components he or she wants to include with the system.

FIGURE 14.3.

Java check boxes.

Furthermore, you can also set the state of a check box explicitly. For example, when a button gets pressed, you can explicitly set the state of check boxes as a result of pressing that button. In the computer-purchasing application, then, a user could select a particular computer system from a list which would in turn set the check boxes representing the defaults of that computer system.

Check Box Groups

At times you might want to use check boxes, but not want the user to select more than one check box from a particular group. In this instance you can instantiate a check box group (see Figure 14.4). A check box group may contain several check boxes, but only one of these check boxes may be selected at a certain time. The check box group enforces the rule that only one of the member check boxes may be selected at a particular time. If a new check box is selected, the previously selected check box will be unchecked.

FIGURE 14.4.

Java check box groups.

A check box that is a member of the check box group may appear different from a normal check box. On some platforms—Windows, for example—it may have the "radio button" appearance, clearly indicating to the user that this button is a member of a group of buttons of which only one at a time can be selected. This visual clue is important because it clearly indicates to the user how that set of buttons will behave.

Something you need to bear in mind, however, is that no constraint forces the members of a check box group to be located in the same region of the screen. Scattering buttons around the screen is confusing to the user. You would need to think out such a design decision very carefully.

Check Box Menu Items

Sometimes—in a pull-down menu, for example—you might want to include items that can be either checked or unchecked. Although you can't add check boxes to menus directly, you can add check box menu items (see Figure 14.5). This class behaves much like the regular Checkbox class; the check boxes can be toggled, and their state can be tested.

FIGURE 14.5.
An example of check box menu items.

Check box menu items do not directly subclass check boxes and cannot be used as entries to check box groups. However, if you know with which menu item check boxes are associated, you can trap the events posted to them and coordinate the states of related menu items and check boxes. In the computer-purchasing application discussed earlier, a check box menu item might allow the user to choose among mutually exclusive peripherals.

Choice Objects

A *choice* is a list of options, one of which may be selected at any given time. A choice is implemented as a pull-down list. When inactivated (unclicked), the choice component is a text box that displays the currently selected choice with an arrow on the right. When the component is selected, a drop-down menu is displayed that enumerates the available selections. If another entry is selected from the list, the choice component returns to its previous state with the new selection displayed as the current selection (see Figure 14.6).

FIGURE 14.6.
An example of choice objects.

An application for this component in the computer-purchasing example might be the user's choice of CPU speeds. The user can select only one of several CPU speeds, but only needs to see the CPU speed selected at any given time. However, if the customer wants to change the selection, he or she can quickly select the desired clock speed from the drop-down list.

File Dialog Boxes

The file dialog box is an example of a component that is too time-consuming to create for just one platform (see Figure 14.7). It allows the user to select a location for saving or loading a file and to navigate through folders to find a file to load or a place in which to save a file.

FIGURE 14.7.

A Java file dialog box.

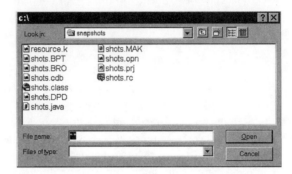

This component is an example of a Java interface that shows the user something familiar. A Macintosh user will see the familiar Macintosh file dialog box; Windows and UNIX users will see what is familiar to them. The operating system determines what actions users can take with the dialog box; for example, they may be able to create new folders or change how the files are displayed. Java application programmers do not need to worry about these actions; they need only create the object and react to the save/load messages it issues.

Images

The Image class represents what it sounds like: images. They can be either graphical bitmaps that are fetched from the disk or images created by drawing commands issued by the programmer. These images can add a lot of visual impact to the display of a program. You can even create animation by flipping through a set of images.

Labels

Labels are critically important for good layout design, especially because some controls are not self-documenting. In other words, the purpose of the control may not be intuitively obvious just from looking at it. Labels are noninteractive text elements that remain as part of the layout (see Figure 14.8).

FIGURE 14.8.

Java labels in action.

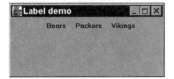

Lists

Lists display options to the user. Unlike the choice component, however, more than one of the available options is displayed at a given time and, depending on how you configure the list, more than one of its elements may be selected (see Figure 14.9).

FIGURE 14.9.

Java lists.

If the list component contains more entries than can be displayed in its area, it will acquire a scrollbar, allowing the user to scroll through the entries to make a choice. This behavior is automatic and requires no special programming when you utilize the List class. The encompassing container object receives notification when a member of the list is selected/unselected and can query the list at any time to see which of the members are currently selected.

Menus

Menu bars are a very convenient way to allow users to access a large number of options quickly. Additionally, the options may be grouped logically to assist the users in finding important options. Menu bars must be added to a frame and are therefore unavailable to applets that reside directly in the browser, although they are still available to applets that open independent frames (see Figure 14.10).

FIGURE 14.10.

A Java menu bar.

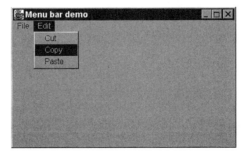

To create menu bars, you must create menu items (which are named) and add them to the menu bar, which is then attached to a certain frame. The menus themselves contain menu items. When the user interacts with a menu bar, events that correspond to the menu items are triggered.

A particular menu item might not be available at a given time because of the state of the program. For example, in a word processor, if no file is present in the program, the Save option in the menu should not be available. In this case, you can disable the particular option, and the AWT library will graphically indicate to the user that the option is not available.

Scrollbars

Scrollbars can enable the user to view an area larger than the area that is physically present in the component (see Figure 14.11). For example, if you want to display a picture that is larger than the available viewing area, you can display only a section of the picture and then allow the user to move the subregion of the picture that he is viewing over the actual area occupied by the picture.

FIGURE 14.11.
Java scrollbars.

It is worth noting, however, that no behavior of the scrollbar is automatic. The programmer utilizing the scrollbar object must trap the user interactions with the scrollbar and adjust the other components of the layout. This type of programming is tedious and time-consuming.

Of course, there are other possible uses for scrollbars, such as setting values across a certain range. For example, a screen that allowed the user to pick a color might have three scrollbars that represent the red, green, and blue components of the color desired. The updating of the scrollbar would display the new color selected.

Text Areas

Text areas are components that represent rectangular areas of text on the screen with scrollbars (see Figure 14.12). You do not need to manage interaction with the scrollbars in this case, as it is handled within the text area component. You can use text areas to display long sets of text in an area too small to show the entire set at once.

FIGURE 14.12.
An example of a text area.

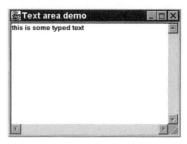

The text area can be set in edit or nonedit mode. In the edit mode the user can select the text area and modify the contents. You can use this technique to allow the user to enter a lot of text in a free-form fashion.

Text Fields

Text fields create one line of text on the display that can be set to a value (a string) and edited by the user (see Figure 14.13). They do not contain scrollbars and have a much smaller screen footprint then the text area widget. Text fields are a very good way to accept one-line text entries. For example, two text fields could accept a user's login name and password.

FIGURE 14.13.
An example of text fields.

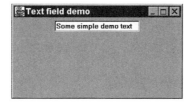

Container Classes

Now that you know about the component classes that are available in the Java AWT, the next elements to examine are the containers into which you can place the components. These containers differ in the way in which they appear to the user, how they treat components added to them, and how they interact with other containers.

All containers are derived from the common base class, Container, to which objects of type component can be added. Containers come with default managers that determine how the internal components are laid out, but the default layout manager can be changed. Containers can also locate internal components and return lists of the components that they contain.

14
AN INTRODUCTION
TO GUI
PROGRAMMING

Dialog Boxes

Dialog boxes are windows that are intended to be short-lived. They must be the children of a frame and can optionally block access to the parent frame while they are open. This container is useful for information that must be either displayed or acquired before a program can continue. For example, you might require users to enter a valid password before allowing them to interact with the program. Or you might want to inform the user of an important event that must be acknowledged before the program continues (see Figure 14.14).

Figure 14.14.

A Java dialog box.

Frames

Frames are independent windows. Frames have a title bar and other widgets that are associated with frames on the operating system running your Java program. For example, the frame in Figure 14.15 is running on Windows 95 and has the normal Windows Minimize, Maximize, and Close buttons.

Figure 14.15.

A Java frame.

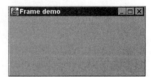

Frames also have a number of useful methods that you can use or override to assist in creating effective interfaces:

- You can change the appearance of the mouse cursor when it is over the window. You can track the location of the mouse cursor and change the mouse cursor when it is over certain components. For example, if the cursor is over a drawable canvas, the mouse cursor can be changed to cross-hairs to indicate that drawing actions can take place.

- You can construct menu bars and attach them to the frame. In this case, the menu bar will be attached to the window in such a fashion that it shows up as part of the window frame, and components will flow in below it.

- You can get and set the icon that will be displayed when the window is iconized.

■ You can set the window to be resizable or unresizable. In resizable windows, the window will be informed of the resize event so that its components can be resized.

■ You can set the text contained in the title bar.

Panels

Panels are not windows in their own right. They must exist in some other kind of window. They are, however, still containers to which components can be added. Their primary purpose is to arrange a set of components in a location. For example, a cluster of buttons that belong together can be placed into a panel, which can then be added to a window. An arbitrary number of panels can then be added to a window.

Your program design can move the panel to a new location, or the layout manager can move it; either way, everything the panel contains will move with it to the new location. This containment feature, once again, simplifies the design and permits quick modification.

Windows

A window by itself is simply a rectangle on the user's screen; Frame and Dialog subclass it to create a window, to which they draw the appropriate image. However, windows can be useful widgets to directly extend to achieve a particular window appearance. You could create a frame with different borders or headers than are usual, for instance.

Layout Managers

Placing components into a window based on absolute pixel locations is typically not appropriate in Java programs because different computer systems use different font sizes, draw components differently, and use different window border widths. To solve this problem, Java uses *layout managers*. Layout managers accept components along with hints of how the components should be laid out in relation to each other.

The layout manager determines how much space each component needs and arranges the components accordingly. For example, when a window is resized, the layout manager intercepts the resize message and lays out the components to accommodate the new space available. Several layout managers are available.

Border Layout

A *border layout* arranges the components along the edges of a container and allows another component to be laid out in the center of the container in the space left over. The terminology is north, south, east, west, and center. Only one component can be added to each area; if you want to have more than one component occupying a region, you can add the components to a panel and then add the panel to the region.

Additionally, when a border layout object is constructed, you can specify how much area to place between the various screen regions. By default, a border layout places no space between the components.

Card Layout

A *card layout* is useful when you need to switch between several sets of components. You can add several panels to a card layout, and it can flip between the panels when signaled.

For example, a program that has to get information from a user may have too many questions to fit comfortably on one screen. You can create several panels that ask for information about a certain topic. The program can flip between the panels to acquire information about the various topics. This method is much faster and easier than erasing and redrawing the components. It is also better than maintaining many separate windows.

Flow Layout

A *flow layout* allows you to place components into a container in a simple fashion, from left to right and from top to bottom, as in English text. You can also tell the container to flow a line of components as centered, aligned left, or aligned right. The flow layout is very useful for laying out buttons in a toolbar.

Grid Bag Layout

A *grid bag layout* allows a number of components to be laid out in a container in relation to each other. The grid bag layout allows components to be placed in a grid cell that extends for a number of cells. They are arranged in relation to each other, but the size of cells in a column may change to accommodate the varying sizes of the components that they contain.

Grid Layout

A *grid layout* is a grid of a fixed number of cells. The grid cells are filled in with components from left to right and from top to bottom, in the order that they are added, and they will occupy the same amount of space.

In the following sections you use the objects that are available in the AWT package to construct some real programs.

Some Sample Programs

This section clarifies the function of the Java components that have been covered in this chapter by creating some simple Java programs. These are Java applications, but you can make them into applets by removing the `main()` function, subclassing `Applet`, and changing the class constructor to an `init()` function.

Java Cash Register

Suppose you have been given the task of writing a cash-register program using the components that you have seen. How will you proceed?

A cash register consists of two entities: a readout that displays the entries and a button pad on which you enter prices and request a sum.

The text display should allow the user to make many entries in a vertical fashion and to scroll through the entries. The buttons should be the same size and arranged neatly in a grid so as to be easy to find.

Do any of these specifications sound familiar? The readout is best implemented as a text area, and the keys should be implemented as buttons placed in a grid layout. The layout of the entire window should be a border layout, with the text area aligned to the north and the keys aligned to the south. Therefore, you will have to place the buttons in a panel, which will then be aligned to the south.

You will need to trap every digit (or decimal) entered, add it to the panel, and place it in an accumulator string.

Aside from the numeric keys, you need three special-case keys:

- The Add key—When the Add key is pressed, you need to convert this string to a real number, add it to the sum, reset the accumulator string, and move to a new line. Whew!

- The Sum key—When the Sum key is pressed, you need to sum in the current term and print out the sum (with a sum line before it).

- The Clear key—When the Clear key is pressed, it zeroes out the accumulator and the current sum and clears out the text window, readying the program for another customer.

Listing 14.2 shows a program that accomplishes these tasks.

Listing 14.2. The Cash class.

```
/*
    Java cash register.
    This program is a simple demonstration of a java application utilizing
    the AWT types Button, TextArea , GridLayout , BorderLayout,
    and not least of all, Frame
*/

import java.awt.*;

public class cash extends Frame
    // This lets us both create a frame and override default messages to intercept
    // the user actions
{
    //The following variables are declared globally to this object because they
    //will be needed in several methods.

    TextArea Readout; //This will be the handle to the cash register 'screen'
    String Current = ""; //This is the line of text currently being entered.
    double Total = 0.0; //This is the sum of the lines thus far entered.

    //These strings will be used as labels for the buttons that will be placed
    //into the grid.  It is important to observe the ordering of these; items are
    //placed into a grid layout in left to right, top to bottom order.

    String [] Symbols =
    {
        "1" , "2" , "3" , "+" ,
        "4" , "5" , "6" , "Clear" ,
        "7" , "8" , "9" , "Quit" ,
        "." , "0" , "="
    };

    //This is the constructor for the cash register.  The initialization takes
    //place by default in this method; it is called when the cash register object
    //is created.
    public cash()
    {
        super("Cash register"); //This initializes the parent of the cash register,
        //the frame.

        setLayout( new BorderLayout() ); //Sets the layout for the whole frame

        //The readout needs only to be added to the north (top) end of the
        //container.
        //It is created empty, and the layout manager will size it for us.
        Readout = new TextArea();
        add( "North" , Readout );

        //The panel will contain all the buttons and will be using a grid layout
        Panel buttonPanel = new Panel();
        buttonPanel.setLayout( new GridLayout( 4 , 3 ) );

        //create all the buttons from the array
        //note that they are added to the panel, and not to the frame.
```

```
        for( int a = 0 ; a < Symbols.length ; ++ a )
        {
            buttonPanel.add( new Button( Symbols[ a ] ) );
        }

        //add the panel( with all its buttons ) to the frame.
        add( "South" , buttonPanel );

        //resize the frame
        resize( 300 , 400 );

        //Now that the frame is done, show it!  This way the user did not see
        //everything being laid out.  Frames are invisible by default
        show();

        //Now we just leave the function.  The AWT will call out action functions
        //when the user has done something.
    }

//Add the current number to the sum.
//If the current is not a number, let the user know and zero out the current
//entry, allowing them to proceed.
void AddCurrent()
{
    try //the code here could throw an exception, which we need to catch,
        //regardless
    {
        Double d = new Double( Current ); //create a real number from our
                                          //string
        Readout.appendText( "\n" ); //insert a carrige
        Total += d.doubleValue();      //add the value to the current
    }
    catch( NumberFormatException e )
    {
        Readout.appendText( "bad entry\n" ); //let the user know she messed up
    }
    Current = ""; //In either case, start a fresh entry
}

//process the user actions
 public boolean action(Event event, Object arg)
{
    //handle quitting elegantly
    if ( arg.equals( "Quit" ) )
    {
        System.exit( 1 );
    }
    else if ( arg.equals( "Clear" ) ) //clear everthing
    {
        Readout.setText( "" );
        Current = "";
        Total = 0.0;
    }
    //add in the current, and show the total.
    //don't clear anything, because the user may want to add more.
    else if ( arg.equals( "=" ) )
    {
```

14

continues

Listing 14.2. continued

```
            AddCurrent();
            Readout.appendText( "---------\n" + Total + "\n" );
        }
        else if ( arg.equals( "+" ) )
        {
            AddCurrent();
            Readout.appendText( "\n" );
        }
        //otherwise, see if its one of our numerical buttons.  If so,
        //tack it into the display and the current accumulator
        else if ( arg instanceof String )
        {
            String str = (String) arg;
            int index = "0123456789.".indexOf( str );
            if ( index != -1 )
            {
                Current += str;
                Readout.appendText( str );
            }
        }
        return true;
    }

    //create this as an object for maximum flexibility.
    public static void main( String [] args )
    {
        new cash();
    }
}
```

Programs like this one will not turn you into the next Bill Gates, but they are good ways to learn the Java AWT.

Java Coffee Shop

Working in the Java motif, the setting of the next program is a Java coffee shop.

The coffee shop should allow the purchaser to do the following:

- Choose several varieties of coffee (for example, regular coffee, cappuccino, latté, and espresso).
- Customers should have a choice of several flavors (for example, chocolate and hazelnut, or regular coffee).
- Customers can choose a small, medium, or large serving.
- Patrons should be able to make special requests (for example, cream, cinnamon, or iced).

The first three choices—coffee type, flavor, and size—can be implemented as choice components. The special requests in the fourth item (cream, cinnamon, or iced) should be check boxes because the user can choose any combination of items from the list of special requests (for example, the customer choosing sugar or cream in her coffee). You will need a button to indicate that the choice has been made and a text area to display the completed order.

The completed program appears in Figure 14.16, and Listing 14.3 shows the source listing.

FIGURE 14.16.

The Java coffee shop.

Listing 14.3. The Coffee class.

```
/*
    A java coffee shop-- utilizing panels, frames, text areas,
    and other cool stuff.
 */


import java.awt.*;

public class coffee extends Frame
{

    Choice type , flavor , size;

    //This is a function to make construction of text boxes easier.
    //It also allows for more rapid modification of properties of several objects.

    Choice MakeChoices( String sbuf[] )
    {
        Choice c = new Choice();
        for( int a = 0 ; a < sbuf.length ; ++ a )
        {
            c.addItem( sbuf[ a ] );
        }
        return c;
    }
```

continues

Listing 14.3. continued

```
//The contents of all the text boxes.  Because they are
//grouped here, they are easy to modify in a consistent
//fashion.


//The types of coffee we have available

String [] types = { "Coffee" , "Latte" , "Mocha" ,
                    "Espresso" , "Cappucino" };


//The flavors of coffee

String [] flavors = { "Plain" , "Hazelnut" , "Amaretto" ,
                      "Almond" , "Chocolate" };


//and the sizes

String [] sizes = { "Small" , "Medium" , "Large" };



//This constructs the choice panel with the drop-down
//boxes that will allow the user to choose the
//kind, flavor, and size of the coffee

void MakeChoicePanel()
{
    Panel p = new Panel();
    type = MakeChoices( types );
    flavor = MakeChoices( flavors );
    size = MakeChoices( sizes );
    p.setLayout( new FlowLayout() );
    p.add( type );
    p.add( flavor );
    p.add( size );
    add( "North" , p );
}


 //these global check boxes will be set to the label of the
 //extra to which they refer.
 //They will be tested for boolean state later.

Checkbox iced , cream , cinnamon , chocolate;

//This function constructs the panel that contains the
//check boxes that represent the various
//coffee options we have available to us.
void MakeOptions()
{
    Panel p = new Panel();
    p.setLayout( new FlowLayout() );
    iced = new Checkbox( "Iced" );
    cream = new Checkbox( "With cream" );
    cinnamon = new Checkbox( "Cinnamon" );
```

```
        chocolate = new Checkbox( "Chocolate" );
        p.add( iced );
        p.add( cream );
        p.add( cinnamon );
        p.add( chocolate );
        add( "South" , p );
    }


    //The members of the ordering region; a text area,
    //and an ordering button.

    TextArea display;
    Button order;


    //Make the ordering panel.

    void MakeOrder()
    {
        Panel p = new Panel();
        p.setLayout( new BorderLayout() );
        display = new TextArea();
        p.add( "Center" , display );
        order = new Button( "Order" );
        p.add( "West" , order );
        add( "Center" , p );
    }


    //The constructor of this function sets up a few basic
    //window elements, build the panels,
    //shows the windows, and exits

    public coffee()
    {
        setTitle( "Java coffee shop" );
        resize( 400 , 300 );
        setLayout( new BorderLayout() );
        MakeChoicePanel();
        MakeOptions();
        MakeOrder();
        show();
    }


    //Handle the user actions--in this case,
    //just showing the order if the order button is pressed.

    public boolean action( Event e , Object o )
    {
        if ( e.target == order ) // if they are ordering coffee!
        {
            //Construct a string describing the order
            String desc = "Okay, you ordered a ";
            desc += size.getSelectedItem() + " ";
```

continues

Listing 14.3. continued

```
            desc += flavor.getSelectedItem() + " ";
            desc += type.getSelectedItem() + "\n";

            //now, consider all the extra stuff the customer
            //may have asked for.
            desc += "And you want that ";
            if ( iced.getState() == true )
            {
                desc += "iced ";
            }
            if ( cream.getState() == true )
            {
                desc += "with cream ";
            }
            if ( cinnamon.getState() == true )
            {
                desc += "with cinnamon";
            }
            if ( chocolate.getState() == true )
            {
                desc += " with chocolate";
            }
            //Add the current order to the display.
            display.appendText( desc + "\n" );
        }
        return true;
    }


    //build a new coffee ordering object.

    public static void main( String [] args )
    {
        new coffee();
    }
}
```

Note that this program demonstrates some new techniques. The constructor of the coffee object does not have sole responsibility for creating all the objects that comprise the coffee shop display. Instead, several helper functions each construct a portion of the display. This technique is important because the code to create the display is fairly complex, and the functions partition the functionality into easy-to-understand segments.

These functions use only a few variables that are global to the object. These global variables are needed so that the action() function can query them to generate its list of what kind of coffee the customer desires.

Note that you are somewhat limited in what you can do with the components. The program is functional, but it is not particularly visually appealing. Making it more attractive would be difficult without a great deal more manual effort. (Chapter 15, "GUI Development Using the Visual J++ Resource Wizard," explains how to create attractive visual interfaces using a more automated approach.)

Implementing Your Own Components: Image Buttons

For your final program, you will create a widget not available in the AWT.

The method for creating new widgets is by subclassing the Canvas class. The Canvas class creates an empty area that can be drawn on. It also receives messages concerning user activities in the area. To create a component, you need to subclass the Canvas class, draw in your component's image, and interpret the user's actions in the appropriate fashion.

The class you construct here is an image button. The image button will behave much like an ordinary button, but it will use an image in its display area instead of a text label. It will respond to user clicks by signaling the containing component that a click has occurred (see Listing 14.4).

Listing 14.4. The ImageButton class.

```
import java.awt.*;

class ImageButton extends Canvas
{
    Image image;
    Dimension ps;

    ImageButton( Image i , int x , int y )
    {
        image = i;
        ps = new Dimension( x , y );
    }

    //The paint function here is quite simple, but it
    //could be more complex.  There could be several
    //version in various states, depressed, active,
    //inactive, and other.
    public void paint( Graphics g )
    {
        if ( image != null )
        {
            g.drawImage( image , 0 , 0 ,
                    ps.width , ps.height , this );
        }
    }

    //The following two functions are 'dummies' here,
    //but they serve an important purpose.  They are
```

continues

Listing 14.4. continued

```
//called when th mouse enters and leaves the component.
//This could be useful to higlight the component
//when entered so as to alert the user for the
//potential for action.
public boolean mouseEnter( Event e , int x , int y )
{
    return true;
}

public boolean mouseExit( Event e , int x , int y )
{
    return true;
}

//This event does nothing here, but it could be
//used to switch to a 'pushed' version of the button
public boolean mouseDown( Event e , int x , int y )
{
    return true;
}

//Ahh.. Now the real work is done.  When the button
//is released, the parent is signaled a button press.


public boolean mouseUp( Event e , int x , int y )
{
    Event evt = new Event( this , Event.ACTION_EVENT , null );
    Container parent = getParent();
    parent.postEvent( evt );
    return true;
}

            //We need to tell the parent what size
            //that the button needs to be.  This
            //is determined upon construction.
    public Dimension preferredSize()
{
    return ps;
}

public Dimension minimumSize()
{
    return ps;
}
}

class Test extends Frame
{
    ImageButton ib;

    Test()
    {
        setTitle( "Image button test" );
        resize( 300 , 300 );
        Toolkit tk = Toolkit.getDefaultToolkit();
```

```
        Image jana = tk.getImage( "Jana2.jpg" );
        System.out.println( "I got " + jana );
        ib = new ImageButton( jana , 150 , 200 );
        setLayout( new FlowLayout() );
        add( ib );
        show();
    }

    public boolean action( Event e , Object o )
    {
        if ( e.target == ib )
        {
            System.out.println( " ->click!<-" );
        }
        return true;
    }

    public static void main( String [] args )
    {
        new Test();
    }
}
```

Figure 14.17 shows what the completed program should look like and gives the test readout.

FIGURE 14.17.

A Java image button.

14

AN INTRODUCTION
TO GUI
PROGRAMMING

Summary

With the information in this chapter you should be able to create forms by using the objects available in the AWT as well as creating your own controls. This approach is code centered. In Chapter 15 you will look at the merits of constructing controls in a form-centered way—that is, by drawing them into a forms designer that generates the code for you.

GUI Development Using the Visual J++ Resource Wizard

by David Hanley

IN THIS CHAPTER

In Chapter 14, "An Introduction to GUI Programming," you learned how to create graphical user interfaces in Java. You did so by creating and subclassing the AWT classes provided with the Java language. The chapter describes the classes available and includes sample programs to demonstrate how to piece together these components to create a functioning program.

You learned something else as well: Creating user interfaces manually is not easy. Creating even a simple interface takes quite a bit of code and is an error-prone endeavor. Also, looking at these user interfaces, you might be unsatisfied with their appearance. The user interfaces work, to be sure, but they are not as visually appealing as the interfaces that users have come to expect from professional programs. A user might pass up your Java program for a non-Java program with a slicker interface.

What is the reason for this design quality gap? Programmers in other, older languages have had access to tools with which they could *draw* the interfaces that they desired. A program would then save this drawing of the user interface in a format typically called a *resource file*. When the program was executing and the user interface was needed, it would be loaded from the disk and presented to the user.

These tools have not been available for Java because of the relative newness of the language, as well as the fact that resource files are typically platform specific. Resources created on, say, a Macintosh will not look good on a Windows machine, and vice versa.

Fortunately, Visual J++ solves this problem. Microsoft has leveraged its development tools for other languages and created a program that lets you draw the user interfaces you desire. Next a Java class that creates the window can be generated. Finally, the generated Java class can be added to the project and invoked to create the window.

This technique is much easier than laying out a window by hand. In addition, changing the layout is easy; instant feedback shows you how the modified layout will look. With Visual J++, an experienced graphic layout artist with no experience programming Java can design/redesign attractive forms for use in the program.

Of course, you will have to accept a few trade-offs. For example, you are limited to what has been provided for you to draw, so you cannot use the full flexibility of the AWT classes. However, you can play some "tricks" with the AWT, which you cannot do with the layout manager.

You cannot use the layout managers to make your designs adjust to the available window size, but if you lay out a window using the grid bag layout and then resize it, the components will adjust to the new window size. This type of flexibility is very important in Java because portable Java programs may run on a variety of platforms with varying resolutions and font sizes. On the whole, however, being able to draw the interfaces you want to use seems to be a good idea, and it is definitely a technique that the programmer should use.

Creating a Login Dialog

In this section you will learn how to create a login dialog that accepts a name and password to verify a user.

In the empty Visual J++ desktop, select File | New. *New* is a blanket term in this environment for creating new entities such as files, projects, and resources.

Visual J++ gives you the option of creating several kinds of files. Choose the option Resource Template from this list and click OK (see Figure 15.1).

FIGURE 15.1.

Creating a new resource.

When this operation is complete, you will see a resource template that resembles Figure 15.2.

FIGURE 15.2.

A blank Java resource template.

Select Insert and then Resource. You will see a list of resources (see Figure 15.3) that can be created and placed in the dialog. In this case you will be creating a dialog, so double-click this entry from the list.

The next window gives you an area on which to draw and a toolbar that presents the items (Java visual components) that you can draw onto the window. The combination of the two is collectively referred to as the *forms designer.* The forms designer will have already placed two buttons in the window (see Figure 15.4), but you can easily remove them or change their names.

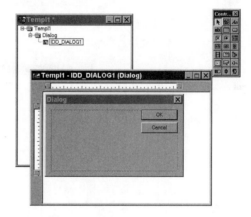

The area on which you can draw can be resized to the dimension that you want your dialog to occupy, both before and during construction of your interface. Try this now: Click on the lower-right corner of the gray window, hold down the mouse button, and move the mouse around. You can control the shape of the dialog.

Now try a few simple actions:

■ Double-click the OK button, and a pop-up window that lets you set pushbutton properties will appear. Click in the Caption text box and replace the word *OK* with *login.* Then close the Push Button Properties window. (See Figure 15.5.)

FIGURE 15.5.

Setting the properties of the button.

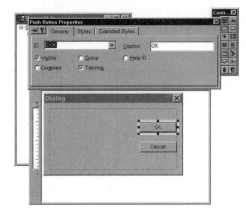

■ Click the new Login button and hold down the mouse button. Drag the Login button to the bottom of the window, toward the left, and leave it there. Similarly, drag the Cancel button to the bottom, but move it toward the right.

Your window should now resemble the window in Figure 15.6.

FIGURE 15.6.

The dialog box after the buttons are moved.

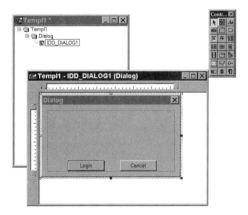

Now do the following to complete the creation of the dialog:

1. Select the Static text button, which appears in the upper-right corner of the toolbar in these figures (use the View | Toolbars menu selection and select controls to make the controls visible), and draw two labels along the left edge of the dialog, evenly spaced. The top label should contain the text User and the bottom one should contain the text Password. You can change the label by right-clicking the labels once they are

drawn and changing the contents of the Label field, or you can start typing the text for the new label, which will also bring up the Text Properties dialog box.

2. Select the text field (or edit box) tool and draw two text fields adjacent to these labels. The text fields should be quite wide but similar in height to their corresponding labels.

3. Double-click the bottom text field (the one associated with the Password label) and select Styles. Check the box labeled Password (see Figure 15.7).

FIGURE 15.7.

Changing the style properties of the Password text box.

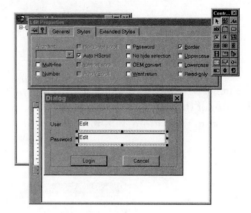

4. Click the switch icon in the lower-left corner of the screen.

Visual J++ will simulate your component actually executing. Your screen should look like Figure 15.8.

FIGURE 15.8.

A preview of your dialog box.

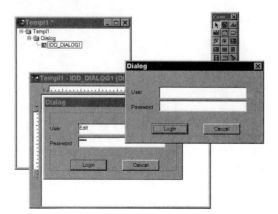

Now that you have designed your first dialog, let's quickly review some of the available components and their major settings available through the various design dialogs. For a complete discussion of these components, see Chapter 14.

Component Properties

You can change the behaviors of the components by setting their properties. For example, you make the text field associated with password display only asterisks when it is filled in by using the Edit Properties dialog. This makes the field suitable for entering passwords or other sensitive data.

Button Properties

Double-click on the Buttons icon to display the now-familiar Push Button Properties window. You can set a number of properties in this window, including

- `Visible`—This setting is on by default; if you turn off the `Visible` property, you can still see the button as you are designing it, but it will be invisible when the window is utilized.
- `Disabled`—A disabled button will be visible (though in a ghosted fashion to make clear its disabled state), but the user will not be able to interact with the button. This setting can be useful for dialog boxes in which certain options are not currently available, but might be available in other situations.

In the special properties section, you get the following properties:

- `Icon & Bitmap`—These settings allow you to use an image for the graphical display of the button. For example, an OK button might have a bitmap with OK in big letters and a check mark used for its image.
- `Client edge & Static edge`—These settings refer to edges that add a slightly different style to a button, drawing attention to a particular button or indicating how a group of buttons should be associated logically.

Text Field Properties

Text fields are the primary way users can enter text into the graphical display, and they have a number of settings.

A text field allows the user to input a single line of text. Here are some of its features:

■ AutoHScroll—If this option is enabled and the user types in more text than can fit in the text field, the text in the field will move to the left, making space for the user to type in more text. Later, the user can move through the text field with the arrow keys. If this option is disabled, once the cursor reaches the right edge of the text field, no more text can be entered. Therefore, disabling this setting might be useful when you want to limit the length of strings entered.

■ Password—When this option is enabled, text that is typed into the field will not be displayed. Rather, asterisks (or some other character) will be displayed to represent the characters the user has entered. This option prevents bystanders from observing the text of passwords as they are being entered.

■ Read Only—With this option enabled, the user cannot enter text into the text field. This option might be used to "lock" certain entries in place after some option has been picked or to achieve a desired visual effect.

■ Want Return—When this option is activated, an event will be sent to the target window when the Enter key is pressed inside this text field. This feature can be very desirable. For example, in a login menu, if the user presses Enter after entering the password, you would like to process the login request instead of forcing the user to click the OK button.

■ Uppercase & Lowercase—This setting changes text that is entered in a field into either uppercase or lowercase, despite what the user tries to enter.

Check Box and Radio Button Properties

Check boxes and radio buttons also have some important properties that can be set by the user.

A check box can be either on or off:

■ Left Text—This option places the text on the left of the component area, with the actual check box on the right. This arrangement is the inverse of the normal ordering of components.

■ Push-like—This gives a check box a button-like appearance, while preserving the semantics of a check box. Although the state is no longer explicitly displayed, you can change the label of the button to reflect its altered state.

■ Icon & Bitmap—These options allow images to be used for check box labels.

Combo Box Properties

You can also set the properties of combo boxes:

- Sort—If Sort is on, the entries of the combo box will be sorted. Sorting can help the user find a desired entry.
- Items—At drawing time, you can enter the list of items that the combo box will display.

List Boxes

List boxes, like combo boxes, allow the selection of selections, but they look different and offer more options:

- Selection—This option lets you choose between single and multiple. In the single-selection scheme, when an item is selected, any item that was previously selected becomes unselected. In the multiple-selection scheme, a new selection does not replace an old selection. Rather, you must click a selected item again to turn it off.
- Disable no scroll—When a list has more items than will fit in the list box, a scrollbar is formed to allow the user to move through the list. Normally, if the display area can accommodate the entire list, the scrollbar will go away. If this setting is selected, however, the scrollbar will not go away. You might want to use this setting when you have several list boxes with differing amounts of content and you want to maintain a uniform look. (They will not look the same if some have default scrollbars and others do not.) Also, having a scrollbar appear as a user is adding items to a list might not be what the user expects.

Static Text (Labels)

Although the user has no direct interaction with the static text, it is a critical component of the visual layout because it identifies the displayed components and guides the user:

- Sunken & Border—These settings change the appearance of labels, making them stand out more from the surrounding screen.
- Align text—The text that you enter can be left aligned, right aligned, or centered in the area that you have drawn.

Integrating Designed Forms into Applications

Now that you have had some experience designing forms and have learned some of the ways controls can be manipulated, you are ready to put the forms into your applications. Of course, you will need to write code to carry out the internal action of the program, and you will have to tie the code that you have written to the forms you have designed. Here is some sample code to get you started:

```
import java.awt.*;
class FormTest extends Frame
{
    FormTest()
    {
        show();
    }

    public static void main( String [] args )
    {
        new FormTest();
    }
}
```

First, create a Java application workspace and import this file into it. Compile and run it. Your display should resemble Figure 15.9.

FIGURE 15.9.

The results of the FormTest *code.*

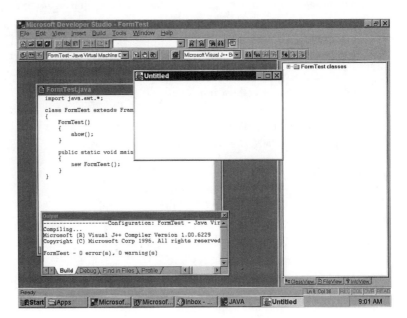

Now create a new resource template and save it into the same directory as the FormTest code example. Choose Insert and select Files into Project. When the file selection dialog box appears, select Files of resource type and pick the resource template you created.

Now that the resource template has been inserted into the project, you can design a form to insert into your program. Select your new resource template (the default name is Templ1; the actual name will be the one you used to save the resource template), click Insert on the top menu bar, and select Resource. When the resource selection comes up, choose Dialog. You will once again be presented with the dialog starting point. In this sample, you create a class registration dialog:

- The class registration should take a name and an ID number. By setting the ID number field's property to Password, you can prevent the actual ID from being displayed.

- Students should enter the appropriate class level and the term for which they are registering. These items should be implemented as choice components.

- Students should be able to enter special requests, such as desiring night classes or not minding intentional conflicts.

- The dialog box should contain a number of text fields in which students enter their desired class list.

Your dialog should resemble the dialog in Figure 15.10.

FIGURE 15.10.

How the student registration might look.

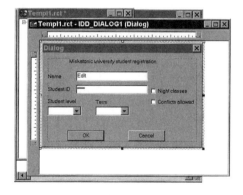

With experience and some practice, designing this screen will take only a few minutes. Creating this layout by hand would be very difficult and would have taken much longer.

The next step is to integrate the object into your program. Choose Tools and select Java Resource Wizard. Then select Browse, the template file you created, and Finish. The next dialog tells you that several files have been created.

Select Insert, choose Files into Project, and insert these files into the project. Now you have the files necessary to display the dialog you have drawn.

Integrating the Generated Classes

The job of integrating the code is not complete until you utilize the created classes.

The classes that Visual J++ creates are designed to interact with your classes, but they are not intended to be modified. This approach enables you, the programmer, to modify all your code without touching the generated code. Also, the code can be regenerated without interfering with the code that you have written. The downside is you have to write more code, but since the Resource Wizard already supplied you with dozens of lines of computer-designed code, you still come out ahead.

The class that the forms designer generates will look pretty much like the following:

```java
    import java.awt.*;
import DialogLayout;

public class IDD_DIALOG1
{
    Container    m_Parent       = null;
    boolean      m_fInitialized = false;
    DialogLayout m_Layout;

    // Control definitions
    //--------------------------------------------------------------------
    Button       IDOK;
    Button       IDCANCEL;
    Label        IDC_STATIC1;
    Label        IDC_STATIC2;
    Label        IDC_STATIC3;
    TextField    IDC_EDIT1;
    TextField    IDC_EDIT2;
    Checkbox     IDC_CHECK1;
    Checkbox     IDC_CHECK2;
    Label        IDC_STATIC4;
    Choice       IDC_COMBO1;
    Label        IDC_STATIC5;
    Choice       IDC_COMBO2;


    // Constructor
    //--------------------------------------------------------------------
    public IDD_DIALOG1 (Container parent)
    {
        m_Parent = parent;
    }

    // Initialization.
    //--------------------------------------------------------------------
    public boolean CreateControls()
    {
        // CreateControls should be called only once
        //----------------------------------------------------------------
        if (m_fInitialized || m_Parent == null)
            return false;
```

```
        // m_Parent must be extended from the Container class
        //---------------------------------------------------------------
        if (!(m_Parent instanceof Container))
            return false;

        // Since a given font may not be supported across all platforms, it
        // is safe to modify only the size of the font, not the typeface.
        //---------------------------------------------------------------
        Font OldFnt = m_Parent.getFont();
        if (OldFnt != null)
        {
            Font NewFnt = new Font(OldFnt.getName(), OldFnt.getStyle(), 8);

            m_Parent.setFont(NewFnt);
        }

        // All positions and sizes are in dialog logical
        // units, so we use a
        // DialogLayout as our layout manager.
        //---------------------------------------------------------------
        m_Layout = new DialogLayout(m_Parent, 217, 124);
        m_Parent.setLayout(m_Layout);
        m_Parent.addNotify();

        Dimension size   = m_Layout.getDialogSize();
        Insets     insets = m_Parent.insets();

        m_Parent.resize(insets.left + size.width  + insets.right,
                        insets.top  + size.height + insets.bottom);

        // Control creation
        //---------------------------------------------------------------
        IDOK = new Button ("OK");
        m_Parent.add(IDOK);
        m_Layout.setShape(IDOK, 34, 103, 50, 14);

        IDCANCEL = new Button ("Cancel");
        m_Parent.add(IDCANCEL);
        m_Layout.setShape(IDCANCEL, 117, 103, 50, 14);

        IDC_STATIC1 = new Label ("Name", Label.LEFT);
        m_Parent.add(IDC_STATIC1);
        m_Layout.setShape(IDC_STATIC1, 7, 27, 36, 12);

        IDC_STATIC2 = new Label ("Miskatonic university student registration.",
Label.LEFT);
        m_Parent.add(IDC_STATIC2);
        m_Layout.setShape(IDC_STATIC2, 36, 7, 142, 13);

        IDC_STATIC3 = new Label ("Student ID", Label.LEFT);
        m_Parent.add(IDC_STATIC3);
        m_Layout.setShape(IDC_STATIC3, 7, 44, 32, 12);
```

```
IDC_EDIT1 = new TextField ("");
m_Parent.add(IDC_EDIT1);
m_Layout.setShape(IDC_EDIT1, 45, 24, 99, 14);

IDC_EDIT2 = new TextField ("");
m_Parent.add(IDC_EDIT2);
m_Layout.setShape(IDC_EDIT2, 45, 42, 99, 13);

IDC_CHECK1 = new Checkbox ("Night classes");
m_Parent.add(IDC_CHECK1);
m_Layout.setShape(IDC_CHECK1, 148, 45, 55, 11);

IDC_CHECK2 = new Checkbox ("Conflicts allowed");
m_Parent.add(IDC_CHECK2);
m_Layout.setShape(IDC_CHECK2, 148, 58, 62, 14);

IDC_STATIC4 = new Label ("Special selections", Label.LEFT);
m_Parent.add(IDC_STATIC4);
m_Layout.setShape(IDC_STATIC4, 153, 35, 57, 8);

IDC_COMBO1 = new Choice ();
m_Parent.add(IDC_COMBO1);
m_Layout.setShape(IDC_COMBO1, 7, 71, 46, 12);

IDC_STATIC5 = new Label ("Student level", Label.LEFT);
m_Parent.add(IDC_STATIC5);
m_Layout.setShape(IDC_STATIC5, 7, 60, 45, 10);

IDC_COMBO2 = new Choice ();
m_Parent.add(IDC_COMBO2);
m_Layout.setShape(IDC_COMBO2, 72, 71, 46, 12);

m_fInitialized = true;
return true;
    }
}
```

You can learn a few things by looking at this class:

- You must pass the handle of a container to this class. The constructed components and attributes are then applied to this parent container.
- Simply constructing this object does nothing for the parent; you must call CreateControls() to actually insert the controls into the parent.
- This class utilizes a standard class named DialogLayout. In this particular framework, DialogLayout can be shared among several dialog components. You must also include DialogLayout in any distribution of your code. DialogLayout is a standard class that is included in Visual J++.

The next step is to modify the frame class to construct the dialog creation object that has been written for you and to call its `CreateControls()` method. The constructor function should now look like the following:

```
IDD_Dialog builder;
    FormTest()
    {
        setFont( new Font( "Helvetica" , Font.PLAIN , 18 ) );
        builder = new IDD_DIALOG1( this );
        builder.CreateControls();
        show();
    }
```

`setFont` is required because all the measurements in the J++-generated `IDD_DIALOG` class are based on font size. If there is no font, there will be a lot of dividing by zero errors. Compilers hate that and will make your life miserable until you fix it. You also need to note that no matter how large you make the font, the Resource Wizard–generated code will set it back to 8, as shown in the following excerpt from `IDD_DIALOG1`:

```
Font OldFnt = m_Parent.getFont();
    if (OldFnt != null)
    {
        Font NewFnt = new Font(OldFnt.getName(), OldFnt.getStyle(), 8);
        m_Parent.setFont(NewFnt);
    }
```

This has the effect of resetting the size of any font you have set to 8. This might be a good place to violate the rule about changing the generated source code if you need larger fonts.

Upon executing this code you should see the dialog in Figure 15.11.

FIGURE 15.11.

The registration program executing.

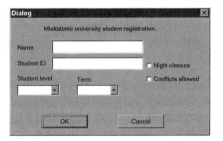

Although you have now created the desired visual display, you can't interact with it yet. You can use the paradigm introduced in Chapter 14, testing the target of the action method against the handles you have to the objects. However, you need to access these widgets through the handle to the IDD_DIALOG object, which is, incidentally, why you made this object global to your function. You should also fill up the choice boxes you created. After making these modifications, your program should look like the following:

```java
import java.awt.*;

//
// This program is a test of the classes you
// can create with the forms designer and
// an example of how you can interact with them.
//
class FormTest extends Frame
{
    IDD_DIALOG1 builder;

    FormTest()
    {
        setFont( new Font( "Helvetica" , Font.PLAIN , 18 ) );
        builder = new IDD_DIALOG1( this );
        builder.CreateControls();

        //
        //fill the class levels into the combo boxes
        //
        builder.IDC_COMBO1.addItem( "Freshman" );
        builder.IDC_COMBO1.addItem( "Sophmore" );
        builder.IDC_COMBO1.addItem( "Junior" );
        builder.IDC_COMBO1.addItem( "Senior" );
        builder.IDC_COMBO1.addItem( "Graduate" );

        //
        //fill the terms into the combo boxes
        //
        builder.IDC_COMBO2.addItem( "Winter" );
        builder.IDC_COMBO2.addItem( "Fall" );
        builder.IDC_COMBO2.addItem( "Summer (ugh)" );

        //
        // Now that you're done, show the window.
        //

        show();
    }

    //
    // create the object.
    //

    public static void main( String [] args )
    {
        new FormTest();
    }

    //
    // This is a dummy object that does nothing now,
```

```
    // but might be filled in to look in the database
    // and register the student into the classes
    // if available.  Along the way, it might open
    // more dialog boxes that would be created
    // with the forms designer.
    //
    void RegisterStudent( String name , String id ,
        String level , String term ,
        boolean night_ok , boolean conflict_ok )
    {
    }


    //
    //This handles the button clicks.  In the
    //case of the 'ok' button being clicked, it
    //pulls out the information filled into the
    //fields and passes it to a registration
    //method.
    //

    public boolean action( Event e , Object o )
    {
        if ( e.target == builder.IDOK )
        {
            RegisterStudent(
                builder.IDC_EDIT1.getText() ,
                builder.IDC_EDIT2.getText() ,
                builder.IDC_COMBO1.getSelectedItem() ,
                builder.IDC_COMBO2.getSelectedItem() ,
                builder.IDC_CHECK1.getState() ,
                builder.IDC_CHECK1.getState()
            );
            dispose();
        }

        //
        // In thic case, the window just goes away.
        //
        if ( e.target == builder.IDCANCEL )
        {
            dispose();
        }
        return true;
    }
}
```

A Side-by-Side Comparison

Let's compare the interface of one of the fairly unattractive programs from the last chapter—the coffee shop program—to a program that you create in the forms builder. This section explains in broad terms how to redesign the interface from the coffee shop example.

One extra trick—changing the IDs of the controls you create to names that describe their functions—makes the programming task easier. The IDs from the last program were hard to remember, and their functions are not obvious from looking at the code. The way to make this
modification is to change the ID property of the component (see Figure 15.12).

FIGURE 15.12.

*Setting the properties of
elements of the coffee
shop.*

You can see the redesigned form in Figure 15.13. Note how much cleaner it is than the original Java coffee shop form in Chapter 14.

FIGURE 15.13.

The coffee shop.

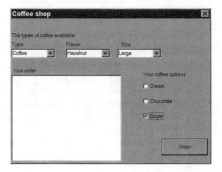

Summary

This chapter examines the tools that Visual J++ provides to the programmer to automate the
creation of graphical user interfaces for Java programs. You have seen the advantages of creating an interface using the Resource Wizard as opposed to hand building the required Java.

III

PART

The Foundation for Visual J++: The Component Object Model

Java and the Component Object Model

by Bryan Morgan

IN THIS CHAPTER

CHAPTER 16

Perhaps the most heavily discussed feature of Microsoft's Internet strategy is a group of technologies collectively referred to as ActiveX. Microsoft introduced this related set of existing and future technologies to allow developers and users to extend their current tools for use across the Internet. For example, although developers once wrote OLE controls for use in building Windows applications, with a few changes these controls can now be downloaded from a Web server and can be displayed and manipulated within a Web browser. Like most other technologies, ActiveX has a well-documented set of advantages and disadvantages. Many developers who have examined ActiveX have concluded that its disadvantages outweigh its advantages, and therefore they have sworn off using it. Other developers with a lot of time and money already invested in ActiveX (through COM and OLE2) plan to make extensive use of its components.

As has been mentioned throughout this book, Visual J++ and the Microsoft Java Virtual Machine (JVM) allow developers to call ActiveX objects (and, in a larger sense, any COM object). COM objects can even be written in Java, compiled by Visual J++, and then called and used within any other Windows application. This versatility opens an entirely new world to Java programmers and raises the Java language to first-class status in the Windows programming world.

The purpose of this chapter is to provide an overview of both COM in general and the capabilities and tools provided with Visual J++. This chapter thoroughly introduces the component object model (COM) and explains its standard capabilities and uses. (The rest of this section of the book discusses Java and the COM in great detail.) In addition, the relative advantages and disadvantages of the COM (and therefore ActiveX) are discussed in detail. (Determining whether the advantages of the COM outweigh the disadvantages is left to the reader.)

Although the classes and tools that come with Visual J++ insulate the user from delving into the COM "plumbing" beneath the surface, good programmers usually understand the foundations of technologies they are working with. Experienced developers know that although GUI environments and class libraries shelter the developer from having to deal with many low-level technical issues, any large development project will invariably require them to get under the hood once in awhile. By the end of this chapter, you will know enough about the COM to visualize what is going on "behind the scenes" in the Microsoft JVM.

An Overview of COM

COM provides a mechanism for software objects, written in any language and running on any platform, to intercommunicate and exchange information. However, because of the heavy marketing behind Microsoft's OLE technologies, until recently most developers almost completely ignored COM.

COM was passed over because it offers no concrete "features" that developers can use within applications, such as GUI components or structured storage mechanisms. OLE 2.0, meanwhile, introduced a number of capabilities that Windows application developers could reuse immediately. On the other hand, COM only defines the *hows* and *whys* of how objects can communicate and be used together. In no way does COM actually specify *what* these objects are supposed to do. (That task is left to the developer!)

To borrow from object-oriented terminology, COM is the *superclass,* or parent, of OLE. OLE defines a large number of objects that possess certain behaviors such as structured storage, drag-and-drop of objects, and monikers. The underlying COM controls the way in which these objects are created and used within an application.

COM is both parts: specification *and* implementation. The COM specification describes, in detail, how component objects are to be created and referenced as well as what characteristics these objects should have. This specification was designed to apply generally to any object-oriented system running on any platform. (In other words, the specification is not a Windows-only specification.) Therefore, if you were an enterprising sort of developer with a lot of time and resources available, Microsoft would be perfectly happy to provide you with assistance in turning the COM specification into an actual implementation for, say, the Apple Macintosh.

The COM implementation is only available for the Windows platform. To verify that your Windows system is indeed "COM aware," do a quick search for the COMPOBJ.DLL file. Within this DLL is a group of functions commonly referred to as the COM Applications Programming Interface, or the COM API. In general, each of these functions begins with the letters *Co* (such as CoCreateInstance(), CoInitialize(), or CoRegisterClassObject()). Keep in mind, however, that at the current time, this implementation of COM exists only for the Windows platform. Heavy work is underway to introduce versions for the UNIX and Macintosh platforms by early 1997.

Identifying COM Objects

COM objects are registered with the system and are given a globally unique identifier (GUID, or CLSID as it is commonly called). Microsoft chose to use the distributed computing environment (DCE) UUID (universally unique ID) algorithm to generate IDs for COM objects. This algorithm uses a combination of a machine's network address, the current date, and the current time to generate a 16-byte identification number. (For developers who are still paranoid about the "uniqueness" of this ID, Microsoft maintains a registry of official CLSIDs and will even generate one for you.) This ID is a 128-bit number and is guaranteed to be unique. Identifying objects in this way frees the programmer from hard-coding library and function ordinals into the source code. Later in this chapter, you will see how to use the JAVAREG tool to generate these CLSIDs for COM objects created in Java.

> **NOTE**
>
> If you are currently using a computer with a Windows operating system, you can examine the Windows Registry to determine the CLSIDs of COM objects. Under Windows 95, run the REGEDIT.EXE program. Under Windows NT, run REGEDT32.EXE. Doing a search for CLSID will locate all of the currently registered objects on your system (or under Windows 95, locate the MY COMPUTER\HKEY_CLASSES_ROOT\CLSID key). As an example, the ActiveMovie control object's CLSID is {05589FA1-C356-11CE-BF01-00AA0055595A}. A Microsoft Word 6 object's CLSID is {00020901-0000-0000-C000-000000000046}.

Programmers familiar with dynamic link libraries (DLLs) in Windows should recall that a function's ordinal number within both a library *and* the library name is indeed hard-coded into the calling application. If the library is ever modified or if a DLL with a duplicate name is copied onto your system, your application will no longer work correctly. COM provides a layer of indirection and additional capabilities to ensure that this problem never occurs. COM objects are referenced by their CLSID numbers and can be queried to determine what features they support. If an older version of a COM object exists on the system (or the COM object does not exist at all!), the application can exit gracefully or prompt the user without crashing. In addition, through the use of distributed COM (DCOM) that is currently available under Windows NT 4.0, COM objects can be located on remote machines as well. Using DCOM, COM objects are communicated with via a remote procedure call (RPC) mechanism. (DCOM is discussed in more detail in Chapter 24, "Distributed Component Object Model.")

COM Interfaces

To understand how COM objects interoperate, you first need to understand the concept of an *interface*. As is the case with the Java language, an interface in COM is simply a related group of methods. Interfaces can inherit from other interfaces to produce added capabilities while reusing existing code. All COM objects must implement at least one interface: IUnknown.

> **NOTE**
>
> By convention, all COM interface names start with the letter I, for example, IUnknown, IClassFactory, and IOleObject. This naming convention allows developers to quickly find interfaces within source code.

The IUnknown interface is discussed in more detail later in the chapter. For now, you just need to know that this interface defines three methods (QueryInterface(), AddRef(), and Release())

that must be implemented by *every* COM object. These methods are responsible for the following:

- Retrieving other interfaces from an object (besides the IUnknown interface)
- Tracking the usage count of an object

A COM object can be accessed only via the set of interfaces that it implements. Because ActiveX controls are COM objects, all ActiveX controls, at a minimum, implement the IUnknown interface. To get at other capabilities supported by the ActiveX control, the IUnknown.QueryInterface() method is called to retrieve other interfaces within the control. Consequently, no method within an object can ever be called without first retrieving a proper interface from the object that contains the method. Conversely, objects can be queried to determine if they support certain interfaces. (As is the case with Java, if a COM object implements an interface, it agrees to implement all the methods within that interface.)

Tracking Reference Counts

Once an interface to an object has been obtained, the interface's methods can be called like any other object method. Each COM object is responsible for tracking the number of users it currently has. As each user of the object finishes using that object's interfaces, the user count is decremented. When the count goes to zero, the COM object is then responsible for freeing itself from memory. This method of memory management removes the burden from the user of the object and forces the object to be responsible for creating and freeing itself from memory. If two objects are dependent on each other (and therefore their reference count never goes to zero), each object will terminate itself when the application using these objects shuts down.

COM Is Not Necessarily OLE

Once again, it is imperative to stress that using COM does not necessarily imply the use of OLE *or* ActiveX within an application. Because many users associate COM with inserting spreadsheets into word processing documents (or other common OLE tasks such as Automation), many developers have become confused over what COM actually is. In short, COM in no way specifies any user interface standards or operating system components. It is simply a specification that defines how objects are registered on a system and how these objects can be incorporated together to build applications. Each COM object is referenced through the use of interfaces and can be written in virtually any programming language. OLE/ActiveX derives from COM in that each ActiveX technology is essentially an implementation of a set of COM interfaces. For instance, OLE controls implement the IUnknown interface as well as a set of interfaces that allow the object to be added to a toolbar or manipulated at design time. As explained in the next section, the Java language is ideally suited for the creation and use of COM objects.

Comparing Java and COM

When Java was initially introduced in 1995, many pundits predicted the imminent fall of Microsoft from its position of market dominance. Others pointed to Microsoft's reluctance to license Java as a sign that Microsoft was indeed threatened by the technology and hoped to simply kill it by refusing to support it. Perhaps the first sign that Java would indeed be successful was when Microsoft agreed to add Java support to the Internet Explorer browser. Additional negotiations eventually led Microsoft to agree to provide the Windows platform reference implementation of the JVM.

Although one can argue that the "networked" nature of Java (and its related component architecture, Java Beans) threatens companies such as Microsoft, which rely largely on the success of the desktop computing market, Microsoft is interested in Java for reasons other than its ability to run code within a Web browser. Microsoft's interest is primarily a result of the synergy between the Java programming language and COM. Because of the excellent fit between Java and COM, Microsoft is presenting Java as a top-notch Windows development language.

> **NOTE**
>
> Although Internet Explorer 3.0 does support the use of Java applets, Microsoft is clearly pushing its own ActiveX controls as *the* tools for supplying active Web content. Because ActiveX controls have complete access to the underlying operating system, they do have some advantages over Java applets. However, these access privileges bring up a number of security and portability concerns that worry many developers. This section of the book does not attempt to answer or defend any of the praise/criticism directed at COM or ActiveX. Instead, the capabilities of Visual J++ will be presented in an objective manner so that you can decide which product is most suitable for your development project.

The two biggest features that allow Java to be used almost seamlessly with COM are

- Class support for multiple interfaces
- Runtime garbage collection

As mentioned earlier, COM objects are defined by which interfaces they implement. In fact, each object is accessed using these interfaces. Although other programming languages are forced to use more difficult pointer notation to access interface tables within an object, the Java language supports the notion of interfaces directly. The following example illustrates the creation of a new COM object in C++ versus that same object being created in Java.

Java and the Component Object Model

CHAPTER 16

381

16

JAVA AND THE
COMPONENT
OBJECT MODEL

In C++:

```
ISurfaceArea pArea;
CoCreateInstance(CLSID_SURFACEAREA, NULL, CLSCTX_SERVER, IID_ISurfaceArea,
    (void**)&pArea );
x=pArea->Calculate();
.
.
.
```

In Java:

```
ISurfaceArea Area = (ISurfaceArea)new SurfaceArea();
x=Area.Calculate();
```

In the case of the C++ example, the COM API function `CoCreateInstance()` is used to retrieve the `ISurfaceArea` interface. This interface is treated as a pointer to another pointer within C++. This syntax becomes fairly cumbersome over the course of an entire program and results in COM API functions being called to instantiate each COM interface.

For programmers who have ever written a line of Java code *or* a line of COM code, the Java statement should be somewhat exciting. For Java programmers, the standard new operator is used to call the `SurfaceArea()` constructor. This line of code is completely indistinguishable from any other Java construction statement. No special syntax or function calls are required thanks to the magic of the Microsoft JVM and the Visual J++ Type Library Wizard (discussed later in this chapter). For COM programmers, this method of retrieving a COM interface is much cleaner and more elegant than traditional methods in C or C++.

Programmers who write in C/C++ must be careful to free all memory that has been allocated when it is no longer used. If memory is not deallocated appropriately, the program could eventually exhaust all of the system memory resources. Meanwhile, recall that programmers can use a variety of garbage collection strategies to dynamically free Java objects at runtime once these objects are no longer being used. This memory management scheme removes the burden from the individual programmer and places the burden on the system garbage collector.

Coincidentally, COM objects are responsible for freeing themselves from memory when they are no longer being used. This similarity enables the Java garbage collector to monitor an object's usage status. When an object is no longer in use, the COM object will free itself from memory as it is supposed to. The difference between Java and C++, for instance, is that this reference counting is completely transparent to the Java programmer. Although the C++ programmer is forced to call the `AddRef` and `Release` methods in the `IUnknown` interface, the Java programmer must simply call the object's constructor. The Microsoft JVM will release the object at the correct time thanks to the Java runtime garbage collection capabilities.

Table 16.1 compares COM and Java, pointing out relevant similarities and differences.

Table 16.1. A comparison of COM and Java.

COM	Java
Uses interfaces to define object protocols.	Uses interfaces to define object protocols.
Binary objects stored in files that can be accessed across a network.	Bytecode objects stored in files that can be accessed across a network.
Each object must support the IUnknown interface at a minimum.	Objects may implement 0 or more interfaces.
Objects can be written in any language.	Objects can be written in the Java language, accessed via native methods, or can be referenced via COM.
Reference counting is used for runtime memory management.	Garbage collection is used for runtime memory management.
Interfaces are grouped within classes.	Interfaces are grouped within classes.
Objects are located and created dynamically at runtime.	Objects are located and created dynamically at runtime.
Objects can be queried to retrieve implemented interfaces.	Objects can be typecast to retrieve implemented interfaces.
Currently platform dependent (Windows only).	Platform independent (requires existence of JVM).
Type library files contain class and interface definitions.	Class files contain class and interface definitions.

As you can see from examining Table 16.1, Java and COM have many things in common. In fact, COM objects appear to be identical to Java objects within Java source code. Although a number of additional events must be accomplished outside of the source code (such as register-ing a COM object, importing a type library), the designers of the Microsoft JVM and Visual J++ deserve some praise for providing Java developers with a truly clean interface to the COM.

Object-Oriented Programming and COM

In addition to sharing some key features with Java, COM is also an object-oriented framework that supports object reuse. You will recall (from Chapter 3, "Object-Oriented Programming with Java") that three key components of an object-oriented programming language are

- Encapsulation
- Polymorphism
- Inheritance

COM fully supports encapsulation through the use of interfaces. All functionality provided by a class is accessed through one of the class's implemented interfaces. All data variables within a class are not visible to the calling application. Instead, this data must be accessed through the use of interface access methods. (You may also remember from Chapter 3 that this method was the preferred means of data access in object-oriented design.) The interface access method of data hiding is the equivalent of making all data members `private` to Java and C++ programmers.

COM objects are also polymorphic. For example, assume that two or more interfaces within a class are derived from a single interface, `IUnknown`. (In fact, all interfaces in COM are required to derive from `IUnknown`!) Once this derivation has been set up, all member functions available in `IUnknown` are also members of all of its derived classes. A parallel can also be drawn for different objects that implement duplicate sets of interfaces. All of these objects are then polymorphic; that is, each object will contain a known set of member methods.

COM has received some criticism from object-oriented purists over the years for not fully supporting inheritance. Although it is true that inside an object a COM interface can inherit from another interface using *language* inheritance (such as is supported in C++ and Java), binary COM objects cannot inherit from one another. In other words, COM does not support *object* inheritance. (Other object models such as CORBA and OpenDoc do support object inheritance.)

Microsoft's reasoning behind this decision is perfectly credible. In its view, COM objects are for use by end users and developers. Because a COM object could have been developed by vendor X and then distributed as part of the operating system, an extremely unstable environment could result when vendor Y decides to override one of the methods within vendor X's object. Unless vendor Y has specific knowledge of the internal workings of vendor X's object (through source code or personal contact), he or she can never be completely sure that overriding vendor X's functionality will cause no problems. On a large-scale basis when hundreds or even thousands of objects are installed on a server operating system, such uncertain behavior could quickly lead to an unreliable environment. In summary, although the designers of COM fully support the notion of inheritance while building an object (using languages such as C++ or Java), their design decision was that the end user of these objects is not really concerned with inheriting from it or overriding certain aspects of the object.

COM objects do support the concept of object/code reuse through the notion of *aggregation*. This topic is discussed later in the chapter. The following section discusses some of the terminology associated with COM that may be unfamiliar to novice COM/Java developers.

Understanding COM Terminology

All Java programs currently consist of one or more class files (denoted by the `.class` file extension). In the near future, programmers will also be able to create binary executable files (using later releases of Visual J++ and other compilers). Java programs are divided into two primary categories: *applets* and *applications*.

> **NOTE**
>
> By now, you should be very familiar with the differences between these two types of Java programs. For more information, see Chapter 8, "Developing Applets and Applications."

The Java applet runs within a Web browser and is therefore *contained* by that Web browser. The applet *serves* its contents to the browser and is displayed to the user via some hidden hooks implemented within the browser. Java applications are similar to applets except for the fact that they run without the aid of a browser. If applets are servers within a container object, then Java applications can be thought of as standalone servers.

The COM uses similar terminology to describe different types of objects. These objects are outlined in Table 16.2.

Table 16.2. COM object-naming conventions.

Name	Description
Container	An object that can contain other COM objects. An example of a COM container is Internet Explorer 3.0.
Server	An object that implements interfaces and exposes them to other objects.
In-Process server	An object server that is implemented within a DLL.
EXE server	An object server that is implemented in an EXE.
Object handler	An in-process server that provides a partial implementation of an object. Most often used for redistribution purposes that do not require editing features.

Another noteworthy feature is that an object can be both a container and a server. For instance, a Microsoft Word document object can contain other COM objects, making Microsoft Word a Container application. Microsoft Word also exposes a number of COM objects for use in other applications (spell checker, mail merge, art, and so on); therefore, Word is also an EXE server. Many ActiveX/OLE controls come in two varieties: in-process servers and object handlers. The in-process server version is for use at design time to set properties and add method handlers. For distribution purposes, a smaller, more efficient version is provided that implements no design-time interfaces.

Using COM Objects

This section discusses the responsibilities of COM objects and the different ways in which they can be used. Keep in mind that many of these details are hidden from the Visual J++ developer thanks to the Visual J++ class library and the Windows JVM. Nevertheless, you should understand what is going on beneath the surface to truly appreciate how COM works.

Each application that uses or creates a new COM object must, at a minimum, initialize and uninitialize the component object library implementation before attempting to access any COM functionality. The COM API provides two methods for doing so: `CoInitialize()` and `CoUninitialize()`.

`CoInitialize()` accepts a pointer to an `IMalloc` interface, although this value can be null if you decide to use the default memory allocator supplied by the COM implementation. Calling `CoInitialize()` will ensure that the `COMPOBJ.DLL` library is loaded along with any additional libraries required to access COM objects. Although calling this method with a `NULL` parameter is perfectly valid, an `IMalloc` interface can be passed should you wish to override the default memory allocation implementation. The `IMalloc` interface defines the following methods:

- `Alloc()`
- `Realloc()`
- `Free()`
- `GetSize()`
- `DidAlloc()`
- `HeapMinimize()`

These methods correspond to normal memory allocation functions found in the Windows API, but in this case they are encapsulated within a COM interface.

`CoUninitialize()` unloads all COM DLLs that were loaded during the course of an application's execution. In addition to other internal functions, this method also calls the `CoFreeAllLibraries()` COM API function in order to unload all COM DLLs from memory.

Dynamically Creating New COM Objects

COM objects, like Java classes, are created and linked at runtime by a calling application. The COM API provides the `CoCreateInstance()` function in order to create an object at runtime. This function accepts a CLSID as input and uses this CLSID to locate the COM object on the local or remote machine. The C calling syntax for the `CoCreateInstance()` function is as follows:

```
HRESULT CoCreateInstance(REFIID clsid, LPUNKNOWN pUnknown, DWORD context,
  REFIID interface_id, LPVOID FAR *iface);
```

Taken individually, these parameters represent the following information:

- `clsid`—The CLSID of the object to be created.
- `pUnknown`—A pointer to the aggregate controlling unknown.
- `context`—Identifies the context in which the object will run. Can be `CLSCTX_LOCAL_SERVER`, `CLSCTX_INPROC_SERVER`, or `CLSCTX_INPROC_HANDLER` (as well as several others).
- `interface_id`—The IID of the interface instance to be created.
- `iface`—A pointer to a memory location that stores the interface pointer.

When the `CoCreateInstance()` function is called, the Registry is searched to determine which object will be created. When this object is located, `CoCreateInstance()` internally retrieves an `IClassFactory` interface from the object. An `IClassFactory` interface is functionally equivalent to a Java class constructor. This interface supplies two methods, `CreateInstance()` and `LockServer()`, which can be used to dynamically create an object and then force that object to stay in memory.

The `CoCreateInstance()` function works fine if you are certain of two things:

1. The object's CLSID
2. The interfaces implemented by that object

Assuming that you know these two things and can retrieve an interface from an object using the `CoCreateInstance()` method, how can you access other interfaces within that object without first shutting down the object and continually calling `CoCreateInstance()` each time you want another interface? The answer lies within the `IUnknown` interface!

The `IUnknown` Interface

Earlier in the chapter, I mentioned that *all* COM objects, at a minimum, must implement the `IUnknown` interface. This interface defines three key methods that supply the fundamental operations common to all COM objects. These three methods are explained in Table 16.3.

Java and the Component Object Model

CHAPTER 16

387

16

JAVA AND THE
COMPONENT
OBJECT MODEL

Table 16.3. The IUnknown interface methods.

Method Name	Purpose
QueryInterface	Accepts a requested interface and returns that interface if it exists within the object
AddRef	Increments the object's reference count (for memory management purposes)
Release	Decrements the object's reference count and frees the object when the count equals zero

The key method in this group is the QueryInterface() method. Because all COM interfaces inherit from the IUnknown interface, once any interface pointer is obtained via a call to CoCreateInstance(), the QueryInterface() method can be called to determine what other interfaces the object supports. (In fact, the IID_IUnknown interface ID itself can be passed directly to CoCreateInstance() if the user wants to return an IUnknown interface directly.) The QueryInterface() method actually does double duty because, if an interface does exist that is the type asked for by the caller, that interface will be returned directly to the calling program. (The AddRef() method will also be automatically called to increment the object's reference count.)

By using the QueryInterface() method, applications can gracefully handle unsupported features in COM objects. In addition, as the system is updated with more capable objects, applications can be written to immediately take advantage of them. COM's use of interfaces as the means of access to an object's capabilities prevents any attempts to access nonexistent features within an object.

The C calling syntax for the QueryInterface() method is as follows:

```
HRESULT QueryInterface(REFIID interface_id, LPVOID FAR *iface);
```

As you can see, the QueryInterface() method accepts an interface ID (IID) and a "pointer to a pointer" that will contain the interface pointer if it exists. Like the CoCreateInstance() method, QueryInterface() returns an HRESULT value. Table 16.4 lists some of the valid values for an HRESULT return value.

Table 16.4. Valid HRESULT values and meanings.

HRESULT Value	Meaning
E_UNEXPECTED	Unexpected failure
E_NOTIMPL	Not implemented
E_OUTOFMEMORY	Ran out of memory

continues

Table 16.4. continued

HRESULT *Value*	*Meaning*
E_INVALIDARG	One or more arguments are invalid
E_NOINTERFACE	No such interface supported
E_POINTER	Invalid pointer
E_HANDLE	Invalid handle
E_ABORT	Operation aborted
E_FAIL	Unspecified error
E_ACCESSDENIED	General access denied error
E_NOTIMPL	Not implemented
DISP_E_UNKNOWNINTERFACE	Unknown interface
DISP_E_MEMBERNOTFOUND	Member not found
DISP_E_PARAMNOTFOUND	Parameter not found
DISP_E_TYPEMISMATCH	Type mismatch
DISP_E_UNKNOWNNAME	Unknown name
DISP_E_NONAMEDARGS	No named arguments
DISP_E_BADVARTYPE	Bad variable type
DISP_E_EXCEPTION	Exception occurred
DISP_E_OVERFLOW	Out of present range
DISP_E_BADINDEX	Invalid index
DISP_E_UNKNOWNLCID	Memory is locked
DISP_E_ARRAYISLOCKED	Memory is locked
DISP_E_BADPARAMCOUNT	Invalid number of parameters
DISP_E_PARAMNOTOPTIONAL	Parameter not optional
DISP_E_BADCALLEE	Invalid callee
DISP_E_NOTACOLLECTION	Does not support a collection

As you will see in Chapter 17, "Encapsulating COM with the Visual J++ Class Library," these HRESULT values are provided for the Visual J++ programmer in the com.ms.com.ComFailException Java class.

Java and the Component Object Model

CHAPTER 16

389

16

JAVA AND THE
COMPONENT
OBJECT MODEL

Retrieving Interfaces

To summarize, each application must at some level go through the following C++ language steps to initialize and use COM objects:

```
HRESULT retValue = CoInitialize(NULL);
if (retValue == S_OK) then
{
  CoCreateInstance(CLSID_SOMEAPP, NULL, CLSCTX_LOCAL_SERVER, IID_IUnknown,
    (void**)&pIUnknown);

  retValue = pIUnknown->QueryInterface(IID_SOMEINTERFACE,
    (void**)&pISomeInterface);
  if (retValue == S_OK) then
  {
    pISomeInterface->Method1();
    pISomeInterface->Method2();

    /* When finished with the interface, call its Release() method! */
    pISomeInterface->Release();
  }
  else
  {
    /* Perform some default operation */
    DisableMenuItem(InterfaceMenu);
  }

  CoUninitialize();
}
```

COM does not have a way to return a list of the interfaces supported by an object. The only real reason to return such a list is to display some sort of interface list to the user (which is not an extremely useful function). Otherwise, if you know that a specific interface is needed, simply calling QueryInterface() for that interface is as easy as scrolling through a list, locating the interface, and then using it. Having such a list would still force you to provide a fallback case because the object could change dynamically over time. Therefore, even if an interface did not exist one day, someone may have installed new software on the machine the next day. Suddenly, the interface now exists! Therefore, your programs should always look for an interface and then provide some default error-handling capability if the interface does not exist.

Reference Counting

Although the QueryInterface() method can return information about an object at runtime, the IUnknown interface supplies the AddRef() and Release() methods to track the number of users an object currently has. At its simplest, the AddRef() method could simply increment an internal counter each time the method was called. The Release() method would decrement the internal counter when called and could free the object when the counter returned to zero.

To make sure that reference counting occurs properly for an object, the following two steps must always occur:

1. Each time a new interface is created at runtime, the AddRef() method must be called using that interface.

2. When the interface goes out of scope (or will be used no longer), the interface's Release() method must be called before the interface is destroyed.

Keep in mind that reference counting applies globally to an entire object, not just to an individual interface. Therefore, you may have cases in which calling AddRef() and Release() is not necessary. These cases occur when an interface is created, used, and freed within the lifetime of another interface, as shown in the following sample code:

```
void *Interface1;
void *Interface2;

CreateTheInterface(&Interface1);

/* Do something with the interface */
Interface1->Method1();
Interface1->Method2();
Interface2 = Interface1;

/* Do something with Interface2 */
Interface2->Method5();
Interface2->Method1();

Interface2 = NULL;

Interface1->Release();
```

In this sample code, Interface2 lives and dies during the lifetime of Interface1. The programmer doesn't have to call the AddRef() and Release() methods of Interface2 because before the beginning and after the end of its lifetime, the reference count stays the same.

A general rule of thumb is that all methods that return an interface pointer should call AddRef() for that interface. All methods that accept an interface as an input parameter or retrieve an interface from some method output should call Release() when they are using that interface. Failing to call the Release() method of an object has important consequences because the object will never be freed as long as the application is running.

Object Reuse Through Containment and Aggregation

Once an object has been created and installed on a file system, implementing inheritance from that object using a new object is not possible. However, *within* the object, using a language such as C++, interfaces can be inherited from or overridden. Using any object-oriented language that supports inheritance, this kind of functionality is possible when building the object. Nevertheless, once the DLL or EXE has been compiled and built and the object has been installed on a system, that object cannot be inherited from in a binary sense because of the unknown nature of objects within a system. Most developers do not feel comfortable blindly overriding methods contained in objects produced by others, especially if they have no idea of what is really going on inside that object. Therefore, object inheritance is not a supported feature of COM.

However, COM does allow objects to reuse the capabilities of other objects through techniques known as *containment* and *aggregation*. Using these techniques, an object does not override another object's interface. Instead, the second object directly uses the first object's interface, and the object that "owns" the interface maintains its own local memory and reference count.

Using Containment

Containment refers to the process whereby one object completely contains another object. When the contained object's interface methods are called, the container object can choose to call the default method or can override that method by calling one of its own. The container object maintains an internal pointer to the contained object's interface. When the container is freed, it will in turn free the contained object. The container object will implement stubs for each method in the contained object. Some of these stubs will override the contained object's methods, whereas others will be passed directly through to the container object. Figures 16.1 and 16.2 illustrate the Book and Dictionary COM objects.

Figure 16.1.
The Book *object.*

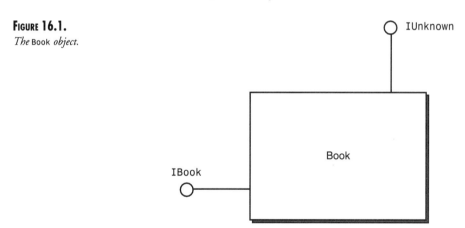

The ways in which these illustrations are drawn serves to illustrate a COM standard. Objects are always drawn as rectangles with an IUnknown "node" showing at the top of the object illustration. The other interfaces are drawn on the left side of the rectangle. Figures 16.3 and 16.4 show how these nodes can connect objects via their exposed interfaces.

FIGURE 16.2.

The Dictionary *object.*

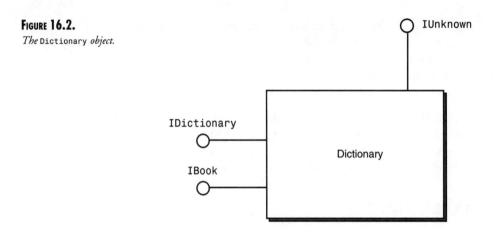

In these illustrations, two objects are being used: the Book object and the Dictionary object. (In object-oriented terms, we could say that Dictionary inherits from Book.) The Book object implements the IUnknown and IBook interface. This IBook interface could supply useful functions such as Read(), Buy(), and TurnPage(). The Dictionary object supplies its own IUnknown interface, but in addition supplies an IReference interface. This interface supplies functions such as LookUp(), FindSynonym(), and CheckSpelling().

The Book object is implemented so that it is completely independent of the Dictionary object. If no Dictionary object is present or if no Dictionary object is passing data to the Book object, the Book object is completely self-contained and will function normally. However, the Dictionary object will implement containment and therefore will create an instance of a Book object when it is created. Recall that this instance can be created via a call such as

```
CoCreateInstance(CLSID_Book, NULL, CLSCTX_LOCAL_SERVER, IID_IBook,
    (void**)&pIUnknown);
```

The IBook interface is stored internally within the Book object. When the Book object is itself destroyed at runtime, the IBook.Release() method will be called to free the Book object as well. Because the Dictionary object plans to always store an internal Book object, it can expose the IBook interface as its own (see Figure 16.3).

If the Dictionary.IBook interface wants to reuse a function exposed by the Book.IBook interface, it can call that function directly. Otherwise, the Dictionary object can override the function by supplying one of its own.

FIGURE 16.3.
*Reusing an object
through containment.*

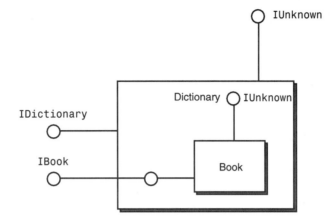

Using Aggregation

Aggregation is different from containment in that the container object (or *aggregate* object, as it is called) does not choose to override any of the methods within the contained object. Instead, it directly exposes the interfaces of the contained object as its own (see Figure 16.4).

FIGURE 16.4.
*Reusing an object
through aggregation.*

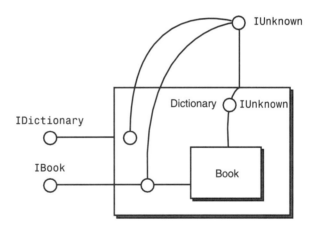

In Figure 16.4, the Dictionary object exposes the Book.IBook interface directly as one of its own. In no way does the Dictionary object attempt to implement any of the IBook functions on its own. This programming device eliminates the need for stub functions (that call the IBook functions directly) but complicates the issue in another sense. Suppose that a user of the Dictionary object retrieves what it thinks is the Dictionary.IBook interface. (In reality, this interface actually belongs to the Book object, but through aggregation it appears to belong to Dictionary.) Using the IBook interface, the following call is made:

```
retValue = pIUnknown->QueryInterface(IID_DICTIONARY, (void**)&pIDictionary);
```

In reality, the Book object is being referenced here, and it has no knowledge of the Dictionary object! How can this possibly work? Aggregation works thanks to the second parameter passed to the CoCreateInstance() function that defines the *controlling unknown* of the aggregate. (So far we have assumed that this parameter would be NULL.) By passing in this controlling unknown, the Dictionary object (the aggregate object) and the Book object (the contained object) agree to work together. If an unknown interface is requested from the Dictionary object, it is passed directly to the Book object for creation. Likewise, a QueryInterface() call to one of the Book object's interfaces can return a Dictionary interface.

Keep in mind that aggregation and containment do not allow binary COM objects to inherit from one another at the system level. In other words, an object cannot simply install itself into the Windows Registry and inform Windows that it is overriding features within another object. Instead, aggregation and containment occur within an object's source code and force an object to have knowledge of another object at compile time in order to be successful.

Connecting Java and COM

The primary facets of COM development have now been covered. The discussion started by showing the many similarities between Java and COM (refer to Table 16.1). An overview of the Microsoft Component Object Model (COM) followed this comparison. Here is a review of the main points:

- The contents of COM objects are accessed and manipulated through a set of published interfaces. A COM interface is functionally equivalent to the interface found in the Java language.
- All COM interfaces must derive from the IUnknown interface. This interface defines three methods: QueryInterface(), AddRef(), and Release().
- Each COM object is identified by a globally unique identifier: the CLSID.
- Each COM interface is identified by a globally unique identifier: the REFIID.
- Capabilities of COM objects can be reused via containment and aggregation.

It is now time to get down to the details that should truly interest the Visual J++ developer. Vague references have been made to operations such as "registering" a COM object with the operating system or "publishing" an object's interfaces. Just as the Java language lends itself to virtually seamless use of COM objects side by side with Java objects, Visual J++ provides several useful tools that greatly ease the Java/COM integration process.

Type Libraries and Object Description Language

The purpose of COM and other object models (such as SOM and CORBA) is to provide a method of reuse for binary objects installed on local or remote operating systems. This world of distributed objects offers many advantages, but it does not necessarily make the developer's life any easier. In terms of advantages, applications are easier to partition (and thus can be scaled when performance reasons call for it). Application components can be upgraded in a transparent manner, and, perhaps most interestingly, these application components can be written in virtually any language. Therefore, if DCOM is successfully ported to the Macintosh and UNIX operating systems, a Windows/Mac/UNIX application could essentially be distributed across a network of computers running the most popular operating systems. In the past, one of the trickiest portions of this design from a software development viewpoint was to develop separate Windows/Mac/UNIX client graphical user interfaces. With Visual J++, even that task should be relatively straightforward in the future!

For simplicity's sake, one part of the puzzle has thus far been ignored. Assume that some of the objects you plan to use in your application will be developed by many different vendors using languages such as C, C++, and Java. How do you begin to determine the contents of the interfaces supplied by these various vendors? To drop down to an even more detailed question, how will your application physically link to these objects? In Java, native methods can be used to tie a Java method to a C language method and standard programming methods exist for linking in a DLL's function. However, linking in methods is quite different from linking in entire interfaces.

Fortunately, this problem has been well researched, and in fact, an entire language has been developed to assist developers in describing the contents of an object. This language, named the Interface Definition Language, or IDL, was originally developed by the Open Software Foundation for use in describing remote procedure call (RPC) interfaces. IDL is also currently used by the CORBA object model. Microsoft has added extensions to standard IDL to produce a description language known as the Object Description Language (ODL). Developers who have used OLE Automation may be familiar with the compiled version of an ODL file: the type library.

Type libraries are used to expose items such as data types, objects, or (of course!) interfaces within binary objects. In essence, these libraries are compiled versions of an ODL source file. These source files were traditionally compiled using a tool such as MKTYPLIB. Once compiled, a type library can exist as a resource within a DLL, OCX, or EXE file just like other resources such as menus, icons, and bitmaps. In addition, a type library can exist as a standalone TBL file that is distributed with a product. A quick search of my hard drive reveals a variety of type library files, including libraries used to access objects within Microsoft Access, PowerPoint, and the Data Access Objects.

COM Tools Included with Visual J++

Visual J++ developers have a variety of tools at their disposal to retrieve information from the type libraries of existing objects. In keeping with the Visual J++ goal of making COM integration as seamless as possible, a tool known as the Java Type Library Wizard automatically extracts type library information from COM objects. Then Java class files are generated and can be imported like any other Java class. (As already noted, COM objects appear identical to Java objects from a language viewpoint.) Unfortunately, creating COM objects in Java using Visual J++ requires a little more effort. The language does not currently contain a "reverse" Type Library Wizard that can produce a type library from a Java object. Instead, the ODL code must be written manually and compiled using the MKTYPLIB or MIDL tools provided by Microsoft. Once this type library has been created, a Java COM object can be registered using the JAVAREG tool provided with Visual J++. The OLE2 Object Viewer included with Visual J++ allows developers to view the contents of a type library quickly, using an intuitive graphical user interface.

The Java Type Library Wizard (JAVATLB)

The Java Type Library Wizard is an extremely handy tool for developers who want to use existing COM objects or to implement existing COM interfaces. However, if you decide to build an application using COM as a foundation, at some point you will have to define and create your own COM objects. The next section discusses the process of physically creating an ODL file and building a type library using MKTYPLIB. Before you can undertake that process, however, you must retrieve a globally unique identifier (GUID) for each interface being defined and for each COM object being built. Visual J++ provides the GUIDGEN.EXE tool to help you.

> **NOTE**
>
> If this tool does not appear in your Visual J++ program group, go to the .\BIN directory of your Visual J++ installation (\MSDEV\BIN by default). The GUIDGEN.EXE executable and help file are located in this directory.

Running the GUIDGEN tool will automatically produce a unique ID that can be used for each interface (see Figure 16.5).

Java and the Component Object Model

CHAPTER 16

397

16

JAVA AND THE
COMPONENT
OBJECT MODEL

FIGURE 16.5.
*GUIDGEN—The
GUID generator tool.*

Several options are available within the GUIDGEN application. For Java development, your concern is in creating a new GUID ID to be associated with a Java class within the Windows Registry. Therefore, click on the fourth option, Registry Format, to retrieve a new GUID. A sample GUID generated using this tool on my current machine was

{1A6D6E81-1421-11d0-B4EE-444553540000}

Of course, because it is globally unique, when this tool is run on your machine, a different ID will be generated. Once this ID has been generated, it can identify objects or interfaces within an ODL file.

Building Type Libraries with MKTYPLIB

The name of the MKTYPLIB tool suggests its function: to make type libraries. Many Java developers may never need to actually build an object description using ODL. Keep in mind that ODL is used to define *new* interfaces. Therefore, if you are only implementing existing COM interfaces, using the Java Type Library Wizard to generate class files for the specified interface is sufficient. Once these class files exist, write the Java class implementing the interfaces in Java and then use the JAVAREG tool to register this Java class and receive a CLSID (see the section on JAVAREG later in the chapter). Assuming that you definitely want to define a new COM interface and implement it in Java, you must take the following steps:

1. Generate a GUID number for the interface and object using the GUIDGEN tool included with Visual J++.
2. Build the interface(s) description using the ODL.
3. Create a type library for the object using MKTYPLIB.
4. Build the Java class to create the interface.
5. Register the new Java COM object using JAVAREG.

Chapter 21, "Building COM Objects with Java," covers in detail the process of creating COM objects using the Java language. The following section briefly describes the ODL and its syntax.

An ODL Primer

This section covers the basic syntax of ODL. (For a more thorough description, consult the Visual J++ documentation.) The basic structure of each library defined within an ODL source file follows:

```
library LibName
{
  importlib "xxx.tlb"

  [attributes] elementname typename {
    memberdescriptions
  };

  [attributes] elementname typename {
    memberdescriptions
  };
}
```

Each ODL source file begins with a `library` statement that relays pertinent information to the type library builder. All statements that apply to a type library must be defined with the `library` block. In addition, all statements within the `library` block are used to build the type library. MKTYPLIB considers all statements outside of the `library` block (except for the actual library attributes) to be IDL file statements. The following example illustrates the use of the `library` statement to create a new type library named `Book`:

```
[
  uuid(1A6D6E81-1421-11d0-B4EE-444553540000),
  helpstring(""),
  lcid(0x0009),
  version(0.1)
]

library Book
{
  importlib("stdole.tlb");

  [
    uuid(1A6D6E82-1421-11d0-B4EE-444553540000),
    helpstring("The Book Interface!"),
    oleautomation,
    dual
  ]
  interface IBook : IUnknown
  {
    void CheckOut([in, string] unsigned char * BookTitle);
      //IUnknown methods omitted here
  };

  [uuid 1A6D6E83-1421-11d0-B4EE-444553540000]
  coclass TheBook
  {
    interface IBook;
  }
}
```

Valid attributes that can be used with the `library` statement are the following: `helpstring`, `helpcontext`, `lcid`, `restricted`, `hidden`, `control`, and `uuid`. Table 16.5 describes some common ODL attributes.

The `importlib` statement imports an exterior type library's contents for compilation purposes. It is similar to the C/C++ language `include` statement or the Java language `import` statement.

The interface statement defines a new interface within the `library` block. An interface is defined as inheriting from a base interface by the use of the colon (:) operator. For example, in the preceding code, interface `IBook` inherits from the `IUnknown` interface. The attributes `dual`, `helpstring`, `helpcontext`, `hidden`, `odl`, `oleautomation`, `uuid`, and `version` are accepted before the interface keyword. The following attributes are accepted on a function in an interface: `helpstring`, `helpcontext`, `string`, `propget`, `propput`, `propputref`, `bindable`, `defaultbind`, `displaybind`, and `vararg`. The `uuid` attribute is required before the interface definition.

The `coclass` statement defines a new class within the library block. The `helpstring`, `helpcontext`, `licensed`, `version`, `control`, `hidden`, and `appobject` attributes are accepted, but not required, before a `coclass` definition. Meanwhile, the `uuid` attribute is required before the `coclass` definition.

Table 16.5. Common ODL attributes.

Attribute	Description
bindable	Property supports data binding
control	Indicates a control item (for display purposes)
defaultbind	Indicates the default bindable property for the object
displaybind	Indicates that the property should be displayed
dual	Interface exposes properties through IDispatch and VTBL
helpcontext	Sets the help file context ID
helpstring	Sets the help string to be displayed
hidden	Indicates the item should not be displayed in an object browser
lcid	Parameter is a locale ID
licensed	Class is licensed
odl	Identifies an interface as an ODL interface
oleautomation	Interface is compatible with OLE Automation
propget	Specifies a property-accessor function
propput	Specifies a property-setting function

continues

Table 16.5. continued

Attribute	Description
propputref	Specifies a property set-by-reference function
restricted	Hides item from use by a macro programmer
string	Specifies a string
uuid	Specifies the GUID of the item
vararg	Indicates a variable number of arguments
version	Specifies an object's version number

Once the ODL file has been built to define your new COM object and its interfaces, you can use the MKTYPLIB tool to compile the ODL definition into a COM type library.

MKTYPLIB Command-Line Syntax

MKTYPLIB is the name of the tool used to "compile" an ODL class definition into a binary type library.

> **NOTE**
>
> If this tool does not appear in your Visual J++ program group, go to the .\BIN directory of your Visual J++ installation (\MSDEV\BIN by default). The MKTYPLIB.EXE executable is located in this directory.

The basic syntax required to use MKTYPLIB is the following:

MKTYPLIB [options] ODLFileName

Table 16.6 lists the MKTYPLIB options as described in the Visual J++ documentation.

Table 16.6. The MKTYPLIB options.

Option	Description
/? or /help	Displays command line Help. In this case, *ODLfile* does not need to be specified.
/align:*alignment*	Sets the default alignment for types in the library. An *alignment* value of 1 indicates natural alignment; *n* indicates alignment on byte *n*.

Option	Description
/cpp_cmd *cpppath*	Specifies *cpppath* as the command to run the C preprocessor. By default, MKTYPLIB invokes CL.
/cpp_opt "*options*"	Specifies *options* for the C preprocessor. The default is /C /E / D__MkTypLib__.
/D *define*[=*value*]	Defines the name *define* for the C preprocessor. The *value* is its optional value. No space is allowed between the equal sign (=) and the value.
/h *filename*	Specifies *filename* as the name for a stripped version of the input file. This file can be used as a C or C++ header file.
/I *includedir*	Specifies *includedir* as the directory where include files are located for the C preprocessor.
/nocpp	Suppresses invocation of the C preprocessor. Specify this option if you do not have the C compiler installed on your machine. (This option means that you cannot use preprocessor directives in your ODL file.)
/nologo	Disables the display of the copyright banner.
/o *outputfile*	Redirects output (for example, error messages) to the specified *outputfile*.
/tlb *filename*	Specifies *filename* as the name of the output TBL file. If not specified, it will be the same name as the *ODLfile*, with the extension .tlb.
/win16 /win32 /mac /mips /alpha /ppc /ppc32	Specifies the output type library to be produced. The default is the current operating system.
/w0	Disables warnings.

Two points need to be made about these options and MKTYPLIB, in general.

First of all, note that some of the options apply specifically to the use of MKTYPLIB in conjunction with a C or C++ compiler. If you are building new type libraries for Java COM objects, you should always use MKTYPLIB with the */nocpp* flag (unless a valid C/C++ compiler is installed on your system). Also, avoid the use of all preprocessor flags.

The second point is that the MKTYPLIB tool will be useful only if you are actually creating new COM objects. You should use the Java Type Library Wizard to extract information from an existing type library if you want to use an existing COM object in your Java code.

Registering Objects with JAVAREG

Once a COM class has been created in Java and its type library has been created as well, you can use the JAVAREG tool to place this object's identification information in the Windows Registry. It is where the linkage takes place between the Java class file name and the CLSID stored in the Registry. The syntax to be used with the JAVAREG tool is as follows:

```
javareg /register /class:JAVACLASSNAME /clsid:{CLSID}
```

Note that in this syntax, the physical name of the Java class file should be substituted for the JAVACLASSNAME symbol, and the CLSID of that class should be substituted for the CLSID symbol.

> **NOTE**
>
> If this tool does not appear in your Visual J++ program group, go to the .\BIN directory of your Visual J++ installation (\MSDEV\BIN by default). The JAVAREG.EXE executable is located in this directory.

To view all of the options available for the JAVAREG tool, run the program from the command line using the following syntax:

```
javareg ?
```

Once run, JAVAREG will add the appropriate keys to the Windows Registry under the HKEY_CLASSES_ROOT\CLSID node (or My Computer\HKEY_CLASSES_ROOT\CLSID under Windows 95).

The OLE2 Object Viewer

One additional tool that is included with Visual J++ is the OLE2 Object Viewer. This tool is extremely useful for examining the contents of all OLE (and therefore COM) objects currently installed on the local system. Although many of the options available within this tool apply specifically to OLE 2.0 concepts, you can also use this tool to view the type libraries of any COM object.

NOTE

If this tool does not appear in your Visual J++ program group, go to the .\BIN directory of your Visual J++ installation (\MSDEV\BIN by default). The OLE2VW32.EXE executable and help file (OLE2VIEW.HLP) are located in this directory.

Figure 16.6 shows the OLE2 Object Viewer tool and the registered COM objects currently available on a system.

FIGURE 16.6.

The OLE2 Object Viewer tool.

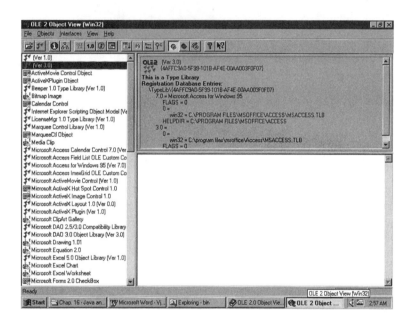

To examine the contents of a specific type library, double-click an object in the left frame within OLE2VW32U. The contents of that object's type library will be displayed in a dialog box resembling Figure 16.7.

Figure 16.7 displays the contents of the type library for the Beeper COM DLL included with the Visual J++ sample applications. In fact, examining the figure closely reveals the definition of the QueryInterface() method itself! Selecting the To File... option will save the contents of the type library to a text file for closer examination. Listing 16.1 shows the equivalent type library information for this object as generated by the OLE2 Object Viewer.

FIGURE 16.7.
Viewing the contents of a COM type library.

Listing 16.1. Type library contents for the Beeper COM object.

```
'================================================================
' Type Library: BeeperLib, Library Version 1.000
' GUID: {6384D582-0FDB-11CF-8700-00AA0053006D}
' LCID: 0X00000000
' Documentation: Beeper 1.0 Type Library
' Help: (o vial)Tx ie *tt'===================================================


'================================================================
' Type Info: Beeper, TypeInfo Version 0.000
' GUID: {6384D586-0FDB-11CF-8700-00AA0053006D}
' LCID: 0X00000000
' TypeKind: coclass
' Documentation: Beeper Object
'_ _ _ _ _ _ _ _ _ _ _ _ _ _ _ _ _ _ _ _ _ _ _ _ _ _ _ _ _ _ _


'================================================================
' Type Info: IBeeper, TypeInfo Version 0.000
' GUID: {6384D584-0FDB-11CF-8700-00AA0053006D}
' LCID: 0X00000000
' TypeKind: dispinterface
' Documentation: IBeeper Interface
'_ _ _ _ _ _ _ _ _ _ _ _ _ _ _ _ _ _ _ _ _ _ _ _ _ _ _ _ _ _ _


' Function: QueryInterface
'
Declare Sub QueryInterface (ByRef riid As Variant, ByRef ppvObj As Variant)

' Function: AddRef
'
Declare Function AddRef () As ULONG

' Function: Release
'
Declare Function Release () As ULONG
```

```
' Function: GetTypeInfoCount
'
Declare Sub GetTypeInfoCount (ByRef pctinfo As Variant)

' Function: GetTypeInfo
'
Declare Sub GetTypeInfo (ByVal itinfo As UINT, ByVal lcid As ULONG,
    ByRef pptinfo As Variant)

' Function: GetIDsOfNames
'
Declare Sub GetIDsOfNames (ByRef riid As Variant, ByRef rgszNames As Variant,
    ByVal cNames As UINT, ByVal lcid As ULONG, ByRef rgdispid As Variant)

' Function: Invoke
'
Declare Sub Invoke (ByVal dispidMember As Long, ByRef riid As Variant,
    ByVal lcid As ULONG, ByVal wFlags As USHORT, ByRef pdispparams As Variant,
    ByRef pvarResult As Variant, ByRef pexcepinfo As Variant,
    ByRef puArgErr As Variant)

' Function: Beep
' Documentation: Play the current sound
'
Declare Sub Beep ()

' Function: Count
' Documentation: Returns number of strings in collection.
'
Declare Function Count () As Long

' Function: Item
' Documentation: Given an index, returns a string in the collection
'
Declare Function Item (ByVal Index As Long) As String

' Function: _NewEnum
'
Declare Function _NewEnum () As LPUNKNOWN
```

Visual Basic developers should be familiar with the syntax of the function declarations in the output listed in Listing 16.1. Because the OLE2 Object Viewer was provided initially to help Visual Basic programmers implement OLE Automation (controlling OLE objects remotely from another application), the output of the OLE2 Object Viewer gives VB-syntax function declarations for each interface function with the Beeper object. Java developers shouldn't feel left out, though. As you will see in Chapter 20, "Calling COM Objects from Java," the Java Type Library Wizard also generates a summary information file containing the function declarations within a COM object. However, these function declarations use Java syntax instead of Visual Basic!

Summary

Microsoft's COM was overshadowed by its child technology, OLE, for several years as Microsoft marketed the prebuilt capabilities available in the OLE 2.0 suite of objects. Although OLE provides a set of implemented interfaces that Microsoft defined to handle a number of common computing concepts (for example, visual editing, structured storage, in-place activation), COM is the flexible object model that underlies all of OLE. Because of Java's popularity, the introduction of distributed COM, and the Internet-aware, streamlined OLE now known as ActiveX, COM has once again become the focus of Microsoft's marketing plan. Visual J++ includes a set of tools to aid the Java developer in integrating and extending COM using the Java language.

Because of the many similarities between Java and COM, integration between the two is nearly seamless for the Java developer. Instead of calling COM API methods directly and passing interface pointers and CLSIDs around an application, COM objects appear to be completely identical to Java objects within Java source code. To create a new COM object for use within an application, the new keyword can be used to call the object's constructor. Microsoft can thank the many similarities between component object models and Java (support for multiple interfaces, dynamic creation and linking, and runtime garbage collection) for this ease of integration.

The following chapters in this part of *Visual J++ Unleashed* explain how to combine Java and COM. The examples show both COM objects built in Java and Java programs calling COM objects. First, however, the items that make the combination of Java and COM possible will be addressed. These items are the Microsoft JVM and the com.ms.com package included with Visual J++.

CHAPTER 17

Encapsulating COM with the Visual J++ Class Library

by Bryan Morgan

IN THIS CHAPTER

Because Java is an object-oriented programming language, new classes can be defined by any Java programmer that extend the capabilities of the language. For example, the Java char data type is used to define a single-character variable. However, the java.lang.String class has been defined within the java package in order to give programmers the ability to use strings of characters. This class is important because the use of strings within programs is much more common than single-character variables.

J++ provides literally hundreds of classes that can handle a wide variety of tasks. Classes contained within the Visual J++ class library give the Java programmer the ability to add networking, multimedia, COM objects, or graphics capabilities to an application. All this functionality can be dropped into an application simply by adding a variable that is of the class type. These classes can also be inherited from through the use of the Java extends keyword.

This chapter provides a general overview of the Java packages that are provided with Visual J++. Some of the classes included with these packages are a standard part of every Java development and runtime environment. Other classes in these packages can only be acquired by purchasing Visual J++. The majority of the Visual J++-specific classes are used to handle the creation or calling of COM objects and are therefore platform dependent. The three primary packages addressed in this chapter are the java, sun, and com packages.

The java Package

Programmers familiar with Visual C++ have probably used the Microsoft Foundation Class (MFC) library to develop Windows applications in C++. Borland C++ programmers should be familiar with Borland's Object Windows Library (OWL). Both of these application frameworks provide a core set of classes that is included with every copy of the compiler. The vast majority of these classes is totally generic and can be reused in a wide variety of application scenarios. The concept of a Java package was introduced in Chapter 3, "Object-Oriented Programming with Java," as a construct that holds a set of related classes and interfaces. A package can contain as few as one class or as many as you wish. Packages can also contain other packages (known as *subpackages*). Visual J++ includes three packages that are contained in the classes.zip file and are installed to the \windows\java\classes directory by default. These packages are the java, sun, and com packages.

NOTE

The classes.zip file also includes the source code for most of these classes. To extract the source code from this file, run the javasrc tool located in the \classes directory using the following syntax: javasrc classes.zip.

The java package makes what is often referred to as the Java Base API or the Java Base Platform. This package is guaranteed to be included with every valid Java compiler and runtime environment. The contents of this package are controlled by JavaSoft. The java package contains the classes that are deemed to be of most importance to Java developers. Included in this package are classes to support graphics, threading, networking, and input/output. The 1.0.2 release of the Java Developer's Kit (JDK) contains the following subpackages:

■ applet

■ awt

■ io

■ lang

■ net

■ util

Each of these subpackages contains a related set of classes and interfaces that share some common functionality. All classes in the applet package, for instance, provide the functionality that is used to create or assist a Java applet. The members of this package are used repeatedly throughout this book, so understanding the capabilities of applet is important. For more detailed information on the java package, refer to Chapter 13, "The Standard Java Packages."

The com Package

The com package contains many classes and interfaces that allow Java code to access Microsoft component object model (COM) objects. Functionality is also provided within these classes to allow COM objects to be implemented in Java. Beginning in Chapter 20, "Calling COM Objects from Java," tools supplied with Visual J++ are introduced to demonstrate how you can use COM objects just as if they were standard Java objects.

The com package contains one subpackage: ms. Most programmers assume that this *ms* stands for Microsoft and that the name is used to differentiate Microsoft's classes from other vendors who may choose to extend the com package with their own subpackages. The com.ms package includes the following subpackages:

■ applet

■ awt

■ lang

■ net

■ com

The following sections provide an overview of the contents of these subpackages. Their contents are explained here so that you will have a clear understanding of the capabilities supported by the com package as it is used in later chapters.

The com.ms.applet Package

The BrowserAppletFrame class within the com.ms.applet package contains functionality used by Internet Explorer to manipulate Java applets. In addition to the standard applet methods such as getDocumentBase(), getCodeBase(), and getParameter(), methods are provided to manage applets within a frame window. The remaining classes within this package provide extended Java support for loading Java classes from within a CAB file. CAB files are files used to contain compressed Java classes. These files can be downloaded from a remote server, then decompressed on the client side. CAB files will be examined in more detail later in the book. Classes such as CabClassLoader and AppletSecurity are used to provide this functionality.

The com.ms.awt Package

The com.ms.awt contains a set of classes that use native methods to create and manipulate Windows GUI components. The CaretX class supplies caret functionality and allows the caret position to be set using x and y coordinates. The FontX class inherits from java.awt.Font and will extend this class by providing TrueType Font support. The MenuX, MenuBarX, and MenuItemX classes extend the traditional Java menus by adding Windows attributes (such as check marks to show toggled menu items).

The com.ms.lang Package

The com.ms.lang package at the current time only contains one class, SystemX. This class contains a large group of methods that deal specifically with retrieving data from the keyboard and also deal with Unicode functionality. Unicode can store and transmit international characters (not just the standard English characters) and is supported under Windows NT. All char variables in Java code are Unicode characters. Specific methods within this class that implement this functionality are LocalStringToJavaString(), JavaStringToLocalString(), getKeyboardLanguage(), and setKeyboardLanguage().

The com.ms.net Package

The com.ms.net package contains classes that directly call WinInet API functions. The com.ms.net.wininet.URLUtils class contains two methods, canonicalizeURL() and combineURL(), that can parse and manipulate URLs. Other classes within the com.ms.net.wininet.http package include HttpInputStream, HttpPostBufferStream, and HttpURLConnection.

The com.ms.com **Package**

The com.ms.com package contains the functionality that is probably of the most interest to Visual J++ developers. In the following chapters, you will begin to explore the various capabilities provided with Visual J++ that allow Java classes to call COM objects and vice versa. Thanks to the Microsoft Java Virtual Machine, COM objects are exposed as a set of properties or methods within a class or interface that fits in very nicely with the Java programming language. Likewise, tools within Visual J++ allow type libraries to be built for Java classes, which opens up the world of COM to Java programmers. Because the Java Virtual Machine is used as a COM in-process server for all Java objects, COM objects can retrieve a CLSID for any Java object, create it using standard COM calls, and then use that object through the set of interfaces it provides.

The IUnknown interface discussed in Chapter 16, "Java and the Component Object Model," is implemented in interface IUnknown. This interface contains the three methods, QueryInterface(), AddRef(), and Release().

COM provides a VARIANT structure type that can store various types of values. This data type is used to pass arguments by reference or by value to interfaces derived from the COM IDispatch interface. The Variant class represents this data type within the com.ms.com package. This class includes many methods that convert the Variant object's data to a wide variety of data types. Examples of these methods are toShort(), toInt(), toFloat(), toDouble(), toCurrency(), toDate(), toString(), toDispatch(), toBoolean(), toObject(), and toByte().

The COM SAFEARRAY data structure is commonly used to save bookmarks when scrolling through lists of values returned from COM objects. An example of a SAFEARRAY type in use is a recordset returned from a Data Access Objects (DAO) query. The recordset can be scrolled forward and backward. Bookmarks can be set using a bookmark that is actually a SAFEARRAY. The com.ms.com package includes a class named SafeArray that implements this functionality in a Java class.

The ComContext class contains a set of constants that represent the different types of COM objects. Constants identified within this class include INPROC_SERVER, INPROC_HANDLER, LOCAL_SERVER, INPROC_SERVER16, REMOTE_SERVER, INPROC_HANDLER16, INPROC_SERVERX86, and INPROC_HANDLERX86.

Finally, the LicenseMgr class allows the instantiation of licensed COM objects from within Java code. This class constructs these objects using the ILicenseMgr interface. Two methods are supplied with this interface: createInstance() and createWithLic(). The method createInstance() will create an object for your use based on a CLSID string that is passed to it. The createWithLic() method requires both a CLSID string and a license string to "unlock" the licensed COM object.

The DAOSAMPLE sample application included with Visual J++ creates a licensed COM object (DAO 3.0) for use within an application. Once this object has been created, it can be used throughout the application to query an underlying Access database.

In the following snippet of code, the string `"mjgcqcejfchcijecpdhckcdjqigdejfccjri"` serves as the license string for the DAO DBEngine. This engine is identified within the Windows Registry using the CLSID `{00025E15-0000-0000-C000-000000000046}`:

> **NOTE**
>
> To verify that this Registry entry is indeed valid, do a quick search through the Registry to determine if it exists on your system. If it doesn't, you will need to install the DAO runtime engine from the Visual J++ CD before you can run the example. On my local machine, the search for this Registry entry turned up a key containing the subkey `InprocServer32`. This key specifies the name of the physical object on the disk to be created. (On my machine, it was `C:\PROGRAM FILES\COMMON FILES\MICROSOFT SHARED\DAO\DAO3032.DLL`.)

```
// Create the License Manager object
ILicenseMgr mgr = new LicenseMgr();

// Use the License Manager to create the DBEngine
result = (_DBEngine) mgr.createWithLic(
// The license key for the DAO DBEngine
"mjgcqcejfchcijecpdhckcdjqigdejfccjri",
// The CLSID for the DAO DBEngine
"{00025E15-0000-0000-C000-000000000046}",
// The aggregation IUnknown* punkOuter
null,
// The ctxFlag to create in inproc server
ComContext.INPROC_SERVER
);
```

The sun Package

The sun package contains a large group of classes and interfaces that have been developed by Sun Microsystems. These classes are subject to change over time and are not part of the Java Base API. In addition, they are not guaranteed to be included in Java runtime environments or development toolkits. However, they are included with Visual J++ and contain many useful objects. The primary subpackages contained within the sun package are

- ■ applet
- ■ audio
- ■ awt
- ■ misc
- ■ net

If some of these package or class names sound suspiciously familiar to packages or classes found in the java package, don't be surprised. Many of the classes found in the sun package are scheduled to be folded into the JDK 1.1 release. At the time of this writing, the 1.1 specification had been finalized, but no working betas have been released to the public. Expect to see updates to all of the major tool sets (including Visual J++) as new versions of the java package are released for public use.

Some of these undocumented, unsupported classes, which contain extremely useful functionality, are briefly described here. (These classes are *not* mentioned anywhere in the Visual J++ documentation.)

The sun.applet Package

The sun.applet package contains some useful classes that may be of interest even to the beginning Java programmer. The AppletCopyright class derives from the java.awt.Frame class and can display a simple copyright splash screen to the user of your application.

The AppletAudioClip class implements the java.applet.AudioClip interface that can play audio clips (sound files).

The AppletProps class also extends from java.awt.Frame in order to create a simple form that can view or set an applet's properties. Specific properties that can be set using this class include proxy servers and security access privileges.

The AppletViewer class is the source code for the appletviewer utility included with Sun's JDK. This utility will correctly run and display Java applets. This functionality can be important given the wide variances between the various Java-capable browsers in terms of Java support. Because something may look fine within Netscape Navigator but may appear incorrectly in Internet Explorer (or vice versa), the appletviewer utility can be used to test an applet to see how it *really* should look.

Finally, the AppletZipClassLoader derives from the sun.applet.AppletClassLoader class. It can retrieve class files from ZIP files stored on a remote server. The ZIP file can be specified using a URL object (java.net.URL), which means that it does not have to exist on the local machine.

The sun.audio Package

From the name of the package, you have probably concluded (correctly) that the classes and interfaces contained in the sun.audio package implement functionality to play and retrieve audio files. The AudioPlayer class derives from java.lang.Thread and implements an audio player within a thread. The AudioDevice class implements a Sun audio device. Because the playing of audio is a platform-specific operation, these classes use native methods to load Windows DLLs (in the case of the Microsoft Java Virtual Machine for Windows).

The sun.awt Package

The sun.awt package contains a number of classes as well as two additional subpackages. Classes within this package provide functionality similar to the classes and interfaces found in the java.awt package. As is the case with other classes found in the sun package, some of these classes are so useful that they are sure to be folded into later releases of the Java Base API.

The FocusingTextField class is a useful text widget that extends the standard java.awt.TextField class by allowing text fields to be tabbed between each other. The setNextField() method can be called to set the "z order" of the TextFields on a form. When a field has the current input focus, it will be highlighted to alert the user.

The VariableGridLayout class extends the java.awt.GridLayout class. Grid layouts are layout managers that can be used to lay out controls on a form without setting specific (x,y) pixel values. The VariableGridLayout class allows controls to be laid out in rows and columns but also allows the relative sizes of these rows and columns to be set.

The sun.awt.image Package

The sun.awt.image package contains a set of classes and interfaces that deal specifically with image file retrieval (in the form of GIF, XBM, or JPEG files). The GifImageDecoder class provides the functionality for reading in GIF files; the JPEGImageDecoder and XBMImageDecoder classes do the same for JPEG and XBM files.

The PixelStore, PixelStore32, and PixelStore8 classes can be used to create a memory cache for pixel data.

The sun.awt.win32 Package

The sun.awt.win32 package provides a set of Win32-specific classes that can encapsulate common graphics features of the Win32 Graphics Device Interface (GDI). Most of these classes are peer interfaces to the Win32 controls. However, several interesting classes that implement portions of the Win32 GDI exist within this package.

The Win32Graphics class encapsulates a Windows graphics device context within a Java class. Many common drawing operations are contained here including methods for drawing shapes, images, and strings on a device context.

The Win32PrintJob class initiates and executes a Win32 print job. Programmers familiar with printing under Windows will realize that a printer's device context can be drawn on using the identical functionality used to draw items on the screen's device context. Therefore, the Win32PrintJob class supplies the getGraphics() method to return a Graphics object to be used for drawing purposes.

Encapsulating COM with the Visual J++ Class Library

CHAPTER 17

415

17

COM AND THE
VISUAL J++
CLASS LIBRARY

The `sun.misc` Package

The `sun.misc` package contains a set of miscellaneous classes. Although these classes don't exactly fit into the other sun subpackages, the `misc` subpackage does not contain a random set of classes. In fact, this subpackage could have just as easily been named `sun.encode`. Many of the classes and interfaces supplied within this subpackage implement some of the more popular encoding/decoding schemes such as Base64 (`Base64Encoder` and `Base64Decoder`) and UUEncode/UUDecode (using `UUEncode` and `UUDecode`). Classes are also supplied to assist in performing cyclic redundancy checks (`CRC16`) and hex dumps (`HexDumpEncoder`).

The `sun.net` Package

The final package contained within the sun package is `sun.net`. As the name implies, this package contains many classes and subpackages that perform various networking operations.

The `MulticastSocket` class can join a multicasting group and open a multicast socket. Also included in the base package are classes that can build network clients and servers. These classes, `NetworkClient` and `NetworkServer`, use sockets to communicate between a client application and a server application. Another interesting class is the `URLCanonicalyzer` class. It takes a partial URL string value, parses it, and produces a valid URL. For instance, if the string `ftp.sun.com` was passed to the `URLCanonicalyzer()` constructor, the string `ftp://ftp.sun.com` would result.

The `sun.net.ftp` Package

The classes within this subpackage allow the Java programmer to provide FTP capabilities within an application. The `FtpClient` class contains methods such as `login()`, `get()`, `put()`, `command()`, `list()`, `cd()`, `ascii()`, and `binary()`. The `IftpClient` class is similar to `FtpClient` except that it allows the use of a proxy server to FTP files from outside of a firewall.

The `sun.net.nntp` Package

If you have ever read messages within an Internet newsgroup, you may be familiar with the term *NNTP*. It stands for Network News Transfer Protocol and is the protocol used to communicate between news reader clients and news servers. The `sun.net.nntp` subpackage contains classes that can be used to create news clients and retrieve articles from a remote server. Specifically, the `NntpClient` class contains methods such as `openServer()`, `getGroup()`, `getArticle()`, `getHeader()`, `startPost()`, and `finishPost()`. You can use the `NewsgroupInfo` class to retrieve information about a specific newsgroup from a news server.

The `sun.net.smtp` Package

E-mail is transferred across the Internet using a protocol known as *Simple Mail Transfer Protocol* (SMTP). Just as Java contains classes for dealing with other networking issues, a client class is included in this package that can create a mail client. Using the capabilities within the `SmtpClient` class, a Java program can send e-mail to a remote address via SMTP. The `to()` method adds destinations; the `from()` method names the sender. Meanwhile, `startMessage()` creates a `PrintStream` object that can be used to send a message to an SMPT mail server.

The `sun.net.www` Package

The `sun.net.www` subpackage contains a variety of classes and subpackages that complement existing Web-related networking classes already found in package `java.net`. Within the www package in particular are classes that can manipulate MIME tables on the Solaris and Win32 platforms.

The `sun.net.www.content.image` Package

The `sun.net.www.content.image` subpackage is a small package that contains wrapper classes used to create or manipulate image files. The `gif`, `jpeg`, `x_xbitmap`, and `x_xpixmap` classes create `URLImageSource` objects and return them as `Object` types to the caller.

The `sun.net.www.http` Package

The `sun.net.www.http` package provides support for using the Hypertext Transport Protocol (HTTP) to communicate between World Wide Web clients and server. The `HttpClient` class can create an HTTP-aware client application. Methods within this class include `openServer()`, `getRequestStatus()`, `getURLFile()`, `getMimeHeader()`, and `getHeaderField()`.

The `sun.net.www.protocol.file` Package

This package may be of interest to Java developers because it contains a class that accepts a URL and allows that file to be open for input. This class, `FileURLConnection`, accepts a URL and returns an `InputStream` object that can write to a file.

The `sun.net.www.protocol.news` Package

One other interesting package hidden deep in the `sun.net` hierarchy is the `sun.net.www.protocol.news` subpackage. This package contains a variety of useful GUI components and classes for building a simple news reader application. The `InlineButton` class extends `java.applet.Applet` and acts similarly to an HTML anchor tag. When clicked, this button retrieves an associated URL. The `ArticlePoster` class extends from `java.awt.Frame` and contains methods for posting articles to a news server. The `ReadIndicator` class also extends `java.applet.Applet` and can display a listing of read and unread news messages within a specific newsgroup.

Summary

The Visual J++ class library includes nearly 500 classes and interfaces that Java programmers can reuse. Although some of these objects were not intended for standard application development tasks, most of these classes provide some useful, generic functionality. The java package contains the core functionality in every Java development tool and runtime environment. Included in this package are classes to create applets, perform networking operations, and read or write streams. The sun package includes many classes with a narrower focus than those in the java package. Many of the objects found within the sun package will eventually make their way into the standard java package. Finally, Microsoft supplies the com package exclusively for use with Visual J++. This package provides the "plumbing" between COM and the Java Virtual Machine. Important classes within this package can instantiate COM objects from within Java code and also create COM objects in Java.

The next two chapters introduce the Microsoft Java Virtual Machine and ActiveX. The Microsoft Java Virtual Machine is a fully compliant virtual machine that extends the standard Java Virtual Machine by allowing Java objects to use COM objects and vice versa. (This extension continues the Microsoft tradition of "embracing and extending" the technologies of other companies.) Following these final overview chapters, you will find working examples that use COM objects within a Java application and also create COM objects in Java that can be called from Visual Basic.

Summary

The Microsoft Java Virtual Machine

by Bryan Morgan

IN THIS CHAPTER

Early in 1996, Microsoft and Sun Microsystems entered into an unusual agreement. The tremendous growth of Java pushed both companies to try to work together after competing against each other for years for sales of operating systems, development tools, and applications. Sun had already released the Java Developer's Kit (version 1.0) and had produced Java Virtual Machines (JVMs) for the Sun Solaris and Windows 95/NT platforms. Work was also under way on a JVM for the Apple Macintosh.

Microsoft had repeatedly said that it supported Java, but in fact it had nothing to show for this oral support. Through their agreement, Sun Microsystems agreed to license the JVM specification to Microsoft. Microsoft agreed to produce the reference implementation of the JVM for the Windows platforms. This essentially means that Microsoft has agreed to provide a complete implementation of the JVM, to be included with future versions of the Windows operating system. Any changes or additions made to the Microsoft Virtual Machine (VM) will be licensed back to Sun for possible inclusion in the official JVM specification.

The Microsoft VM

After several months of work, Microsoft has now released its JVM. It is currently available in Microsoft's Internet Explorer 3.0 (or higher) Web browser and is used by Visual J++ to compile and run Java code. This Virtual Machine has been dubbed the "Microsoft Windows Virtual Machine for Java." Besides being a mouthful of words, this title also hints that there is something different under the hood that separates this JVM from the Sun specification. (Those familiar with Microsoft have probably already suspected this.)

Before immediately dismissing the Microsoft VM and Visual J++ in general because of these differences, remember that the Microsoft VM is a complete JVM built according to the Sun specification. Every feature in a standard virtual machine is included in the Microsoft VM. All packages included in the Sun JVM (such as `java.awt`, `java.io`, `java.net`, and `java.util`) are present in the Microsoft VM. Because of Sun's licensing requirements, developers should feel secure that any Java code written using Visual J++ will run just fine within any Java-aware browser on any platform.

> **CAUTION**
>
> Although code written using Visual J++ and the Microsoft VM can run unmodified in any Web browser that supports Java, this is not to say that all Web browser implementations are perfect. The Sun VM specification has a few gray areas that have yet to be cleared up. This has resulted in Java code that runs fine under one browser (such as MSIE) but will not run in another (such as Netscape Navigator). This has nothing to do with the Visual J++ compiler; rather, the problem lies in the Web browser implementation itself.

In addition to providing a complete implementation of the JVM, Microsoft also chose to extend its virtual machine so that it could be used by all Windows applications, not just the Web browser. This extension gives the Microsoft VM the capability to load component object model (COM) classes and expose COM interfaces of Java classes. This means that the Microsoft VM allows Java classes to exist as both standard Java classes and COM objects. ActiveX controls are examples of COM objects that could be created using Java. (It should also be pointed out that the Microsoft VM itself is implemented as an ActiveX control.) In short, the Microsoft VM allows Java classes to be reused by nearly all popular Windows programming environments.

The remainder of this chapter introduces the Sun JVM specification and explains the Microsoft VM extensions. This discussion is not intended to discuss the actual "plumbing" details, but rather to give you an idea of what goes on when a JVM interprets and runs Java code.

The JVM Specification

As the creator of Java and the Virtual Machine, Sun Microsystems owns the specification for the JVM. Sun currently works with other virtual machine builders (such as Apple, IBM, and Microsoft) to ensure that all versions of the JVM remain true to the overall Sun specification. This specification lays out in detail the Java runtime architecture, bytecodes and their format, and Java class-file format. All capabilities described in the specification must be included by every licensee of the JVM.

> **NOTE**
>
> Although every feature must be implemented by a licensee, how that feature is implemented is generally left up to the individual licensees. For instance, the Microsoft VM performs garbage collection of objects in memory; however, it uses a "stop and copy" scheme instead of the standard "mark and sweep" paradigm.

Some abstractions are completely left up to the implementor, such as the following:

- Garbage collection algorithms (such as "mark and sweep" versus "stop and copy")
- Specific tools used such as compiler, interpreter, and operating system
- Runtime optimizations of Java code
- Runtime organization of the data areas

The initial specification also says that all compliant JVMs will initially provide the capability to interpret and run Java classes. Although this does not rule out the production of machine code by Java compilers, it does ensure the capability to run interpreted Java applets and applications. (Tools currently used to interpret and run Java applications include Sun's `java` interpreter and the Microsoft `jview` interpreter.)

Components of the JVM

The JVM, like a true computer hardware machine, uses several components to manage and run programs. Readers familiar with microprocessor organization will notice some similarities between these machines and the JVM. The following components make up the JVM:

- Java instruction set
- Primitive data types
- Virtual machine registers
- Virtual machine stack
- Virtual machine garbage-collected heap

Each of these components is used to track and manage Java code at runtime.

Java Instruction Set

Think of the Java instruction set as a set of bytecodes that are Java "machine code." Java compilers take Java source code and produce class files whose contents are made up of Java instruction set commands. A Java instruction set command consists of an opcode specifying the operation to be performed and zero or more operands supplying parameters that will be used by the operation. Instruction set opcodes are always one byte long. The operand's size may vary. If an operand's size is greater than one byte, it is stored in "big-endian" order with the high-order byte first. (The section "The Java Instruction Set" lists the common Java opcodes and their meanings.)

Primitive Data Types

Each JVM must natively support a set of primitive data types, including `int`, `boolean`, `char`, `short`, `byte`, `float`, `double`, and `long`. These data types are managed by the compiler; the programmer does not have to create them specifically. In other words, operations involving the primitive data types are supported at the opcode level.

JVM Registers

The JVM maintains a set of internal registers used to store the machine state while a program is executing. This set of registers is analogous to the hardware registers in a microprocessor. Some examples of the JVM registers follow:

- `pc`—The Java program counter
- `optop`—A pointer to the top of the Java operand stack
- `frame`—A pointer to the execution environment of the currently executing method
- `vars`—A pointer to the 0th local variable of the currently executing method

Each register is defined to be 32 bits wide.

JVM Stack

The JVM stack is used to track the state of a single method invocation and is made up of local variables, an execution environment, and the operand stack.

Local variables are all 32 bits wide. In the case of long integers or double precision floating-point values (that is, 64-bit numbers), two local variables are addressed by the index of the first local variable. Specific opcodes are defined to load the values of local variables onto the stack and also to store variables from the stack into local variables. Local variables are addressed as indices from the vars register and therefore can be treated as an array.

The execution environment is used to maintain the operations of the Java stack itself. The environment maintains pointers to the previous stack frame, its own local variables, and operand stack base and top.

When compiled, each Java method defines a list of "catch clauses" to describe the instruction range for which the method is active and the type of exception that it is to handle. The catch clause list for the current method is searched for a match each time an exception is thrown by the executing program. Before the system can branch to the exception handler, the exception must be verified against the catch clause. If the exception is within the instruction range and the exception is a subtype of the type of exception that the clause handles, the program branches to the exception handler. When no handler is found, the stack frame is popped and the exception is raised again.

JVM Garbage-Collected Heap

The JVM garbage-collected heap is the area from which runtime objects are allocated. Unlike traditional system heaps of memory, the JVM monitors which objects are in use. When an object is determined to be unused throughout the remainder of the program, the JVM automatically frees the memory for that object. The JVM specification does not specify how the memory is to be freed up. Many garbage collection strategies use the mark-and-sweep algorithm, which goes through the following steps:

1. Every object in memory is examined.
2. Objects that are in use are marked.
3. The virtual machine sweeps back through memory. All objects left unmarked are freed.

The Sun Microsystems implementation of the JVM uses this algorithm. Although it is fast, it often results in the fragmentation of memory. The Microsoft VM uses a different algorithm known as "stop and copy," which goes through the following steps:

1. Every object in memory is examined.
2. Objects that are in use are copied immediately to another area in memory.
3. At the end, all objects that were not copied are freed.

Stop and copy requires a greater amount of memory to accomplish the same result achieved by the mark-and-sweep algorithm. However, it does not result in memory fragmentation.

The Constant Pool

When a Java applet or application is run, all the objects are loaded into the *constant pool* (or *class constant pool*). This pool of data contains the names of all fields and methods and other such information that is used by methods in the class. When the class is first read in from memory, the class structure has two fields related to the constant pool, nconstants, which indicates the number of constants contained in this class's constant pool, and constant_into.constants_offset., which contains an integer offset (in bytes) from the start of the class to the data that describes the constants in the class.

The constant pool is treated as an array named constant_pool. constant_pool[0] can be used by the implementor for anything. The remainder of the constant_pool array is used to store the sequence of bytes in the class object beginning at the constant_info.constants_offset byte location.

The Java Instruction Set

The Java instruction set, as described earlier, is a set of bytecodes that is equivalent to compiled languages' machine code. These bytecodes are interpreted by the JVM at runtime and are subsequently converted into the machine code for whichever platform the JVM is running on. Table 18.1 contains descriptions of some of the more common Java instructions.

Table 18.1. A partial listing of the Java instruction set.

Opcode	Description
bipush	Push 1-byte signed integer onto the stack
sipush	Push 2-byte signed integer onto the stack
ldc1	Push 1-byte value from constant pool
ldc2	Push 2-byte value from constant pool
ldc2w	Push long or double from constant pool
aconst_null	Push null object
iconst_m1	Push integer constant −1 onto the stack
iload	Load integer from local variable
lload	Load long from local variable
fload	Load float from local variable
dload	Load double from local variable

Opcode	Description
aload	Load local object variable
istore	Store integer into local variable
lstore	Store long into local variable
fstore	Store float into local variable
dstore	Store double into local variable
astore	Store object reference into local variable
iinc	Increment local variable by constant
newarray	Allocate new array
anewarray	Allocate new array of objects
multianewarray	Allocate new multidimensional array
arraylength	Get length of array
iaload	Load integer from array
laload	Load long from array
faload	Load float from array
iastore	Store into integer array
lastore	Store into long array
fastore	Store into float array
dastore	Store into double array
nop	Do nothing (no-op)
pop	Pop top stack word
pop2	Pop top two stack words
dup	Duplicate top stack word
dup2	Duplicate top two stack words
swap	Swap top two stack words
iadd	Integer add
ladd	Long add
fadd	Float add
dadd	Double add
isub	Integer subtract
lsub	Long subtract
fsub	Float subtract

18

THE MICROSOFT
JAVA VIRTUAL
MACHINE

continues

Table 18.1. continued

Opcode	Description
dsub	Double subtract
imul	Integer multiply
lmul	Long multiply
fmul	Float multiply
dmul	Double multiply
idiv	Integer division
ldiv	Long division
fdiv	Float division
ddiv	Double division
imod	Integer modulus
lmod	Long modulus
fmod	Float modulus
dmod	Double modulus
ineg	Integer negate
lneg	Long negate
fneg	Float negate
dneg	Double negate
ishl	Integer shift left
ishr	Integer shift right
iushr	Integer logical shift right
lshl	Long shift left
lshr	Long shift right
lushr	Long logical shift right
iand	Integer boolean and
land	Long boolean and
ior	Integer boolean or
lor	Long boolean or
ixor	Integer boolean xor
lxor	Long boolean xor
i2l	Integer to long conversion
i2f	Integer to float conversion

Opcode	Description
i2d	Integer to double conversion
l2i	Long to integer conversion
l2f	Long to float conversion
l2d	Long to double conversion
f2i	Float to integer conversion
f2l	Float to long conversion
f2d	Float to double conversion
d2i	Double to integer conversion
d2l	Double to long conversion
d2f	Double to float conversion
int2byte	Integer to byte conversion
int2char	Integer to char conversion
int2short	Integer to short conversion
ireturn	Return integer from method
lreturn	Return long from method
freturn	Return float from method
dreturn	Return double from method
areturn	Return object reference from method
return	Return void from method
tableswitch	Access jump table by index and jump
lookupswitch	Access jump table by key match and jump
putfield	Set field in object
getfield	Get field in object
putstatic	Set static field in class
getstatic	Get static field in class
invokevirtual	Invoke class method
invokenonvirtual	Invoke nonvirtual method
invokestatic	Invoke static method
invokeinterface	Invoke interface method
athrow	Throws an exception
new	Creates a new object
newfromname	Creates a new object from a given name

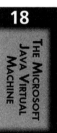

18

THE MICROSOFT
JAVA VIRTUAL
MACHINE

continues

Table 18.1. continued

Opcode	Description
checkcast	Make sure object is of a given type
instanceof	Determine whether object is of given type
verifystack	Verify that stack is empty
breakpoint	Calls the breakpoint handler

The instructions listed in Table 18.1 are used to manipulate primitive data types and objects (classes and interfaces) using the JVM registers, stack, and heap. When Java source code is compiled by Visual J++, each line of Java code is then converted into an associated set of instructions from the instruction set listed in Table 18.1. These instructions are combined and placed into a class file for the JVM to interpret into machine code.

Class Files

Class files receive their names from several sources. The most obvious source is that each Java class object, when compiled, is stored in one of these files. These files also always end with the .class extension. Each public or private class or interface is compiled into a class file with the name *objectname.class.*

The JVM specification describes the actual format of a class file. Whereas other portions of the specification allow for some variance, the class file format is very exact in its specifications.

The format of this file groups class fields into a structure that closely resembles a C language struct programming structure. The types u1, u2, and u4 are used to designate unsigned 1-, 2-, or 4-byte quantities.

> **NOTE**
>
> Each class file begins with the magic field. For a JVM to interpret the class file, the value of this field must be 0xCAFEBABE.

The remainder of the class file contains a large number of fields used to describe the variables and methods used in the class. Also contained in the file are the opcodes that make up each method.

Limitations of the JVM

Because Java's designers intentionally force virtual machine implementors to work with a set of constraints, the JVM has a few restrictions. These restrictions are necessary to ensure a high level of portability of executable content across multiple platforms (the goal of Java). The following are some inherent restrictions:

- Because the JVM uses 32-bit pointers and addressing, the maximum amount of memory that can be addressed is 4GB.
- All branch and jump instructions use signed 16-bit offsets. This limits the size of a single method to 32KB.
- Local variable indices are stored as 8-bit values. This limits the number of variables per stack frame to 256.
- Constant pool indices are stored as signed 16-bit values. This limits the number of entries in the constant pool to 32KB.
- The number of methods in a class is limited to 256.
- The number of parameters to a method is limited to 256 32-bit words.

Most of these restrictions are of no consequence to the average developer. (Have you ever passed more than 256 parameters to a method? If so, and you were working on a development team, you probably were not employed for long!) The only serious restrictions that could cause problems are perhaps the 256-method-per-class limit and the overall memory addressing limit of 4GB. These limits are mentioned here so that the Visual J++ developer is aware of the limits of the underlying Microsoft VM.

Integrating Java and COM Using the Microsoft VM

As mentioned at the beginning of the chapter, the Microsoft VM is the reference implementation of the JVM for the Windows platform. Any Java bytecodes produced by any compiler on any platform should be able to run without modification using the Microsoft JVM in Internet Explorer. (In reality, bugs in the Internet Explorer browser may prevent a few select operations from working properly. However, this is not because of any Microsoft extensions to the JVM.)

There are some major features in the Microsoft JVM that separate it from every other virtual machine built by all the other major manufacturers (IBM, Sun, Apple, Netscape, and so on). Because of the many similarities between COM and Java, the Microsoft VM also supports the integration of COM objects (such as ActiveX controls) and Java classes. This is possible because the Microsoft VM is capable of loading COM objects and exposing their interfaces. Because of the many similarities between COM and Java, COM objects can be created and used in Java classes. In fact, to the Java programmer, there is really no difference between the two. All the details involved with binding to the native COM code are hidden from the developer.

18

THE MICROSOFT
JAVA VIRTUAL
MACHINE

If COM objects can be used in Java code, it makes sense that the Microsoft VM would be able to expose Java classes as COM objects as well. (It does!) This capability allows Java classes to be exposed as COM objects and therefore to be reused by applications written in other programming languages such as Visual Basic, C++, or Delphi.

Combining COM and Java

The fact that COM objects can be used in Java programs (and vice versa) is a cause of concern to many professional software developers and Java enthusiasts. When COM and Java are mixed together using tools such as Visual J++ and the Microsoft VM, Java loses one of its greatest assets: platform independence. In return, the Java developer gains access to a huge base of existing code written in a variety of languages. Throughout this book, it has been (and will continue to be) emphasized that programmers who want to use ActiveX/COM and Java should think carefully about the potential users of their applications. In the intranet case, in which all users are using Windows95/NT and the Internet Explorer browser, a strong argument can be made for a combination of ActiveX and Java. In the Internet case, in which a variety of platforms and browsers exist, Java allows the developer to reach the broadest audience.

Another way of looking at this same issue is to view Java as just a great programming language. This is the basis of Microsoft's Java strategy. If you have been actively involved with building Windows applications and plan to do so for some time, the Visual J++ compiler combined with the Microsoft VM gives you a powerful new tool to use in building these applications.

Using COM Objects in Java

Chapter 7, "Advanced Java Programming," introduces the concept of *native methods*. Native methods in Java allow Java code to indirectly call methods written in other languages such as C or C++. This native code interface is supplied by every JVM, including the Microsoft VM. The Microsoft VM also provides another method for reusing existing methods written in other programming languages: by using COM objects in Java.

From the programming language level, COM objects look identical to Java objects when used in Java code. This is because COM, like Java, supports the following:

- Memory management of objects
- Dynamically created and linked objects
- Classes that can contain variables and methods and can implement interfaces
- Multiple interfaces per class
- Error handling

Because of these similarities, it was clear early on that COM and Java could be integrated using extensions to the JVM. To start, the virtual machine must understand how to extract class and interface information from COM objects. Fortunately, COM object information is stored in a file known as a *type library* (similar in purpose to a Java class file). After the type library has been examined, it is converted to Java class files. Special attributes are added to the class files so that the Microsoft VM will know that the objects represented by these class files are COM objects, not simply Java objects. (This is an example of a Microsoft extension that would render a class file useless on other platforms.)

Identifying COM Objects

Recall that regular Java class files can be imported by a class using statements such as the following:

```
import java.awt.*;
import sun.tools.debug;
import activex.*;
```

When the Java compiler encounters the `import` keyword, it examines the CLASSPATH environment variable on the local machine to determine which directories contain Java classes. Using these three statements, these class files would be located in the following directories:

```
$CLASSPATH/java/awt/*
$CLASSPATH/sun/tools/debug
$CLASSPATH/activex/*
```

If the classes are not found in the specified directory, most Java compilers would generate an error. The Microsoft Visual J++ compiler goes a step further, however, to try to locate potential COM objects using the following methodology:

1. It examines the directories listed in the CLASSPATH environment variable for Java class files.

2. If no class files are found, these same directories are searched for type library files (`*.tlb`) or interface definition language files (`*.idl`).

3. If none of these files is found, the Windows Registry is examined to retrieve type library information about the referenced objects.

When the COM information is obtained from the type library, interface definition file, or Registry entries, corresponding Java class files are built that allow the COM objects to be used in Java code.

Memory Management of COM Objects

Because Java frees you from having to deallocate memory when objects are no longer used, this same capability must be present for COM objects as well. Fortunately, COM objects support a similar memory management scheme known as *reference counting*. Reference counting is a COM object's process of maintaining an internal count of how many other objects are currently referencing it. An object's reference count is decremented whenever its `release()` method is called. When the reference count goes to 0, the COM object will free itself. Java differs slightly from this model because the JVM is responsible for tracking the reference count of objects, not the individual objects themselves.

The Microsoft VM performs double duty in this area. It still tracks the usage of all Java objects and frees them when they are no longer used. In addition, it also calls each COM object's `release()` method when it detects another object is no longer using it. When the COM object's reference count goes to 0, it removes itself from memory.

Limitations of Java/COM Integration

One of the primary reasons that Java and COM could be integrated so smoothly and quickly is that Java provides the capability for an object to implement multiple interfaces. As explained in Chapter 16, "Java and the Component Object Model," ActiveX relies heavily on interfaces that objects must implement so that other objects can reuse them. Without the notion of multiple interfaces, it would be very difficult to integrate Java and COM in a transparent manner.

Despite this advantage, Java does differ from COM in some respects. These differences put some restrictions on the level of integration between Java and COM. First, recall that the key to using Java and COM objects together is the COM objects' *type library*. The Microsoft VM imports the COM type library and subsequently constructs a Java class file. In theory, this is a wonderful concept. However, some COM objects cannot be described within a type library because of limitations of the type library model. Therefore, COM objects that fall into this category cannot be implemented in Java.

Also recall that Java only supports single inheritance of objects. COM supports a type of inheritance known as *aggregation*. An object can aggregate a set of interfaces obtained from another object and present them as its own. (Note that it did not inherit from these interfaces.) This set of interfaces is known as an *aggregate*. There can be multiple aggregates within a single COM object. To the Java programmer, this would appear as a single class inheriting methods from multiple classes, which is not allowed. Because this goes against the fundamental concepts of Java, multiple aggregation in imported COM objects is not allowed.

Summary

The true magic of Java is the underlying JVM. It is this virtual machine that converts the platform-independent bytecodes into platform-*dependent* machine code at runtime. The JVM specification is controlled by Sun Microsystems. This specification lists the capabilities that an implementor must support to produce a compliant virtual machine.

All virtual machines resemble hardware machines in some respects. They all include support for an instruction set, primitive data types, registers, program stack, and object heap.

The instruction set for a JVM contains a large group of instructions that are responsible for loading and unloading objects and their members. In addition, the JVM specification defines in detail the format of the Java class file. Any extensions to the specification in this area can be ignored by virtual machines that do not support these extensions. Therefore, Microsoft's class file extensions that provide information about COM objects will be ignored by other virtual machines that do not support these COM extensions. Unfortunately, it is impossible to predict how each environment will react when these extensions are encountered. Be prepared to witness your ActiveX-enabled Java code crash a browser (such as Netscape Navigator) that does not support ActiveX. (All it takes is one null memory address or a bad pointer reference and the whole browser can come crashing down.)

The Microsoft VM provides the standard functionality described in the JVM specification. In addition, Microsoft also allows Java objects to use COM objects, and vice versa, because the object models of Java and COM are extremely similar. Both support inheritance, multiple interfaces, and dynamically created and linked objects. Java class definitions are compiled and stored as bytecodes within *class files*; COM objects' definitions are compiled and stored as *type libraries*. One of the primary tasks of the Microsoft VM is to translate between class files and type libraries so that neither COM nor Java can tell the difference between the other's objects and its own.

For the developer, the advantage of this COM/Java integration is that he or she can easily re-use existing ActiveX controls in Java applications. Java classes can also be included as programming objects in standard Windows programming languages such as Visual Basic, C++, and Delphi. The result of this is that Visual J++ should not be viewed as just a Web development tool. Instead, the Microsoft VM allows Visual J++ to claim the same status and level of support as Microsoft's other flagship products: Visual Basic and Visual C++.

18

THE MICROSOFT
JAVA VIRTUAL
MACHINE

Extending Java Using ActiveX

by Bryan Morgan

IN THIS CHAPTER

CHAPTER 19

The purpose of this chapter is to point out the strengths and weaknesses in Microsoft's ActiveX technology. A key point to remember is that with Microsoft Visual J++, the Java developer has two options to play with: pure Java and ActiveX. In other words, the topic of ActiveX and Java is no longer an either/or discussion. Therefore, developers have the responsibility of picking the best tool for the job (which is the way it is supposed to be).

The Advantages of ActiveX

In any fair discussion, nearly every new technology has a set of advantages and disadvantages. ActiveX has been praised by many and criticized by just as many others. (This type of debate usually at least indicates that the technology does something interesting!) Nonetheless, with the advent of the Microsoft Internet Explorer 3.0 browser, the Microsoft Virtual Machine for Java, and Visual J++, ActiveX is going to be around for quite some time. This discussion focuses on the advantages of ActiveX and its benefits for Web programmers. The starting point is that ActiveX enables Web programmers to do some things that they simply cannot do using any other technology. Consequently, ActiveX is often the only game in town.

High Performance

The ActiveX technologies are all *binary* technologies. Therefore, unlike Java, they don't require a runtime interpreter that translates bytecodes into machine code. Downloaded components (ActiveX controls) are able to run at true machine speeds, and consequently, ActiveX controls run much faster than comparable Java applets.

Persistence

A dynamically loaded object can be said to be *persistent* if that object remains on the local system after it has been used. Although in some instances persistence can be a disadvantage, when ActiveX controls are initially downloaded, they are installed on the local system and remain there. (Future versions of Internet Explorer will allow the user to set defaults that control how ActiveX controls are saved.) The next time the user visits a page containing this ActiveX control, no downloading needs to be done. Instead, the ActiveX control is embedded immediately within the form. Java applets, meanwhile, are only cached on the local file system during the Web browser's current session. The next time the user visits the Web site (after closing the browser), the applet most likely will have to be downloaded again. Downloading an applet may not seem like a big deal, but because many applets inherit and use a wide variety of other classes, many of these additional classes also have to be downloaded. It is not unusual for a single applet to download 50 separate class files before it can be used within the Web page.

Huge Existing Code Base

Although Java is an extremely exciting technology and may be the language of choice for many in the coming years, ActiveX technologies have been around since 1990. An extremely large base of code currently exists in the thousands of ActiveX controls available on the market today. Because of the component object model (COM) foundation, all OLE controls available before the introduction of ActiveX can be downloaded and used within a Web browser just like ActiveX controls. The primary difference between ActiveX controls and OLE controls is that ActiveX controls are *required* to implement only one interface: Iunknown. Therefore, ActiveX controls can be much smaller than OLE controls, although in some cases ActiveX controls are no different in size than their OLE counterparts.

ActiveX controls are hugely popular, and an entire industry already exists and thrives on their production and sales. Among the ActiveX controls currently installed on my machine are

- Map Display
- Chart
- Spreadsheet
- Spellchecker
- RealAudio
- Stock Ticker
- Movie Player
- Image Viewer
- Date and Calendar
- Progress Bar

Although existing Java applets can perform some of the functionality mentioned above, some of the operations are beyond the scope of Java-applet technology. For instance, it is possible to write a stock ticker Java applet to retrieve stock quotes. However, that applet will be unable to save the data it retrieves to a local file. In addition, many of the available Java spreadsheet and chart classes (to pick some examples) suffer from extremely poor performance and low functionality.

Meanwhile, the market has pretty much sorted out the winners from the losers in the ActiveX control arena. Companies such as Sheridan, Micro-Help, and Visual Components have established excellent reputations for building high-performance, high-functionality ActiveX objects. When you purchase components from these companies, you have some assurance that they will work as advertised.

The following applications can be built with Visual J++ and the controls listed previously:

- A Web page containing HTML and an ActiveX control to display mapping coverages.
- A Windows application written in Java to show a spreadsheet.
- A Web application containing Java applets and ActiveX controls side-by-side to plot data to a screen based on input coming from a real-time stock ticker. Data from this application could be printed to a local printer in the form of customized reports (not just a mirror of the Web page sent to the printer).

The Windows Virtual Machine for Java makes all this functionality possible. You may be surprised to learn that even the Microsoft Virtual Machine itself was built as an ActiveX object! Thousands of developers have spent huge amounts of time and money investing in application development using ActiveX components. It is wishful to expect all these developers to simply stop everything they have been doing for the past two years, retool, and begin developing Web-based Java applications. ActiveX acts as a bridge between the two technologies by allowing existing components to be reused while new components are added to applications. These components could be written in Java, Visual Basic, Delphi, C++, or any other language that supports the creation of ActiveX controls.

Language Independence

ActiveX objects have one additional advantage: They can be written in any language and can be called from any other language.

> ### NOTE
>
> Before continuing with this topic, let me take a moment to define the word *any* in the world of Microsoft. Developers cannot simply sit down with a FORTRAN compiler and immediately start using ActiveX controls. Instead, the compiler needs to be able to support the linkages between ActiveX and standard code. Likewise, for a language to call an ActiveX object, the compiler must be "ActiveX aware" and support the hooks necessary to dynamically link together ActiveX objects with binary code.

Under Windows 95/NT, the development tools that control the lion's share of the PC software development market all support the usage of ActiveX controls. As mentioned earlier, this list includes Visual Basic and C++, Delphi, PowerBuilder, FoxPro, and Access. C++, Delphi, and Visual Basic also support the creation of ActiveX controls. Therefore, an ActiveX object written in C++ could be dropped onto a Delphi form (or an HTML page for viewing in Microsoft Internet Explorer). The word *object* is intentionally used here to mean a programming construct that encapsulates data and methods in an atomic object.

Programs written in Java, meanwhile, can have only limited communication with code written in other languages through the use of *native methods*. Once these methods are used, Java classes cannot "travel" to remote machines as they do when they are downloaded to a client browser. Because native methods can link only to static object code, Java does not have a way to dynamically update the linked-in code; in contrast, ActiveX objects have such a mechanism.

Distributed COM

With the advent of distributed COM (DCOM) in Windows NT 4.0, ActiveX objects also have the capability of communicating with objects located on remote machines. These objects could be placed on other machines for a variety of reasons:

- Maintainability—Objects could be updated once on the server and all clients would immediately "see" the update.

- Network performance—Each individual object would not need to be downloaded in its entirety over the network; instead, remote procedure calls (RPCs) are used to communicate among the objects.

- Scalability—DCOM allows objects to be mirrored across multiple machines to improve performance for the end user.

Much attention has been paid to the two-tier design of traditional client/server applications. In this development mode, all display and application logic resides on the client (Web browser containing applets/controls or a normal GUI application), and the database operations reside on the server. Several problems arise with this development paradigm. The biggest problem is that the display code and the application code often become so intertwined that code maintenance is extremely difficult. If a screen needs to be dramatically changed, a huge amount of reworking is involved. Breaking applications into logical portions and distributing these segments across multiple tiers (often called *n-tiers*) leads to better maintainability, performance, and scalability.

The Flip Side: The Disadvantages of ActiveX

Believe it or not, despite the marketing hype surrounding ActiveX, it does have some real disadvantages. These disadvantages are outlined in an unbiased manner in the following sections.

Platform Dependence

Microsoft advertises ActiveX as having "cross-platform support." Although versions of ActiveX are being readied for the Macintosh and UNIX operating systems, the fact remains that today ActiveX can be used only on Microsoft's own operating system (Windows). To Microsoft's credit, the COM in no way specifies any vendor- or platform-specific implantation features. However, thus far no one besides Microsoft has stepped forward and built an implementation on top of COM.

A discussion seems to continually rage in the Java newsgroup (comp.lang.java) over whether the words *cross-platform* even matter. After all, Microsoft owns nearly a 90 percent share of the personal computing operating system market—so who cares about cross-platform? In other words, what good does being cross-platform do you if all of your customers' platforms are the same? This point is extremely interesting, and like all good questions, it doesn't have an easy answer. In an ideal world, individual users could choose their computing environment based on their personal preferences. That is, the software would come to the user, rather than the user being forced to go to the software.

Java itself is not completely above this discussion. Although Java code may be able to run unmodified on virtually any platform, it is unable to interoperate with other parts of the operating system. In a generic Web-centric environment, the Web browser could act as the operating system and applet execution environment. However, this approach excludes all applications that take advantage of operating system features to provide more value to the end user (for example, printing, file access, interapplication data sharing).

Microsoft has announced its intention to develop ActiveX-aware versions of the Internet Explorer browser for the Macintosh and UNIX operating systems. The time frame in which these browsers are introduced combined with the success of the Mac and UNIX ports of ActiveX will play key roles in the success of Microsoft's cross-platform ActiveX strategy.

Security Model

Java was designed from the ground up to ensure that a client machine running Java code could be nearly certain that the code would not harm the local system. Java applets have no ability to read or write to the local file system or to make any operating system calls whatsoever (a security technique known as *sandboxing*). No matter who the developer of the Java applet is, a user can download an applet, run it, and never really think about the security implications of doing so. Although no system connected to the outside world via the Internet can ever be 100 percent secure, the Java language and runtime environment go a long way to preventing security flaws.

ActiveX controls, meanwhile, have full system privileges. Once an ActiveX control is downloaded, your Windows Registry may be updated and the component will be installed onto your local system. The ActiveX control is able to perform a directory search of the file system, change video resolutions, reboot your computer, or even grab files and send them over the Internet to a remote server. With these capabilities, no security model on earth will ever make users feel completely comfortable. Microsoft is trying, however, to convince the computer industry and the public in general of the virtues of its ActiveX security model. This model uses a technique known as *code signing* to verify the contents of ActiveX controls before they are downloaded.

Code signing is provided by an independent software testing facility (called a certification authority) that tests code to verify that it does what it says it does. When this software has been tested, the code is signed using a *digital signature,* which contains information that can be examined by software that supports the Microsoft Trust Verification service (Internet Explorer, for example). Using this service, a Web browser can determine whether a control had been modified since being assigned a digital signature. If tinkering has occurred, the Web browser can alert the user or disallow downloading.

> **CAUTION**
>
> Keep in mind that ActiveX components, unlike Java applets, do not undergo any runtime verification. Therefore, once the control is installed on a machine, it is free to do whatever it wants.

ActiveX controls are not required to use code signing. In fact, Internet Explorer 3.0 allows users to control the security level at which they wish to operate (see Figure 19.1).

FIGURE 19.1.
The Internet Explorer security Options dialog.

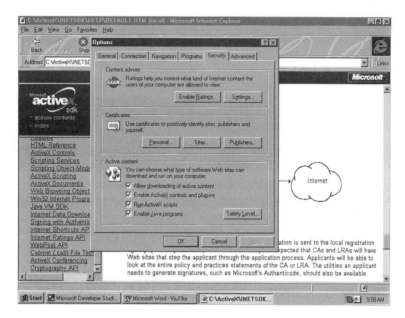

Security can mean different things in different contexts. Java is secure in that Java code is unable to access the local operating system when running within a Web browser. ActiveX security, though not as foolproof, can still provide the same level of security that is found today in shrink-wrapped software. Perhaps the biggest problem with ActiveX security is that it leads the public to trust only software produced by the major software manufacturers. A tiny, brand-new software company may have difficulty convincing people to download and run their ActiveX code, especially when a major manufacturer (such as Microsoft) offers a comparable product.

Network Performance

One other disadvantage of ActiveX controls that is often ignored is their size. Going back to the partial list of ActiveX controls currently installed on my machine, the following list shows these controls and their size. Some of these controls are OLE controls; others are actual ActiveX controls, and they are noticeably smaller (the `Stock Ticker` and `RealAudio` controls, in particular). The following list illustrates the file sizes of some typical ActiveX controls:

- `Map Display`—374KB
- `Chart`—294KB
- `Spreadsheet`—623KB

19

EXTENDING JAVA
USING ACTIVEX

- `Spellchecker`—84KB
- `RealAudio`—114KB
- `Stock Ticker`—88KB
- `Movie Player`—187KB
- `Image Viewer`—96KB
- `Date and Calendar`—325KB and 228KB
- `Progress Bar`—208KB

In contrast, the 469 Java classes included in the Visual J++ `classes.zip` file take up a total of 769KB, or approximately 1.75KB each. Although some applets also download a number of additional classes in order to be interpreted and run, all 469 files in the Visual J++ class library will be included on the local Windows machine as part of the Microsoft Virtual Machine. (In other words, they don't need to be downloaded.) Microsoft has gone a step further with the Visual J++ product and allowed developers to package all of the required class files for an applet together into a single CAB file. This file is compressed on the server side, and the individual class files are extracted from the CAB file as the Java Virtual Machine needs them. Compressing files in this way greatly reduces download time of Java classes.

Some ActiveX controls also require dynamic link libraries (DLLs) and other files to be installed along with the ActiveX control. When these controls are downloaded, an installation routine will often start and install the control on the local machine. Although this process has to be completed only once, it still causes a long enough wait that many users may just cancel the operation altogether. Developers who have built OLE controls should obtain the ActiveX SDK and really look at converting these controls to true ActiveX controls in order to save download time.

Browser Dependence

As you are probably well aware by now, ActiveX is supported natively only in Microsoft's Internet Explorer 3.0 browser. A Netscape plug-in from nCompass Labs also allows the Netscape Navigator to display pages containing ActiveX controls, but Netscape does not support this product. Through the 4.0 release of the Navigator, Netscape has no plans to add ActiveX support to its browser either. Therefore, if you were to build Web pages containing ActiveX controls or Java applets communicating with ActiveX components (as you will see later in this chapter in the section titled "Combining Java and COM Using Visual J++"), those pages would display properly only within Microsoft Internet Explorer.

As new ActiveX-enabled versions of Microsoft Internet Explorer become available for the Macintosh and UNIX platforms, the situation is sure to change. At that point an overwhelming majority of operating systems would feature support for ActiveX and Java; then all bets are off. However, developers interested in ActiveX should realize that a growing contingent of users are worried about ActiveX's security drawbacks as well as its platform dependence. If you are making development choices, you need to consider all these concerns.

What Does ActiveX Mean for the Web Developer?

All this jockeying for position in the Web sweepstakes has left many developers' heads spinning. Microsoft continues to release a barrage of related ActiveX technologies with little explanation of the benefits and drawbacks inherent in each technology's usage. What's worse, the real-time nature of the Web has led to the reporting of new features and products before these features are actually solidified.

ActiveX and the Intranet Setting

In the near term, the success of ActiveX will be found in the intranet setting. At the department or division level, software and hardware resources can be quantified and controlled to a much larger degree than the entire Internet. Therefore, organizations that have already chosen Windows 95 or NT as part of their standard desktop should be able to implement ActiveX solutions with relative ease. The advantages of ActiveX really show up in this situation because the department's information services staff can continue to work with the development tools they've been using. Web servers can be set up to provide replication, if necessary, and objects on servers can be updated so that users see the changes in real-time. In fact, existing OLE controls and ActiveX controls can even be reused. At this point the professional developer should look at encapsulating application logic in the form of distributed objects on servers. The user interface can be generated fairly rapidly using standard Web publishing tools. Java can also be used throughout development projects in combination with ActiveX to match the best tool with the job.

ActiveX and the Internet

On the other hand, ActiveX faces a much more daunting task before it can claim success across the World Wide Web. Because of security concerns and the fact that a large minority of World Wide Web clients are non-Windows machines, most developers voice skepticism about ActiveX on the Internet. As Microsoft demonstrates the effectiveness of its code-signing solution, and as ActiveX is ported to other platforms, ActiveX should slowly gain a larger measure of support than it is currently receiving.

In any case, to reach the lowest common denominator, pure Java is still the best choice for providing active Web applications to the greatest number of clients. Despite its flaws, the Java language and runtime environment were designed with the Web in mind (not retrofitted for the Web after the fact) and contain a number of advantages simply not found in any other technology on the market today. Other chapters in this book (Chapters 25, "Browser Support for Active Content," 26, "HTML and Web Page Design," and 29, "Embedding Components Within Web Pages") demonstrate how to use Java to build applets for display in Web pages.

The following example illustrates the use of Java (using Microsoft Visual J++) to build a COM-aware Java applet.

Combining Java and COM Using Visual J++

Web developers skilled in Java and COM/ActiveX have the best of the desktop and the Internet at their fingertips. The Visual J++ development tool allows Java programmers to call COM objects using Java code. These COM objects look exactly the same to the developer as every other Java class. In fact, using tools included with Visual J++, actual Java class files are generated for each COM object. These classes can then be imported and used as if they were a standard class.

This "magic" is made possible through the use of the Microsoft Virtual Machine for Java. Microsoft has licensed the JVM specification from Sun Microsystems and has signed an agreement to build the "reference implementation" of the JVM for the Windows platform. Any additions that Microsoft makes to the Windows JVM can be given back to Sun for inclusion in its Java Virtual Machine specification. Unlike the Virtual Machine included with most Web browsers such as Netscape Navigator, the Microsoft Virtual Machine actually becomes part of the operating system after installation. Therefore, it becomes available to *all* Windows applications. Because it is implemented as a COM object, the Microsoft Virtual Machine can be utilized by any application that supports the same COM interfaces. Thus, objects created in Java can appear as COM objects to other Windows applications. With this provision, Microsoft has elevated Java to the same programming status as its other flagship languages: C++ and Visual Basic.

The javabeep example included with Visual J++ demonstrates a Java class calling a COM object (located in the beeper.dll file). This simple object is used to build a Java applet and application that will beep and print a message each time the user clicks the mouse on the application's client window.

Using the Java Type Library Wizard in Visual J++, standard Java classes are generated from the COM object's type library.

> **NOTE**
>
> A *type library* in COM is simply a "definition" file that lists all of the methods, variables, and interfaces supported by the object that the type library represents. A type library is similar in nature to a C++ header file.

These classes provide a mapping between the variables, methods, and interfaces used in the COM object and the variables, methods, and interfaces in the new Java class. When the Type Library Wizard is finished, two new classes will have been created for your usage in the `\windows\java\lib\beeper` directory:

- `Beeper.class`
- `IBeeper.class`

To access these two objects (actually contained in the `beeper.dll` COM library), add the following line of code to your Java applet or application:

```
import beeper.*;
```

This line will import both classes in the `Beeper` package. To create a new `beeper` object for use within your Java class, the following code is sufficient:

```
IBeeper m_Beeper = null;
…
if(m_Beeper==null)
  m_Beeper = (IBeeper) new Beeper();
```

Once the object has been created, the following statement will call into the `beeper.dll` and issue a beep:

```
m_Beeper.beep();
```

Programmers with some Java experience will notice that syntactically everything here is standard Java code. The real work is being done at the Virtual Machine level. Figure 19.2 shows the `JavaBeep` project running as an application.

Figure 19.3 shows the `JavaBeep` project running as an applet.

FIGURE 19.2.

A Java application calling a COM object.

19

EXTENDING JAVA
USING ACTIVEX

FIGURE 19.3.

A Java applet calling a COM object.

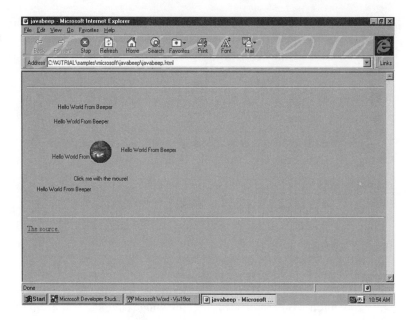

Summary

The ActiveX technologies are extremely powerful and have the potential to allow Web-based applications to do things that were previously impossible. You can develop truly interactive, interesting applications using ActiveX controls, ActiveX scripting, and ActiveX documents; HTML and Java applets; and the Web browser as the operating environment. With a tool such as Visual J++, the ActiveX controls can even be built using Java, and Java applets can contain ActiveX controls. This combination provides the professional software developer with the best desktop and Internet technologies.

ActiveX itself has a number of advantages and disadvantages. It has the advantages of being language independent, demonstrating good performance, and having a large existing code base. Some of its drawbacks include its platform dependence (Windows only at the current time), its access to the local operating system, and its limited browser support (Internet Explorer only at the current time).

Microsoft is taking steps to address each of these issues, but many developers are comfortable with the capabilities of Java as it currently exists. To port ActiveX to a small number of desktop operating systems requires an extensive effort, whereas the Java Virtual Machine already exists on nearly every operating platform in use today. ActiveX security (via code signing) requires an independent certification authority (that is, bureaucracy) to certify and verify a control's behavior.

Tools such as Visual J++ allow Java developers to pick and choose among different Java, COM, and ActiveX objects and build applications using the best features of all three technologies. Visual J++ comes with three wizards designed to greatly enhance your productivity as a Java programmer:

- Java Applet Wizard
- Java Resource Wizard
- Java Type Library Wizard

These wizards, combined with a visual debugger, online documentation, and excellent development environment, provide an extremely flexible tool that you can use for standard Java programming as well as ActiveX programming.

Over time, the question of whether ActiveX's strengths are enough to overcome its inherent weaknesses will be resolved. Until then, both technologies will probably coexist and continue to improve. This situation will be to the software developer's benefit.

Calling COM Objects from Java

by Bryan Morgan

IN THIS CHAPTER

What separates Visual J++ and the Microsoft Virtual Machine from all other Java tools is the integration between Java and Microsoft's component object model (COM). Previous chapters provide an introduction to those readers new to using COM projects or, in particular, programming with COM objects. This chapter is primarily example oriented, illustrating how Java code can be written to call COM objects using Visual J++ and the Microsoft Virtual Machine.

A Mix of COM with Your Java (or Java with Your COM!)

When you have to use some combination of COM and Java (whether through COM objects, ActiveX controls, or some other means), you have three options:

- Build a Java applet or application that uses an existing COM object. This COM object could even be written in Java!
- Create a Java applet to work with an existing ActiveX control. This can be done to build a Web page that equals a standalone Windows application in its power and sophistication.
- Write a COM object in Java for use by other programs written in any popular language (C++, VB, Delphi, and so on).

Examples in this chapter examine the first two of these options. Both specifically deal with calling a COM object from within a Java program. The third option is presented in Chapter 21, "Building COM Objects with Java."

Ground Rules for Calling COM Objects from Java

Whenever software components are integrated to form a working application, some setup and system configuration are required to ensure that the various components work together correctly. For instance, when a Visual Basic developer uses an OCX control on a form, this control must be registered with the operating system. When a UNIX programmer distributes a set of shared objects for use by one or more applications, the system path must be set to include the directory containing these libraries. Likewise, Java programmers must go through two primary steps before a COM object can be successfully compiled and used in a Java program. First, the COM object must be registered on the local system. Following this, the contents of the COM object's type library must be extracted using tools provided with Visual J++. Another step is required to actually distribute the completed Java classes to other users. This step requires the classes to be digitally signed for security purposes.

Registering the Object

The first step applies to not only Java programmers, but programmers developing in any language: You need to register the COM object in the Windows Registry using the CLSIDs stored in the object. (Recall from Chapter 15, "GUI Development Using the Visual J++ Resource Wizard," that CLSIDs are globally unique identification numbers that are used to identify a COM object.) You can register COM objects several different ways.

At the simplest, you can record and manually add the required Registry settings using the Registry tool, named REGEDIT.EXE under Windows 95 and REGEDT32.EXE under Windows NT. You can also write and run registration script files that will automatically register the script's settings into the Registry. Perhaps the simplest way to register many COM objects is by using the REGSVR32.EXE tool.

> **NOTE**
>
> Under Windows 95, REGSVR32.EXE is in your \WINDOWS\SYSTEM directory. Under Windows NT, REGSVR32.EXE is in the \WINDOWS\SYSTEM32 directory.

REGSVR32 takes advantage of the fact that all COM in-process servers (DLLs and OCXs) are required to be self-registering by definition. REGSVR32 simply calls the necessary commands in the object to register it in the Registry. If an application is run without a corresponding COM object being registered, it is common to see an error message such as "Object Not Found" or something along those lines. When an application using OLE controls is originally run with errors, it is common to find that the set of controls was not registered.

REGSVR32 is a command-line tool that has a simple set of options (see Table 20.1).

Table 20.1. REGSVR32 command-line options.

Option	Description
/u	Unregister the specified COM server
/s	Register the COM server silently (with no visible output)
/c	Register the COM server with output to the console

The REGSVR32 tool is used with the following command-line syntax:

```
regsvr32 <options> filename.xxx
```

The /s option is commonly used during an application's installation process to register a control in the background without alerting the user. Microsoft Internet Explorer uses the silent registration option to register ActiveX components as they are downloaded from remote locations.

20

CALLING COM
OBJECTS FROM
JAVA

Creating Java Classes Using the Java Type Library Wizard

After a COM object has been registered with the system, it is still simply a DLL/OCX/EXE binary object residing on the hard drive. To allow the Java programmer to use this object, Microsoft could have simply added a thinly disguised native method interface to COM objects. However, because of the many similarities between Java and COM (see Chapter 16, "Java and the Component Object Model"), Microsoft provides a method to seamlessly combine COM and Java objects in source code. In other words, COM objects can be instantiated and used side by side with other Java objects with no special syntax or keywords required. This magic was accomplished by creating a tool that could examine the contents of a COM type library, extract them, and produce the corresponding Java class files to match the contents of the type libraries. As you know by now, after the class files are created, the import statement can be used to import a package or class into another Java class.

The *Java Type Library Wizard* is used to build these class files in Visual J++. This wizard can be run from the Visual J++ IDE by selecting the Tools | Java Type Library Wizard main menu option. The application that responds to this menu selection is actually JAVATLB.EXE, located in your installation directory's \bin subdirectory. The Type Library Wizard can also be run from the command line with a set of extended options using the following syntax:

```
javatlb <options> type_library_filename
```

Keep in mind that a type library can exist in a standalone .tlb file. It can also be stored as a resource within a COM object (.exe, .dll, .ocx, .olb). When run on a type library, a directory (named with the type library's filename) will be created in the trusted libraries directory on the local machine.

> **NOTE**
>
> To determine which directory is currently being used to store trusted classes, examine the registry key HKEY_LOCAL_MACHINE\Software\Microsoft\Java VM\TrustedLibsDirectory using the Registry Editor.

One Java class file is created for each class or interface in the type library. Options that can be used in combination with the Java Type Library Wizard are listed in Table 20.2.

Table 20.2. JAVATLB command-line options.

Option	Description
@list	Displays @ symbol + filename containing list of type library files
/U	Displays signatures for all public methods for each class file
/U:T	Displays signatures for all public methods for each class file and writes the information to a text file
/p package_name	Specifies which package the output class files will be placed into

When run from the Developer Studio menu selection, the Java Type Library Wizard always produces a file named SUMMARY.TXT and places that file in the type library's trusted directory. This file contains the signatures for each method in the class file. In effect, the Java Type Library Wizard runs JAVATLB with the following syntax:

```
javatlb /U:T library.tlb > SUMMARY.TXT
```

Handling Security During Distribution

Security options become significantly more complex when Java classes are combined with COM objects to build applications. First, using ActiveX controls implies an entirely new set of security precautions that may be new even to the veteran Java programmer. Second, Java class files generated from a COM type library must be contained in a CAB file and digitally signed using Microsoft's Code Signing standard. Applets or applications that make use of these Java classes will not run outside the Visual J++ Developer Studio unless they are contained in a CAB file and have been signed. Security issues are addressed in detail in Chapter 23, "Security with ActiveX Authenticode." For now, let's assume that the samples shown in this chapter (and Chapters 21, "Building COM Objects with Java," 22, "Using ActiveX Documents to Convey Information," and 23) will be run from Developer Studio to avoid this problem.

> **NOTE**
>
> When loading ActiveX controls embedded in an HTML page using Internet Explorer 3.0, make sure that IE's security options are set to the Medium level. This is done by selecting the View menu and then the Options item. Select the Security tab and then the Safety button. Finally, select either the None or Medium options to enable the downloading and display of ActiveX components.

Again, be sure to run all Java/COM examples included with Visual J++ or with this book from the Developer Studio environment. Because none of these classes have been signed and are not contained in a CAB file, a java.lang.VerifyError error may occur.

Calling a COM Object from Java

This section gives an example to illustrate how a COM object can be called from a Java applet or application. It would have been possible to create a COM in-process server DLL that exported a class or interface to be called from Java. However, the topic of creating COM objects using C or C++ is outside the scope of this book. (In addition, creating COM objects in Java is not discussed until Chapter 21.) Therefore, for purposes of illustration, the JavaCallingCOM sample included with Visual J++ is studied.

The JavaCallingCOM sample application consists of a COM automation server DLL, Java applet, and set of HTML files used to display and document the sample application. The server DLL,

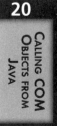

comserver.dll, contains a set of available system sound IDs (stored as constants) along with the ICOmBeeper interface, which provides helper functions to select and play the sounds.

Although it might seem a little odd because of the underlying complexity of what is actually happening, when the object's structure has been extracted into Java class files, it is extremely easy to use that object in Java source code. Following the steps outlined in "Registering the Object" before the COM DLL can be accessed from a Java program, the DLL must be registered and class files must be generated using the Java Type Library Wizard. Therefore, take the following steps: First, execute the following statement in the directory containing the COMServer DLL: c:\windows\system\regsvr32 comserver.dll. Following this exercise, use the Java Type Library Wizard to select the COMServer 1.0 Type Library to generate class files (see Figure 20.1).

FIGURE 20.1.

The Java Type Library Wizard.

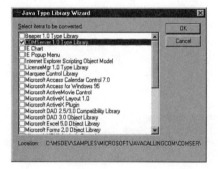

When the wizard has successfully generated the class files for the COMServer DLL, you can verify the classes by examining the \WINDOWS\SYSTEM\JAVA\TRUSTLIB\COMSERVER directory (or the trusted classes directory on your machine). In this directory, the following class files should have been created:

    BeeperConstants.class

    CCOMBeeper.class

    ICOMBeeper.class

A file named SUMMARY.TXT also should have been created. This file will contain the signatures for all public methods and variables contained in each class or interface in the DLL of the COM. Listing 20.1 shows the contents of the generated SUMMARY.TXT file.

Listing 20.1. The contents of the COMSERVER.DLL summary file.

```
public interface comserver/ICOMBeeper extends com.ms.com.IUnknown
{
    public abstract void putSound(int);
    public abstract int getSound();
    public abstract java.lang.String getSoundName();
    public abstract void Play();
```

```
}

public class comserver/CCOMBeeper extends java.lang.Object
{
}

public interface comserver/BeeperConstants extends com.ms.com.IUnknown
{
    public static final int Default;
    public static final int Asterisk;
    public static final int Exclamation;
    public static final int Hand;
    public static final int Question;
    public static final int StandardBeep;
}
```

Each constant defined in the BeeperConstants interface represents a system sound that will be played by calling the Play() method found in the IComBeeper interface.

As described in Chapter 16, COM objects are always referenced by one of their exposed interfaces. This particular COM object can be accessed by the ICOMBeeper interface. By examining the usecom applet class in the usecom.java source file, you can see the COM object declared exactly like any other Java object:

```
ICOMBeeper m_beeper;
```

Later on, the COM object is instantiated using the standard Java new keyword:

```
m_beeper = new CCOMBeeper();
```

From there, the Java list box is simply filled with text, and the sound associated with that list's index is set using the following lines of code:

```
m_beeper.putSound(BeeperConstants.Asterisk);
m_nameList[1].name = m_beeper.getSoundName();
m_nameList[1].value = m_beeper.getSound();
```

As you can see, the putSound(), getSoundName(), and getSound() methods are all defined in the ICOMBeeper interface in Listing 20.1. Figure 20.2 shows the JavaCallingCOM applet being run in Internet Explorer 3.0.

By selecting one of the sounds displayed in the list box and pressing the Play the Sound button, you will play the default sounds currently registered under Windows. This is an example of integrating Java with a COM object to do something that is simply not possible using Java alone. Because of security restrictions the Java security model places on Java applets, system resources such as hard drives, audio, or printers cannot be accessed using Java.

FIGURE 20.2.

The JavaCallingCOM
applet.

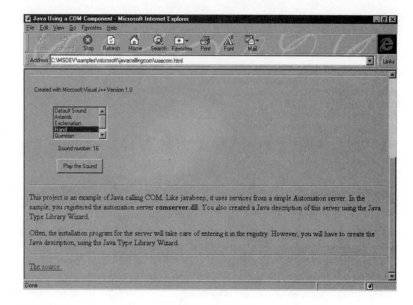

Providing Active Content with Java Applets and ActiveX Controls

Because ActiveX controls are compliant with the COM, you can also access them from Java code. This functionality gives you a huge existing base of ActiveX controls that can be used to build powerful Web pages. To provide truly active functionality to the user, several approaches can be used.

Perhaps the most obvious starting point for a Java programmer is to build a Web page consisting entirely of Java classes. This allows you to design a page that can be viewed on many operating systems, including Windows, Macintosh, OS/2, and UNIX. This is a huge advantage that does not exist for the ActiveX developer. However, hundreds if not thousands of production-quality ActiveX controls currently exist that you can immediately use. The same cannot be said for third-party Java classes. Therefore, under certain circumstances, it may be necessary to build a Web-based application using existing ActiveX components. When this decision has been reached, you can choose to script the controls on a page using VBScript or some other ActiveX scripting language. For many ActiveX developers, this may be a viable option. However, this will not be a cure-all for many others.

When ActiveX controls must be used in conjunction with some other powerful user-interface capabilities, a combination of Java and ActiveX offers the widest range of opportunities. The example used throughout the remainder of this chapter illustrates the use of Java with an ActiveX control to build an interactive charting application.

Introduction to the Java/ActiveX Example

The program developed in this chapter makes use of an ActiveX control that can be down-loaded from the Microsoft Web site at no cost. This control is combined with Java to build a charting application. Data is plotted in an ActiveX charting control based on a variety of user selections in the Java applet. As is shown in the example, a tiny bit of VBScript is used to "glue" the Java applet and ActiveX control together. A knowledge of VBScript is not necessary to understand the example; when the scripting language is used, it is explained.

To download the ActiveX component and run this application, you must use Microsoft Internet Explorer 3.0 (or higher). If another browser appears on the market with ActiveX support, how-ever, this example still might not work. Remember that the Java/COM integration is made possible with the Microsoft Virtual Machine. Any browser that does not support Microsoft's extensions to the Java Virtual Machine will not be able to run the sample application. (For the foreseeable future, it appears that the Internet Explorer is the only browser with ActiveX *and* Java support.)

Retrieving the ActiveX Control

The control used to build this example is available free from Microsoft's ActiveX Web site. To download this control, go to http://www.microsoft.com/activex/gallery/default.htm and select the Chart control listed with the other Microsoft entries. When downloading the control, make sure that your security settings in Microsoft Internet Explorer are set correctly. When loading ActiveX controls embedded in an HTML page or installing these controls over the Internet using Internet Explorer 3.0, make sure that IE's security options are set to the Medium level.

While the control is downloading, a digital certificate displays to verify that the software has been signed (see Figure 20.3).

FIGURE 20.3.

The Chart *control's verification certificate.*

When downloaded, the Chart control is automatically registered onto your local system. Whereas Java classes are only temporarily cached to the local drive for a finite period of time by most browsers, ActiveX controls are permanently installed to your hard drive. Because this "feature" is unpopular with many users, Microsoft has stated that the permanent installation of ActiveX controls will be a user-configurable option in the future.

To look at it from another angle, ActiveX controls have a temporary advantage over Java classes in this area for intranet developers: One of the frustrating aspects of Java development is that each time a user loads a page, he or she may have to reload entire Java classes even if the user just visited the site recently. This happens often with intranet applications, where corporate users are visiting a page constantly. ActiveX controls must be downloaded only once and are then installed on the user's system. The next time the user visits the page, the control loads instantly with no download time.

Fortunately for "pure" Java developers, the Java Beans 1.0 specification provides for items known as *jars*, which store groups of Java classes to the local hard drive. This should greatly improve the startup performance of most Web-based Java applications. While Microsoft's Internet Explorer browser does not allow users to disable persistent caching of ActiveX controls, hopefully Java-enabled browsers will allow users to disable the caching of Java classes if they choose to do so.

Also note that the documentation for this ActiveX control is available at `http://www.microsoft.com/activex/gallery/ms/ieprog/chart.htm`. This document includes a description of the properties, events, and methods supported by this object.

Building Java Classes from the Control's Type Library

After retrieving the ActiveX Chart control from the Microsoft Web site, you must retrieve the contents of its type library for a Java class to be able to converse with the control at runtime. To do this, use the Java Type Library Wizard, as described in the section "Calling a COM Object from Java." In Visual J++, select the Tools|Java Type Library Wizard menu option and then select the IE Chart object when prompted by the dialog box shown in Figure 20.1. When completed, the following class files will be located in the \iechart subdirectory in your \windows\java\trustlib directory (or the current trusted libraries directory on your machine):

```
DiechartEvents.class

enumBackStyle.class

enumChartStyle.class

enumChartType.class

enumColorScheme.class

enumGridPlacement.class

enumGridStyle.class

enumLegendStatus.class
```

```
enumLineStyle.class

iechart.class

Iiechart.class
```

The contents of the SUMMARY.TXT file (see Listing 20.2) show the properties, classes, and interfaces exposed in the Chart control.

Listing 20.2. The SUMMARY.TXT file for the IEChart ActiveX control.

```
public class iechart/iechart extends java.lang.Object
{
}
public interface iechart/DiechartEvents extends com.ms.com.IUnknown
{
}
public interface iechart/Iiechart extends com.ms.com.IUnknown
{
    public abstract float getDataItem();
    public abstract void putBackColor(int);
    public abstract void putDataItem(float);
    public abstract void putChartType(int);
    public abstract void putForeColor(int);
    public abstract java.lang.String getColumnName();
    public abstract int getColumns();
    public abstract void putColumns(int);
    public abstract void putColorScheme(int);
    public abstract int gethgridStyle();
    public abstract int getvgridStyle();
    public abstract void Reload();
    public abstract void putVerticalAxis(short);
    public abstract int getColorScheme();
    public abstract int getRowIndex();
    public abstract void putRowIndex(int);
    public abstract void putColumnIndex(int);
    public abstract int getRows();
    public abstract void putRows(int);
    public abstract void putGridPlacement(int);
    public abstract void putDisplayLegend(int);
    public abstract short getHorizontalAxis();
    public abstract int getColumnIndex();
    public abstract java.lang.String getRowName();
    public abstract void putRowName(java.lang.String);
    public abstract void putColumnName(java.lang.String);
    public abstract java.lang.String getURL();
    public abstract void putURL(java.lang.String);
    public abstract void puthgridStyle(int);
    public abstract void putvgridStyle(int);
    public abstract int getGridPlacement();
    public abstract void AboutBox();
    public abstract int getDisplayLegend();
    public abstract float getChartData();
    public abstract void putHorizontalAxis(short);
    public abstract int getBackStyle();
    public abstract short getVerticalAxis();
```

20

CALLING COM
OBJECTS FROM
JAVA

continues

Listing 20.2. continued

```
    public abstract void putChartData(float[]);
    public abstract void putBackStyle(int);
    public abstract short getScale();
    public abstract void putScale(short);
    public abstract int getBackColor();
    public abstract int getForeColor();
    public abstract int getChartType();
}
public interface iechart/enumLineStyle extends com.ms.com.IUnknown
{
    public static final int Solid;
    public static final int Dash;
    public static final int Dot;
    public static final int DashDot;
    public static final int DashDotDot;
}
public interface iechart/enumGridPlacement extends com.ms.com.IUnknown
{
    public static final int Bottom;
    public static final int Top;
}
public interface iechart/enumLegendStatus extends com.ms.com.IUnknown
{
    public static final int Off;
    public static final int On;
}
public interface iechart/enumBackStyle extends com.ms.com.IUnknown
{
    public static final int Transparent;
    public static final int Opaque;
}
public interface iechart/enumColorScheme extends com.ms.com.IUnknown
{
    public static final int ColorScheme1;
    public static final int ColorScheme2;
    public static final int ColorScheme3;
    public static final int ColorScheme4;
    public static final int ColorScheme5;
}
public interface iechart/enumGridStyle extends com.ms.com.IUnknown
{
    public static final int NoGrid;
    public static final int SolidGrid;
    public static final int BoldGrid;
    public static final int DottedGrid;
    public static final int BoldDottedGrid;
}
public interface iechart/enumChartStyle extends com.ms.com.IUnknown
{
    public static final int Simple;
    public static final int Stacked;
    public static final int Full;
}
public interface iechart/enumChartType extends com.ms.com.IUnknown
{
    public static final int SimplePieChart;
    public static final int SpecialPieChart;
```

```
        public static final int SimplePointChart;
        public static final int StackedPointChart;
        public static final int FullPointChart;
        public static final int SimpleLineChart;
        public static final int StackedLineChart;
        public static final int FullLineChart;
        public static final int SimpleAreaChart;
        public static final int StackedAreaChart;
        public static final int FullAreaChart;
        public static final int SimpleColumnChart;
        public static final int StackedColumnChart;
        public static final int FullColumnChart;
        public static final int SimpleBarChart;
        public static final int StackedBarChart;
        public static final int FullBarChart;
        public static final int HLCSimpleStockChart;
        public static final int HLCWsjStockChart;
        public static final int OHLCSimpleStockChart;
        public static final int OHLCWsjStockChart;
}
```

As you can see, the majority of the classes defined in the Chart control are used to provide constants that the Chart control uses for display purposes. All the functionality contained in the control can be accessed through the Iiechart interface. Note the naming convention used for the methods in the Iiechart interface. Thanks to the propget and propput keywords used in the type library definition, the Java Type Library Wizard can determine whether these methods are get or put methods.

> **NOTE**
>
> For more information on the propget and propput keywords, see the section on ODL syntax titled "An ODL Primer" in Chapter 16.

In short, methods that begin with get are property-accessor methods. Those that begin with put are property-setting methods.

Building an HTML Page Using the ActiveX Control

Chances are very good that by now you have built your own HTML page for viewing in a Web browser. Possibly you have even added Java applets to a page or are at least aware of the <APPLET> HTML tag used to embed Java applets in a page. However, it is far less likely that you have ever actually built Web pages containing ActiveX controls. Although this chapter is not intended to be an HTML tutorial (see Chapter 26, "HTML and Web Page Design," for that), you can use the contents of Listing 20.3 to build a "starter" Web page using the ActiveX Chart control.

20

CALLING COM
OBJECTS FROM
JAVA

Listing 20.3. The contents of `Example1.html`.

```
<html>

<Title>Visual J++ Unleashed - Java/COM Integration Example</Title>

<CENTER>
<H1>Integrating Java and COM</H1><br>
<H3>Example One</H3>
</CENTER>

<CENTER>
<table cellpadding=15>
<tr>

<td>
<applet
    code=ChartApplet.class
    codebase=ChartApplet
    id="TheApplet"
    width=0
    height=0>
</applet>
</td>

<td>
<object
    classid="clsid:FC25B780-75BE-11CF-8B01-444553540000"
    id="TheChart"
    width=400
    height=200
    align=center
    hspace=0
    vspace=0
>
<param name="ChartType" value="5">
<param name="hgridStyle" value="0">
<param name="vgridStyle" value="0">
<param name="colorscheme" value="0">
<param name="DisplayLegend" value="1">
<param name="BackColor" value="#ffffff">
<param name="ForeColor" value="#0000ff">
<param name="Rows" value="12">
<param name="Columns" value="3">
<param name="RowNames" value="Jan Feb Mar Apr May Jun Jul Aug Sep Oct Nov Dec">
<param name="ColumnNames" value="Sales Overhead Profit">
<param name="data[0]" value="500 100 400">
<param name="data[1]" value="600 100 500">
<param name="data[2]" value="750 100 650">
<param name="data[3]" value="400 100 300">
<param name="data[4]" value="250 100 150">
<param name="data[5]" value="800 100 700">
<param name="data[6]" value="875 100 775">
<param name="data[7]" value="1000 100 900">
<param name="data[8]" value="700 100 600">
```

```
<param name="data[9]" value="625 100 525">
<param name="data[10]" value="550 100 450">
<param name="data[11]" value="800 100 700">
</object>
</td>

</tr>
</table>
</CENTER>

<hr>

By the end of the chapter, this example will use the
<a href="http://www.microsoft.com/activex/gallery/ms/ieprog/chart.htm">
Microsoft ActiveX Chart control</a> and a Java applet to demonstrate how a
COM object can be used within a Java program.  For now, the chart will be filled
with a set of
values passed to the control as parameters.

</html>
```

This HTML source code constructs a page using an HTML table to contain the Java applet (nonexistent at this point) and the ActiveX Chart control. Note the large number of param tags passed to the ActiveX object. These parameters directly correspond to various properties of the control. Passing these parameters allows you to set some properties at design time so that there is not a lot of initialization when the Java applet starts up. Among the properties being set are ChartType, BackColor and ForeColor, Rows, Columns, and ColorScheme.

> **NOTE**
>
>
> If you are curious about how these properties work, experiment with the Example1.html source file on the CD-ROM with this book. Again, the documentation for this control's properties and methods is available at http://www.microsoft.com/activex/gallery/ms/ieprog/chart.htm.

Figure 20.4 shows the Example1.html file loaded and running in Internet Explorer 3.0.

This small amount of HTML coding constitutes virtually all the COM work you have to do to build the remainder of the example. From this point on, except for one line of VBScript code to be added to the Web page, the application is written entirely in Java.

FIGURE 20.4.

Example1.html *in*
Internet Explorer 3.0.

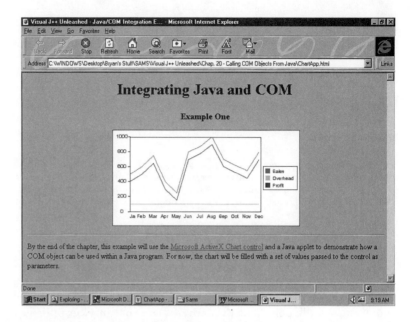

FIGURE 20.4.

Example1.html *in Internet Explorer 3.0.*

Creating an ActiveX-Aware Java Applet

Listing 20.3 is used to demonstrate how ActiveX properties are set at startup through parameter passing. You now have an ActiveX (COM) object sitting all alone on a Web page. Earlier the Java Type Library Wizard was used to build class files corresponding to the contents of the ActiveX Chart control. Before you can simply import these classes and begin writing Java code, one last hurdle must be cleared: Java applets cannot directly trap ActiveX control events; instead, these controls must be "hooked" together using VBScript. When an event is fired by the Chart control, VBScript must trap that event and send it to the applet. Likewise, a Java applet cannot directly access an ActiveX control's properties or methods without a little help from VBScript. For a Java class to access a control (using a COM interface), that control must be passed to the applet using VBScript as an object of type java.lang.Object. The applet can then typecast this Object parameter to the appropriate interface.

Accessing the Chart control from within a Java class is rather straightforward because the Chart control only supports properties and methods, not events. Therefore, you must simply create a Java applet that has a method that accepts an Object as a parameter. Inside this method, the Object parameter is typecast to an object of type Iiechart. The following method demonstrates what your applet's method will look like:

```
public void setCtrl(Object oc)
{
  m_Chart = (Iiechart)oc;
}
```

When this method is created, a single VBScript function is declared that will pass the control to the Java applet. This function is contained in the HTML source file and looks like this:

```
<script language=VBScript>
<!--

' Send the controls to the applet
Sub window_onLoad
  document.TheApplet.setCtrl TheChart
end sub

!-->
</script>
```

The onLoad() VBScript method is called after the page has been loaded in Internet Explorer. The one line of code in this method calls the applet's setCtrl() method and passes it the ActiveX Chart control as a parameter.

Creating a Java Applet to Control the Chart

All the pieces are now in place. The ActiveX control has been downloaded and registered. Java class files have been generated to provide access to the ActiveX object. The HTML file has been created to contain the Java applet and ActiveX control. All that is left is to build an applet to control the chart!

> **NOTE**
>
> Before you start this process, if you are re-creating the HTML files by hand, make sure you add the VBScript onLoad() method described previously to the HTML form. In addition, be sure to reset the Java applet's width and height parameters. (In Example1.html, they are both set to 0.)

First, the ChartApplet applet performs two basic operations:

- Allows the user to select one of the three chart color schemes
- Allows the user to select the chart type

When the user changes either of these specifications, the chart is automatically updated. The three chart color schemes are presented as radio button selections (java.awt.Checkbox components), and the various chart types are displayed in a list box. An Update button is provided; when clicked, it updates the chart with the user's settings. Listing 20.4 shows the source code for the ChartApplet class.

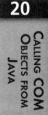

20

CALLING COM
OBJECTS FROM
JAVA

Listing 20.4. The ChartApplet class.

```java
//*************************************************************************
// ChartApplet.java:     Applet
//
//*************************************************************************
import java.applet.*;
import java.awt.*;
import iechart.*;


//========================================================================
// Main Class for applet ChartApplet
//
//========================================================================
public class ChartApplet extends Applet
{
  Iiechart m_Chart;

  // The button used to update the chart
  Button btnUpdateChart = new java.awt.Button("Update Chart");

  //The list used to display the chart types
  List lstChartTypes = new java.awt.List();

  //The Checkbox Group used to select the color scheme
  CheckboxGroup grpScheme = new java.awt.CheckboxGroup();

  //The Panel used to contain the checkbox group
  Panel m_Group = new Panel();

  // ChartApplet Class Constructor
  //-----------------------------------------------------------------------
  public ChartApplet()
  {
  }

  // APPLET INFO SUPPORT:
  // The getAppletInfo() method returns a string describing the applet's
  // author, copyright date, or miscellaneous information.
  //-----------------------------------------------------------------------
  public String getAppletInfo()
  {
    return "Name: ChartApplet\r\n" +
      "Author: Bryan Morgan\r\n" +
      "Created with Microsoft Visual J++ Version 1.0";
  }

  public void init()
  {
    setLayout(new BorderLayout());
    add("North", m_Group);
    m_Group.add(new Label("Color Scheme:"));
    m_Group.add(new Checkbox("0", grpScheme, true));
    m_Group.add(new Checkbox("1", grpScheme, false));
    m_Group.add(new Checkbox("2", grpScheme, false));

    //Add the list to the BorderLayout
    add("Center", lstChartTypes);
```

```
    //Add the button to the BorderLayout
    add("South", btnUpdateChart);

    //Now fill the list with Chart Types
    lstChartTypes.addItem("Simple Pie");
    lstChartTypes.addItem("Pie with wedge out");
    lstChartTypes.addItem("Simple Point Chart");
    lstChartTypes.addItem("Stacked Point Chart");
    lstChartTypes.addItem("Full Point Chart");
    lstChartTypes.addItem("Simple Line Chart");
    lstChartTypes.addItem("Stacked Line Chart");
    lstChartTypes.addItem("Full Line Chart");
    lstChartTypes.addItem("Simple Area Chart");
    lstChartTypes.addItem("Stacked Area Chart");
    lstChartTypes.addItem("Full Area Chart");
    lstChartTypes.addItem("Simple Column Chart");
    lstChartTypes.addItem("Stacked Column Chart");
    lstChartTypes.addItem("Full Column Chart");
    lstChartTypes.addItem("Simple Bar Chart");
    lstChartTypes.addItem("Stacked Bar Chart");
    lstChartTypes.addItem("Full Bar Chart");
    lstChartTypes.addItem("HLC Stock Chart");
    lstChartTypes.addItem("HLC Stock Chart WSJ");
    lstChartTypes.addItem("OHLC Stock Chart");
    lstChartTypes.addItem("OHLC Stock Chart WSJ");
  }

  public void setCtrl(Object oc)
  {
    m_Chart = (Iiechart)oc;
  }

  public boolean action(Event evt, Object what)
  {
    if (evt.target == btnUpdateChart)
    {
      m_Chart.putChartType(lstChartTypes.getSelectedIndex());
      Integer caption = new Integer((grpScheme.getCurrent()).getLabel());
      m_Chart.putColorScheme(caption.intValue());
      // Event handled
      return true;
    }
    return false;
  }
}
```

The majority of the `ChartApplet` class is a standard Java program. A Layout Manager is added to handle the layout of components on the applet. Again, the VBScript calls the `setCtrl()` method so that the applet can access the ActiveX object in the HTML page. The `action()` method is used to trap the button click, and this is where the `Chart`'s methods are called (`putChartType()` and `putColorScheme()`). Using these two methods, the chart's type and color scheme can be set remotely in Java.

Figure 20.5 shows the Example2.html file loaded in Internet Explorer 3.0. Changing any of the options on the left side and then clicking the Update Chart button automatically updates the chart.

FIGURE 20.5.

A Java applet and an ActiveX control coexisting.

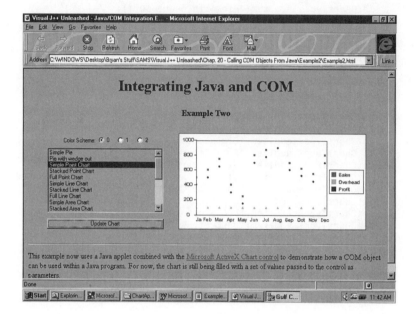

Summary

COM objects can be easily integrated into Java applets or applications, thanks to the Java Type Library Wizard included with Visual J++. This tool extracts the type library information stored in a COM object (such as an ActiveX control) and creates the corresponding Java class files for the COM interfaces, classes, and constants contained in the type library. When these class files have been created, they can be imported into a Java class. From that point, these classes appear to the Java programmer to be identical to standard Java classes. Of particular interest to many Java developers is the ability to integrate existing ActiveX/OLE controls and Java applets in Web pages. This integration is made possible with the Microsoft Virtual Machine and the Java Type Library Wizard.

Building COM Objects with Java

by Bryan Morgan

IN THIS CHAPTER

CHAPTER 21

Chapter 20, "Calling COM Objects from Java," gives examples showing COM objects being used in code written in the Java programming language. Because of the similarities between COM and Java, the two technologies can work together in a seamless fashion. When Java classes have been built to "wrap" the COM object, these classes can be treated like any other Java class in a Java program.

Chapter 20 gives examples showing Java code calling a COM dynamic link library as well as an ActiveX control in a Web page. This chapter addresses the opposite situation: Just as Java code can be written to call COM objects, it can also be written to implement COM objects. Because COM is a language-independent object model, when a COM object has been implemented in Java and registered on the system, this Java COM object can be used by programmers writing in Visual Basic, C++, Delphi, or other popular Windows programming languages. This chapter examines the process of designing and constructing COM objects as well as the issues involved with their use. The examples demonstrate building a COM object that is used in a Java applet, a Java application, and a Visual Basic application to demonstrate the power of combining Java and COM.

A Brief Review of COM

Several topics discussed in Chapter 16, "Java and the Component Object Model," help lay the groundwork for the material covered here. COM provides the "plumbing" that is used by objects implemented in various programming languages. Using the rules laid down by COM, these objects can coexist and interact in a predictable fashion—even if the objects were developed by different vendors in different years! However, much of the material introduced in Chapter 16 remains unseen by the COM developer programming in Java.

For instance, recall the rule that each COM object must implement, at a minimum, the IUnknown interface. This remains true for COM objects implemented in Java; however, thanks to the methods by which COM and Java were integrated using the Microsoft Virtual Machine, the developer is shielded from the details of implementing this interface (and many other details). Whereas programmers in other languages are forced to use the API functions in COM to initialize COM and retrieve interface pointers, Java programmers can create a COM object by simply using the new() operator. This is identical to the way that standard Java classes are instantiated in Java.

Reference counting is normally accomplished through calls to the AddRef() and Release() methods of the IUnknown interface. However, thanks to Java's garbage-collected memory-management model, the Java runtime environment handles the freeing of any memory associated with an allocated COM object. Finally, containment and aggregation using COM objects is presented in Chapter 16 as a way to support code reuse. The Java programmer can extend an existing COM class through aggregation by using the extends keyword when defining the new class.

To sum up programming COM objects in Java, it is fair to say that the integration between COM and Java is so seamless that another Java programmer could read your completed source code and not even know that COM was being used. In fact, the differences would only show up if someone wanted to use your Java COM object on a platform other than Windows.

Developing COM Objects for Programmers Using Other Languages

Chapter 20 mentions that calling COM/ActiveX objects from Java has its disadvantages. For instance, the charting example given in Chapter 20 will only run within the Microsoft Internet Explorer browser and (currently) on the Windows platform. This can be viewed as a disadvantage in the Internet environment, where many users using many platforms will routinely access your Web-based information or application. However, developing COM objects in Java in no way puts you at such a disadvantage because COM objects are typically developed to accomplish tasks other than providing active content within a Web browser. If you write a powerful, well-designed COM object in Java, your end result will be a standalone object that can be used by programmers coding in Visual Basic, C++, and Delphi. Using distributed COM (DCOM), this object can even be on a remote machine across a network. Therefore, instead of limiting the Java programmer, it opens up the Java language to a whole new world of users. Although Java is still in its infancy, one of its chief criticisms is that is does not "play well" with other languages. Building a Java class as a COM object opens its use up to programmers in many other languages (including Java).

Designing a Simple COM Object

Before worrying about the implementation details involved with constructing a COM or Java object, take a moment to think about the design issues. As mentioned before, the following Java constructs remain the same when constructing COM objects:

- The programmer uses the new() operator to instantiate an object.
- The object is automatically garbage collected.
- The object can be typecast to an appropriate interface.
- Objects can be inherited from by using the extends keyword.
- Objects can be tested for equality using the == operator.
- Underlying globally unique identifiers (GUIDs) of the COM classes and interfaces are transparent to the Java programmer.

Knowing these things, you can set out to design a COM class just as you would design a Java class. The only possible difference is that all methods used to put or get object information must be defined in an interface in the COM class.

NOTE

Although it is possible to design interfaces and then construct classes by implementing those interfaces, most object-oriented programmers simply define all methods as class members by default instead of defining interfaces. Whereas Java allows classes to be used in this way, COM requires it.

In the examples used throughout this chapter, a COM class is created to perform string manipulation functions equivalent to the functionality found in the `java.lang.String` class. (Keep in mind that although Java programmers may take this class for granted, programmers in other languages do not have these built-in capabilities!) When completed, the example demonstrates a generic COM object that programmers can use in any language to perform common string operations.

Examining the `java.lang.String` class reveals a wide variety of useful functionality that will be implemented in our string object (we'll call it `CString`). Table 21.1 is a list of the `CString` class's methods.

Table 21.1. Methods contained in `CString`.

Method Name	Description
StringLength	Determines the length of a string
HashCode	Computes the hash code for a string
CharAtPos	Returns the character at a specified position within a string
GetChars	Returns a substring based on the specified start and stop positions within a string
EqualsIgnoreCase	Performs string comparison that is not case sensitive
CompareTo	Performs a lexicographic comparison of two strings
RegionMatches	Compares substrings within two strings
RegionMatchesIgnoreCase	Performs a comparison of substrings within two strings that is not case sensitive
StartsWith	Determines whether a string starts with a specified prefix
EndsWith	Determines if a string ends with a specified suffix
IndexOf	Returns the index of the first specified character within a string
IndexWithinIndex	Returns the index of the first specified character within a string within the specified interval

Method Name	*Description*
LastIndexOf	Returns the last index of the specified character within a string
SubString	Returns a portion of a string from a specified index to the end
SubStringFromTo	Returns a portion of a string from a specified starting index to an ending index
Concat	Concatenates a string to a specified string
Replace	Replaces all characters within a string with a specified new character
ToLowerCase	Converts a string to lower case
ToUpperCase	Converts a string to upper case
Trim	Trims all leading and trailing white space from a string
BoolToStr	Returns the string representation of a boolean value (true or false)
IntToStr	Returns the string value of an integer
LongToStr	Returns the string value of a long
FloatToStr	Returns the string value of a float
DoubleToStr	Returns the string value of a double

These methods will be implemented in Java and packaged as a COM object. Listing 21.1 shows the Java method definitions for each of the methods contained in Table 21.1.

Listing 21.1. Java definitions for the methods in Table 21.1.

```
public int Length(String str);
public int HashCode(String str);
public char CharAtPos(String str, int index);
public void GetChars(String str, int srcBegin, int srcEnd, char dst[],
    int dstBegin);
public boolean EqualsIgnoreCase(String str, String anotherString);
public int CompareTo(String str, String anotherString);
public boolean RegionMatches(String str, int toffset, String other, int offset,
    int len);
public boolean RegionMatchesIgnoreCase(String str, int toffset, String other,
    int ooffset, int len);
public boolean StartsWith(String str, String prefix);
public boolean EndsWith(String str, String suffix);
public int IndexOf(String str, int ch);
public int IndexOfIndex(String theString, String  str, int  fromIndex);
public int LastIndexOf(String str, int ch);
public String Substring(String str, int beginIndex);
```

continues

Listing 21.1. continued

```
public String SubstringFromTo(String str, int beginIndex, int endIndex);
public String Concat(String str1, String str2);
public String Replace(String str, char oldChar, char newChar);
public String ToLowerCase(String str);
public String ToUpperCase(String str);
public String Trim(String str);
public String BoolToStr(boolean b);
public String IntToStr(int i);
public String LongToStr(long l);
public String FloatToStr(float f);
public String DoubleToStr(double d);
```

Creating the Type Library

As mentioned in this chapter and originally discussed in Chapter 16, COM classes are defined within a type library. This type library is created from an object description language (ODL) object specification file containing the definition of a COM class and its interfaces. This section demonstrates how to create the ODL definition for the CString object using the MKTYPLIB tool included with Visual J++ to build the type library.

To review, the following steps must be completed to build a COM object for use by other applications:

1. Generate GUIDs for each class and interface to be defined within a type library.
2. Create an ODL file containing method definitions for all the interfaces within a class.
3. Compile the ODL file using MKTYPLIB to produce a COM type library.
4. Generate the Java interface classes to the COM object using JavaTLB (included with Visual J++).
5. Implement the interfaces in a Java class (or classes).
6. Register the created Java class (or classes) using JAVAREG (included with Visual J++).

After completing these steps, the COM object is ready to be used by any application capable of calling COM objects. We are now ready to begin the actual construction of the object.

Generating GUIDs for the COM Object

Before generating GUIDs for the COM object, you must first decide how many interfaces and classes will be contained in the defined ODL library. You will be defining one class, CString, that could contain one or more interfaces. For simplicity's sake, group all the methods listed in Table 21.1 into one interface named IString. Although it would be possible to group all the different types of methods into smaller, separate interfaces, nothing would be gained from that exercise from a learning standpoint. (The same effort and knowledge required to create one COM interface is basically duplicated when creating two or more.)

Building COM Objects with Java

CHAPTER 21

475

21

BUILDING COM
OBJECTS WITH
JAVA

Therefore, the COM object to be built in this chapter consists of a class named `CString` containing an interface named `IString`. The contents of the `IString` interface are the methods listed in Table 21.1. Three GUIDs must be generated to define the elements within the type library: The first will be used to define the library itself; the second will be used to identify the COM class `CString`; and the third will be used to identify the `IString` interface.

Chapter 16 introduces the `GUIDGEN` tool, which is capable of generating GUIDs. This tool is included with Visual J++ and can be run from the Tools | Create GUID main menu option. Running this tool three times on my machine produced the following three GUIDs for the type library:

```
{0AD2C500-18A5-11d0-B4EE-444553540000}
{0AD2C501-18A5-11d0-B4EE-444553540000}
{0AD2C502-18A5-11d0-B4EE-444553540000}
```

If you run this tool on your machine, you will retrieve a different set of IDs. Therefore, unless you are planning to re-create the entire example, simply use these GUIDs in any code you create throughout the remainder of the chapter.

Building the Shell of a Type Library

Now that the GUIDs have been generated for the `CString` class, the shell of the COM object can be created. This empty shell is listed in Listing 21.2 and contains no method definitions as of yet.

Listing 21.2. The initial attempt at the CString type library.

```
// This describes the library Chapter21Lib
[
  uuid (0AD2C500-18A5-11d0-B4EE-444553540000),
  version (1.0),
  helpstring("Visual J++ Unleashed Chapter21 Type Library")
]
library Chapter21Lib
{
  // Chapter21Lib imports the interfaces, classes, structures,
  // types, and so forth from STDOLE32.TLB.
  importlib("stdole32.tlb");

  // This describes the interface IString, a dispinterface.
  // A dispinterface is an IDispatch-type interface.
  // Making this interface derive from IDispatch allows
  // this interface to be used via OLE Automation
  [
    uuid (0AD2C501-18A5-11d0-B4EE-444553540000),
    helpstring("Visual J++ Unleashed IString Interface")
  ]
  dispinterface IString
```

continues

Listing 21.2. continued

```
  {
    properties:
    methods:
  }

  // The coclass that implements the interface
  [
    uuid (0AD2C502-18A5-11d0-B4EE-444553540000),
    helpstring("Visual J++ Unleashed CString Class")
  ]
  coclass CString
  {
    dispinterface IString;
  };
};
```

What is accomplished in Listing 21.2? Basically, the entire ODL definition for the CString class is created except for the method declarations. The class definition, in fact, is complete. It simply defines dispinterface IString as a member of the CString class.

Two things should be noted about the definition in Listing 21.2. First, note the use of the GUIDs throughout the class definition. As stated earlier, one GUID was generated to be used by the library, the interface, and the class. The second item to note is the dispinterface keyword used to define the IString interface. Declaring an interface in ODL using the dispinterface keyword means that this interface will derive from the IDispatch interface rather than directly from the IUnknown interface. Deriving from the IDispatch interface enables the object to be accessed directly through OLE Automation. In the C programming language, the contents of the IDispatch interface appear as follows:

```
interface IDispatch : IUnknown
{
  HRESULT GetTypeInfoCount(unsigned int *pctinfo);
  HRESULT GetTypeInfo(unsigned int itinfo, LCID lcid, ITypeInfo **pptinfo);
  HRESULT GetIDsOfNames(REFIID riid, OLECHAR **rgszNames, unsigned int cNames,
    LCID lcid, DISPID *rgdispid);
  HRESULT Invoke(DISPID dispID, REFIID riid, LCID lcid, unsigned short wFlags,
    DISPPARAMS *pDispParams, VARIANT *pVarResult, EXCEPINFO *pExcepInfo,
    unsigned int *puArgErr);
};
```

The Invoke() method is used by OLE Automation controllers (such as Visual Basic) to call a method or access a property within a dispatch interface. The GetIDsOfNames() method converts the physical names of properties or methods to logical dispatch IDs within the dispatch interface. The GetTypeInfoCount() method determines whether type library information is available for the interface. Finally, the GetTypeInfo() method returns type information for the dispatch interface. Fortunately for the Java programmer, the plumbing involved with implementing the IDispatch interface is handled by the Microsoft Virtual Machine. The Java developer must simply implement the additional functions defined in the interface that derives from IDispatch.

Building COM Objects with Java

CHAPTER 21

477

21

BUILDING COM
OBJECTS WITH
JAVA

Mapping Java Types to ODL Types

Now that you have laid down the outline of the `CString` class, it is time to start defining the methods in the `IString` interface. Each method declaration has the following general syntax:

```
[id(#)]return_type method_name([in/out] data_type param1,
    [in/out] data_type param2 ...);
```

Before randomly assigning ID numbers to identify a specific method within `dispinterface`, note that the `id` flag is a 32-bit integer number. The first 16 bits (0–15) are open for the developer to use. Bits 16–31 are reserved to pass additional information to the calling object. (Consult the COM documentation included with Visual J++ to learn more about the `id` flag.)

The ODL defines its own set of data types, all of which map, in one way or another, to corresponding Java data types (see Table 21.2).

Table 21.2. ODL data types and their Java counterparts.

ODL Data Type	Java Data Type
boolean	boolean
char	char
double	double
int	int
int64	long
float	float
long	int
short	short
unsigned char	byte
BSTR	class java.lang.String
CURRENCY/CY	long (divide by 10,000 to get the original value as a fixed-point number)
DATE	double
SCODE/HRESULT	int
VARIANT	class com.ms.com.Variant
IUnknown *	interface com.ms.com.IUnknown
IDispatch *	class java.lang.Object
SAFEARRAY(*typename*)	class com.ms.com.SafeArray
typename *	single-element array of *typename*
void	void

For instance, nearly all the methods to be declared in the IString interface use Java String objects in one way or another. To declare a java.lang.String parameter in ODL, the parameter would be declared as type BSTR.

Now that you know the syntax for each method's definition and have an understanding of the available ODL data types, it is time to actually build the ODL definitions for the IString methods. Because these methods were originally defined in Java (refer to Listing 21.1), it is a relatively easy step to convert them to their ODL equivalents. The Example21 library is fully defined in Listing 21.3.

Listing 21.3. The complete definition of the IString interface.

```
// This describes the library Chapter21Lib
[
  uuid (0AD2C500-18A5-11d0-B4EE-444553540000),
  version (1.0),
  helpstring("Visual J++ Unleashed Chapter21 Type Library")
]
library Chapter21Lib
{
  // Chapter21Lib imports the interfaces, classes, structures,
  // types, and so forth from STDOLE32.TLB.
  importlib("stdole32.tlb");

  // This describes the interface IString, a dispinterface.
  // A dispinterface is an IDispatch-type interface.
  // Making this interface derive from IDispatch allows
  // this interface to be used via OLE Automation
  [
    uuid (0AD2C501-18A5-11d0-B4EE-444553540000),
    helpstring("Visual J++ Unleashed IString Interface")
  ]
  dispinterface IString
  {
    properties:
    methods:
      [id(0)] long Length([in] BSTR str);
      [id(1)] long HashCode([in] BSTR str);
      [id(2)] char CharAtPos([in] BSTR str, [in] long index);
      [id(3)] void GetChars([in] BSTR str, [in] long srcBegin,
        [in] long srcEnd, [in,out] char* dst, [in] long dstBegin);
      [id(4)] boolean EqualsIgnoreCase([in] BSTR str, [in] BSTR anotherString);
      [id(5)] long CompareTo([in] BSTR str, [in] BSTR anotherString);
      [id(6)] boolean RegionMatches([in] BSTR str, [in] long toffset,
        [in] BSTR other, long offset, [in] long len);
      [id(7)] boolean RegionMatchesIgnoreCase([in] BSTR str, [in] long toffset,
        [in] BSTR other, [in] long ooffset, [in] long len);
      [id(8)] boolean StartsWith([in] BSTR str, [in] BSTR prefix);
      [id(9)] boolean EndsWith([in] BSTR str, [in] BSTR suffix);
      [id(10)] long IndexOf([in] BSTR str, [in] long ch);
      [id(11)] long IndexOfIndex([in] BSTR theString, [in] BSTR str,
        [in] long fromIndex);
      [id(12)] long LastIndexOf([in] BSTR str, [in] long ch);
      [id(13)] BSTR Substring([in] BSTR str, [in] long beginIndex);
      [id(14)] BSTR SubstringFromTo([in] BSTR str, [in] long beginIndex,
```

```
        [in] long endIndex);
      [id(15)] BSTR Concat([in] BSTR str1, [in] BSTR str2);
      [id(16)] BSTR Replace([in] BSTR str, [in] char oldChar,
        [in] char newChar);
      [id(17)] BSTR ToLowerCase([in] BSTR str);
      [id(18)] BSTR ToUpperCase([in] BSTR str);
      [id(19)] BSTR Trim([in] BSTR str);
      [id(20)] BSTR BoolToStr([in] boolean b);
      [id(21)] BSTR IntToStr([in] long i);
      [id(22)] BSTR LongToStr([in] CURRENCY l);
      [id(23)] BSTR FloatToStr([in] float f);
      [id(24)] BSTR DoubleToStr([in] double d);
  }

  // The coclass that implements the interface
  [
    uuid (0AD2C502-18A5-11d0-B4EE-444553540000),
    helpstring("Visual J++ Unleashed CString Class")
  ]
  coclass CString
  {
    dispinterface IString;
  };
};
```

The ODL file containing the contents of Listing 21.3 is named Example21.ODL. It can be found in the \TypeLib directory for this chapter on the CD-ROM included with this book.

Using MKTYPLIB to Build the Type Library

When the ODL source code has been created for the IString interface, the type library can be created using the MKTYPLIB tool included with Visual J++. For Java programmers, this tool can be utilized using the following syntax:

```
mktyplib /nocpp filename.odl
```

The /nocpp option must be specified on the command line, or else MKTYPLIB will try to use a C preprocessor. In addition to the /nocpp option, MKTYPLIB also accepts several other useful command-line options. For a complete list of these options, see the documentation on MKTYPLIB in Chapter 16.

Before using MKTYPLIB, make sure its directory is in your system PATH. By default, this directory will be C:\MSDEV\BIN. To build the Example21.TLB type library file, simply execute the following command:

```
mktypelib /nocpp Example21.odl
```

Running this command creates the EXAMPLE21.TLB file. This file will be utilized by the JAVATLB file to create skeleton Java classes based on the contents of the type library. You may receive warnings about using the char data types in the ODL, because the char data type is not directly supported by the IDispatch::Invoke() method. Therefore, you cannot invoke any methods using this data type through an OLE Automation controller. Because neither the Java nor the Visual Basic examples use these methods, in this example these warnings will be ignored. However, if you were building an application to use these methods, it would be wiser to use the unsigned char data type instead. When this happens, the Java class files that are generated treat the unsigned char data type as a byte value. It would be the programmer's responsibility in the Java implementation to convert this byte value to a character value. For our purposes, however, the example continues as is.

Generating the Java Interface to the COM Object Using JAVATLB

In Chapter 20, the Java Type Library Wizard is used from within the Visual J++ development environment to build Java class files for registered COM objects. The JAVATLB tool is the command-line version of the Java Type Library Wizard that performs a similar task. However, when JAVATLB is used from the command prompt, it can generate class files from a type library even if that type library has not yet been registered. In the previous section, "Using MKTYPLIB to Build the Type Library," you should have built a type library correctly for your CString class. Therefore, at this point you will generate trusted class files from this type library. After making sure that the directory containing JAVATLB.EXE is included in your system PATH statement, run the following command to generate the Java class files:

```
javatlb Example21.tlb
```

When this command has been completed successfully, examine the contents of your Java \Trustlib directory. By default, this directory should be c:\windows\java\Trustlib. To determine the exact location of the Trustlib directory on your machine, examine the following registry key:

```
HKEY_LOCAL_MACHINE\Software\Microsoft\Java VM\TrustedLibsDirectory
```

A new directory should have been created within your \Trustlib directory named Example21. This directory will contain two Java class files: CString.class and IString.class.

To receive a SUMMARY.TXT file containing the interface method definitions in Java, run JAVATLB with the following syntax:

```
javatlb /U:T Example21.tlb
```

This produces the SUMMARY.TXT file shown in Listing 21.4.

Listing 21.4. Example21.TLB summary information created by JAVATLB.

```
public class example21/CString extends java.lang.Object
{
}
```

```
public interface example21/IString extends com.ms.com.IUnknown
{
    public abstract boolean RegionMatches(java.lang.String, int,
        java.lang.String, int, int);
    public abstract boolean RegionMatchesIgnoreCase(java.lang.String, int,
        java.lang.String, int, int);
    public abstract int IndexOf(java.lang.String, int);
    public abstract int IndexOfIndex(java.lang.String, java.lang.String, int);
    public abstract java.lang.String ToLowerCase(java.lang.String);
    public abstract java.lang.String SubstringFromTo(java.lang.String, int,
        int);
    public abstract int LastIndexOf(java.lang.String, int);
    public abstract java.lang.String ToUpperCase(java.lang.String);
    public abstract int Length(java.lang.String);
    public abstract boolean EndsWith(java.lang.String, java.lang.String);
    public abstract boolean StartsWith(java.lang.String, java.lang.String);
    public abstract boolean EqualsIgnoreCase(java.lang.String,
        java.lang.String);
    public abstract java.lang.String Concat(java.lang.String,
        java.lang.String);
    public abstract java.lang.String Trim(java.lang.String);
    public abstract int HashCode(java.lang.String);
    public abstract char CharAtPos(java.lang.String, int);
    public abstract void GetChars(java.lang.String, int, int, char[], int);
    public abstract java.lang.String BoolToStr(boolean);
    public abstract java.lang.String IntToStr(int);
    public abstract java.lang.String LongToStr(long);
    public abstract java.lang.String FloatToStr(float);
    public abstract java.lang.String Replace(java.lang.String, char, char);
    public abstract java.lang.String DoubleToStr(double);
    public abstract int CompareTo(java.lang.String, java.lang.String);
    public abstract java.lang.String Substring(java.lang.String, int);
}
```

A quick comparison of the summary file contents with the Java methods defined in Listing 21.1 reveals an exact match! Therefore, the type library was created correctly *and* the JAVATLB tool was able to accurately build Java classes based on the contents of this type library. Now all that is left to do is to actually implement the IString interface in Java and then register the Java class as a COM object. When this is done, sample applications will be built in Java and Visual Basic that make use of this COM object.

Implementing the COM Object in Java

The "new" work is now behind you. You have made use of the JAVATLB and MKTYPLIB tools to build a COM type library and create Java classes based on the contents of that type library. Now you must climb back on familiar ground and implement the IString interface in Java. Because the methods in this interface very closely resemble the member methods of the java.lang.String class, nearly all of these methods will consist of a single line of code.

Listing 21.5 contains the actual implementation of the CString class in Java. This Java class will be named COMString to avoid name conflicts with the CString.class file.

Listing 21.5. Contents of the COMString Java class.

```
/*
 *
 * COMString
 *
 */

import java.lang.String;

// Import the generated COM interface
import example21.*;

public class COMString implements IString
{
  public int Length(String str)
  {
    return (str.length());
  }

  public int HashCode(String str)
  {
    return (str.hashCode());
  }

  public char CharAtPos(String str, int index)
  {
    return (str.charAt(index));
  }

  public void GetChars(String str, int srcBegin, int srcEnd,
    char dst[], int dstBegin)
  {
    str.getChars(srcBegin, srcEnd, dst, dstBegin);
  }

  public boolean EqualsIgnoreCase(String str, String anotherString)
  {
    return (str.equalsIgnoreCase(anotherString));
  }

  public int CompareTo(String str, String anotherString)
  {
    return (str.compareTo(anotherString));
  }

  public boolean RegionMatches(String str, int toffset, String other,
      int offset, int len)
  {
    return (str.regionMatches(toffset, other, offset, len));
  }

  public boolean RegionMatchesIgnoreCase(String str, int toffset,
      String other, int ooffset, int len)
```

Building COM Objects with Java

CHAPTER 21

483

21

BUILDING COM
OBJECTS WITH
JAVA

```
{
  return (str.regionMatches(true, toffset, other, toffset, len));
}

public boolean StartsWith(String str, String prefix)
{
  return (str.startsWith(prefix));
}

public boolean EndsWith(String str, String suffix)
{
  return (str.endsWith(suffix));
}

public int IndexOf(String str, int ch)
{
  return (str.indexOf(ch));
}

public int IndexOfIndex(String theString, String  str, int fromIndex)
{
  return (str.indexOf(str, fromIndex));
}

public int LastIndexOf(String str, int ch)
{
  return (str.lastIndexOf(ch));
}

public String Substring(String str, int beginIndex)
{
  return (str.substring(beginIndex));
}

public String SubstringFromTo(String str, int beginIndex, int endIndex)
{
  return (str.substring(beginIndex, endIndex));
}

public String Concat(String str1, String str2)
{
  return (str1.concat(str2));
}

public String Replace(String str, char oldChar, char newChar)
{
  return (str.replace(oldChar, newChar));
}

public String ToLowerCase(String str)
{
  return (str.toLowerCase());
}

public String ToUpperCase(String str)
{
  return (str.toUpperCase());
}
```

continues

Listing 21.5. continued

```
public String Trim(String str)
{
  return (str.trim());
}

public String BoolToStr(boolean b)
{
  return (String.valueOf(b));
}

public String IntToStr(int i)
{
  return (String.valueOf(i));
}

public String LongToStr(long l)
{
  return (String.valueOf(l));
}

public String FloatToStr(float f)
{
  return (String.valueOf(f));
}

public String DoubleToStr(double d)
{
  return (String.valueOf(d));
}
}
```

Each method in this class simply calls the corresponding method within the java.lang.String class. This class implements the IString interface and therefore implements all the IString methods. If any of these methods were left off, the compiler would generate an error.

Registering the Java Classes Using JAVAREG

One last step remains before the COMString class can be used as a COM object by any other application: registering the new COM object in the Windows Registry. Visual J++ comes with a command-line tool named JAVAREG that will insert the proper entries into the Registry based on the options passed to it by the user. (See Chapter 16 for a complete listing of the JAVAREG options.) The two most important options for registering a Java class as a COM object are /class:class_name and /clsid:{xxxxx}.

To register a new class, use the /register option. Likewise, to unregister a class, use the /unregister option. Using this set of commands, register the COMString class using the following syntax:

```
javareg /register /class:COMString /clsid:{0AD2C502-18A5-11d0-B4EE-444553540000}
```

Building COM Objects with Java

CHAPTER 21

485

21

BUILDING COM
OBJECTS WITH
JAVA

The `CLSID` used when registering the Java class should *always* be the `CLSID` of the `coclass` defined in the ODL file. To verify that the `COMString` class was correctly registered, search through the Registry for the string `COMString`. Notice that the value of the `HKEY_CLASSES_ROOT\CLSID\0AD2C502-18A5-11d0-B4EE-444553540000\InprocServer32` Registry key is `MSJAVA.DLL`. This is the in-process server for the Microsoft Virtual Machine. This value will remain the same for all Java classes registered as COM objects.

Calling the COM Object from a Java Applet

Now that a COM object has been created in Java, you must test it out to ensure that things are working the way they are supposed to. The remainder of the chapter demonstrates thoroughly testing the COM object using a Java applet and a Visual Basic application. Each of these applications looks virtually identical; the only difference is that one of them is written in Java and runs in a Web browser, whereas the other one is written in Visual Basic and runs as a standalone Windows application. What these applications have in common is that they both will call the same COM object: `CString`.

To demonstrate that the Java/COM object actually works as promised, five methods will be called and results will be displayed to the screen:

- `Length()`
- `ToLowerCase()`
- `Trim()`
- `EqualsIgnoreCase()`
- `StartsWith()`

To call a COM object from Java, you will have to reuse the knowledge gained in Chapter 20. However, the only tricky material covered in that chapter involved registering the COM object and generating the Java class files from the COM object's type library. In the case of the `COMString` class, both operations have already been accomplished. Therefore, you are free to dive right in and begin building a Java applet to test the five candidate methods. This applet simply needs to import the `CString` classes using the following statement:

```
import example21.*;
```

The source code for the Java tester applet is shown in Listing 21.6. The interesting portion of this sample program occurs during the `action()` method, where the contents of the text components are retrieved based on button-push events. The text retrieved is passed to one of the COM object's member methods. The output from these methods is displayed in the text boxes on the right side.

Listing 21.6. The Java/COM tester applet.

```java
//*****************************************************************************
// COMTester.java:  Applet
//
//*****************************************************************************
import java.applet.*;
import java.awt.*;
import example21.*;
import COMString;
import COMTesterFrame;


//=============================================================================
// Main Class for applet COMTester
//
//=============================================================================
public class COMTester extends Applet
{
    // STANDALONE APPLICATION SUPPORT:
    // m_fStandAlone will be set to true if applet is run standalone
    //-------------------------------------------------------------------------
    boolean m_fStandAlone = false;
    TextField LengthL, LengthR, LowerL, LowerR, TrimL, TrimR, EqualsTL, EqualsBL,
        EqualsR, StartsTL, StartsBL, StartsR;
    Button bLength, bLower, bTrim, bEquals, bStarts;
    IString StringObj;


    // STANDALONE APPLICATION SUPPORT
    // The main() method acts as the applet's entry point when it is run
    // as a standalone application. It is ignored if the applet is run from
    // within an HTML page.
    //-------------------------------------------------------------------------
    public static void main(String args[])
    {
        // Create Toplevel Window to contain applet COMTester
        //---------------------------------------------------------------------
        COMTesterFrame frame = new COMTesterFrame("COMTester");
        // Must show Frame before we size it so insets() will return valid values
        //---------------------------------------------------------------------
        frame.show();
        frame.hide();
        frame.resize(frame.insets().left + frame.insets().right  + 480,
        frame.insets().top  + frame.insets().bottom + 200);

        // The following code starts the applet running within the frame window.
        // It also calls GetParameters() to retrieve parameter values from the
        // command line, and sets m_fStandAlone to true to prevent init() from
        // trying to get them from the HTML page.
        //---------------------------------------------------------------------
        COMTester applet_COMTester = new COMTester();

        frame.add("Center", applet_COMTester);
        applet_COMTester.m_fStandAlone = true;
        applet_COMTester.init();
        applet_COMTester.start();
        frame.show();
    }
```

Building COM Objects with Java

CHAPTER 21

487

21

BUILDING COM
OBJECTS WITH
JAVA

```
// COMTester Class Constructor
//--------------------------------------------------------------------------
public COMTester()
{
  StringObj = new COMString();
  LengthL = new TextField(25);
  LengthR = new TextField(25);
  LowerL  = new TextField(25);
  LowerR  = new TextField(25);
  TrimL   = new TextField(25);
  TrimR   = new TextField(25);
  EqualsTL = new TextField(25);
  EqualsBL = new TextField(25);
  EqualsR = new TextField(25);
  StartsTL = new TextField(25);
  StartsBL = new TextField(25);
  StartsR = new TextField(25);
  bLength = new Button("Length ->");
  bLower = new Button("ToLowerCase ->");
  bTrim = new Button("Trim ->");
  bEquals = new Button("Equals ->");
  bStarts = new Button("StartsWith ->");
}

// APPLET INFO SUPPORT:
// The getAppletInfo() method returns a string describing the applet's
// author, copyright date, or miscellaneous information.
//--------------------------------------------------------------------------
public String getAppletInfo()
{
  return "Name: COMTester\r\n" +
      "Author: Bryan Morgan\r\n" +
      "Created with Microsoft Visual J++ Version 1.0";
}

public void init()
{
  Panel p1, p2, p3, p4, p5, p6, p7;
  resize(480, 200);
  setLayout(new GridLayout(7, 1));
  p1 = new Panel(); add(p1); p1.setLayout(new FlowLayout(FlowLayout.LEFT));
  p2 = new Panel(); add(p2); p2.setLayout(new FlowLayout(FlowLayout.LEFT));
  p3 = new Panel(); add(p3); p3.setLayout(new FlowLayout(FlowLayout.LEFT));
  p4 = new Panel(); add(p4); p4.setLayout(new FlowLayout(FlowLayout.LEFT));
  p5 = new Panel(); add(p5); p5.setLayout(new FlowLayout(FlowLayout.LEFT));
  p6 = new Panel(); add(p6); p6.setLayout(new FlowLayout(FlowLayout.LEFT));
  p7 = new Panel(); add(p7); p7.setLayout(new FlowLayout(FlowLayout.LEFT));

  p1.add(LengthL);
  p1.add(bLength);
  p1.add(LengthR);
  p2.add(LowerL);
  p2.add(bLower);
  p2.add(LowerR);
  p3.add(TrimL);
  p3.add(bTrim);
  p3.add(TrimR);
  p4.add(EqualsTL);
```

continues

Listing 21.6. continued

```
    p4.add(bEquals);
    p4.add(EqualsR);
    p5.add(EqualsBL);
    p6.add(StartsTL);
    p6.add(bStarts);
    p6.add(StartsR);
    p7.add(StartsBL);
    LengthL.reshape(10, 10, 75, 25);
    bLength.reshape(95, 10, 75, 25);
    LengthR.reshape(180, 10, 75, 25);
}

public boolean action(Event evt, Object arg)
{
  String str1, str2;
  String result;
  int strlen;
  boolean streq;

  if (evt.target.equals(bLength))
  {
    str1 = LengthL.getText();
    strlen = StringObj.Length(str1);
    LengthR.setText(StringObj.IntToStr(strlen));
  }
  else if (evt.target.equals(bLower))
  {
    LowerR.setText(StringObj.ToLowerCase(LowerL.getText()));
  }
  else if (evt.target.equals(bTrim))
  {
    TrimR.setText(StringObj.Trim(TrimL.getText()));
  }
  else if (evt.target.equals(bEquals))
  {
    str1 = EqualsTL.getText();
    str2 = EqualsBL.getText();
    streq = StringObj.EqualsIgnoreCase(str1, str2);
    EqualsR.setText(StringObj.BoolToStr(streq));
  }
  else if (evt.target.equals(bStarts))
  {
    str1 = StartsTL.getText();
    str2 = StartsBL.getText();
    streq = StringObj.StartsWith(str1, str2);
    StartsR.setText(StringObj.BoolToStr(streq));
  }
  return true;
  }
}
```

The following COMString methods are called in Listing 21.6:

- ■ Length()
- ■ IntToStr()
- ■ ToLowerCase()
- ■ Trim()
- ■ EqualsIgnoreCase()
- ■ BoolToStr()
- ■ StartsWith()

Figure 21.1 illustrates what the applet looks like in the Internet Explorer 3.0 Web browser.

FIGURE 21.1.

The tester applet in Internet Explorer 3.0.

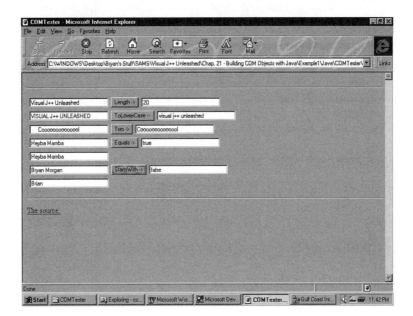

This example demonstrates that it is possible to call a COM object from within a Java application. However, one of COM's best features is its language independence. The example in the following section builds a sample application that is very similar to the first except that it is created in Visual Basic.

Calling the COM Object from Visual Basic

For a Visual Basic application to retrieve a Java/COM interface and call that interface's methods, two steps are required. First, the Visual Basic application must declare a variable whose data type is defined to be the interface name. For instance, in the previous sections you created a COM interface named IString. To use this interface in Visual Basic, you would declare a variable using the following syntax:

```
Dim StringObj As IString
```

Continuing with the objects created in the previous example, to initialize the StringObj variable, you would issue the following statement:

```
Set StringObj = New CString
```

From that point on, the interface methods can be called using the standard Visual Basic dot notation (.) syntax.

> **NOTE**
>
> Make sure to put the COMSTRING.CLASS Java class file somewhere in the Java class path before running the Visual Basic application. The class path directories can be determined by examining the HKEY_LOCAL_MACHINE\SOFTWARE\Microsoft\Java VM\Classpath Registry key. The application will also work if the Java class file is located in the \trustlib directory with the generated CString and IString COM stub classes.

If you plan to build a Visual Basic application from scratch that calls an existing COM object, add a reference to that object's type library by selecting the Tools | References menu option and then selecting the COM object's type library in the ensuing dialog. When this is done, Visual Basic adds a CLSID and type library name internally in the project. When this is done, you can create and use an object of that type freely within the program.

The StringObj parameter can be initialized by issuing the following command in the Form_Load() method:

```
Set StringObj = New CString
```

When this variable has been initialized, it is simply a matter of calling the COMString object's methods and returning their results to the screen. Listing 21.7 contains a partial code listing of the COMServer Visual Basic application. It shows the syntax used to call the various COM functions from Visual Basic.

Listing 21.7. Visual Basic code used to call COM interface methods.

```
Private Sub bEquals_Click()
  EqualsR.Text = StringObj.EqualsIgnoreCase(EqualsTL.Text, EqualsBL.Text)
End Sub

Private Sub bLength_Click()
  Dim length As Integer
  length = StringObj.length(LengthL.Text)
  LengthR.Text = length
End Sub
```

```
Private Sub bLower_Click()
  LowerR.Text = StringObj.ToLowerCase(LowerL.Text)
End Sub

Private Sub bStarts_Click()
  StartsR.Text = StringObj.StartsWith(StartsTL.Text, StartsBL.Text)
End Sub
Private Sub bTrim_Click()
  TrimR.Text = StringObj.Trim(TrimL.Text)
End Sub
```

Figure 21.2 shows the Visual Basic application running with outputs sent from the COMString Java/COM object.

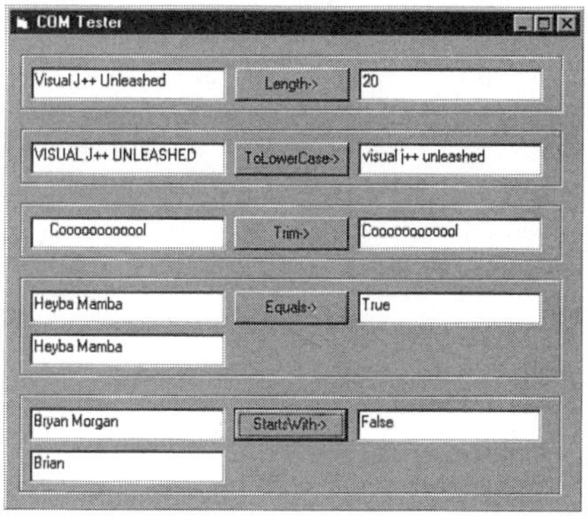

FIGURE 21.2.

The Visual Basic COMTester *application.*

Although the examples here use only Java and Visual Basic, similar functionality is possible using languages such as Delphi or C++. Keep in mind that to call Java COM objects from a Visual Basic (or other language) application, you must have the Microsoft Virtual Machine installed on the local system. It then follows that for the Virtual Machine to be installed, Microsoft's Internet Explorer browser must also be installed. The reality of the situation now is that few people will probably choose to implement a COM object using Java because Java is an interpreted language. To avoid this performance hit, COM objects will probably continue to be built using C or C++ until Java can be compiled to machine code in future versions of Visual J++.

Summary

Using tools such as JavaTLB and JAVAREG, the Visual J++ developer can develop COM objects that can then be used by programmers using other languages such as Visual Basic, Delphi, and C++. The ODL is used to build a COM class definition. After the definition has been completed, the ODL source file can be compiled to create a COM type library using the MKTYPLIB tool included with Visual J++. When the type library has been built, Java classes can be generated using the JavaTLB tool. The Java code for the COM object can be written to utilize COM without adding any new Microsoft-proprietary extensions to the Java language. A COM object can be created for use within an application simply by using the new keyword. Methods and properties within that object can then be utilized using standard Java syntax. After the class has been successfully built using Visual J++, it can be registered in the Windows Registry using JAVAREG. When the object has been registered, it can be used by any Windows application that can dynamically allocate and create a COM object.

Using ActiveX Documents to Convey Information

by Bryan Morgan

IN THIS CHAPTER

Microsoft's ActiveX technologies give developers the ability to build Internet applications using an existing base of programming objects and Application Programming Interfaces (APIs). In Chapter 20, "Calling COM Objects from Java," you learned how to use ActiveX controls to develop powerful Java applications or applets. Later chapters will discuss an entire suite of server technologies from Microsoft, some of which are based on ActiveX/COM, as well as how objects can be distributed across a network using DCOM. These objects can be called by other objects without the need to download anything to a local machine. All these technologies use the component object model (COM) as their basis. The Microsoft Internet Explorer browser supports another ActiveX technology known as ActiveX documents. This chapter explains what ActiveX documents are and how they can be used to enhance existing Web-based information.

From OLE 1.0 to ActiveX Documents

ActiveX documents is the name for one of the newest ActiveX technologies from Microsoft. For readers who have had experience working with OLE2, ActiveX documents are the next logical extension of a subset of OLE 2.0 known as *visual editing*. Under OLE 2.0, visual editing allows a client object embedded in a server object to take over that server's menus and frame when the client object is clicked ActiveX documents take that idea a step further by allowing the client object to completely take over the server's frame window. The result is that the client application *appears* to have been called up in its own window. In actuality, however, the server application is still running; it is simply acting as a temporary container. Before delving into ActiveX documents and how they apply to the Java/Web developer, the first part of this chapter focuses on the parent of ActiveX documents: OLE 2.0 visual editing.

Visual Editing, OLE 1.0, and OLE 2.0

The purpose of OLE 1.0 was to allow objects to be linked and embedded within other objects (thus the name *object linking and embedding*, or OLE). When one of these objects is double-clicked under OLE 1.0, an entirely separate application is brought up to handle this object activation. Figure 22.1 shows an example of this procedure. In this figure, an OLE 1.0 object (Sound Recorder, in this case) is embedded in an OLE 2.0 document (Microsoft Word).

Although a lot of work is done behind the scenes in OLE 1.0 to allow objects to be linked and embedded within other objects, the user does not receive that much added value. However, OLE 2.0 expands greatly on this idea. OLE 2.0 has a host of new capabilities, including structured file storage, in-place activation, and visual editing. ActiveX documents are an outgrowth of visual editing. Figure 22.2 shows visual editing in action; two OLE 2.0 applications (Microsoft Word and Excel) are working together to form an OLE compound document.

FIGURE 22.1.

An OLE 1.0 object embedded in an OLE 2.0 document.

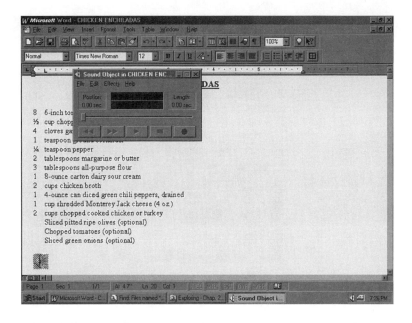

22

USING ACTIVEX
DOCUMENTS

FIGURE 22.2.

OLE 2.0 in-place activation.

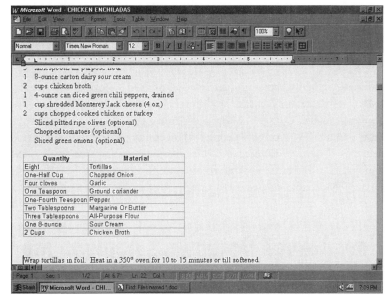

In this figure, a Microsoft Excel spreadsheet is embedded within a Microsoft Word document. Clicking on the Excel spreadsheet automatically changes the Microsoft Word menus and toolbars to the Microsoft Excel menus and toolbars (see Figure 22.3).

FIGURE 22.3.

Editing an Excel spreadsheet within Microsoft Word.

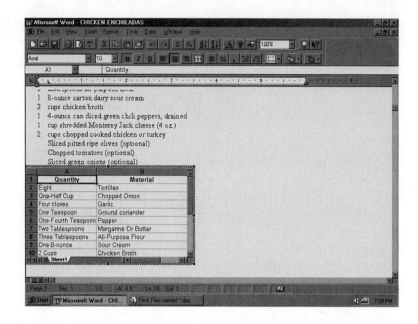

All this activity takes place through OLE 2.0 (using COM as the underlying foundation for object intercommunication) without requiring you to switch applications. Although OLE 2.0 was demonstrated earlier in the book, you now know enough about COM and interfaces to go beneath the surface and examine the process.

What is essentially happening is a large amount of handshaking between the client application (Microsoft Excel, in this case) and the server application (Microsoft Word). Saying that both applications are "OLE 2.0 compliant" means that they both have implemented a set of interfaces that allow objects to be edited while contained in other objects (known as *container* objects). In this case, Microsoft Excel implements a set of interfaces so that it can be drawn and controlled within another application's window. In addition, Microsoft Word has a set of interfaces that enable it to query the Microsoft Excel objects and determine if the required interfaces have been implemented. If they have, the document will be shown to the user.

How ActiveX Documents Apply to the Web

OLE 2.0 has given users of desktop software (such as spreadsheets, word processors, and presentation builders) added functionality and power. Many users like working with applications that support the OLE 2.0 components because they can focus on the document at hand without being forced to switch manually from application to application. From a presentation viewpoint, documents have a much richer appearance both when displayed on the screen and when printed out. The ability to mingle presentations, multimedia, and spreadsheets within a single document gives the appearance of a sophisticated desktop publishing effort when, in fact, standard software was used to lay out the objects.

However, the OLE 2.0 visual editing paradigm does not apply exactly to the World Wide Web. On the desktop, the container application (Microsoft Word in Figures 22.2 and 22.3) is always the "main" application that the user starts. This application contains the parent document that the user of the application physically opens. In the case of documents displayed on the World Wide Web, the container application is the Web browser. In addition, all information on the Web is generally for display only.

> **NOTE**
>
> Of course, some pages allow the user to update fields in order to post information back to the server. However, the primary purpose of the Web in its current form is to disseminate information to viewers in the form of HTML documents.

These documents are always displayed in a read-only fashion by the browser; therefore, the user doesn't have to dynamically insert objects into the document.

Missing from the Web, however, is the ability of Web browsers to automatically display documents of types other than HTML. HTML provides an excellent way to lay out static content such as text and graphics, as well as interactive content in the form of Java applets or ActiveX controls.

The problem is that not all information available in the world today exists in the form of HTML. An ideal solution would be for the Web browser to support all standards dealing with the display of HTML documents. In addition, however, the Web browser should be able to load other document types (such as the compound document displayed in Figures 22.2 and 22.3). Currently the two major browser developers, Microsoft and Netscape, have introduced competing ways of achieving this result.

Relatively early in its life cycle, the Netscape Navigator introduced the idea of Netscape "plug-ins" to allow file types to be displayed within the Netscape browser. Currently, plug-ins are available for Progressive Network's RealAudio, Macromedia Shockwave, VRML, and many other uses. Once the RealAudio plug-in is installed, clicking on a hyperlink to a RealAudio file causes that audio file to be played on your hard drive, using the installed RealAudio application. A Shockwave file can be displayed directly within the HTML page itself, using the Shockwave plug-in (similar to a Java applet being embedded within a Web page). By writing a Netscape plug-in and conforming to the Netscape APIs, developers of software products can be sure that their application's output will be displayed within the Netscape browser (assuming that the appropriate plug-in is installed on the user's computer).

The problem with this approach, according to Microsoft, is that it is a browser-only solution. In other words, although the downloaded file may be displayed correctly within the browser, no other applications on the local system can access that plug-in for their own uses.

ActiveX documents are similar in some respects to Netscape plug-ins. Files can be downloaded from remote servers and will be displayed automatically within Microsoft's Internet Explorer browser. However, instead of being simple add-ons to a Web browser, ActiveX documents use applications that currently exist on the user's local system to display the file within the browser. Because COM provides the basis for how the ActiveX document container (the browser) and the ActiveX document server (the application associated with the downloaded file) interface, *any* application can be written to become an ActiveX document container or server. The next version of Windows (currently code-named "Nashville" and probably slated to be named Windows 97) will support ActiveX documents extensively. In fact, the Explorer itself will be an ActiveX document container with the capability to display views of the current system, as well as the local network and Internet at large, to the user. Clicking on any document that supports these extensions will allow the user to view the document within the Explorer. In short, the Web browser and the local file-system browser will become one integrated tool.

Viewing ActiveX Documents

Believe it or not, ActiveX documents actually grew out of a little-used tool included with Microsoft Office for Windows 95 named the Office Binder (see Figure 22.4). Before the advent of "doc objects," as they were called when Microsoft introduced them, OLE 2.0 visual editing was the closest users could come to mixing different types of data within a single application. The Office Binder application modified this paradigm slightly by providing a generic container application that could display multiple types of documents, all of which were stored in separate files.

FIGURE 22.4.

The Microsoft Office Binder application.

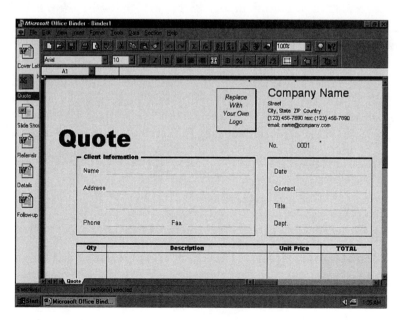

Shortly after the introduction of this product, Microsoft extended the idea to include content served over the Internet. Thus ActiveX documents were born. The release of the Internet Explorer 3.0 Web browser marked the first actual implementation of an ActiveX document container application. Using Internet Explorer, clicking on a hyperlink to a file will result in a request for one of two possible actions:

- Save the file to the local drive for examination later
- Have Internet Explorer open the file as an ActiveX document

The HTML file in Listing 22.1 displays some text on the screen. Clicking on the hyperlink at the bottom of the page will display a Microsoft Word file within the browser (if Microsoft Word is installed on your local system).

Listing 22.1. An HTML listing containing a hyperlink to a Microsoft Word document.

```
<html>
<head>
<title>Visual J++ Unleashed</title>
</head>
<body>
<center>
<h1>Visual J++</h1><br>
<h2>Unleashed</h2><br>
<br>
<br>
<h3>Chapter 22</h3>
<h4>ActiveX Documents</h4>
</center>
<hr>
<a href="Example1.doc">
Click here to view this as a Word file.</a>
</body>
</html>
```

Loading the `Example1.html` file into the Microsoft Internet Explorer 3.0 (or later) Web browser should result in a display that resembles Figure 22.5.

Clicking on the hyperlink at the bottom of the page displayed in Figure 22.6 will load the ActiveX document, `Example1.doc`, using its associated application, Microsoft Word 7.0.

To see something else cool, grab a folder (either from the desktop or from within the Windows Explorer) and drag it over the Internet Explorer client area. Dropping the folder into the client area will result in that folder itself being displayed as an ActiveX document (see Figure 22.7).

FIGURE 22.5.

The contents of Listing 22.1 in Internet Explorer 3.0.

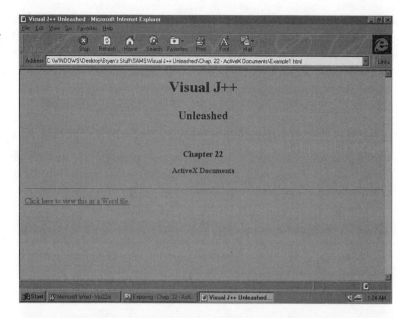

FIGURE 22.6.

An ActiveX document in Internet Explorer 3.0.

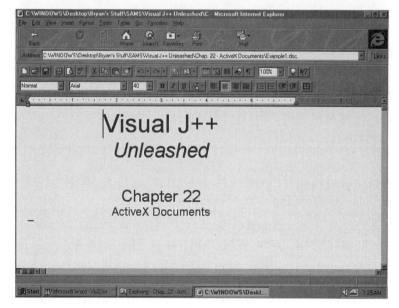

FIGURE 22.7.
*Windows folders
displayed as documents.*

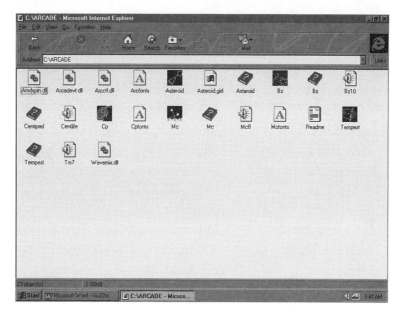

Like all other ActiveX client-side extensions, at the time of this writing, ActiveX documents can be viewed only within an application that can act as an ActiveX document container. The only Web browser that supports this functionality is Microsoft's Internet Explorer.

Adding ActiveX Document Support

Although you will probably not be creating an ActiveX document container such as Internet Explorer or the Office Binder application, chances are that you may have an application that could be improved by its integration with ActiveX. The following examples illustrate the type of applications that could be improved by adding the ActiveX document interfaces:

■ Any current Windows-based database-access application that uses many screens and links various actions within a program to screen call-ups. Each of these links could be replaced by hyperlinks in HTML, and the actual program screens could be driven by user-selected hyperlinks within a browser. All screens within the application would then appear as ActiveX documents to the user.

■ Any application that saves its information in a single, fixed-format file. These files, when opened, could be viewed as ActiveX documents, allowing the application to be integrated with other Web capabilities (FTP, HTTP, e-mail, and so on) and providing an easy-to-use interface (Web browser).

To make an application an ActiveX document server, a set of 10 interfaces needs to be implemented. Table 22.1 briefly describes these interfaces.

Table 22.1. ActiveX document interfaces.

Interface Name	Description
IPersistStorage	Enables the use of OLE structured storage.
IPersistFile	Enables the use of OLE compound files for file storage.
IOleObject	Must be implemented by all OLE objects.
IDataObject	Must be implemented to define data-transfer capabilities.
IOleInPlaceObject	Must be implemented by all in-place servers.
IOleInPlaceActiveObject	Must be implemented by all in-place activation servers.
IOleDocument	Used to verify that the application can be an ActiveX document.
IOleDocumentView	Implements an ActiveX document view.
IOleCommandTarget	(Optional) Used for container/server interactions.
IPrint	(Optional) Enables support of print automation.

Once the application implements these interfaces, file types associated with that application can be viewed within Internet Explorer or any other ActiveX document container.

Summary

This chapter provides a glimpse at the capabilities that currently exist within Microsoft's ActiveX client-side technologies. The purpose here is to define the term *ActiveX documents* and explain how developers can use this technology to complement existing Web-based solutions.

Despite some of the problems with ActiveX (security, platform-dependence, and daunting learning curve), many of its components are available today and are designed to fully integrate the Web with the Windows desktop. In situations where most, if not all, systems are running 32-bit Windows operating systems, ActiveX must be considered as a development option. However, until ActiveX is commercially available on other popular operating systems, such as the Apple Macintosh and UNIX, it cannot be considered to be a perfect solution for the Internet as a whole. This is because a large number (if not a majority) of the computers currently being used to access information on the Internet are non-Windows machines.

ActiveX documents allow Web-site designers and application builders to become suppliers of Web-based content without having to learn the complexities of HTML. Because applications written to implement the required ActiveX document interfaces can be viewed within the Internet Explorer browser, developers can distribute Microsoft Office data, for instance, without attempting to format it in HTML. Future versions of Windows promise to use ActiveX documents extensively throughout the system.

Security with ActiveX Authenticode

by Mahendra Palsule

IN THIS CHAPTER

CHAPTER 23

Just as there are constructors and destructors in an object-oriented language, there are creators and destroyers of software. While software developers invest millions of dollars in creating sophisticated applications, anonymous hackers and authors of software viruses expend their effort in modifying, reverse engineering, and corrupting original software.

The Internet explosion in this decade has turned this key concern of the information technology industry into a pressing issue. While the ubiquitous World Wide Web offers unprecedented capabilities for software developers, its fundamentally insecure framework offers a similar opportunity for those with unscrupulous intentions.

When today's Web surfers browse enhanced Web sites, they often download software either in the form of Java applets and ActiveX controls or as software applications, shareware demos, and so on. Software is also distributed or delivered across the Internet via e-mail attachments or by using File Transfer Protocol (FTP).

To ensure that this software is indeed from a reliable source and has not been tampered with in any way, a security mechanism is required to verify the genuineness and integrity of the code before it is installed and executed on the user's system.

In this chapter you will see how Microsoft's Authenticode technology addresses these concerns using digital signatures and Software Publisher Certificates.

Introduction to Code Signing

Code-signing technology is used to verify the identity of the software publisher and check the integrity of the software so that users can be assured of the trustworthiness of the code. *Code signing* involves bundling digital signatures along with the original code, which remains unchanged.

> **NOTE**
>
> From the perspective of verifying the source and integrity of code, understand that the executable code, or software component, is akin to a chunk of data. Hence, in the context of code signing, the software component is frequently referred to as the data that is signed.

Before I explain about Authenticode and the tools used to sign code, a discussion of some key concepts related to code signing is in order. The nuts and bolts of the Authenticode security model are digital signatures and certificates. Although you do not need to delve deep into encryption technology, a clear grasp of the fundamental concepts would go a long way toward using the code-signing tools productively.

Digital Signatures

A *digital signature* is a fixed-length piece of binary data that is created as part of the code-signing process. Digital signatures can be used along with software code as well as with any data such as messages or documents. The identity of the signer and the integrity of the data since it was signed can be verified by the receiver of the message or the end user of a software component.

Digital signatures use public-key algorithms that are designed to work with a key pair. A *key pair* consists of a private key that is used to encrypt the data and a public key that is used to decrypt the encrypted data. The private key is kept confidential by the signer, whereas the public key is made available along with the signed data. The public key is distributed with a certificate, which I will explain in the next section.

Because the original software component may be of a huge size, a fixed-length encrypted digest is first created before using the private key to sign it. The digest is created using a one-way hashing algorithm, which means that the original data can never be retrieved from the digest using the hashing algorithm.

The *digest* or *hash value* is like the fingerprint of the original data. The hashing algorithm is sensitive to any discrepancies in the original data at the bit level, so reapplying the hash algorithm to a modified version of the data creates a different digest. The creation of a digital signature is illustrated in Figure 23.1.

FIGURE 23.1.

The process of creating a digital signature.

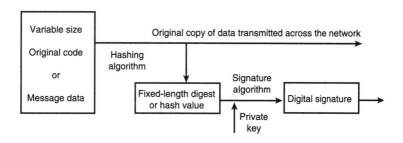

Using a signature algorithm and the private key of the signer, the encrypted digest is transformed to create the digital signature that is transmitted along with the original code. The hashing algorithm used to create the digest and the signature algorithm used to sign the digest should be the same at both ends of the code transfer.

The recipient of the signed code uses the hashing algorithm on the code to create a digest. Then, using the digital signature algorithm with the public key of the signer, he decrypts the digest in the accompanying signature. The process of verifying digital signed code is illustrated in Figure 23.2.

FIGURE 23.2.
The process of verifying a digital signature.

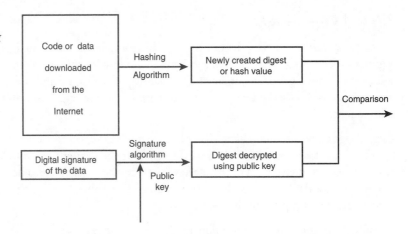

If the two digests are identical, the source and integrity of the code are verified. If there is a mismatch, it indicates that the received code does not match the one originally signed by the signer.

Hashing Algorithms

Two common hashing algorithms used are the MD5 Message Digest and the Secure Hash Algorithm (SHA) algorithms.

The MD5 hashing algorithm, which generates a 128-bit hash value, was developed by RSA Data Security, Inc. The SHA was co-developed by the National Institute of Standards and Technology (NIST) and the National Security Agency (NSA).

Digital Certificates

With the digital-signature technology I've outlined, the public key that is freely distributed may be used by unscrupulous individuals to impersonate others. If a software component allows a user to enter his user ID and public key, for example, an impersonator can substitute his own public key while entering another person's user ID.

Public-key certificates are documents issued and signed by a trusted authority containing someone's user ID and public key. The trusted authority is known as a *certification authority* (CA). The CA is responsible for verifying the credentials of a user before issuing the certificate. Figure 23.3 shows the certificate for the Microsoft Certificate Enrollment ActiveX Control, issued by VeriSign.

FIGURE 23.3.

The certificate for the Microsoft Certificate Enrollment ActiveX Control, issued by VeriSign.

Trust Hierarchy

Different entities may take on the role of the CA in different environments. For example, the IT department of a company may be the CA for users of the company's network, and an Internet service provider may act as the CA for its subscribers. The situation in which the recipient does not trust a particular CA is handled by the concept of a trust hierarchy.

A *trust hierarchy* is similar to how you are more likely to trust a friend's friend rather than a complete stranger. If a complete stranger established a chain of individuals starting from a friend you trust, with each trusting the next in the chain, you would find yourself able to place your trust in that stranger.

Ideally, there would be a root trusted authority whom everybody trusted—perhaps a federal government agency or a trustworthy company. Digital certificates could then be easily created from the linear chain of the trusted authorities leading to the root CA.

How are certificates digitally represented? Public-key certificates are in the industry-standard X.509 format discussed in the following section.

The X.509 Certificate

The industry-standard X.509 protocol specification includes a structure for public-key certificates. The X.509 certificate is a cryptographic certificate containing the unique name of the vendor and the public key of the vendor. The certificate is signed by the CA issuing the certificate. The format of the X.509 certificate is shown in Figure 23.4.

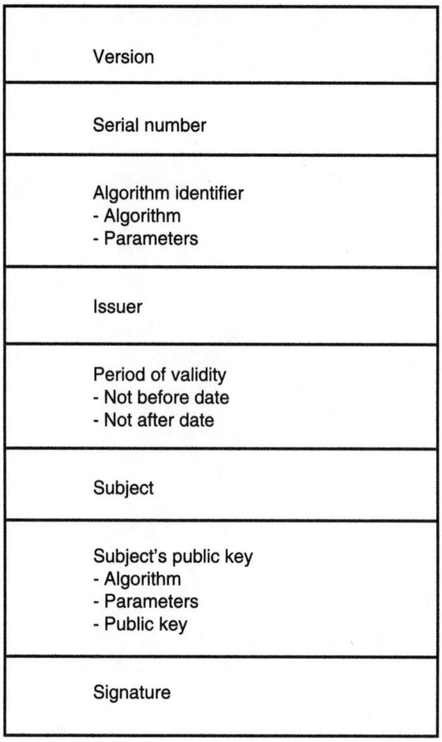

FIGURE 23.4.

The X.509 certificate format.

Version
Serial number
Algorithm identifier - Algorithm - Parameters
Issuer
Period of validity - Not before date - Not after date
Subject
Subject's public key - Algorithm - Parameters - Public key
Signature

The Software Publisher Certificate

The *Software Publisher Certificate* (SPC) is the document issued by the CA that conforms to the industry-standard X.509 certificate with Version 3 extensions. Each digital certificate is linked to the certificate of the CA that signed it, thus forming a linked chain of certificates.

Multiple X.509 certificates are encapsulated in a format defined by the Public Key Cryptography Standard #7 (PKCS#7). Among other things, this standard defines a standard representation of a signature block. The PKCS#7 signature block can contain multiple certificates along with the data that is signed. This signature block is also referred to as a *signed-data object*.

The SPC is a PKCS#7 signed-data object containing the X.509 certificates of the signer, the root certificate supplied by the CA, and the signer's public key. The signer or software publisher is the *subject* of the certificate.

This SPC is used to create the final signature file containing a PKCS#7 signed-data object that is distributed along with the code. For code that is downloaded in the portable executable (PE) format, this signature file is stored in the binary file in a separate section.

Now that you have an understanding of the fundamental concepts of code signing, I will now discuss Microsoft's Authenticode code-signing technology.

Authenticode

Authenticode is a security mechanism that puts end users in control of what software is allowed to run on their system. Authenticode is currently implemented in Microsoft Internet Explorer 3.0. All Microsoft development tools will incorporate support for code signing using Authenticode in future releases. I will first present an overview of Authenticode and then discuss its relevance from the perspective of Java developers.

The User's Perspective

The Authenticode technology implemented in Internet Explorer 3.0 alerts users before downloading and executing software from the Internet. Authenticode currently supports signed Win32 Portable Executable (PE) format files, which may be in the form of Java applets, ActiveX controls, plug-ins, executables, cabinet files, and so on. If the code has been signed by a CA, the certificate is displayed to the user. If the code has not been digitally signed, Internet Explorer by default does not download the code.

The user can set the safety level of this security mechanism to one of three settings by choosing Safety Level from the Security tab in the dialog accessed from the View | Options menu, as shown in Figure 23.5.

FIGURE 23.5.

Safety-level settings in Internet Explorer 3.0.

With the default security setting of High, Internet Explorer avoids downloading any unsigned code and displays a dialog box to the user noting that a potential security hazard was avoided. With this default setting, users cannot view any Web page that contains unsigned code, thus preventing malicious code from being downloaded to the average user's system.

A Medium security setting warns expert users and developers if Internet Explorer encounters unsigned code, but gives them the option of downloading the unsigned code. A security setting of None assumes all code to be safe and downloads all code whether signed or unsigned.

Users can also configure Authenticode in Internet Explorer using Personal, Site, and Publisher certificate options found in the Security tab of the Options dialog box, as shown in Figure 23.6.

FIGURE 23.6.

*Security options in
Internet Explorer 3.0.*

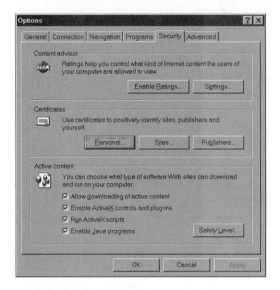

The Publisher's Perspective

The Authenticode code-signing technology can be used by software developers to build a trusted relationship with their customers. The code-signing process ensures that customers always use original software. Using Software Publisher Certificates for code signing builds brand recognition among the developer community.

Code-signed software can also be used by Web sites that host software libraries and shareware programs on the Internet. If Web sites host code-signed software, they will have an enhanced reputation and can ensure that users download authentic code.

NOTE

Authenticode does not guarantee that the signed software component is bug free. Also, it cannot be used for software copy protection.

As you have seen, the Authenticode code-signing technology is not restricted to ActiveX components, but also can be used to sign Java `.class` files and `.CAB` cabinet files. Because the underlying digital-signature technology is independent of the file format, future Authenticode releases will support documents with embedded macros and Macintosh executables. Microsoft is also exploring possibilities for signing HTML code and entire Web pages.

In the corporate environment, the Internet Explorer Administration Kit allows administrators to preconfigure Internet Explorer security settings and control which settings can be changed by users.

Java and Authenticode

Java uses a security model based on the concept of a trusted computing base, commonly referred to as a *sandbox*. I'll review the basic properties of the sandbox before looking at how Authenticode works with Java.

The Java Sandbox

Java applets downloaded from the Internet are executed in a restricted environment in the Java Virtual Machine (JVM) on the client system. The JVM considers these downloaded applets as *untrusted*, in contrast with *trusted* applets that are loaded from the local file system. The following restrictions apply to untrusted applets:

- File Access—Untrusted applets do not have access to the file system on the client system. Therefore these applets cannot read, write, or modify the properties of any files on the user's system.

- Network Access—Untrusted applets cannot make network connections except to the host from which they were downloaded.

- Native Code—Untrusted applets cannot load libraries present on the client's system, nor can they start other programs or make native method calls.

- System Properties—Apart from a specific set of system properties like the operating-system name and Java version number, untrusted applets cannot read or access sensitive system properties like the user's account name or current working directory.

This restricted environment is likened to a sandbox because it is supposed to be difficult to get out of one. There are two limitations in the sandbox security model, however.

First, the sandbox approach limits the functionality of downloaded Java applets. File-system access and the capability to use libraries and other programs on the client system are essential features of most useful software. Java has yet to deliver much of its promise due to these restricting features of the sandbox security model.

Secondly, the sandbox acts as the sole barrier between possibly hostile code and precious system resources. A single barrier, however impenetrable, is not recommended for today's needs of electronic commerce. Responsibility for security should be distributed.

Sun Microsystems plans to include support for digital signatures, digests, and key management in the next major release of the Java Developer's Kit, version 1.1. Microsoft has taken the initiative in resolving the problem of trusting downloaded code with the Authenticode code-signing technology.

Stepping Out of the Sandbox

Authenticode can be used in conjunction with the sandbox for overcoming the limitations of the sandbox security model. Authenticode provides the mechanism for accountability that gives the user the freedom to decide whether a Java applet can step out of the sandbox.

Authenticode enables digitally signed Java code to use system resources, perform file I/O, make system calls, and invoke other programs on the client system. Java programs can also use component object model (COM) services of a COM object on the client system.

Internet Explorer 3.0 considers downloaded Java code that is digitally signed with a valid Software Publisher Certificate as trusted and allows it to step out of the sandbox. Unsigned Java applets downloaded from the Internet can still execute within the sandbox supported by Internet Explorer 3.0. Thus Authenticode technology incorporated in Internet Explorer 3.0 enhances the Java sandbox security model and works in conjunction with it.

Using Authenticode with Java

Now let's look at how you can create signed Java code that can be downloaded and used as trusted code.

The `Cab&Sign` directory on the Visual J++ CD-ROM contains the self-extracting file `Codesign.exe` that contains the code-signing tools, utilities, and documentation.

> **TIP**
>
> You can get the latest version of the toolkit from the Microsoft Web site. The code-signing tools are included as part of the ActiveX Software Development Kit (SDK), which is available for free download at `http://www.microsoft.com/activex/`.

The tools are not installed automatically by the Visual J++ setup program. You should copy the self-extracting executables and install them yourself in the directory of your choice. The next sections discuss how to use these tools.

Using the Code-Signing Tools

The self-extracting `Codesign.exe` file installs the programs listed in Table 23.1.

Table 23.1. Programs installed by `Codesign.exe`.

Program	Purpose
MakeCert	Creates a certificate for testing purposes only
Cert2SPC	Creates a test Software Publisher Certificate
SignCode	Uses a Software Publisher Certificate to sign code
PeSigMgr	Inspects the certificate in a signed file
ChkTrust	Checks the validity of a signed file

All of the programs listed in the table, except for `SignCode`, are command-line tools. As noted, the `MakeCert` and `Cert2SPC` programs are provided for testing purposes only and should not be used after you obtain a valid Software Publisher Certificate from a Certification Authority.

The following sections discuss the use of each program in detail.

Creating a Test Certificate with `MakeCert`

As its name suggests, the `MakeCert` program is used to generate a test certificate. The `MakeCert` program can generate a public/private key pair and associate it with a name you choose. It creates an X.509 certificate that contains your name bound to the public key in the signature.

You can view the options and their syntax for `MakeCert` by typing `makecert -?` or simply `makecert` at the command prompt. The syntax for using `MakeCert` is

`makecert [options]` *outputCertificateFile*

The various options for `MakeCert` are shown in Table 23.2.

Table 23.2. `MakeCert` options.

Option	Purpose
-u:*subjectKey*	Specifies the publisher's key-pair name. If the key pair does not exist, it will be generated.
-U:*subjectCertFile*	You can use an existing public key in a certificate with this option. Specifies the filename of the certificate to use.

continues

Table 23.2. continued

Option	Purpose
-k:*subjectKeyFile*	Specifies the location of the subject's private-key (.pvk) file. The private-key file contains the publisher's private key. This option can also be used to create the file if it does not exist.
-n:*name*	Specifies the name for the publisher's certificate, conforming to the X.509 standard.
-d:*displayname*	Specifies the name of the publisher that is displayed in the user interface of the certificate.
-s:*issuerKeyFile*	Specifies the location of the issuer's key; defaults to the root key provided for testing purposes.
-i:*issuerCertFile*	Specifies the location of the issuer's certificate.
-#:*serialNumber*	Specifies the serial number of the certificate. Specifying this value is optional; the maximum value is 2 raised to the power of 31. The default value generated is guaranteed to be unique.
-l:*policyLink*	Specifies a hyperlink to SPC Agency policy information that will be created in the certificate.
-I	Explicitly specifies that the certificate would be used by individual software publishers.
-C	Explicitly specifies that the certificate would be used by commercial software publishers.
-C:f	Explicitly specifies that the publisher met the minimal financial criteria of the CA.
-S:*session*	Specifies the session name for the enrollment session.
-P:*purpose*	Specifies why the certificate is to be generated. The possible values are CodeSigning (default) and ClientAuth for client authentication.
-x:*providerName*	Specifies the cryptographic service provider to use.
-y:*nProviderType*	Specifies the cryptographic provider type to use.
-K:*keyspec*	Specifies the key. The possible values are S for a signature key (default) and E for a key-exchange key.
-B:*dateStart*	Specifies the start date of the validity period. The default is when the certificate is generated.
-D:*nMonths*	Specifies the duration of the validity period.

Security with ActiveX Authenticode
CHAPTER 23   515

Option	Purpose
-E:*dateEnd*	Specifies the certificate expiration date. The default value is the year 2039.
-h:*numChildren*	Specifies the maximum number of certificates that can be linked below this certificate in the certificate chain of the trust hierarchy.
-t:*types*	Specifies the type of certificate. Possible values are E for end-entity and C for certification authority. You can use either or both values.
-g	This option will not be supported in future versions of makecert and should not be used.
-r	Creates a self-signed certificate.
-m	Specifies that the MD5 hash algorithm should be used. MD5 is the default algorithm used.
-a	Specifies that the SHA1 hash algorithm should be used.
-N	Includes the Netscape client-authentication extension in the certificate.

You do not need to use most of the options to create an X.509 certificate with default values. A typical invocation of MakeCert would be

```
c:>MakeCert -u:MyUniqueKey -k:MyUniqueKeyFile -n:CN=MyCompany myCert.cer
```

This generates a certificate file myCert.cer with a signature in which the public part of the key pair MyUniqueKey is bound to the publisher MyCompany. If the key pair MyUniqueKey does not already exist, it is generated along with the MyUniqueKeyFile file in which the key pair is stored.

> **NOTE**
>
> The myCert.cer certificate just created cannot be used to actually sign code using the CodeSign program. You must use a valid SPC before you begin actually signing your code.

Creating an SPC with Cert2SPC

You can create a test Software Publisher Certificate from the certificate created by MakeCert using the Cert2SPC (certificate-to-SPC) program.

This program encapsulates the certificate created with MakeCert and the root certificate into a PKCS#7 signed-data object. It is also possible to include additional certificates into the SPC. The syntax for using Cert2SPC is

```
Cert2SPC cert1.cer cert2.cer ... certN.cer output.spc
```

where *cert1 ...certN* are the names of the certificates to be included in the SPC, and *output.spc* is the name of the PKCS#7 signed-data object that is created.

A typical invocation of the Cert2SPC program would be

```
c:>Cert2SPC root.cer myCert.cer myCert.spc
```

This generates a Software Publisher Certificate myCert.spc including the root.cer and myCert.cer certificates.

NOTE

The Software Publisher Certificate myCert.spc just created is not a valid SPC and cannot be used to actually sign code using the CodeSign program. You need a valid SPC from an appropriate CA to begin signing your code.

Signing Code with SignCode

SignCode is the actual code-signing program you use to sign your code. Before you begin using SignCode, you must obtain a valid Software Publisher Certificate from a trusted Certification Authority.

You can use SignCode either by specifying options on the command line or by starting SignCode without any parameters to invoke the Code Signing Wizard.

The syntax for using SignCode from the command line is

```
SignCode -prog ProgramFile -spc Credentials -pvk PrivateKeyFile/KeySet Name
    -name opusName -info opusInfo -gui -nocerts -provider CryptoProviderName
-providerType n [-commercial¦-individual] [-sha¦-md5]
```

In this syntax

- -prog *ProgramFile* is the name of the program to sign.
- -spc *Credentials* is the file containing your credentials, usually the Software Publisher Certificate file.
- -pvk *privateKeyFile* is the name of the file containing your private key, typically a private-key (.pvk) file.
- -name *opusName* is the name for your published program.

- ▪ `-info` *opusInfo* is the location for obtaining more information about your program, such as a URL.
- ▪ `-gui` invokes the Code Signing Wizard.
- ▪ `-provider` *CryptoProviderName* is the name of the cryptographic service provider to use.
- ▪ `-providerType` *n* is the type of the cryptographic service provider to use.
- ▪ `-commercial` indicates that the code being signed was created by a commercial software publisher.
- ▪ `-individual` indicates that the code being signed was created by an individual software publisher. This is the default.
- ▪ `-sha` specifies that the SHA hashing algorithm should be used.
- ▪ `-md5` specifies that the MD5 hashing algorithm should be used. This is the default.
- ▪ `-?` displays the available options.

Here's how you can use `SignCode` from the command line to sign your Java applet's `.class` file:

```
c:>SignCode -prog myApplet.class -spc myCert.spc -pvk MyKey
```

`SignCode` does the following in response to the preceding command:

1. Creates a 128-bit hash value or digest of `myApplet.class` using the MD5 hashing algorithm.
2. Encrypts (or signs) the digest with the private key of the `MyKey` key pair.
3. Creates a PKCS#7 signature block containing the digest and the `myCert.spc` certificate.
4. The signature block is then added to the `myApplet.class` file in a reserved section, thus digitally signing it.

If you like wizards, you can use the Code Signing Wizard by executing `SignCode` without any parameters. The Code Signing Wizard starts, as shown in Figure 23.7.

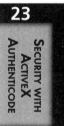

FIGURE 23.7.

The Code Signing Wizard's welcome screen.

Press the Next button to proceed with signing your program. The wizard asks you the program you want to sign, the name you want to give to the signed program, and the location where additional information about your program can be obtained. Figure 23.8 shows the next screen of the wizard after the relevant information has been entered.

FIGURE 23.8.

The Code Signing Wizard, Step 1: program information.

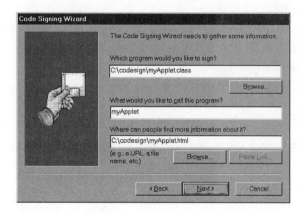

The information you specify in this step maps to the `-prog`, `-name`, and `-info` command-line parameters.

Clicking the Next button takes you to the next step of the Code Signing Wizard. You need to specify the credentials that would be used to sign the program, the location of the private key with which the program would be signed, and the hashing algorithm you want to use to create the cryptographic digest from your program. Figure 23.9 shows this step of the Code Signing Wizard with the relevant information supplied.

FIGURE 23.9.

The Code Signing Wizard, Step 2: security information.

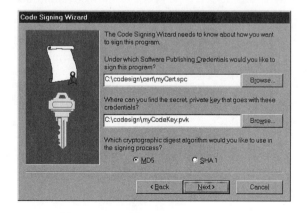

The information you specify in this step maps to the `-spc`, `-pvk`, and either `-sha` or `-md5` of the `SignCode` command-line parameters.

Pressing the Next button brings up the Code Signing Wizard's information review screen. (See Figure 23.10.)

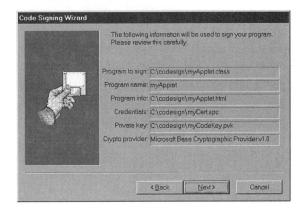

FIGURE 23.10.

The Code Signing Wizard, Step 3: information review.

Observe that the information in the first five fields is what you entered in the previous two steps. The bottom field of the list shows the cryptographic service provider that the Code Signing Wizard uses, which is the Microsoft Cryptographic Base Provider version 1.0 supplied along with the Windows 95 and Windows NT operating systems. The Cryptography API Provider module provides the implementation for encryption, hashing, and signature-verification algorithms.

Press Next after you finish reviewing the information, and the Code Signing Wizard comes to the final step in the code-signing process. (See Figure 23.11.)

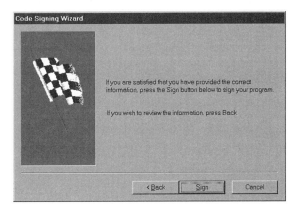

FIGURE 23.11.

The Code Signing Wizard, Step 4: signing code.

Click the Sign button to sign your code. If the Code Signing Wizard successfully signed your code, a message box pops up, as shown in Figure 23.12.

FIGURE 23.12.

The Code Signing Wizard's success message.

You are finished using the code-signing tool. Now you need to verify that your code has indeed been signed correctly.

Checking Certificates with PeSigMgr

The `PeSigMgr` (portable executable signature manager) program can check a portable executable image file to verify that it contains a PKCS#7 signature block. It can also list, add, and remove the certificates from a signed file.

The syntax of `PeSigMgr` is

```
PESIGMGR [options] signedFile
```

where `signedFile` is your signed program file. The various options are

- `-?` lists the available options.
- `-l` lists the certificates in an image.
- `-a:Filename` adds a certificate file to an image.
- `-r:index` removes the certificate at position *index* in the chain of certificates in an image.
- `-s:Filename` used with `-r` to save the removed certificate.
- `-t:CertType` used with `-a` to specify the type of the certificate— X.509 or PKCS#7. Default is X.509.

If you signed the `mySoftware.exe` file, you can check the existence of the certificate in `mySoftware.exe` by entering

```
c:>PeSigMgr -l mySoftware.exe
```

If a certificate is found in `mySoftware.exe`, `PeSigMgr` gives the number, revision, and type of the certificate. A typical output of the `PeSigMgr` program is

```
>Certificate 0 Revision 256 Type PKCS#7
```

Note that `PeSigMgr` only checks for the existence of a certificate in the signed code. It does not verify the signature in any way. It is only used for checking whether `SignCode` really signed the program.

To check the validity of a signed software component, you should use the `ChkTrust` program, which is explained in the following section.

Checking Validity with `ChkTrust`

The `ChkTrust` program is used to check the validity of a signed file. The syntax for `ChkTrust` is

```
c:>ChkTrust [-c¦-i¦-j] signedfile
```

In this syntax

- `-c` indicates a cabinet file.
- `-i` indicates a PE image file. This is the default option.
- `-j` indicates a Java class file.
- `-N` indicates that if the program is not signed, the dialog box alerting the possible danger should not be displayed.

For example, `ChkTrust` could be invoked to verify the signed file `myApplet.class`:

```
c:>ChkTrust -j myApplet.class
```

When you invoke `ChkTrust` like this, it does the following:

1. Extracts the PKCS#7 signature block from `myApplet.class`.
2. Extracts the X.509 certificates from the PKCS#7 signature block.
3. Applies the hashing algorithm specified in the X.509 certificate to the file data and creates a new digest.
4. Uses the public key specified in the X.509 certificate to decrypt the signed hash in the PKCS#7 signature block, thus obtaining another copy of the digest.
5. Compares the two digests.

   If the digests do not match, it means either the digest was modified or the public and private keys do not match.

   If the digests are identical, it verifies that the signer's X.509 certificate points back to the root certificate and that the correct root key was used. If this succeeds, it signifies that the original code has not been modified and the vendor was authorized to publish the file by the root CA. `ChkTrust` returns a success result code of `0` in this situation.

A successful response gives the following output:

```
Result:0
```

In this section, I have discussed the tools you need to sign your Java applets. There is a better method to embed signed Java code in a Web page, which is discussed in the next section.

Introduction to Cabinet Files

Enhanced Java applets are large, use multiple `.class` files, and typically require a set of image and audio files. Normally, each file required for the applet is downloaded individually. Further, the `.class` files and the audio and image data are downloaded in uncompressed format. Individually downloading multiple uncompressed files results in longer download times for large applets.

Cabinet (CAB) files can be used to compress multiple files into a single `.CAB` file. CAB file technology has been used for distributing Microsoft software such as Windows 95. Individual files required by a Java applet can be stored in a single CAB file, resulting in faster download and execution of Java applets.

Signed CAB files are well suited for the distribution of class libraries. Developers of class libraries can incorporate the complete directory hierarchy of their classes in the CAB file. The mechanism for downloading CAB files also provides support for version control and vendor conflict.

> **NOTE**
>
> Sun Microsystems plans to include Java archive (JAR) file technology in the next major release of the Java Developer's Kit, version 1.1. The features of JAR and CAB files are quite similar.

Creating Cabinet Files

 Along with the `Codesign.exe` file, there is an accompanying self-extracting executable file `CabDevKi.exe` in the `Cab&Sign` directory on the Visual J++ CD-ROM.

The `CabDevKi.exe` installs the files listed in Table 23.3 to the directory you specify.

Table 23.3. Files installed by CabDevKi.exe.

Filename	Purpose
diamond.exe	The compression tool to make cabinets
cabarc.exe	Alternative, simpler tool for making cabinets
classpck.ddf	Template file for including applet files in the CAB file
master.ddf	Template files for including Java libraries in the CAB file
master.inf	Setup information file for libraries in the CAB file
README.txt	Release documentation provided with the cabinet development toolkit

Filename	Purpose
overview.htm	Overview of the cabinet file technology
outline.gif	Image file used in overview.htm
diamond.doc	Overview of the compression used for CAB files

There are two ways to create CAB files. The simpler method is to use the cabarc utility. There is another method using templates, which involves additional steps in creating CAB files. Here I will discuss the cabarc utility, which is recommended for applet developers.

The syntax for the cabarc utility is

```
CABARC [<options>] <command> <cabfile> [<filelist...>] [dest_dir]
```

There are three commands to list and extract files from CABs and create new cabinets:

- l lists the contents of a CAB file.
- n creates a new CAB file.
- x extracts files from a CAB file.

Here are some sample invocations of these commands:

- cabarc l contents.cab lists the contents of the file contents.cab.
- cabarc n mynewfile.cab *.class *.gif creates a new cabinet file called mynewfile.cab containing all .class and .gif files in the current directory.
- cabarc x myfile.cab my*.* extracts all files matching my*.* from the cabinet file myfile.cab.

You can use the following options with these commands:

- -c to confirm files to be operated on.
- -o to overwrite without confirmation, when extracting.
- -m to set compression type. You can specify MSZIP for compression or NONE for no compression. Default is MSZIP.
- -p to preserve relative pathnames.
- -P to strip a specified prefix from a path of files when added.
- -r to recurse into subdirectories (usually used with -p).
- -s to reserve space in cabinet for code signing.
- -i to set cabinet set ID when creating a cabinet set of multiple CAB files (default is 0).
- -- to stop option parsing.

The two significant uses of these options are support for parsing a directory structure and support for embedding digital signatures in the CAB file.

The simple applet with animation support developed using the Applet Wizard can be a case study for seeing the benefits of CAB file technology. Developing a sample applet with multithreading and animation support using the Applet Wizard creates a single class file and a subdirectory for images. Using cabinet file compression, there is a 30 percent reduction in the number of bytes that need to be downloaded. In situations involving a larger number of class files and other audio and image data, there can be remarkable savings in download time.

The CAB file technology supports the following API calls made by the applet for loading image and audio data:

- `java.lang.Applet.getImage(URL)`
- `java.lang.Applet.getAudioClip(URL)`

These are the most common methods used to load images and audio data from the Internet. When an applet from a CAB file calls these APIs, the system first tries to find the requested files in the local CAB file that is already downloaded. If it does not find the necessary files within the CAB file, the system tries to fetch it in the normal way across the Internet.

Using Cabinet Files in Web Pages

Applet developers can use the CABBASE parameter of the <APPLET> tag to make use of cabinet files. Internet Explorer versions 3.0 beta 3 and later support the CABBASE parameter. Using the CODEBASE parameter as well ensures that browsers that do not support the CABBASE parameter will also be able to download the code. Thus, here's a sample HTML code using the cabinet file for the Java applet when the .class files are located in a different directory than the HTML page:

```
<APPLET CODE="myApplet.class" CODEBASE="/java/classes/" WIDTH=m
    HEIGHT=n>
<PARAM NAME="cabbase" VALUE="myApplet.cab">
</APPLET>
```

You have now seen how you can use cabinet files effectively in conjunction with Authenticode to decrease download times and enhance the performance of Java applets.

Summary

The Authenticode code-signing technology is the leading initiative toward software accountability on the Internet. More than 40 companies have endorsed the Authenticode proposal. Companies such as VeriSign and GTE are providing the underlying infrastructure of Trusted Authorities for the digital signature and certificates initiative. Standard policies for issuing digital certificates for individual and commercial software publishers are being framed.

As the code-signing initiative gains momentum, Internet users will be in control of what software is allowed to run on their system. Whether an umbrella organization evolves to ensure standardized policies for Certification Authorities remains to be seen.

CHAPTER 24

Distributed Component Object Model

by Hiro Ruo

IN THIS CHAPTER

This chapter introduces the reader to the future of computing according to Microsoft: the distributed component object model (DCOM). DCOM allows COM objects to be distributed across remote servers and for the entire operating system to consist of COM objects.

Information "Not-so-Super" Highway

The Information Superhighway is indeed a power tool, giving a user access to a plethora of resources and information all over the world. This is especially evident in the exponential explosion of the number and variety of Web sites on the World Wide Web. The Web is a set of encyclopedias, a mail system, an enormous database, a museum, a newsroom, a telephone, an entertainment system, a broadcast network, a worldwide address book, and many more things. However, its true potential has yet to be exploited.

The technology growth on the Web is tremendous. Just yesterday, a text browser was a piece of software only a doctoral student could manage. Information available on the Internet was limited to the most obscure scientific research topics. Today, anyone with a modern PC can view high-quality art and maneuver the Internet at the touch of a mouse button. Video, audio, and interactive play are all part of the Internet technology toolkit. Technologies such as COM will make the Internet more powerful and flexible. But a superhighway it is not. Why not?

The limiting factor is the connection. Today's typical home computer consists of PCI video, Soundblaster-compatible audio, storage space close to 1GB, and the latest and greatest modem, which transmits and receives at an unimpressive 28Kbps (kilobits per second). This is because the only ubiquitous connection available in the typical house is a telephone line, so a typical home user connecting to the Internet must wait excruciatingly for the information to download to his or her local computer in order to use it. This situation will only worsen as the amount of information increases.

So, what is the solution? Installing ISDN or T-1 lines in a home is unreasonable for the average home computer owner. New communications technologies will take years to become ubiquitous. A better connectivity model for the Web that can utilize the currently available hardware is required, and the answer may be distributed computing.

The Current Programming Model

A good place to start in understanding the distributed computing model is to look at the current programming model. The average program requires three major components: a way for the user to interface with the program, a functional body that actually performs the tasks required by the program, and a method of storing the program. Figure 24.1 illustrates this model.

FIGURE 24.1.

The current program-ming model.

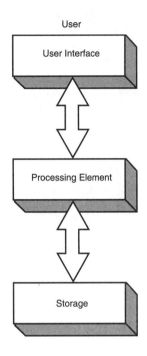

A user accesses the program through the user interface, which can be as simple as "Press Any Key to Continue" or as complex as a window graphical user interface. With this interface, the user has control of where to take the program next, as well as a method of entry to and exit from the program.

The processing element is the main computational component of the program. Any task that the program actually performs resides in this block. These tasks can range from the actual mathematical operations in a calculator program to the rendering of complex 3D images in a virtual reality program. The processing element takes instructions from the user through the user interface to determine what tasks to perform and how they will be carried out. It also returns the results of the computation to the user through the user interface.

The storage component is where the program itself and any transient data and information the program needs is kept. This includes the memory used to run the program or the hard drive where the program is kept. The user can access storage through the user interface and the processing element.

This model applies to any program run on a standalone computer. The user starts the program stored on his PC. He controls the program, enters any data, receives the results, and exits the program through the user interface. The program runs in the memory contained in the PC and utilizes the swap space and file system for storage of intermediate and final results.

24

DISTRIBUTED COMPONENT OBJECT MODEL

This programming model is also implemented in the environment of the Web as a local phenomenon. For example, to run a nifty game found while surfing the Web, the user must download the program to his or her local computer's memory in order to run it. In this case, the Web is used only as an information retrieval system. And with the low bandwidth of a telephone line, this retrieval can be inefficient and lengthy. Therein lies the unnecessarily imposed limitations on the use of the Web today: Programmers are writing applications intended for local use only and distributing them across the Web as is.

Distributed Computing

So, what is distributed computing? And how can it help solve the bandwidth problem of today's Web?

The word "distributed" gives an image of many pieces of an item strewn in all directions, possibly in a well-organized manner. And that is the essence of the concept of distributed computing: the capability to utilize a dispersed set of resources to perform the act of computation.

In the current programming model described earlier, a program will run on the local computer on which the program was started. The local computer will multitask all the different functionalities of the program to emulate the simultaneous occurrence of all the events happening. In distributed computing, each task of the program may be assigned to another computer connected to the local computer. In this way, the execution of the program is shared by the local computer and others on the network on which it is connected. This is distributed computing.

Let's look at writing a book as an example to demonstrate this concept. Say you want to write a book to teach people how to use Visual J++. You could sit down, parse through the enormous amount of information required to understand how to use Visual J++, and then proceed with typing the hundreds of pages, drawing the many diagrams and figures, writing the numerous example programs for the book, authoring the CD-ROM of examples and help files, formatting the entire set of text and graphics into the finished product, drawing the catchy cover art, and compiling a listing of all the related books and articles to read. Obviously, this is not the most efficient way to accomplish the goal of writing a book. But writing a standalone program is performing just such a task: The writer probably does not have the resources to perform all the tasks necessary in a timely manner, even if he or she were superhuman.

Using a distributed computing model to write your book, you could seek out several other writers and have them write as many chapters in which they have expertise as they can. Then you could make arrangements with a publisher to communicate with the distributors, hire a trucking company and an airline pilot, have a lawyer work out the contract details, and so on. You get the picture.

In a similar manner, a program can run on multiple computers using the same programming model described previously. The local user interface is used to call various processing elements stored on different remote storage components to execute a program. This distribution across multiple computers allows more flexibility, more efficient resource allocation/sharing, more modularity, and more computing power. Figure 24.2 illustrates the distributed computing environment.

FIGURE 24.2.
The distributed programming model.

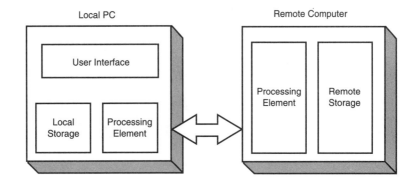

Distributed Web

The distributed computing model can be easily integrated into the Web. The Internet is a perfect infrastructure for such a model. A Web browser, or any program that facilitates access to the Internet, is the user interface. From here, the Web and all its resources are at the user's disposal.

The Web is distributed in the sense that it is a means by which one computer can connect to many other computers to access these computers' information. Too often, however, the resources on the Web act only as storage media. A user should have the processing power and storage capacity of any resource on the Internet. A local PC is not tailored to perform highly computationally intensive tasks such as large searches or database management, but there are many servers and other comparable nodes out there that have this capability. It would only be logical to utilize these resources. The Web PC and other similar low-cost Internet boxes were designed with the intent of harnessing this capability.

Figure 24.3 shows a possible collaboration of several Web servers to perform a complex 3D modeling requested by the PC connecting to the Internet. The search engine Web server is utilized to parse the resources of the Web for graphical objects to be used in the 3D model. The database Web server stores and facilitates the processing of the graphical object definition used. The graphical Web server generates the actual 3D model, collecting information found by the search and database servers. The computational Web server is utilized to perform the complex calculations required in the rendering of the 3D model. Although incomplete, this example demonstrates the potential of a distributed program on the Web.

FIGURE 24.3.

An example of a distributed program on the World Wide Web.

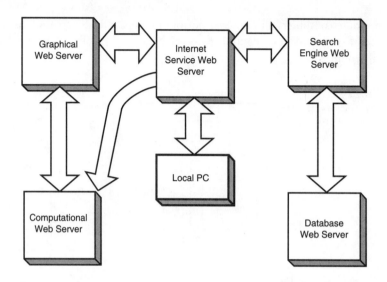

Currently, the de facto method for using the Web in a somewhat distributed manner is with common gateway interface (CGI) programs. CGI programs are run on remote servers that give users additional processing power to run computing-intensive applications such as database access and searching algorithms. The intent of this protocol is to enable access to security-restricted information that otherwise cannot be utilized by the PC. It is also a good first step toward implementing and utilizing the potential of distributed computing power on the Web.

As the Internet evolves into a more ideal distributed computing environment, better methods of sharing resources are needed. The distributed Web model is a possible solution. At a logical block level, this concept seems simple, but as we know, its implementation is no trivial matter. There are many questions to be answered regarding security, protocol, communication services, and operating system design. A possible answer to these questions is DCOM.

DCOM

DCOM is currently being developed by Microsoft Corporation as a follow-up to its COM implementations. DCOM is an application-level protocol for object-oriented remote procedure calls (RPCs) intended for a distributed system. It is based on the distributed computing environment (DCE) RPC specification developed by the Open Software Foundation (OSF). Through the use of COM, DCOM will support standard functionality of any distributed environment, including the Web, regardless of computer platform, communication protocol, and operating system.

The vision of Microsoft for COM, as previously described in this section, is a universal infrastructure for implementing highly portable, object-oriented software that can be used by any of its operating systems, including future versions of Windows 95 and Windows NT. All software, including operating system modules, applications, and networking, will be written so that they conform to the COM specification and therefore can be easily transplanted to any platform without customization.

DCOM is an extension of this idea. Just as future software implementations will use COM to access the local features of a computer, DCOM will allow these same software implementations to use remote features of other connected computers. Any resource, barring security restrictions, available to a local PC can then also be made available to remote PCs over a connection. A perfect implementation would be on the World Wide Web.

DCOM Key Features

DCOM implementation is synonymous to an RPC implementation that conforms to the DCE specification. Key features of DCOM are portability, runtime binding across the network, transparency to requesting applications, and most importantly, a well-defined interface to allow remote task execution. Some details of DCOM features follow.

DCOM utilizes the network data representation (NDR) for any arbitrary data types supported by DCE RPC. This implementation eliminates the need for increased complexity required with the development to support the growing number of formats and task-specific syntax. With today's explosion of new formats and syntax, the effort to upgrade existing software for these features is tremendous. DCOM will allow one common method to support these and future technologies.

Another feature of DCOM is the inherent support for a secure distributed environment. DCOM implements the security provided by DCE RPC, including its capability for authentication, authorization, and data integrity. This is an absolute requirement in today's Web, due to the popularity of applications to transmit confidential data and the adoption of intranets by companies requiring limited, monitored access to confidential information.

Today, information is updated on the Web by simply overwriting existing data and programs. To keep the integrity of the existing interface, both server and client software must be updated simultaneously. With DCOM, this is not necessary. You can label an interface version with universally unique IDs (UUIDs). You can then update an existing interface by publishing a new UUID with the interface, so that both the old and new interfaces can be supported. And two parties can simultaneously update an existing interface without fear of conflict between the two updates. To understand the implementation of DCOM, one must first understand the RPC protocol as defined by the DCE. The following is a list of terminology that requires definition and clarification:

- Binding—Establishing a connection between a client and a server that facilitates the actual calling of the RPC.
- Endpoint—A protocol-specific interface used by servers to listen for RPC requests.
- Entry Point Vector (EPV)—Entry points to the operations supported by managers within the application.

24

DISTRIBUTED COMPONENT OBJECT MODEL

- Manager—A set of routines that implements the operations of an interface. Multiple managers for the same interface can coexist to facilitate multiple revisions.

- Name Service—The RPC API that allows applications, on both client and server, to transfer binding information.

- Universally unique identifier (UUID)—An identifier used by RPC to determine the characteristics of an RPC interface or object.

The basis for RPC protocol is in a client/server implementation. An RPC is the protocol by which a client can call a resource available at a remote node (server) through its local RPC manager. The following steps illustrate how a client interacts with the server using RPC (see Figure 24.4):

FIGURE 24.4.

RPC client perspective.

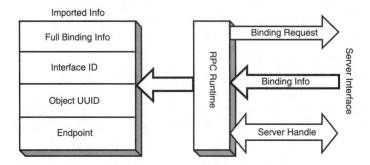

1. Before making the actual RPC call, the client must get a compatible binding, one that provides the interface required using mutually supported protocol; it does this by searching a name service called by RPC API routines. Typically, the client first specifies the interface desired, and the RPC runtime uses this information to find bindings with compatible protocol sequences. The client can also specify a protocol sequence or a particular object UUID.

2. After finding such a binding, the client must then import the binding information from that element. For each binding the client imports, the runtime provides a handle to the indexed server binding that refers to the binding information maintained by the client RPC runtime. A server binding handle, in this client case, may also include a pointer to a particular object UUID, if requested.

3. If a compatible binding is found, the client can then make the actual RPC call using the server binding handle returned.

4. The client runtime now has the binding information and any object UUID involved in the establishment of the binding handle, as well as the interface ID and the operation number of the requested routine.

Now let's look at the same RPC call from the perspective of the server (see Figure 24.5):

FIGURE 24.5.

RPC server perspective.

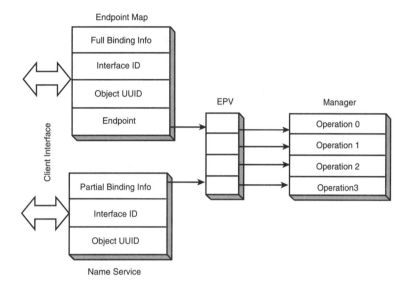

1. The server API defines a manager EPV for each manager available on the server. When an RPC request arrives from a client, the operation number for the request is used to index an element from one of the manager EPVs.

2. The server registers object UUID, interface ID, type UUID, and EPV associations with the RPC runtime to establish an interface mapping that allows the correct selection of the manager.

3. The server returns the appropriate protocol sequences for the request, and the runtime establishes a set of endpoints for these sequences. The runtime will also return a set of binding handles that refer to this set of endpoints if requested to do so.

4. If a call is received with a partial binding (one that lacks an endpoint), the endpoint mapper can use information registered by the server, including interface ID, binding information, and object UUID, to select an endpoint capable of handling the call.

5. The server can export the binding information, minus an endpoint if one was available, through one or more name service entries.

The binding information is a key element of the transactions that occur during an RPC call. It is the method by which a client can access the server and its resources. The binding information format is not a rigid definition, however; Figure 24.6 illustrates the difference between different sets of binding information.

FIGURE 24.6.

Binding information.

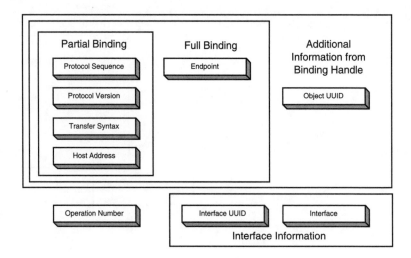

DCOM Functionality

A DCOM call, also called object RPC (ORPC), is actually an RPC call as specified by the DCE. With this implementation, DCOM inherits the security, reliability, and robustness inherent in the RPC protocol. This section discusses the few minor differences between DCOM and RPC.

DCOM utilizes an interface pointer identifier (IPID). This 128-bit identifier is synonymous with the UUID of RPC and is used to identify a specific interface of an object on a server. In fact, the static type of IPID is a UUID.

In a DCOM implementation, the interface ID contains two additional arguments: ORPCTHIS and ORPCTHAT. An ORPCTHAT argument may also be present in a "fault," which is the result of calling an ORPC on a server that does not support the specified interface to the requested object.

The IPID may contain pertinent information to identify the server, object, and interface requested with a ORPC, but it cannot specify the binding information required to execute the ORPC. An additional object exporter identifier (OXID) is used to indicate the scope of an object. An OXID is used to determine the RPC string binding necessary to complete a ORPC by connection to the desired IPID. The OXID is translated into a map of bindings that the referenced application can use to determine whether it is within the scope of the object. Attached to each OXID is an OXID object through which remote management of interface requests are returned.

An extension of DCOM is the concept of marshaled interface reference of an object. There are several types of marshaled interfaces: NULL, a reference to nothing; STANDARD, a standard reference to a remote object; CUSTOM, which gives an object control of references to itself; and HANDLER, which allows a reference through a proxy.

The DCOM protocol also allows remote reference counting on a per-interface methodology. The incrementing and decrementing of the reference count are implemented using the `RemAddRef` and `RemRelease` calls. These calls are not processed immediately but are cached until all local references to a remote object are released for processing. This allows a more efficient network communications protocol, resulting in lower network traffic.

To handle abnormal termination of remote objects, DCOM supports a pinging system. Associated with an object are a `pingPeriod` and `numPingsToTimeOut`. These values allow a certain number of pings and lapse of time before an object that isn't responding is considered terminated. DCOM also supports Delta Pinging, which allows pings to be grouped into sets; a ping is then performed on a set of IDs instead of pinging for each ID requested. Again, this greatly reduces network traffic.

DCOM also utilizes causality IDs, in which a string of ORPCs can be linked by this UUID to indicate that they are causally related. With this information, an application receiving a string of ORPCs will have visibility into the transient relations of ORPCs, so the application can have some knowledge of possible deadlocks due to misprocessing an ORPC of a causal set.

Table 24.1 shows the DCOM data types and structures. Refer to the DCOM specification for a more detailed explanations.

Table 24.1. DCOM data types and structures.

OBJREF	*Marshaled Object Reference*
OBJREF_STANDARD	Standard Marshaled Object Reference
OBJREF_HANDLER	Handler Marshaled Reference
OBJREF_CUSTOM	Custom Marshaled Reference
OBJREF_NULL	NULL Marshaled Reference
STDOBJREF	Marshaled COM Interface Pointer
SORFLAGS	Object Exporter Flags
ORPCINFOFLAGS	ORPC Flags
ORPCTHIS	Request Marshaled Arguments
ORPCTHAT	Response Marshaled Arguments
HRESULTS	ORPC Return Value

24

DISTRIBUTED
COMPONENT
OBJECT MODEL

Summary

This chapter presents an overview of the concept of distributed computing and how DCOM can be implemented on today's Web infrastructure to facilitate faster, more modular, more powerful Internet activities. The implementation of the DCOM protocol may help with some inefficiencies of the current Internet by allowing applications to be distributed and shared across the abundant resources available.

So, where does DCOM take us next? It is evident from all the hype over the Internet that Microsoft wishes to be a key contributor in the future of the Internet. The announcement of the availability of COM brings Microsoft's product line closer to a fully portable set of codes that will allow for the proliferation of Microsoft products, including Windows 95 and Windows NT. At this writing, Microsoft has announced the transition of ActiveX and DCOM to an industry standards body. With the addition of DCOM, users can now take advantage of the built-in support for portability and modularity of COM and DCOM to the next level— the Internet as single body. As DCOM becomes a predominant implementation of Internet software, applications will be able to access any resource anywhere on the Web just as they access the resources of the local PC/operating system. This will allow flexibility and seamless functionality like never before. This is the vision of Microsoft and the future of the World Wide Web.

IV

PART

Activating the Internet with Visual J++

CHAPTER 25

Browser Support for Active Content

by David Blankenbeckler

IN THIS CHAPTER

The Web browser is the vehicle by which you will be able to share your Java applets. With the Internet craze of the past year or two, almost everyone has used a Web browser. However, you may not be fully aware of the features available in the latest Web browsers and the differences between the two most widely used browsers, Microsoft Internet Explorer and Netscape Navigator.

This chapter describes the key functionality of the most common Web browsers and covers the following topics:

- A definition of the term *Web browser*
- A discussion of the Internet strategies adopted by rivals Microsoft and Netscape
- Descriptions of many Web browser features
- A comparison of Netscape Navigator and Microsoft Internet Explorer

What Is a Web Browser?

The first Web browsers were much simpler than the popular, feature-rich browsers that companies such as Microsoft and Netscape have developed. In fact, the first Web browsers were designed for scientists who wanted to exchange information with colleagues. Those early browsers simply supported text and hyperlinks; they did not offer multimedia features such as the active content enabled by Java.

Tim Berners-Lee and the other founders of the Web could not have guessed the widespread mania their point-and-click Web interface would create. This type of interface allowed non-technical users to gain access to the wealth of information being exchanged over the Internet. The essential function of the first Web browsers was to simply read special HTML files from other computers (Web servers) on the Internet. These HTML files had two components:

- The information that was being communicated (as text)
- Special formatting and hyperlink codes

The special HTML codes, or *tags*, would tell the browser how to format the text to allow for such things as **bold** and *italics*. Additional HTML tags would tell the browser to treat certain words as links to other HTML files (hyperlinks), which could be on the same computer or any other computer attached to the Internet. Listing 25.1 shows an example of a very simple HTML file.

Listing 25.1. An example of an HTML file.

```
<HTML>
<HEAD>
<TITLE>An HTML Example!</TITLE>
</HEAD>
<BODY>
This is a very simple HTML file.
</BODY>
</HTML>
```

HTML stands for Hypertext Markup Language. HTML is an open specification that is maintained by the World Wide Web Consortium (W3C). For a more detailed discussion of HTML, refer to Chapter 26, "HTML and Web Page Design." For more information about the W3C, refer to `http://www.w3.org/`.

The protocol that allows Web clients and servers to communicate is known as HTTP, or Hypertext Transfer Protocol. In order to understand HTTP, you also need to understand TCP/IP—a discussion that is beyond the scope of this book. The following are some resources for more information about TCP/IP and HTTP:

> *TCP/IP Unleashed* from Sams.net Publishing
>
> *Teach Yourself TCP/IP in 14 Days* from Sams.net Publishing
>
> `http://www.cis.ohio-state.edu/hypertext/information/rfc.html`, the Web site of the Internet Architecture Board, the definitive source for the standards of TCP/IP
>
> `http://www.ietf.cnri.reston.va.us/`, Internet Engineering Task Force, which designs and develops protocols for the Internet

Web browsers have "learned" to do much more than simply display text and hyperlinks. As a matter of fact, some industry watchers predict that Web browsers may soon become the primary software interface on computers, replacing the operating systems of today.

The Great Browser War

The popularity of the Internet has fueled severe competition for the Web browser market. The competition is so fierce that hardly a day goes by without an announcement about a new browser feature or a new business deal concerning one of the key browser vendors.

The primary contenders in this struggle are Microsoft and Netscape. This rivalry has been both good and bad for the public at large. The rate at which new functionality has been added has been very exciting, and the fight for market share has reduced the effective price of browsers to zero dollars. However, the rate of change has also spawned many incompatibilities, since the standards-making bodies cannot keep up with the need for new functionality. This has caused confusion and frustration among the users as they unsuccessfully attempt to access content on the Internet.

Netscape Navigator and Microsoft Internet Explorer currently own approximately 90 percent of the browser market. The rest of this chapter discusses the primary features of and differences between these products with an emphasis on topics of interest to the Visual J++ developer.

A useful introduction to the topic of browsers is a discussion of the Internet in general and the browser strategies of Microsoft and Netscape.

Microsoft's Strategy: ActiveX

No one is surprised that Microsoft's strategy involves migrating the Web browser capability to the operating system itself. Microsoft would like to make Web browsing simply an extension of the operating system. The user would then be able to use Windows Explorer to view his or her local or network file system as well as the Internet.

Microsoft is pursuing its strategy with three key components:

- Shell extensions
- WinInet API extensions
- ActiveX

Shell Extensions

The first part of the Microsoft strategy is to add a new shell extension to the desktop, which would integrate browsing capability with the operating system. Browsing the Internet and your local hard drive may become a unified process.

WinInet Extensions

The second new technology from Microsoft is WinInet extensions. These extensions to the Win32 API give programmers access to the Internet protocols through a simple interface, enabling them to integrate Internet capability into applications with ease. WinInet extensions hide the complexities of TCP/IP and HTTP from the application developer.

ActiveX

The third, and most talked about component of the Microsoft Internet strategy, is ActiveX. Born out of object linking and embedding (OLE), ActiveX is based on the common object model (COM), a component architecture that allows code to be modularized and abstracted in such a way that other programs can use it without having to know anything about the internal workings of the component itself. It essentially delivers the promise of object-oriented programming—reusable code.

The real power and benefit of ActiveX is the installed base of ActiveX components and the use of these components in other development environments. ActiveX components are based on the widely used OCX (OLE custom control) model in Microsoft Visual Basic and Visual C++. These same components are now being positioned as Internet application building blocks. Because a large number of developers are already familiar with ActiveX and because its components are widely available, ActiveX will most likely become a popular and successful Web application development tool. In addition, ActiveX controls can be created in many different development environments, including Microsoft Visual J++, Visual Basic, and Visual C++.

A Powerful Combination

The combination of Microsoft's shell and WinInet extensions along with ActiveX is powerful indeed. In particular, ActiveX will make useful Web applications a reality because ActiveX, unlike Java, has access to the client's resources, such as the file system. Microsoft (and I) believe that being able to access the client's resources is necessary in order for applications to be useful on the Web. A wealth of content already exists on the Web, and it is extremely useful, but interactive applications, such as a word processor or spreadsheet, require access to some of the client's resources if they are to be truly functional.

Of course, any talk of Web applications having access to client resources immediately raises security concerns. What if a rogue application formats your hard disk or deletes important files? The purist response and the road taken by the Java developers was to simply make client resources inaccessible (except in a limited sense through the Web browser). On the other hand, Microsoft has a strategy to deal with this issue. Microsoft's approach to security uses code signing. With this method, the user is warned by the browser when a new ActiveX component that does not have a proper authorization code is being installed. The user then has the opportunity to cancel the loading of the new, unknown software.

In addition to these three key components, Microsoft also supports both JavaScript and VBScript. These scripting languages form the glue that developers can use to integrate the various components of an application. You can use either of these scripting languages to control the objects and applets in your HTML files. In addition, you can use both JavaScript and VBScript for communication between applets and objects. This communication capability will allow cohesiveness between the various pieces that make up a Web application.

The Microsoft strategy has a few problems. The most notable is that ActiveX is platform-specific code. This is in contrast to Java, which is interpreted by the browser and is thus platform independent for any Java-enabled environment.

Netscape's Strategy: Netscape ONE

Netscape's strategy is reflected in its name Netscape ONE (or Open Network Environment). Netscape's position is that Internet applications should be completely open and platform independent. The key components to Netscape's strategy are

- Java
- Netscape ONE plug-ins
- LiveConnect
- Netscape Internet foundation classes

Java

Netscape was the first company to recognize and implement Java in a Web browser, and Java is a cornerstone in Netscape's strategy. Java provides the platform independence that is promoted as the solution for Internet applications by Netscape. Inherent in the security features of Java is the inability to access client resources such as the file system. Netscape realizes that this security feature limits the types of applications that can be created and is working with Sun Microsystems to implement code-signing security features for Java applets. If implemented, these security features will provide the capability to grant certain access rights to Java applets that have been cleared by the security system.

Netscape Plug-ins

Ironically, Netscape also supports native, platform-dependent code in the form of Netscape plug-ins. The interface to the Netscape plug-ins, however, is platform independent. Even though the plug-in interface is platform independent, the plug-ins are compiled to native code and must be developed for each platform that is to be supported. Netscape claims that because the interface is platform independent, to recompile to different platforms is extremely simple.

The purpose of the Netscape plug-ins is very similar to that for ActiveX components—for some applications access to system resources is critical. (Examples of Netscape plug-ins include the RealAudio plug-in and the Apple QuickTime plug-in.) The user will notice two primary differences between Netscape plug-ins and ActiveX components.

The first difference is that the user must install plug-ins manually before using them. An ActiveX component, on the other hand, will be automatically installed, in a process invisible to the user (assuming, of course, that the code-signing check passed). The other difference is that the ActiveX model is based on the widely used OCX model. Therefore, ActiveX components can be used in environments other than the browser, including Microsoft Visual Basic, Visual C++, and Visual J++. As a side note, Microsoft Internet Explorer supports Netscape plug-ins.

LiveConnect

Netscape's LiveConnect software layer is the glue that binds the various objects in an HTML document, such as Java applets, Netscape plug-ins, JavaScript, and HTML itself. This layer allows the different objects to work together through the JavaScript scripting language. Microsoft Internet Explorer has a competing interface standard known as COM.

Netscape plans to extend the LiveConnect model by adding support for distributed messaging with the Internet Inter-ORB Protocol (IIOP). The IIOP is part of the common object request broker architecture (CORBA), which is an open standard for connecting applications over the Internet. IIOP will allow Netscape Navigator applications to communicate with other CORBA-compliant network applications.

Netscape Internet Foundation Classes

In order to provide platform-independent access to the client, Netscape has developed its Internet foundation classes. These objects allow Java applets, JavaScript, or other objects to access client services through a platform-independent layer. The first release supports user-interface controls and services. This support provides access to advanced controls that are not part of standard HTML, such as sliders, and supports richer content display, such as multifont text.

Netscape may add the following support to its Internet foundation classes in the near future:

- Messaging services
- Security services
- Distributed object services

Browser Features

Now that you understand the basic strategies behind the Microsoft and Netscape browsers, you are ready to continue with a discussion of the key features of a Web browser. The section on each feature also highlights any differences in implementation between Netscape and Microsoft.

HTML 3.2 Support

HTML is the foundation of a Web document and is constantly being improved with additional features. The newest version is release 3.2. Both Internet Explorer 3.0 and Netscape Navigator 3.0 support HTML 3.2. The major new features of this version are support for tables, the <APPLET> tag (which supports Java applets), and the capability for text to flow around images.

Both browsers support additional HTML features that are not yet released by the W3C. In particular, Internet Explorer supports cascaded style sheets, which allow HTML authors to add styles to their documents much as they do in a word processor. Navigator supports the <MULTICOL> tag that allows the author to create multiple columns of text without having to use tables.

Both browsers support frames, which are not a part of HTML 3.2. Frames break the browser display into two or more windows that can independently display an HTML document. Each frame has its own scrollbar and can be advanced or moved backward independently. Figure 25.1 shows an example of a frame.

FIGURE 25.1.
An HTML frame example.

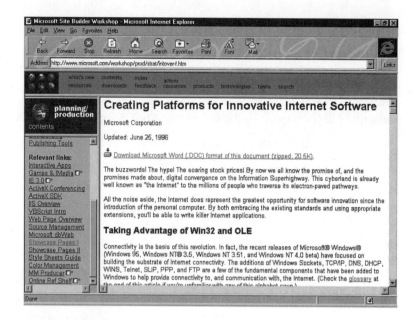

Just-in-Time Java Compiling

Of course, both Navigator and Internet Explorer support Java applets. The platform-independent nature of Java means that the Java Virtual Machine must interpret the code before it can run on the client platform. Understandably, this requirement creates a performance problem for Java applets. However, the recent advent of just-in-time (JIT) Java compiling reduces the performance hit.

With JIT Java compiling, the Java bytecodes are compiled before being used. The bytecodes have been simplified to the point that the compiling process is very fast. Although this will not provide a performance improvement for code that runs only once, it will significantly speed up loops in the code or code that is called several times.

Both Internet Explorer and Navigator support JIT Java compiling.

ActiveX Controls

As mentioned previously, Internet Explorer supports the use of ActiveX controls. Netscape does not directly support ActiveX controls, but instead supports a third-party Netscape plug-in (from NCompass Labs) that provides ActiveX support. The support provided by NCompass Labs is not 100 percent compatible, however. The incompatibility is created because the NCompass Labs plug-in, ScriptActive, only supports ActiveX controls that are placed in HTML files with the <EMBED> tag. Microsoft, and all of its tools, support the <OBJECT> tag instead. This means that HTML documents that use the <OBJECT> tag will not work with the ScriptActive plug-in for Netscape Navigator. For more information about ScriptActive see http://www.ncompasslabs.com/.

ActiveX Documents

Microsoft Internet Explorer 3.0 supports ActiveX documents. This feature enables a user to view and edit richly formatted documents such as those from Microsoft Excel or Microsoft Word. ActiveX documents are based on OLE documents and work in much the same way. For example, if a user opens a page containing a Word document, the Word toolbars and menus will appear. The user can then view and edit the document exactly as if he or she were actually running Word. The browser controls are available as well, and the user can move to another page at any time. If a user does not have the appropriate application installed on his or her system, ActiveX viewers that allow users to display richly formatted documents are available for many document types. Figure 25.2 shows an example of a Word document being edited in Internet Explorer 3.0.

FIGURE 25.2.

An example of an ActiveX document.

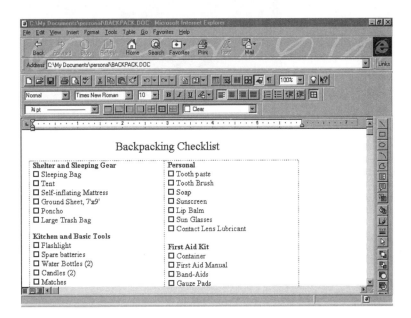

The ActiveX documents specification is an open standard, and most major application vendors will most likely support it in the near future. Although Netscape Navigator does not currently support ActiveX documents, Navigator 3.0 will launch the appropriate application and open the document. In addition, a plug-in is available from NCompass Labs called DocActive that provides comparable support to ActiveX documents.

Netscape Plug-in Support

Like ActiveX, Netscape plug-ins provide a way for developers to add native code applications to a browser. Both Internet Explorer and Netscape Navigator support Netscape plug-ins.

In order to support LiveConnect, the plug-ins must be recompiled with the SDK (Software Development Kit) provided by Netscape. Microsoft Internet Explorer does not support LiveConnect. Therefore, you will not be able to control plug-ins with JavaScript in Microsoft Internet Explorer. The plug-ins themselves should still work, however.

An example of an interesting plug-in from Starfish Software, called EarthTime, appears in Figure 25.3.

FIGURE 25.3.

An example of a Netscape plug-in.

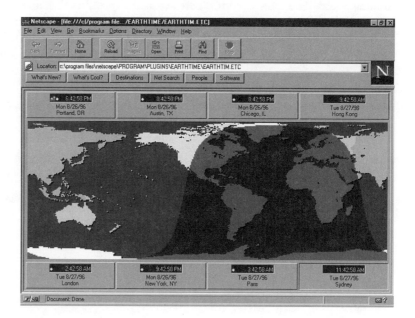

Multimedia Support

Both Microsoft Internet Explorer and Netscape Navigator have a broad array of support for multimedia.

Video Playback

The ability to play back video clips is appearing as a standard feature in the latest generation of Web browsers. Support of video playback is available in varying degrees in both Navigator and Internet Explorer.

Netscape Navigator accomplishes video playback through the LiveVideo feature. (LiveVideo supports only AVI playback at this time.) Microsoft's ActiveMovie provides greater support than LiveVideo does. This ActiveX component currently supports AVI, MPEG, MOV, and QuickTime playback. Figure 25.4 shows an example of the video playback feature for Internet Explorer.

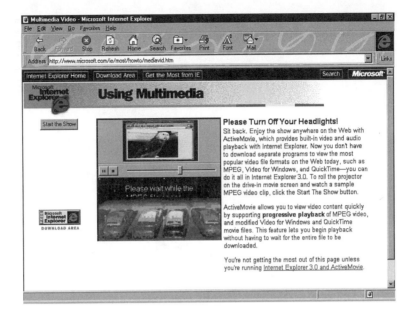

FIGURE 25.4.
*An example of
ActiveMovie.*

Audio Playback

Both browsers support audio playback in the following formats: AIFF, AU, MIDI, and WAV. Microsoft Internet Explorer supports MPEG audio also.

RealAudio

RealAudio provides the ability to receive live broadcast audio over the Internet. For example, many radio stations now use RealAudio to broadcast live over the Internet. For more information on RealAudio, go to `http://www.realaudio.com`.

Both Microsoft and Netscape support RealAudio through the use of a plug-in. Figure 25.5 shows the RealAudio plug-in.

Shockwave

A browser that supports Macromedia's Shockwave can display interactive multimedia programs created with Macromedia's Director software. This capability is one means of creating interactive games on the Web. To find out more about Shockwave, see `http://www.macromedia.com`.

Internet Explorer supports Shockwave through an ActiveX control available from Macromedia. Netscape Navigator supports Shockwave through a plug-in, also available from Macromedia (again at `http://www.macromedia.com`). Figure 25.6 shows an example of the Shockwave plug-in. This example is a game called Galactic Marauders from Matt's Shockwave Spectacular at `http://www.onramp.net/joker/Galactic_ Marauders/`.

FIGURE 25.5.

A RealAudio plug-in.

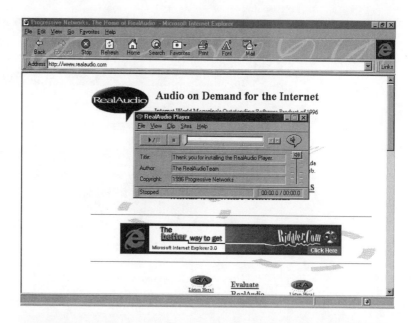

FIGURE 25.6.

A Shockwave plug-in example.

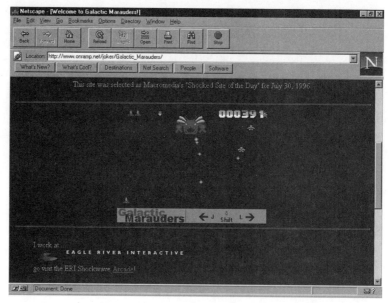

VRML and 3D Animation

Virtual Reality Modeling Language, or VRML, enables you to create 3D worlds in Web pages. As you might imagine, this language is very useful for creating games on the Internet, but its use is not limited to games. For example, you can design a Web page to resemble a 3D store in which visitors can wander up and down the aisles to inspect the merchandise.

Both Internet Explorer and Netscape Navigator offer built-in support for VRML. (Internet Explorer uses Direct3D and Navigator uses Live3D.) The example of VRML in Figure 25.7 is from Intel's home page at http://www.intel.com/procs/ppro/intro/vrml/mma.wrz.

FIGURE 25.7.

An example of VRML.

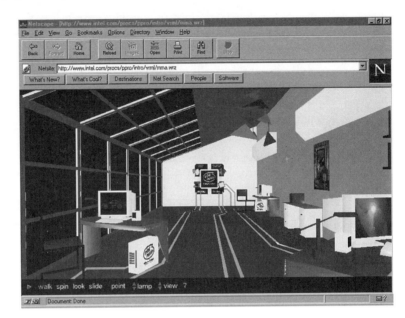

Script Support

Support for scripting in a Web browser is important because it is the primary means by which the objects in an HTML document are integrated. Two major scripting languages are available:

- JavaScript
- VBScript

Both Netscape Navigator 3.0 and Microsoft Internet Explorer 3.0 support JavaScript, a scripting language developed by Netscape. (Do not confuse JavaScript with Java, the programming language.) Netscape originally called its scripting language LiveScript, but renamed it JavaScript to capitalize on the enormous popularity and press coverage of the Java programming language. You can find a detailed discussion of JavaScript in Chapter 27, "Manipulating Web Components Using JavaScript."

The other scripting choice is VBScript. This scripting language was developed by Microsoft and is actually a subset of Visual Basic. VBScript is fully upward compatible with Visual Basic, which is a major competitive advantage because of the large number of developers who are already familiar with Visual Basic. The only browser that currently supports VBScript is Microsoft Internet Explorer. You'll find a detailed explanation of VBScript in Chapter 28, "Manipulating Web Components Using VBScript."

Security Features

The Java Virtual Machine includes security features that prevent a Java applet from harming or accessing data on the user's computer. For example, Java applets cannot access the user's file system or execute any programs on the local system. This security feature is known as *sandboxing* because the Java Virtual Machine essentially builds a sandbox in which Java applets can execute. The Java Virtual Machine will not allow Java applets to perform operations outside of this sandbox. Of course, Navigator and Internet Explorer support this standard security model for Java applets. In addition, both browsers provide support for secure communications over the Internet.

Navigator and Internet Explorer provide support for secure communications through the Secure Socket Layer (SSL) protocol. SSL 2.0 and SSL 3.0 permit users to conduct secure communications over the Internet. This provides the ability to safely exchange information such as credit card numbers.

NOTE

The Secure Socket Layer, or SSL, protocol was developed by Netscape to facilitate secure communications over the Internet. This is accomplished by encryption of the data as well as authentication of the server. The data encryption is done at a low level that is independent of the higher level protocol being used. This allows SSL to be used with all the common Internet protocols such as HTTP, FTP, Telnet, and so on. The encryption key is agreed upon by client and server and is unique for communications between the two. The server is always authenticated before each transaction takes place. Optionally, the client can also be authenticated.

The latest version, SSL 3.0, was published in March of 1996. The following URL provides more details about SSL:

    http://home.netscape.com/newsref/std/SSL.html

Microsoft Internet Explorer offers a new security feature called Authenticode, which verifies that ActiveX controls are from a legitimate source. This security level is especially important if ActiveX controls have access to all of the client's resources, including the file system. While this measure does not protect against poorly written or mischievous code, it does provide a level of accountability to the developer of the software. See Chapter 23, "Security with ActiveX Authenticode," for a detailed discussion of Authenticode.

Comparison Summary

The features of Netscape Navigator 3.0 and Microsoft Internet Explorer 3.0 are very similar. Instead of comparing all the features, this section focuses on the major differences. Table 25.1 summarizes the major differences between the two browsers.

Table 25.1. Feature comparison of Microsoft Internet Explorer 3.0 and Netscape Navigator 3.0.

Feature	Internet Explorer	Navigator
Scripting support	VBScript, JavaScript	JavaScript only
ActiveX	Yes	Plug-in only[1]
ActiveX documents	Yes	Plug-in only[1]
LiveConnect	N/A	Yes
ActiveX code signing	Yes	Plug-in only[1]
Multicolumn tag	No	Yes
Style sheets	Yes	No
Video playback formats	AVI, MPEG, MOV, QuickTime	AVI only[2]
Audio playback formats	AIFF, AU, MIDI, MPEG audio, WAV	AIFF, AU, MIDI, WAV[2]

[1]Note that ActiveX support in Netscape Navigator is limited to HTML documents that use the `<EMBED>` tag to place the control. Microsoft and all of its development tools use the `<OBJECT>` tag.

[2]Other audio and video formats may be available through plug-ins.

Browser Considerations for Developers

This chapter explains the key functions of the newest Web browsers. As a developer of Web applications, you need to understand the capabilities of browsers because they contain and present your applications to the user.

The first step in developing a Web application is to define your audience. Will the entire population of Web users be using your application, or will it be used only inside your company? Will all the users of your application have the same operating system, or will people be using a variety of different system platforms (for example, Macintosh, UNIX, Windows 95)?

The next step is to identify the technologies that you will be using in your application. Will you be using ActiveX? What multimedia capabilities do you intend to use? RealAudio? VRML? Shockwave? Your answers might depend on the browsers available to your audience. Alternatively, you might decide on the technologies first and then choose the appropriate Web browser.

For example, if you are developing a database application for an intranet, you might have full control over the browser that your audience will be using. In this case, you can use whatever browser best supports the technologies that you require. At the other extreme, you might need to support the entire population of Web users. In this case, you will need to limit the technologies that you use to the most widely deployed features. Because you are reading this book (and therefore probably working in Java), you most likely do not expect to support every browser out there, since not all browsers support Java.

Understanding the audience and the browsers that the users will be using is extremely important to the developer. This information must be a top consideration when you design a Web application.

Summary

The purpose of this chapter is to explain the key features of Web browsers. In particular, the discussion centers on the market leaders, Netscape Navigator and Microsoft Internet Explorer. These two products together own more than 90 percent of the browser market.

The next few chapters cover some of the features of today's Web browsers in more detail, beginning with a discussion and tutorial of HTML. Subsequent chapters discuss the scripting languages JavaScript and VBScript.

HTML and Web Page Design

by David Blankenbeckler

IN THIS CHAPTER

CHAPTER 26

HTML, or Hypertext Markup Language, is the glue that binds all the content on the Internet so that it can be properly presented on your Web browser. The name itself, Hypertext Markup Language, accurately describes the primary purposes of the language:

- To provide *hypertext* links that allow the reader to jump to a different position inside a document or to other documents
- To provide a *markup* method for defining the structure and formatting of the text in the document

HTML was originally designed to allow people to share static content. However, the demand for active content has extended HTML far beyond these humble beginnings to include support for scripting (see Chapter 27, "Manipulating Web Components Using JavaScript," and Chapter 28, "Manipulating Web Components Using VBScript") as well as support for ActiveX objects and Netscape plug-ins. HTML's simplicity and ease of use allow it to prevail as the content framework for the Web, tying all the pieces together for presentation in your Web browser.

The purpose of this chapter is to

- Explain the basic concepts of HTML
- Describe the most commonly used HTML features
- Discuss browser support and the future of HTML

This chapter gives you a basic understanding of HTML and serves as a reference for the most commonly used features of HTML. The information presented in this chapter is compliant with HTML version 3.2.

The next two chapters discuss the two powerful HTML scripting languages, JavaScript and VBScript. Scripting allows a page to become dynamic by making a page programmable. For example, you can have an input validation script that will run when information has been entered into a form. Scripting also allows communication between the HTML document and Java applets or ActiveX controls. ActiveX controls and Java applets are placed into a document with the <OBJECT> and <APPLET> tags, respectively. The <OBJECT> and <APPLET> tags are covered in Chapter 29, "Embedding Components Within Web Pages."

An Overview of HTML

You might be wondering why to bother to learn HTML when several commercial packages that generate HTML code for you are available. Products such as Microsoft FrontPage and Netscape Navigator Gold will allow you to enter content in a WYSIWYG ("what you see is what you get") environment just as if you were using a good word processor. As a matter of fact, you should use these products to enter more than just a few lines of content. Unfortunately, these packages have not evolved to the point that they can support all the latest features necessary to build active, multimedia Web pages. Therefore, you really can't avoid learning how to get around inside an HTML file.

Required Tools for HTML Development

An HTML file is not compiled; it is simply a text file that the Web browser interprets. Consequently, the only tools you need to design a Web page are an ASCII text editor, such as Notepad, to write the code and a Web browser to test your creation.

This is all you need to design a Web page, but you can also use HTML authoring software such as Microsoft FrontPage, Anawave Software HotDog Pro, or Netscape Navigator Gold.

> **NOTE**
>
> Most Web browsers have an option that enables you to view HTML source code. This feature is a very useful way to see how other Web pages have been designed. In Microsoft Internet Explorer, select Source from the View menu. In Netscape Navigator 3.0, select Document Source from the View menu.

What Are HTML Tags?

When a Web browser reads an HTML file, the text is parsed sequentially for special instructions that tell the browser what to do with the content of the file. The special instructions in an HTML file are known as *tags*. Tags are enclosed inside the < and > characters. For example, when the browser reads the example file in Listing 26.1, the first text it finds is <HTML>. This tag told the browser that the code to follow was HTML and to treat it as such. Generally, a set of tags marks off the relevant portion of the document. The start and end tags are the same except that the final one includes a slash (/) character.

Listing 26.1. A simple HTML example.

```
<HTML>
<HEAD>
<TITLE>A Simple Example of HTML</TITLE>
</HEAD>
<BODY>
This is a simple example of an HTML document.
</BODY>
</HTML>
```

The result of this example is shown in Figure 26.1.

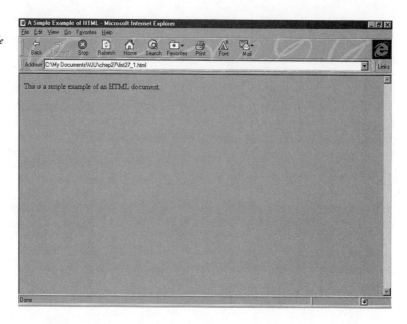

The third line in Listing 26.1 tells the browser to treat the text between `<TITLE>` and `</TITLE>` as a title. Microsoft Internet Explorer and Netscape Navigator will display the text in the top of the window. The text between `<BODY>` and `</BODY>` will be displayed in the body of the document.

NOTE

Tags do not have to be in uppercase; that is, they are not case sensitive. However, the general practice is to use uppercase for all tags simply to improve readability.

HTML Attributes

Some HTML tags have specific attributes that can be set to specify a certain behavior. An *attribute* is a type of extension to an HTML tag that allows you to specify additional information. Examples include

- Specifying a graphics file to load and display, such as `SRC` in the following tag:
  `<IMG SRC='http://www.blankenbeckler.com/images/pic1.gif'>`

- Specifying a URL for a hyperlink, such as `HREF` in the following tag: `<A HREF='http://www.blankenbeckler.com'>`

A tag can have more than one attribute. Each attribute must be followed by at least one space. A single space is generally used, but is not required.

The Basic Structure of an HTML File

An HTML file is broken into several sections. For example, there is a section for the document heading as well as the document body. Refer to Listing 26.2 as I discuss the structural tags for HTML.

Listing 26.2. The basic structure of an HTML file.

```
<HTML>
<HEAD>
<TITLE>This appears in the title bar.</TITLE>
</HEAD>
<BODY>
This appears in the body of the document
</BODY>
</HTML>
```

Required Tags

While there is a wide array of HTML tags available, only a few are actually required per the HTML specification. These required tags are essentially the tags that define the structure of the document. While these tags are required by the specification, both Internet Explorer and Netscape Navigator will properly display a file without them. For example, a plain-text file will be displayed properly in either browser.

<HTML>...</HTML>

An HTML document must begin with the <HTML> tag and end with the </HTML> tag. This tag set tells the browser that the file being read is an HTML document and everything between <HTML> and </HTML> should be parsed for other tags.

Attributes

VERSION="Version info"—This attribute is used to indicate HTML Document Type Definition (DTD). For example, a document supporting version 3.2 would use "-//IETF//DTDHTML//EN//3.2".

Example

See Listing 26.2.

<HEAD>...</HEAD> Header of Document

The purpose of the <HEAD> section is to contain information about the document, such as the title.

Attributes

None

Example

See Listing 26.2.

<TITLE>...</TITLE>—Title of Document

The title should describe the contents of the page. This text will be displayed in the title bar of the browser. In addition, the title will typically be used in the bookmark and history list implemented in most, if not all, browsers. Therefore, titles should be relatively short and summarize the contents of the page.

Attributes

None

Example

See Listing 26.2.

<BODY>...</BODY>—Body of Document

The body contains the content of the document. Many other types of tags within the body format text, insert pictures, and create tables, hyperlinks, and lists.

Attributes

None

Example

See Listing 26.2.

Other General Page Tags

There are two general page tags that are used in HTML documents, <BASE> and the comment tag.

<BASE>—Base Address

The <BASE> tag indicates a base address for relative references in the document. This tag should be included in the <HEAD> section.

Attributes

> HREF="..."—Indicates the base address

Example

```
<BASE HREF="http://www.blankenbeckler.com/main/">
```

In this example, a hyperlink later in the document could use `<A HREF="computer.html">Computer Products</A>` to reference `http://www.blankenbeckler.com/main/computer.html`. This allows the HTML author to specify addresses without having to type in the full address.

`<!-...->`—Comment

The comment tag encloses comments within the HTML file. The browser does not display any text inside these tags.

Attributes

None

Example

The following text could be anywhere inside the HTML document:

```
<!- This is a comment. It will not be interpreted or displayed by the browswer. ->
```

Basic HTML Formatting Tags

There are many different HTML tags available to specify the format and content of a document. For example, there are text-formatting tags to specify that text be bold or italics. In addition, there are tags that are used to insert images or hyperlinks.

Text-Formatting Tags

There are many different types of HTML tags to control the format of text. The HTML Specification only provides guidelines about how each of these should be handled by the browser. For this reason, some of the tags may be implemented slightly differently on various browsers.

`<B>...</B>`—Bold

`<B>` creates **bold** text between `<B>` and `</B>`.

Attributes

None

Example

```
<HTML><HEAD><TITLE>A Bold Example</TITLE></HEAD><BODY>
<B>This text is bold.</B><BR>
This text is not.
</BODY></HTML>
```


—Break

This <BR> tag specifies a line break.

Attributes

None

Example

The following example causes the two sentences to appear on separate lines:

```
<HTML><HEAD><TITLE>A Break Example</TITLE></HEAD><BODY>
This is line one.<BR>This is line two.
</BODY></HTML>
```

<CITE>—Citation

<CITE> indicates a citation or title of a book.

Attributes

None

Example

```
<HTML><HEAD><TITLE>A CITE Example</TITLE></HEAD><BODY>
<CITE>This is CITE text!</CITE>
<BR>This is normal text.
</BODY></HTML>
```

<CODE>—Code

The <CODE> tag indicates programming code.

Attributes

None

Example

```
<HTML><HEAD><TITLE>A CODE Example</TITLE></HEAD><BODY>
The line <CODE>if x=5 then y=0</CODE> sets y to 0 if x is 5.
</BODY></HTML>
```

<EM>...</EM>—Emphasis

The text between <EM> and </EM> is emphasized. This is generally implemented by the browser as italicized text.

Attributes

None

Example

```
<HTML><HEAD><TITLE>A Emphasize Example</TITLE></HEAD><BODY>
<EM>This text is emphasized.</EM><BR>
This text is not.
</BODY></HTML>
```

<H1>, <H2>, <H3>, <H4>, <H5>, <H6>—Headings

The tags <H1> through <H6> are heading tags. <H1> is the topmost level, while <H6> indicates the lowest level. These tags are completely independent of each other and can be used in any order; for example, you could use <H1>, then <H3>, then <H5>; or you could use only <H3>.

Attributes

None

Example

The code example in Listing 26.3 contains three heading levels. You can see the results of this code in Figure 26.2.

Listing 26.3. A heading example.

```
<HTML><HEAD><TITLE>A Heading Example</TITLE></HEAD><BODY>
<H1>Plants</H1><P>
<H2>Trees</H2><P>
<H3>Oak</H3><P>
<H3>Maple</H3><P>
<H2>Grasses</H2><P>
<H3>Bermuda</H3><P>
<H3>Centipede</H3><P>
<H1>Animals</H1><P>
<H2>Mammals</H2><P>
<H3>Elephant</H3><P>
<H3>Lion</H3><P>
<H2>Birds</H2><P>
<H3>Eagle</H3><P>
<H3>Sparrow</H3><P>
</BODY></HTML>
```

FIGURE 26.2.

The results of the code in Listing 26.3.

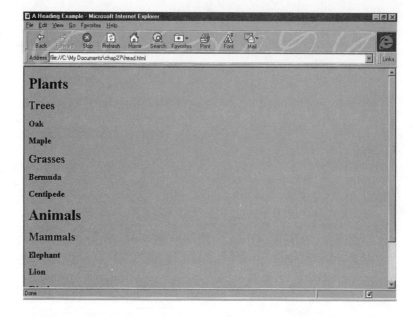

<I>...</I>—Italics

Creates *italic* text between <I> and </I>.

Attributes

None

Example

```
<HTML><HEAD><TITLE>A Italics Example</TITLE></HEAD><BODY>
<I>This text is italic.</I><BR>
This text is not.
</BODY></HTML>
```

<KBD>...</KBD>—Keyboard

The keyboard tag indicates keyboard input. For example, instructions for installing software might ask the user to type SETUP.

Attributes

None

Example

```
<HTML><HEAD><TITLE>A Keyboard Format Example</TITLE></HEAD><BODY>
To install the software, please type <KBD>SETUP</KBD>.
</BODY></HTML>
```

\<P\>–Paragraph

\<P\> represents a new paragraph.

Attributes

None

Example

See the example for \<H1\> through \<H6\>.

\<PRE\>...\</PRE\>–Preformatted

The \<PRE\> tag set creates preformatted text that maintains the spacing of the characters. Text is displayed in a nonproportional font.

Attributes

WIDTH=—Can be used to specify the maximum number of characters per line. The browser uses WIDTH= to determine a suitable font size.

Example

The following example shows text that is preformatted:

```
<HTML><HEAD><TITLE>A Pre-formatted Example</TITLE></HEAD><BODY>
<PRE>
Left side
                   In the middle
                                     Right side
</PRE>
</BODY></HTML>
```

\<SAMP\>...\</SAMP\>–Sample

\<SAMP\> indicates a sequence of literal characters, data output, or programming code. In most browsers this is implemented similarly to the \<CODE\> tag.

Attributes

None

Example

```
<HTML><HEAD><TITLE>A SAMPLE Example</TITLE></HEAD><BODY>
<SAMP>This is SAMPLE text!</SAMP>
<BR>This is normal text.
</BODY></HTML>
```

<STRONG>—Strong Emphasis

<STRONG> indicates strong emphasis.

Attributes

None

Example

```
<HTML><HEAD><TITLE>A Strong Example</TITLE></HEAD><BODY>
<STRONG>This is strongly emphasized!</STRONG>
<BR>This is normal text.
</BODY></HTML>
```

<SUB>—Subscript

<SUB> indicates a subscript.

Attributes

None

Example

```
<HTML><HEAD><TITLE>A Subscript Example</TITLE></HEAD><BODY>
This is an example of a sub<SUB>script</SUB><BR>
</BODY></HTML>
```

<SUP>—Superscript

<SUP> indicates superscript.

Attributes

None

Example

```
<HTML><HEAD><TITLE>A Superscript Example</TITLE></HEAD><BODY>
This is an example of a super<SUP>script</SUP><BR>
</BODY></HTML>
```

<TT>...</TT>—Teletype

The <TT> tag set indicates a typewriter or teletype-style text. This tag is generally implemented by the browser as a nonproportional font, such as Courier.

Attributes

None

Example

```
<HTML><HEAD><TITLE>A TT Example</TITLE></HEAD><BODY>
<TT>This is TT text!</TT>
<BR>This is normal text.
</BODY></HTML>
```

A Text-Formatting Example

Listing 26.4 illustrates the use of each of the text-formatting tags, and Figure 26.3 shows the corresponding output.

Listing 26.4. A text-formatting example.

```
<HTML><HEAD><TITLE>A Text-Formatting Example</TITLE></HEAD>
<BODY>
The purpose of this example is to show you the various text-formatting tags.
<P>
<B>Bold Text</B><BR>
<CITE>This is a citation</CITE><BR>
The following is a code sample: <CODE>if x = 3 then y = 0</CODE><BR>
<EM>Emphasized Text</EM><BR>
<I>Italicized Text</I><BR>
<KBD>This text should be typed at the keyboard</KBD><BR>
<SAMP>This is sample text</SAMP><BR>
<STRONG>This text is STRONGLY emphasized</STRONG><BR>
This is an example of a sub<SUB>script</SUB><BR>
This is an example of a super<SUP>script</SUP><BR>
<TT>Typewriter text</TT><BR>
</BODY>
</HTML>
```

FIGURE 26.3.

A text-formatting example.

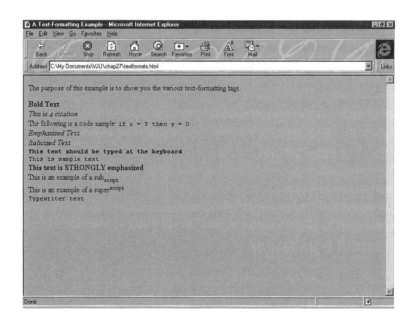

Tags to Create Lists

HTML provides support for creating lists in two different forms, ordered and unordered lists.

<UL>...</UL>—Unordered List

The unordered list tag creates a list. The browser will display the list with bullets. The `<LI>` tag precedes each list item.

Attributes

COMPACT—Suggests that the browser use a more compact style when displaying the list.

TYPE—Specifies the type of bullet to be used. Valid values are `disc`, `square`, and `circle`.

Example

The following example shows a list of three items, and the result of this code appears in Figure 26.4:

```
<HTML><HEAD><TITLE>A List Example</TITLE></HEAD><BODY>
<UL>
<LI>Item 1
<LI>Item 2
<LI>Item 3
</UL>
</BODY></HTML>
```

FIGURE 26.4.

A bulleted list example.

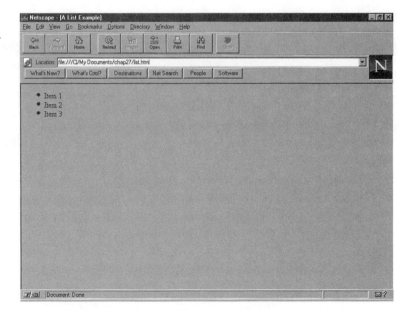

<OL>—Ordered List

The ordered list tag creates a numbered list, as shown in Figure 26.5.

Attributes

COMPACT— Suggests that the browser use a more compact style when displaying the list.

TYPE—Specifies the type of numbering to be used. Valid values are

TYPE	*Numbering Style*
1	1, 2, ...
a	a, b, ...
A	A, B, ...
I	i, ii, ...
I	I, II, ...

Example

```
<HTML><HEAD><TITLE>An Ordered List Example</TITLE></HEAD><BODY>
<OL TYPE=A>
<LI>Apples
<LI>Peaches
<LI>Oranges
</OL>
</BODY></HTML>
```

FIGURE 26.5.

An ordered list example.

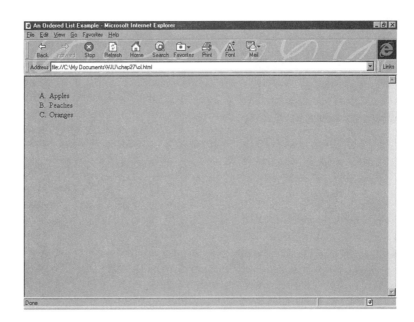

Creating a Hyperlink

A hyperlink is a link between a specific text or image in one document to either another location in the same document or to another document. When a user clicks the hyperlink, the new location will be displayed.

`<A>...</A>`—Anchor

The anchor tag creates a hyperlink anchor. The text between `<A>` and `</A>` will become a hyperlink to the specified location.

Attributes

`HREF="..."`—Specifies the location for the hyperlink (for example, `HREF="www.microsoft.com"`).

`NAME="..."`—Identifies a name for another link to reference. This attribute allows another hyperlink to access this spot in the document by referring to that name. For example, to set an anchor in a document to `CHAP5` you would use `<A NAME="CHAP5">`. Then to access the anchor that was named `CHAP5` from another location in the document, you would use `<A HREF="#CHAP5">`.

`TITLE="..."`—Provides the title of the destination document. The browser can use this attribute to show the title when the mouse is over the hyperlink. However, this attribute does not appear to have any effect in Netscape Navigator 3.0 or Microsoft Internet Explorer 3.0. It may be supported in future versions of these browsers.

Example

Follow this link to Microsoft:

```
<HTML><HEAD><TITLE>A Hyperlink Example</TITLE></HEAD><BODY>
<A HREF="http://www.microsoft.com/">Microsoft's Homepage</A>
</BODY></HTML>
```

Adding Graphics

Adding graphics to an HTML document is accomplished with the `<IMG>` tag. A horizontal rule can be added with the `<HR>` tag.

`<IMG>`—Image

The `<IMG>` tag is used to insert a GIF or JPEG graphic into the document.

Attributes

`SRC="..."`—Specifies the location and file name for the image file.

`ALT="..."`—Specifies a string of text to display in case the browser does not support graphical output.

ALIGN="TOP"¦"MIDDLE"¦"BOTTOM"—Aligns the image either top, middle, or bottom relative to the current line of text. You can also use the WIDTH and HEIGHT settings to specify the width and height in pixels.

ISMAP—Indicates that the image is a clickable map. This attribute usually involves a CGI program to handle the request.

Example

The following example shows the Sams Publishing logo, which appears in Figure 26.6:

```
<HTML><HEAD><TITLE>IMG Example</TITLE></HEAD><BODY>
<IMG SRC="sams16.gif">
</BODY></HTML>
```

FIGURE 26.6.
An <IMG> example.

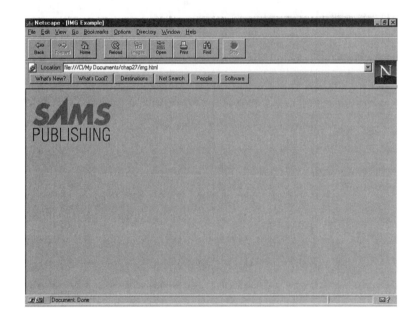

<HR>—Horizontal Rule

<HR> draws a thin horizontal rule across the page, as shown in Figure 26.7.

Attributes

None

Example

```
<HTML><HEAD><TITLE>Horizontal Rule Example</TITLE></HEAD><BODY>
This text is above the line.
<HR>
This text is below the line.
</BODY></HTML>
```

FIGURE 26.7.

A horizontal rule example.

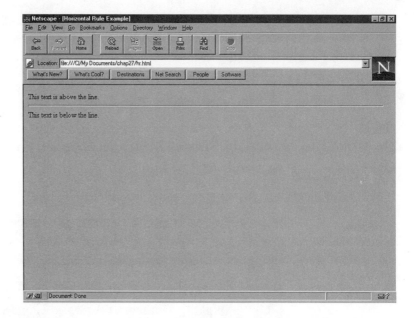

Creating Tables

Although popular Web browsers have supported tables for quite some time, tables didn't become official until the recent release of the HTML 3.2 standard. This section shows you how to use tables in your HTML pages. It starts by explaining the requisite table tags and concludes with a detailed example.

<TABLE>...</TABLE>—Table

The <TABLE> tag surrounds the entire table portion of the HTML file.

Attributes

ALIGN=LEFT¦CENTER¦RIGHT—Specifies the horizontal position of the table with respect to the left and right margins.

WIDTH=—Specifies the width of the table. The value of this attribute can be specified in pixels or as a percentage of the space between the current left and right margins. For example, to make the table occupy 60 percent of the space between the two margins, use WIDTH="60%". If the width parameter is not used, then the default value is 100 percent.

BORDER=—Specifies the border thickness in pixels.

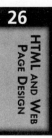

CELLSPACING—Specifies the spacing between each cell as well as the spacing between the table frame and the outside cells. This attribute provides backward compatibility.

CELLPADDING—Specifies the spacing between the border of each cell and the contents of that cell.

Example

See Listing 26.5.

<CAPTION>...</CAPTION>—Caption

The caption tag specifies a caption for the table.

Attributes

ALIGN=TOP¦BOTTOM—Controls the position of the caption relative to the table. The default position is unspecified, but appears to be TOP for both Microsoft Internet Explorer 3.0 and Netscape Navigator 3.0.

Example

See Listing 26.5.

<TD>—Table Data Cell

The <TD> tag precedes each data cell in the table. An end tag, </TD>, is optional.

Attributes

ALIGN=LEFT¦CENTER¦RIGHT—Specifies the horizontal position of the cell contents for a table row.

COLSPAN=—Specifies the number of columns that this cell spans. The default value is 1.

NOWRAP—Disables automatic text wrapping for a data cell.

ROWSPAN=—Specifies the number of rows that this cell spans. The default value is 1.

VALIGN=TOP¦MIDDLE¦BOTTOM—Specifies the vertical alignment of the cell contents.

WIDTH=—Suggests a width (in pixels) for the browser to use when rendering the cell.

HEIGHT=—Suggests a height (in pixels) for the browser to use when rendering the cell.

Example

See Listing 26.5.

<TH>—Table Head Cell

<TH> specifies a heading cell in the table and should precede each heading cell. Browsers usually use a bold font (or some other emphasis) for heading cells to distinguish them from data cells. An end tag, </TH>, is optional.

Attributes

Same as <TD> attributes previously defined.

Example

See Listing 26.5.

<TR>—Table Rows

<TR> indicates the start of a new row in the table.

Attributes

ALIGN=LEFT¦CENTER¦RIGHT—Specifies the horizontal position of the cell contents for a table row.

VALIGN=TOP¦MIDDLE¦BOTTOM—Specifies the vertical alignment of the cell contents.

Example

See Listing 26.5.

Using Tags to Form a Table

Tables are a little more difficult to understand than some of the other elements of HTML simply because they contain so many different tags. The HTML file in Listing 26.5 shows you how to fit together all these pieces to form a table.

Listing 26.5. A table example.

```
<HTML><HEAD><TITLE>A Table Example</TITLE></HEAD>
<BODY>
<TABLE><CAPTION>Yearly Sales</CAPTION>
<TR><TH>Salesperson<TH>1994<TH>1995<TH>1996
<TR><TD>D. Blankenbeckler<TD>$125,000<TD>$115,000<TD>$187,000
<TR><TD>B. Morgan<TD>$165,000<TD>$130,000<TD>$177,000
<TR><TD>H. Ruo<TD>$110,000<TD>$133,000<TD>$165,000
</TABLE>
</BODY>
</HTML>
```

The browser output from this file is shown in Figure 26.8.

FIGURE 26.8.

A browser's version of the table created in Listing 26.5.

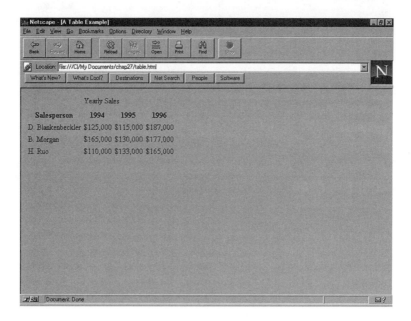

The first line in the body of the file starts with <TABLE>. This tag is required so that the browser knows that a table structure will follow. Note that the table structure must end with a </TABLE> tag. Everything between the <TABLE> and </TABLE> tags is part of the table.

The first item in the table structure is the caption text, or title of the table; it must be followed by the </CAPTION> tag. You can use text-formatting tags to change the appearance of the caption.

The next line starts with <TR> to define the first row in the table. This row will contain headings, so it takes the <TH> tag. The <TH> tag precedes each heading (for example, Salesperson). The closing </TH> and </TR> tags are optional and are not used in this example. Omitting the optional closing tags enhances the readability of the HTML source code.

The next line starts with another <TR> tag, which tells the browser that a new row has begun. This row contains data elements, each of which begins with a <TD> tag. Like the <TH> and <TR> tags, the closing </TD> tag is not necessary and therefore not used.

The following two lines are also data lines and are structured exactly the same. A </TABLE> closing tag indicates the end of the table.

The next element to add to the table is a border. An easy way to add a border is to include the BORDER=1 attribute in the <TABLE> tag (that is, <TABLE BORDER=1>). The modified code is shown in Listing 26.6.

Listing 26.6. Another table example.

```
<HTML><HEAD><TITLE>A Table Example</TITLE></HEAD>
<BODY>
<TABLE BORDER=1><CAPTION>Yearly Sales</CAPTION>
<TR><TH>Salesperson<TH>1994<TH>1995<TH>1996
<TR><TD>D. Blankenbeckler<TD>$125,000<TD>$115,000<TD>$187,000
<TR><TD>B. Morgan<TD>$165,000<TD>$130,000<TD>$177,000
<TR><TD>H. Ruo<TD>$110,000<TD>$133,000<TD>$165,000
</TABLE>
</BODY>
</HTML>
```

The output for this example is shown in Figure 26.9.

FIGURE 26.9.

Another table example; this table includes a border.

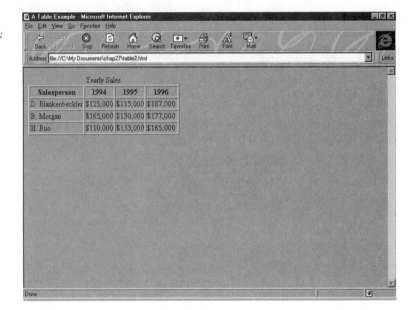

Creating Forms

HTML provides a means for the user to enter information, send it back to the server, and receive a customized page of information in return. An example that you might be familiar with is a stock quote page. You can enter a stock ticker symbol, and the server will create a page with the stock's current price and other information. This type of customization is typically accomplished through the use of HTML forms and a common gateway interface (CGI) program that runs on the server. The form sends the user-supplied information back to the server, where the CGI program creates a customized page based on the user's information.

Read on to learn how to use HTML forms. The discussion starts with a review of the tags used to create forms and concludes with an analysis of a sample form.

> **NOTE**
>
> The topic of CGI programming is not discussed here. The interested reader is referred to one of the many books on the subject, such as Sams Publishing's *CGI Programming Unleashed*.

<FORM>...</FORM>

The <FORM> tag set encloses the entire form. <FORM> is required at the beginning of the form structure, and </FORM> marks its end.

Attributes

ACTION="..."—Specifies the URL of the program that executes as a result of the submit button being clicked. This program is typically a CGI program on the server.

METHOD="GET"¦"POST"—If GET is selected, the browser will form a query URL that includes the location of the current form and the values entered into the form. The server will then use this information to process the query. If POST is selected, the form data is sent to the server as a data block to the standard input service.

ENCTYPE=—Specifies the format of the data to be sent to the server.

Example

See Listing 26.7.

<INPUT>

<INPUT> specifies an input object on the form. Several different types of input objects are available, such as text box, radio button, and check box. The attributes available depend on the type of input object selected (with TYPE=).

Attributes

TYPE="TEXT"¦"PASSWORD"¦"CHECKBOX"¦"HIDDEN"¦"RADIO"¦"IMAGE"¦"SUBMIT"¦"RESET"—
Specifies the type of input object to use. The following options are available:

- TEXT—Used to specify a single line of text input. The NAME= attribute is required, but MAXLENGTH, SIZE, and VALUE are optional.

- PASSWORD—Identical to the TEXT field above, except that the input is hidden.

- ◼ CHECKBOX—Used to represent a boolean choice. The required attributes are NAME= and VALUE=. The CHECKED attribute is optional. Several different check boxes can have the same NAME but different VALUEs. In this case, the data returned will simply be the name and value pair for each check box that is selected by the user.

- ◼ RADIO—Used to represent a boolean choice and can be grouped with other RADIO buttons to form a group of buttons in which only one can be selected at a time. Use the same NAME for each radio button to create this type of group. The required attributes are NAME= and VALUE=. The CHECKED= attribute is optional.

- ◼ IMAGE—Allows an image to be used as an input object when the x and y coordinates of the mouse click are the values returned or when a point is selected by a mouse click and SUBMIT is generated. The required attributes are SRC= and NAME=. The ALIGN= attribute is optional.

- ◼ HIDDEN—Hides a field so that the user cannot see it. You can use a hidden field to carry information forward through a series of forms. The NAME= and VALUE= attributes are required.

- ◼ SUBMIT—Specifies a button that, when clicked, submits the results of the form. Optional attributes include NAME= and VALUE=.

- ◼ RESET—Specifies a button that, when clicked, clears the form and resets the values to the initial state. The VALUE= attribute is optional. If present, VALUE= indicates a label for the button.

NAME=—Specifies a name for a particular input object.

VALUE=—Specifies and initializes a value for a particular input object.

SIZE=—Specifies the amount of display space allocated for a particular input object.

MAXLENGTH=—Specifies the maximum length of data for a particular input object.

CHECKED—Indicates that the initial state of a CHECKBOX or RADIO button is on.

ALIGN=—Aligns the image input object with the text, the same way as <IMG> does.

Example
See Listing 26.7.

<SELECT>

<SELECT> creates a list of items from which the user can make a selection. You need to use the <OPTION> tag to create the list of items.

Attributes

MULTIPLE—Indicates that multiple items can be selected from the list.

NAME=—Specifies the name of the field.

SIZE=—Specifies the number of visible items. The other items can be seen by using the scrollbar. If the size is set to 1, the result is generally a drop-down list.

Example

See Listing 26.7.

<OPTION>

The <OPTION> tag specifies the choices for a <SELECT> object.

Attributes

SELECTED—Indicates that this value is initially selected.

VALUE=—Indicates the value that is returned if this option is selected. The default value is the OPTION item text (the text following <OPTION>).

Example

See Listing 26.7.

<TEXTAREA>...</TEXTAREA>

The <TEXTAREA> tag set creates a multiline text field.

Attributes

COLS=—Indicates the number of columns wide the field should be.

NAME=—Specifies the name of the field.

ROWS=—Indicates the number of rows for the field.

Example

See Listing 26.7.

Building a Form

Listing 26.7 builds a simple form that contains most of the common elements used in forms. The screen output is shown in Figure 26.10.

Listing 26.7. A form example.

```
<HTML><HEAD><TITLE>A Form Example</TITLE></HEAD>
<BODY>
<FORM>
Please enter your name:<BR>
First<INPUT TYPE=TEXT NAME="FNAME" MAXLENGTH=15 SIZE=10>
MI<INPUT TYPE=TEXT NAME="MI" MAXLENGTH=1 SIZE=1>
Last<INPUT TYPE=TEXT NAME="LNAME" MAXLENGTH=20 SIZE=15>
<P>
Please select your favorite season of the year:<BR>
Spring<INPUT TYPE=RADIO NAME="SEASON" VALUE="Spring">
Summer<INPUT TYPE=RADIO NAME="SEASON" VALUE="Summer">
Fall  <INPUT TYPE=RADIO NAME="SEASON" VALUE="Fall">
Winter<INPUT TYPE=RADIO NAME="SEASON" VALUE="Winter">
<P>
Please check all of the outdoor activities that you enjoy:<BR>
Hiking<INPUT TYPE=CHECKBOX NAME="ACT" VALUE="Hiking">
Skiing<INPUT TYPE=CHECKBOX NAME="ACT" VALUE="Skiing">
Water Sports<INPUT TYPE=CHECKBOX NAME="ACT" VALUE="Water">
Cycling<INPUT TYPE=CHECKBOX NAME="ACT" VALUE="Cycling">
<P>
Please enter any additional outdoor activities that you enjoy below:<BR>
<TEXTAREA NAME="Other" COLS=60 ROWS=4></TEXTAREA>
<P>
<INPUT TYPE=SUBMIT><INPUT TYPE=RESET>
</FORM>
</BODY>
</HTML>
```

FIGURE 26.10.

The form created by the code in Listing 26.7.

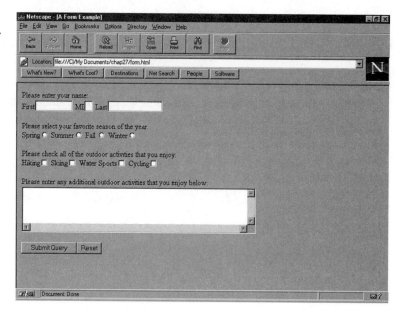

The form definition begins with the <FORM> tag at the beginning of the body of Listing 26.7. You can also see that the </FORM> tag marks the end of the form. The first three fields are text input boxes, created by the <INPUT TYPE=TEXT...> tags.

The next four fields are radio buttons, created with <INPUT TYPE=RADIO...>. Because all four buttons have the same name, "SEASON", they are grouped together. Therefore, only one of the buttons can be selected at any one time.

The check boxes were created with the <INPUT TYPE=CHECKBOX...> tags. Check boxes are different from radio buttons in that check boxes can be selected independently of each other even though they all have the same name. When the check boxes have the same name, as in this example, each NAME and VALUE pair will be returned. For example, depending on the choice made by the user, the following data might have been returned:

```
ACT, Hiking
ACT, Cycling
```

The <TEXTAREA NAME="Other" COLS=60 ROWS=4></TEXTAREA> line creates the multiline text input box. The text box should be 60 columns wide and 4 rows deep. If desired, default text can be inserted before the </TEXTAREA> tag. For example, the following line would insert None as the default text:

```
<TEXTAREA NAME="Other" COLS=60 ROWS=4>None</TEXTAREA>
```

The following short example illustrates the use of the <SELECT> tag. The code appears in Listing 26.8. Notice the use of the MULTIPLE key to allow the selection of multiple items on the ordered list. Selecting multiple items typically requires that the user press the Ctrl key while clicking on the desired items. Figure 26.11 displays the corresponding screen output.

Listing 26.8. A form that uses <SELECT>.

```
<HTML><HEAD><TITLE>A Form Example</TITLE></HEAD>
<BODY>
<FORM>
Please select the items you wish to order:<BR>
<SELECT NAME="ITEMS" SIZE="3" MULTIPLE>
<OPTION>Coffee Mug
<OPTION>Coffee Warmer
<OPTION>Drip Coffee Maker
<OPTION>Standard Expresso Maker
<OPTION>Deluxe Expresso Maker
</SELECT>
<P>
Select your form of payment:<BR>
<SELECT NAME="PAYMENT" SIZE="1">
<OPTION>Cash
<OPTION>Check
<OPTION>Credit Card
</SELECT>
```

continues

Listing 26.8. continued

```
<P>
<INPUT TYPE=SUBMIT><INPUT TYPE=RESET>
</FORM>
</BODY>
</HTML>
```

FIGURE 26.11.

The screen display generated by the code in Listing 26.8.

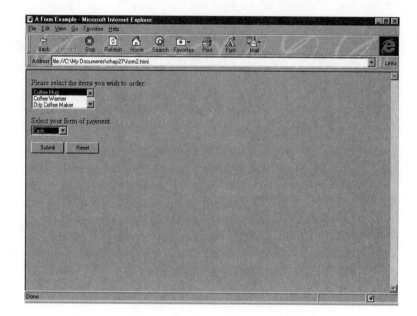

Summary

The official, released version of the World Wide Web Consortium (W3C) HTML specification at the time of this writing is 3.2. The W3C will continue to add new features to HTML. The group is currently working on support for the following types of improvements to HTML:

- Form functionality
- Frames
- Cascading style sheets

However, the most popular browsers are already adding support for these types of features. If you are developing Web pages, you need to consider your audience. If your expected audience is the entire world, you might wish to limit HTML use to the most recently approved specification. In addition, you should test your pages on all the popular Web browsers, in particular, Netscape Navigator 3.0 and Microsoft Internet Explorer 3.0.

You can find information on the latest released and proposed HTML standards on the World Wide Web Consortium's home page, which is located at http://www.w3.org/pub/WWW/.

Manipulating Web Components Using JavaScript

by David Blankenbeckler

CHAPTER 27

In Chapter 26, "HTML and Web Page Design," you learned how to use HTML to create Web pages. This is fine for presenting information, but it does not really provide for a dynamic page that can respond to user events. Netscape created a scripting language called LiveScript to add this functionality. This language was later renamed JavaScript to capitalize on the popularity of the Java programming language. Though there are some similarities between Java and JavaScript, they are two separate languages.

JavaScript was designed to be a scripting language that can be embedded in HTML files. It is not compiled but instead interpreted by the browser. Unlike Java, which is first converted to easy-to-compile bytecodes, JavaScript is read by the browser as source code. This makes it easy for you to learn JavaScript by example because you can see how others are using JavaScript in their pages.

JavaScript is an object-based language, which means it includes many types of objects. An example is the Math object, which provides all sorts of mathematical functionality. However, JavaScript is not object oriented like C++ or Java because it does not support classes or inheritance.

JavaScript can respond to events such as form loading or unloading. This allows JavaScript to be a dynamic, interactive scripting language as opposed to a linear scripting language like MS-DOS batch files.

Like HTML and Java, JavaScript is designed to be platform independent; it will run on any platform that has a JavaScript-capable browser. Also like Java, JavaScript is designed to be secure. It is not possible for JavaScript to read or write to the user's files.

This chapter introduces the JavaScript programming language so that you can successfully implement JavaScript into your HTML files.

Using Scripts in HTML Files

Scripts are embedded in HTML files using the <SCRIPT>...</SCRIPT> pair of tags. The <SCRIPT> tags can appear in either the <HEAD> or <BODY> section of the HTML file. The advantage of placing it in the <HEAD> section is that it will be loaded and ready before the rest of the document loads.

The only attribute currently defined for the <SCRIPT> tag is LANGUAGE=, which is used to specify the scripting language. There are currently two values defined: "JavaScript" and "VBScript". For your JavaScript programs, use the following syntax:

```
<SCRIPT LANGUAGE="JavaScript">
// INSERT ALL JavaScript HERE
</SCRIPT>
```

> **NOTE**
>
> You might have noticed that the comment is not enclosed in normal <- and -> tags for HTML comments. This is because JavaScript supports the same style of comments as C and Java. Both the single-line // syntax and the /* ... */ syntax for multiple lines are supported.

The difference in commenting syntax between HTML and JavaScript allows you to hide the JavaScript code inside an HTML comment so that older browsers that don't support it won't read it, as in the following example:

```
<SCRIPT LANGUAGE="JavaScript">
<!-- From here the JavaScript code is hidden
// INSERT ALL JavaScript HERE
// this is where the hiding ends -->
</SCRIPT>
```

The // is necessary on the last line of the script so that the browser will not try to interpret the line as JavaScript code. The examples in this chapter do not include the JavaScript hiding feature simply to make the code a little more readable.

A Simple <SCRIPT> Example

Let's start with a simple example to show you the JavaScript language and give you an idea of some of the things that are possible. The following program prompts the user for his name and then displays a short message using the name that was entered:

```
<HTML><HEAD>
<TITLE>A JavaScript Example</TITLE>
<SCRIPT LANGUAGE="JavaScript">
var name = window.prompt("Hello! What is your name?","");
document.write("Hello " + name + "! I hope you like JavaScript!");
</SCRIPT>
</HEAD>
<BODY>
</BODY>
</HTML>
```

Figure 27.1 shows the input prompt, and Figure 27.2 shows the output to the screen after you enter your name.

This example displays a prompt with the window.prompt method. The value obtained is stored in a variable called name. The variable is then combined with other strings and displayed in the browser's window using the document.write method.

Now that you have briefly glimpsed the functionality available through JavaScript, let's continue with a tutorial of the language itself.

FIGURE 27.1.

A JavaScript example before you enter your name.

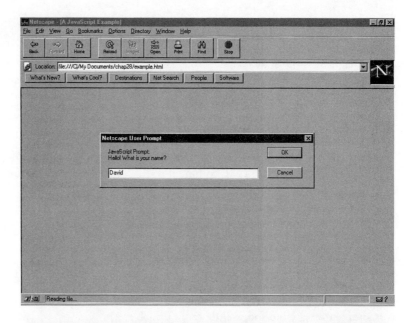

FIGURE 27.2.

A JavaScript example after you enter your name.

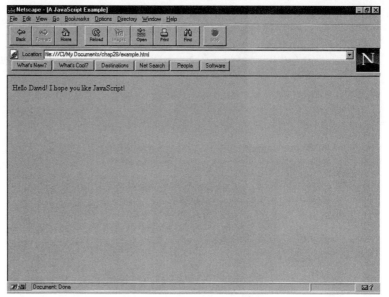

Variables in JavaScript

A JavaScript variable must start with a letter or an underscore. A number cannot be used as the first character of a variable name but can be used after the first character. JavaScript is case sensitive.

There are two scopes available for variables: global and local. A global variable can be accessed anywhere in the application (HTML file). A local variable can be accessed only in the current function. Global variables are declared as follows:

```
x = 0;
```

A local variable is declared inside a function with the var keyword, as in the following:

```
var x = 0;
```

A global variable may use the var statement as well, but it is not necessary.

The following section discusses the types of data that can be assigned to variables in JavaScript.

Data Types

Unlike C++ or Java, JavaScript is a loosely typed language, meaning that you do not have to specify a data type when a variable is declared. The data types are automatically converted to the appropriate type as necessary.

Consider the following example:

```
<HTML><HEAD>
<TITLE>A Data Type Example</TITLE>
<SCRIPT LANGUAGE="JavaScript">
var fruit = 'apples';
var numfruit = 12;
numfruit = numfruit + 20;
var temp = "There are " + numfruit + " " + fruit + ".";
document.write(temp);
</SCRIPT>
</HEAD>
<BODY>
</BODY>
</HTML>
```

JavaScript-enabled browsers will correctly handle this example with the following output:

```
There are 32 apples.
```

The JavaScript interpreter will treat the numfruit variable as an integer when 20 is added, and then as a string when it is combined with the temp variable.

The next section discusses the representation of values in JavaScript. The representation of a specific value is known as a *literal.*

Expressing Literals in JavaScript

Literals are values in a program that don't change. The following are examples of literals:

```
8
```

```
"The dog ate my shoe."
```

```
true
```

> **NOTE**
>
> In JavaScript there is no CONST type, as in Visual Basic and C, that can be used to represent some constant value; instead, it simply uses a variable.

The way in which values are represented in JavaScript is broken into four categories: integers, floating points, booleans, and strings. Each of these is discussed in the following sections.

Integer

Integers in JavaScript can be represented in three ways:

- Base 10—You can represent integers in base 10 by expressing the number without a leading zero.
- Octal—You can express integers in octal by prefixing with 0.
- Hexadecimal—You can express integers in hexadecimal by prefixing with 0x.

Floating Point

A floating point literal is composed of the following parts:

- A decimal integer
- A decimal point (.)
- A fractional integer
- An exponent

To be classified as a floating-point literal as opposed to an integer, there must be at least one digit followed by either a decimal point or E. The following are some examples of floating-point literals:

```
9.87
-0.85E4
9.87E14
.98E-3
```

Boolean

The boolean literal is used to indicate a true or false condition. There are two values:

```
true
false
```

String

A string literal is represented by zero or more characters enclosed in either single or double quotes (they must match at both ends!). The following are examples of string literals:

```
"the cat ran up the tree"
'the dog barked'
"100"
```

In order to represent a double quote in a string, simply use \ ". The following line of JavaScript code provides an example:

```
Document.Write("\"This text is inside quotes.\"");
```

Building Expressions in JavaScript

A set of literals, variables, or operators that evaluates to a single value is an *expression*. The single value can be a string, number, or boolean value. There are essentially three types of expressions in JavaScript:

- Arithmetic—Evaluates to a number. For example, (3 + 4) * (84.5 / 3) would evaluate to 197.1666666667.
- String—Evaluates to a string. For example, "The dog barked" + barktone + "!" might evaluate to The dog barked ferociously!.
- Logical—Evaluates to a boolean. For example, temp > 32 might evaluate to false. JavaScript supports a conditional expression as well. The syntax for this follows:

  ```
  (condition) ? valTrue : valFalse
  ```

  If the condition evaluates to true, then the expression evaluates to valTrue; if false, the expression evaluates to valFalse. Here's an example:

  ```
  state = (temp > 32) ? "liquid" : "solid"
  ```

  In this example, the variable state would be assigned the value "liquid" if the variable temp were greater than 32; otherwise the value of state would be set to "solid".

Operators

Operators are used to perform some operation on data. An operator can return either a numeric value, a string value, or a boolean value to indicate true or false. The JavaScript operators are grouped into the following categories: assignment, comparison, arithmetic, string, logical, and bitwise logical.

Assignment

The assignment operator is the equal sign (=), which assigns the value of the right operand to the left operand. In addition, JavaScript supports several shortcut operators:

Normal Assignment	Shorthand Method
x = x + y	x += y
x = x - y	x -= y
x = x * y	x *= y
x = x / y	x /= y
x = x % y	x %= y

Comparison

The purpose of a comparison operator is to compare two operands and return `true` or `false` based on the comparison. The following comparison operators are supported by JavaScript:

Syntax	Description
==	Returns `true` if the operands are equal.
!=	Returns `true` if the operands are not equal.
>	Returns `true` if the left operand is greater than the right operand.
>=	Returns `true` if the left operand is greater than or equal to the right operand.
<	Returns `true` if the left operand is less than the right operand.
<=	Returns `true` if the left operand is less than or equal to the right operand.

Arithmetic

In addition to the standard operators (+, -, *, /) for addition, subtraction, multiplication, and division, JavaScript supports the following arithmetic operators:

Syntax	Description
var1 % var2	The modulus operator returns the remainder of the integer division of var1 by var2.
-	The unary negation operator negates its operand.
var++	The increment operator adds one to var. This can also be represented by ++var.
var--	The decrement operator subtracts one from var. This can also be represented by --var.

NOTE

If you are assigning the result of an increment or decrement to another variable such as y = x++, there are different results depending on whether the ++ or -- appears before or after the variable name (x in this case). If the ++ or -- is used before x, then x would be incremented or decremented before the value of x is assigned to y. If the ++ or -- is after x, the value of x is assigned to y before it is incremented or decremented.

String

When used with a string, the + operator becomes the concatenation operator and concatenates the two strings, as in the following:

```
"abc" + "xyz"
```

This code evaluates to abcxyz.

Logical

JavaScript supports the following logical operators:

Syntax	Description
expr1 && *expr2*	The logical AND operator, returns true if both *expr1* and *expr2* are true.
expr1 ¦¦ *expr2*	The logical OR operator, returns true if either *expr1* or *expr2* is true. Only if both are false will false be returned.
!*expr*	The logical NOT operator negates *expr*. It causes *expr* to become false if it was true and true if it was false.

Bitwise

For bitwise operations, the values are first converted to 32-bit integers and then evaluated bit by bit. The following operators are supported:

Syntax	Description
&	The bitwise AND operator compares each bit and returns 1 if both bits are 1.
¦	The bitwise OR operator compares each bit and returns 1 if either of the bits is 1.
^	The bitwise XOR operator compares each bit and returns 1 if one and only one of the bits is 1.

There are also several bitwise shift operators. The value is converted to 32 bits before the shift operation. After the shift operation, the value is converted to the type of the left operand. The bitwise shift operators are as follows:

Syntax	Description
<<	The left shift operator, shifts the left operand the right operand number of bits to the left. For example, 4<<2 becomes 16 (100 binary becomes 10000 binary). Bits shifted to the left are discarded and zeros appear on the right in their place.
>>	The right shift operator, shifts the left operand the right operand number of bits to the right. For example, 16>>2 becomes 4 (10000 binary becomes 100 binary). Bits shifted to the right are discarded, and the sign of the left operator is preserved.
>>>	The zero-fill right shift operator, shifts the left operand the right operand number of bits to the right. The sign bit is shifted in from the left (unlike with the >> operator). Bits shifted to the right are discarded. For example, -8>>>2 becomes 1073741822 because the sign bit becomes part of the number. Of course, >>> and >> will yield the same result for positive numbers.

There are also some shortcut bitwise operators:

Normal Assignment	Shorthand Method
x = x << y	x <<= y
x = x >> y	x >>= y
x = x >>> y	x >>>= y
x = x & y	x &= y
x = x ^ y	x ^= y
x = x ¦ y	x ¦= y

Statements

The statements that are available in JavaScript can be grouped into the following categories:

- Conditional
- Loop
- Object manipulation

Conditional Statements

Conditional statements provide the ability for a program to make a decision and perform specific actions based on the result of that decision. JavaScript provides this support through the `if...else` statement.

if...else

The `if...else` statement allows you to check for a certain condition and execute statements based on that condition. The optional `else` statement allows you to specify a set of statements to execute if the condition is not true.

Syntax

```
if (condition) {
    // statements for true condition
}
else {
    // statements for false condition
}
```

Example

```
if (x == 10) {
    document.write("x is equal to 10, setting x=0.");
    x = 0; }
else
    document.write("x is not equal to 10.");
```

> **NOTE**
>
> The { and } characters are used to separate blocks of code. For example, notice that the { and } are used for the `true` condition in the previous example because there are two lines of statements. The `false` condition is only a one-line statement, so the { and } are not necessary.

Loop Statements

Loop statements are a means of looping through a section of code until an expression evaluates to `true`. JavaScript provides two types of loop statements:

- `for` loop
- `while` loop

for

The for loop sets an initial expression, *initExpr*, then loops through a section of JavaScript statements as long as a *condition* expression evaluates to true. Each time through the loop the expression *incrExpr* is executed.

Syntax

```
for (initExpr; condition; incrExpr) {
   // statements to execute while looping
}
```

Example

```
for (x=1; x<=10; x++){
y = x * 25;
document.write("x="+ x + " y=" + y + "<BR>");
}
```

This example loops through the code until x is greater than 10. Figure 27.3 shows the output.

FIGURE 27.3.

A for *loop example.*

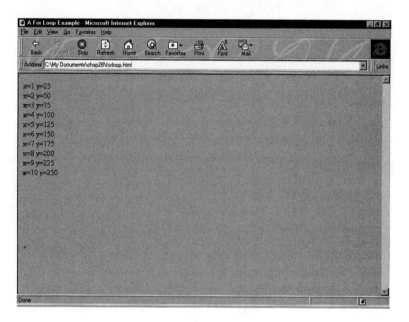

while

The while loop continues as long as a specified *condition* evaluates to true.

Syntax

```
while (condition) {
   // statement to execute while looping
}
```

Example

```
x = 1;
while (x <= 10) {
y = x * 25;
document.write("x="+ x + " y=" + y + "<BR>");
x++;
}
```

This produces the same result as the for loop example in Figure 27.3.

break

The break statement can be used to terminate the execution of a for or while loop. The program flow will continue at the statement following the end of the loop.

Syntax

```
break;
```

The following example loops until x is greater than or equal to 100. However, if the loop is entered with a value less than 50, the loop terminates and execution continues after the loop:

```
while (x < 100) {
   if (x < 50) break;
   x++;
}
```

continue

The continue statement is similar to the break statement except that execution is terminated and restarted at the beginning of the loop. For a while loop, control is returned to the *condition*. For a for loop, control is returned to the *incrExpr*.

Syntax

```
continue;
```

Example

The following example increments x from 0 to 5 and then skips to 8 and continues incrementing to 10:

```
x = 0;
while (x <= 10) {
  document.write("The value of x is " + x + "<BR>");
   if (x == 5) {
      x = 8;
      continue;
   }
   x++;
}
```

Object Manipulation Statements

As mentioned at the beginning of this chapter, JavaScript is an object-based language. JavaScript includes several statements that are designed to work with objects. The objects included in JavaScript are discussed later in this chapter.

for...in

The for...in statement is used to loop through all the properties of an object. The variable can be any arbitrary variable name; it is needed simply as something to refer to as you use the property in statements inside the loop. The following example should help you understand this statement.

Syntax

```
for (variable in object) {
   // statements
   }
```

Example

The following example cycles through all the properties of the Window object and prints the name of each property. Figure 27.4 shows the output:

```
<HTML><HEAD>
<TITLE>A For In Example</TITLE>
<SCRIPT LANGUAGE="JavaScript">
document.write("The properties of the Window object are: <BR>");
for (var x in window){
    document.write(x + "<BR>");
}
</SCRIPT>
</HEAD>
<BODY>
</BODY>
</HTML>
```

new

The new variable is used to create a new instance of an object.

Syntax

```
objectvar = new objecttype ( param1 [, param2] … [,paramN] )
```

The following example creates an object called person that has the properties firstname, lastname, age, and sex. Note that the this keyword is used to refer to the object in the person function. Then two instances of person are created using the new statement:

```
<HTML><HEAD>
<TITLE>A New Example</TITLE>
<SCRIPT LANGUAGE="JavaScript">
```

```
function person(firstname, lastname, age, sex){
   this.firstname = firstname;
   this.lastname = lastname;
   this.age = age;
   this.sex = sex;
}
person1= new person("David", "Blankenbeckler", "27", "Male");
person2= new person("Kimberly", "Blankenbeckler", "27", "Female");
document.write("The first person's name is ", person1.firstname + ". <BR>");
document.write("The second person's name is ", person2.firstname + ".");
</SCRIPT>
</HEAD>
<BODY>
</BODY>
</HTML>
```

FIGURE 27.4.

Output from the
for...in example.

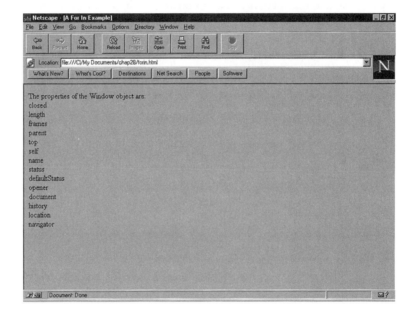

27

WEB
COMPONENTS
AND JAVASCRIPT

this

The this keyword is used to refer to the current object. The calling object is generally the current object in a method or function.

Syntax

`this[.property]`

Example

See the example for the new statement.

with

The `with` statement is used to set the default object for a series of statements so that you can refer to the properties without using the parent object.

Syntax

```
with(object){
    // statements
}
```

Example

The following example shows the use of the `with` statement to set the default object to document so that the `write` method can be used without having to refer to the document object itself, that is, `document.write`:

```
<HTML><HEAD>
<TITLE>A With Example</TITLE>
<SCRIPT LANGUAGE="JavaScript">
with (document) {
    write("This is an example of the things that can be done <BR>");
    write("with the <B>with</B> statement.<P>");
    write("This can really save some typing!");
}
</SCRIPT>
</HEAD>
<BODY>
</BODY>
</HTML>
```

Functions

JavaScript supports the use of functions. While it's not necessary, a function can have one or more parameters and one return value. Because JavaScript is a loosely typed language, you do not need to define parameters or return types for a JavaScript function. A function can also be a property of an object, in which case it will act as a method for that object.

The `function` statement is used to create a function in JavaScript.

Syntax

```
function fnName([param1][,param2]…[,paramN]){
    // function statements
}
```

Example

The following example shows how to create and use a function as a member of an object. The `printStats` function is created as a method of the object `person`:

```
<HTML><HEAD>
<TITLE>A Function Example</TITLE>
```

```
<SCRIPT LANGUAGE="JavaScript">
function person(firstname, lastname, age, sex){
   this.firstname = firstname;
   this.lastname = lastname;
   this.age = age;
   this.sex = sex;
   this.printStats = printStats;    //makes printStats a method of person
}
function printStats(){
   document.write(this.firstname + " " + this.lastname + "'s stats are:<BR>");
   document.write("Age: " + this.age + "<BR>");
   document.write("Sex: " + this.sex + "<BR>");
}
person1= new person("David", "Blankenbeckler", "27", "Male");
person2= new person("Kimberly", "Blankenbeckler", "27", "Female");
person1.printStats();
</SCRIPT>
</HEAD>
<BODY>
</BODY>
</HTML>
```

Built-In Functions

JavaScript contains several built-in functions, that is, functions that are built into the language itself and are not a part of an object:

- eval
- parseInt
- parseFloat

These built-in functions are described in the following sections.

eval

The eval function is used to evaluate expressions or statements. Any expression, statement, or object properties can be evaluated. This is useful for evaluating expressions that are entered by the user (otherwise it could be evaluated directly).

Syntax

```
returnval = eval( any legal Java expressions or statements )
```

Example

```
<HTML><HEAD>
<TITLE>An Eval Example</TITLE>
<SCRIPT LANGUAGE="JavaScript">
var string = "10 + Math.sqrt(64)";
document.write(string + " = " + eval(string));
</SCRIPT>
```

```
</HEAD>
<BODY>
</BODY>
</HTML>
```

parseInt

The parseInt function takes a string value and attempts to convert it to an integer of a base that's specified by an optional second parameter. This function can be used to convert different bases back to base 10 or to ensure that character-entered data is converted to integer before being used in calculations. In the case of bad input data, the parseInt function reads and converts a string until the point where it finds non-numeric characters. In addition, parseInt truncates floating-point numbers.

Syntax

```
parseInt(string [, radix]);
```

Example

```
<HTML><HEAD>
<TITLE>An parseInt Example</TITLE>
<SCRIPT LANGUAGE="JavaScript">
document.write("Converting 0xC hex to base-10: " + parseInt(0xC, 10) + "<BR>");
document.write("Converting 1100 binary to base-10: " + parseInt(1100, 2));
</SCRIPT>
</HEAD>
<BODY>
</BODY>
</HTML>
```

parseFloat

This built-in function is similar to the parseInt function except that it returns a floating point representation of string input.

Syntax

```
parseFloat(string);
```

Example

The following example shows how parseFloat works for several types of strings. Figure 27.5 shows the output:

```
<HTML><HEAD>
<TITLE>An parseFloat Example</TITLE>
<SCRIPT LANGUAGE="JavaScript">
```

```
document.write("This script will show how different strings are ");
document.write("converted using parseFloat.<BR>");
document.write("137 = " + parseFloat("137") + "<BR>");
document.write("137abc = " + parseFloat("137abc") + "<BR>");
document.write("abc137 = " + parseFloat("abc137") + "<BR>");
document.write("1abc37 = " + parseFloat("1abc37") + "<BR>");
</SCRIPT>
</HEAD>
<BODY>
</BODY>
</HTML>
```

FIGURE 27.5.

Screen output from the parseFloat example.

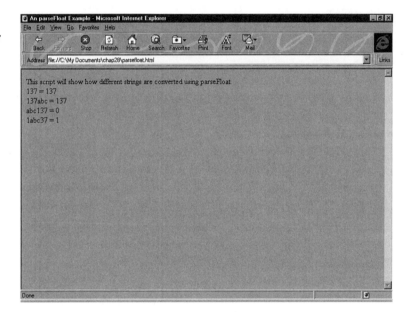

Arrays

Although JavaScript has no explicit support for arrays, Netscape has published a method that allows you to make your own by creating a function that initializes the array as follows:

```
function InitArray(numElements) {
   this.length = numElements;
   for (var x = 1; x <= numElements; x++) {
       this[x] = 0 }
   return this;
}
```

This creates an array of the specified size and fills it with 0. Note that the first element is the length of the array and should not be used.

To create an array, type the following:

```
myArray = new InitArray(10);
```

This creates `myArray[1]` through `myArray[10]`, with each element containing a `0`. The array can be populated with data as follows:

```
myArray[1] = "South Carolina";
myArray[2] = "Oregon";
```

Here's a full example:

```
<HTML><HEAD>
<TITLE>An Array Example</TITLE>
<SCRIPT LANGUAGE="JavaScript">
function InitArray(numElements) {
    this.length = numElements;
    for (var x = 1; x <= numElements; x++) {
        this[x] = 0 }
    return this;
}
myArray = new InitArray(10);
myArray[1] = "South Carolina";
myArray[2] = "Oregon";
document.write(myArray[1] + "<BR>");
document.write(myArray[2] + "<BR>");
</SCRIPT>
</HEAD>
<BODY>
</BODY>
</HTML>
```

Events

JavaScript is an event-driven language, which means it can respond to certain events, such as a mouse click or the loading of a document. An event can cause a section of code (known as an event handler) to execute to allow the program to respond appropriately.

Event Handlers

The section of code, or function, that responds to an event is called an *event handler.* The event handler is specified as an attribute of an HTML tag:

```
<tagName eventHandler="JavaScript Code or Function">
```

The following example calls the `CheckAge()` function when the value of the text field is changed:

```
<INPUT TYPE=TEXT NAME="AGE" onChange="CheckAge()">
```

The event handler code does not have to be a function; it can be JavaScript statements separated by semicolons. However, for purposes of modularity and code "cleanliness," it is typically a separate function.

The following event handlers are available in JavaScript:

Event	Description
onBlur	Occurs when the input focus is removed from form element.
onClick	Occurs when the user clicks form element or link.
onChange	Occurs when the text, text area, or select element value is changed.
onFocus	Occurs when the form element gets the focus.
onLoad	Occurs when the page is loaded.
onMouseOver	Occurs when the mouse is moved over a link or anchor.
onSelect	Occurs when the user selects a form element's input field.
onSubmit	Occurs when the user submits a form.
onUnload	Occurs when the user exits a page.

The following example shows a simple event handler script that validates a value entered into a text field. The user's age is entered in the field, and the event handler checks whether a valid age was entered. If not, a message will appear asking the user to re-enter the value. The event handler is called when the AGE field is changed and the focus is moved to another field. Figure 27.6 shows the screen output for the following code:

```
<HTML>
<HEAD>
<TITLE>An Event Handler Example</TITLE>
<SCRIPT LANGUAGE="JavaScript">
function CheckAge(form) {
   if ((form.age.value < 0) ¦¦ (form.age.value > 120)) {
      alert("Please enter your real age!");
      form.age.value = 0;
   }
}
</SCRIPT>
</HEAD>
<BODY>
<FORM NAME="SURVEY">
Please enter your name and age:<BR>
First<INPUT TYPE=TEXT NAME="FNAME" MAXLENGTH=15 SIZE=10>
MI<INPUT TYPE=TEXT NAME="MI" MAXLENGTH=1 SIZE=1>
Last<INPUT TYPE=TEXT NAME="LNAME" MAXLENGTH=20 SIZE=15><BR><BR>
Age<INPUT TYPE=TEXT NAME="AGE" MAXLENGTH=3 SIZE=2 onChange="CheckAge(SURVEY)">
<P>
Please select your favorite season of the year:<BR>
Spring<INPUT TYPE=RADIO NAME="SEASON" VALUE="Spring">
Summer<INPUT TYPE=RADIO NAME="SEASON" VALUE="Summer">
Fall  <INPUT TYPE=RADIO NAME="SEASON" VALUE="Fall">
Winter<INPUT TYPE=RADIO NAME="SEASON" VALUE="Winter">
<P>
Please check all of the outdoor activities that you enjoy:<BR>
Hiking<INPUT TYPE=CHECKBOX NAME="ACT" VALUE="Hiking">
Skiing<INPUT TYPE=CHECKBOX NAME="ACT" VALUE="Sking">
```

```
Water Sports<INPUT TYPE=CHECKBOX NAME="ACT" VALUE="Water">
Cycling<INPUT TYPE=CHECKBOX NAME="ACT" VALUE="Cycling">
<P>
<INPUT TYPE=SUBMIT><INPUT TYPE=RESET>
</FORM>
</BODY>
</HTML>
```

FIGURE 27.6.

An event handler example.

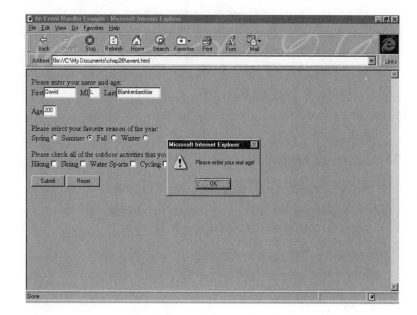

JavaScript Objects

As mentioned at the beginning of the chapter, JavaScript is an *object-based*, not *object-oriented*, programming language, primarily because it does not support classes or inheritance. This section presents the objects available for your JavaScript programs. Figure 27.7 shows the JavaScript object hierarchy.

In the JavaScript object hierarchy, the descendant objects are actually properties of the parent object. For example, in the example for the event handler, the form, named SURVEY, would be a property of the document object, and the text field, named AGE, a property of the form. To reference the value of AGE, you could use the following:

```
document.SURVEY.AGE.value
```

Objects in JavaScript have properties, methods, and event handlers associated with them. For example, the document object has a title property. This property reflects the contents of the <TITLE> tag for the document. In addition, you have seen the document.write method used in many of the examples. This method is used to output text to the document.

FIGURE 27.7.
The JavaScript object hierarchy.

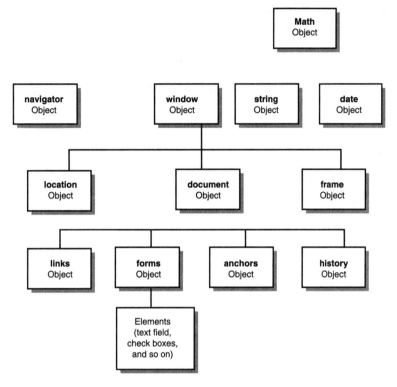

Objects can also have event handlers. For example, the links object has two event handlers, onClick and onMouseOver. The onClick event handler is invoked when a link object is clicked, and the onMouseOver is invoked when the mouse pointer passes over the link.

The properties, methods, and event handlers for each JavaScript object are described in the following sections.

The navigator Object

The navigator object is used to obtain information about the browser, such as the version number. It does not have any methods or event handlers associated with it.

Properties

appCodeName—Used to specify the internal code name of the browser (for example, Atlas).

AppName—Used to specify the name of the browser.

AppVersion—Used to specify version information for the navigator object.

userAgent—Used to specify the user-agent header.

Example

The following example displays each property of the `navigator` object:

```
<HTML><HEAD>
<TITLE>A Navigator Object Example</TITLE>
<SCRIPT LANGUAGE="JavaScript">
document.write("appCodeName = " + navigator.appCodeName+ "<BR>");
document.write("appName = " + navigator.appName + "<BR>");
document.write("appVersion = " + navigator.appVersion + "<BR>");
document.write("userAgent = " + navigator.userAgent + "<BR>");
</SCRIPT>
</HEAD>
<BODY>
</BODY>
</HTML>
```

The window Object

The `window` object is a top-level object. The document, frame, and location objects are all properties of the `window` object.

Properties

`defaultStatus`—The default message that is displayed in the window's status bar.

`Frames`—An array that reflects all the frames in a window.

`Length`—The number of frames in a parent window.

`Name`—The name of the current window.

`Parent`—The parent window object.

`Self`—The current window.

`Status`—Used for a temporary status message for the window's status bar. This is used to get or set the status message and overrides `defaultStatus`.

`Top`—The topmost window.

`Window`—The current window.

Methods

`alert("message")`—Displays a dialog box with the string `"message"` and an OK button.

`clearTimeout(timeoutID)`—Clears a timeout set by `SetTimeout`. `SetTimeout` returns `timeoutID`.

`windowReference.close`—Closes the window referred to by `windowReference`.

`confirm("message")`—Displays a dialog box with the string `"message"`, an OK button, and a Cancel button. Returns `true` for OK and `false` for Cancel.

`[windowVar = ][window].open("URL", "windowName", ["windowFeatures"])`—Opens a new window.

prompt("*message*" [,"*defaultInput*"])—Opens a dialog box with a text field for input.

TimeoutID = setTimeout(*expression*, *msec*) —Evaluates *expression* after *msec* has elapsed.

Event Handlers

onLoad—Occurs when a window finishes loading.

OnUnload—Occurs when a window is unloaded.

The `location` Object

The location object's properties contain information about the URL of the current document. This object does not have any methods or event handlers. Refer to the following sample URL in the property descriptions that follow:

http://www.abc.com/chap1/page2.html#topic3

Properties

hash—The current location's anchor name (for example, topic3).

Host—The hostname:port portion of the URL (for example, www.abc.com). Note that the port is typically the default port and is not shown.

Hostname—The host and domain name (for example, www.abc.com).

href—The entire URL for the current document.

Pathname—The path portion of the URL (for example, /chap1/page2.html).

port—The communications port used on the host computer, typically the default port.

Protocol—The protocol being used (with the colon) (for example, http:).

Search—A search query that may be at the end of a URL for a CGI script.

The `frame` Object

A window can have several frames. The frames can be scrolled independently, and each can have a unique URL. There are no event handlers for a frame. The onLoad and onUnload events are for the window object.

Properties

frames—An array of all the frames in a window.

Name—The <FRAME> tag's NAME attribute.

Length—The number of child frames within a frame.

Parent—The window or frame containing the current frameset.

`self`—The current frame.

`Window`—The current frame.

Methods

`clearTimeout(`*timeoutID*`)`—Clears a timeout set by `SetTimeout`. `SetTimeout` returns *timeoutID*.

TimeoutID = `setTimeout(`*expression, msec*`)`—Evaluates *expression* after *msec* has elapsed.

The document Object

The `document` object contains information about the current document and provides methods for writing information to the screen. The `document` object is created by using the `<BODY>`... `</BODY>` tag pair. Several of the properties reflect attributes associated with the `<BODY>` tag.

The `anchors`, `forms`, `history`, and `links` objects are properties of the document object. There are no event handlers for a frame. The `onLoad` and `onUnload` events are for the `window` object.

Properties

`alinkColor`—Same as the `ALINK` attribute.

`anchors`—Array of all the anchors in a document.

`bgColor`—Same as the `BGCOLOR` attribute.

`cookie`—Used to specify a cookie.

`fgColor`—Same as the `TEXT` attribute.

`forms`—An array of all the forms in a document.

`lastModified`—The date a document was last modified.

`linkColor`—Same as the `LINK` attribute.

`links`—An array of all the links in a document.

`location`—The complete URL of a document.

`referrer`—The URL of the calling document.

`title`—The contents of the `<TITLE>` tag.

`vlinkColor`—The `VLINK` attribute.

Methods

`document.clear`—Clears the current document.

`document.close`—Closes an output stream and forces data sent to layout to display.

`document.open([`*`"mimeType"`*`])`—Opens a stream to collect the output of `write` or `writeln` methods.

`document.write(`*`expression1`* `[,`*`expression2`*`], ...[,`*`expressionN`*`])`—Writes HTML expressions to a document in the specified window.

`document.writeln(`*`expression1`* `[,`*`expression2`*`], ...[,`*`expressionN`*`])`—Writes HTML expressions to a document in the specified window and follows them with a newline.

The anchors Object

An anchor is text in a document that can be the target of a hyperlink. It is defined by using the `<A>...</A>` tag pair. The `anchors` object has no properties, methods, or event handlers. The `anchors` array references each named anchor in a document. Anchors are referenced as follows:

`document.anchors[`*`index`*`]`

The `anchors` array has a single property, `length`, which stores the number of named anchors in the document. This can be referred to as follows:

`document.anchors.length`

The forms Object

Forms are created with the `<FORM>...</FORM>` tag pair. Most of the `forms` object properties reflect attributes of the `<FORM>` tag. There are also several objects that are properties of the `forms` object:

    button

    checkbox

    hidden

    password

    radio

    reset

    select

    submit

    text

    textarea

If a document contains several forms, they can be referenced by the `forms` array. The number of forms is found with the following:

`document.forms.length`

Each form can be referenced as follows:

`document.forms[index]`

Properties

> `action`—The ACTION attribute.
>
> `elements`—An array reflecting all the elements in a form.
>
> `encoding`—The ENCTYPE attribute.
>
> `length`—The number of elements on a form.
>
> `method`—The METHOD attribute.
>
> `target`—The TARGET attribute.

Method

> `formName.submit()`—Submits the form named `formName`

Event Handler

> `onSubmit`—Occurs when a form is submitted

The `history` Object

The `history` object is used to store information about the previous URLs visited by the user. The list of URLs is stored in chronological order. There are no event handlers associated with the `history` object.

Property

> `length`—The number of entries in the `history` object

Methods

> `history.back()`—Used to reference the previous URL visited; for example, the previous URL in the history list.
>
> `history.forward()`—Used to reference the next URL in the history list. Until either the user or a script moves backward on the history list, this will have no effect.
>
> `history.go(delta ¦ "location")`—Used either to move forward or backward `delta` number of entries on the history list or to go to a specific URL on the history list referred to by `location`. If `delta` is used, the reference is backward if negative and forward if positive. If `location` is used, the closest URL containing `location` as a substring is called.

The `links` Object

A `links` object is text or a picture that is specified as a hyperlink. The properties of the `links` object deal primarily with the URL of the hyperlink. The `links` object does not have any methods.

The `links` array contains a list of all the links in a document. The number of links can be found using the following:

```
document.links.length()
```

A specific link can be referenced by the following array:

```
document.links[index]
```

To describe the properties of the `links` object, use the following fictional URL:

```
http://www.abc.com/chap1/page2.html#topic3
```

Properties

`hash`—The anchor name of the link, for example, `topic3`.

`Host`—The `hostname:port` portion of the URL (for example, *www.abc.com*). Note that the port is typically the default port and not shown.

`Hostname`—The host and domain name (for example, *www.abc.com*).

`href`—The entire URL for the link.

`Pathname`—The path portion of the URL (for example, `/chap1/page2.html`).

`port`—The communications port used on the host computer, typically the default port.

`Protocol`—The protocol being used (with the colon) (for example, `http:`).

`Search`—A search query that can be at the end of a URL for a CGI script.

`Target`—The same as the `TARGET` attribute of `<LINK>`.

Event Handlers

`onClick`—Occurs when user clicks the link.

`onMouseOver`—Occurs when the mouse is moved over the link.

The `Math` Object

The `Math` object is a built-in object in JavaScript. This object's properties contain many common mathematical constants and trigonometric and other mathematical functions. There are no event handlers for the `Math` object.

The reference to *number* in the methods can be either a number or an expression that evaluates to a valid number.

Properties

E—Euler's constant, approximately 2.718.

LN2—The natural logarithm of 2, approximately 0.693.

LN10—The natural logarithm of 10, approximately 2.302.

LOG2E—The base 2 logarithm of e, approximately 1.442.

LOG10E—The base 10 logarithm of e, approximately 0.434.

PI—The value of π, approximately 3.14159.

SQRT1_2—The square root of one-half, approximately 0.707.

SQRT2—The square root of 2, approximately 1.414.

Methods

Math.abs(*number*)—Returns the absolute value of *number*.

Math.acos(*number*)—Returns the arc cosine (in radians) of *number*. The value *number* must be between –1 and 1.

Math.asin(*number*)—Returns the arc sine (in radians) of *number*. The value *number* must be between –1 and 1.

Math.atan(*number*)—Returns the arc tan (in radians) of *number*.

Math.ceil(*number*)—Returns the lowest integer equal to or greater than *number*.

Math.cos(*number*)—Returns the cosine of *number*.

Math.exp(*number*)—Returns e^*number*, where e is Euler's constant.

Math.floor(*number*)—Returns the highest integer equal to or less than *number*.

Math.log(*number*)—Returns the natural log of *number*.

Math.max(*num1*, *num2*)—Returns the greater of *num1* and *num2*.

Math.min(*num1*, *num2*)—Returns the lesser of *num1* and *num2*.

Math.pow(*base*, *exponent*)—Returns the value of base to the exponent power.

Math.random() – Returns random number between 0 and 1. Note that this only works on UNIX platforms.

Math.round(*number*)—Returns the value of *number* rounded to the nearest integer.

Math.sin(*number*)—Returns the sine of *number*.

Math.sqrt(*number*)—Returns the square root of *number*.

Math.tan(*number*)—Returns the tangent of *number*.

The Date Object

The Date object is a built-in object in JavaScript. It provides many useful methods for getting and dealing with the time and date. The Date object has no properties or event handlers associated with it.

Most of the date methods have `Date` objects associated with them. The methods defined in this section use the `Date` object *dateVar*. The examples for many of the methods use the value stored in *dateVar* as follows:

```
dateVar = new Date("August 16, 1996 20:45:04");
```

Methods

> `dateVar.getDate()`—Returns the day of the month (1–31) for *dateVar* (for example, 16).
>
> `dateVar.getDay()`—Returns the day of the week (0=Sunday through 6=Saturday) for *dateVar* (for example, 5).
>
> `dateVar.getHours()`—Returns the hour (0–23) for *dateVar* (for example, 20).
>
> `dateVar.getMinutes()`—Returns the minutes (0–59) for *dateVar* (for example, 45).
>
> `dateVar.getMonth()`—Returns the month (0–11) for *dateVar* (for example, 7).
>
> `dateVar.getSeconds()`—Returns the seconds (0–59) for *dateVar* (for example, 4).
>
> `dateVar.getTime()`—Returns the number of milliseconds since January 1, 1970 00:00:00.
>
> `dateVar.getTimezoneOffset()`—Returns the offset in minutes of the current local time to GMT.
>
> `dateVar.getYear()`—Returns the year for *dateVar* (for example, 96).
>
> `Date.parse(dateStr)`—Parses the string *datestr* and returns the number of milliseconds since January 1, 1970 00:00:00.
>
> `dateVar.setDate(day)`—Sets the day of the month to *day* for *dateVar*.
>
> `dateVar.setHours(hours)`—Sets the hours to *hours* for *dateVar*.
>
> `dateVar.setMinutes(minutes)`—Sets the minutes to *minutes* for *dateVar*.
>
> `dateVar.setMonth(month)`—Sets the month to *month* for *dateVar*.
>
> `dateVar.setSeconds(seconds)`—Sets the seconds to *seconds* for *dateVar*.
>
> `dateVar.setTime(value)`—Sets the time to *value*, which represents the number of milliseconds since January 1, 1970, 00:00:00.
>
> `dateVar.setYear(year)`—Sets the year to *year* for *dateVar*.
>
> `dateVar.toGMTString()`—Returns a string representing *dateVar* as GMT.
>
> `dateVar.toLocaleString()`—Returns a string representing *dateVar* in the current time zone.
>
> `Date.UTC(year, month, day [,hours] [,minutes] [,seconds])`—Returns the number of milliseconds since January 1, 1970, 00:00:00 GMT.

The String Object

The `String` object is a built-in object in JavaScript and provides many string manipulation methods. The only property for the `String` object is the length (`length`).

There are no event handlers for the `String` object.

Methods

`str.anchor(name)`— Used to dynamically create an `<A>` tag. The `name` parameter is the NAME attribute of the tag.

`str.big()`—Creates the same effect as the `<BIG>` tag on the string `str`.

`str.blink()`—Creates the same effect as the `<BLINK>` tag on the string `str`.

`str.bold()`—Creates the same effect as the `<BOLD>` tag on the string `str`.

`str.charAt(a)`—Returns the *a*th character from `str`.

`str.fixed()`—Creates the same effect as the `<TT>` tag on the string `str`.

`str.fontcolor(color)`—Creates the same effect as the `<FONT COLOR=color>` tag.

`str.fontsize(size)`—Creates the same effect as the `<FONTSIZE=size>` tag.

`str.indexOf(srchStr [,index])`—Returns the offset into `str` of the first appearance of `srchStr`. The string is searched from left to right. The `index` parameter can be used to start the search somewhere other than the beginning of the string.

`str.italics()`—Creates the same effect as the `<I>` tag on the string `str`.

`str.lastIndexOf(srchStr [, index])`—Returns the offset into `str` of the last occurrence of `srchStr`. The string is searched from right to left. The `index` parameter can be used to start the search somewhere other than the end of the string.

`str.link(href)` —Used to create a HTML link dynamically for the string `str`. The `href` parameter is the destination URL for the link.

`str.small()`—Creates the same effect as the `<SMALL>` tag on the string `str`.

`str.strike()`—Creates the same effect as the `<STRIKE>` tag on the string `str`.

`str.sub()`—Creates a subscript for string `str`, just like the `<SUB>` tag.

`str.substring(a, b)`—Returns the substring of `str` indicated by the characters between the *a*th and *b*th character. The character count is from left to right starting at 0.

`str.sup()`—Creates a superscript for string `str`, just like the `<SUP>` tag.

`str.toLowerCase()`—Converts `str` to lowercase.

`str.toUpperCase()`—Converts `str` to uppercase.

Summary of Reserved Words

The following words are defined as part of the JavaScript language and cannot be used as variable names:

abstract	eval	int	static
boolean	extends	interface	super
break	false	long	switch
byte	final	native	synchronized
case	finally	new	this
catch	float	null	throw
char	for	package	throws
class	function	parseFloat	transient
const	goto	parseInt	true
continue	if	private	try
default	implements	protected	var
do	import	public	void
double	in	return	while
else	instanceof	short	with

27

WEB
COMPONENTS
AND JAVASCRIPT

Summary

This chapter provides a brief introduction to the JavaScript language. In addition, it should serve as a useful reference during the development of your JavaScript applications.

While this chapter provides a concise reference to the JavaScript language, the subject is broad enough that entire books have been written about it. One useful book is *Teach Yourself JavaScript in 14 Days* by Sams.net Publishing.

Because JavaScript is still a new and changing language, you should also refer to Netscape's Web site for the latest information concerning the language. Netscape is located at `http://www.netscape.com/`.

CHAPTER 28

Manipulating Web Components Using VBScript

by David Blankenbeckler

IN THIS CHAPTER

In Chapter 27, "Manipulating Web Components Using JavaScript," you learned how to use JavaScript in your Web pages. There is another choice for writing scripts for your HTML documents: VBScript. The VBScript language works in much the same manner as JavaScript: The code is written and saved in text format in your HTML documents. When the browser sees VBScript code, it automatically interprets and runs it.

Many programmers are familiar with Microsoft's Visual Basic programming language. This is one of the key benefits that VBScript has over JavaScript; VBScript is a subset of the Visual Basic programming language. It is fully upward compatible with Visual Basic.

VBScript is currently only supported by Microsoft Internet Explorer. This is a major drawback because Netscape has such a large user base and does not currently support VBScript.

This chapter presents the VBScript programming language so that you can successfully implement VBScript into your HTML files. This chapter should also serve as a convenient reference to the VBScript language.

Differences Between VBScript and Visual Basic

As mentioned, VBScript is a subset of Visual Basic. Readers who are very familiar with Visual Basic may simply need to know what Visual Basic features are not available in VBScript. This section briefly discusses the major differences between the two. Readers who are unfamiliar with Visual Basic should skip ahead to the next section, "Using Scripts in HTML Files."

The following list identifies the most significant features of Visual Basic that are not supported by VBScript:

- All data types except `Variant`
- The `Const` statement
- The `Like` operator
- The `On Error GoTo` statement
- The `Resume` and `Resume Next` statements
- The `End` and `Stop` statements
- The `DoEvents` function
- The `Date` and `Time` statements
- The `Timer` function
- All file I/O ability
- All the financial functions
- Array lower bound other than zero

As you may notice, most of the exclusions from VBScript were made because they didn't make sense in an HTML scripting language or they violated the security features necessary for Web use. For example, the file I/O capabilities of Visual Basic would clearly cause security violations with Web applications.

Using Scripts in HTML Files

Scripts are embedded in HTML files using the `<SCRIPT>`...`</SCRIPT>` pair of tags. The `<SCRIPT>` tags can appear either in the `<HEAD>` or `<BODY>` section of the HTML file. The advantage of placing them in the `<HEAD>` section is that they will be loaded and ready before the rest of the document loads.

The only attribute currently defined for the `<SCRIPT>` tag is `LANGUAGE=`. This attribute is used to specify the scripting language. There are currently two values defined: `"JavaScript"` and `"VBScript"`. The following syntax should be used for your VBScript applications:

```
<SCRIPT LANGUAGE="VBScript">
' INSERT ALL VBScript HERE
</SCRIPT>
```

> **NOTE**
>
> You might have noticed that the comment is not enclosed in normal `<--` and `-->` tags for HTML comments. This is because VBScript supports the same comment style as Visual Basic. A single apostrophe or the Rem statement is used to indicate a comment in VBScript (and Visual Basic).

The difference in commenting syntax between HTML and VBScript allows you to hide the VBScript code inside an HTML comment so that older browsers that don't support it won't read it, as in the following example:

```
<SCRIPT LANGUAGE="VBScript">
<!-- From here the VBScript code is hidden
' INSERT ALL VBScript HERE
' this is where the hiding ends
-->
</SCRIPT>
```

The examples in this chapter do not include the script hiding feature simply to make the code a little more readable. However, you should always include this in your code so that non-VBScript-enabled browsers can be handled properly.

Let's start with a simple example to show you the VBScript language and give you an idea of some of the things that are possible. The following program prompts the user for his or her name and then displays a short message using the name that was entered:

```
<HTML><HEAD>
<TITLE>A VBScript Example</TITLE>
<SCRIPT LANGUAGE="VBScript">
dim name
```

```
name = InputBox("Hello! What is your name?")
Document.Write "Hello " & name & "! I hope you like VBScript!"
</SCRIPT>
</HEAD>
<BODY>
</BODY>
</HTML>
```

Figure 28.1 shows the input prompt. Figure 28.2 shows the output to the screen after the name was entered.

FIGURE 28.1.

A VBScript example, before you've entered your name.

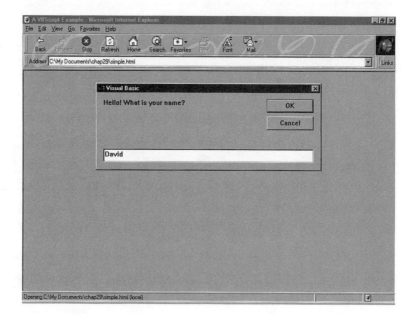

This example displays a prompt with the InputBox function. The value obtained is stored in a variable called *name*. The variable is tfeç sol:Aned with other text and displayed in the browser's window using the Document.Write method.

Now that you have briefly glimpsed the functionality available with VBScript, the chapter continues with a tutorial of the language itself.

Variables in VBScript

A VBScript variable must start with a letter. A number cannot be used as the first character of a variable name but can be used after the first character. VBScript is not case sensitive.

A variable is declared in VBScript with the Dim statement, as in the following:

```
Dim myvariable
```

FIGURE 28.2.

A VBScript example, after you've entered your name.

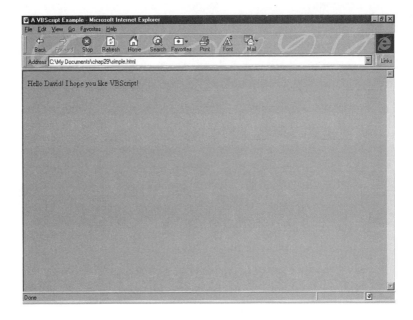

Multiple variables can be declared together if you separate each variable name by a comma, as in the following:

```
Dim myvariable, x, y, AVeryLongVariableNameWithANumberInIt8
```

> **NOTE**
>
> Like Visual Basic, VBScript supports the use of variables without first declaring them with `Dim`. However, this is generally not considered good programming practice. The `Option Explicit` statement will force all variables to require declaration with the `Dim` statement. This statement should be placed at the beginning of VBScript code to ensure that the variable names you have chosen are spelled consistently throughout your program; an error message will appear the first time you try to run the script if there are any undeclared variables being used.

There are two scopes available for variables: global and local. A global variable can be accessed anywhere in the script and lasts as long as the script is running. A local variable is declared inside a procedure or function and can be accessed only in that procedure or function. In addition, local variables only last as long as you are executing that procedure.

The following section discusses the types of data that can be assigned to variables in VBScript.

28

WEB
COMPONENTS
AND VBSCRIPT

Data Types

Like JavaScript, VBScript is a loosely typed language, meaning that you do not have to specify a data type when a variable is declared. All variables are of type Variant. The Variant is automatically converted to the following subtypes as necessary:

Boolean—True or false

Byte—Integer from 0 to 255

Date—Represents a date or time from January 1, 100, to December 31, 9999.

Double—A floating point number from +/– 4.94065645841247E–324 to +/– 1.79769313486232E308

Empty—Indicates that a value has not been assigned yet

Error—Indicates an error number

Integer—An integer from –32,768 to 32,767

Long—An integer from –2,147,483,648 to 2,147,483,647

Null—Purposefully set to no valid data

Object—An object

Single—A floating-point number from +/– 1.401298E–45 to +/– 3.402823E38.

String—A string

As mentioned, VBScript automatically converts a Variant to the appropriate subtype as needed. Consider the following example:

```
<HTML><HEAD>
<TITLE>A Data Type Example</TITLE>
<SCRIPT LANGUAGE="VBScript">
dim fruit
dim numfruit
dim temp
fruit = "apples"
numfruit = 12
numfruit = numfruit + 20
temp = "There are " & numfruit & " " & fruit & "."
Document.Write temp
</SCRIPT>
</HEAD>
<BODY>
</BODY>
</HTML>
```

VBScript-enabled browsers will correctly handle this example with the following output:

```
There are 32 apples.
```

The VBScript interpreter will treat the numfruit variable as an integer when 20 is added and then as a string when it is combined into the temp variable.

Expressing Literals in VBScript

Literals are values in a program that don't change. In VBScript there isn't a CONST statement, as in Visual Basic, that can be used to represent some constant value; rather you simply use a variable.

The way that values are represented in VBScript can be broken into five categories: integers, floating points, booleans, dates, and strings. Each of these is discussed in the following sections.

Integers

Integers in VBScript are represented in base 10. Integers are expressed as numbers without a decimal point, e, or E. The following are examples of integer literals:

```
10

4920056843
```

Floating Point

A floating-point literal is comprised of the following parts:

- A decimal integer
- A decimal point (.)
- A fractional integer
- An exponent

In order to be classified as a floating-point literal, as opposed to an integer, there must be at least one digit followed by either a decimal point, e, or E. Examples of floating-point literals are

```
9.87

-0.85e4

0.98E-3
```

Boolean

The boolean literal is used to indicate a true or false condition. There are simply two values:

```
True

False
```

Date and Time

A date or time can be expressed in VBScript by enclosing it within the # character. The following are examples of date literals:

```
#2-12-69#
#9-4-1996#
#2/12/69#
#10:35:00#
#20:45:30#
#8:45:30p#
#2/12/69 8:45:30p#
#8:45:30p 2/12/69#
```

String

A string literal is represented by zero or more characters enclosed in double quotes. The following are examples of string literals:

```
"the cat ran up the tree"
"100"
```

Arrays

Unlike JavaScript, the VBScript language has direct support for arrays. This section assumes that you already have a basic understanding of arrays.

Declaring arrays is very similar to declaring other types of variables. To do so, you use the Dim statement and follow the array name by the upper bound in parentheses. For example, the following line would create an array of 12 elements, called monthlySales:

```
Dim monthlySales(11)
```

Notice that 11 is used but there are 12 elements. This is because the first element of an array in VBScript is always 0. (The feature of Visual Basic that allows you to declare arrays with a lower bound other than 0 is not supported in VBScript.)

To access an array element, use the variable name followed by the element in parentheses. For example, to reference the fifth element, you would use the following:

```
monthlySales(4)
```

Multidimensional arrays (up to 60 dimensions) are supported in VBScript. To declare a multidimensional array, add an upper bound parameter for each dimension, separated by commas. For example, consider the following 3D array declaration:

```
ThreeDCoord(99,99,99)
```

VBScript also supports dynamic arrays with the ReDim statement. For an array to be declared dynamic, it must initially be declared without upper bounds (that is, empty parentheses). The ReDim statement can then be used to set the upper bounds later in the script. The

ReDim statement can be used as often as necessary. Unless the `Preserve` keyword is used, the contents of the array will be lost after each `ReDim`. Also, if an array is redimensioned to a smaller size with the `Preserve` keyword, the excess contents will be lost. Consider the following example:

```
Dim monthlySales()
' VBScript code can go here
' Later a ReDim statement is used
ReDim monthlySales(11)
monthlySales(7) = 20000
ReDim Preserve montlySales(23)
' The monthlySales(7) value is preserved
' and the array is enlarged to 24 elements
ReDim monthlySales(35)
' All monthlySales contents are lost since Preserve was not used
```

Building Expressions in VBScript

A set of literals, variables, and/or operators that evaluates to a single value is an *expression*. The single value can be a string, number, or boolean value. There are four types of expressions in VBScript:

- Arithmetic
- String
- Date
- Logical

Arithmetic

An expression that evaluates to a number is an arithmetic expression, as in the following:

```
( 3 + 4 ) * (84.5 / 3)
```

This expression would evaluate to `197.1666666667`.

String

An expression can also evaluate to a string. Literal strings are enclosed in double quotes, as in the following:

```
"The dog barked" & barktone & "!"
```

This expression might evaluate to `"The dog barked ferociously!"`.

Date

A date can be used in an expression as well. To assign a literal date to a variable, enclose the date in # characters. The date can then be used in an expression. For example, the following code will assign a date to a variable and then use the variable in an expression to add 5 days:

```
Dim thisDay
thisDay = #8/17/96#
Document.Write "In 5 days it will be " & (thisDay + 5)
```

The output from this code follows:

```
In 5 days it will be 8/22/96
```

This capability, combined with the many date functions in VBScript, makes working with dates easy. The VBScript date functions are covered in the "Date and Time Functions" section.

Logical

VBScript also supports logical expressions. These expressions evaluate to either `true` or `false`. They are then typically used with conditional statements. An example of a logical expression follows:

```
temp > 32
```

This expression can evaluate to `true` or `false`, depending on the value of `temp`.

Operators

Operators are used to perform some operation on data. Operators can return either a numeric value, a string value, or a boolean value to indicate true or false. The VBScript operators are grouped into the following categories: assignment, comparison, arithmetic, string, logical, and bitwise logical.

Assignment

The assignment operator is the equal sign, which assigns the value of the right operand to the left operand. For example, the following line assigns the value of 3 to the variable `x`:

```
x = 3
```

Comparison

The purpose of a comparison operator is to compare two operands and return `true` or `false` on the basis of the comparison. The following comparison operators are supported by VBScript:

  = returns `true` if the operands are equal.

  <> returns `true` if the operands are not equal.

  > returns `true` if the left operand is greater than the right operand.

  >= returns `true` if the left operand is greater than or equal to the right operand.

  < returns `true` if the left operand is less than the right operand.

  <= returns `true` if the left operand is less than or equal to the right operand.

  Is returns `true` if the left object is the same as the right object.

Arithmetic

In addition to the standard operators (+, -, *, /) for addition, subtraction, multiplication, and division, VBScript supports the following arithmetic operators:

num1*num2*—The integer division operator will divide *num1* by *num2* and return an integer result.

var1 Mod *var2*—The modulus operator returns the remainder of the integer division of *var1* by *var2*.

-num—The unary negation operator simply negates *num*.

num^exp—The exponentiation operator will raise *num* to the power of *exp*.

String

VBScript has a special operator, &, that is used for concatenating strings: *str1* & *str2* combines *str1* with *str2*.

Logical

VBScript supports the following logical operators, which return a boolean value:

- *expr1* And *expr2*—The logical And operator will return true if both *expr1* and *expr2* are true.

- *expr1* Or *expr2*—The logical Or operator will return true if either *expr1* or *expr2* is true. Only if both are false will false be returned.

- Not *expr*—The logical Not operator negates *expr*. It causes *expr* to become false if it was true and true if it was false.

- *expr1* Xor *expr2*—The logical Xor operator will return true if either *expr1* or *expr2* is true, but not both. If both *expr1* and *expr2* are true, then false will be returned.

- *expr1* Eqv *expr2*—The equivalence operator will return true if either *expr1* and *expr2* are both true or *expr1* and *expr2* are both false.

- *expr1* Imp *expr2*—The implication operator will return a value based on Table 28.1.

Table 28.1. The logical implication operator.

expr1	*expr2*	*Result*
False	False	true
False	True	true
True	False	false
True	True	true
Null	False	null

continues

28

WEB
COMPONENTS
AND VBSCRIPT

Table 28.1. continued

expr1	expr2	Result
Null	True	true
False	Null	true
True	Null	null
Null	Null	null

Bitwise

If two numeric expressions are used with the logical operators defined in the previous section, then a bitwise comparison will be performed. The following operators are supported:

- *expr1* And *expr2*—The bitwise And operator compares each bit and returns 1 if both bits are 1.

- *expr1* Or *expr2*—The bitwise Or operator compares each bit and returns 1 if either of the bits is 1.

- *expr1* Xor *expr2*—The bitwise Xor operator compares each bit and returns 1 if one and only one of the bits is 1.

- Not *expr*—The bitwise Not operator will invert the value of each bit. A 0 will become a 1 and a 1 will become a 0.

- *expr1* Eqv *expr2*—The bitwise Eqv operator compares each bit and returns 1 if either both bits are 0 or both are 1.

- *expr1* Imp *expr2*—The implication operator will compare each bit and return a value based on Table 28.2 when used with numeric expressions.

Table 28.2. The bitwise implication operator.

expr1	expr2	Result
0	0	1
0	1	1
1	0	0
1	1	1

Statements

Statements form the underlying structure of a program and are used to specify the path of execution. Statements are used for branching based on conditions and looping through a section of code until a specified condition is met. VBScript statements are divided into two categories: conditional and looping.

Conditional Statements

Conditional statements provide the ability to perform steps based on the outcome of a comparison. VBScript provides this support through the `If...Else` and `Select Case` statements.

If...Then...Else

The `If...Then...Else` statement allows you to check for a certain condition and execute statements based on that condition. The optional `Else` statement allows you to specify a set of statements to execute if the condition is not true.

Syntax

```
If condition Then
'    statements for true condition
Else
'    statements for false condition
End If
```

The `End If` statement is only necessary if there is more than one line of statement following the true or false condition.

Example

```
If x = 10 Then
   Document.Write "x is equal to 10, setting x = 0."
   x = 0
Else
   Document.Write "x is not equal to 10."
End If
```

Note that the `End If` statement is not necessary in this simple comparison:

```
If myVar = True Then yourVar = false
```

Select Case

The `Select Case` statement is useful when a single condition needs to be checked and there are multiple outcomes based on the result.

Syntax

```
Select Case expr
   Case n
      ' statements for this case
   Case m
      ' statements for this case
   '... additional case statements as necessary
   [Case Else]
      ' statements for the default case
End Select
```

28

WEB
COMPONENTS
AND VBSCRIPT

Example

The following example would evaluate the variable *Day* and print to the screen the appropriate message:

```
Select Case Day
    Case 0
        Document.Write "Today is Sunday.<BR>"
    Case 1
        Document.Write "Today is Monday.<BR>"
    Case 2
        Document.Write "Today is Tuesday.<BR>"
    Case 3
        Document.Write "Today is Wednesday.<BR>"
    Case 4
        Document.Write "Today is Thursday.<BR>"
    Case 5
        Document.Write "Today is Friday.<BR>"
    Case 6
        Document.Write "Today is Saturday.<BR>"
    Case Else
        Document.Write "ERROR: Invalid value for Day!<BR>"
End Select
```

Loop Statements

Loop statements provide a means for looping through a section of code until an expression evaluates to true. VBScript provides three types of loop statements:

- For...Next
- While...Wend
- Do

For...Next

The For loop will set *var* to *init*, then loop through a section of VBScript statements incrementing *var* by 1 before each loop. When *var* = *final*, the loop executes one final time, the loop ends, and the statement following Next is executed. If *var* is incremented to a value greater than *final*, the loop will also terminate.

If Step is specified, *var* will be incremented (or decremented) by the value of *step* each loop. When *step* is negative, the value of *var* will be decremented by *step* each loop. In this case, when *var* is less than *final*, the loop will terminate.

An optional Exit For statement can be used to terminate the loop at any time by placing one or more Exit For statements inside the loop.

Syntax

```
For var = init To final [Step step]
' statements to execute while looping
Next
```

Example

```
For x=0 To 10 Step 2
    y = x * 25
    Document.Write "x=" & x & " y=" & y & "<BR>"
Next
```

This example will loop through the code until x is equal to 10. Figure 28.3 shows the output.

FIGURE 28.3.

A For...Next *loop example.*

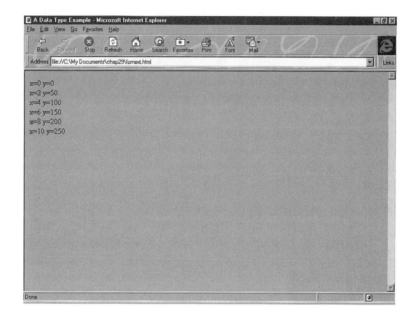

While...Wend

The While loop will continue as long as a specified *condition* evaluates to true. When *condition* no longer evaluates to true, the loop will immediately exit and the statement following Wend will be executed.

Syntax

```
While condition
' statements to execute while looping
Wend
```

Example

```
x = 0
While x <= 10
    y = x * 25
    Document.Write "x="+ x + " y=" + y + "<BR>"
    x = x + 2
Wend
```

This will produce the same result as the For loop example in Figure 28.3.

Do

The Do loop provides several forms, depending on how the loop is exited. You can exit the loop with either a While or an Until condition. In addition, an optional Exit Do can be used either as the sole means of exiting the loop or in combination with While or Until.

A Do While loop will continue to execute as long as a certain *condition* remains true.

A Do Until loop will continue to execute until a certain *condition* is true.

Syntax

```
Do While condition
' statements to execute while looping
[Exit Do]
' statements to execute while looping
Loop

Do Until condition
' statements to execute while looping
[Exit Do]
' statements to execute while looping
Loop
```

The Until or While keyword can also be placed at the end of the loop. It is simply a matter of taste; the same result will be obtained:

```
Do
' statements to execute while looping
Loop [Until¦While]
```

Examples

```
Do
    y = x * 25
    Document.Write "x="+ x + " y=" + y + "<BR>"
    x = x + 2
Loop Until x > 10

Do While x <= 10
    y = x * 25
    Document.Write "x="+ x + " y=" + y + "<BR>"
    x = x + 2
Loop
```

These two examples will produce the same result as the For...Next loop and the While...Wend loop examples in Figure 28.3.

Procedures

A procedure is a set of statements that can be called as needed from your main code or other procedures. VBScript supports the use of two types of procedures: Sub, which does not have a return value, and Function, which does.

Both types of procedure can have one or more parameters passed to it. Because VBScript is a loosely typed language, it is not necessary to define parameter or return types for a VBScript procedure.

Because procedures must be defined before they are called, they should always be placed at the beginning of an HTML document in the <HEAD> section.

Sub Procedure

The Sub procedure should be used when a procedure does not have a return value.

Syntax

```
Sub SubName([param1][,param2]...[,paramN])
    ' sub procedure statements
End Sub
```

To call this procedure, use the following syntax:

```
SubName [param1][,param2]...[,paramN]
```

Example

The following example shows the use of the Sub procedure by creating a procedure to calculate and display the area of a circle:

```
<HTML><HEAD>
<TITLE>A Sub Procedure Example</TITLE>
<SCRIPT LANGUAGE="VBScript">
Sub PrintAreaOfCircle(radius)
    Document.Write "A circle of radius " & radius & " cm has an area of "
    Document.Write 3.14159 * radius^2
    Document.Write " cm<SUP>2</SUP>.<BR>"
End Sub
' Now we will call the Sub
PrintAreaOfCircle(4)
PrintAreaOfCircle(6)
PrintAreaOfCircle(10.5)
</SCRIPT>
</HEAD>
<BODY>
</BODY>
</HTML>
```

Figure 28.4 shows the output from this example.

Function Procedure

The Function procedure should be used when there is value returned at the exit of the procedure.

FIGURE 28.4.

An example of a Sub *procedure.*

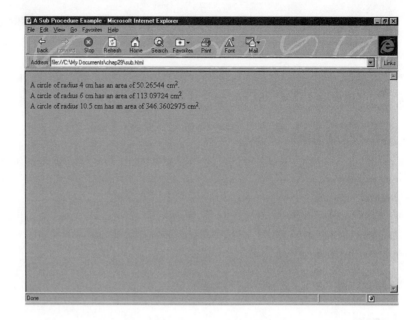

Syntax

```
Function fnName([param1][,param2]...[,paramN])
    ' function statements;
    fnName = expr
End Function
```

Notice that the return value for a function is given by setting the function name, *fnName*, equal to some value before the end of the function.

The syntax for calling a function follows:

```
returnVar = fnName([param1][,param2]...[,paramN])
```

Example

The following example shows the use of the Function procedure by creating a procedure to calculate and display the area of a circle. The output from this example is the same as the output from the Sub example in Figure 28.4:

```
<HTML><HEAD>
<TITLE>A Function Procedure Example</TITLE>
<SCRIPT LANGUAGE="VBScript">
Function AreaOfCircle(radius)
    AreaOfCircle = 3.14159 * radius^2
End Function
' Now we will call the Function three times like before
Document.Write "A circle of radius 4 cm has an area of " & AreaOfCircle(4)
Document.Write " cm<SUP>2</SUP>.<BR>"
Document.Write "A circle of radius 6 cm has an area of " & AreaOfCircle(6)
Document.Write " cm<SUP>2</SUP>.<BR>"
```

```
Document.Write "A circle of radius 10.5 cm has an area of "
Document.Write AreaOfCircle(10.5) & " cm<SUP>2</SUP>.<BR>"
</SCRIPT>
</HEAD>
<BODY>
</BODY>
</HTML>
```

Built-In Functions

VBScript contains a wide selection of built-in functions. It is useful to categorize them as follows:

- Math
- Dates and time
- String manipulation
- User interface
- Data type (conversions)

The following sections discuss the functions for each of these categories.

Math Functions

VBScript provides a wide range of mathematical functions. In the following function declarations, numExpr can be either a number or an expression that evaluates to a number:

Abs(*numExpr*)—Returns the absolute value of *numExpr*.

Atn(*numExpr*)—Returns the arctangent of *numExpr*.

Cos(*numExpr*)—Returns the cosine of *numExpr*.

Exp(*numExpr*)—Returns $e^{numExpr}$, where e is Euler's constant.

Fix(*numExpr*)—Returns the integer portion of *numExpr*. If the number is negative, the next greater integer will be returned.

Int(*numExpr*)—Returns the integer portion of *numExpr*. If the number is negative, the next lower integer will be returned.

Log(*numExpr*)—Returns the natural log of *numExpr*.

Rnd([*numExpr*])—Returns a pseudorandom number. The number is not really random because the same seed will always produce the same result. If *numExpr* is used, the result will be as follows: If *numExpr* = 0, then Rnd returns the last random number generated.

If *numExpr* > 0, then Rnd returns the next random number in the sequence.

If *numExpr* < 0, then Rnd returns a random number based on the seed, *numExpr*. The same seed will always return the same number.

The `Randomize` statement will generate a seed for the `Rnd` function based on the system clock. This will provide for a much better illusion of randomness, as in the following example:

```
Randomize
x = Rnd()
```

`Sgn(numExpr)`—Returns 1 if *numExpr* is greater than 0, -1 if *numExpr* is less than 0, and 0 if *numExpr* is equal to 0.

`Sin(numExpr)`—Returns the sine of *numExpr*.

`Sqr(numExpr)`—Returns the square root of *numExpr*.

`Tan(numExpr)`—Returns the tangent of *numExpr*.

Date and Time Functions

`Date`—Returns the current date from the system clock.

`DateSerial(year, month, day)`—Returns a value of subtype Date to represent the *year*, *month*, and *day* that were passed.

`Day(date)`—Returns an integer between 1 and 31 to represent the day for the *date* that was passed.

`Hour(time)`—Returns an integer between 0 and 23 to represent the hour for the *time* that was passed.

`Minute(time)`—Returns an integer between 0 and 59 to represent the minute for the *time* that was passed.

`Month(date)`—Returns an integer between 1 and 12 to represent the month for the *date* that was passed.

`Now`—Returns the current date and time based on the system clock.

`Second(time)`—Returns an integer between 0 and 59 to represent the second for the *time* that was passed.

`Time`—Returns the current time from the system clock.

`TimeSerial(hour, minute, second)`—Returns a value of subtype Date to represent the *hour*, *minute*, and *second* that were passed.

`Weekday(date [, firstday])`—Returns an integer between 1 and 7 that represents the current day of the week for *date*. By default, Sunday is represented by 1, Monday 2, and so on. If a *firstday* parameter is passed, then another day can be set to be represented by 1. For example, if 2 is passed as the *firstday* parameter, then Monday would be represented by 1.

`Year(date)`—Returns an integer that represents the year in *date*; for example, 1996.

String Manipulation Functions

VBScript has a wide array of built-in functions to assist you in dealing with strings. In the following function declarations, *strExpr* can be either a string or an expression that evaluates to a string:

Asc(*strExpr*)—Returns an integer representing the ANSI code for the first character of *strExpr*.

Chr(*ANSICode*)—Returns the character represented by *ANSICode*.

Hex(*number*)—Returns a string that represents *number* in hexadecimal.

InStr([*startPos*,] *string, srchstr* [, *compType*])—Returns the position of the first occurrence of *srchstr* in *string*. If *startPos* is specified, then the search will begin at that position. The *compType* parameter can be either 0 or 1. The default value of 0 is case sensitive. A *compType* of 1 indicates that the search should not be case sensitive.

LCase(*strExpr*)—Converts *strExpr* to lowercase and returns it as a string.

Left(*strExpr, numChars*)—Returns a substring of *strExpr* that begins at the first position (on the left) and is *numChars* in length.

Len(*strExpr ¦ varName*)—If a string expression is passed, Len returns the length of that string. If a variable name is passed, Len returns the number of bytes required to store that variable.

LTrim(*strExpr*)—Removes all leading spaces from *strExpr* and returns it as a string.

Mid(*strExpr, startPos, numChars*)—Returns a substring of *strExpr* that begins at *startPos* and is *numChars* in length.

Oct(*number*)—Returns a string that represents *number* in octal.

Right(*strExpr, numChars*)—Returns a substring of *strExpr* that begins at the last position (on the right) and is *numChars* in length.

RTrim(*strExpr*)—Removes all trailing spaces from *strExpr* and returns it as a string.

StrComp(*strExpr1, strExpr2* [,*compType*])—Compares *strExpr1* and *strExpr2*. If they are equal, 0 is returned. -1 is returned if *strExpr1* is less than *strExpr2*. 1 is returned if *strExpr1* is greater than *strExpr2*. If either string is null, Null is returned.

> The *compType* parameter can be either 0 or 1. The default value of 0 is case sensitive. A *compType* of 1 indicates that the search should not be case sensitive.

String(*length, character*)—Returns a string of repeating *character* that is *length* in length.

Trim(*strExpr*)—Removes all leading and trailing spaces from *strExpr* and returns it as a string.

UCase(*strExpr*)—Converts *strExpr* to uppercase and returns it as a string.

User Interface Functions

InputBox(*prompt* [, *title*][, *default*][, *xPos*][, *yPos*][, *helpFile*, *context*])—
This function will display a dialog box with a text field. The contents of the text field
will be returned. The parameters are defined as follows:

> *prompt*—The prompt displayed in the dialog box.

> *title*—The text displayed on the title bar of the dialog box.

> *default*—The default contents of the text field.

> *xPos*—The distance (in twips) of the dialog box from the left edge of the screen.

> *yPos*—The distance (in twips) of the dialog box from the top of the screen.

> *helpFile*—The filename of the help file that should be used for context-
> sensitive help.

> *context*—The context number for the appropriate help topic in *helpFile*.

The following code is an example of how to use InputBox. Figure 28.5 shows the screen
output:

```
<HTML><HEAD>
<TITLE>A InputBox Example</TITLE>
<SCRIPT LANGUAGE="VBScript">
dim Name
Name = InputBox("Please enter your name.", "This is an InputBox!", "John Doe")
</SCRIPT>
</HEAD>
<BODY>
</BODY>
</HTML>
```

FIGURE 28.5.

*An example of an
input box.*

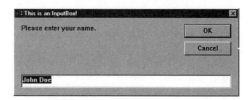

MsgBox(*prompt*[, *buttons*][, *title*][, *helpfile*, *context*])—The MsgBox function
will display a dialog box with one or more buttons, as configured by the *buttons*
parameter. The parameters are defined as follows:

> *prompt*—The prompt displayed in the dialog box.

> *buttons*—A number that specifies the number and type of buttons to display in
> the dialog box. The number is arrived at by adding together four numbers to
> specify the number and type of buttons, the icon style, the default button, and
> the modality of the dialog box. The *buttons* configurations are as follows:

Number/Type Buttons	Effect
0	OK button
1	OK and Cancel buttons
2	Abort, Retry, and Ignore buttons
3	Yes, No, and Cancel buttons
4	Yes and No buttons
5	Retry and Cancel buttons

Icon Style	Effect
0	No icon
16	Critical Message icon
32	Warning Query icon
48	Warning Message icon
64	Information Message icon

Default Button	Effect
0	First button
256	Second button
512	Third button
768	Fourth button

Modality	Effect
0	Application Modal
4096	System Modal

title—The text displayed on the title bar of the dialog box.

helpFile—The filename of the help file that should be used for context-sensitive help.

context—The context number for the appropriate help topic in *helpFile*.

The return value provides the button that was selected:

Return Value	Button Selected
1	OK
2	Cancel
3	Abort
4	Retry
5	Ignore

28

WEB
COMPONENTS
AND VBSCRIPT

Return Value	Button Selected
6	Yes
7	No

The following code is an example of how to use the MsgBox function:

```
<HTML><HEAD>
<TITLE>A MsgBox Example</TITLE>
<SCRIPT LANGUAGE="VBScript">
dim answer
answer = MsgBox("You are about to become a VBScript expert!" & Chr(13) &
    "Are you ready?", 36 , "This is a MsgBox!")
if answer = 6 then Document.Write "That is great! <BR>"
if answer = 7 then Document.Write "Oh, that's too bad. <BR>"
</SCRIPT>
</HEAD>
<BODY>
</BODY>
</HTML>
```

This script will display a dialog box with Yes and No buttons (4) and a Warning Query icon (32). This is specified by the value 36 (32+4). The Chr(13) will create a carriage return after the first sentence of the prompt. The script will then respond depending on whether Yes or No was returned. Figure 28.6 shows the screen output.

FIGURE 28.6.

An example of a message box.

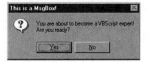

Data Type Functions

VBScript provides many functions to help in dealing with data types. The functions in the following list prefixed with C are used to convert a value to a Variant of a specific subtype. Those prefixed with Is can be used to determine if an expression can be converted to a specific subtype:

CBool(*expr*)—Returns *expr* converted to subtype Boolean. If *expr* is 0, then false will be returned. True will be returned if *expr* is unequal to 0. A type mismatch runtime error will occur if *expr* does not represent a numeric value.

CByte(*expr*)—Returns *expr* converted to subtype Byte. If *expr* cannot be converted to subtype Byte, a type mismatch runtime error will occur.

CDate(*expr*)—Returns *expr* converted to subtype Date. If *expr* cannot be converted to subtype Date, a type mismatch runtime error will occur.

CDbl(*expr*)—Returns *expr* converted to subtype Double. If *expr* cannot be converted to subtype Double, a type mismatch or overflow runtime error will occur.

`CInt(`*expr*`)`—Returns *expr* converted to subtype Integer. If *expr* cannot be converted to subtype Integer, a type mismatch or overflow runtime error will occur.

`CLng(`*expr*`)`—Returns *expr* converted to subtype Long. If *expr* cannot be converted to subtype Long, a type mismatch or overflow runtime error will occur.

`CSng(`*expr*`)`—Returns *expr* converted to subtype Single. If *expr* cannot be converted to subtype Single, a type mismatch or overflow runtime error will occur.

`CStr(`*expr*`)`—Returns *expr* converted to subtype String.

> If *expr* is `Boolean`, then either `true` or `false` is returned.
>
> If *expr* is a `Date`, then a string will be returned in the short date format for the particular system.
>
> If *expr* is subtype `Error`, then a string containing the word *Error* and the error number will be returned.
>
> If *expr* is `Null`, a runtime error occurs.

`DateValue(`*string*`)`—Returns a variant of subtype Date to represent the date in *string*.

`IsArray(`*expr*`)`—Returns a boolean indicating whether *expr* is an array.

`IsDate(`*expr*`)`—Returns a boolean indicating whether *expr* can be converted to a date.

`IsEmpty(`*expr*`)`—Returns a boolean indicating whether *expr* is empty. The intent of this function is to pass a variable name as *expr* to determine if it has been initialized.

`IsNull(`*expr*`)`—Returns a boolean indicating whether *expr* contains `Null`.

`IsNumeric(`*expr*`)`—Returns a boolean indicating whether *expr* can be evaluated to a numeric value.

`IsObject(`*expr*`)`—Returns a boolean indicating whether *expr* references a valid object.

`LBound(`*arrayName[, dimension]*`)`—Returns the lower bound of *arrayName* for the *dimension* indicated. VBScript does not support lower bounds other than zero, so this function is not very useful.

`TimeValue(`*string*`)`—Returns a variant of subtype Date to represent the time in *string*.

`UBound(`*arrayName[, dimension]*`)`—Returns the upper bound of *arrayName* for the *dimension* indicated.

`Val(`*strExpr*`)`—Returns the first numeric value found in *strExpr*. The numeric value must be at the beginning of *strExpr*. Spaces, tabs, and line feeds will be removed and periods converted to decimal points. The prefixes `&O` and `&H` in *strExpr* can be used to specify octal or hexadecimal values.

`VarType(`*varName*`)`—Returns a number that indicates the `Variant` subtype of *varName* according to the following table:

28

WEB
COMPONENTS
AND VBSCRIPT

Returned Value	Subtype
0	Empty
1	Null
2	Integer
3	Long
4	Single
5	Double
7	Date
8	String
9	Automation object
10	Error
11	Boolean
12	Variant
13	Non-automation object
17	Byte
8192	Array

Events and Event Handlers

VBScript is an event-driven language, which means it can respond to certain events, such as a mouse click or the loading of a document. An event can cause a section of code (known as an event handler) to execute to allow the program to respond appropriately.

The program that responds to an event is called an event handler. The event handler is specified as an attribute of an HTML tag:

```
<tagName eventHandler="VBScript Statement or Procedure">
```

The following example calls the CheckAge Sub when the text field is changed:

```
<INPUT TYPE=TEXT NAME="AGE" onChange="CheckAge">
```

The event handler code does not have to be a procedure; it can be a single VBScript statement. Because only a single statement can be used and a separate procedure is more readable, the event handler is typically a separate procedure.

The following list describes the event handlers available in VBScript:

- onBlur occurs when the input focus is removed from a form element.
- onClick occurs when the user clicks a form element or link.

■ onChange occurs when a text, text area, or select element value is changed.

■ onFocus occurs when a form element gets the focus.

■ onLoad occurs when the page is loaded.

■ onMouseOver occurs when the mouse is moved over a link or anchor.

■ onSelect occurs when the user selects a form element's input field.

■ onSubmit occurs when the user submits a form.

■ onUnload occurs when the user exits a page.

The following example shows a simple event handler script that will validate a value entered into a text field. The user's age is entered in the field, and the event handler will check whether a valid age was entered. If not, a message will appear asking the user to reenter the value. The event handler is called when the AGE field is changed and the focus is moved to another field. Figure 28.7 shows the screen output:

```
<HTML>
<HEAD>
<TITLE>An Event Handler Example</TITLE>
<SCRIPT LANGUAGE="VBScript">
Sub CheckAge(form)
    If ((form.age.value < 0) Or (form.age.value > 120)) Then
        alert "Please enter your real age!"
        form.age.value = 0
    End If
End Sub
</SCRIPT>
</HEAD>
<BODY>
<FORM NAME="SURVEY">
Please enter your name and age:<BR>
First<INPUT TYPE=TEXT NAME="FNAME" MAXLENGTH=15 SIZE=10>
MI<INPUT TYPE=TEXT NAME="MI" MAXLENGTH=1 SIZE=1>
Last<INPUT TYPE=TEXT NAME="LNAME" MAXLENGTH=20 SIZE=15><BR><BR>
Age<INPUT TYPE=TEXT NAME="AGE" MAXLENGTH=3 SIZE=2 onChange="CheckAge(SURVEY)">
<P>
Please select your favorite season of the year:<BR>
Spring<INPUT TYPE=RADIO NAME="SEASON" VALUE="Spring">
Summer<INPUT TYPE=RADIO NAME="SEASON" VALUE="Summer">
Fall  <INPUT TYPE=RADIO NAME="SEASON" VALUE="Fall">
Winter<INPUT TYPE=RADIO NAME="SEASON" VALUE="Winter">
<P>
Please check all of the outdoor activities that you enjoy:<BR>
Hiking<INPUT TYPE=CHECKBOX NAME="ACT" VALUE="Hiking">
Skiing<INPUT TYPE=CHECKBOX NAME="ACT" VALUE="Skiing">
Water Sports<INPUT TYPE=CHECKBOX NAME="ACT" VALUE="Water">
Cycling<INPUT TYPE=CHECKBOX NAME="ACT" VALUE="Cycling">
<P>
<INPUT TYPE=SUBMIT><INPUT TYPE=RESET>
</FORM>
</BODY>
</HTML>
```

28

WEB
COMPONENTS
AND VBSCRIPT

FIGURE 28.7.

*A VBScript event
handler example.*

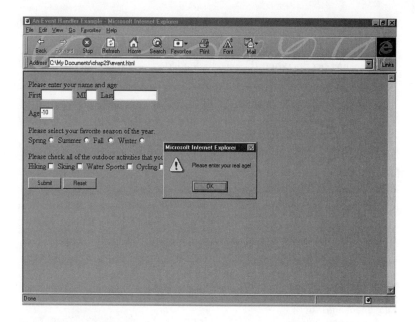

VBScript Object Model

The object hierarchy for Microsoft Internet Explorer and VBScript is very similar to and compatible with the JavaScript object hierarchy. The primary difference is that there is no built-in Math, Date, or String object. Of course, these are not needed because there are built-in functions to handle these types of operations.

The reader should refer to Chapter 27 for descriptions of each object and its associated properties, methods, and event handlers. As mentioned, each of these objects applies equally to VBScript except for the Math, String, and Date objects.

Summary of Reserved Words

The following words are defined as part of the VBScript language and cannot be used as variable names:

Abs	Erase	Len	Set
And	Err	Log	Sgn
Asc	Error	Loop	Sin
Atn	Exit	Ltrim	Sqr
Call	Exp	Mid	Step
Case	Fix	Minut	Str

Cbool	For	Mod	StrComp
Cbyte	Function	Month	String
Cdate	Hex	MsgBox	Sub
CDbl	Hour	Next	Tan
Chr	If	Not	Then
Cint	Imp	Now	Time
Clear	InputBox	Oct	TimeSerial
CLng	InStr	On	TimeValue
Cos	Int	Or	Trim
CSng	Is	Preserve	UBound
CStr	IsArray	Raise	UCase
Date	IsDate	Randomize	Until
DateSerial	IsEmpty	ReDim	Val
DateValue	IsNull	Rem	VarType
Day	IsNumeric	Right	Weekday
Dim	IsObject	Rnd	Wend
Do	Lbound	RTrim	While
Else	Lcase	Second	Xor
Eqv	Left	Select	Year

28

WEB
COMPONENTS
AND VBSCRIPT

Summary

This chapter provides a brief introduction and reference to the VBScript language. Although this chapter is a concise guide to the language, VBScript could easily be the subject of an entire book. One such book is *Teach Yourself VBScript in 21 Days* by Sams.net Publishing.

The creator of VBScript, Microsoft, maintains information on its Web site, http://www.microsoft.com. A particularly useful page for Web developers is http://www.microsoft.com/workshop.

Embedding Components Within Web Pages

by David Blankenbeckler

IN THIS CHAPTER

Part IV, "Activating the Internet with Visual J++," discusses HTML, JavaScript, and VBScript. You might be wondering what all this stuff has to do with Java and Java applets. This chapter answers this question by introducing the `<APPLET>` and `<OBJECT>` tags. These tags are used to insert Java applets and objects (such as ActiveX controls) into your HTML documents.

The chapter begins with a description of the `<APPLET>` tag. It then demonstrates building a simple Java applet and inserting it into an HTML file. The example is extended to show how to pass parameters to the applet from within the HTML file.

The example is then expanded further to show how to use JavaScript and VBScript to access the applet's methods and variables. Finally, ActiveX controls are introduced to the example and everything is glued together with JavaScript and VBScript.

Using the `<APPLET>` and `<OBJECT>` Tags

Embedding applets and objects into HTML is accomplished through the use of two tags, the `<APPLET>` tag and the `<OBJECT>` tag.

The `<APPLET>` Tag

The `<APPLET>` tag is used to insert Java applets into an HTML document. The applet definition begins with `<APPLET>` and ends with `</APPLET>`. The following attributes are available:

ALIGN="LEFT"¦"CENTER"¦"RIGHT"—Aligns the applet either LEFT, CENTER, or RIGHT relative to the current line of text. The values are defined as follows:

LEFT—The object is positioned to the left and subsequent text is flowed past the right side of the object.

CENTER—The object is centered after the current line. Subsequent text begins on the line following the object.

RIGHT—The object is positioned to the right and subsequent text is flowed past the left side of the object.

ALT=*textstring*—Displays *textstring* on browsers that do not support Java.

CODE=*applet*—Specifies the Java applet, for example, myApplet.class.

CODEBASE=*appletURL*—Specifies a base URL for the applet if it is not in the same location as the calling HTML.

HEIGHT=*value*—Specifies the suggested height of the applet in standard units.

HSPACE=*value*—Specifies the horizontal space of the applet in standard units. This is the amount of space between the object and text before and after the object.

NAME=*name*—Provides the applet with a name so that other objects or applets can refer to it.

VSPACE=*value*—Specifies the vertical space of the applet in standard units. This is the amount of space above and below the object.

WIDTH=*value*—Specifies the suggested width of the applet in standard units.

In addition to the attributes, an applet can have parameters passed to it through the <PARAM> tag. The <PARAM> tag is used as follows:

```
<PARAM NAME=paramName VALUE=paramValue>
```

For example, if the applet has a parameter named myParameter and you wanted to pass the string "David" to it, you could use the following applet definition:

```
<APPLET CODE=myApplet.class WIDTH=50 HEIGHT=100>
<PARAM NAME=myParameter VALUE=David>
</APPLET>
```

The <OBJECT> Tag

The <OBJECT> tag is used to insert objects into an HTML document. An object can be a Java applet, an ActiveX control, an AVI file, and so on. Because the <APPLET> tag was introduced before the <OBJECT> tag, it is still generally used for adding applets. However, the <OBJECT> tag could also be used and actually has greater functionality.

The object definition begins with <OBJECT> and ends with </OBJECT>. The following attributes are available:

ALIGN="LEFT"¦"CENTER"¦"RIGHT"¦"BASELINE"¦"MIDDLE"¦"TEXTBOTTOM"¦"TEXTMIDDLE"¦"TEXTTOP"— Used to align the object in the document. The values are defined as follows:

LEFT—The object is positioned to the left and subsequent text is flowed past the right side of the object.

CENTER—The object is centered after the current line. Subsequent text begins on the line following the object.

RIGHT—The object is positioned to the right and subsequent text is flowed past the left side of the object.

BASELINE—The bottom of the object is aligned vertically with the baseline.

MIDDLE—The middle of the object is aligned vertically with the baseline.

TEXTBOTTOM—The bottom of the object is aligned vertically with the bottom of the text.

TEXTMIDDLE—The middle of the object is aligned vertically halfway between the baseline and the x-height of the text. The x-height is the top of a lowercase x in the current font.

TEXTTOP—The top of the object is aligned vertically with the top of the text.

BORDER=*width*—When an object is defined as a hyperlink, this attribute specifies the suggested width of the border.

CLASSID=*object*—The URL that identifies the object implementation.

CODEBASE=*objectURL*—Used to specify a base URL for the object if it is not in the same location as the calling HTML.

CODETYPE=*mediaType*—Used to specify the Internet media type of the object specified by CLASSID. This is used by some browsers to speed network access.

DATA=*dataURL*—The URL that identifies the object's data, if necessary. If the object consists entirely of data, such as an AVI file, the browser can determine the media type from the TYPE attribute and load the appropriate object implementation. A CLASSID is not necessary in this case.

DECLARE—Indicates that the object should be declared but not instantiated. This can be used when you are referencing the object later in the document.

HEIGHT=*value*—Specifies the suggested height of the object in standard units.

HSPACE=*value*—Specifies the horizontal space of the object in standard units. This is the amount of space between the object and text before and after the object.

ID=*idName*—Used to specify an identifier that can be used inside the current document to refer to the object.

NAME=*value*—Used to provide a name for the object when it is used as part of a form.

SHAPES—Used to indicate that the object has hyperlinks associated with shapes on the object.

STANDBY=*message*—Used to specify a short message to display while the object is loading.

TYPE=*mediaType*—Used to specify the Internet media type of the data specified by DATA.

USEMAP=*mapURL*—Used to specify an image map.

VSPACE=*value*—Specifies the vertical space of the object in standard units. This is the amount of space above and below the object.

WIDTH=*value*—Specifies the suggested width of the object in standard units.

Like the applet, an object can have parameters passed to it. This is done using the same method as the applet, through the <PARAM> tag. The <PARAM> tag is used as follows:

```
<PARAM NAME=paramName VALUE=paramValue>
```

Now that you understand how to use the <APPLET> and <OBJECT> tags, you can put them to use. First, let's create a simple Java applet to use in the examples for this chapter.

Creating a Simple Java Applet

This example demonstrates how to create a simple Java applet that draws a circle. The applet has three parameters that are used to control the color of the circle: R, G, and B, used to indicate the red, green, and blue components for the color of the circle. The valid range of values for each color component is 0 to 255.

First the applet is built using Visual J++. It is then integrated into HTML and the color of the circle set by passing parameters.

The first step is to run Applet Wizard to create a new applet. (See Chapter 11, "Building a Simple Java Applet with Visual J++," for a review of Applet Wizard.)

Create a New Project

Create a new project workspace by selecting New from the File menu. Name the project Circle and select Java Applet Wizard for the type of project. Follow the steps in Table 29.1 as you run the wizard.

Table 29.1. The steps for creating a new project.

Wizard Step	What You Do
Step 1	Keep the defaults and select Next.
Step 2	Enter 60 for both the width and height and select Next.
Step 3	Turn off multithreading support and select Next.
Step 4	Enter three parameters of type int and call them r, g, and b.
Step 5	Select Finish.

The generated code is shown in Listing 29.1. A few of the comments have been removed for simplicity.

Listing 29.1. Creating a new project.

```
//****************************************************************************
// Circle.java:      Applet
//
//****************************************************************************
import java.applet.*;
import java.awt.*;

//============================================================================
// Main Class for applet Circle
//
```

continues

29

EMBEDDING
COMPONENTS IN
WEB PAGES

Listing 29.1. continued

```
//===============================================================================
public class Circle extends Applet
{
    //--------------------------------------------------------------------------
    // Members for applet parameters
    // <type>          <MemberVar>     = <Default Value>
    //--------------------------------------------------------------------------
      private int m_r = 0;
      private int m_g = 0;
      private int m_b = 0;

    // Parameter names.  To change a name of a parameter, you need only make
    // a single change.  Simply modify the value of the parameter string below.
    //--------------------------------------------------------------------------
      private final String PARAM_r = "r";
      private final String PARAM_g = "g";
      private final String PARAM_b = "b";

    // Circle Class Constructor
    //--------------------------------------------------------------------------
    public Circle()
    {
          // TODO: Add constructor code here
    }

    // APPLET INFO SUPPORT:
    //    The getAppletInfo() method returns a string describing the applet's
    // author, copyright date, or miscellaneous information.
     //--------------------------------------------------------------------------
    public String getAppletInfo()
    {
          return "Name: Circle\r\n" +
                 "Author: David Blankenbeckler\r\n" +
                 "Created with Microsoft Visual J++ Version 1.0";
    }

    // PARAMETER SUPPORT
    //    The getParameterInfo() method returns an array of strings describing
    // the parameters understood by this applet.
    //
     // Circle Parameter Information:
     //  { "Name", "Type", "Description" },
     //--------------------------------------------------------------------------
    public String[][] getParameterInfo()
    {
          String[][] info =
          {
                { PARAM_r, "int", "Parameter description" },
                { PARAM_g, "int", "Parameter description" },
                { PARAM_b, "int", "Parameter description" },
          };
          return info;
    }

    // The init() method is called by the AWT when an applet is first loaded or
```

```
    // reloaded.  Override this method to perform whatever initialization your
    // applet needs, such as initializing data structures, loading images or
    // fonts, creating frame windows, setting the layout manager, or adding UI
    // components.
    //--------------------------------------------------------------------------
    public void init()
    {
            // PARAMETER SUPPORT
            //    The following code retrieves the value of each parameter
            // specified with the <PARAM> tag and stores it in a member
            // variable.
            //--------------------------------------------------------------------------
            String param;

            // r: Parameter description
            //--------------------------------------------------------------------------
            param = getParameter(PARAM_r);
            if (param != null)
                m_r = Integer.parseInt(param);

            // g: Parameter description
            //--------------------------------------------------------------------------
            param = getParameter(PARAM_g);
            if (param != null)
                m_g = Integer.parseInt(param);

            // b: Parameter description
            //--------------------------------------------------------------------------
            param = getParameter(PARAM_b);
            if (param != null)
                m_b = Integer.parseInt(param);

//--------------------------------------------------------------------------
            resize(60, 60);

            // TODO: Place additional initialization code here
    }

    // Place additional applet clean up code here.  destroy() is called
    // when your applet is terminating and being unloaded.
    //--------------------------------------------------------------------------
    public void destroy()
    {
            // TODO: Place applet cleanup code here
    }

    // Circle Paint Handler
    //--------------------------------------------------------------------------
    public void paint(Graphics g)
    {
            g.drawString("Created with Microsoft Visual J++ Version 1.0", 10, 20);
    }

    //    The start() method is called when the page containing the applet
    // first appears on the screen. The AppletWizard's initial implementation
    // of this method starts execution of the applet's thread.
    //--------------------------------------------------------------------------
```

continues

Listing 29.1. continued

```
public void start()
{
        // TODO: Place additional applet start code here
}

//    The stop() method is called when the page containing the applet is
// no longer on the screen. The AppletWizard's initial implementation of
// this method stops execution of the applet's thread.
//-------------------------------------------------------------------------
public void stop()
{
}

// TODO: Place additional applet code here
}
```

The Java applet is almost complete. All you have to do now is add a few lines of code to draw a circle using a function in the java.awt.Graphics class. To use this class you must first import it into your source. Visual J++ has already done this with the following line at the beginning of the source:

```
import java.awt.*;
```

So all you have to do is add the code to set the color and draw the circle. (For more information about the java.awt.Graphics class, refer to Chapters 13, "The Standard Java Packages," and 14, "An Introduction to GUI Programming.")

Before drawing the circle you need to set the color using the setColor() method. Then simply draw the circle using the fillOval() method. Add these two lines to Circle's paint() method as follows:

```
public void paint(Graphics g)
{
    g.setColor(new Color(m_r, m_g, m_b));
    g.fillOval(10, 10, 40, 40);
}
```

Note that you can also remove the filler code that the wizard inserted into the paint() method. As you can see, the setColor() function will use the parameters that you passed for red, green, and blue to set the color.

You can now build the Java applet and view it in your Java-enabled Web browser. Use the Circle.html file that was created automatically by the Applet Wizard. The output should appear similar to Figure 29.1.

FIGURE 29.1.

The Circle *applet.*

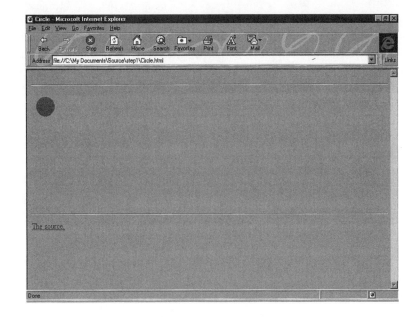

Integrating a Java Applet into HTML

The Applet Wizard automatically created an HTML file because you selected the option to do so. To learn more about the `<APPLET>` tag, you should review this HTML file. It appears as follows:

```
<html>
<head>
<title>Circle</title>
</head>
<body>
<hr>
<applet
    code=Circle.class
    id=Circle
    width=60
    height=60 >
    <param name=R value=0>
    <param name=G value=0>
    <param name=B value=0>
</applet>
<hr>
<a href="Circle.java">The source.</a>
</body>
</html>
```

The applet that you created, `Circle`, is included in the document by the `<APPLET>` tag. The `code=` attribute is used to specify the `Circle` class. In addition, you can see the initial `height` and `width` of the applet are set to `60`.

The ID attribute that was automatically inserted by Applet Wizard is not a standard attribute for the <APPLET> tag. Instead the NAME attribute should be used. The ID or NAME attribute is used when referencing the applet elsewhere in the HTML file, such as in a script. Although the ID attribute will work properly for Internet Explorer 3.0, it will not work correctly with Netscape Navigator 3.0. Therefore, the ID attribute should be changed to NAME, which will work properly for both browsers. Change the ID attribute to NAME as follows:

```
<applet
    code=Circle.class
    name=Circle
    width=60
    height=60 >
    <param name=R value=0>
    <param name=G value=0>
    <param name=B value=0>
</applet>
```

The three parameters that you created—R, G, and B—were also automatically created in the HTML file by Applet Wizard. As you can see, all three of these were set to 0, which represents the color black.

Passing Parameters to a Java Applet

To change the initial color of the circle, simply set the parameters to different values. For example, the following HTML code will create a green circle, because parameter G is set to 255 and the other two are set to 0:

```
<html>
<head>
<title>Circle</title>
</head>
<body>
<hr>
<applet
    code=Circle.class
    name=Circle
    width=60
    height=60 >
    <param name=R value=0>
    <param name=G value=255>
    <param name=B value=0>
</applet>
<hr>
<a href="Circle.java">The source.</a>
</body>
</html>
```

Although this is useful for specifying the default color, it does not give you dynamic control over the color of the circle. To change the color of the circle dynamically, you must use a scripting language such as VBScript or JavaScript (or build that functionality into the Java applet itself). The next section explores the use of VBScript and JavaScript in controlling a Java applet.

Controlling a Java Applet with VBScript

Now you'll add buttons to the form so that the user can change the color of the circle. But first you need to add a method to the applet to provide access to the variables m_r, m_g, and m_b. These three variables are private variables that the applet sets to the values of the passed parameters, r, g, and b.

You could simply make the m_r, m_g, and m_b variables public. However, this is not good object-oriented programming practice. Instead, an accessor method should be used to change the values of these variables. Instead of creating three different accessor methods (one for each of r, g, and b), you can simply create a single method called setCircleColor:

```
public void setCircleColor(int red, int green, int blue)
{
m_r = red;
m_g = green;
m_b = blue;
}
```

You also need to create a means to make the applet repaint. Simply changing the member variables for the colors will not cause the circle to be repainted. This is easily accomplished, however, by adding a call to the repaint() method in the setCircleColor method. Here's an example:

```
public void setCircleColor(int red, int green, int blue)
{
m_r = red;
m_g = green;
m_b = blue;
repaint();
}
```

Since you have declared the setCircleColor method as public, you can access it from a script in an HTML document. The new version of the Circle applet can now be rebuilt.

> **NOTE**
>
> After rebuilding your applet you will most likely need to restart the Web browser since the old version will still be in the cache.

With these changes you can now access the private member variables, m_r, m_g, and m_b, from the script using the accessor method (setCircleColor) you created. You will add three buttons to the HTML document to change the color to either red, green, or blue. You can add these buttons by placing the following form definition after the applet definition in Circle.html:

```
<FORM>
<INPUT TYPE="BUTTON" NAME="cmdRED" VALUE="RED"><P>
<INPUT TYPE="BUTTON" NAME="cmdGREEN" VALUE="GREEN"><P>
<INPUT TYPE="BUTTON" NAME="cmdBLUE" VALUE="BLUE"><P>
</FORM>
```

This will create three buttons named cmdRED, cmdGREEN, and cmdBLUE. You now need an event handler script for the onClick event for each button. Each of the onClick event handlers will simply set the color variables to the appropriate values using the setCircleColor method that you created. For example, to handle the clicking of the red button you would use the following:

```
Sub cmdRED_onClick
    call document.Circle.setCircleColor(255, 0, 0)
End Sub
```

As you can see, accessing the private variables of an applet through a public accessor method is fairly easy. While it is similarly easy to access the variables directly by defining them as public, this is generally not good programming practice. However, if it is desired, it is simply a matter of defining the variable with the public modifier. The variable can then be defined just like the method. Here's an example:

```
' DO NOT ADD THIS TO THE SCRIPT WE ARE BUILDING
' THIS IS JUST AN EXAMPLE OF ACCESSING PUBLIC VARIABLES OF AN APPLET
Sub directVariableAccess
    document.Circle.m_r = 255
    document.Circle.m_g = 0
    document.Circle.m_b = 0
End Sub
```

Adding the event handlers for the green and blue buttons is accomplished in a similar manner, calling the setCircleColor method with the appropriate parameters. Listing 29.2 shows the modified HTML file after the addition of the buttons and their associated event handlers.

Listing 29.2. The modified HTML file for the Circle applet with VBScript.

```
<html>
<head>
<title>Circle</title>
</head>
<body>
<hr>
<applet
    code="Circle.class"
    name=Circle
    width=60
    height=60 >
    <param name=R value=0>
    <param name=G value=0>
    <param name=B value=0>
</applet>
<SCRIPT LANGUAGE="VBScript">

Sub cmdRED_onClick
    call document.Circle.setCircleColor(255, 0, 0)
End Sub
```

```
Sub cmdGREEN_onClick
    call document.Circle.setCircleColor(0, 255, 0)
End Sub

Sub cmdBLUE_onClick
    call document.Circle.setCircleColor(0, 0, 255)
End Sub

</SCRIPT>
<FORM>
<INPUT TYPE="BUTTON" NAME="cmdRED" VALUE="RED"><P>
<INPUT TYPE="BUTTON" NAME="cmdGREEN" VALUE="GREEN"><P>
<INPUT TYPE="BUTTON" NAME="cmdBLUE" VALUE="BLUE"><P>
</FORM>

<hr>
<a href="Circle.java">The source.</a>
</body>
</html>
```

You can now view the changes to `Circle.html` in your Web browser. Clicking one of the three buttons changes the color of the circle. The output should now appear similar to Figure 29.2.

FIGURE 29.2.

The Circle *applet with VBScript.*

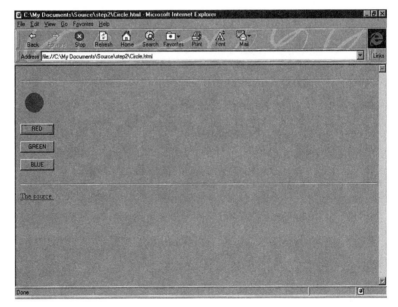

29

EMBEDDING
COMPONENTS IN
WEB PAGES

Controlling a Java Applet with JavaScript

Controlling an applet with JavaScript is very similar to using VBScript; the only difference is related to the syntax of the language. The form definition for JavaScript is slightly different: You specify the event handler code in the form control tag. For example, the form definition would be as follows:

```
<FORM>
<INPUT TYPE="BUTTON" NAME="cmdRED" VALUE="RED" onClick="setRED()"><P>
<INPUT TYPE="BUTTON" NAME="cmdGREEN" VALUE="GREEN" onClick="setGREEN()"><P>
<INPUT TYPE="BUTTON" NAME="cmdBLUE" VALUE="BLUE" onClick="setBLUE()"><P>
</FORM>
```

As you can see, the first button, named cmdRED, has an onClick event handler called setRED(). There are similar onClick event handlers for the green and blue buttons. The event handlers would then be added as follows:

```
function setRED() {
    document.Circle.setCircleColor(255,0,0);
}
```

The setGREEN() and setBLUE() event handlers should be added in a similar fashion, changing the calling parameters appropriately. The complete HTML listing should now look as shown in Listing 29.3.

Listing 29.3. The complete HTML code for the Circle applet with JavaScript.

```
<html>
<head>
<title>Circle</title>
</head>
<body>
<hr>
<applet
    code="Circle.class"
    name=Circle
    width=60
    height=60 >
    <param name=R value=0>
    <param name=G value=0>
    <param name=B value=0>
</applet>

<SCRIPT LANGUAGE="JavaScript">
function setRED() {
    document.Circle.setCircleColor(255,0,0);
}

function setGREEN() {
    document.Circle.setCircleColor(0,255,0);
}
```

```
function setBLUE() {
   document.Circle.setCircleColor(0,0,255);
}
</SCRIPT>

<FORM>
<INPUT TYPE="BUTTON" NAME="cmdRED" VALUE="RED" onClick="setRED()"><P>
<INPUT TYPE="BUTTON" NAME="cmdGREEN" VALUE="GREEN" onClick="setGREEN()"><P>
<INPUT TYPE="BUTTON" NAME="cmdBLUE" VALUE="BLUE" onClick="setBLUE()"><P>
</FORM>

<hr>
<a href="Circle.java">The source.</a>
</body>
</html>
```

This HTML document should now appear and work like the VBScript file in Figure 29.2.

Integrating ActiveX Controls into HTML

Now that you have learned about the structure and parameters of the <OBJECT> tag, let's put it to use in our Circle.html document to add scrollbar controls for changing the three colors. You can use Microsoft's ActiveX controls for the scrollbars. Microsoft also provides a very useful tool to assist with inserting ActiveX controls into HTML documents called the ActiveX Control Pad. In the following example, you will use the VBScript HTML file that you developed earlier in this chapter.

ActiveX Control Pad

The ActiveX Control Pad provides a nice user interface for inserting ActiveX controls and other objects into your HTML file. The following seven steps demonstrate the process of inserting the scrollbar control for red (refer to Figure 29.3 when performing the first four steps):

1. Run the ActiveX Control Pad and open the Circle.html file.
2. Position the cursor before the beginning of the form and select Insert ActiveX Control from the Edit menu.
3. Select Microsoft Forms 2.0 ScrollBar from the list.
4. Select OK.

   The Properties dialog box and another box showing the size and orientation of the control will now appear. (See Figure 29.4.) Now modify a few of the properties using the dialog box, and then change the orientation of the scrollbar in the other box.

   First change the ID attribute to a more meaningful name, sbRED. Then change the upper and lower limits of the scrollbar to the upper and lower limits for the red setting, 0 and 255.

FIGURE 29.3.

Inserting an ActiveX control with the ActiveX Control Pad.

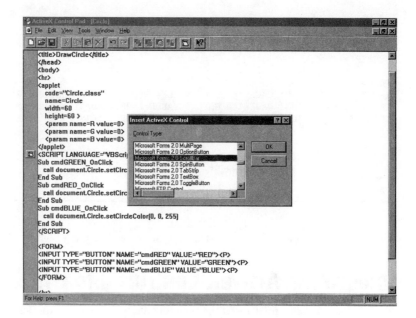

5. In the Properties dialog box, change the following properties:

```
ID = sbRED
Min = 0
Max = 255
```

The scrollbar defaults to a vertical position. You can easily change this by using the mouse to adjust the orientation and size of the control in the other dialog box.

6. Use the mouse to turn the scrollbar to a horizontal position, as shown in Figure 29.4.

7. Close the Properties dialog box, and the <OBJECT> tag will automatically be added to the HTML document.

That's all it takes to add an ActiveX scrollbar control to your HTML file! All that's left is to add the event handler code to respond to the scrollbar events.

Repeat the instructions to insert two more scrollbars for control of green, sbGREEN, and blue, sbBLUE.

To clean things up a bit and provide captions for the scrollbars, add the following HTML code after each </OBJECT> tag:

   Red<P>

This will add two nonbreaking spaces and a color identifier followed by a paragraph break. Replace Red with Green and Blue for the other two scrollbar captions.

FIGURE 29.4.

Modifying an ActiveX control with the ActiveX Control Pad.

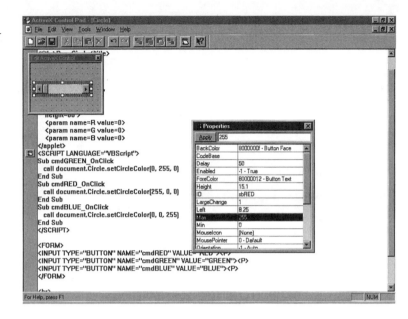

The resulting HTML file should now appear as in Listing 29.4.

Listing 29.4. The `Circle` HTML file with ActiveX controls.

```
<html>
<head>
<title>Circle</title>
</head>
<body>
<hr>
<applet
    code="Circle.class"
    name=Circle
    width=60
    height=60 >
    <param name=R value=0>
    <param name=G value=0>
    <param name=B value=0>
</applet>
<SCRIPT LANGUAGE="VBScript">

Sub cmdRED_onClick
   call Document.Circle.setCircleColor(255,0,0)
End Sub

Sub cmdGREEN_onClick
   call Document.Circle.setCircleColor(0,255,0)
End Sub
```

29

EMBEDDING
COMPONENTS IN
WEB PAGES

continues

Listing 29.4. continued

```
Sub cmdBLUE_onClick
   call Document.Circle.setCircleColor(0,0,255)
End Sub

</SCRIPT>
<P>

<OBJECT ID="sbRED" WIDTH=104 HEIGHT=20
 CLASSID="CLSID:DFD181E0-5E2F-11CE-A449-00AA004A803D">
    <PARAM NAME="Size" VALUE="2752;529">
    <PARAM NAME="Max" VALUE="255">
</OBJECT>   Red<P>

<OBJECT ID="sbGREEN" WIDTH=104 HEIGHT=20
 CLASSID="CLSID:DFD181E0-5E2F-11CE-A449-00AA004A803D">
    <PARAM NAME="Size" VALUE="2752;529">
    <PARAM NAME="Max" VALUE="255">
</OBJECT>   Green<P>

<OBJECT ID="sbBLUE" WIDTH=104 HEIGHT=20
 CLASSID="CLSID:DFD181E0-5E2F-11CE-A449-00AA004A803D">
    <PARAM NAME="Size" VALUE="2752;529">
    <PARAM NAME="Max" VALUE="255">
</OBJECT>   Blue <P>

<FORM>
<INPUT TYPE="BUTTON" NAME="cmdRED" VALUE="RED"><P>
<INPUT TYPE="BUTTON" NAME="cmdGREEN" VALUE="GREEN"><P>
<INPUT TYPE="BUTTON" NAME="cmdBLUE" VALUE="BLUE"><P>
</FORM>

<hr>
<a href="Circle.java">The source.</a>
</body>
</html>
```

Controlling ActiveX with Scripting

The final task is to provide scripting to support the ActiveX controls you added. There are essentially two things to add for each control:

1. A Change event handler for each scrollbar to change the color of the circle. This event handler will update the color of the circle when the user changes the position of a scrollbar.

2. Modifications to the onClick event handlers for the buttons so that they can set the scrollbars to correspond to changes caused by pressing the buttons. For example, if the scrollbars are all set midway and the Red button is pressed, then the Red scrollbar should be set to 255 and the Green and Blue scrollbars to 0.

First, add the three event handlers to change the color of the circle when the scrollbar is changed. Actually, the only difference between these event handlers and the ones created for the buttons are that these modify only a single color because they allow for incremental adjustments of color. For example, the event handler for the Red scrollbar would look like this:

```
Sub sbRED_Change
    call Document.Circle.setCircleColor(sbRED.Value, sbGREEN.Value, sbBLUE.Value)

End Sub
```

This event handler will respond to changes to sbRED, which is the red scrollbar. When a change occurs the setCircleColor method is called with the current values of the red, green, and blue scrollbars. This will cause the m_r, m_g, and m_b variables in the Circle Java applet to be updated and the repaint() method called. The color of the circle will then change to reflect the new amount of each color specified by the scrollbars.

Add two similar functions to support the change event of the other two scrollbars, sbGREEN and sbBLUE.

Now modify the event handlers for the button's onClick events. Add three statements to each handler to update the current value of each of the scrollbars. For example, the cmdRED_onClick event handler should have the following three lines added to it:

```
sbRED.Value = 255
sbGREEN.Value = 0
sbBLUE.Value = 0
```

Now when the red button is clicked, the scrollbars will be updated to reflect the correct color of the circle. Similar statements should be added to the cmdGREEN_onClick and cmdBLUE_onClick handlers. The complete code listing is shown in Listing 29.5. The final screen output is shown in Figure 29.5.

Listing 29.5. The complete Circle applet.

```
<html>
<head>
<title>Circle</title>
</head>
<body>
<hr>
<applet
    code="Circle.class"
    name=Circle
    width=60
    height=60 >
    <param name=R value=0>
    <param name=G value=0>
    <param name=B value=0>
</applet>
<SCRIPT LANGUAGE="VBScript">
```

continues

Listing 29.5. continued

```
Sub cmdRED_onClick
    call Document.Circle.setCircleColor(255,0,0)
    sbRED.Value = 255
    sbGREEN.Value = 0
    sbBLUE.Value = 0
End Sub

Sub sbRED_Change
    call Document.Circle.setCircleColor(sbRED.Value, sbGREEN.Value, sbBLUE.Value)
End Sub

Sub cmdGREEN_onClick
    call Document.Circle.setCircleColor(0,255,0)
    sbRED.Value = 0
    sbGREEN.Value = 255
    sbBLUE.Value = 0
End Sub

Sub sbGREEN_Change
    call Document.Circle.setCircleColor(sbRED.Value, sbGREEN.Value, sbBLUE.Value)
End Sub

Sub cmdBLUE_onClick
    call Document.Circle.setCircleColor(0,0,255)
    sbRED.Value = 0
    sbGREEN.Value = 0
    sbBLUE.Value = 255
End Sub

Sub sbBLUE_Change
    call Document.Circle.setCircleColor(sbRED.Value, sbGREEN.Value, sbBLUE.Value)
End Sub

</SCRIPT>
<P>

<OBJECT ID="sbRED" WIDTH=104 HEIGHT=20
 CLASSID="CLSID:DFD181E0-5E2F-11CE-A449-00AA004A803D">
    <PARAM NAME="Size" VALUE="2752;529">
    <PARAM NAME="Max" VALUE="255">
</OBJECT>   Red<P>

<OBJECT ID="sbGREEN" WIDTH=104 HEIGHT=20
 CLASSID="CLSID:DFD181E0-5E2F-11CE-A449-00AA004A803D">
    <PARAM NAME="Size" VALUE="2752;529">
    <PARAM NAME="Max" VALUE="255">
</OBJECT>   Green<P>

<OBJECT ID="sbBLUE" WIDTH=104 HEIGHT=20
 CLASSID="CLSID:DFD181E0-5E2F-11CE-A449-00AA004A803D">
    <PARAM NAME="Size" VALUE="2752;529">
    <PARAM NAME="Max" VALUE="255">
</OBJECT>   Blue <P>
```

```
<FORM>
<INPUT TYPE="BUTTON" NAME="cmdRED" VALUE="RED"><P>
<INPUT TYPE="BUTTON" NAME="cmdGREEN" VALUE="GREEN"><P>
<INPUT TYPE="BUTTON" NAME="cmdBLUE" VALUE="BLUE"><P>
</FORM>

<hr>
<a href="Circle.java">The source.</a>
</body>
</html>
```

FIGURE 29.5.

The final Circle *applet with ActiveX controls.*

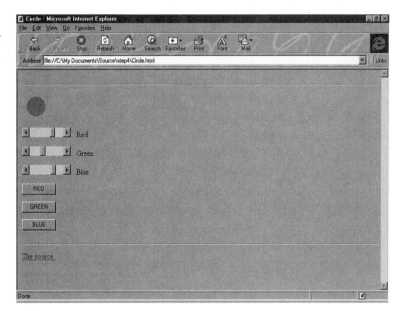

You should now be able to change the color of the circle by either pressing one of the three color buttons or changing one of the three color scrollbars. In addition, pressing the buttons should cause the scrollbars to be updated to reflect the current color of the circle.

This example could also be created using JavaScript instead of VBScript. Listing 29.6 shows this same example created with JavaScript.

Listing 29.6. The Circle **applet, created with JavaScript.**

```
<html>
<head>
<title>Circle</title>
</head>
<body>
<hr>
```

continues

Listing 29.6. continued

```
<applet
    code="Circle.class"
    name=Circle
    width=60
    height=60 >
    <param name=R value=0>
    <param name=G value=0>
    <param name=B value=0>
</applet>

<SCRIPT LANGUAGE="JavaScript">
function setRED(){
   Document.Circle.setCircleColor(255,0,0);
   sbRED.Value = 255;
   sbGREEN.Value = 0;
   sbBLUE.Value = 0;
}

function sbRED_Change(){
   Document.Circle.setCircleColor(sbRED.Value, sbGREEN.Value, sbBLUE.Value)
}

function setGREEN(){
   Document.Circle.setCircleColor(0,255,0);
   sbRED.Value = 0;
   sbGREEN.Value = 255;
   sbBLUE.Value = 0;
}

function sbGREEN_Change(){
   Document.Circle.setCircleColor(sbRED.Value, sbGREEN.Value, sbBLUE.Value)
}

function setBLUE(){
   Document.Circle.setCircleColor(0,0,255);
   sbRED.Value = 0;
   sbGREEN.Value = 0;
   sbBLUE.Value = 255;
}

function sbBLUE_Change(){
   Document.Circle.setCircleColor(sbRED.Value, sbGREEN.Value, sbBLUE.Value)
}

</SCRIPT>
<P>

<OBJECT ID="sbRED" WIDTH=104 HEIGHT=20
 CLASSID="CLSID:DFD181E0-5E2F-11CE-A449-00AA004A803D">
    <PARAM NAME="Size" VALUE="2752;529">
    <PARAM NAME="Max" VALUE="255">
</OBJECT>   Red<P>

<OBJECT ID="sbGREEN" WIDTH=104 HEIGHT=20
 CLASSID="CLSID:DFD181E0-5E2F-11CE-A449-00AA004A803D">
```

```
      <PARAM NAME="Size" VALUE="2752;529">
      <PARAM NAME="Max" VALUE="255">
</OBJECT>   Green<P>

<OBJECT ID="sbBLUE" WIDTH=104 HEIGHT=20
  CLASSID="CLSID:DFD181E0-5E2F-11CE-A449-00AA004A803D">
      <PARAM NAME="Size" VALUE="2752;529">
      <PARAM NAME="Max" VALUE="255">
</OBJECT>   Blue <P>

<FORM>
<INPUT TYPE="BUTTON" NAME="cmdRED" VALUE="RED" onClick="setRED()"><P>
<INPUT TYPE="BUTTON" NAME="cmdGREEN" VALUE="GREEN" onClick="setGREEN()"><P>
<INPUT TYPE="BUTTON" NAME="cmdBLUE" VALUE="BLUE" onClick="setBLUE()"><P>
</FORM>

<hr>
<a href="Circle.java">The source.</a>
</body>
</html>
```

Summary

This chapter concludes Part IV. These chapters provide information about the glue that bonds your Visual J++ creations together into their final form: an HTML document. Although Visual J++ can be used to create standalone Java applications, it will most likely be used to create Java applets. Through the use of HTML and the two scripting languages, applets can be generalized and modularized. This is a powerful concept because it creates the opportunity for reusable modules.

As an example, consider the following: You are designing a Web document that requires graphing and database capabilities. You could approach this task in two ways. First, you could design everything into a Java applet. This would definitely work, but it doesn't create nice, clean generic modules that can be used again in future projects. Or you could create generic modules and glue them together using scripts. The graphing capability could be provided by a generic graphing ActiveX control. The database might be a custom applet that you design. These two components can then communicate with each other through a scripting language such as VBScript or JavaScript. When used in this way, scripting is a powerful concept.

V

PART

Visual J++
Development Topics

Querying Databases with Data Access Objects

by Mike Cohn

IN THIS CHAPTER

In this chapter you'll learn how to use the Microsoft Data Access Objects (DAOs) in your Visual J++ programs. The DAO is an entire database engine that includes a set of objects and methods capable of performing just about any database operation you're likely to need. Although the database native to the DAO is the Jet engine used in Microsoft Access, the DAO can also be used to access ODBC data sources. DAO programming could be the topic of an entire book, so this chapter only scratches the surface. It does, however, provide sufficient information to get you started and includes examples of reading, updating, deleting, adding, and searching.

Overview of the Data Access Objects

The Microsoft DAO and Jet database engine get around more than the Beach Boys do in that song of theirs. Jet was introduced in November 1992 in Access 1.0. Since then, the Jet engine and DAO have been used in Access, Visual Basic, Visual Basic for Applications (including Word and Excel), and Visual C++. Because the DAO is used in so many other Microsoft products, you should not be surprised to discover that it can be useful in your Visual J++ efforts.

Figure 30.1 shows the relationships among the DAO elements. This figure does not show inheritance relationships. Instead it shows container relationships. In other words, from this figure you can tell that a database contains recordsets and that recordsets contain fields.

FIGURE 30.1.

The relationships among the DAO elements.

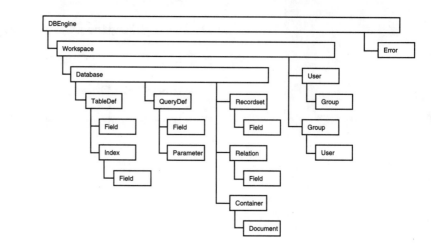

As you can see from Figure 30.1, the DAO contains many objects. Because these are ActiveX objects, you will access them from Visual J++ through Java interfaces. Java Type Library Wizard creates these interfaces.

Generating the Class Files

Before you can use the DAO in your Java programs, you must create the class files that will be linked into your programs. To create these files, select Java Type Library Wizard from the Tools menu in the Developer Studio. You will see a list of ActiveX items installed on your system (see Figure 30.2). Select Microsoft DAO 3.0 Object Library and click the OK button. This step generates Java class files for you to use. It also creates a file named SUMMARY.TXT, which contains a brief list of each object and method that was generated. The file is normally placed in C:\WINDOWS\JAVA\TRUSTLIB\DAO3032\SUMMARY.TXT.

FIGURE 30.2.

You must run the Java Type Library Wizard to generate class files for DAO.

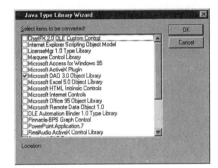

Using _DBEngine Objects

Although more than 30 DAO interfaces are available, you do not need to know or use all of them. In fact, this chapter focuses on only a handful of them. Knowing about just these few interfaces will enable you to add powerful database access to your Java programs.

The first object you need to know about is the _DBEngine interface. This object is at the top of the DAO hierarchy and is the first object you construct when writing a program that uses DAO. To construct a _DBEngine object you should use the method DBEngine_create in the class dao_dbengine. The dao_dbengine class handles the low-level tasks of constructing a COM object. This class is shown in Listing 30.1 and is also provided with Visual J++.

> **NOTE**
>
> Although dao_dbengine.java is included with Visual J++, it is installed only when you install the DAOSample applet. To install DAOSample, open the InfoView. Select Samples, Microsoft Samples, and finally DAOSample. Follow the instructions that appear in the right pane of the InfoView.

Listing 30.1. dao_dbengine.java.

```
// Create a DAO DBEngine object with the license

import dao3032._DBEngine;
import com.ms.com.*;

public class dao_dbengine
{
    // The static public method creates the DBEngine object
    static public _DBEngine create()
    {
        // The return value
        _DBEngine result;

        // Create the License Manager object
        ILicenseMgr mgr = new LicenseMgr();

        // Use the License Manager to create the DBEngine
        result = (_DBEngine) mgr.createWithLic(

            // The license key for the DAO DBEngine
            "mjgcqcejfchcijecpdhckcdjqigdejfccjri",

            // The CLSID for the DAO DBEngine
            "{00025E15-0000-0000-C000-000000000046}",

            // The aggregation IUnknown* punkOuter
            null,

            // The ctxFlag to create in inproc server
            ComContext.INPROC_SERVER
            );

        return result;
    }
}
```

The DBEngine_create method uses the Java LicenseMgr class to construct the new component object model (COM) component. To construct a _DBEngine object in your code, write the following line:

```
_DBEngine dbengine = dao_dbengine.create();
```

Useful Methods

Although many methods are available for use with _DBEngine objects, the following sections describe the most useful.

OpenDatabase

This method opens a new database. Its signature is as follows:

```
Database OpenDatabase(String dbname, Variant exclusive,
    Variant readonly, Variant source);
```

The `dbname` parameter is the filename of the database being opened. The remaining three parameters are each variants. The `Variant` class passes data to COM objects and each `Variant` object can hold any type of data—`string`, `numeric`, or `boolean`. The `exclusive` parameter needs to hold a boolean value indicating whether this program requires exclusive access to the database. The `read-only` parameter is a boolean value indicating whether the database is to be opened in read-only or in read-write mode. The `source` parameter holds string data such as `"PWD=ROSEBUD"` that can be used when opening an ODBC data source. As an example of using `OpenDatabase`, consider the following:

```
// create Variants that will hold parameters that will be
// passed to OpenDatabase
Variant var1 = new Variant();
Variant var2 = new Variant();
Variant var3 = new Variant();

// set parameters for call to OpenDatabase
var1.putBoolean(false);
var2.putBoolean(false);
var3.putString("");

// Open the database for non-exclusive, read-write access
Database db = dbengine.OpenDatabase(filename, var1, var2, var3);
```

In this case, three new variants are constructed. The first two are set to false. The third is set to hold an empty string. `OpenDatabase` is then called with these parameters, and the database is opened in nonexclusive, read-write mode.

getVersion

The `getVersion` method does not require any parameters and will return a string representing the version of the Jet engine in use. Table 30.1 shows the various Jet engine versions and the versions of other Microsoft products with which they were released.

Table 30.1. The versions of the Jet engine and the products with which they were released.

Engine Version	Access	Visual Basic	Excel	Visual C++	Visual J++
1.0 (1992)	1.0				
1.1 (1993)	1.1	3.0			
2.2 (1994)	2.0				
2.5 (1995)		4.0 (16 bit)			
3.0 (1995)	7.0	4.0 (32 bit)	7.0	4.0	1.0

30
QUERYING DATABASES WITH DAO

Using Database Objects

You have already seen how to create a database object with the OpenDatabase method of _DBEngine. In the following sections you will learn about the most useful methods for using database objects.

Controlling Transactions

The three methods BeginTrans, CommitTrans, and Rollback are used to manage transactions. Transactions are useful because they assist in managing the integrity of a database. You use BeginTrans to indicate the start of a transaction block. You can then use CommitTrans to commit the database activity since the transaction began or Rollback to undo the activity. These methods have the following signatures:

```
void BeginTrans();
void CommitTrans();
void Rollback();
```

Why would you want to use these methods? By thinking of your database activity in terms of transactions instead of atomic events (inserts, updates, and deletes), you can prevent some data problems. For example, suppose you are writing an order entry system for taking online orders. When customers access your Web page, they fill in a spreadsheet with a column for the product code and the quantity needed. They can enter as many items as desired but must click a Submit button before the order is sent to the shipping department.

If the customer enters an order for 100 units of product ABC, the program should check the database for stock on hand and reduce the available quantity by 100. Once the customer clicks the Submit button, the transaction is committed to the database. However, if the customer selects the Cancel button instead of Submit, the transaction can be rolled back.

OpenRecordset

The OpenRecordset method creates a recordset. A recordset is a collection of records. Recordset objects are among the most important in the DAO and are discussed in detail later in this chapter. The signature for OpenRecordset is as follows:

```
Recordset OpenRecordset(String source, Variant type,
    Variant options);
```

The source parameter can hold either the name of the table in the database or an SQL statement that returns a set of rows. The type parameter must hold one of the following values:

- dbOpenTable
- dbOpenDynaset
- dbOpenSnapshot

Each of these parameters indicates a different type of recordset. A table recordset corresponds to a single table in the underlying database. Records may be added, updated, or deleted in a table recordset. A dynaset recordset is the result of a query and may include columns from more than one table. Records may be added, updated, or deleted in a dynaset. Finally, a snapshot recordset is a static copy of the records at the moment the recordset was created. A snapshot may contain fields from more than one table but adds, updates, and deletes are not allowed.

The options parametercan hold any of the values shown in Table 30.2.

Table 30.2. Valid values for the options parameter to OpenRecordset.

Value	*Description*
dbAppendOnly	Records may be added but not updated or deleted. Applies only to dbOpenDynaset.
dbConsistent	When using a recordset created from joined tables, only those fields not involved in the join can be updated. Applies only to dbOpenDynaset.
dbDenyRead	Prevents other users from reading any records in the recordset. Applies only to dbOpenTable.
dbDenyWrite	Prevents other users from writing to any records in the recordset.
dbForwardOnly	The recordset supports only the MoveNext movement method.
dbInconsistent	When using a recordset created from joined tables, all fields, including those involved in the join, can be updated. Applies only to dbOpenDynaset.
dbReadOnly	No changes can be made to the recordset.
dbSeeChanges	Generates an error if another program attempts to make a change to the record that is being edited.
dbSQLPassThrough	When using an ODBC data source, passes SQL code directly to the server for execution.

As an example of creating a table recordset, consider Listing 30.2. First a database is opened. Then two variants, var4 and var5, are constructed. The values dbOpenTable and dbReadOnly are placed into the variants and are passed to OpenRecordset. The name Programmer is also passed to OpenRecordset, which causes the Programmer table to be opened in read-only mode.

Listing 30.2. Opening a table recordset.

```
// create Variants that will hold parameters that will be
// passed to OpenDatabase
Variant var1 = new Variant();
Variant var2 = new Variant();
Variant var3 = new Variant();

// set parameters for call to OpenDatabase
var1.putBoolean(false);
var2.putBoolean(false);
var3.putString("");

// open the database for nonexclusive access
Database db = dbengine.OpenDatabase(filename, var1, var2, var3);

// create Variants that will hold parameters that will be
// passed to OpenDatabase
Variant var4 = new Variant();
Variant var5 = new Variant();

var4.putShort(Constants.dbOpenTable);
var5.putShort(Constants.dbReadOnly);

// create the recordset
recordset = db.OpenRecordset("Programmer", var4, var5);
```

Close

This method closes a database object. It requires no parameters and has no return value.

Using Field Objects

The Field object represents the individual columns in a database table. Although many methods are available for use with Field objects, the two you will use most frequently are putValue and getValue. These methods move data into and out of Field objects. The signatures of these methods are as follows:

```
Variant getValue();
void putValue(Variant);
```

As an example of how to retrieve a value from a Field object, consider the following:

```
Variant value = new Variant();
value = salaryField.getValue();
int salary = value.toInt();
```

First a new Variant object is constructed. Then the getValue method retrieves the value of salaryField. Because value is a Variant, it is converted to a more useful data type. In this case, value.toInt is used to load the integer variable, salary.

You can move data in the opposite direction—*into* a `Field` object— in a similar manner, using `putValue`. For example, the following code doubles the value stored in the salary field:

```
Variant value = new Variant();
value.putInt(oldSalary * 2);
salaryField.putValue(value);
```

Using Recordset Objects

In the section "Using Database Objects" you were introduced to recordsets. In this section you learn how to use a recordset to view, add, update, delete, and find records. The following sections describe how to perform some of the most common operations on recordsets.

Reading Records Sequentially

To move through a recordset, you can use the `MoveFirst`, `MoveNext`, `MovePrevious`, and `MoveLast` methods, whose signatures are as follows:

```
void MoveFirst();
void MoveNext();
void MovePrevious();
void MoveLast();
```

Each of these methods will reposition the current record of the recordset. As an example of how these methods are used, consider Listing 30.3. This example iterates through all of the rows in the Programmer table of the supplied Access database. Information about each programmer is displayed in a text area, as shown in Figure 30.3.

Listing 30.3. The class DAORead demonstrates moving through a recordset sequentially.

```
import java.applet.*;
import java.awt.*;
import java.net.*;
import dao_dbengine;
import dao3032.*;
import com.ms.com.Variant;

public class DAORead extends Applet
{
    Recordset recordset;
    TextArea output;
    Database db;

    public void init()
    {
        resize(500, 400);
        output = new TextArea(20, 50);
        add(output);
    }
```

continues

Listing 30.3. continued

```java
public void start()
{
    OpenDatabase();
}

public void stop()
{
    // Close the recordset and database
    recordset.Close();
    db.Close();
}

private boolean OpenDatabase()
{
    URL dbURL;
    try {
        // otherwise generate it relative to the applet
        dbURL = new java.net.URL(getDocumentBase(),
                "sample.mdb");
    }
    catch(Exception e) {
        showStatus("Error: " + e.getMessage());
        return false;
    }

    // strip "file:/" from dbURL
    String filename = dbURL.getFile().substring(1);

    // create the database engine
    _DBEngine dbengine = dao_dbengine.create();

    // create Variants that will hold parameters that will be
    // passed to OpenDatabase
    Variant var1 = new Variant();
    Variant var2 = new Variant();
    Variant var3 = new Variant();

    // set parameters for call to OpenDatabase
    var1.putBoolean(false);
    var2.putBoolean(false);
    var3.putString("");

    // Open the database for nonexclusive access
    db = dbengine.OpenDatabase(filename, var1, var2, var3);

    // create Variants that will hold parameters that will be
    // passed to OpenDatabase
    Variant var4 = new Variant();
    Variant var5 = new Variant();

    var4.putShort(Constants.dbOpenTable);
    var5.putShort(Constants.dbReadOnly);

    // create the recordset
    recordset = db.OpenRecordset("Programmer", var4, var5);
```

```
    // display all the records in this dynaset
    DisplayAllRecords();

    return true;
}

private void DisplayAllRecords()
{
    // create variants and assign the names of each column
    Variant varFirstName = new Variant();
    varFirstName.putString("FirstName");

    Variant varLastName = new Variant();
    varLastName.putString("LastName");

    Variant varSalary = new Variant();
    varSalary.putString("Salary");

    Variant varKnowsJava = new Variant();
    varKnowsJava.putString("KnowsJava");

    Variant varJobTitle = new Variant();
    varJobTitle.putString("JobTitle");

    // determine how many records in the recordset
    int count = recordset.getRecordCount();

    // position recordset at the first record
    recordset.MoveFirst();

    // loop through the recordset, displaying each record
    for(int recNum = 0; recNum < count; recNum++)
    {
        // get the fields in this recordset
        Fields fields = recordset.getFields();
        _Field fld;

        // create a Variant that will hold each the value
        // read from each column
        Variant value;

        // get the LastName field
        fld = fields.getItem(varLastName);
        // get its value
        value = fld.getValue();
        // display the value
        output.appendText(value.toString() + ", ");

        // get the FirstName field
        fld = fields.getItem(varFirstName);
        // get its value
        value = fld.getValue();
        // display the value
        output.appendText(value.toString() + "\r\n");

        // get the JobTitle field
        fld = fields.getItem(varJobTitle);
```

30

QUERYING
DATABASES WITH
DAO

continues

Listing 30.3. continued

```
              // get its value
              value = fld.getValue();
              // display the value
              output.appendText("\t" + value.toString() + "\r\n");

              // get the Salary field
              fld = fields.getItem(varSalary);
              // get its value
              value = fld.getValue();
              // display the value
              output.appendText("\t" + value.toString() + "\r\n");

              // get the KnowsJava field
              fld = fields.getItem(varKnowsJava);
              // get its value
              value = fld.getValue();
              // display the value
              Boolean knowsJava = new Boolean (value.toBoolean());
              output.appendText("\tKnows Java: " +
                      knowsJava.toString() + "\r\n");
              recordset.MoveNext();
          }
      }
}
```

FIGURE 30.3.

The DAORead *example displays information about each programmer in the database.*

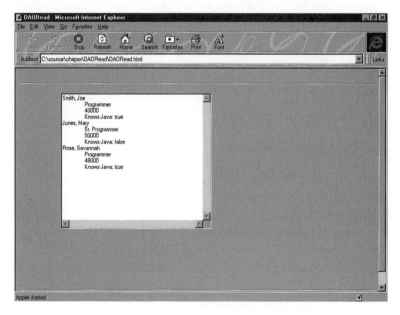

The init method of class DAORead simply resizes the screen and then places a TextArea component on the screen. The start method invokes the OpenDatabase method. OpenDatabase constructs a URL from the document base and name of the Access database file to be opened. Next `dao_dbengine.create` creates the database engine. The database is opened using `OpenDatabase` and three variants. Finally, the Programmer table is opened as a table record-set in read-only mode. The `DisplayAllRecords` method is then called to display the record contents.

`DisplayAllRecords` begins with a series of lines such as these:

```
Variant varFirstName = new Variant();
varFirstName.putString("FirstName");
```

These lines create a `Variant` variable for each column in the Programmer table and then store the name of the column in the variant. After each variant is created, `getRecordCount` retrieves the number of records in the recordset. The `getRecordCount` method will always return the correct number of records in a table-type recordset. For a dynaset or snapshot, `getRecordCount` will return the correct value only after all records in the set have been retrieved.

The recordset is initially positioned on the first record with `MoveFirst`. At this point a loop begins that will iterate through each of the records in the recordset based on the quantity returned by `getRecordCount`. Each time through the loop the contents of the row will be displayed. In order to access the fields stored in a recordset, you need to use the `getFields` method. In Listing 30.3 the fields are retrieved as follows:

```
Fields fields = recordset.getFields();
```

The `getFields` method will create a collection of fields. To get at an individual item within the collection, use the `getItem` method. In Listing 30.3 the contents of the `LastName` field are retrieved with the following code:

```
// get the LastName field
fld = fields.getItem(varLastName);
// get its value
value = fld.getValue();
// display the value
output.appendText(value.toString() + ", ");
```

The method `fields.getItem` is passed the variant that contains the string `"LastName"`. This step will cause `fld` to contain a reference to the specific field that contains data from the `LastName` column of the database. Next `fld.getValue` retrieves the value of this field and places it in the variant `value`. Finally, `value.toString` converts the variant into a string that is passed to `appendText`, thus adding the contents of the `LastName` column to the `TextArea` on the applet.

After similar code is repeated for each of the columns in the database—`FirstName`, `LastName`, `JobTitle`, `Salary`, and `KnowsJava`—the `MoveNext` method selects a new current record. Once the user closes the applet, the `stop` method is invoked and the recordset and database are closed.

The `MoveLast` and `MovePrevious` methods work in an analogous manner. If you need to move backwards through a recordset, you can use these methods instead of `MoveFirst` and `MoveNext`.

30

QUERYING
DATABASES WITH
DAO

> **NOTE**
>
> You should notice from this example that it is necessary to use the following three import statements:
>
> ```
> import dao_dbengine;
> import dao3032.*;
> import com.ms.com.Variant;
> ```
>
> These lines import the dao_dbengine class described earlier in the chapter, the DAO objects generated by the Java Type Library Wizard, and the Variant class that is used with all COM objects.

Updating Records

Before the contents of a record can be updated with new values, the record must be placed in edit mode, which is done with the Edit method. In edit mode, you can use the Resultset.getFields and the Field.putValue methods to alter the values in a record. Once the desired changes have been made, the record can be updated with the Update method. Once a record is updated, it is automatically taken out of edit mode. If, instead of updating a record, you need to take a record out of edit mode without committing any changes to the record, you can use CancelUpdate. The signatures of these new methods are as follows:

```
void Edit();
void Update();
void CancelUpdate();
```

 As an example of how to update the values in a record, consider the GiveBonuses method shown in Listing 30.4. This method is from the DAOUpdate example provided on the CD-ROM that accompanies this book. The GiveBonuses method is similar to DisplayAllRecords from Listing 30.3 in that it also uses getRecordCount, MoveFirst, and MoveNext to loop through the records in the recordset. However, in this example, each programmer who knows Java will have his or her salary doubled.

Listing 30.4. Updating the salaries of all Java programmers in the database.

```
private void GiveBonuses()
{
    // determine how many records in the recordset
    int count = recordset.getRecordCount();

    // create a variant for each column
    Variant varSalary = new Variant();
    Variant varKnowsJava = new Variant();

    // set the name of each column
    varSalary.putString("Salary");
    varKnowsJava.putString("KnowsJava");
```

```
    // position recordset at the first record
    recordset.MoveFirst();

    // loop through the recordset, displaying each record
    for(int recNum = 0; recNum < count; recNum++)
    {
        // get the fields in this recordset
        Fields fields = recordset.getFields();
        _Field fld;

        // create a variant that will hold each the value
        // read from each column
        Variant value;

        // get the KnowsJava field
        fld = fields.getItem(varKnowsJava);
        // get its value
        value = fld.getValue();

        // if the programmer knows Java, give a good raise
        if (value.toBoolean() == true)
        {
            // get the Salary field
            fld = fields.getItem(varSalary);
            // get its value
            value = fld.getValue();
            // store the salary
            int salary = value.toInt();

            // double the programmer's salary
            int newSalary = salary * 2;

            // put the recordset into edit mode
            recordset.Edit();

            // assign the new salary to the current record
            value.putInt(newSalary);
            fld.putValue(value);

            // update the recordset
            recordset.Update();

            // display the salary change
            DisplayRaise(fields, salary, newSalary);
        }
        else
            DisplayNoRaise(fields);

        recordset.MoveNext();
    }
}
```

30
QUERYING
DATABASES WITH
DAO

Inside the `for` loop of `GiveBonuses`, the value of the `KnowsJava` field is retrieved and converted to a boolean value. If this value is `true`, the `salary` field is retrieved from the database and stored in the integer variable salary. This value is doubled and then stored in newSalary. The actual updating of the record in the database takes place with the following lines:

```
recordset.Edit();
value.putInt(newSalary);
fld.putValue(value);
recordset.Update();
```

Depending on whether or not the programmer received a raise, either the method DisplayRaise or the method DisplayNoRaise will be called. These methods are as follows:

```
private void DisplayRaise(Fields fields, int oldSalary, int newSalary)
{
    String firstName = GetField(fields, "FirstName");
    String lastName  = GetField(fields, "LastName");

    output.appendText(firstName + " " + lastName +
            " got a raise from " +
            String.valueOf(oldSalary) +
            " to " + String.valueOf(newSalary) + "\r\n");
}

private void DisplayNoRaise(Fields fields)
{
    String firstName = GetField(fields, "FirstName");
    String lastName  = GetField(fields, "LastName");

    output.appendText(firstName + " " + lastName +
            " didn't get a raise.\r\n");
}
```

Rather than construct and manipulate their own Variant variables, each of these methods calls the GetField method. GetField was written as follows:

```
private String GetField(Fields fields, String fldName)
{
    // create a new variant using fldName
    Variant var = new Variant();
    var.putString(fldName);

    // get the field
    _Field fld = fields.getItem(var);
    // get its value
    Variant value = fld.getValue();

    return value.toString();
}
```

GetField works on a generic Fields container and field name. A variant is constructed and set to hold the field name. The corresponding field is then retrieved from the Fields container and its value is returned as a string.

Figure 30.4 shows the result of running DAOUpdate.

FIGURE 30.4.

The DAOUpdate *example doubles the salaries of all Java programmers.*

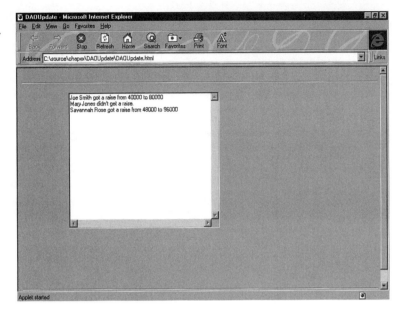

Deleting Records

Deleting a record is as simple as calling the Delete method when the record to be deleted is the current record in the recordset. For example, Listing 30.5 shows the FireProgrammers method from the example DAODelete that is included on the CD-ROM. This method loops through all of the programmers in the Programmer table, examining the value of the KnowsJava column. When it finds a programmer who does not know Java, he or she is deleted from the database.

Listing 30.5. DAODelete illustrates how to fire anyone who doesn't know Java.

```
private void FireProgrammers()
{
    // determine how many records in the recordset
    int count = recordset.getRecordCount();

    // create a variant for the KnowsJava column
    Variant varKnowsJava = new Variant();
    varKnowsJava.putString("KnowsJava");

    // position recordset at the first record
    recordset.MoveFirst();

    // loop through the recordset, displaying each record
    for(int recNum = 0; recNum < count; recNum++)
    {
```

continues

Listing 30.5. continued

```
        // get the fields in this recordset
        Fields fields = recordset.getFields();
        _Field fld;

        // create a variant that will hold the values
        // read from the columns
        Variant value;

        // get the KnowsJava field
        fld = fields.getItem(varKnowsJava);
        // get its value
        value = fld.getValue();

        // fire the programmer if he doesn't know Java
        if (value.toBoolean() == false)
        {
            // display a message about the fired programmer
            DisplayFiring(fields);

            // delete the current record
            recordset.Delete();
        }

        recordset.MoveNext();
    }
}
```

The Delete method does not automatically advance the recordset to the next record. It is still necessary to use MoveNext to advance to the next record in the set. Figure 30.5 shows the results of running DAODelete.

FIGURE 30.5.

The DAODelete example fires any programmers who do not know Java.

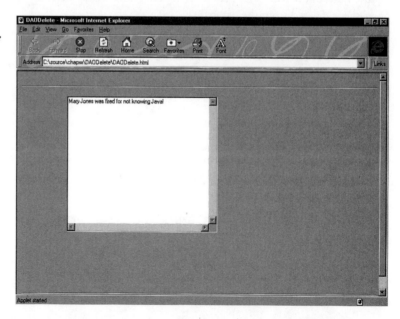

Adding New Records

Adding a record is similar to editing a record. However, instead of placing the database into edit mode with the `Edit` method, the database is placed into add mode with the `AddNew` method. The `DAOAdd` example provided on the CD-ROM shows how to add a new programmer to the database. Listing 30.6 shows the `AddNewHire` method from the `DAOAdd` class.

Listing 30.6. DAOAdd shows how to add a new programmer to the database.

```
private void AddNewHire()
{
    // create a variant for each column
    Variant varFirstName = new Variant();
    Variant varLastName = new Variant();
    Variant varSalary = new Variant();
    Variant varKnowsJava = new Variant();
    Variant varJobTitle = new Variant();

    // set the name of each column
    varFirstName.putString("FirstName");
    varLastName.putString("LastName");
    varSalary.putString("Salary");
    varKnowsJava.putString("KnowsJava");
    varJobTitle.putString("JobTitle");

    // tell the recordset its about to get a new record
    recordset.AddNew();

    // retrieve the fields for this recordset
    Fields fields = recordset.getFields();
    _Field fld;

    // create a variant to hold temporary values
    Variant value = new Variant();

    // set the FirstName field
    fld = fields.getItem(varFirstName);
    value.putString("Napoleon");
    fld.putValue(value);

    // set the LastName field
    fld = fields.getItem(varLastName);
    value.putString("Solo");
    fld.putValue(value);

    // set the Salary field
    fld = fields.getItem(varSalary);
    value.putInt(63000);
    fld.putValue(value);

    // set the KnowsJava field
    fld = fields.getItem(varKnowsJava);
    value.putBoolean(true);
    fld.putValue(value);
```

continues

Listing 30.6. continued

```
    // set the JobTitle field
    fld = fields.getItem(varJobTitle);
    value.putString("Lead Programmer");
    fld.putValue(value);

    // commit the new record to the recordset
    recordset.Update();
}
```

In order to add a new programmer, a variant is created for each column in the database and AddNew puts the database into add mode. The fields in the recordset are retrieved with getFields. Then, for each column in the database, the following actions occur:

- The variant containing the field name retrieves the field.
- The value variant is loaded with the desired value.
- putValue puts the value into the field.
- Update commits the new record.

If an error had occurred or this method was interactive and the user changed his or her mind, CancelUpdate could be used to cancel the new record. Figure 30.6 shows the results of running DAOUpdate.

FIGURE 30.6.

The DAOAdd example shows how to add a new programmer to the database.

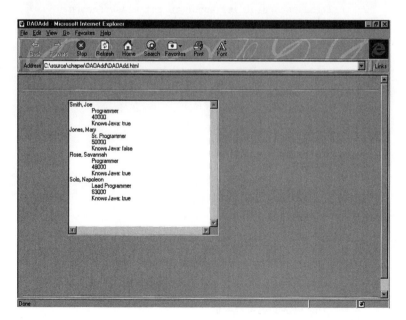

Finding Records

Sometimes you've created a resultset and need to scan through it to find one or more records that match certain criteria. The DAO engine provides a set of methods for doing exactly this. To find the first record that meets your criteria, you can use the FindFirst method. Other methods you can use are FindNext, FindPrevious, and FindLast, which have the following signatures:

```
void FindFirst(String);
void FindNext(String);
void FindPrevious(String);
void FindLast(String);
```

The string parameter passed to these methods is the search criteria. For example, the following two examples show valid search criteria:

```
FindFirst("Salary < 50000");
FindLast("FirstName = 'Savannah'");
```

In order to determine if a record was found that matched the search criteria, you use the method getNoMatch whose signature is as follows:

```
boolean getNoMatch();
```

This method will return true if no match was found or false otherwise. By combining these methods, you can write code that will loop through a recordset to find all records that match the desired criteria. For example, consider the following FindProgrammers method:

```
private void FindProgrammers()
{
    // setup the search criteria
    String criteria = "Salary < 50000";

    // find the first matching record
    recordset.FindFirst(criteria);

    // while there are matching records keep going
    while (recordset.getNoMatch() == false)
    {
        // display the programmer's name
        DisplayProgrammer();

        // and search for another one
        recordset.FindNext(criteria);
    }
}
```

 This method is from the example class DAOFind that is included on the accompanying CD-ROM. FindProgrammers searches for all programmers who make less than the specified salary. For each record that matches, the DisplayProgrammer method will be called. This method displays information about the underpaid programmers, as shown in Figure 30.7.

30

QUERYING
DATABASES WITH
DAO

FIGURE 30.7.

The DAOFind *example
identifies underpaid
programmers.*

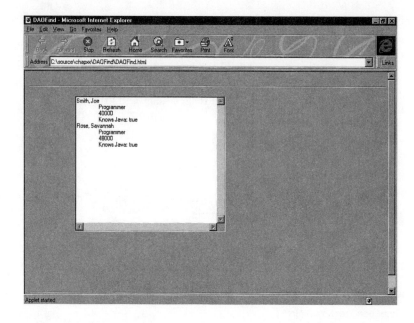

The FindFirst and other Find methods work only when the database is opened as a dynaset.
Therefore, the OpenDatabase method needs to specify dbOpenDynaset instead of dbOpenTable,
as shown in the following code fragment:

```
Variant var4 = new Variant();
Variant var5 = new Variant();

var4.putShort(Constants.dbOpenDynaset);
var5.putShort(Constants.dbEditAdd);

// create the recordset
recordset = db.OpenRecordset("Programmer", var4, var5);
```

Summary

This chapter introduces the DAO and shows you how to use these objects in your Java programs. You learn about Database, Recordset, and Field objects and how to combine these objects
to perform useful tasks. The examples use the DAO to browse a database, add new records,
update existing records, delete records, and search for records. Armed with the information
from this chapter, you are now prepared to write your own programs using the DAO.

CHAPTER 31

Basic Java Multimedia Capabilities

by Hiro Ruo

IN THIS CHAPTER

This chapter presents the basic multimedia capabilities provided with the Java Developer's Kit (JDK). The following topics are discussed:

- Image retrieval and display
- Audio retrieval and playback
- Animation using standard Java animation techniques

Multimedia Web

One of the most popular uses of the Web is as a publishing tool. The Web is a plethora of corporate propaganda, product advertisements, and information distribution. To aid in the presentation of this information, multimedia content is widely used.

Multimedia is the integration of several types of media. It is typically associated with the combination of graphics and audio contents, and ultimately full animation. This sensually stimulating form of media can be a powerful tool when implemented as content for a Web page.

Java provides facilities to implement graphics and audio in an applet. These features are explored in Chapter 32, "Extending Multimedia Capabilities Through ActiveX." First you will look at how graphical images can be retrieved and displayed from within an applet. Then, you will explore how audio content can be added to an applet so that sound files will be playing when the Web page is opened. Finally, you will integrate these features in an applet to create animation with audio simultaneously.

Image Retrieval

To display an image, the image must first be retrieved. Java supports the retrieval of images with a few commands.

GetGraphics

`GetGraphics()` creates a graphics context for drawing to an offscreen image. This method can only be called for offscreen images, which are created with the `createImage` method with two integer arguments. In the code shown in the examples in this chapter, `getGraphics()` is called to create a graphics context while downloading the images offscreen. The return values of `getGraphics()` is a graphics context to draw to the off-screen image. If for some reason the graphics were not loaded properly, `getGraphics().drawString` can be called to visually notify that an error condition has occurred.

GetImage

GetImage(*filename*) is the command called to retrieve the actual image files. Given the filename in String format, getImage will retrieve the specified files. In the following example, the getImage command is called in different contexts. In a standalone applet, the toolkit getImage is called with the filename as the parameter. In an applet, getImage should be called with the getDocumentBase return values as a parameter. The getDocumentBase command will return the URL of the referencing document that contains the applet. You can also call a similar command, getCodeBase, which returns the URL of the applet.

These commands set up the environment by which filenames can be indexed in the code. Upon a successful call to getImage, the image with the pixel data referenced by the filename is returned. Note also that the filename does not have to be locally stored; the getImage syntax allows a URL to a remote filename to be the parameter passed. This is how an image can be retrieved remotely to be displayed on the Web page being developed.

Image Retrieval Status Checking

To check the status of the image retrievals, the m_fAllLoaded flag is provided. This flag is updated as files—in this case, images—are downloaded. If the required images are not yet completely downloaded, the m_fAllLoaded flag is FALSE (0). When all the required files have completely downloaded successfully, the flag is then set to TRUE (1). This can be used as an error checking mechanism: If the point in the code at which the files should have been downloaded is reached and the m_fAllLoaded flag is still false, then an error during the download has occurred, and the user should be notified.

The first example examines the implementation of these functions and flags. Note that the examples in this chapter list only the main classes. The Visual J++ Applet Wizard also creates a *Frame.class file associated with the project workspace. No modifications were done to this file for these examples, but this class is required for the applet to function correctly.

Image Display

When the required images are downloaded for the applet/application, the images will be displayed accordingly. The following sections describe this process.

Establishing a Display Window

First, you must define a window where the image or any other screen content will be displayed. This is accomplished with a resize(x,y) command. Resize() will create an active window of horizontal size x pixels and vertical size y pixels for the applet/application. Any subsequent calls to put content on the display should be directed to this window. Any image larger than the defined size will not be displayed on the screen completely.

In addition, a Graphic Context must be referenced (denoted by the variable g in Listing 31.1). The *graphics context* is the space in which any commands to display something on the screen are performed. For example, if you wish to display text on the screen, g.drawImage(String,x,y) will be called to display the text String in the window defined at coordinate (x,y).

Listing 31.1. An image retrieval and display applet.

```java
import java.applet.*;
import java.awt.*;
import ImageSortFrame;

public class ImageSort extends Applet implements Runnable
{
    Thread      m_ImageSort = null;
    private Graphics m_Graphics;
    private Image    m_Images[];
    private int      m_nCurrImage;
    private int      m_nImgWidth  = 0;
    private int      m_nImgHeight = 0;
    private boolean  m_fAllLoaded = false;
    private final int NUM_IMAGES = 9;
    boolean m_fStandAlone = false;
    private String m_ImageFile[] = new String[NUM_IMAGES];
    private final String PARAM_ImageFile1 = "ImageFile1";
    private final String PARAM_ImageFile2 = "ImageFile2";
    private final String PARAM_ImageFile3 = "ImageFile3";
    private final String PARAM_ImageFile4 = "ImageFile4";
    private final String PARAM_ImageFile5 = "ImageFile5";
    private final String PARAM_ImageFile6 = "ImageFile6";
    private final String PARAM_ImageFile7 = "ImageFile7";
    private final String PARAM_ImageFile8 = "ImageFile8";
    private final String PARAM_ImageFile9 = "ImageFile9";

    String GetParameter(String strName, String args[])
    {
        if (args == null)
        {
            return getParameter(strName);
        }

        int    i;
        String strArg    = strName + "=";
        String strValue = null;

        for (i = 0; i < args.length; i++)
        {
            if (strArg.equalsIgnoreCase(args[i].substring(0, strArg.length())))
            {
                strValue= args[i].substring(strArg.length());
                if (strValue.startsWith("\""))
                {
```

```
                    strValue = strValue.substring(1);
                    if (strValue.endsWith("\""))
                        strValue = strValue.substring(0, strValue.length() - 1);
                }
            }
        }
        return strValue;
    }

    void GetParameters(String args[])
    {
        String param;

        param = GetParameter(PARAM_ImageFile1, args);
        if (param != null)
            m_ImageFile[0] = param;
        param = GetParameter(PARAM_ImageFile2, args);
        if (param != null)
            m_ImageFile[1] = param;
        param = GetParameter(PARAM_ImageFile3, args);
        if (param != null)
            m_ImageFile[2] = param;
        param = GetParameter(PARAM_ImageFile4, args);
        if (param != null)
            m_ImageFile[3] = param;
        param = GetParameter(PARAM_ImageFile5, args);
        if (param != null)
            m_ImageFile[4] = param;
        param = GetParameter(PARAM_ImageFile6, args);
        if (param != null)
            m_ImageFile[5] = param;
        param = GetParameter(PARAM_ImageFile7, args);
        if (param != null)
            m_ImageFile[6] = param;
        param = GetParameter(PARAM_ImageFile8, args);
        if (param != null)
            m_ImageFile[7] = param;
        param = GetParameter(PARAM_ImageFile9, args);
        if (param != null)
            m_ImageFile[8] = param;
    }

    public static void main(String args[])
    {
        ImageSortFrame frame = new ImageSortFrame("ImageSort");

        frame.show();
            frame.hide();
        frame.resize(frame.insets().left + frame.insets().right  + 320,
                    frame.insets().top  + frame.insets().bottom + 240);
        ImageSort applet_ImageSort = new ImageSort();
        frame.add("Center", applet_ImageSort);
        applet_ImageSort.m_fStandAlone = true;
        applet_ImageSort.GetParameters(args);
        applet_ImageSort.init();
```

continues

Listing 31.1. continued

```java
            applet_ImageSort.start();
                frame.show();
    }

    public ImageSort()
    {
    }

    public String getAppletInfo()
    {
        return "Name: ImageSort\r\n" +
                "Author: Hiro Yueh-Hung Ruo\r\n" +
                "Created with Microsoft Visual J++ Version 1.0";
    }

    public String[][] getParameterInfo()
    {
        String[][] info =
        {
            { PARAM_ImageFile1, "String", "Parameter description" },
            { PARAM_ImageFile2, "String", "Parameter description" },
            { PARAM_ImageFile3, "String", "Parameter description" },
            { PARAM_ImageFile4, "String", "Parameter description" },
            { PARAM_ImageFile5, "String", "Parameter description" },
            { PARAM_ImageFile6, "String", "Parameter description" },
            { PARAM_ImageFile7, "String", "Parameter description" },
            { PARAM_ImageFile8, "String", "Parameter description" },
            { PARAM_ImageFile9, "String", "Parameter description" },
        };
        return info;
    }

    public void init()
    {
    int i;

        if (!m_fStandAlone)
            GetParameters(null);
        resize(320, 240);
    }

    private void displayImage(Graphics g)
    {
        if (!m_fAllLoaded)
            return;

        g.drawImage(m_Images[m_nCurrImage],
            (size().width - m_nImgWidth[m_nCurrImage]) / 2,
            (size().height - m_nImgHeight[m_nCurrImage]) / 2, null);     }

    public void paint(Graphics g)
    {
        if (m_fAllLoaded)
        {
            Rectangle r = g.getClipRect();
```

```
                g.clearRect(r.x, r.y, r.width, r.height);
                displayImage(g);
        }
        else
                g.drawString("Loading images...", 10, 20);
}

public void start()
{
        if (m_ImageSort == null)
        {
                m_ImageSort = new Thread(this);
                m_ImageSort.start();
        }
}

public void stop()
{
        if (m_ImageSort != null)
        {
                m_ImageSort.stop();
                m_ImageSort = null;
        }
}

public void run()
{
        m_nCurrImage = 0;

                if (!m_fAllLoaded)
        {
         repaint();
         m_Graphics = getGraphics();
         m_Images   = new Image[NUM_IMAGES];

         MediaTracker tracker = new MediaTracker(this);
         String strImage;

                for (int i = 1; i <= NUM_IMAGES; i++)
                    {
                    strImage = "images/" + m_ImageFile[i-1];
                        if (m_fStandAlone)
                            m_Images[i-1] = Toolkit.getDefaultToolkit()
                                            .getImage(strImage);
                        else
                            m_Images[i-1] = getImage(getDocumentBase(), strImage);

                            tracker.addImage(m_Images[i-1], 0);
                    }
        try
        {
            tracker.waitForAll();
            m_fAllLoaded = !tracker.isErrorAny();
        }
        catch (InterruptedException e)
        {
        }
```

continues

Listing 31.1. continued

```
            if (!m_fAllLoaded)
            {
                stop();
                m_Graphics.drawString("Error loading images!", 10, 40);
                return;
            }

            for (int i = 0; i < NUM_IMAGES; i++)
            {
                m_nImgWidth[i]  = m_Images[i].getWidth(this);
                 m_nImgHeight[i] = m_Images[i].getHeight(this);
            }
        }
        repaint();

        while (true)
        {
            try
            {
                displayImage(m_Graphics);
                Thread.sleep(50);
            }
            catch (InterruptedException e)
            {
                stop();
            }
        }
    }
    public boolean mouseDown(Event evt, int x, int y)
    {
        repaint();
        m_nCurrImage++;
        if (m_nCurrImage == NUM_IMAGES)
            m_nCurrImage = 0;
        return true;
    }
}
```

Creating an Image Object

For each image to be displayed, there must be a corresponding Image object associated with it. This Image object is the reference to the image to be displayed. With each image is a corresponding Image Observer. This is the construct that contains the attributes of the image, including the Width, Height, and other properties of the image. The Image Observer is accessed to obtain the pixel size of the image after it is loaded.

Basic Java Multimedia Capabilities

CHAPTER 31

705

31

BASIC JAVA
MULTIMEDIA
CAPABILITIES

Putting the Image on the Screen

When the `Image` is defined by a reference to a certain image file, it can be displayed. The command to put the image on the screen in the active window of the applet/application is the `drawImage()` command. Its syntax follows:

```
drawImage(Image, x, y, backgroundColor, Image Observer);
```

The image object `Image` is displayed at coordinates `(x,y)` in reference to the active window from the upper-left corner. The optional parameter `backgroundColor` can be specified to indicate what color the transparent pixels in the image will display. The `Image Observer` is set to this to indicate the current image context. `DrawImage()` is called within the realm of the graphics context g.

Currently, standard Java will support the display of GIF and JPEG files. Files can be converted to these formats using a variety of graphics tools available today, such as PaintShop Pro or CorelDRAW!.

Note that in the following example, a function `paint()` is called. This command is a primitive for repainting the screen and is used when displaying images for animation. Also, note that a `Frame` is defined for the applet/application. This is to support running this program as a standalone application. This is how an image file can be displayed.

Now let's look at Listing 31.2. In this example of a program, a series of image files are displayed in the active window while giving the user control of the sequence of display. Using the `mouseDown()` primitive, you can allow the user to parse through an array of `Images`. This example shows a common method by which image files can be retrieved and displayed. In addition, it demonstrates using parameters to pass image filenames to the applet/application, so that any change in which image to display can be implemented simply by editing the HTML file's parameter entries. Listing 31.2 also sets the stage for animation. It constantly repaints the image, awaiting input from the user. This is the method in which a series of images can be displayed to form animation.

The HTML file in Listing 31.2 is used to run the applet/application of Listing 31.1. It passes the applet a set of image files. The images are displayed in the sequence from `ImageFile1` to `ImageFile9` and repeated.

Listing 31.2. An image retrieval and display HTML.

```
<html>
<head>
<title>ImageSort</title>
</head>
<body>
<hr>
```

continues

Listing 31.2. continued

```
<applet
    code=ImageSort.class
    id=ImageSort
    width=320
    height=240 >
    <param name=ImageFile1 value="img0001.gif">
    <param name=ImageFile2 value="img0002.gif">
    <param name=ImageFile3 value="img0003.gif">
    <param name=ImageFile4 value="img0004.gif">
    <param name=ImageFile5 value="img0005.gif">
    <param name=ImageFile6 value="img0006.gif">
    <param name=ImageFile7 value="img0007.gif">
    <param name=ImageFile8 value="img0008.gif">
    <param name=ImageFile9 value="img0009.gif">
</applet>
<hr>
<a href="ImageSort.java">The source.</a>
</body>
</html>
```

The resulting Web page displayed by accessing the above HTML file with a Web browser (in this case, Netscape 2.0) is shown in Figure 31.1. With each mouse click in the applet window, a different image as indexed by the HTML file is displayed. This is a simple application that allows you to present graphical content in a Web page using an applet/application.

FIGURE 31.1.
Image retrieval and display applet.

Basic Java Multimedia Capabilities

CHAPTER 31

707

31

BASIC JAVA
MULTIMEDIA
CAPABILITIES

With a few modifications to the above code ImageSort.java, you can display images in a more flexible manner. An example would be to pass an additional integer parameter to indicate how many parameters, or image filenames, will be passed to the applet. The applet then must be modified to accept this first parameter to determine the size of the parameter and Image arrays to create so that the files can then be retrieved properly.

> **NOTE**
>
> The image in Figure 31.1 and others used in this example were obtained from the LAL Aviation Archives located at http://lal.cs.byu.edu/planes/planes.html.

Now that you can retrieve images and display them, let's look at another aspect of multimedia—the audio content.

Audio Retrieval and Playback

The retrieval and playback of audio is quite a bit simpler than the image display support. There are three simple, common ways to retrieve, play, and manipulate audio clips.

Playing

Play() is the command used to play an audio clip once. This command is demonstrated in Listing 31.3. On each instance of this function in a program, the audio clip is started. The standalone syntax of play()follows:

```
play(URL, audiofile);
```

Listing 31.3. An audio retrieval and play applet.

```
import java.applet.*;
import java.awt.*;
import AudioPlayFrame;

public class AudioPlay extends Applet implements Runnable
{
    Thread      m_AudioPlay = null;
    boolean m_fStandAlone = false;
    private String m_AudioFile = "";
AudioClip backmusic;
    private final String PARAM_AudioFile = "AudioFile";
    String GetParameter(String strName, String args[])
    {
        if (args == null)
        {
```

continues

Listing 31.3. continued

```java
            return getParameter(strName);
        }
        int    i;
        String strArg    = strName + "=";
        String strValue = null;
        for (i = 0; i < args.length; i++)
        {
            if (strArg.equalsIgnoreCase(args[i].substring(0, strArg.length())))
            {
                strValue= args[i].substring(strArg.length());
                if (strValue.startsWith("\""))
                {
                    strValue = strValue.substring(1);
                    if (strValue.endsWith("\""))
                        strValue = strValue.substring(0, strValue.length() - 1);
                }
            }
        }
        return strValue;
    }
    void GetParameters(String args[])
    {
        String param;

        param = GetParameter(PARAM_AudioFile, args);
        if (param != null)
            m_AudioFile = param;
    }
    public static void main(String args[])
    {
        AudioPlayFrame frame = new AudioPlayFrame("AudioPlay");
        frame.show();
        frame.hide();
        frame.resize(frame.insets().left + frame.insets().right  + 320,
                     frame.insets().top  + frame.insets().bottom + 240);
        AudioPlay applet_AudioPlay = new AudioPlay();
        frame.add("Center", applet_AudioPlay);
        applet_AudioPlay.m_fStandAlone = true;
        applet_AudioPlay.GetParameters(args);
        applet_AudioPlay.init();
        applet_AudioPlay.start();
        frame.show();
    }
    public AudioPlay()
    {
    }
    public String getAppletInfo()
    {
        return "Name: AudioPlay\r\n" +
               "Author: Hiro Yueh-Hung Ruo\r\n" +
               "Created with Microsoft Visual J++ Version 1.0\r\n" +
               "Example for Chapter 31, Visual J++ Unleashed";
    }
    public String[][] getParameterInfo()
    {
```

```
        String[][] info =
        {
            { PARAM_AudioFile, "String", "Parameter description" },
        };
        return info;
    }
    public void init()
    {
        if (!m_fStandAlone)
            GetParameters(null);
        resize(320, 240);
            backmusic = getAudioClip(getDocumentBase(),"bomb.au");
    }
    public void destroy()
    {
    }
    public void paint(Graphics g)
    {
        g.drawString("Click in Window to Hear Sound", 10, 20);
    }
    public void start()
    {
        if (m_AudioPlay == null)
        {
            m_AudioPlay = new Thread(this);
            m_AudioPlay.start();
        }
            backmusic.loop();
    }
    public void stop()
    {
        if (m_AudioPlay != null)
        {
            m_AudioPlay.stop();
            m_AudioPlay = null;
        }
    }
    public void run()
    {
        while (true)
        {
            try
            {
                repaint();
                Thread.sleep(50);
            }
            catch (InterruptedException e)
            {
                stop();
            }
        }
    }
    public boolean mouseDown(Event evt, int x, int y)
    {
        play(getCodeBase(),m_AudioFile);
        return true;
    }
```

continues

Listing 31.3. continued

```
public boolean mouseUp(Event evt, int x, int y)
{
    return true;
}
}
```

A URL can be obtained by using either the getCodeBase() or getDocumentBase() functions, as described in the "Image Retrieval" and "Image Display" sections. Again, this is the simple method by which remote files, in this case audio files, can be indexed by an application.

Stopping

stop() is the command used to stop the play of an audio file that is currently playing. This function is useful to allow larger audio files to be loaded but stopped, depending on the context of the applet.

Repeating

The loop() command is used if an audio file is to be played continuously. When a loop() is used to initiate the play of an audio file, the file will play from the beginning once again after the file has completed playing. The standalone syntax of loop() follows:

```
loop(URL, audiofile);
```

An example of using this function is to play an audio file while a Web page is being used. Listing 31.3 demonstrates this by opening an audio file for play when it starts.

Single Audio Clips

When either loop() or play() is called, the audio file will download. This audio file is then loaded into memory, so that on future instances of calling this audio file, downloading is not necessary. A better method of retrieving audio clips is with the getAudioClip() command. If an object AudioClip is defined within a program, any calls of play(), stop(), or loop() to that object will result in manipulation of only that audio clip. The getAudioClip() is called as follows:

```
getAudioClip(audiofile);
```

Again, audiofile can be either a local file or a remote file accessed with a URL.

Multiple Audio Clips

Multiple audio clips can be played simultaneously. With each instance of play() or loop(), an audio file specified will be loaded (if it is not already) and played. While this audio file is

Basic Java Multimedia Capabilities

CHAPTER 31

711

31

BASIC JAVA
MULTIMEDIA
CAPABILITIES

playing, any additional instances of the same file or other audio files can also be called. The simultaneous play of audio clips is limited only by the audio subsystem in your PC.

Note also that the AU audio format is the default and only support. If a WAV or other audio file is to be played, it must be converted into the AU format. The sampling rate of the AU file supported should also be set to 8K. Tools to do this are available on the Web. Check out the Windows 95 Shareware Web site at `http://www.windows95.com/apps/sound.html` for some shareware audio utilities.

Listing 31.3 presents an applet that opens a window of 320×240 pixels in which bomb bursts, or any other audio file, are played continuously when the applet opens. This is accomplished by calling `getAudioClip()` in the `init()` function and `loop()` in `start()`. If the mouse button is clicked anywhere in the active window, the audio file specified by the parameter plays. This simple example illustrates the flexibility with which audio files can be used: either as background music or as a sensory indicator of an action taking place (in this case, the mouse click). This audio model is used in the next section to illustrate the integration of both audio and video content into an animated multimedia applet.

Animation

The sections "Image Retrieval" and "Image Display " demonstrate how a series of image files can be displayed with the user controlling progress with the mouse. The section "Audio Retrieval and Playback," shows how audio files can be loaded and played within the context of an applet. Let's now combine these two multimedia primitives into an animation applet/ application.

What Is It?

What is animation? It is simply a series of images presented in a continuous sequence. In cartoons, the pictures are not actually moving; rather, a large number of images closely related to the previous and following images are displayed at a high enough sequential speed that the result is the semblance of motion. Animation on a computer is similarly accomplished. *Animation* is simply one image after another displayed in sequence without any interaction from the user.

What gives us the pseudomotion in animation is the relationships of the images within the sequence. This can be accomplished either by creating distinct images frame by frame and selecting the sequence in which they will be displayed, or by manipulating a single image file. This section demonstrates the use of animation utilizing the methods previously demonstrated in image retrieval and display.

Integrating Audio

The integration of audio content enhances the animation with sound, giving an applet/application true multimedia presentation features. In the following example, audio file retrieval and playback are synchronized with the animation.

The secret to animation is the capability to constantly refresh the screen and display a new image; so you must find a way to display images one after the other without interruption. To accomplish this, all the images must be completely loaded to ensure that the image can be displayed using the `imageUpdate()` command. The `imageUpdate()` command will check if the image files are loaded before display, returning a `false` if the image files required are not loaded yet. This will ensure that the images are in memory and ready for use.

Painting and Repainting

In addition to ensuring that the images are available, there must be a method to refresh the screen so that any previous content is cleared off the screen. The `paint()` command is then required. This command is called on any `repaint()` call. The operations in a `paint()` call determine how the screen will be refreshed. In the following example, `paint()` will clear the active window with the selected background color and repaint the current image. Therefore, on any `repaint()` issued, the screen is cleared back to just the background color, and the current image being displayed is repainted, giving the display a clean image.

All that needs to be done now is to create the sequence of animation.

First, Listing 31.4 "slides" the image file display from the left side of the active window to the center of the screen. This is accomplished by dynamically changing the location at which the image file is displayed. Recall from the previous sections that `drawImage()` is passed the coordinates `(x,y)`. Changing these values in an organized, premeditated fashion will allow you to manipulate where the image shows on the screen. In this case, x is increased from `0` to the center value (calculated with the `Image` attribute `Width` in relation to the active window size) while keeping y constant. This is a simple example of how to animate objects by manipulating a single image file.

Next, Listing 31.4 creates animation by displaying several images in a predetermined sequence with predetermined timing. The variable `m_ImageFlag` determines this sequence. In the example, the images are displayed according to the index of this array. The program sequentially indexes each `m_ImageFlag` array item to determine which of the `ImageFiles` to display. In this sequence, the animation is created because the images are related to the previous and following images.

To add audio content, we used the same method as described in the "Audio Retrieval and Playback" section. However, in this case, the audio initiation must be synchronized to the images being displayed. This is done by calling `play()` at the appropriate location in the program. It is

Basic Java Multimedia Capabilities

CHAPTER 31

713

31

BASIC JAVA
MULTIMEDIA
CAPABILITIES

predetermined which image file changes will result in an animation action that will have an audio content associated with it. On these change sequences, `play()` is called and the `AudioClip` indexed. To properly time the audio end to the next animation sequences, additional still frames are inserted until the audio file has completed playing. This will require some experimentation. A better method would be to use shorter `AudioClips` and trigger the playback within the code. In this example, the `bomb.au` file can be broken into two pieces, and the actual explosion can be played back using `play()` at the appropriate indexed image of `m_ImageFlag`.

Listing 31.4. An animation applet.

```java
import java.applet.*;
import java.awt.*;
import java.awt.image.*;
import AnimationFrame;

public class Animation extends Applet implements Runnable
{
    Thread      m_Animation = null;
    private Graphics m_Graphics;
    private Image     m_Images[];
    private int       m_nCurrImage;
    private boolean   m_fAllLoaded = false;
    private final int NUM_IMAGES = 8;
    private final int NUM_AUDIO = 2;
    private final int NUM_ITERATION = 80;
    private int       m_nImgWidth[]  = new int[NUM_IMAGES];
    private int       m_nImgHeight[] = new int[NUM_IMAGES];
    private AudioClip sound1;
    private AudioClip sound2;
    private boolean StopFlag;
    boolean m_fStandAlone = false;
    private String m_ImageFile[] = new String[NUM_IMAGES];
    private String m_AudioFile[] = new String[NUM_AUDIO];
    private int m_ImageFlag[] = {0,1,2,1,2,1,2,1,2,1,2,0,0,0,0,0,0,0,3,4,5,
                                 0,0,0,0,0,0,0,0,0,0,0,0,0,0,0,0,0,0,0,0,0,0,
                                 0,0,0,0,0,0,0,0,0,0,0,0,0,0,0,0,0,6,7,6,7,
                                 6,7,6,7,6,7,6,7,6,7,6,7,0,0};

private final String PARAM_AudioFile1 = "AudioFile1";
    private final String PARAM_AudioFile2 = "AudioFile2";
    private final String PARAM_ImageFile1 = "ImageFile1";
    private final String PARAM_ImageFile2 = "ImageFile2";
    private final String PARAM_ImageFile3 = "ImageFile3";
    private final String PARAM_ImageFile4 = "ImageFile4";
    private final String PARAM_ImageFile5 = "ImageFile5";
    private final String PARAM_ImageFile6 = "ImageFile6";
    private final String PARAM_ImageFile7 = "ImageFile7";
    private final String PARAM_ImageFile8 = "ImageFile8";

    String GetParameter(String strName, String args[])
    {
        if (args == null)
        {
```

continues

Listing 31.4. continued

```
            return getParameter(strName);
        }
        int     i;
        String strArg    = strName + "=";
        String strValue = null;

        for (i = 0; i < args.length; i++)
        {
            if (strArg.equalsIgnoreCase(args[i].substring(0, strArg.length())))
            {
                strValue= args[i].substring(strArg.length());
                if (strValue.startsWith("\""))
                {
                    strValue = strValue.substring(1);
                    if (strValue.endsWith("\""))
                        strValue = strValue.substring(0, strValue.length() - 1);
                }
            }
        }
        return strValue;
    }
    void GetParameters(String args[])
    {
        String param;

        param = GetParameter(PARAM_AudioFile1, args);
        if (param != null)
            m_AudioFile[0] = param;
        param = GetParameter(PARAM_AudioFile2, args);
        if (param != null)
            m_AudioFile[1] = param;
        param = GetParameter(PARAM_ImageFile1, args);
        if (param != null)
            m_ImageFile[0] = param;
        param = GetParameter(PARAM_ImageFile2, args);
        if (param != null)
            m_ImageFile[1] = param;
        param = GetParameter(PARAM_ImageFile3, args);
        if (param != null)
            m_ImageFile[2] = param;
        param = GetParameter(PARAM_ImageFile4, args);
        if (param != null)
            m_ImageFile[3] = param;
        param = GetParameter(PARAM_ImageFile5, args);
        if (param != null)
            m_ImageFile[4] = param;
        param = GetParameter(PARAM_ImageFile6, args);
        if (param != null)
            m_ImageFile[5] = param;
        param = GetParameter(PARAM_ImageFile7, args);
        if (param != null)
            m_ImageFile[6] = param;
        param = GetParameter(PARAM_ImageFile8, args);
        if (param != null)
            m_ImageFile[7] = param;
    }
```

```java
public static void main(String args[])
{
    AnimationFrame frame = new AnimationFrame("Animation");
    frame.show();
        frame.hide();
    frame.resize(frame.insets().left + frame.insets().right  + 320,
                 frame.insets().top  + frame.insets().bottom + 240);
    Animation applet_Animation = new Animation();
    frame.add("Center", applet_Animation);
    applet_Animation.m_fStandAlone = true;
    applet_Animation.GetParameters(args);
    applet_Animation.init();
    applet_Animation.start();
        frame.show();
}
public Animation()
{
}
public String getAppletInfo()
{
    return "Name: Animation\r\n" +
           "Author: Hiro Yueh-Hung Ruo\r\n" +
           "Created with Microsoft Visual J++ Version 1.0";
}
public String[][] getParameterInfo()
{
    String[][] info =
    {
        { PARAM_AudioFile1, "String", "Parameter description" },
        { PARAM_AudioFile2, "String", "Parameter description" },
        { PARAM_ImageFile1, "String", "Parameter description" },
        { PARAM_ImageFile2, "String", "Parameter description" },
        { PARAM_ImageFile3, "String", "Parameter description" },
        { PARAM_ImageFile4, "String", "Parameter description" },
        { PARAM_ImageFile5, "String", "Parameter description" },
        { PARAM_ImageFile6, "String", "Parameter description" },
        { PARAM_ImageFile7, "String", "Parameter description" },
        { PARAM_ImageFile8, "String", "Parameter description" },
    };
    return info;
}
public void init()
{
int i;

    if (!m_fStandAlone)
        GetParameters(null);
    resize(320, 240);
    sound1 = getAudioClip(getDocumentBase(),m_AudioFile[0]);
    sound2 = getAudioClip(getDocumentBase(),m_AudioFile[1]);
    StopFlag = true;
}
public void destroy()
{
}
public boolean imageUpdate(Image img, int flags, int x, int y, int w, int h)
{
```

continues

Listing 31.4. continued

```
            if (m_fAllLoaded)
                return false;
            if ((flags & ALLBITS) == 0)
                return true;
            if (++m_nCurrImage == NUM_IMAGES)
            {
                m_nCurrImage = 0;
                m_fAllLoaded = true;
            }
            return false;
        }
private void displayImage(Graphics g)
    {
            if (!m_fAllLoaded)
                return;
            g.drawImage(m_Images[m_ImageFlag[m_nCurrImage]],
                    (size().width - m_nImgWidth[m_ImageFlag[m_nCurrImage]]) / 2,
(size().height - m_nImgHeight[m_ImageFlag[m_nCurrImage]]) / 2,
 null);
    }
private void displayImage2(Graphics g, int x)
{
    if (!m_fAllLoaded)
        return;
    g.drawImage(m_Images[m_ImageFlag[m_nCurrImage]],
        x, (size().height - m_nImgHeight[m_ImageFlag[m_nCurrImage]]) / 2, null);
}
public void paint(Graphics g)
    {
            if (m_fAllLoaded)
            {
                Rectangle r = g.getClipRect();

                g.clearRect(r.x, r.y, r.width, r.height);
                displayImage(g);
            }
            else
                g.drawString("Loading images...", 10, 20);
    }
    public void start()
    {
        if (m_Animation == null)
        {
            m_Animation = new Thread(this);
            m_Animation.start();
        }
    }
    public void stop()
    {
        if (m_Animation != null)
        {
            m_Animation.stop();
            m_Animation = null;
        }
    }
```

```java
public void run()
{
    m_nCurrImage = 0;
        if (!m_fAllLoaded)
    {
            repaint();
            m_Graphics = getGraphics();
            m_Images   = new Image[NUM_IMAGES];
            MediaTracker tracker = new MediaTracker(this);
            String strImage;

        for (int i = 1; i <= NUM_IMAGES; i++)
            {
            strImage = "images/" + m_ImageFile[i-1];
                if (m_fStandAlone)
                    m_Images[i-1] = Toolkit.getDefaultToolkit()
                                    .getImage(strImage);
                else
                    m_Images[i-1] = getImage(getDocumentBase(), strImage);
                    tracker.addImage(m_Images[i-1], 0);
        }
        try
        {
            tracker.waitForAll();
            m_fAllLoaded = !tracker.isErrorAny();
        }
        catch (InterruptedException e)
        {
        }
        if (!m_fAllLoaded)
        {
            stop();
            m_Graphics.drawString("Error loading images!", 10, 40);
            return;
        }
        for (int i = 0; i < NUM_IMAGES; i++)
        {
            m_nImgWidth[i]  = m_Images[i].getWidth(this);
             m_nImgHeight[i] = m_Images[i].getHeight(this);
        }
    }
    repaint();
    for (int i=32; i>0; i—)
    {
        displayImage2(m_Graphics,
            (size().width - m_nImgWidth[m_ImageFlag[m_nCurrImage]])-(10*i));
    }
    repaint();
    while (StopFlag)
    {
        try
        {
            m_nCurrImage++;
            if (m_nCurrImage == NUM_ITERATION)
                m_nCurrImage = 0;
            displayImage(m_Graphics);
```

continues

Listing 31.4. continued

```
            if ((m_nCurrImage==1) || (m_nCurrImage==3) || (m_nCurrImage==5))
                sound1.play();
            if (m_nCurrImage==14)
                sound2.play();
            Thread.sleep(50);
        }
        catch (InterruptedException e)
        {
            stop();
        }
    }
}
public boolean mouseDown(Event evt, int x, int y)
{
    sound1.stop();
    sound2.stop();
    StopFlag = false;
    return true;
}
}
```

The HTML file described in Listing 31.5 is used by the selected Web browser (in this case, Netscape 2.0) to run the applet. It again passes the filenames of the audio and image files to the applet as parameters, making this program flexible enough that other images and audio files can also be used to create the animation. With some minor changes to the code, the animation sequence can also be passed through this method. This additional implementation can make this a generic animation program, in which the content developer can select the sequence and audio and image used without recompiling the code. Listing 31.5 shows the HTML file created that can be used to run the applet of Listing 31.4 in a Web page.

Listing 31.5. An animation applet HTML.

```
<html>
<head>
<title>Animation</title>
</head>
<body>
<hr>
<applet
    code=Animation.class
    id=Animation
    width=320
    height=240 >
    <param name=AudioFile1 value="Audio/gun-shot.au">
    <param name=AudioFile2 value="Audio/bomb.au">
    <param name=ImageFile1 value="img0001.gif">
```

Basic Java Multimedia Capabilities

CHAPTER 31

719

31

BASIC JAVA
MULTIMEDIA
CAPABILITIES

```
        <param name=ImageFile2 value="img0002.gif">
        <param name=ImageFile3 value="img0003.gif">
        <param name=ImageFile4 value="img0004.gif">
        <param name=ImageFile5 value="img0005.gif">
        <param name=ImageFile6 value="img0006.gif">
        <param name=ImageFile7 value="img0007.gif">
        <param name=ImageFile8 value="img0008.gif">
</applet>
<hr>
<a href="Animation.java">The source.</a>
</body>
</html>
```

Figure 31.2 illustrates the animation accomplished in the sample program by manipulating the single image file. As you can see, the image appears to "slide" onto the screen.

FIGURE 31.2.

*Animation with a
single image file.*

Figure 31.3 illustrates the animation of the sample program by sequentially displaying several related image files. Although not shown here, with certain frames (the second image with the firing of the gun, and the third and fourth frames of dropping and exploding the bomb), audio files are played and synchronized.

FIGURE **31.3.**
*Animation with
multiple image files.*

Summary

The use of image files and audio files can result in a powerful applet to be used in a Web page. With animation, or even simply displaying image files or playing back audio files, you can liven up the content of your Web page and help make it more noticeable. These techniques can be easily applied to a business environment, where advertisements can be sequentially displayed, potential customers can parse through a series of photos of the product being marketed, or "welcome" messages by the company president can be played. Or you can use these multimedia techniques to make your own personal Web page that much cooler.

Extending Multimedia Capabilities Through ActiveX

by Hiro Ruo

IN THIS CHAPTER

This chapter presents the multimedia capabilities that currently exist in the form of ActiveX controls and discusses how they can be used in conjunction with Visual J++.

ActiveX

Chapter 31, "Basic Java Multimedia Capabilities," investigates how multimedia content can be added to a Java applet/application using the built-in support for multimedia in the Java language and Visual J++. This is a powerful and flexible capability of Java that can greatly enhance the appeal and content of Web pages. However, there are plenty of other forms of multimedia available on the Web today.

Although Java in its original form supported multiple platforms transparently, it could not natively support the multiple formats of multimedia written in many languages. Implementing these contents still depended on having the proper application and browser extensions installed locally on the computer. If a computer were to support every content format, it would become a tangled mess of software from the many different vendors of these formats.

This problem is addressed with ActiveX extensions defined by Microsoft Corporation. ActiveX is a platform definition based on COM. (Refer to Part III, "The Foundation for Visual J++: The Component Object Model," for more information about COM.) ActiveX controls are COM objects, or a form of object linking and embedding (OLE) objects. This chapter investigates how ActiveX and Java can work hand in hand, with the help of Visual J++. (For more information about ActiveX and Microsoft's strategy for the Internet, see Chapter 19, "Extending Java Using ActiveX.")

The OLE Object Viewer

Visual J++ provides several tools and facilities to help with the integration of ActiveX controls into a Java project. One of these is the OLE Object Viewer.

The OLE Object Viewer provides a simple interface that allows the Visual J++ developer to parse the OLE objects , including ActiveX controls, that are available for implementation into a Java program. The OLE Object Viewer uses information stored in the registry of the operating system to give you a thorough understanding of all the OLE objects that are enabled in your system and the interfaces to each object. It also allows you to verify the behavior of the objects. The Object Viewer provides the following information:

- A list of OLE objects installed
- Interfaces supported by the objects
- Whether the object is an inproc or local server or handler
- The object's registry entries

- Status of object support of the listed interface
- Information available through the listed interfaces
- Version of the OLE dynamic link libraries
- Location of the OLE dynamic link libraries
- The Type Library export functions, subroutines, constants, and variables

The OLE Object Viewer is started by selecting OLE Object View from the Tools menu in Visual J++. Figure 32.1 shows the OLE Object View window.

FIGURE 32.1.

The OLE Object View window.

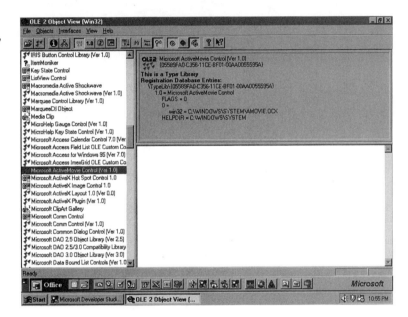

You can see a list of objects in the Object window on the left. Note in Figure 32.1 that the selected object is an ActiveMovie control. The registered interfaces of the object are listed in the Interface window on the bottom right. Additional information about the object is detailed in the upper-right window. The icons preceding the object name indicate the type of object; the ActiveMovie control icon indicates that it is an OLE object. Figure 32.2 is an index to the types of objects and the icons displayed in the Object Viewer.

You can use this tool and the interface information when implementing ActiveX controls to help decide which ActiveX controls can be embedded and how to integrate the object into the program.

Figure 32.2.

OLE object types.

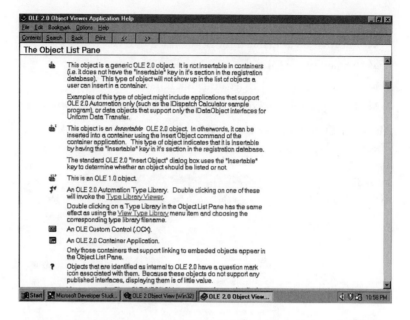

Clicking the type definition within the Object Viewer lists the names of all the types defined for this object. Selecting one of these will display an object and all of its pertinent interface function information. Figure 32.3 illustrates the information displayed by the Type Interface Viewer for `IActiveMovie`. The information displayed is the function information and format for the `FileName` function for `IActiveMovie` objects.

Figure 32.3.

The Type Interface Viewer.

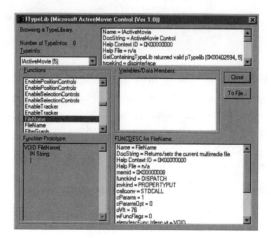

Selecting `FileName()`, as shown in Figure 32.3, illustrates the use of the function `FileName` in a Java program. This function is used to set the multimedia file to be played in an `IActiveMovie` object within a Java applet. Similarly, each function for `IActiveMovie` can be parsed in the Functions box, and the description viewed in the FUNCDESC box. These functions are used and implemented in an example in this chapter. The information provided by this interface will allow the correct reuse of the object selected.

The To File... button can be selected to save the object interface and function information into a text file so that it can be used as a ready reference.

As you can see, the OLE Object Viewer is a powerful tool that allows you to use existing objects and their interfaces to embed these objects into a Java program. The interfaces and functions associated with these objects can be readily looked up and used within any program.

Customizing ActiveX Controls

Another facility that Visual J++ provides is an interface to customize the objects and components of ActiveX and other COM objects: the Component Gallery.

The Component Gallery allows you to get a iconized list of available components in the system, including any programs that were written using Visual J++. ActiveX controls installed in the system are such reusable components that can be manipulated and parsed using the Component Gallery. The Component Gallery is started by selecting Component from the Insert menu. Figure 32.4 shows the Component Gallery window.

FIGURE 32.4.

The Component Gallery window.

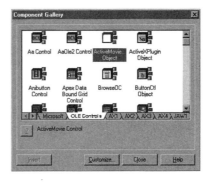

The Component Gallery lists all available categories, including Microsoft-defined components, OLE controls (including ActiveX components), and separate tabs for folders containing components of previously written Visual J++ projects. Wherever available, there is also a Help button that is enabled to provide more information about the component selected.

Clicking on the Customize button will open the Customize Component Gallery dialog box. This tool provides an interface for you to create new categories, move components between categories, add components to a category, and delete components or categories. This functionality gives you flexibility to define new categories of components for reuse in future projects. Figure 32.5 illustrates the Customize Component Gallery dialog box.

FIGURE 32.5.

The Customize Component Gallery dialog box.

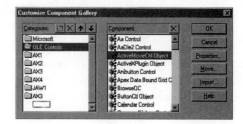

Clicking on the Properties button will display general information about the component selected. The Move option allows you to move the component selected to a different category. The Import option allows you to add an external component to the category selected.

The Java Type Library Wizard

To allow a Java program to refer to a COM object, such as an ActiveX control, Visual J++ provides the Java Type Library Wizard. This makes ActiveX controls available from any Java program. This is how multimedia content in the form of ActiveX controls can be embedded in a program developed using Visual J++.

Type libraries are defined by COM to store information, including the classes and interfaces about the COM entity. This chapter demonstrates an application in which a multimedia ActiveX control is embedded into a Java program using the Type Library Wizard in Visual J++.

First, you will create a simple applet using the Java Applet Wizard, as described in Chapter 11, "Building a Simple Java Applet with Visual J++." The template program created, AX2, will be both an applet and an application so that the Java Viewer (JVIEW) can be used. At the writing of this chapter, Visual J++ is still in beta release and does not fully support integration of all COM types. Future releases of Visual J++ will have this function enabled. Therefore, this example is a simple applet with only the addition of the ActiveX content.

After creating the starting template code, choose the Java Type Library Wizard from the Tools menu of the Microsoft Developer Studio, as shown in Figure 32.6.

FIGURE 32.6.

The Java Type Library Wizard.

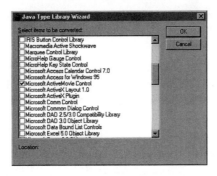

From the Java Type Library Wizard, select the item to be implemented in the Java program—in this case, an ActiveMovie control.

When you click on OK, the output window will display the `import` statement that should be used to refer to the selected item and its interfaces. For this example, the `import` statement looks like this:

```
import amovie.*;
```

Note that the `import` statement is not absolutely required. Any class that must be referenced within the program can be referenced with the complete name of the class. The `import` statement is used to facilitate easier references using the short name.

The information provided by the Object Viewer, as described in the "OLE Object Viewer" section, can now be used to correctly utilize the functionality of this object as embedded in this example Java program.

First, a new instance of this `IActiveMovie` object must be defined. The following line of code is added to perform this task:

```
IActiveMovie AXMovie = new ActiveMovie();
```

Any future references to interfaces and functions associated with the ActiveMovie object can now be done through `AXMovie`. For this example using the ActiveMovie control, some basic settings are required. The filename of the video clip to be played must be specified by inserting the following statement:

```
AXMovie.putFileName("AX1.mov");
```

Note that calling the function `FileName` is performed with the prefix `put`. As described in the "OLE Object Viewer" section, the function is of invocation type `PROPERTYPUT`. This means the function is called as a sub of `AXMovie`, or any other name used to reference the ActiveMovie object, with a `put`.

In addition, the window size of the video playback is set as follows:

```
AXMovie.putMovieWindowSize(0);
```

The size settings are described by the WindowSizeConstant() type found when viewing the ActiveMovie object with the OLE Object Viewer. The parameter to the MovieWindowSize() function is a USERDEFINED parameter. The values that are accepted are as follows:

Function	Value
amvOriginalSize (int)	= 0
amvDoubleOriginalSize (int)	= 1
amvOneSixteenthScreen (int)	= 2
amvOneFourthScreen (int)	= 3
amvOneHalfScreen (int)	= 4
amvMaximized (int)	= 5

These values can be defined as constants in the Java program example. I have elected to set the value with an integer only.

You can invoke the command Run() to play back the selected video clip. This is accomplished simply by including the following statement in the program source code:

```
AXMovie.Run();
```

This is a very simple example that does not take full advantage of all the controls available with this ActiveX control. The source code in Listing 32.1 can now be compiled as a complete Java applet/application that embeds the ActiveX control ActiveMovie.

Listing 32.1. The ActiveMovie control.

```java
import java.applet.*;
import java.awt.*;
import AX2Frame;
import amovie.*;

public class AX2 extends Applet implements Runnable
{
    Thread      m_AX2 = null;
    IActiveMovie AXMovie = new ActiveMovie();
    private Graphics m_Graphics;
    boolean m_fStandAlone = false;

    public static void main(String args[])
    {
        AX2Frame frame = new AX2Frame("AX2");
        frame.show();
                frame.hide();
        frame.resize(frame.insets().left + frame.insets().right  + 320,
                    frame.insets().top  + frame.insets().bottom + 240);
```

```
        AX2 applet_AX2 = new AX2();
        frame.add("Center", applet_AX2);
        applet_AX2.m_fStandAlone = true;
        applet_AX2.init();
        applet_AX2.start();
            frame.show();
    }

    public AX2()
    {
    }

    public String getAppletInfo()
    {
        return "Name: AX2\r\n" +
               "Author: Hiro Yueh-Hung Ruo\r\n" +
               "Created with Microsoft Visual J++ Version 1.0";
    }


    public void init()
    {
        resize(320,240);
        AXMovie.putFileName("AX1.mov");
        AXMovie.putMovieWindowSize(0);
    }

    public void destroy()
    {
    }

    private void displayImage(Graphics g)
    {
    }

    public void paint(Graphics g)
    {
    }

    public void start()
    {
        if (m_AX2 == null)
        {
            m_AX2 = new Thread(this);
            m_AX2.start();
        }
    }

    public void stop()
    {
        if (m_AX2 != null)
        {
            m_AX2.stop();
            m_AX2 = null;
        }
    }
```

continues

Listing 32.1. continued

```
public void run()
{
        m_Graphics = getGraphics();
        MediaTracker tracker = new MediaTracker(this);
        String strImage;

        try
        {
            AXMovie.Run();
            Thread.sleep(50);
        }
        catch (InterruptedException e)
        {
            stop();
        }
}

public boolean mouseDown(Event evt, int x, int y)
{
    AXMovie.Pause();
    return true;
}
}
```

The resulting applet/application opens a frame and plays the selected Quicktime for Windows video clip AX1.MOV (other video formats are also supported). Again, the example uses the JVIEW.EXE real-mode Java viewer included with the Java Developer's Kit to play the video clip. Because the beta release of Visual J++ does not fully support implementation of COM objects, a browser could not be used to play back the video clip. However, the functionality of the integration of ActiveMovie can be demonstrated with JVIEW. The resulting window of the applet is shown in Figure 32.7.

FIGURE 32.7.

An AX2 *program example with ActiveMovie.*

The ActiveMovie control provides an extensive interface to control the movie content to be played back. These are not used in the example for simplicity's sake, but are shown in Listing 32.2.

Listing 32.2. ActiveMovie control functions.

```
QueryInterface (ByRef riid As Variant, ByRef ppvObj As Variant)
AddRef ()
Release ()
GetTypeInfoCount (ByRef pctinfo As Variant)
GetTypeInfo (ByVal itinfo As UINT, ByVal lcid As ULONG, ByRef pptinfo As Variant)
GetIDsOfNames (ByRef riid As Variant, ByRef rgszNames As Variant,
               ByVal cNames As UINT, ByVal lcid As ULONG,
               ByRef rgdispid As Variant)
Invoke (ByVal dispidMember As Long, ByRef riid As Variant,
        ByVal lcid As ULONG, ByVal wFlags As USHORT,
        ByRef pdispparams As Variant, ByRef pvarResult As Variant,
        ByRef pexcepinfo As Variant, ByRef puArgErr As Variant)
AboutBox ()
Run ()
Pause ()
Stop ()
ImageSourceWidth ()
ImageSourceHeight ()
Author ()
Title ()
Description ()
FileName ()
FileName (ByVal  String)
Duration ()
CurrentPosition ()
CurrentPosition (ByVal  Double)
PlayCount ()
PlayCount (ByVal  Long)
SelectionStart ()
SelectionStart (ByVal  Double)
SelectionEnd ()
SelectionEnd (ByVal  Double)
CurrentState ()
Rate ()
Rate (ByVal  Double)
Volume ()
Volume (ByVal  Long)
Balance ()
Balance (ByVal  Long)
EnableContextMenu ()
EnableContextMenu (ByVal  Boolean)
ShowDisplay ()
ShowDisplay (ByVal  Boolean)
ShowControls ()
ShowControls (ByVal  Boolean)
ShowPositionControls ()
ShowPositionControls (ByVal  Boolean)
ShowSelectionControls ()
ShowSelectionControls (ByVal  Boolean)
ShowTracker ()
ShowTracker (ByVal  Boolean)
EnablePositionControls ()
EnablePositionControls (ByVal  Boolean)
EnableSelectionControls ()
EnableSelectionControls (ByVal  Boolean)
```

32

MULTIMEDIA
CAPABILITIES AND
ACTIVEX

continues

Listing 32.2. continued

```
EnableTracker ()
EnableTracker (ByVal  Boolean)
AllowHideDisplay ()
AllowHideDisplay (ByVal  Boolean)
AllowHideControls ()
AllowHideControls (ByVal  Boolean)
DisplayMode ()
DisplayMode (ByVal  USERDEFINED)
AllowChangeDisplayMode ()
FilterGraph ()
FilterGraph (ByVal  LPUNKNOWN)
FilterGraphDispatch ()
DisplayForeColor ()
DisplayForeColor (ByVal  USERDEFINED)
DisplayBackColor ()
DisplayBackColor (ByVal  USERDEFINED)
MovieWindowSize (ByVal  USERDEFINED)
FullScreenMode ()
FullScreenMode (ByVal  Boolean)
AutoStart ()
AutoStart (ByVal  Boolean)
AutoRewind ()
AutoRewind (ByVal  Boolean)
hWnd ()
Appearance ()
Appearance (ByVal  USERDEFINED)
BorderStyle ()
BorderStyle (ByVal  USERDEFINED)
Enabled ()
Enabled (ByVal  Boolean)
Info ()
```

Note that there are several functions with duplicate names. They are actually not the same functions, however, because they are called by different methods. As previously described, `FileName` is called with put to set the filename of the video clip file. Calling `FileName` with get instead retrieves the filename of the video file being played.

These functions can be implemented in your Java program in conjunction with the ActiveMovie control to provide more flexibility and capabilities to the interface to the ActiveX content. This opens the door for truly interactive ActiveX content on a Web page using Java.

The Dialog Box Editor

Another simple method for integrating ActiveX content, or any other OLE control objects, into a Web page using Java is with the Dialog box editor provided with Visual J++. Similar to those in Visual Basic, this drag-and-drop development tool allows you to graphically determine the type and location of the controls to implement into the program.

The Dialog box editor is invoked by selecting Resources from the Insert menu item, as shown in Figure 32.8.

FIGURE 32.8.

Inserting resources.

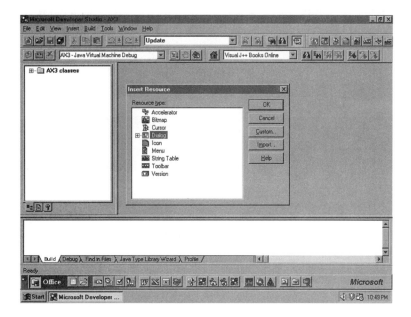

Selecting Dialog in this dialog box will open the Dialog box editor of Visual J++, as shown in Figure 32.9.

FIGURE 32.9.

The Dialog box editor.

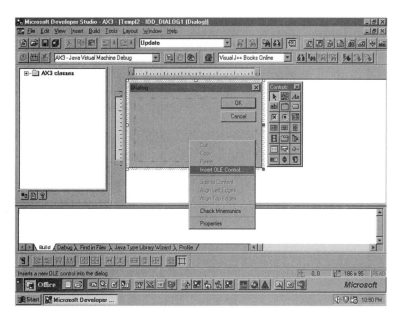

The default dialog box created contains two buttons: OK and Cancel. The dialog box is stretchable, allowing you to determine the size of the window to be used in the program.

To the right of the dialog box is the Control toolbox. This toolbox allows you to drag-and-drop any of a set of controls, including radio buttons, movie clips, and images, onto the dialog box's working window.

A right-click in the working area of the dialog box will bring up a menu, as illustrated in Figure 32.9. Selecting Insert OLE Control will bring up the window shown in Figure 32.10.

Figure 32.10.

The OLE Object Selector window.

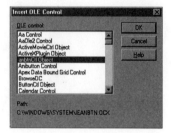

A list of all available OLE control objects is displayed in a scroll box. Highlighting any of these items will display the path to the OLE control object in the PATH field at the bottom of the OLE Object Selector dialog box. In Figure 32.10, the Microsoft Internet Explorer Animated Button Object is selected. The OLE control file is IEANBTN.OCX, installed in the default Windows 95 directory.

Selecting the OK button embeds a workspace within the dialog box being developed. This will provide the infrastructure necessary to customize the ActiveX, or other OLE objects, in the Java program. The working window of the dialog box appears as shown in Figure 32.11. The working space of the selected OLE object is displayed with a text description of the object inserted.

The ActiveX object, Microsoft Internet Explorer Animated Button object, is now implemented in the dialog box being created. Note the lack of actual content of the working space of the OLE control object. This is because the object is not completely defined yet. In this example, the animated button does not have any animation or graphical content associated with it.

Following the previously listed steps allows you to use a graphical interface to easily embed any available OLE control object into a project under development. This dialog box can now be included in a Java application and enabled with some minor changes to the resulting source code.

While in the Dialog box editor, you can further customize the embedded object. Right-clicking within the workspace of the embedded object and selecting the Properties item will result in the window shown in Figure 32.12.

FIGURE 32.11.
*ActiveX object
embedding.*

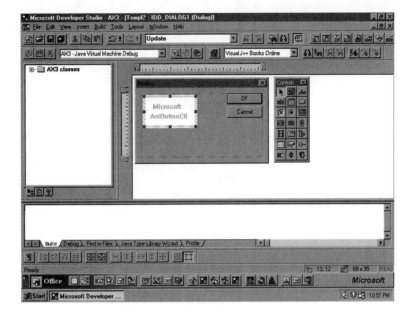

FIGURE 32.12.
*ActiveX object
properties.*

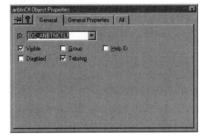

The Object Properties window allows you to configure certain default options of the object. For the animated button example, the object ID and options relating to the display of the button on the screen are available for change. Figure 32.12 shows the default options for the animated button.

Now save the dialog box entry. Closing the working window of the Dialog Box editor in Visual J++ (or manually selecting the Save or Save As option in the File menu) will allow you to custom name the dialog box template.

Next, you must create the Java files associated with this dialog box using the Java Resource Wizard. The Java Resource Wizard (see Figure 32.13) is run by selecting Java Resource Wizard from the Tools menu.

FIGURE 32.13.

The Java Resource Wizard.

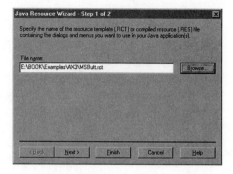

The Resource File created with the Dialog Box editor is entered into the File name box in Step 1 of the Java Resource Wizard. Note that the Resource File was saved in the directory of the Java project in which the dialog box will be added.

Selecting Next completes the creation of the source code for the dialog box. If a resource has a duplicate name, there will be an additional step here that allows you to rename the resource. Figure 32.14 illustrates the completion of the Java Resource Wizard.

FIGURE 32.14.

The dialog box created.

In the final window of the Java Resource Wizard, the files that were made as a result of creating the dialog box are listed. These files can now be implemented into a Java project to include the dialog box in the program.

The dialog box and its associated source code are implemented into the Java project as follows. First, you must select File in Project from the Insert menu. Select the IDD_DIALOG2 file to be added to the Java project.

Next, lines of code similar to those added for the previous example of implementing an ActiveMovie object must be added to this Java program. Instead of importing the amovie class, you will import the IDD_DIALOG2 class. This will allow simple references to the interfaces of the dialog box. The lines of code are as follows:

```
import IDD_DIALOG2;
...
IDD_DIALOG2 Abutt;
...
init() {
Abutt = new IDD_DIALOG2(this);
```

Because you used the Java Resource Wizard to create the `IDD_DIALOG2` class, the controls associated with the dialog box can be created with the `CreateControls()` command, like this:

```
Abutt.CreateControls();
```

If a `resize()` command is included in the `init()` function, it must be removed.

Now add the interfaces and functions to the Microsoft Internet Explorer Animated Button to the source code within the dialog box Java files, as described in the ActiveMovie example.

Additional ActiveX Content

In addition to the ActiveMovie and Animated Button ActiveX objects, there are many more that you can use in your Java programs. These include not only those developed by Microsoft, but also a plethora of options from other companies. Table 32.1 is just a sample of such controls.

Table 32.1. ActiveX control providers.

Company	ActiveX Controls
Adobe Systems, Inc.	Acrobat Control for ActiveX
Black Diamond Consulting, Inc.	Surround Video
Brilliance Labs, Inc.	CyberGO ActiveX Control
Citrix Systems, Inc.	Citrix WinFrame ICA Control
Farallon Communications, Inc.	Look@Me
Macromedia	Shockwave ActiveX Control
Microsoft	Animated Button
	ActiveMovie
	Chart
	Gradient
	Label
	Marquee
	Menu
	Popup Menu
	Popup Window
	Preloader
	Stock Ticker

continues

Table 32.1. continued

Company	ActiveX Controls
	Timer
	View Tracker
Vivo Software, Inc.	VivoActive Player for ActiveX

In all, there are more than 1,000 ActiveX products out there at your disposal. These ActiveX controls can be used and reused to enhance the multimedia contents of the modern Web page. And with the advent of COM and its wide acceptance, ActiveX content will be accessed by almost everyone on the Web.

Summary

This chapter demonstrates how simple it can be to implement multimedia content using ActiveX. Chapter 31 demonstrates using the default Java support for video, audio, and animation to enhance the sensory impact of your Java applets/applications. However, the "old" method requires extensive creation of image content (not an easy task for those of us who are artistically impaired programmers) and coordination of video and audio to create animation.

With ActiveX as the basis for multimedia, content and interfaces can easily be reused with simple changes to the files being accessed. With COM support, these Java programs can become a de facto standard for distributing multimedia with ActiveX. It also allows developers and programmers everywhere to be able to use their own favorite language and multimedia format without worry of conflicting with the desired content of the Web page or end users' machines.

Multimedia is the defining measure for the quality of Web page content pages today, and ActiveX is the future by which multimedia content can become ubiquitous across the entire Internet.

Appendixes

VI
PART

JavaScript Language Reference

by David Blankenbeckler

IN THIS APPENDIX

This appendix is a quick reference for the JavaScript language.

Language keywords and symbols are shown in a monospace font. Arguments and other parts to be substituted are in *italic monospace*.

Optional parts are indicated by brackets. If there are several options that are mutually exclusive, they are shown separated by pipes (¦) like this:

```
[ public ¦ private ¦ protected ] type varname
```

Reserved Words

The following words are defined as part of the JavaScript language and cannot be used as variable names:

abstract	extends	interface	synchronized
boolean	false	long	this
break	final	native	throw
byte	finally	new	throws
case	float	null	transient
catch	for	package	true
char	function	private	try
class	goto	protected	var
const	if	public	void
continue	implements	return	while
default	import	short	with
do	in	static	
double	instanceof	super	
else	int	switch	

Literals

Literals in JavaScript are represented as follows:

Syntax	*Description*
number	Integer (Base10)
0number	Integer (Octal)
0xnumber	Integer (Hex)
num1.num2	Floating point

Syntax	Description
`num1Enum2`	Exponential floating point
`'characters'`	String
`"characters"`	String
`\b`	Backspace
`\f`	Form feed
`\n`	New line
`\r`	Carriage return
`\t`	Tab
`\"`	Double quote
`true`	Boolean
`false`	Boolean

Operators

The JavaScript operators are grouped into the following categories: assignment, comparison, arithmetic, string, logical, and bitwise.

Assignment

The following assignment operators are supported in JavaScript:

Syntax	Description
`variable = value`	Assignment of `value` to `variable`
`variable += expression`	`variable = variable + expression`
`variable -= expression`	`variable = variable - expression`
`variable *= expression`	`variable = variable * expression`
`variable /= expression`	`variable = variable / expression`
`variable %= expression`	`variable = variable % expression`
`variable <<= expression`	`variable = variable << expression`
`variable >>= expression`	`variable = variable >> expression`
`variable >>>= expression`	`variable = variable >>> expression`
`variable &= expression`	`variable = variable & expression`
`variable ^= expression`	`variable = variable ^ expression`
`variable ¦= expression`	`variable = variable ¦ expression`

Comparison

The following comparison operators are supported in JavaScript:

Syntax	Description
==	Equal
!=	Not equal
>	Greater than
>=	Greater than or equal to
<	Less than
<=	Less than or equal to

Arithmetic

The following arithmetic operators are supported in JavaScript:

Syntax	Description
var1 + var2	Addition
var1 - var2	Subtraction
var1 * var2	Multiplication
var1 / var2	Division
var1 & var2	Modulus
-	Negation
var++	Postfix increment
++var	Prefix increment
var--	Postfix decrement
--var	Prefix decrement

String

The following string operator is supported in JavaScript:

Syntax	Description
string1 + string2	String concatenation

Logical

The following logical operators are supported in JavaScript:

Syntax	Description
expr1 && expr2	Logical AND
expr1 ¦¦ expr2	Logical OR
!expr	Logical NOT

Bitwise

The following bitwise logical operators are supported in JavaScript:

Syntax	Description
arg1 & arg2	Bitwise AND
arg1 ¦ arg2	Bitwise OR
arg1 ^ arg2	Bitwise XOR
arg1 << arg2	Left shift
arg1 >> arg2	Right shift
arg1 >>> arg2	Zero-fill right shift

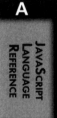

Statements

JavaScript provides the traditional conditional and loop statements as well as a set of object manipulation statements.

Conditional Statements

Conditional statements provide the ability to perform steps based on the outcome of a comparison. JavaScript provides this support through the if...else statement.

if...else

The syntax for the if...else statement is as follows:

```
if (condition) {
    // statements for true condition
}
else {
    // statements for false condition
}
```

Loop Statements

Loop statements provide a means for looping through a section of code until an expression evaluates to true (or false).

The for Loop

The for loop will set an initial expression, initExpr, and then loop through a section of JavaScript statements as long as a condition evaluates to true. Each time through the loop, the expression incrExpr is executed:

```
for (initExpr; condition; incrExpr) {
   // statements to execute while looping
   [break;]
   [continue;]

}
```

The while Loop

The while loop will continue as long as a specified condition evaluates to true:

```
while (condition) {
   // statement to execute while looping
   [break;]
   [continue;]
}
```

Object Manipulation Statements

JavaScript includes several statements that are designed to work with objects.

The for...in Statement

The for...in statement is used to loop through all the properties of an object:

```
for (variable in object) {
   // statements
   }
```

The new Statement

The new variable is used to create a new instance of an object:

```
objectvar = new objecttype ( param1 [, param2] … [,paramN] )
```

The with Statement

The with statement is used to set the default object for a series of statements. The properties can then be referred to without using the parent object:

```
with(object){
    // statements
}
```

The this Keyword

The this keyword is used to refer to the current object:

```
this[.property]
```

The JavaScript Object Hierarchy

The object hierarchy for JavaScript is shown in Figure A.1.

FIGURE A.1.
The JavaScript object hierarchy.

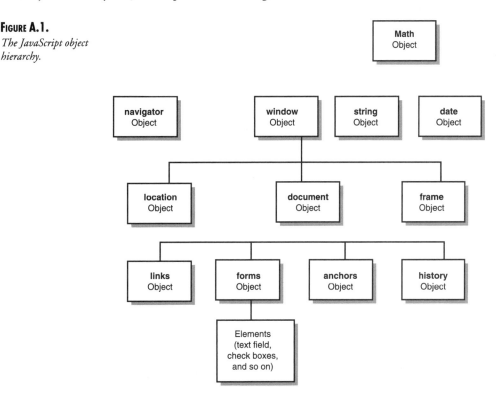

The Navigator Object

The Navigator object is used to obtain information about the browser, such as the version number. The Navigator object does not have any methods or event handlers associated with it.

Properties

appCodeName—Used to specify the internal code name of the browser; for example, Atlas.

appName—Used to specify the name of the browser.

appVersion—Used to specify version information for the Navigator object.

userAgent—Used to specify the user-agent header.

The Window Object

The Window object is a top-level object. The Document, Frame, and Location objects are all properties of the Window object.

Properties

defaultStatus—The default message that is displayed in the window's status bar.

frames—An array that reflects all of the frames in a window.

length—The number of frames in a parent window.

name—The name of the current window.

parent—Refers to the parent Window object.

self—Refers to the current window.

status—Used for a temporary status message for the window's status bar. This is used to get or set the status message and overrides defaultStatus.

top—Refers to the topmost window.

window—Refers to the current window.

Methods

alert("*message*")

Displays a dialog box with the string *message* and an OK button.

clearTimeout(*timeoutID*)

Clears a timeout set by SetTimeout. SetTimeout returns *timeoutID*.

```
windowReference.close
```

Closes the window referred to by *windowReference*.

```
confirm("message")
```

Displays a dialog box with the string *"message"*, an OK button, and a Cancel button. Returns `true` for OK and `false` for Cancel.

```
[windowVar = ][window].open("URL", "windowName", ["windowFeatures"])
```

Opens a new window.

```
prompt("message" [,"defaultInput"])
```

Opens a dialog box with a text field for input.

```
TimeoutID = setTimeout(expression, msec)
```

Evaluates *expression* after *msec* has elapsed.

Event Handlers

`onLoad`—Occurs when a window finishes loading.

`onUnload`—Occurs when a window is unloaded.

The Location Object

The `Location` object contains properties with information about the URL of the current document. This object does not have any methods or event handlers.

Refer to the following sample URL in the property descriptions that follow:

```
http://www.abc.com/chap1/page2.html#topic3
```

Properties

`hash`—The current location's anchor name; in this example, `topic3`.

`host`—The `hostname:port` portion of the URL; in this example, `www.abc.com` (note that the port is typically the default port and is not shown).

`hostname`—The host and domain name; in this example, `www.abc.com`.

`href`—The entire URL for the current document.

`pathname`—The path portion of the URL; in this example, `/chap1/page2.html`.

`port`—The communications port used on the host computer. Typically the default port.

`protocol`—The protocol being used (with the colon); in this example, `http:`.

`search`—A search query that may be at the end of a URL for a CGI script.

The Frame Object

A window can have several frames. There are no event handlers for a frame.

Properties

frames—An array of all the frames in a window.

name—The <FRAME> tag's NAME attribute.

length—The number of child frames within a frame.

parent—The window or frame containing the current frameset.

self—The current frame.

window—The current frame.

Methods

clearTimeout(*timeoutID*)

Clears a timeout set by SetTimeout. SetTimeout returns *timeoutID*.

TimeoutID = setTimeout(*expression*, *msec*)

Evaluates *expression* after *msec* has elapsed.

The Document Object

The Document object contains information about the current document and provides methods for writing information to the screen.

Properties

alinkColor—Same as the ALINK attribute.

anchors—Array of all the anchors in a document.

bgColor—Same as the BGCOLOR attribute.

cookie—Used to specify a cookie.

fgColor—Same as the TEXT attribute.

forms—An array of all the forms in a document.

lastModified—The date a document was last modified.

linkColor—The same as the LINK attribute.

links—An array of all the links in a document.

location—The complete URL of a document.

referrer—The URL of the calling document.

title—The contents of the <TITLE> tag.

vlinkColor—The VLINK attribute.

Methods

document.clear

Clears the current document.

document.close

Closes an output stream and forces data sent to layout to display.

document.open(["*mimeType*"])

Opens a stream to collect the output of write or writeln methods.

document.write(*expression1* [,*expression2*], ...[,*expressionN*])

Writes HTML expressions to a document in the specified window.

document.writeln(*expression1* [,*expression2*], ...[,*expressionN*])

Writes HTML expressions to a document in the specified window and follows them with a newline.

The anchors Object

An anchor is text in a document that can be the target of a hyperlink. The anchors object has no properties, methods, or event handlers.

Anchors are referenced as follows:

document.anchors[*index*]

The anchors array has a single property, length, that stores the number of named anchors in the document. This can be referred to as follows:

document.anchors.length

The forms Object

If a document contains several forms, they can be referenced by the forms array. The number of forms is found with the following:

document.forms.length

Each form can be referenced as follows:

```
document.forms[index]
```

Properties

> action—The ACTION attribute.
>
> elements—An array reflecting all the elements in a form.
>
> encoding—The ENCTYPE attribute.
>
> length—Reflects the number of elements on a form.
>
> method—The METHOD attribute.
>
> target—The TARGET attribute.

Method

```
formName.submit()
```

Submits the form named *formName*.

Event Handler

> onSubmit—Occurs when a form is submitted.

The History Object

The History object is used to store information about the previous URLs visited by the user. The list of URLs is stored in chronological order. There are no event handlers associated with the History object.

Property

> length—The number of entries in the History object.

Methods

```
history.back()
```

Used to reference the previous URL visited (the previous URL in the history list).

```
history.forward()
```

Used to reference the next URL in the history list. Until either the user or a script moves backward on the history list, this will have no effect.

```
history.go(delta ¦ "location")
```

Used to either move forward or backward *delta* number of entries on the history list or to go to a specific URL on the history list referred to by *location*. If *delta* is used, the reference will be backward if negative and forward if positive. If *location* is used, the closest URL containing *location* as a substring will be called.

The `links` Object

A `links` object is text or a picture that is specified as a hyperlink. The properties of the `links` object deal primarily with the URL of the hyperlink. The `links` object does not have any methods.

The `links` array contains a list of all the links in a document. The number of links can be found by:

```
document.links.length
```

A specific link can be referenced by the array, like this:

```
document.links[index]
```

For the descriptions of properties in the following section, the following sample URL is used:

```
http://www.abc.com/chap1/page2.html#topic3
```

Properties

hash—The anchor name of the link; in this example, topic3.

host—The hostname:port portion of the URL; in this example, www.abc.com (note that the port is typically the default port and is not shown).

hostname—The host and domain name; in this example, www.abc.com.

href—The entire URL for the link.

pathname—The path portion of the URL; in this example, /chap1/page2.html.

port—The communications port used on the host computer. Typically the default port.

protocol—The protocol being used (with the colon); in this example, http:.

search—A search query that may be at the end of a URL for a CGI script.

target—The same as the TARGET attribute of <LINK>.

Event Handlers

onClick—Occurs when user clicks on the link.

onMouseOver—Occurs when the mouse is moved over the link.

The Math Object

The Math object is a built-in object in JavaScript. The Math object has no event handlers associated with it.

Properties

E—Euler's constant, e, approximately 2.718.

LN2—The natural logarithm of 2, approximately 0.693.

LN10—The natural logarithm of 10, approximately 2.302.

LOG2E—The base 2 logarithm of e, approximately 1.442.

LOG10E—The base 10 logarithm of e, approximately 0.434.

PI—The value of π, approximately 3.14159.

SQRT1_2—The square root of one-half, approximately 0.707.

SQRT2—The square root of 2, approximately 1.414.

Methods

`Math.abs(number)`

Returns the absolute value of *number*.

`Math.acos(number)`

Returns the arc cosine (in radians) of *number*. The value of *number* must be between -1 and 1.

`Math.asin(number)`

Returns the arc sine (in radians) of *number*. The value of *number* must be between -1 and 1.

`Math.atan(number)`

Returns the arc tangent (in radians) of *number*.

`Math.ceil(number)`

Returns the lowest integer equal to or greater than *number*.

`Math.cos(number)`

Returns the cosine of *number*.

`Math.exp(number)`

Returns e^{number}, where e is Euler's constant.

`Math.floor(number)`

Returns the highest integer equal to or less than *number*.

`Math.log(`*`number`*`)`

Returns the natural log of *number*.

`Math.max(`*`num1, num2`*`)`

Returns the greater of *num1* and *num2*.

`Math.min(`*`num1, num2`*`)`

Returns the lesser of *num1* and *num2*.

`Math.pow(base, exponent)`

Returns the value of `base` to the exponent power.

`Math.random()`

Returns a random number between 0 and 1. Note that this works only on UNIX platforms.

`Math.round(`*`number`*`)`

Returns the value of *number* rounded to the nearest integer.

`Math.sin(`*`number`*`)`

Returns the sine of *number*.

`Math.sqrt(`*`number`*`)`

Returns the square root of *number*.

`Math.tan(`*`number`*`)`

Returns the tangent of *number*.

The Date Object

The `Date` object is a built-in object in JavaScript. The `Date` object has no event handlers or properties associated with it.

Some of the following method examples use the value stored in `dateVar` as follows:

`dateVar = new Date("August 16, 1996 20:45:04");`

Methods

`dateVar``.getDate()`

Returns the day of the month (1–31) for *dateVar*; in this example, `16`.

`dateVar``.getDay()`

Returns the day of the week (0=Sunday through 6=Saturday) for *dateVar*; in this example, `5`.

`dateVar.getHours()`

Returns the hour (0–23) for `dateVar`; in this example, 20.

`dateVar.getMinutes()`

Returns the minutes (0–59) for `dateVar`; in this example, 45.

`dateVar.getMonth()`

Returns the month (0–11) for `dateVar`; in this example, 7.

`dateVar.getSeconds()`

Returns the seconds (0–59) for `dateVar`; in this example, 4.

`dateVar.getTime()`

Returns the number of milliseconds since Jan. 1, 1970, 00:00:00.

`dateVar.getTimezoneOffset()`

Returns the offset in minutes of the current local time to GMT.

`dateVar.getYear()`

Returns the year for `dateVar`; in this example, 96.

`Date.parse(dateStr)`

Parses the string `datestr` and returns the number of milliseconds since Jan. 1, 1970, 00:00:00.

`dateVar.setDate(day)`

Sets the day of the month to `day` for `dateVar`.

`dateVar.setHours(hours)`

Sets the hours to `hours` for `dateVar`.

`dateVar.setMinutes(minutes)`

Sets the minutes to `minutes` for `dateVar`.

`dateVar.setMonth(month)`

Sets the month to `month` for `dateVar`.

`dateVar.setSeconds(seconds)`

Sets the seconds to `seconds` for `dateVar`.

`dateVar.setTime(value)`

Sets the time to `value`, which represents the number of milliseconds since Jan. 1, 1970, 00:00:00.

dateVar.setYear(*year*)

Sets the year to *year* for *dateVar*.

dateVar.toGMTString()

Returns a string representing *dateVar* as GMT.

dateVar.toLocaleString()

Returns a string representing *dateVar* in the current time zone.

Date.UTC(*year*, *month*, *day* [,*hours*] [,*minutes*] [,*seconds*])

Returns the number of milliseconds since Jan. 1, 1970, 00:00:00 GMT.

The String Object

Property

length—The length of the string.

Methods

str.anchor(*name*)

Used to dynamically create an <A> tag. The *name* parameter is the NAME attribute of the tag.

str.big()

Creates the same effect as the <BIG> tag on the string *str*.

str.blink()

Creates the same effect as the <BLINK> tag on the string *str*.

str.bold()

Creates the same effect as the <BOLD> tag on the string *str*.

str.charAt(*a*)

Returns the character at position *a* from the string *str*.

str.fixed()

Creates the same effect as the <TT> tag on the string *str*.

str.fontcolor(*color*)

Creates the same effect as the <FONT COLOR=*color*> tag.

`str.fontsize(size)`

Creates the same effect as the `<FONTSIZE=size>` tag.

`str.indexOf(srchStr [,index])`

Returns the offset into `str` of the first appearance of `srchStr`. The string is searched from left to right. The `index` parameter can be used to start the search somewhere other than the beginning of the string.

`str.italics()`

Creates the same effect as the `<I>` tag on the string `str`.

`str.lastIndexOf(srchStr [, index])`

Returns the offset into `str` of the last occurrence of `srchStr`. The string is searched from right to left. The `index` parameter can be used to start the search somewhere other than the end of the string.

`str.link(href)`

Used to create an HTML link dynamically for the string `str`. The `href` parameter is the destination URL for the link.

`str.small()`

Creates the same effect as the `<SMALL>` tag on the string `str`.

`str.strike()`

Creates the same effect as the `<STRIKE>` tag on the string `str`.

`str.sub()`

Creates a subscript for string `str`, just like the `<SUB>` tag.

`str.substring(a, b)`

Returns the substring of `str` indicated by the characters between the character at position `a` and the character at position `b`. The character count is from left to right starting at 0.

`str.sup()`

Creates a superscript for string `str`, just like the `<SUP>` tag.

`str.toLowerCase()`

Converts `str` to lowercase.

`str.toUpperCase()`

Converts `str` to uppercase.

VBScript Language Reference

by David Blankenbeckler

IN THIS APPENDIX

This appendix is a summary and quick reference for the VBScript language.

Language keywords and symbols are shown in a monospaced font. Arguments and other parts to be substituted are in *italic monospace*.

Optional parts are indicated by brackets. If there are several options that are mutually exclusive, they are shown separated by pipes (¦) like this:

```
[ public ¦ private ¦ protected ] type varname
```

Summary of Reserved Words

The following words are defined as part of the VBScript language and cannot be used as variable names:

Abs	Erase	Len	Set
And	Err	Log	Sgn
Asc	Error	Loop	Sin
Atn	Exit	Ltrim	Sqr
Call	Exp	Mid	Step
Case	Fix	Minute	Str
Cbool	For	Mod	StrComp
Cbyte	Function	Month	String
Cdate	Hex	MsgBox	Sub
CDbl	Hour	Next	Tan
Chr	If	Not	Then
Cint	Imp	Now	Time
Clear	InputBox	Oct	TimeSerial
CLng	InStr	On	TimeValue
Cos	Int	Or	Trim
CSng	Is	Preserve	UBound
CStr	IsArray	Raise	UCase
Date	IsDate	Randomize	Until
DateSerial	IsEmpty	ReDim	Val
DateValue	IsNull	Rem	VarType
Day	IsNumeric	Right	Weekday

Dim	IsObject	Rnd	Wend
Do	Lbound	RTrim	While
Else	Lcase	Second	Xor
Eqv	Left	Select	Year

Literals

Literals in VBScript are represented as follows:

Syntax	Description
`number`	Integer (base 10)
`num1.num2`	Floating point
`num1Enum2`	Exponential floating point
`"characters"`	String
`#m/d/y#`	Date
`#m-d-y#`	Date
`#hour:min:sec#`	Time
`#m-d-y hour:min:sec#`	Date and Time
`#hour:min:sec m/d/y#`	Date and Time
`True`	Boolean
`False`	Boolean

Operators

The VBScript operator is grouped into the following categories: assignment, comparison, arithmetic, string, logical, and bitwise.

Assignment

The following assignment operator is supported in VBScript:

Syntax	Description
`variable = value`	Assignment of `value` to `variable`

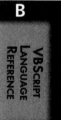

B

VBSCRIPT
LANGUAGE
REFERENCE

Comparison

The following comparison operators are supported in VBScript:

Syntax	*Description*
=	Equal
<>	Not equal
>	Greater than
>=	Greater than or equal to
<	Less than
<=	Less than or equal to
Is	Equal (objects)

Arithmetic

The following arithmetic operators are supported in VBScript:

Syntax	*Description*
var1 + var2	Addition
var1 - var2	Subtraction
var1 * var2	Multiplication
var1 / var2	Division
var1 & var2	Modulus
var1 \ var2	Integer division
-	Negation
var1^exp	Exponentiation

String

The following string operator is supported in VBScript:

Syntax	*Description*
string1 & string2	String concatenation

Logical

The following logical operators are supported in VBScript:

Syntax	Description
`expr1 And expr2`	Logical AND
`expr1 Or expr2`	Logical OR
`Not expr`	Logical NOT
`expr1 Xor expr2`	Logical exclusive OR
`expr1 Eqv expr2`	Equivalence
`expr1 Imp expr2`	Implication

Bitwise Logical

The following bitwise logical operators are supported in VBScript:

Syntax	Description
`arg1 And arg2`	Bitwise AND
`arg1 Or arg2`	Bitwise OR
`arg1 Xor arg2`	Bitwise XOR
`Not arg1`	Bitwise Not
`expr1 Eqv expr2`	Bitwise equivalence
`expr1 Imp expr2`	Bitwise implication

Statements

VBScript statements are divided into two categories: conditional and looping.

Conditionals

Conditional statements provide the ability to perform steps based on the outcome of a comparison. VBScript provides this support through the `If...Else` and `Select Case` statements.

If...Else

The syntax for the `If…Else` statement is as follows:

```
If condition Then
'   statements for true condition
[Else]
'   statements for false condition
End If
```

Select Case

The syntax for the Select Case statement is as follows:

```
Select Case expr
   Case n
      ' statements for this case
   Case m
      ' statements for this case
   '… additional case statements as necessary
   [Case Else]
      ' statements for the default case
End Select
```

Loops

Loop statements provide a means for looping through a section of code until an expression evaluates to true (or false).

For...Next

The syntax for the For…Next statement is as follows:

```
For var = init To final [Step step]
' statements to execute while looping
Next
```

While...Wend

The syntax for the While...Wend statement is as follows:

```
While condition
' statements to execute while looping
Wend
```

Do While

The syntax for the Do While statement is as follows:

```
Do While condition
' statements to execute while looping
[Exit Do]
' statements to execute while looping
Loop
```

Do Until

The syntax for the Do Until statement is as follows:

```
Do Until condition
' statements to execute while looping
[Exit Do]
' statements to execute while looping
Loop
```

Alternate Form of Do loop

The `Do Until` and `Do While` loops can also be used with the following syntax:

```
Do
' statements to execute while looping
Loop [Until¦While]
```

Procedures

VBScript provides two different types of procedures, `Sub` and `Function`. When there is no return value, `Sub` should be used. When there is a return value, `Function` should be used.

Subroutine

The syntax for a `Sub` procedure is as follows:

```
Sub SubName([param1][,param2]…[,paramN])
    ' sub procedure statements
End Sub
```

Function

The syntax for a `Function` procedure is as follows:

```
Function fnName([param1][,param2]…[,paramN])
    ' function statements;
    fnName = expr
End Function
```

Built-in Functions

VBScript contains a number of built-in functions. Each of the VBScript functions is summarized in the following sections.

Math

VBScript provides many different built-in functions for performing mathematical operations.

In the following function declarations, *numExpr* can be either a number or an expression that evaluates to a number.

`Abs(numExpr)`

Returns the absolute value of *numExpr*.

`Atn(numExpr)`

Returns the arc tangent of *numExpr*.

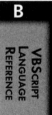

`Cos(`*numExpr*`)`

Returns the cosine of *numExpr*.

`Exp(`*numExpr*`)`

Returns $e^{numExpr}$ where e is Euler's constant.

`Fix(`*numExpr*`)`

Returns the integer portion of *numExpr*. If the number is negative, the next greater integer is returned.

`Int(`*numExpr*`)`

Returns the integer portion of *numExpr*. If the number is negative, the next lower integer is returned.

`Log(`*numExpr*`)`

Returns the natural log of *numExpr*.

`Rnd([`*numExpr*`])`

Returns a pseudo-random number. The number is not really random because the same seed will always produce the same result. If *numExpr* is used, the result is as follows:

> If *numExpr* = `0`, `Rnd` returns the last random number generated.
>
> If *numExpr* > `0`, `Rnd` returns the next random number in the sequence.
>
> If *numExpr* < `0`, `Rnd` returns a random number based on the seed, *numExpr*. The same seed always returns the same number.

The `Randomize` statement will generate a seed for the `Rnd` function based on the system clock. This will provide a much better illusion of randomness. Here's an example:

```
Randomize
x = Rnd()
```

`Sgn(`*numExpr*`)`

Returns `1` if *numExpr* is greater than 0, `-1` if *numExpr* is less than 0, and `0` if *numExpr* is equal to 0.

`Sin(`*numExpr*`)`

Returns the sine of *numExpr*.

`Sqr(`*numExpr*`)`

Returns the square root of *numExpr*.

`Tan(`*numExpr*`)`

Returns the tangent of *numExpr*.

Dates and Time

VBScript contains a number of built-in functions to work with dates and time.

`Date`

Returns the current date from the system clock.

`DateSerial(year, month, day)`

Returns a value of subtype `Date` to represent the *year*, *month*, and *day* that were passed.

`Day(date)`

Returns an integer between 1 and 31 to represent the day for the *date* that was passed.

`Hour(time)`

Returns an integer between 0 and 23 to represent the hour for the *time* that was passed.

`Minute(time)`

Returns an integer between 0 and 59 to represent the minute for the *time* that was passed.

`Month(date)`

Returns an integer between 1 and 12 to represent the month for the *date* that was passed.

`Now`

Returns the current date and time based on the system clock.

`Second(time)`

Returns an integer between 0 and 59 to represent the second for the *time* that was passed.

`Time`

Returns the current time from the system clock.

`TimeSerial(hour,minute,second)`

Returns a value of subtype `Date` to represent the *hour*, *minute*, and *second* that were passed.

`Weekday(date [, firstday])`

Returns an integer between 1 and 7 that represents the current day of the week for *date*. By default, Sunday is represented by 1, Monday 2, and so on. If a *firstday* parameter is passed, another day can be set to be represented by 1. For example, if 2 is passed as the *firstday* parameter, Monday would be represented by 1.

`Year(date)`

Returns an integer that represents the year in *date*; for example, 1996.

B

VBScript
Language
Reference

String Manipulation

VBScript contains many built-in functions to assist in dealing with strings.

In the function declarations below, *strExpr* can be either a string or an expression that evaluates to a string.

`Asc(strExpr)`

Returns an integer representing the ANSI code for the first character of *strExpr*.

`Chr(ANSICode)`

Returns the character represented by *ANSICode*.

`Hex(number)`

Returns a string that represents *number* in hexadecimal.

`InStr([startPos,] string, srchstr [, compType])`

Returns the position of the first occurrence of *srchstr* in *string*. If *startPos* is specified, the search begins at that position. The *compType* parameter can be either 0 or 1. The default value of 0 is case sensitive. A *compType* of 1 indicates that the search should not be case sensitive.

`LCase(strExpr)`

Converts *strExpr* to lowercase and returns it as a string.

`Left(strExpr, numChars)`

Returns a substring of *strExpr* that begins at the first position (on the left) and is *numChars* in length.

`Len(strExpr ¦ varName)`

If a string expression is passed, Len returns the length of that string. If a variable name is passed, Len returns the number of bytes required to store that variable.

`LTrim(strExpr)`

Removes all leading spaces from *strExpr* and returns it as a string.

`Mid(strExpr, startPos, numChars)`

Returns a substring of *strExpr* that begins at *startPos* and is *numChars* in length.

`Oct(number)`

Returns a string that represents *number* in octal.

`Right(strExpr, numChars)`

Returns a substring of *strExpr* that begins at the last position (on the right) and is *numChars* in length.

RTrim(*strExpr*)

Removes all trailing spaces from *strExpr* and returns it as a string.

StrComp(*strExpr1*, *strExpr2* [,*compType*])

Compares *strExpr1* and *strExpr2*. If they are equal, 0 is returned. -1 is returned if *strExpr1* is less than *strExpr2*. 1 is returned if *strExpr1* is greater than *strExpr2*. If either string is null, Null is returned.

The *compType* parameter can be either 0 or 1. The default value of 0 is case sensitive. A *compType* of 1 indicates that the search should not be case sensitive.

String(*length*, *character*)

Returns a string of repeating *character* that is *length* in length.

Trim(*strExpr*)

Removes all leading and trailing spaces from *strExpr* and returns it as a string.

UCase(*strExpr*)

Converts *strExpr* to uppercase and returns it as a string.

User Interface

VBScript provides two built-in functions that provide easy access to the user interface: InputBox and MsgBox.

InputBox(*prompt* [, *title*][, *default*][, *xPos*][, *yPos*][, *helpFile*, *context*])

This function displays a dialog box with a text field. The contents of the text field are returned. The parameters are defined as follows:

Parameter	Description
prompt	The prompt that is displayed in the dialog box.
title	The text that is displayed on the title bar of the dialog box.
default	The default contents of the text field.
xPos	The distance (in twips) of the dialog box from the left edge of the screen.
yPos	The distance (in twips) of the dialog box from the top of the screen.
helpFile	The filename of the help file that should be used for context-sensitive help.
context	The context number for the appropriate help topic in *helpFile*.

B

```
MsgBox(prompt[, buttons][, title][, helpfile, context])
```

The `MsgBox` function displays a dialog box with one or more buttons, as configured by the *buttons* parameter. The parameters are defined as follows:

Parameter	*Description*
`prompt`	The prompt that is displayed in the dialog box.
`buttons`	A number that specifies the number and type of buttons to display in the dialog box. The number is arrived at by adding together four numbers to specify the number and type of buttons, the icon style, the default button, and the modality of the dialog box. The *buttons* configurations are as follows:

Number/Type Buttons	*Effect*
`0`	An OK button
`1`	OK and Cancel buttons
`2`	Abort, Retry, and Ignore buttons
`3`	Yes, No, and Cancel buttons
`4`	Yes and No buttons
`5`	Retry and Cancel buttons

Icon	*Style*
`0`	No icon
`16`	Critical Message icon
`32`	Warning Query icon
`48`	Warning Message icon
`64`	Information Message icon

Default	*Button*
`0`	First button
`256`	Second button
`512`	Third button
`768`	Fourth button

Modality	Description
0	Application Modal
4096	System Modal
title	The text that is displayed on the title bar of the dialog box.
helpFile	The filename of the help file that should be used for context-sensitive help.
context	The context number for the appropriate help topic in *helpFile*.

The return value provides the button that was selected:

Return Value	Button Selected
1	OK
2	Cancel
3	Abort
4	Retry
5	Ignore
6	Yes
7	No

Data Type

VBScript provides several built-in functions for dealing with data types.

CBool(*expr*)

Returns *expr* converted to subtype Boolean. If *expr* is 0, False is returned. True is returned if *expr* is unequal to 0. A type mismatch runtime error occurs if *expr* does not represent a numeric value.

CByte(*expr*)

Returns *expr* converted to subtype Byte. If *expr* cannot be converted to subtype Byte, a type mismatch runtime error occurs.

CDate(*expr*)

Returns *expr* converted to subtype Date. If *expr* cannot be converted to subtype Date, a type mismatch runtime error occurs.

CDbl(*expr*)

Returns *expr* converted to subtype Double. If *expr* cannot be converted to subtype Double, a type mismatch or overflow runtime error occurs.

`CInt(expr)`

Returns *expr* converted to subtype `Integer`. If *expr* cannot be converted to subtype `Integer`, a type mismatch or overflow runtime error occurs.

`CLng(expr)`

Returns *expr* converted to subtype `Long`. If *expr* cannot be converted to subtype `Long`, a type mismatch or overflow runtime error occurs.

`CSng(expr)`

Returns *expr* converted to subtype `Single`. If *expr* cannot be converted to subtype `Single`, a type mismatch or overflow runtime error occurs.

`CStr(expr)`

Returns *expr* converted to subtype `String`.

If *expr* is boolean, either `True` or `False` is returned.

If *expr* is a `Date`, a string will be returned in the short date format for the particular system.

If *expr* is of the subtype `Error`, a string containing the word *Error* and the error number is returned.

If *expr* is `Null`, a runtime error occurs.

`DateValue(string)`

Returns a `Variant` of subtype `Date` to represent the date in *string*.

`IsArray(expr)`

Returns a boolean indicating whether *expr* is an array.

`IsDate(expr)`

Returns a boolean indicating whether *expr* can be converted to a `Date`.

`IsEmpty(expr)`

Returns a boolean indicating whether *expr* is empty. The intent of this function is to pass a variable name as *expr* to determine if it has been initialized.

`IsNull(expr)`

Returns a boolean indicating whether *expr* contains `Null`.

`IsNumeric(expr)`

Returns a boolean indicating whether *expr* can be evaluated to a numeric value.

`IsObject(expr)`

Returns a boolean indicating whether *expr* references a valid object.

`LBound(arrayName[, dimension])`

Returns the lower bound of *arrayName* for the *dimension* indicated. Because VBScript does not support lower bounds other than zero, this function is not very useful.

`TimeValue(string)`

Returns a `Variant` of subtype `Date` to represent the time in *string*.

`UBound(arrayName[, dimension])`

Returns the upper bound of *arrayName* for the *dimension* indicated.

`Val(strExpr)`

Returns the first numeric value found in *strExpr*. The numeric value must be at the beginning of *strExpr*. Spaces, tabs, and linefeeds will be removed and periods converted to decimal points. The prefixes `&0` and `&H` in *strExpr* can be used to specify octal or hexadecimal values.

`VarType(varName)`

Returns a number that indicates the `Variant` subtype of *varName* according to the following:

Returned Value	Subtype
0	Empty
1	Null
2	Integer
3	Long
4	Single
5	Double
7	Date
8	String
9	Automation object
10	Error
11	Boolean
12	Variant
13	Non-automation object
17	Byte
8192	Array

B

VBSCRIPT
LANGUAGE
REFERENCE

INDEX

Symbols

A

You Already Smelled The Coffee.
Now Move On To The Hard Stuff...

Web Informant will get you there.

Developing successful applications for the Web is what you really like to do. You like your information straight. You want it bold and to the point.

Web Informant Magazine is the only source you need, offering nuts and bolts programming solutions, specific coding techniques, actual code and downloadable files—no gimmicks, trends or fluff.

It's a powerful source of information, and it's the only source of information challenging enough to keep you on the edge. It's tough. It's Java®, Perl, JavaScript, HTML, and VRML. It's unexplored territory, and you like it that way.

Web Informant will get you there.

You can get there from here. To order, and receive THREE free issues call 1.800.88.INFORM or 916.686.6610. FAX: 916.686.8497. Ask for offer #SAMS8001.

To get there via a direct link to our Web site page:
HTTP://WWW.INFORMANT.COM/WI/INDEX.HTM

THREE FREE ISSUES! YES! I want to sharpen my Web development skills. Sign me up to receive three FREE issues of *Web Informant*, The Complete Monthly Guide to Web Development. If I choose to subscribe, I'll get 11 additional BIG issues (14 in all) for the super low price of $49.95.* That's a savings of 40% off the single-copy price. If I don't, I'll simply write "cancel" on the invoice and owe nothing, with no further obligation on my part.

Name

Company

Address

City/State/Zip
(City/Province/Postal Code)

Country _____ Phone

FAX

E-Mail

*International rates: $54.95/year to Canada, $74.95/year to Mexico, $79.95/year to all other countries. **SAMS 8001**
Informant Communications Group ■ 10519 E Stockton Blvd ■ Ste 142 Elk Grove, CA 95624-9704

Java Unleashed, Second Edition

Michael Morrison, et al.

Java Unleashed, Second Edition is an expanded and updated version of the largest, most comprehensive Java book on the market.

Price: $49.99 USA/$70.95 CDN   *User level: Intermediate—Advanced*
ISBN: 1-57521-197-1   *1,200 pages*

Teach Yourself Java in 21 Days, Professional Reference Edition

Laura Lemay, Charles L. Perkins & Michael Morrison

Introducing the first, best, and most detailed guide to developing applications with the hot new Java language from Sun Microsystems. Provides detailed coverage of the hottest new technology on the World Wide Web. Shows readers how to develop applications using the Java language. Includes coverage of browsing Java applications with Netscape Navigator and other popular Web browsers.

Price: $59.99 USA/$84.95 CDN   *User level: Casual—Accomplished—Expert*
ISBN: 1-57521-183-1   *900 pages*

Web Programming Unleashed

Breedlove, et al.

This comprehensive tome explores all aspects of the latest technology craze—Internet programming. Programmers will turn to the proven expertise of the *Unleashed* series for accurate, up-to-date information on this hot new programming subject.

Price: $49.99 USA/$70.95 CDN   *User level: Accomplished—Expert*
ISBN: 1-57521-117-3   *1,200 pages*

Java Developer's Reference

Mike Cohn, et al.

This is the information- and resource-packed development package for professional developers. It explains the components of the Java Developer's Kit (JDK) and the Java programming language. Everything needed to program Java is included within this comprehensive reference, making it the tool developers will turn to over and over again for timely, accurate information on Java and the JDK.

Price: $59.99 USA/$84.95 CDN   *User level: Accomplished—Expert*
ISBN: 1-57521-129-7   *1,200 pages*

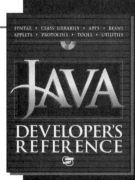

Teach Yourself SunSoft Java WorkShop in 21 Days

Rogers Cadenhead, Laura Lemay, and Charles E. Perkins

Written in Java itself, the Java WorkShop included with this book is a cross-platform tool that provides a rich set of tools for the beginner or professional Java programmer. The WorkShop combines with the book to provide the most comprehensive way to learn SunSoft Java.

Price: $39.99 USA/$56.95 CDN   User level: Casual—Accomplished
ISBN: 1-57521-159-9   600 pages

Developing Intranet Applications with Java

Jerry Ablan

This book shows developers the intricacies of Java intranet development. It teaches how to create interactive databases, multimedia, animation, and sound for use on an intranet. It also teaches how to add interactivity to Web databases.

Price: $45.00 USA/$70.95 CDN   User level: Accomplished—Expert
ISBN: 1-57521-166-1   528 pages

Microsoft FrontPage 97 Unleashed, Second Edition

William Stanek

FrontPage 97 works directly with the Microsoft Office 97 suite of products. Its built-in WYSIWYG (What You See Is What You Get) editor is the best and most popular Web authoring tool on the market. Having FrontPage 97 work with Office 97 will increases its market potential, because Web publishing now will be open to the millions of Office 97 registered users. New and experienced FrontPage users need this book to show them how to use the new version's power to add multimedia, sound, animation, and Office 97 documents to a Web site.

Price: $49.99 USA/$70.95 CDN   User level: Accomplished—Expert
ISBN: 1-57521-226-9   1,000 pages

Microsoft Office 97 Unleashed

Paul McFedries and Sue Charlesworth

Microsoft has brought the Web to its Office suite of products. Hyperlinking, Office Assistants, and Active Document Support lets users publish documents to the Web or an intranet site. It also completely integrates with Microsoft FrontPage, making it possible to point-and-click a Web page into existence. This book details each of the Office products—Excel, Access, PowerPoint, Word, and Outlook—and shows the estimated 22 million registered users how to create presentations and Web documents.

Price: $39.99 USA/$49.95 CDN   User level: Accomplished—Expert
ISBN: 0-672-31010-4   1,200 pages

Add to Your Sams.net Library Today
with the Best Books for Internet Technologies

ISBN	Quantity	Description of Item	Unit Cost	Total Cost
1-57521-197-1		Java Unleashed, Second Edition (book/CD-ROM)	$49.99	
1-57521-183-1		Teach Yourself Java in 21 Days, Professional Reference Edition (book/CD-ROM)	$59.99	
1-57521-117-3		Web Programming Unleashed (book/CD-ROM)	$49.99	
1-57521-129-7		Java Developer's Reference (book/CD-ROM)	$59.99	
1-57521-159-9		Teach Yourself SunSoft Java WorkShop in 21 Days (book/CD-ROM)	$39.99	
1-57521-166-1		Developing Intranet Applications with Java (book/CD-ROM)	$49.99	
1-57521-226-9		Microsoft FrontPage 97 Unleashed, Second Edition (book/CD-ROM)	$49.99	
0-672-31010-4		Microsoft Office 97 Unleashed, Second Edition (book/CD-ROM)	$35.00	
		Shipping and Handling: See information below.		
		TOTAL		

Shipping and Handling: $4.00 for the first book, and $1.75 for each additional book. If you need to have it NOW, we can ship product to you in 24 hours for an additional charge of approximately $18.00, and you will receive your item overnight or in two days. Overseas shipping and handling adds $2.00. Prices subject to change. Call between 9:00 a.m. and 5:00 p.m. EST for availability and pricing information on latest editions.

201 W. 103rd Street, Indianapolis, Indiana 46290

1-800-428-5331 — Orders   1-800-835-3202 — FAX   1-800-858-7674 — Customer Service

Book ISBN 1-57521-161-0

What's on the CD-ROM?

- Visual J++ Publisher's Edition from Microsoft: Create your own J++ programs!
- Java Generic Library from ObjectSpace, Inc.: The ultimate brew of containers and algorithms
- HotDog 32* from Sausage Software: One of the most popular HTML editors
- Paint Shop Pro 3.12* from JASC Software: Perfect for image conversions and creating or modifying all types of images
- NetFerret collection from Vironix: Easily find anything on the Web with this great search collection
- Adobe Acrobat Reader: Browse portable document-formatted files with this reader
- Nico Mak's WinZip* for Windows 95/NT: The most popular compression program for Windows!
- Internet Explorer 3.0 from Microsoft: Check your VBScripts with this browser!
- ActiveX Control Pad from Microsoft: Easily insert ActiveX controls into your HTML!
- Source code from the authors: Easy-to-follow examples in electronic form
- The HTML version of *Java Developer's Guide*: A full electronic book online!

Windows 95/NT 4 Installation Instructions

1. Insert the CD-ROM disc into your CD-ROM drive.
2. From the Windows desktop, double-click on the My Computer icon.
3. Double-click on the icon representing your CD-ROM drive.
4. Double-click on the icon titled SETUP.EXE to run the installation program.
5. Installation creates a program group named Visual J++ Unleashed. This group will contain icons to browse the CD-ROM.

NOTE

If Windows 95/NT 4.0 is installed on your computer and you have the AutoPlay feature enabled, the SETUP.EXE program starts automatically whenever you insert the disc into your CD-ROM drive.

the date of receipt. Some states and jurisdictions do not allow limitations on duration of an implied warranty, so the above limitation may not apply to you. To the extent allowed by applicable law, implied warranties on the SOFTWARE PRODUCT and hardware, if any, are limited to ninety (90) days and one year, respectively.

CUSTOMER REMEDIES. Microsoft's and its suppliers' entire liability and your exclusive remedy shall be, at Microsoft's option, either (a) return of the price paid, or (b) repair or replacement of the SOFTWARE PRODUCT or hardware that does not meet Microsoft's Limited Warranty and which is returned to Microsoft with a copy of your receipt. This Limited Warranty is void if failure of the SOFTWARE PRODUCT or hardware has resulted from accident, abuse, or misapplication. Any replacement SOFTWARE PRODUCT or hardware will be warranted for the remainder of the original warranty period or thirty (30) days, whichever is longer. Outside the United States, neither these remedies nor any product support services offered by Microsoft are available without proof of purchase from an authorized international source.

NO OTHER WARRANTIES. To the maximum extent permitted by applicable law, Microsoft and its suppliers disclaim all other warranties, either express or implied, including, but not limited to, implied warranties of merchantability AND fitness for a particular purpose, with regard to the SOFTWARE PRODUCT, and any accompanying hardware. This limited warranty gives you specific legal rights. You may have others, which vary from state/jurisdiction to state/jurisdiction.

NO LIABILITY FOR CONSEQUENTIAL DAMAGES. TO THE MAXIMUM EXTENT PERMITTED BY APPLICABLE LAW, IN NO EVENT SHALL MICROSOFT OR ITS SUPPLIERS BE LIABLE

FOR ANY special, incidental, indirect, or consequential DAMAGES WHATSOEVER (INCLUDING, WITHOUT LIMITATION, DAMAGES FOR LOSS OF BUSINESS PROFITS, BUSINESS INTERRUPTION, LOSS OF BUSINESS INFORMATION, OR ANY OTHER PECUNIARY LOSS) ARISING OUT OF THE USE OF OR INABILITY TO USE THE SOFTWARE PRODUCT, EVEN IF MICROSOFT HAS BEEN ADVISED OF THE POSSIBILITY OF SUCH DAMAGES. BECAUSE SOME STATES and JURISDICTIONS DO NOT ALLOW THE EXCLUSION OR LIMITATION OF LIABILITY FOR CONSEQUENTIAL OR INCIDENTAL DAMAGES, THE ABOVE LIMITATION MAY NOT APPLY TO YOU.

countries currently include, but are not necessarily limited to Cuba, Iran, Iraq, Libya, North Korea, Syria, and the Federal Republic of Yugoslavia (Serbia and Montenegro, U.N. Protected Areas and areas of Republic of Bosnia and Herzegovina under the control of Bosnian Serb forces). You warrant and represent that neither the U.S.A. Bureau of Export Administration nor any other federal agency has suspended, revoked or denied your export privileges.

9. NOTE ON JAVA SUPPORT. THE SOFTWARE PRODUCT CONTAINS SUPPORT FOR PROGRAMS WRITTEN IN JAVA. JAVA TECHNOLOGY IS NOT FAULT TOLERANT AND IS NOT DESIGNED, MANUFACTURED OR INTENDED FOR USE OR RESALE AS ONLINE CONTROL EQUIPMENT IN HAZARDOUS ENVIRONMENTS REQUIRING FAIL-SAFE PERFORMANCE, SUCH AS IN THE OPERATION OF NUCLEAR FACILITIES, AIRCRAFT NAVIGATION OR COMMUNICATIONS SYSTEMS, AIR TRAFFIC CON-TROL, DIRECT LIFE SUPPORT MACHINES, OR WEAPONS SYSTEMS, IN WHICH THE FAILURE OF JAVA TECHNOLOGY COULD LEAD DIRECTLY TO DEATH, PERSONAL INJURY, OR SEVERE PHYSICAL OR ENVIRON-MENTAL DAMAGE.

Miscellaneous

If you acquired this product in the United States, this EULA is governed by the laws of the State of Washington.

If you acquired this product in Canada, this EULA is governed by the laws of the Province of Ontario, Canada. Each of the parties hereto irrevocably attorns to the jurisdiction of the courts of the Province of Ontario and further agrees to commence any litigation which may arise hereunder in the courts located in the Judicial District of York, Province of Ontario.

If this product was acquired outside the United States, then local law may apply.

Should you have any questions concerning this EULA, or if you desire to contact Microsoft for any reason, please contact the Microsoft subsidiary serving your country, or write: Microsoft Sales Information Center/One Microsoft Way/Redmond, WA 98052-6399.

LIMITED WARRANTY

LIMITED WARRANTY. Except with respect to Microsoft Internet Explorer and the REDISTRIBUTABLES, which are provided "as is," without warranty of any kind, Microsoft warrants that (a) the SOFTWARE PRODUCT will perform substantially in accordance with the accompanying written materials for a period of ninety (90) days from the date of receipt, and (b) any hardware accompanying the SOFTWARE PRODUCT will be free from defects in materials and workmanship under normal use and service for a period of one (1) year from

transfer all your rights under this EULA that pertain to the Microsoft Internet Explorer only in conjunction with a permanent transfer of your validly licensed copy of a Microsoft operating system product.

e. Termination. Without prejudice to any other rights, Microsoft may terminate this EULA if you fail to comply with the terms and conditions of this EULA. In such event, you must destroy all copies of the SOFTWARE PRODUCT. In addition, your rights under this EULA that pertain to the Microsoft Internet Explorer software shall terminate upon termination of your Microsoft operating system product EULA

6. REDISTRIBUTABLE COMPONENTS.

a. Redistributable Files. In addition to the license granted in Section 1, Microsoft grants you a nonexclusive, royalty-free right to reproduce and distribute the object code version of those portions of the SOFTWARE designated in the SOFTWARE as: (i) the files identified in the REDISTRB.WRI file located in the \MSDev\Redist subdirectory on the "Microsoft Visual J++ version 1.00" CD-ROM (collectively, "REDISTRIBUTABLES"), provided you comply with Section 6.b.

b. Redistribution Requirements. If you redistribute the REDISTRIBUTABLES, you agree to: (i) distribute the REDISTRIBUTABLES in object code form only in conjunction with and as a part of your software application product which adds significant and primary functionality and which is designed, developed, and tested to operate in the Microsoft Windows and/or Windows NT environments; (ii) not use Microsoft's name, logo, or trademarks to market your software application product; (iii) include a valid copyright notice on your software product; (iv) indemnify, hold harmless, and defend Microsoft from and against any claims or lawsuits, including attorney's fees, that arise or result from the use or distribution of your software application product; and (v) not permit further distribution of the REDISTRIBUTABLES by your end user. Contact Microsoft for the applicable royalties due and other licensing terms for all other uses and/or distribution of the REDISTRIBUTABLES.

7. U.S. GOVERNMENT RESTRICTED RIGHTS. The SOFTWARE PRODUCT and documentation are provided with RESTRICTED RIGHTS. Use, duplication, or disclosure by the Government is subject to restrictions as set forth in subparagraph (c)(1)(ii) of the Rights in Technical Data and Computer Software clause at DFARS 252.227-7013 or subparagraphs (c)(1) and (2) of the Commercial Computer Software—Restricted Rights at 48 CFR 52.227-19, as applicable. Manufacturer is Microsoft Corporation/One Microsoft Way/Redmond, WA 98052-6399.

8. EXPORT RESTRICTIONS.

You agree that you will not export or re-export the SOFTWARE PRODUCT to any country, person, entity or end user subject to U.S.A. export restrictions. Restricted

continued on preceding page

Solely with respect to electronic documents included with the SOFTWARE, you may make an unlimited number of copies (either in hardcopy or electronic form), provided that such copies shall be used only for internal purposes and are not republished or distributed to any third party.

2. UPGRADES. If the SOFTWARE is an upgrade, whether from Microsoft or another supplier, you may use or transfer the SOFTWARE only in conjunction with upgraded product. If the SOFTWARE is an upgrade from a Microsoft product, you may now use that upgraded product only in accordance with this EULA.

3. SUBSCRIPTION UPDATES. If you have acquired the SOFTWARE PRODUCT as part of a subscription package, then you must treat as an upgrade any subsequent versions of SOFTWARE PRODUCT received as an update to your subscription package.

4. COPYRIGHT. All title and copyrights in and to the SOFTWARE PRODUCT (including but not limited to any images, photographs, animations, video, audio, music, text, and "applets" incorporated into the SOFTWARE PRODUCT), the accompanying printed materials, and any copies of the SOFTWARE PRODUCT are owned by Microsoft or its suppliers. The SOFTWARE PRODUCT is protected by copyright laws and international treaty provisions. Therefore, you must treat the SOFTWARE PRODUCT like any other copyrighted material except that you may either (a) make one copy of the SOFTWARE PRODUCT solely for backup or archival purposes or (b) install the SOFTWARE PRODUCT on a single computer provided you keep the original solely for backup or archival purposes. You may not copy the printed materials accompanying the SOFTWARE PRODUCT.

5. DESCRIPTION OF OTHER RIGHTS AND LIMITATIONS.

   a. Limitations on Reverse Engineering, Decompilation, and Disassembly. You may not reverse engineer, decompile, or disassemble the SOFTWARE PRODUCT, except and only to the extent that such activity is expressly permitted by applicable law notwithstanding this limitation.

   b. No Separation of Components. The SOFTWARE PRODUCT is licensed as a single product and neither the software programs making up the SOFTWARE PRODUCT nor any UPDATE may be separated for use by more than one user at a time.

   c. Rental. You may not rent or lease the SOFTWARE PRODUCT.

   d. Software Transfer. You may permanently transfer all of your rights under this EULA, provided that you retain no copies, you transfer all of the SOFTWARE PRODUCT (including all component parts, the media and printed materials, any upgrades, this EULA, and, if applicable, the Certificate of Authenticity), and the recipient agrees to the terms of this EULA. If the SOFTWARE PRODUCT is an upgrade, any transfer must include all prior versions of the SOFTWARE PRODUCT. Notwithstanding the foregoing, you may permanently

End-User License Agreement for Microsoft Software

Microsoft Visual J++, Publisher's Edition

IMPORTANT—READ CAREFULLY: This Microsoft End-User License Agreement ("EULA") is a legal agreement between you (either an individual or a single entity) and Microsoft Corporation for the Microsoft software product identified above and Microsoft Internet Explorer, which include computer software and associated media and printed materials, and may include "online" or electronic documentation (together, the "SOFTWARE PRODUCT" or "SOFTWARE"). By installing, copying, or otherwise using the SOFTWARE PRODUCT, you agree to be bound by the terms of this EULA. If you do not agree to the terms of this EULA, promptly return the unused SOFTWARE PRODUCT to the place from which you obtained it for a full refund.

Software product LICENSE

The SOFTWARE PRODUCT is protected by copyright laws and international copyright treaties, as well as other intellectual property laws and treaties. The SOFTWARE PRODUCT is licensed, not sold.

1. GRANT OF LICENSE. This EULA grants you the following rights:

   You may use one copy of the Microsoft Software Product identified above on a single computer. The SOFTWARE is in "use" on a computer when it is loaded into temporary memory (i.e., RAM) or installed into permanent memory (e.g., hard disk, CD-ROM, or other storage device) of that computer. However, installation on a network server for the sole purpose of internal distribution to one or more other computer(s) shall not constitute "use" for which a separate license is required, provided you have a separate license for each computer to which the SOFTWARE is distributed.

   You may only use copies of the Microsoft Internet Explorer software only in conjunction with a validly licensed copy of Microsoft operating system products (e.g., Windows® 95 or Windows NT®). You may make copies of the SOFTWARE PRODUCT for use on all computers for which you have licensed Microsoft operating system products.

continued on preceding page